Methods in Behavioral Research

Methods in Behavioral Research

FIFTEENTH EDITION

PAUL C. COZBY

California State University, Fullerton

SCOTT C. BATES

Utah State University

Mc
Graw
Hill

METHODS IN BEHAVIORAL RESEARCH

mheducation.com/highered

For Paul Rosenblatt

—PCC

For my grandmother, Marcile Lottie Yastrop, who had a teacher's heart.

—SCB

Guide to Diversity, Equity, and Inclusion

Since our first edition, *Methods in Behavioral Research* has helped students learn to think like behavioral scientists. Scientists rely on observations to uncover the truth. Historically, most of the scholarship in the behavioral sciences was conducted by White men with White male research participants; it is a discipline built on a single, segmented, incomplete view of humanity. While systemic inequality in society and science has held our collective understanding of humanity back, the persistence, talent, and hard work of many scholars have resulted in a more diverse, equitable, and inclusive science. Now behavioral research is being conducted worldwide, with diverse participants, by researchers with diverse backgrounds and experiences. We are a better science today than we were yesterday and must continue striving to be better. Because *Methods in Behavioral Research* is dedicated to helping students learn about the foundation of the behavioral sciences, it is our responsibility to shine a light on this history and help illuminate a more inclusive path forward.

We use inclusive language, even if original texts do not. Language evolves and changes over time. In *Methods of Behavioral Research*, we describe some classic studies in the behavioral sciences. We will often modify the language used in those studies to reflect an inclusive sensibility. We are guided by the American Psychological Association's Inclusive Language Guidelines because we agree that, "by embracing inclusive language… we firmly believe that we will not only communicate effectively with more people but also better adapt to a diversifying society and globe" (American Psychological Association, 2021b). We also laud the APA's conceptualization of this living document and believe that language guidelines—like language itself—change over time.

We engage with diversity, equity, and inclusion. When discussing studies, we will describe their limitations regarding diversity, equity, and inclusion. One of the essential concepts in behavioral science—the idea that a study can be generalized beyond the population studied—will be emphasized when we talk about research. We will be careful about discussing a study conducted at a specific time and place with a particular group of research participants. When describing one of psychology's most famous studies, the Milgram obedience studies, we note that Milgram's sample mainly consisted of White people from New England. And we will draw attention to replications that expand those findings beyond their narrow origin.

We cite research conducted with diverse populations and researchers from diverse backgrounds. Research has not always represented diverse viewpoints (Roberts et al., 2020). We will not always succeed—behavioral science has a long way to go before it can represent the diversity of humanity—but we are trying (Buchanan, 2021). We foreground research conducted with diverse people by researchers who represent the diversity of humanity—such as Dr. Changwon Son and his colleagues, who studied the effects of COVID-19 on college students' mental health in the United States; or Drs. Aurino, Wolf, and Tsinigo's (2020) study of household food insecurity and early childhood development in Ghana, Africa; and Dr. Nada Goodrum and her colleagues' longitudinal study of mothers' disclosure of their HIV status to their children (Goodrum et al., 2021).

This book is a product of its authors and their environment. We welcome feedback and hope you will reach out to us directly if you have a critique, suggestion, or thought.

Contents

FUNDAMENTAL RESEARCH ISSUES   83

MEASUREMENT CONCEPTS   111

14 GENERALIZATION 326

Preface

Methods in Behavioral Research guides students toward success by helping them study smarter and more efficiently. Supported by SmartBook®, McGraw Hill's adaptive and personalized reading experience, this Fifteenth Edition provides helpful pedagogy, rich examples, and a clear voice in its approach to methodological decision making.

In this Fifteenth Edition, we strive for an accessible presentation and continue looking for opportunities to drive home foundational concepts and reinforce students' understanding of the material. We have reimagined end-of-chapter content. We chose concepts that students have traditionally found most challenging and designed exercises that ask them to reflect, recall, and organize the material. We have also aligned with the *Publication Manual of the American Psychological Association* (7th ed.). Focused organization combined with clear and direct writing remains a hallmark of *Methods in Behavioral Research*. Chapters follow the arc of a research investigation, from planning through conducting and presenting.

ORGANIZATION

Methods in Behavioral Research moves carefully through the major concepts in behavioral research, from the foundations of scientific study through practical issues in research design and implementation.

"Scientific Understanding of Behavior" grounds students in the scientific approach, emphasizing the distinction between basic and applied research. "Where to Start" discusses sources of ideas for research and the importance of library research. "Ethics in Behavioral Research" focuses on research ethics; ethical issues are covered in depth here and emphasized throughout the book. "Fundamental Research Issues" introduces validity and examines psychological variables and the distinction between experimental and nonexperimental approaches to studying relationships among variables. "Measurement Concepts" focuses on measurement issues, including reliability and validity. Nonexperimental research approaches—including naturalistic observation, case studies, and content analysis—are described in "Observational Methods." "Asking People About Themselves: Survey Research" covers sampling as well as the design of questionnaires and interviews. "Experimental Design" and "Conducting Experiments" present the basics of designing and conducting experiments. Factorial designs are emphasized in "Complex Experimental Designs." "Single-Case, Quasi-Experimental, and

Developmental Research" discusses the designs for special applications: single-case experimental designs, developmental research designs, and quasi-experimental designs. "Understanding Research Results: Description and Correlation" and "Understanding Research Results: Statistical Inference" focus on the use of statistics to help students understand research results. These chapters include material on effect size and confidence intervals. Finally, "Generalization" discusses external validity, meta-analyses, open science, and the importance of replications.

FEATURES

Methods in Behavioral Research includes the following features to enhance learning:

NEW! APA Style Resources. New, easy-to-use guides on APA style formatting for the title page, page and section format, citations, and the reference page. The title page guide includes both professional and student versions. The citations guide includes how-to guides for many common in-text and parenthetical citations as well as formats for commonly used sources. The page and section guide guides students through APA headers, font choices, margins, and running heads. The reference page guide includes global formatting as well as source-level formatting.

NEW! Sample Paper. A new, fully annotated sample paper—written by an undergraduate researcher—provides an accessible example of good APA style. Annotation points to common questions and common misperceptions and connects students back to the APA Style Resources sections for additional information. The new sample paper and annotations were designed to be easy to use in both e-book and print formats.

Engaging with Research. This feature has been refined to include authors from diverse backgrounds and topic-of-study that reflect the diversity of the behavioral sciences. These boxes include published journal articles with questions and exercises designed to focus on chapter-related material. In addition, the articles help students become familiar with the structure and language of journal articles in psychology. Most important, we have provided links to online copies of the articles whenever possible.

Being a Skilled Consumer of Research. These exercises are designed to get students out of the textbook and out of their classrooms and into the broader world in which we all move. These exercises ask students to look at examples of research—such as studies on the predictors of happiness and the causes and effects of sitting in the front of the classroom—to compare what they've learned in class or the text with what they see. Applying the concepts they have learned will help them expand their understanding of the content.

Fully updated according to the Publication Manual of the American Psychological Association (7th ed.): This edition includes and supports new guidelines on ethical and bias-free writing, adopts the new standard for in-text citations, updates rules for manuscript formatting, and adopts the APA's final resolution to the eternal question: One space or two after a period? (Answer: One!)

Check Your Learning: Practice Exercises. In previous editions, these Check Your Learning boxes were placed within the body of the chapter. We learned that students often found this placement distracting and preferred to be able to control when to complete the exercises. Feature includes an in-text callout to place the content; the actual exercises and answers are at the end of the chapter.

Solid pedagogy. Each chapter opens with a set of learning objectives that serve as reading guides and ends with a review of major concepts and key terms.

Practical examples. Thought-provoking examples help students interpret challenging concepts and complex research designs. For instance, the concept of diversity of ideas is examined through the lens of biases regarding rap music, and theory article formats are introduced by discussion of a recent study on suicide.

Emphasis on decision-making. Distinguishing among a variety of research designs helps students understand when to use one type of design over another.

FLEXIBLE

Chapters are designed to work independently, so that they can be adapted to any curriculum or syllabus. Sections are clearly defined, and relevant practice exercises are called out within each, making it easy to reorder or skip topics.

In addition, two appendices related to communicating research findings and conducting statistical analyses can be used at any time throughout the course. Appendix A includes an annotated version of a published paper and provides firm instructions for organizing research. Appendix B includes a bank of statistical tests that can be applied to a variety of research designs.

Methods in Behavioral Research is available to instructors and students in traditional print format as well as online within McGraw Hill Connect, a digital assignment and assessment platform. Connect includes assignable and assessable videos, quizzes, exercises, and interactive activities, all associated with learning objectives for *Methods in Behavioral Research.* These online tools make managing assignments easier for instructors, and learning and studying more motivating and efficient for students.

Power of Process, available in Connect for Research Methods, guides students through the process of critical reading, analysis, and writing. Faculty can select or upload their own content, such as journal articles, and assign analysis strategies to gain insight into students' application of the scientific method. For students, Power of Process offers a guided visual approach to exercising critical thinking strategies to apply before, during, and after reading published research.

Power of Process for
PSYCHOLOGY

A PERSONALIZED EXPERIENCE THAT LEADS TO IMPROVED LEARNING AND RESULTS

Students study more effectively with Connect and SmartBook. How many students think they know everything about introductory psychology, but struggle on the first exam?

With more than a decade of collecting data from billions of questions answered across 90+ disciplines, we've learned a lot about adaptive learning's impact on student performance. We've created a secure space for learning that balances intentional rigor with the freedom to make mistakes. This is an environment that develops self-awareness through meaningful, immediate feedback that improves student success. SmartBook builds on our market-leading technology with enhanced capabilities that deliver a more personalized, productive, and accessible learning experience for students and instructors.

SmartBook helps students study more efficiently by highlighting what to focus on in the chapter, asking review questions, and directing them to resources until they understand. SmartBook creates a personalized study path customized to individual student needs, continually adapting to pinpoint knowledge gaps and focus learning on concepts requiring additional study. By taking the guess-work out of what to study, SmartBook fosters more productive learning and helps students better prepare for class. With SmartBook, instructors have the flexibility to tailor assignments to their courses. Pick the topics, depth of coverage, or even the length of time students spend on an assignment. SmartBook assignments can help students build foundational knowledge, while review assignments can focus on multiple chapters or previously assigned concepts to help students prepare for exams.

With McGraw Hill's free ReadAnywhere app, students can read or study when it's convenient for them—anytime, anywhere. Available for iOS or Android smartphones or tablets, ReadAnywhere gives users access to McGraw Hill tools, including the eBook and SmartBook in Connect. Students can take notes, highlight, and complete assignments offline, and their work will sync when they open the app with WiFi access. SmartBook also provides a more accessible student experience with improved color contrast, descriptions for images, increased keyboard navigation, and enhanced screen reader support. Work is ongoing to improve the user experience for all.

POWERFUL REPORTING

Whether a class is face-to-face, hybrid, or entirely online, McGraw Hill Connect provides the tools needed to reduce the amount of time and energy instructors spend administering their courses. Easy-to-use course management tools allow instructors to spend less time administering and more time teaching, while reports allow students to monitor their progress and optimize their study time.

- The **At-Risk Student Report** provides instructors with one-click access to a dashboard that identifies students who are at risk of dropping out of the course due to low engagement levels.
- The **Category Analysis Report** details student performance relative to specific learning objectives and goals, including APA learning goals and outcomes and levels of Bloom's taxonomy.
- **The SmartBook Reports** allow instructors and students to easily monitor progress and pinpoint areas of weakness, giving each student a personalized study plan to achieve success.

ADDITIONAL RESOURCES

Achieve simplicity in assigning and engaging your students with course materials. Craft your teaching resources to match the way you teach! With McGraw Hill Create, you can easily rearrange chapters, combine material from other content sources, and quickly upload content you have written, such as your course syllabus or teaching notes. Find the content you need in Create by searching through thousands of leading McGraw Hill textbooks. Arrange your book to fit your teaching style. Create even allows you to personalize your book's appearance by selecting the cover and adding your name, school, and course information. Order a Create book and you'll receive a complimentary electronic review copy (eComp) via email in about an hour. Experience how McGraw Hill Create empowers you to teach your students *your* way: http://create.mheducation.com

CONTENT CHANGES IN THE FIFTEENTH EDITION

The Fifteenth Edition of *Methods in Behavioral Research* reflects global and specific chapter level changes.

Global changes

- We've adopted APA's inclusive language guidelines.
- We engage with diversity, equity, and inclusion in examples.
- We cite research conducted with diverse populations and researchers from diverse backgrounds.
- Engaging with Research was refined to include authors from diverse backgrounds and topics of study that reflect the diversity of the behavioral sciences.
- Appendix A was significantly revised to focus on usability for students: new sections related to APA style (7th edition) were created, and a new sample paper was designed to connect students to APA style guidelines and help them learn effective APA style writing.
- Being a Skilled Consumer of Research was refined to specifically enhance critical thinking skills.

Chapter 1

- "Being a Skilled Consumer of Research" has been revised to include eight key questions to help students evaluate "any research study that will reveal a lot about how much the study should be trusted."
- Repositioned "Engaging with Research" chapter-ending features are explained in chapter 1 and align with the eight questions to ask of a study to be a Being a Skilled Consumer of Research.
- The new "Engaging with Research" chapter feature is a study of ethnic variation in gratitude and well-being, and asks students to evaluate this study using the eight questions that lead to being a skilled consumer of research.

Chapter 2

- Analysis of the impact of the pandemic on research and academic conferences.
- A new key example related to Latina identity safety in STEM environments anchors the chapter.

Chapter 3

- Discussion on how exploitation of minority groups in research has contributed to COVID-19 vaccine resistance.

- Explanation of the informed consent procedure used in the Milgram study, which allowed for participants to withdraw at any time without penalty.
- Description of the Greenspan and Loftus (2021) study on misinformation and "enhanced debriefing."
- Examination of "debriefing" as a researcher's obligation to treat participants with dignity and respect.
- Significantly revised section on Research with Nonhuman Animal Subjects.

Chapter 4

- Several new examples, including Schreer's 2009 study of how Black customers were subject to suspicion in a customer scenario, Weijers and de Koning's 2021 study of how subjects reacted to varying reminders to sanitize hands. Guntzviller et al. 2020 found that stress is related to poor mental health among young adult Hispanics and that social support can help mitigate the effects of stress.
- Expanded discussion of predictive validity, with the construct of "grit" as an example.
- New Engaging with Research study examining workplace discrimination using a "lost email" experiment (Agerström et al., 2021).

Chapter 5

- A new section, *Measurement Validity: For Whom*, focuses on measurement validity across populations in an effort to draw attention to measurement biases that intersect with the diversity of study populations.

Chapter 6

- A significantly revised section introducing qualitative and quantitative approaches.
- Discussion of the Goodrum et al. 2021 study using mixed-methods research design to study what happens after mothers diagnosed with HIV disclose their HIV status to their children.
- A new section on Sampling Behaviors and Experiences describes the Experience Sampling Method (ESM) and Day Reconstruction Method (DRM).
- Description of the Halstead et al. 2021 study on PTSD resulting from racial discrimination and sexual abuse during childhood.
- Definition of *psychobiography* as a case study in which the researcher applies psychological theory to explain the life of a historical figure.
- Discussion of Stout et al. 2020 study that tried two different mentors for recruiting Black and non-Hispanic White older adults for research investigation on Alzheimer's disease.

- Explanation of the National Longitudinal Mortality Study as a database for studying the effects of demographic and socioeconomic characteristics on mortality rates.
- New examples of archival research studies using written, audio, and video records: Kruspe et al. (2020), who analyzed Twitter messages during the first months of the COVID-19 pandemic; Corbett and Savarimuthu (2022), who analyzed 6,528 tweets about sustainable energy; Trivedi et al. (2021), who examined suicide prevention using Google-search trends; and Lewis et al. (2020), who analyzed the content of books for young children to detect and quantify gender biases.
- The new Engaging with Research study examines meal service and feeding practices among Mexican American fathers and mothers (Penilla et al., 2022).

Chapter 7

- Updated section on using pictorial scales in behavioral research.
- New information on conducting surveys in large randomly selected samples, especially online, and the Pew Research Center's *American Trends Panel*.
- Discussion of the McBride et al. (2021) study on the impact of concerns about climate change on psychological well-being.
- Explanation of convenience samples through online participant recruitment services such as Amazon Mechanical Turk and Prolific.
- The new "Engaging with Research" study examines the effects of COVID-19 on U.S. college students' mental health (Son et al., 2020).

Chapter 8

- Discussion of education reform, especially emphasis on STEM and the Educational Robotics approach and its impact on cognitive development.
- A new example of the Solomon four-group design studied the effect of an intervention to promote responsible substance use, safe sex, and other positive behaviors in a diverse sample of 18- to 24-year-olds experiencing homelessness (Rew et al. 2022).
- Debate on the manipulation check as a potential demand characteristic that alerts subjects to the study's purpose.
- The new Engaging with Research study examines executive functions in 5- and 6-year-old typically developing children through educational robotics in a randomized control trial study (Di Lieto et al., 2020).

Chapter 9

- Examination of the methods used to study memory and cognition, including the Cushing and Bodner 2022 study on improving proofreading accuracy.

- Hies and Lewis (2022) used a face database to obtain stimuli for a study on perceptions of people wearing masks during the COVID pandemic.
- Forrin et al. (2021) studied whether and how the behavior of one student in a learning situation might affect the behavior of another. They proposed that inattention (or attention) to learning could spread, a phenomenon called "attention contagion."
- Randall et al. (2017) investigated weight discrimination in a field experiment conducted on a college campus.
- Wang et al. (2021) used a technology called the Contain Intelligent Facial Expression Recognition System (CIFERS) to explore real-time emotions (joy and anxiety) of college students.
- De Vita et al. (2021) conducted research to examine the pain-reducing effects of cannabidiol (CBD) and determine the degree to which observed pain reduction is due to the effects of CBD as opposed to the psychological expectancies associated with this substance.
- Introduction of the "examiner" expectancy effect using the Sodos et al. 2018 study in which examiners first rated whether or not they believed an examinee was a cannabis user.
- Discussion of the debate about the use of manipulation checks (Ejelöv and Luke, 2020; Hauser et al., 2018). One concern is that the manipulation check might serve as a demand characteristic, alerting subjects to the purpose of the study.
- A new section on Open Science and Preregistration.
- The new Engaging with Research study examines Instagram influencer posts using eye-tracking technology to see how specific tags on posts (#ad versus #sponsored) would impact people's visual attention to those ads (Klein et al., 2020).

Chapter 10

- A new example of a mixed factorial design. Pan et al. (2020), for example, were interested in identifying factors that might help college students pay attention to the material presented in a recorded lecture.
- A new Engaging with Research study reported on an experiment with Instagram users in the United States to test whether hiding "likes" would affect the users' mood and loneliness (Wallace and Buil, 2020).

Chapter 11

- Enhanced discussion of the ex post facto design and selection differences that can arise.
- Discussion of the Rathje et al. (2021) study on empathy

- The new Engaging with Research Study (Aurino et al., 2020) reported on a longitudinal study of children in Ghana, in sub-Saharan Africa.

Chapter 12

- Significantly revised section on multiple correlation and regression.
- A new section on mediating and moderating variables.
- A revised section on advanced statistics that creates a gentle introduction to the more sophisticated statistical approaches that students see in recently published work.

Chapter 14

- A deeply revised section on Generalizing Across People that focuses on identities (including sex, gender, sexual orientation, race, and ethnicity) and culture, threats to external validity.
- A deeply revised section on Generalizing Across Situations focuses on research conducted in a laboratory setting and researcher expectancy effects.
- A new example of meta-analysis that examined the effectiveness of psychotherapy delivered remotely for children and adolescents (Venturo-Conerly et al., 2022).
- A new book-ending section, Using Research to Improve Lives, frames the behavioral sciences in terms of "There is a lot of work left to do" and our hope that students "feel more prepared to do it."
- The new Engaging with Research study investigated the experiences of economically disadvantaged mothers during the COVID-19 pandemic (Haskett et al., 2022).

Appendix A

- Updated and aligned with the *Publication Manual of the American Psychological Association* (7th ed.).
- An enhanced organization designed to provide useful and accessible resources for students as they learn to write in APA style.
- The section Avoiding Biased Language now refers to the APA *Inclusive Language Guidelines* (APA, 2021b).
- A new annotated sample paper—written by an undergraduate—provides an accessible example of good APA style.
- New APA Style Resources pages provide students will easy-to-use guidance on the title page, page and section format, citations, and the reference page.

INSTRUCTOR RESOURCES

Methods in Behavioral Research also includes the following instructor resources:

Instructor's Manual: Designed to provide a wide variety of resources for presenting the course, the instructor's manual includes learning objectives, ideas for lectures and discussions, laboratory demonstrations, and activities aligned specifically to facilitate a clearer knowledge of research methods.

Test Bank: By increasing the rigor of the test bank development process, McGraw Hill has raised the bar for student assessment. A coordinated team of subject-matter experts methodically vetted each question and each set of possible answers for accuracy, clarity, and effectiveness. Each question is further annotated for level of page difficulty, Bloom's taxonomy, APA learning outcomes, and corresponding coverage in the text. Structured by chapter, the questions are designed to test students' conceptual, applied, and factual understanding.

Test Builder: New to this edition and available within Connect, Test Builder is a cloud-based tool that enables instructors to format tests that can be printed or administered within a Learning Management System. Test Builder offers a modern, streamlined interface for easy content configuration that matches course needs, without requiring a download.

Test Builder enables instructors to:

- Access all test bank content from a particular title
- Easily pinpoint the most relevant content through robust filtering options
- Manipulate the order of questions or scramble questions and / or answers
- Pin questions to a specific location within a test
- Determine your preferred treatment of algorithmic questions
- Choose the layout and spacing
- Add instructions and configure default settings

Lecture Presentation: Accessibility compliant, PowerPoint slides are provided that present key points of the chapter, along with supporting visuals. All of the slides can be modified to meet individual needs.

Image Gallery: The complete set of figures and tables from the text are available for download and can be easily embedded into PowerPoint slides.

Remote proctoring and browser-locking capabilities: Hosted by Proctorio within Connect, remote proctoring provides control of the assessment environment by enabling security options and verifying the identity of the student. Seamlessly integrated within Connect, these services allow instructors to control students' assessment experience by restricting browser activity, recording students' activity, and verifying students are doing their own work. Instant and detailed reporting gives instructors an at-a-glance view of potential academic integrity concerns, thereby avoiding personal bias and supporting evidence-based claims.

Writing Assignment: The Writing Assignment tool delivers a learning experience to help students improve their written communication skills and conceptual understanding. As an instructor you can assign, monitor, grade, and provide feedback on writing more efficiently and effectively

ACKNOWLEDGMENTS

Many individuals helped to produce this and previous editions of this book. The portfolio manager at McGraw Hill was Jason Seitz; we are also indebted to the editors of previous editions, Franklin Graham, Ken King, Mike Sugarman, and Krista Bettino, for their guidance. We are extremely grateful for the input from numerous students and instructors:

Marina Bornovalova
University of South Florida

Kristy Boyce
The Ohio State University

Blaine Browne
Valdosta State University

Robert Christman
Mohawk Valley Community College

Emily Cohen-Shikora
Washington University at St. Louis

Paul Curran
Grand Valley State University

Robert O. Deaner
Grand Valley State University

Christopher Dickinson
Appalachian State University

Melanie Domenech Rodríguez
Utah State University

Dana S. Dunn
Moravian College

Mario Fific
Grand Valley State University

Stephen Gabbard
Wright State University, Dayton

Leslie A. Gill
Eastern New Mexico University

Suzanne Helfer
Adrian College

Charles M. Huffman
Georgia Southwestern State University

Christopher Howard
Husson University

Ashley Jordan
University of Arizona

Ruthellen Josselson
Society for Qualitative Inquiry in Psychology The Fielding Graduate University

Jeff Kibler
Nova Southeastern University

Cecile Lardon
University of Alaska Fairbanks

Mindy Ma
Nova Southeastern University

Hajime Otani
Central Michigan University

Mary K. Radeke
Central Washington University

Theodore M. Singelis
California State University, Chico

Lynda Villaneuva
University of Houston

About the Authors

Paul C. Cozby is Emeritus Professor of Psychology at California State University, Fullerton. Dr. Cozby was an undergraduate at the University of California, Riverside, and received his PhD in psychology from the University of Minnesota. He is a fellow of the American Psychological Association and a member of the Association for Psychological Science. He served as an officer of the Society for Computers in Psychology and as Executive Officer of the Western Psychological Association. He is the author of *Using Computers in the Behavioral Sciences* and co-editor with Daniel Perlman of *Social Psychology*.

Scott C. Bates is a Professor and Department Head of the Psychology Department at Utah State University in Logan, Utah. He earned a BS in Psychology from Whitman College, an MS in Psychology from Western Washington University, and a PhD in social psychology from Colorado State University. His research interests and experiences are varied. He has conducted research in areas as wide-ranging as adolescent problem behavior and problem-behavior prevention, teaching and learning in higher education, and the psychological consequences of growing and tending plants in outer space.

We are always interested in receiving comments and suggestions from students and instructors. Please email us at scott.bates@usu.edu or cozby@fullerton.edu.

fizkes/Shutterstock

1

Scientific Understanding of Behavior

LEARNING OBJECTIVES

- Describe why it is essential to understand research methods.
- Explain the scientific approach to learning about behavior and be able to compare and contrast it with other ways of knowing.
- Identify and explain key features of the scientific approach to understanding behavior, and be able to compare and contrast it with a pseudoscientific approach.
- Describe and give examples of the four goals of scientific research: description, prediction, determination of cause, and explanation of behavior.
- Summarize the three elements for inferring causation: temporal order, covariation of cause and effect, and elimination of alternative explanations. Be able to generate an example.
- Determine if a study is basic or applied research.

DOES INSTAGRAM IMPACT HOW WE FEEL ABOUT OURSELVES? Why do we help some people in need and not others? How do our early childhood experiences affect our later lives? What causes depression? Why do some people experience anxiety so intense that it disrupts their lives? What is the impact of racism? How is gender identity formed? What can we do to promote human flourishing?

Students often cite a curiosity about questions like these as their motivation for taking courses in the behavioral sciences. Science is the best way to explore and answer these sorts of questions. In this book, we examine scientific research methods in the behavioral sciences. This introductory chapter will focus on how knowledge of research methods can help us understand the world around us. We will also review the characteristics of a scientific approach to studying behavior and some general types of research studies that behavioral scientists conduct.

CONSUMING RESEARCH

Newspapers, television, and websites are daily sources of information about the latest research on human and even animal behavior. You might have seen these articles in the New York Times: "Does Instagram Harm Girls? No One Actually Knows," or "An Overlooked Cure for Loneliness." A headline in theweek.com is intriguing: "Your Dog Yawns When You Yawn Because He Loves You." Cable news CNN shows us "How to become more resilient, according to the research." Frequent reports of survey results describe people's views on various topics ranging from politics to the economy, health, education, and the environment. And you might wonder if your grandfather might benefit from a "brain training" app advertised to improve cognitive functioning.

The critical question is: How do you evaluate such reports? Do you accept the information because they are supposed to be scientific? A background in research methods will help you read these reports critically, evaluate the methods employed, and decide whether the conclusions are reasonable. Learning about research methods will help you think critically; learning about research methods will help you be a skilled consumer of research.

Why Learn about Research Methods?

Learning about research methods is essential for many reasons. First, many professions use research findings. For example, mental health professionals must make decisions about treatment methods, medications, and testing procedures. Such decisions are made using research findings; to make good decisions, mental health professionals must be able to read the research literature in the field and apply it to their professional lives. Similarly, people working in business environments frequently rely on research to make decisions about marketing strategies, ways of improving employee productivity and morale, and methods of selecting and training new employees. Educators must keep up with research on topics such as the effectiveness of various teaching strategies or programs to deal with special student problems. It is useful to know research methods and the ability to evaluate research reports in many fields.

It is also important to recognize that scientific research has become increasingly prominent in public policy decisions. Legislators and political leaders at all levels of government frequently take political positions and propose legislation based on research findings. Research may also influence judicial decisions: A classic example is the *Social Science Brief* prepared by psychologists and accepted as evidence in the landmark 1954 case *Brown v. Board of Education,* in which the U.S. Supreme Court banned school segregation in the United States. One of the studies cited in the brief was conducted by Clark and Clark (1947), who found that when allowed to choose between light-skinned and dark-skinned dolls, both Black and White children preferred to play with the light-skinned dolls (see Stephan, 1983, for a further discussion of the implications of this classic study).

Behavioral research on human development has influenced U.S. Supreme Court decisions related to juvenile crime. In 2005, for instance, the Supreme Court decided that juveniles could not face the death penalty (*Roper v. Simmons*), and the decision was informed by neurological and behavioral research showing that in juveniles, the level of development of their brains, social relationships, and character make juveniles less culpable than adults for the same crimes. Similarly, in 2010, in *Graham v. Florida,* the U.S. Supreme Court decided that juvenile offenders could not be sentenced to life without parole for nonhomicide offenses. This decision was influenced by research in developmental psychology and neuroscience. The Court majority pointed to this research in their conclusion that assessment of blame and standards for sentencing should be different for juveniles and adults because juveniles lack adults' maturity, ability to resist pressures from peers and others, and personal sense of responsibility (Clay, 2010).

Research is also important when developing and assessing the effectiveness of programs designed to achieve specific goals—for example, improving high school graduation rates in a community, influencing people to be vaccinated, teaching employees how to reduce the effects of stress, or making a workplace welcoming and productive for everybody. We need to determine whether these sorts of programs are successfully meeting their goals.

Finally, research methods are important because they can provide us with the best way to find answers to questions like those we posed at the outset of this chapter. Research methods can be the way to satisfy our native curiosity about ourselves, our world, and those around us.

WAYS OF KNOWING

We opened this chapter with several questions about human behavior and suggested that scientific research is a valuable means of answering them. There are, of course, other ways of knowing. People have always observed the world around them and sought explanations for what they see and experience. So, the question must be asked: How does the scientific approach differ from other ways of learning about behavior?

Intuition

People planning to adopt after unsuccessful attempts to become pregnant often report that friends and co-workers say that the adoption will soon be followed by a pregnancy. Pregnancy does sometimes follow adoption, and can lead to the belief that adoption increases the likelihood of pregnancy for people who are having difficulties conceiving a child. People who hold this belief usually go one step further and offer an explanation for this effect—such as, that the adoption reduces a major source of stress, and the stress reduction, in turn, increases the chances of conception (see Gilovich, 1991).

This example illustrates the use of **intuition** and anecdotal evidence to draw general conclusions about the world around us. When you rely on intuition, you accept unquestioningly what your own personal judgment or a single story (anecdote) about one person's experience tells you. The intuitive approach takes many forms. Often it involves finding an explanation for our own behaviors or the behaviors of others. For example, you might develop an explanation for why you keep having conflicts with your roommate, such as "My roommate hates me" or "Having to share a bathroom creates conflict." Other times, intuition is used to explain events that you observe, as in the case of concluding that adoption increases the chances of conception for people who are having difficulty conceiving a child.

A problem with intuition is that numerous cognitive and motivational biases affect our perceptions, and so we may draw erroneous conclusions about cause and effect (cf. Fiske & Taylor, 2021; Gilovich, 1991). Gilovich points out that there is in fact no relationship between adoption and subsequent pregnancy, according to scientific research investigations. So why do we hold this belief? Most likely it is because of a cognitive bias called *illusory correlation* that occurs when we focus on two events that stand out and occur together. When an adoption is closely followed by a pregnancy, our attention is drawn to the situation, and we are biased to conclude that there must be a causal connection. Such illusory correlations are also likely to occur when we are highly motivated to believe in the causal relationship. Although this is a natural thing for us to do, it is not scientific. A scientific approach requires much more evidence before conclusions can be drawn.

Authority

Humans are often persuaded by those in **authority**. The philosopher Aristotle said: "We believe good men more fully and readily than others." The obvious exclusion of more than half of humanity aside, Aristotle would argue that we are more likely to be persuaded by a speaker who seems prestigious, trustworthy, and respectable than by one who appears to lack such qualities.

Many of us might accept Aristotle's arguments simply because *he* is considered a prestigious authority—a convincing and influential source—and his writings remain important. Similarly, many people are all too ready to accept anything they learn from the internet, news media, books, government officials, celebrities, religious figures, or even a professor because they believe that statements made by such authorities must be true.

The problem, of course, is that the statements might not be true. The scientific approach rejects the notion that one can accept *on faith* the statements of any authority; again, more evidence is needed before we can draw scientific conclusions.

Empiricism

The scientific approach to acquiring knowledge recognizes that intuition, anecdote, and authority can be sources of ideas about behavior. However, scientists do not unquestioningly accept anyone's intuitions—including their own. Scientists recognize that *their* ideas are just as likely to be wrong as anyone else's. Also, scientists do not accept on faith anyone's pronouncements, regardless of that person's prestige or authority. Thus, scientists are very skeptical about what they see and hear. Scientific skepticism means that ideas must be evaluated on the basis of careful logic and results from well-executed scientific investigations.

If scientists reject intuition and blind acceptance of authority as ways of knowing about the world, how do they go about gaining knowledge? How does the scientist know anything?

The fundamental characteristic of the scientific approach is **empiricism**—the idea that knowledge comes from observations. Data are collected and analyzed, and the data form the basis of conclusions about the nature of the world. The scientific method embodies a number of rules for collecting and evaluating data; these rules will be explored throughout this book.

The Scientific Approach

The power of the scientific approach can be seen all around us. Whether you look at biology, chemistry, medicine, physics, anthropology, or psychology, you will see amazing advances over the past 5, 25, 50, or 100 years. We have a greater understanding of the world around us, and the applications of that understanding have kept pace. Goodstein (2000) describes an "evolved theory of science" that defines the characteristics of scientific inquiry. These characteristics are summarized below.

- **Data play a central role.** For scientists, knowledge is primarily based on observations. Scientists enthusiastically search for observations that will verify or reject their ideas about the world. They develop theories, argue that existing data support their theories, and conduct research that can increase our confidence that the theories are correct. Observations can be criticized, alternatives can be suggested, and data collection methods can be called into question. But in each of these cases, the role of data is central and fundamental. Scientists have a "show me, don't tell me" attitude.

- **Scientists are not alone.** Scientists make observations and are trained to accurately report to other scientists and the public. You can be sure that many other scientists will follow up on the findings by conducting research that replicates and extends these observations.

- **Science is adversarial.** Science is a way of thinking in which ideas do battle with other ideas in order to move ever closer to the truth. Research can be conducted to test any idea; supporters of the idea and those who disagree with the idea can report their research findings, and these can be evaluated by others. Some ideas, even some very good ideas, may prove to be wrong if the research fails to provide support for them. Good scientific ideas are testable, which means that they can be either supported or falsified by data—the latter concept is called **falsifiability** (Popper, 2002). If an idea is falsified when it is tested, science advances because this result can spur the development of new and better ideas.

- **Scientific evidence does not rely solely on authority—it is peer-reviewed.** Before a study is published in a top-quality scientific journal, it is reviewed by other scientists who have the expertise to carefully evaluate the research. This process is called **peer review.** The role of these reviewers is to recommend whether the research should be published. This review process ensures that research with major flaws will not become part of the scientific literature. In essence, science exists in a free market of ideas in which the best ideas are supported by research, and scientists can build upon the research of others to make further advances.

Skepticism

The advantage of the scientific approach over other ways of knowing about the world is that it provides an objective set of rules for gathering, evaluating, and reporting observations. It is an open system that allows ideas to be refuted or supported by other scientists, with other data. This does not mean that intuition, anecdote, and authority are unimportant, however. As noted previously, scientists often rely on intuition and assertions of authorities for ideas for research. Moreover, there is nothing wrong with accepting the assertions of an authority as long as we do not accept them as scientific evidence. Scientific evidence is not obtainable for many things, such as certain beliefs that religious figures or texts ask us to accept on faith. Some beliefs cannot be tested and thus are beyond the scope of science. In science, however, ideas must be evaluated on the basis of available evidence that can be used to support or refute the ideas.

There is also nothing wrong with having opinions or beliefs as long as they are presented simply as opinions or beliefs. However, we should always ask whether the opinion can be tested scientifically or whether scientific evidence exists that relates to the opinion. For example, opinions on whether exposure to violent movies, TV, and video games increases aggression are only opinions until scientific evidence on the issue is gathered.

As you learn more about scientific methods, you will become increasingly **skeptical** of the research results reported in the media and the assertions of scientists as well. You should be aware that scientists often become authorities when they express their ideas. When someone claims to be a scientist, should we be more willing to accept what they say? First, ask about the individual's credentials.

It is usually wise to pay more attention to someone with an established reputation in the field and attend to the reputation of the institution represented by the person. It is also worthwhile to examine the researcher's funding source; you might be a bit suspicious when research funded by a drug company supports the effectiveness of a drug manufactured by that company, for example. Similarly, when an organization with a particular social-political agenda funds the research that supports that agenda, you should be skeptical of the findings and closely examine the methods of the study. In fact, you should always closely examine the methods of studies!

You should also be skeptical of pseudoscientific research. **Pseudoscience** is the use of seemingly scientific terms and demonstrations to substantiate claims that are not based on scientific research. The claim may be that a product or procedure will enhance your memory, relieve depression, or treat autism or post-traumatic stress disorder. The fact that these are all worthy outcomes makes us very susceptible to believing pseudoscientific claims and forgetting to ask whether there is a valid scientific basis for the claims.

A good example comes from a procedure called *facilitated communication* that has been used by therapists working with children with severe autism. Some children with severe autism spectrum disorder lack verbal skills for communication; to help them communicate, a facilitator holds the child's hand while the child presses keys to type messages on a keyboard. This technique produces impressive results, indicating that the children are now able to express themselves. Of course, well-designed studies revealed that the facilitators, not the children, controlled the typing. The problem with all pseudoscience is that creates false hopes and makes promises that will not be fulfilled. Often the techniques can be dangerous as well. In the case of facilitated communication, a number of facilitators typed messages accusing a parent of physically or sexually abusing the child. Some parents were actually convicted of child abuse. In these legal cases, the scientific research on facilitated communication was used to help the defendant parent. Cases such as this have led to a movement to promote the exclusive use of evidence-based therapies—therapeutic interventions grounded in scientific research findings that demonstrate their effectiveness (Brown, 2016; cf. Lilienfeld et al., 2004).

So how can you tell if a claim is pseudoscientific? It is not easy. In fact, a philosopher of science noted that "the boundaries separating science, nonscience, and pseudoscience are much fuzzier and more permeable than ... most scientists ... would have us believe" (Pigliucci, 2010). Here are a few indicators that claims are not based on science:

- Claims that are untestable and therefore cannot be refuted
- Claims that rely on imprecise, biased, or vague language
- Evidence that is based on anecdotes and testimonials rather than scientific data
- Evidence that is from "experts" who have only vague qualifications and do not support their claims with sound scientific evidence

- Claims based only on confirmatory evidence, ignoring conflicting evidence
- Reliance on "scientific" evidence that cannot be independently verified because the methods used to establish that evidence have not been described

Finally, we are all increasingly susceptible to false reports of scientific findings circulated online. Many of these reports claim to be associated with a reputable scientist or scientific organization, and then they take on a life of their own. A widely covered report, supposedly from the World Health Organization, claimed that the gene for blond hair was being selected out of the human gene pool. Blond hair would be a disappearing trait! General rules to follow when reading internet sites: (1) Be highly skeptical of "scientific" assertions that are supported by only vague or improbable evidence. And (2) take the time to do an internet search for supportive evidence. At internet sites like snopes.com, truthorfiction.com, and fact-check.org/askscicheck/ you can check many of the claims that are on the internet.

BEING A SKILLED CONSUMER OF RESEARCH

How much trust we should place in a study depends upon the methods that were used to conduct the study. Sometimes study authors overreach, coming to conclusions that are not justified. Here are eight key questions you can ask of any research study that will reveal a lot about how much the study should be trusted. The better the answers to these questions, the more confident you can be of the study:

1. **"What is the primary goal of this study? Description, Prediction, Determining Cause, or Explaining? Do the authors achieve their goals?"** Every study has a goal. As you have seen in this chapter, the goals vary. For any study you read, it is important to try to understand the overall goal. Are the authors trying to describe a phenomenon? Are they trying to make a prediction? Are they trying to show that one thing causes another?
2. **"What did these researchers do? What was the method?"** Published research always includes a description of how the research was conducted. A skillful consumer of research will review a study's methodology carefully to see if the researchers' method is well connected to their goal.
3. **"What was measured?"** All studies in the behavioral sciences start with measurement: identifying the concepts to be studied and figuring out how to measure them. This is related to the idea of construct validity, which will be covered in depth in other chapters.
4. **"To what or whom can we generalize the results?"** Generalization involves making broad or general inferences based on the procedures and findings in a specific study. Humans are a very diverse species. Do results based on one population apply (generalize) to other populations? Are the methods that were used applicable to other settings? This is related to the concept of external validity, which will be covered in later chapters.

5. **"What did they find? What were the results?"** After a study author justifies what they are doing in the *Introduction* section and describes what they did in the *Method* section, they will spend time explaining what they found. It is easy to be intimated by complex statistics. In peer-reviewed research, you can assume that the analyses were probably correctly conducted, and you can attend more closely to "what they found" and not become bogged down in the statistics.

6. **"Have other researchers found similar results?"** A single study can be interesting, but scientific progress involves accumulating studies. We can be more confident in a study if other studies have found the same results.

7. **"What are the limitations of this study?"** Researchers will often include a statement about the limitations of a study—often in the *Discussion* section. You may be able to think of other limitations: Is there another variable at play? Is there a better measure of a variable? Can we generalization the results to other people?

8. **"What are the ethical issues present in this study?"** Every study of human and animal participants poses risks. As such, every study should be evaluated for the ethical treatment of its participants.

GOALS OF BEHAVIORAL SCIENCE

Scientific research on behavior is guided by four general goals: (1) description, (2) prediction, (3) determining causes, and (4) understanding or explanation.

Description

Description is the first goal of science. Psychologists and other behavioral scientists can describe behavior, which can often be directly observed (such as the amount of food consumed, running speed, eye gaze, or loudness of laughter), or mental states (such as happiness, sadness, or boredom), which are often less observable.

A group of researchers studied the amount of digital media use (screen use) by 5,412 adolescents in the United States during the COVID-19 pandemic (Nagata et al., 2022). The participants provided self-reports of screen time (excluding school-related activities)—watching television/streaming, playing games, social media, and so on. Figure 1 shows that the average number of hours of daily screen time for the entire sample was 7.70 hours. This finding illustrates description of behavior. The researchers next decided to separately describe screen use for participants categorized as Asian American, Hispanic/Latinx, Black, and White. As you can see, Asian American and White adolescents report fewer hours of screen time than do Blacks or Hispanic/Latinx. Further research would be needed to explain this finding; explanation is another goal of science.

Researchers are often interested in describing the ways in which events are systematically related to one another. Do the adolescents who report high amounts of screen use have a lower grade point average than peers who report less screen use?

FIGURE 1
Adolescent
screen time
use during
COVID-19
pandemic

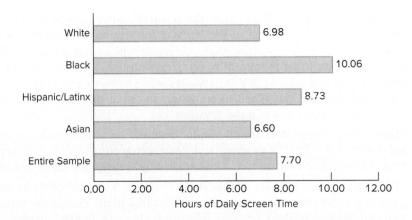

Do jurors judge physically attractive defendants more leniently than unattractive defendants? Are people more likely to be persuaded by a speaker who has high credibility? In what ways do cognitive abilities change as people grow older? Do children living in low-income households perform poorly in school? Do students who study in a room with a television on score lower on exams than students who study in a quiet environment?

Prediction

The second goal of behavioral science is to make accurate predictions. Once events have been shown to be related to one another—for example, that early-childhood poverty is related to lower school achievement—predictions can be made. Children growing up in poverty are predicted to have fewer indicators of academic achievement. It also becomes possible to make other, follow-on, predictions. If early-childhood poverty is related to school achievement, then it may predict educational attainment such as graduating from high school and adult income.

It is worth noting that such predictions are probabilistic; there is only a higher likelihood that a child in a low-income household will not be a high achiever in school. But many of those children will not fit that pattern. When thinking about any particular child, there is no way to be certain, based on low family income, that the child will or will not demonstrate achievement in school.

Determining Causes

The third goal of science is to determine the causes of behavior. Although we might accurately predict the occurrence of a behavior, we might not correctly identify its cause. Research shows that a child's aggressive behaviors can be partially predicted by knowing how much violence the child is exposed to via video games and television. Unfortunately, unless we know that exposure to screen violence is a cause of behavior, we cannot assert that aggressive behavior can be reduced by limiting time spent viewing scenes of violence. A child who is highly aggressive may prefer to watch violence when choosing video games and television programs. We are now confronting questions of cause and effect: To know how to change behavior, we need to know the causes of behavior.

There are three types of evidence used to identify the cause of behavior (Cook & Campbell, 1979). It is not enough to know that two events occur together, as in the case of knowing that viewing screen violence is a predictor of actual aggression. In the most simple case, where a change in one variable causes a change in another, three things must hold true (see Figure 2):

1. There is a temporal order of events in which the cause *precedes* the effect. This is called **temporal precedence.** Thus, we need to know that viewing violence occurred first and aggression followed.

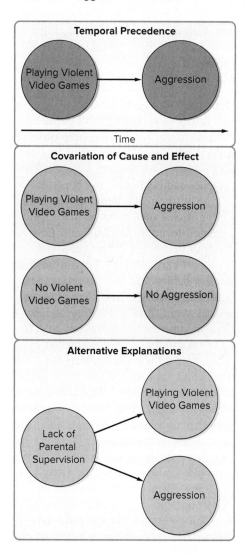

FIGURE 2
Determining cause and effect

2. When the cause is present, the effect occurs; when the cause is not present, the effect does not occur. This is called **covariation of cause and effect.** We need to know that children who watch television violence behave aggressively and that children who do not watch television violence do not behave aggressively.

3. Nothing other than a causal variable could be responsible for the observed effect. This is a process of eliminating **alternative explanations.** There should be no other plausible alternative explanation for the relationship. This third point about alternative explanations is very important: Suppose that the children who spend a lot of time viewing game and television violence are left alone more than are children who do not view screen violence. In this case, the increased aggression could have an alternative explanation: lack of parental supervision. Causation will be discussed again in other chapters.

Explaining Behavior

Even if we know that viewing screen violence causes aggression, we still need to explain this relationship. Is it due to becoming desensitized to violence? Is it learning that violence is a way to achieve goals? Further research is necessary to shed light on possible explanations of what has been observed. Usually, additional research like this is carried out by testing theories that are developed to explain particular behaviors.

The final goal of science is to explain—to understand why a behavior occurs. Consider the relationship between childhood poverty and school achievement (Duncan et al., 2010). One such explanation for the relationship between poverty and school success is related to brain development. Early childhood poverty has been observed in research to be related to structural and functional differences in parts of the brain that support skills that we rely on in school. If that's true, then we should see differences in babies' brains—poverty should impact brain development. A research project called Baby's First Years has set out to study just that. Over the course of several years, Troller-Renfree and her colleagues have been giving one group of low-income mothers $20 per month and another group of low-income mothers $333 per month (Troller-Renfree et al., 2022). These researchers are studying the impact of these cash transfers on babies' brains. They concluded that "monthly unconditional cash transfer given to low-income families may have a causal impact on infant brain activity." That is still not a complete explanation. Additional research is always necessary to build a complete explanatory case.

Description, prediction, determination of cause, and explanation are all closely intertwined. Determining cause and explaining behavior are particularly closely related because it is difficult ever to know the true cause or all the causes of any behavior. An explanation that appears satisfactory may turn out to be inadequate when other causes are identified in subsequent research.

In short, there is a certain amount of ambiguity in the enterprise of scientific inquiry. New research findings almost always pose new questions that must be addressed by further research; explanations of behavior often must be discarded or revised as new evidence is gathered. Such ambiguity is part of the excitement and fun of science.

Check Your Learning

Check Your Learning: Practice Exercise #1 gives you a chance to test your understanding of the distinctions among these four goals of science.

BASIC AND APPLIED RESEARCH

In this section, we will explore the differences and similarities between basic research, which tries to answer fundamental questions about the nature of behavior, and applied research, which addresses issues in which there are practical problems and potential solutions.

Basic Research

Basic research tries to answer fundamental questions about the nature of behavior. Studies are often designed to address theoretical issues concerning phenomena such as cognition, emotion, motivation, learning, personality, development, and social behavior. Here are descriptions of a few journal articles that pertain to some basic research questions:

> Brothers, T., & Traxler, M. J. (2016). Anticipating syntax during reading: Evidence from the boundary change paradigm. *Journal of Experimental Psychology: Learning, Memory, and Cognition, 42*(12), 1894–1906. https://doi.org/10.1037/xlm0000257
>
> When reading, you focus on text in the center of your visual field. However, you may also "preprocess" words that are just beyond the central focus; this is called the parafovea. This effect occurs even though the text lacks the clarity of the text in the center of the field of vision. The Brothers and Traxler (2016) study demonstrated that participants process not just the words in the parafovea but also their meaning. For example, sentences with valid syntax in the parafovea, such as "The admiral would not confess," were read more quickly than sentences with invalid syntax, such as "The admiral would not surgeon."
>
> Tierney, A., Patel, A. D., Jasmin, K., & Breen, M. (2021). Individual differences in perception of the speech-to-song illusion are linked to musical aptitude but not musical training. *Journal of Experimental Psychology: Human Perception and Performance, 47*(12), 1681–1697. https://doi.org/10.1037/xhp0000968
>
> The speech-to-song illusion occurs when a sequence of spoken words is heard as speech on the first presentation but is perceived as music after a few repetitions. Deutsch (2021) discusses this illusion and provides an example

using the phrase "sometimes behave so strangely." Research has demonstrated that individuals differ in the likelihood that they will report hearing the phrase as a song. Tierney et al. (2021) found that experiencing the illusion was not related to an individual's amount of musical training; however, those most likely to experience the phrase as music did possess several musical skills, including perception of beat and tonality.

Applied Research

The research articles listed above were concerned with basic processes of behavior and cognition rather than any immediate practical implications. In contrast, **applied research** is conducted to address issues in which there are practical problems and potential solutions. To illustrate, here are two summaries of journal articles about applied research:

Rosen, C. C., Simon, L. S., Gajendran, R. S., Johnson, R. E., Lee, H. W., & Lin, S.-H. (Joanna). (2019). Boxed in by your inbox: Implications of daily e-mail demands for managers' leadership behaviors. *Journal of Applied Psychology, 104*(1), 19–33. https://doi.org /10.1037/apl0000343

A common source of work stress is the overwhelming demands of incoming email messages. This study measured email demands among 48 managers enrolled in a university Executive Master of Business Administration program. Using the Experience Sampling Method (ESM), the researchers asked participants to complete two surveys each day for 10 consecutive workdays. The first survey arrived at the end of the morning and asked about the morning email demands and the manager's progress in meeting work goals up to that point in the day. Another survey at the end of the day measured the extent to which the managers had engaged in behaviors reflecting outstanding leadership. As predicted, higher morning email demands were related to perceptions of lower goal progress. And the end-of-day surveys revealed that the morning demands were associated with fewer leadership behaviors.

Mekawi, Y., Carter, S., Packard, G., Wallace, S., Michopoulos, V., & Powers, A. (2022). When (passive) acceptance hurts: Race-based coping moderates the association between racial discrimination and mental health outcomes among Black Americans. *Psychological Trauma: Theory, Research, Practice, and Policy, 14*(1), 38–46. https://doi.org/10.1037/tra0001077.supp

Is the type of race-based coping style used following racial discrimination a factor in whether an individual suffers negative mental health outcomes? The researchers used a measure of coping styles to classify Black American adults as using passive or active coping (e.g., when treated unfairly, was the individual's response style "keep it to yourself" or "talk to others about it"). The participants with an active coping style were less likely to experience symptoms of depression or posttraumatic stress as a response to racial discrimination.

A major area of applied research is called **program evaluation,** which assesses the social reforms and innovations that occur in government, education, the criminal justice system, industry, health care, and mental health institutions. In an influential paper on "reforms as experiments," Campbell (1969) noted that social programs are really experiments designed to achieve certain outcomes. He argued persuasively that social scientists should evaluate each program to determine whether it is having its intended effect. If it is not, alternative programs should be tried. This is an important point that people in all organizations too often fail to remember when new ideas are implemented; the scientific approach dictates that new programs should be evaluated. Here are two sample journal articles about program evaluation:

Haynes, N. J., Vandenberg, R. J., Wilson, M. G., DeJoy, D. M., Padilla, H. M., & Smith, M. L. (2021). Evaluating the impact of the Live Healthy, Work Healthy program on organizational outcomes: A randomized field experiment. *Journal of Applied Psychology*. https://doi.org/10.1037/apl0000977

The Live Healthy, Work Healthy program was designed to provide to workers with chronic health conditions the skills and self-efficacy to improve their health-related behaviors such as physical activity, nutrition, sleep, and effectively dealing with negative emotions. The workers participated in a series of small-group workshops that took place during regular work hours. Previous research describes positive effects of the program on health behaviors. The Haynes et al. (2021) study describes the effects of the program on organizational outcomes. Workers participating in the program showed increased perceptions of organizational support, lower feelings of burnout, and greater organizational commitment and work commitment.

Manlove, J., Cook, E., Whitfield, B., Johnson, M., Martínez-García, G., & Garrido, M. (2020). Short-term impacts of Pulse: An app-based teen pregnancy prevention program for Black and Latinx women. *Journal of Adolescent Health, 66*(2), 224–232. https://doi.org/10.1016/j.jadohealth.2019.08.017

Pulse is an app-based pregnancy prevention program designed to address needs and preferences of young Black and Latinx women. The specific target population in this study consists of 18- to 20-year-old women; the researchers note that these women have a high rate of unplanned pregnancy and lack of access to prevention programs. Participants in the study were randomly assigned to the Pulse app intervention or a control group given a general health app. After six weeks, the Pulse users were more likely to be using contraception and had greater knowledge of birth control effectiveness.

Much applied research is conducted in settings such as large business firms, marketing research companies, government agencies, and public polling organizations and is not published but instead is used within the company or by clients of the company. Whether or not such results are published, however, they are used to help people make better decisions concerning problems that require immediate action.

Comparing Basic and Applied Research

Both basic and applied research are important, and neither can be considered superior to the other. In fact, progress in science is dependent on a fundamental interplay between basic and applied research. Much applied research is guided by the theories and findings of basic research investigations. For example, one of the most effective treatment strategies for specific phobia—an anxiety disorder characterized by extreme fear reactions to specific objects or situations—is called *exposure therapy* (Chambless et al., 1996). In exposure therapy, people who suffer from a phobia are exposed to the object of their fears in a safe setting while a therapist trains them in relaxation techniques in order to counterprogram their fear reaction. This behavioral treatment emerged from the work of Pavlov and Watson, who studied the processes by which animals acquire, maintain, and—critically—lose reflexive reactions to stimuli (Wolpe, 1982). Today this work has been extended even further, as the use of virtual reality technologies to treat anxiety disorders has been studied and found to be as effective as traditional exposure treatment (Opris et al., 2012).

In recent years, many in our society, including legislators who control the budgets of research-granting agencies of the government, have demanded that research be directly relevant to specific social issues. The problem with this attitude toward research is that we can never predict the ultimate applications of basic research. Psychologist B. F. Skinner, for example, conducted basic research in the 1930s on operant conditioning, which carefully described the effects of reinforcement on such behaviors as bar pressing by rats. Years later this research led to many practical applications in treatments, education, and industry. Research with no apparent practical value at one point in time can ultimately can be very useful. The fact that no one can predict the eventual impact of basic research leads to the conclusion that support of basic research is necessary both to advance science and to benefit society.

Check Your Learning

Check Your Learning: In Practice Exercise #2, test your understanding of the distinction between basic and applied research.

This chapter has introduced you to the major goals and general types of research. All researchers use scientific methods, whether they are interested in basic research or applied research. The themes and concepts in this chapter will be expanded in the remainder of the book. They will be the basis on which you evaluate the research of others and plan your own research projects.

ENGAGING WITH RESEARCH: INTRODUCTION

Most chapters in this book include a chapter-closing feature called Engaging with Research, which is designed to relate some of the critical points in the chapter to a published journal article. In each case, you will be asked to obtain a copy of the article using some of the skills presented in the chapter "Where to Start." Then, you will be asked to read the article and answer some questions that are closely aligned with the material in the chapter.

For our first Engaging with Research activity, acquire and read this article:

> Corona, K., Senft, N., Campos, B., Chen, C., Shiota, M., & Chentsova-Dutton, Y. (2020). Ethnic variation in gratitude and well-being. *Emotion, 20*(3), 518–524. https://doi.org/10.1037/emo0000582

Tip: You will find an online copy of the article using this link: https://cpb-us-e2.wpmucdn.com/faculty.sites.uci.edu/dist/6/103/files/2019/10/2019-Corona-Senft-Campos-Chen-Shiota-Chentsova-Dutton-2019.pdf. You may also have access to the article via your online databases.

After reading the article, answer the following questions (which will be familiar to you from earlier in this chapter!):

1. **What is the primary goal of this study? Description, Prediction, Determining Cause, or Explanation? Do the authors achieve their goals?**
   a. Did these researchers discuss cause and effect? Did they make claims about how the things they measured cause changes in one another? Did they claim that being Latinx *caused* differences in gratitude?
   b. Would you describe this study as applied research or basic research? Why?
2. **What did these researchers do? What was the method?**
3. **What was measured?**
4. **To what or whom can we generalize the results?**
   a. Corona et al. (2021) collected data from a group of Latino, East Asian, and European men in their first study, and Latino and East Asian men in their second. In both cases, the research participants were from American universities. Do you think the results would be different if the researchers collected data from other populations? What about men from universities in other countries? Or women? Or people who were not university students? Do you think their results would be different?
5. **What did they find? What were the results?**

6. **Have other researchers found similar results?**
7. **What are the limitations of this study?**
   a. What did the authors say about the limitations of the study in the discussion section?
8. **What are the ethical issues present in this study?**
   a. Review the methods section: What ethical issues or procedures were addressed in the study?

BEING A SKILLED CONSUMER OF RESEARCH

1. Imagine a debate on the following statement: "Knowledge of research methods is unnecessary for students who intend to pursue careers in clinical and counseling psychology." Develop "pro" and "con" arguments—arguments that support or oppose the assertion.

2. Read several editorials in the your college's newspaper or in the *New York Times,* the *Wall Street Journal, USA Today,* the *Washington Post,* or another major metropolitan news publication, and identify the sources used to support the assertions and conclusions. Did the writer use intuition, appeals to authority, scientific evidence, or a combination of these? Give specific examples.

3. Imagine a debate on the following statement: "Behavioral scientists should only conduct research that has immediate practical applications." Develop "pro" and "con" arguments—arguments that support or oppose the assertion.

4. You read a social media post that says, "Childhood poverty has a stronger impact on academic achievement among Black children as compared to White children." The study itself collected data from a sample of White children in the Northwest, and Black children in Texas. How strongly should researchers make a case for effect? Why?

Check Your Learning: Practice Exercises

Practice Exercise #1

For the five studies briefly described below, identify the primary goal of science that the study seems designed to achieve: (a) description, (b) prediction, (c) determination of cause, or (d) understand/explain.

Study	Primary Goal of Science			
	Description	Prediction	Determination of Cause	Understand / Explain
1. A researcher studies sleep habits of college students in order to identify those who will graduate in four years and those who will not.				
2. A researcher uses a survey to collect information about the sleeping habits of college students in order to see if sleep has an impact on grades.				
3. A researcher conducts interviews of college students about their sleep habits in order to figure out why college students struggle to get enough sleep.				
4. A researcher uses a survey to collect information about the sleeping habits of college students.				
5. A researcher has some college students drink a caffeinated soda at 11 p.m. and has others drink a decaffeinated version of the same soda, in order to see if sleep is affected by caffeine intake.				

Practice Exercise #2

Basic and Applied Research

Examples of research questions	Basic	Applied
1. What is the impact of stress on cardiovascular health?		
2. What role does race play in the relationship between stress and cardiovascular health?		
3. How do neurons generate neurotransmitters?		
4. How do we process visual images?		
5. How can a city increase recycling by residents?		
6. Which strategies are best for coping with climate change?		

(Answers are provided at the end of this chapter.)

CHAPTER REVIEW

Review Questions

1. Why is it important for anyone in our society to have knowledge of research methods?
2. How does the scientific approach differ from other ways of gaining knowledge about behavior?
3. Why is scientific skepticism useful in furthering our understanding of behavior?
4. Provide (a) definitions and (b) examples of description, prediction, determination of cause, and explanation as goals of scientific research.
5. Describe the three types of evidence necessary in order to infer causation (Cook and Campbell, 1979).
6. Describe the characteristics of scientific inquiry, according to Goodstein (2000).
7. How does basic research differ from applied research?

Study Terms

Alternative explanations (p. 12)

Applied research (p. 14)

Authority (p. 4)

Basic research (p. 13)

Covariation of cause and effect (p. 12)

Empiricism (p. 5)

Falsifiability (p. 6)

Generalization (p. 8)

Goals of behavioral science
(Description, Prediction, Determining
Causes, and Explaining) (p. 9)

Intuition (p. 4)

Peer review (p. 6)

Program evaluation (p. 14)

Pseudoscience (p. 7)

Skepticism (p. 6)

Temporal precedence (p. 11)

Check Your Learning: Answers

Practice Exercise #1

1. b; 2. c; 3. d; 4. a; 5. c

Practice Exercise #2

basic = 1, 3, 4; applied = 2, 5, 6

Zephyr_p/Shutterstock

2

Where to Start

LEARNING OBJECTIVES

- Explain how research questions, hypotheses, and predictions are related.
- Describe the different sources of ideas for research that are outlined in this chapter, including common sense, practical problems, observation of the world around us, theories, and past research.
- Explain the two functions of a theory.
- Compare and contrast the three kinds of journal articles: literature reviews, theory articles, and empirical research.
- Summarize what is commonly included in the major sections of an empirical research article: the abstract, introduction, method, results, and discussion sections.
- Demonstrate an ability to conduct searches of past research using APA PsycInfo, Web of Science, Scopus, and Google Scholar.

THE MOTIVATION TO CONDUCT SCIENTIFIC RESEARCH COMES FROM A NATURAL CURIOSITY ABOUT THE WORLD. Most people have their first experience with research when their curiosity leads them to ask, "I wonder what would happen if …" or "I wonder why …," followed by an attempt to answer the question. What are the sources of inspiration for such questions? How do you find out about other people's ideas and past research? In this chapter, we will explore some sources of scientific ideas. We will also consider the nature of research reports published in professional journals.

RESEARCH QUESTIONS, HYPOTHESES, AND PREDICTIONS

Curiosity is expressed in the form of questions. A **research question** is the first and most general step in designing and conducting a research investigation. A good research question must be specific so that it can be answered with a research project. So, you might initially be motivated to want to answer a question like "What causes depression?" This question is much too general, given the complexity of the topic. After becoming familiar with the theories and research on depression, your interest might focus on a more specific question, such as "Is depression related to unhelpful ways of thinking about the causes of success and failure?" That is a more specific, testable question.

A hypothesis can be thought of as one of the possible answers to a research question. In research, a **hypothesis** is a tentative answer to a research question. Once a hypothesis is proposed, data must be gathered and evaluated in terms of whether the evidence is consistent or inconsistent with the hypothesis.

In our example, the hypothesis might be: "Depression is related to the types of attributions made about success and failure experiences." More specifically, the hypothesis might be that individuals who are diagnosed with depression will attribute success to good luck but will attribute failure to their personal shortcomings. Once the hypothesis is stated, the researcher can design a study to test it. This will require making decisions about how to choose the people who will participate, the nature of the tasks that they might work on, and how to devise a way to have the participants experience success or failure. There would need to be a way to measure attributions of luck versus personal factors as the cause of the success or failure.

Once the study is designed, the researcher can make a specific prediction about the outcome of the study. A **prediction** follows directly from a hypothesis, is directly testable, and includes specific variables and methodologies. The prediction in our example might be: "In comparison to those with minimal or mild depression, participants categorized as having moderate or severe depression, based on the Beck Depression Inventory score, will score higher on luck when responding to a success experience and higher on personal causes when responding to a failure experience."

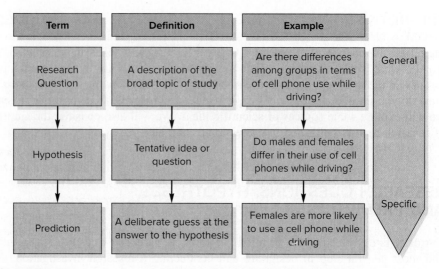

FIGURE 1
Relationships among research questions, hypotheses, and predictions

If a prediction is confirmed by the results of the study, the hypothesis is supported. If the prediction is not confirmed, the researcher will either reject the hypothesis or conduct further research using different methods to study the hypothesis. It is important to note that when the results of a study confirm a prediction, the hypothesis is only supported, not proven. Researchers study the same hypothesis using a variety of methods, and each time this hypothesis is supported by a research study, we become more confident that the hypothesis is correct.

Figure 1 shows the relationships among research questions, hypotheses, and predictions, using an actual study of cell phone use. Cramer et al. (2007) had general questions about use of cell phones while driving, such as "What impact do passengers have on cell phone use while driving?" The researchers developed some specific hypotheses, such as "Having a passenger in the car reduces cell phone use." They then designed a procedure for observing student driving on campus and made predictions about the outcome. For example, "Drivers with a passenger in the car will be less likely to be using a cell phone than those driving alone."

Check Your Learning

Check Your Learning: Practice Exercise #1 will help you tease apart question, hypothesis, and prediction.

SOURCES OF IDEAS

Each day seems to bring us some type of information about a phenomenon related to human behavior. This information may arrive on an internet news site, a tweet or Facebook post, a television program, or even a printed magazine. The topic might be a description of an individual's experience of trauma with a discussion of possible effects, the potential benefits of delaying age of first marriage, or an assertion that a vegetarian diet improves cognitive functioning. It is not easy to say where good ideas come from. Many people are capable of coming up with worthwhile ideas but find it difficult to verbalize the process by which they are generated. Cartoonists know this—they show a brilliant idea as a lightbulb flashing over the person's head. But where does the electricity come from? Let's consider five sources of ideas: common sense, practical problems, observation of the world around us, theories, and past research.

Common Sense

One source of ideas that can be tested is the body of knowledge called common sense—the things we all believe to be true. Do "opposites attract"? Do "birds of a feather flock together"? If you "spare the rod," do you "spoil the child"? Is "a picture worth a thousand words"? Asking questions such as these can lead to research programs studying attraction, the effects of punishment, and the role of visual images in learning and memory.

Testing a commonsense idea can be valuable because it can confirm the commonsense expectation or it can confirm that such notions do not always turn out to be correct. The actual research on memory for information in pictures or words supports what is called the Picture Superiority Effect—memory for pictures is superior to memory for words (Madigan, 2014). However, the research also shows that the real world is more complicated than our commonsense ideas would have it. For example, pictures can aid memory when they are highly distinctive, but distinctive words can prove superior to less distinctive pictures (Ensor et al., 2019). Conducting research to test commonsense ideas often forces us to go beyond a commonsense theory of behavior.

Practical Problems

Research is also stimulated by practical problems that can have immediate applications. On a larger scale, researchers have guided public policy by conducting research on obesity and eating disorders, as well as other social and health issues. Such problems may be local and highly specific; for example, groups of city planners and citizens might survey bike riders to determine the most desirable route for a bike path. Other problems, such as early childhood education, substance abuse, domestic violence, and suicide prevention, may be applicable to much larger problems and populations.

Observation of the World Around Us

Observations can provide many ideas for research. The curiosity sparked by your observations and experiences can lead you to ask questions about all sorts of phenomena. In fact, this type of curiosity is what drives many students to engage in their first research project.

Have you ever had the experience of storing something away in a "special place" where you were sure you could find it later (and where no one else would possibly look for it), only to later discover that you could not recall where you had stored it? Such an experience could lead to systematic research on whether it is a good idea to put things in special places. In fact, Winograd and Soloway (1986) conducted a series of experiments on this very topic. Their research demonstrated that people are likely to forget where something is placed when two conditions are present: (1) The location where the object is placed is judged to be highly memorable *and* (2) the location is considered a very unlikely place for the object. Thus, although it may seem to be a good idea at the time, storing something in an unusual place is generally not a good idea.

A more recent example is obvious: Research ideas generated by the COVID-19 pandemic. To illustrate, we searched the APA PsycInfo database for any publications with titles that included COVID or COVID-19 or coronavirus or pandemic. As you might expect, a 2019 search found only 11 items and these did not address the coming COVID-19 pandemic (there was one book by Steven Taylor (2019) with the prescient title *The psychology of pandemics: Preparing for the next global outbreak of infectious disease*). The following year brought us a "lockdown" along with 4,168 COVID-19 publications (the first one to appear in our particular search had this intriguing title: *Less sex, but more sexual diversity: Changes in sexual behavior during the COVID-19 coronavirus pandemic* (Lehmiller et al., 2020). In 2021, even more entries appeared: A total of 5,824. To appreciate the impact of the pandemic on research, compare those numbers to the number of articles with "extraversion" in the title. The total for 2019 through 2021 was only 95 publications. Further, we should note that our search for research on the COVID-19 pandemic did not include papers that were presented at academic conferences during those years.

Observations of the world around us may even lead to an academic career. When he was an undergraduate, psychologist Michael Lynn worked in restaurants, and much of his compensation consisted of tips from customers. That experience sparked an interest in studying tipping. For many years Lynn has studied tipping behavior in restaurants and hotels in the United States and in other countries (Tipping Expert, 2013). He has looked at factors that increase tips, such as posture, touching, and phrases written on a check, and his research has had an impact on the hotel and restaurant industry. If you have ever worked in restaurants, you have undoubtedly formed many of your own hypotheses about tipping behavior. Lynn went one step further and took a scientific approach to testing his ideas. His research illustrates that taking a scientific approach to a problem can lead to new discoveries and important applications.

Finally, we should mention the role of serendipity—sometimes the most interesting discoveries are the result of accident or sheer luck. Ivan Pavlov is best known for discovering what is called *classical conditioning,* wherein a neutral stimulus (such as a tone), if paired repeatedly with an unconditioned stimulus (such as food) that produces a reflex response (such as salivation), will eventually produce the response when presented alone. Pavlov did not set out to discover classical conditioning. Instead, he was studying the digestive system in dogs by measuring their salivation when given food. He accidentally discovered that the dogs were salivating prior to the actual feeding and then studied the ways in which the stimuli preceding the feeding could produce a salivation response. Of course, such accidental discoveries are made only when viewing the world with an inquisitive eye.

Theories

Much research in the behavioral sciences tests theories of behavior. A **theory** consists of a systematic body of ideas about a particular topic or phenomenon. Psychologists have theories relating to human behavior, learning, memory, and personality, for example. These ideas form a coherent and logically consistent structure that serves two important functions.

First, theories *organize and explain* a variety of specific facts or descriptions of behavior. Such facts and descriptions are not very meaningful by themselves, and so theories are needed to impose a framework on them. This framework makes the world more comprehensible by providing a few abstract concepts around which we can organize and explain a variety of behaviors. As an example, consider how Charles Darwin's theory of evolution organized and explained a variety of facts concerning the characteristics of animal species. Similarly, in psychology one classic theory of memory asserts that there are separate systems of short-term memory and long-term memory. This theory accounts for a number of specific observations about learning and memory, including such phenomena as the different types of memory deficits that result from a blow to the head versus damage to the hippocampus area of the brain and the rate at which a person forgets material they have just read.

Second, theories *generate new knowledge* by focusing our thinking so that we notice new aspects of behavior—theories guide our observations of the world. The theory generates hypotheses about behavior, and the researcher conducts studies to test the hypotheses. If the studies confirm the hypotheses, the theory is supported. As more and more evidence accumulates that is consistent with the theory, we become more confident that the theory is correct.

Sometimes people describe a theory as "just an idea" that may or may not be true. We need to separate this use of the term—which implies that a theory is essentially the same as a hypothesis—from the scientific meaning of *theory.* A scientific theory consists of much more than a simple "idea." A scientific theory is grounded in actual data from prior research as well as numerous hypotheses that are consistent with the theory. These hypotheses can be tested through further research. Such testable hypotheses are falsifiable—the data can either support or refute the hypotheses. As a theory develops with more and more evidence that supports the theory, it is wrong to say that it is "just an idea." Instead, the theory becomes well established as it enables us to explain a great many observable facts. It is true that research may reveal a weakness in a theory when a hypothesis generated by the theory is not supported. When this happens, the theory can be modified to account for the new data. Sometimes a new theory will emerge that accounts for both new data and the existing body of knowledge. This process defines the way in which science continually develops with new data that expand our knowledge of the world around us.

Evolutionary theory has influenced our understanding of sexual attraction and mating patterns (Buss, 2011). For example, Buss describes a well-established finding that males experience more intense feelings of jealousy when a partner has a sexual relationship with someone else (sexual infidelity) than when the partner has developed an emotional bond only (emotional infidelity); females, in contrast, are more jealous when the partner has engaged in emotional infidelity rather than sexual infidelity. This finding is consistent with evolutionary theory, which asserts that males and females have evolved different strategies for mate selection. All individuals have an evolutionary interest in passing their genes on to future generations. However, females have relatively few opportunities to reproduce, have a limited age range during which to reproduce, and traditionally have had to assume major child-care responsibilities. Males, in contrast, can reproduce at any time from puberty onward and have a reproductive advantage in that they can produce more offspring than a given female can. Because of these differences, the theory predicts that females and males will have different perspectives on infidelity. Females will be more threatened if the partner might no longer provide support and resources for childrearing by developing an emotional bond with another partner. Males are more distressed if it is possible that they will be caring for a child who does not share their genes. Although research supports evolutionary theory, alternative theories can be developed that may better explain the same findings.

Levy and Kelly (2010) suggest that attachment theory may provide a better explanation. They point out that males and females differ in their level of attachment in relationships. Also, females in general show greater attachment than males do. From the perspective of attachment theory, the amount of attachment will be related to the distress experienced by an instance of emotional infidelity. Research by Levy and Kelly found that high-attachment individuals were most upset by emotional infidelity; individuals with low attachment to the relationship were more distressed by sexual infidelity. These findings will lead to more research to test the two theoretical perspectives.

Theories are usually modified as new research defines the scope of the theory. The necessity of modifying theories is illustrated by the theory of short-term versus long-term memory. In the original conception, the long-term memory system was described as a storehouse of permanent, fixed memories. However, now-classic research by cognitive psychologists, including Loftus (1979), has shown that memories are easily reconstructed and reinterpreted. In one study, participants watched a film of an automobile accident and later were asked to tell what they saw in the film. Loftus found that participants' memories were influenced by the way they were questioned. For example, participants who were asked whether they saw "the" broken headlight were more likely to answer yes than were participants who were asked whether they saw "a" broken headlight. Results such as these have required a more complex theory of how long-term memory operates.

Past Research

Another source of ideas is past research. Becoming familiar with a body of research on a topic is perhaps the best way to generate ideas for new research. Because the results of research are published, researchers can use the body of past literature on a topic to continually refine and expand our knowledge. Virtually every study raises questions that can be addressed in subsequent research. The research may lead to an attempt to apply the findings in a different setting, to study the topic with a different age group, or to use a different methodology to replicate the results. In the Cramer et al. (2007) study on cell phone use while driving, trained observers noted cell phone use of 3,650 students leaving campus parking structures during a 3-hour period on two different days. They reported that 11% of all drivers were using cell phones. Females were more likely than males to be using a cell phone, and drivers with passengers were less likely than solitary drivers to be talking on a phone. Knowledge of this study might lead to research on ways to reduce students' cell phone use while driving.

In addition, as you become familiar with the research literature on a topic, you may see inconsistencies in research results that need to be investigated, or you may want to study alternative explanations for the results. Also, what you know about one research area often can be successfully applied to another research area.

Let's look at a concrete example of a study that was designed to address methodological flaws in previous research. Recall from the chapter "Scientific Understanding of Behavior" the procedure called "facilitated communication." Facilitated communication was intended to help children who are diagnosed with autism spectrum disorder (ASD). Autism spectrum disorder is characterized by a number of symptoms. Some children diagnosed with ASD show severe impairments in language and communication. Parents and care providers were greatly encouraged by facilitated communication, which allowed a child with ASD to communicate with others by pressing keys on a keyboard showing letters and other symbols. A facilitator held the child's hand to facilitate the child's ability to determine which key to press. With this technique, many autistic children seemed to begin communicating their thoughts and feelings and answering questions posed to them. Most people who saw facilitated communication in action regarded the technique as a miraculous breakthrough.

The conclusion that facilitated communication was effective was based on a comparison of the child with ASD's ability to communicate with and without the facilitator. The difference is impressive to most observers. Recall, however, that scientists are by nature skeptical. They examine all evidence carefully and ask whether claims are justified. In the case of facilitated communication, Montee et al. (1995) noted that the facilitator might have been unintentionally guiding the child's fingers to type meaningful sentences. In other words, the facilitator, and not the autistic individual, might be controlling the communication. Montee et al. conducted a study to test this idea. In one condition, both the facilitator and the autistic child were shown a picture, and the child was asked to indicate what was shown in the picture by typing a response with the facilitator. This was done on a number of trials. In another condition, only the child saw the pictures. In a third condition, the child and facilitator were shown different pictures (but the facilitator was unaware of this fact). Consistent with the hypothesis that the facilitator is controlling the child's responses, the pictures were correctly identified only in the condition in which both saw the same pictures. Moreover, when the child and facilitator viewed different pictures, the child never made the correct response, and usually the picture the facilitator had seen was the one identified.

As you can see, previous research and thinking on a topic can be a critical source of ideas for a study. So, then, the next questions are: What does published work look like? What sorts of research reports are there?

TYPES OF JOURNAL ARTICLES

There are many types of journal articles (American Psychological Association, 2020b), but most fall into three categories: literature reviews that summarize research, theory articles that describe theories, and empirical articles that describe specific research projects.

Literature Reviews

Literature reviews provide summaries of previous research on a particular topic. The journal *Psychological Bulletin* and the *Annual Review of Psychology* specialize in publishing literature reviews. However, you will now find reviews in many different publications in all areas of research. Traditionally, literature reviews were narrative descriptions of individual research investigations along with conclusions, controversies, and directions for future research. This is one such review:

> Storer, H. L., Casey, E., & Herrenkohl, T. (2016). Efficacy of bystander programs to prevent dating abuse among youth and young adults: A review of the literature. *Trauma, Violence, & Abuse, 17*(3), 256–269. https://doi.org/ 10.1177/1524838015584361
>
> These authors review research on "bystander" programs that are designed to prevent dating violence and abuse. Bystander programs focus on developing skills for people to intervene when they witness dating abuse or behaviors that can lead to dating abuse. This article describes bystander programs and summarizes their impact on bystander attitudes and behaviors.

Today you are likely to see the terms *systematic review* or *systematic literature review* in the titles of literature review articles. These terms signify that the author used specific methods for searching past literature along with criteria for including a study in the review. Systematic reviews often use published "preferred reporting items" that provide consistency across reviews and allow others to replicate the procedures (Moher et al., 2009).

> García-Vera, M. P., Sanz, J., & Gutiérrez, S. (2016). A systematic review of the literature on posttraumatic stress disorder in victims of terrorist attacks. *Psychological Reports, 119*(1), 328–359. https://doi.org/10.1177/0033294116658243
>
> These researchers reviewed the literature on post-traumatic stress disorder (PTSD) among victims of terrorist attacks. Having identified 35 studies of PTSD among such victims, they report that across studies, 33% to 39% of direct victims of a terrorist attack developed PTSD. They also reported rates for others (e.g., community members, emergency workers, and relatives and friends of victims). They discussed their results in the context of treatment for victims of terrorism.

Because literature reviews summarize research across many studies, they are an important part of the research landscape. A more quantitative review method for comparing a large number of studies in a specific research area is called **meta-analysis** (Borenstein et al., 2009). In meta-analysis, researchers analyze the results of a number of studies using statistical procedures. Thus, rather than relying solely on judgments obtained in a narrative literature review, meta-analysis allows researchers to draw statistical conclusions. In short, with meta-analysis researchers attempt to determine if a research finding is the same across multiple studies. Here is one example of a meta-analysis:

> Moshe, I., Terhorst, Y., Philippi, P., Domhardt, M., Cuijpers, P., Cristea, I., Pulkki-Råback, L., Baumeister, H., & Sander, L. B. (2021). Digital interventions for the treatment of depression: A meta-analytic review. *Psychological Bulletin, 147*(8), 749–786. https://doi.org/10.1037/bul0000334
>
> Digital interventions for treatment of depression consist of software programs delivered via computer, internet, or smartphones and are designed to provide information and exercises along with practice assignments.

Theory Articles

Some published research reports are the culmination of work that describes a theory. A theory, as we described earlier, consists of a systematic body of ideas about a particular topic or phenomenon. While literature reviews summarize, theory articles generally summarize and integrate research to provide a new framework for understanding a phenomenon.

The following three articles are examples of theory articles:

Ajzen, I. (1991). The theory of planned behavior. *Organizational Behavior and Human Decision Processes, 50*(2), 179–211. https://doi.org/10.1016/0749-5978(91)90020-T

Ajzen's very influential theory of planned behavior has been cited in other articles more than 10,000 times. The article describes the theory of planned behavior, which links behavior to attitudes toward a given behavior, the social norms surrounding the behavior, and intention to engage in the behavior. Thus, an attitude like "College is good" and a social norm like "All of my friends want me to go college" predict intention to go to college, which in turn predicts applying to college.

Bandura, A. (1977). Self-efficacy: Toward a unifying theory of behavioral change. *Psychological Review, 84*(2), 191–215. https://doi.org/10.1037/0033-295X.84.2.191

Bandura's influential theory article defined self-efficacy as our belief in our own ability to be successful and hypothesized that self-efficacy would predict many behavioral outcomes. If I believe that I can lose 20 pounds or stop smoking, I am more likely to be able to successfully do so.

Klonsky, E. D., & May, A. M. (2015). The Three-Step Theory (3ST): A new theory of suicide rooted in the "ideation-to-action" framework. *International Journal of Cognitive Therapy, 8*(2), 114–129. https://doi.org/10.1521/ijct.2015.8.2.114

This theory article is related to suicide. The authors theorize that suicide ideation—as opposed to a suicide attempt—is the result of psychological pain and hopelessness, and that for people who are experiencing pain and hopelessness, connections to other people are critical to keeping them safe.

Empirical Research Articles

The empirical research article is a report of a study in which data were gathered to help answer a research question.

Empirical research articles usually have five sections: (1) an *Abstract,* such as the ones found in APA PsycINFO; (2) an *Introduction or literature review* that explains the problem under investigation and the specific hypotheses being tested; (3) a *Method* section that describes in detail the exact procedures used in the study; (4) a *Results* section in which the findings are presented; and (5) a *Discussion* section in which the researcher may speculate on the broader implications of the results, propose alternative explanations for the results, discuss reasons a particular hypothesis may not have been supported by the data, and/or make suggestions for further research on the problem. In addition to the five major sections, you will find a list of all the references that were cited. Review the summary of the sections in Figure 2 as you read about each section in greater detail.

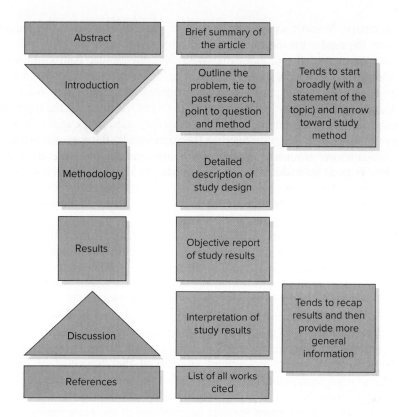

FIGURE 2
Major sec-
tions of a
research
article

Abstract The *Abstract* is a summary of the research report and typically runs between 150 and 250 words in length. It includes information about the hypothesis, the procedure, and the broad pattern of results. Generally, little information is abstracted from the Discussion section of the paper. Some journals are now including a special summary along with a traditional abstract. You may see a "Public Significance," "Impact," or "Statement of Relevance" section, or a similar statement that will be useful to readers who may not be familiar with the technical aspects of the study but do want to understand its importance.

Introduction In the *Introduction,* the researcher outlines the problem that has been investigated. Past research and theories relevant to the problem are described in detail. The researcher's specific expectations are noted, often as formal hypotheses. In other words, the investigator introduces the research in a logical format that shows how past research and theory are connected to the current research problem and the expected results.

Method The *Method section* is divided into subsections, with the number of subsections determined by the author and dependent on the complexity of the research design. Sometimes the first subsection presents an overview of the design to prepare the reader for the material that follows. The next subsection describes the characteristics of the participants. What was the gender composition of the participants? What was the ethnic composition of the participants? What was the average age? How many participants were included? If the study used human participants, some mention of how participants were recruited for the study would be needed. The next subsection details the procedure used in the study. In describing any stimulus materials presented to the participants, the way the behavior of the participants was recorded, and so on, it is important that no potentially crucial detail be omitted. Such detail allows the reader to know exactly how the study was conducted, and it provides other researchers with the information necessary to replicate the study. Other subsections may be necessary to describe in detail any equipment or testing materials that were used.

We have been using the term *participants* to refer to the individuals who are studied in research projects. An equivalent term in psychological research is *subjects*. The *Publication Manual of the American Psychological Association* (APA, 2020) allows the use of either *participants* or *subjects* when describing humans who are studied in psychological research. You will see both terms when you read about research; both terms will be used in this book. Other terms that you may encounter include *respondents* and *informants*. The individuals who take part in survey research are often called *respondents. Informants* are the people who help researchers understand the dynamics of particular cultural and organizational settings—this term originated in anthropological and sociological research, and is now being used by psychologists as well. Many research reports will use more specific descriptions of the participants—such as *employees* in an organization, *students* in a classroom, or *residents* of an assisted living facility.

Results   In the *Results section,* the researcher presents the findings, usually in three ways. First, there is a description in narrative form—for example, "The location of items was most likely to be forgotten when the location was both judged to be highly memorable and an unusual place for the item to be stored." Second, the results are described in statistical language. Third, the material is often depicted in tables and graphs.

The statistical terminology of the Results section may appear formidable. However, lack of knowledge about the calculations is not really a deterrent to understanding the article or the logic behind the statistics. Statistics are only a tool the researcher uses in evaluating the outcomes of the study.

Discussion   In the *Discussion section,* the researcher reviews the research described in the *Method section* and the *Results section* from various perspectives. Do the results support the hypothesis? If they do, the author should give all possible explanations for the results and discuss why one explanation is superior to another. If the hypothesis has not been supported, the author should suggest potential reasons. What might have been wrong with the methodology, the hypothesis, or both? The researcher may also discuss how the results compare with past research results on the topic. Also, particular limitations of the study may be described; for example, a sample consisting of young college students may limit the generalization of the results. Finally, the discussion section may include suggestions for possible practical applications of the research and for future research on the topic.

You should familiarize yourself with some actual research articles. Appendix A ends with an entire article in manuscript form. An easy way to find more articles in areas that interest you is to visit the websites of the American Psychological Association (APA) at www.apa.org/pubs/journals and the Association for Psychological Science (APS) at www.psychologicalscience.org/publications. When you select a journal that interests you, you will go to a page that allows you to read the abstracts—and sometimes the full text—of recent articles published in the journal. Read articles to become familiar with the way information is presented in reports. As you read, you will develop ways of efficiently processing the information in the articles. It is usually best to read the abstract first, then skim the article to decide whether you can use the information provided. If you can, go back and read the article carefully. Note the hypotheses and theories presented in the introduction, write down anything that seems unclear or problematic in the method, and read the results in view of the material in the introduction. Be critical when you read the article; students often generate the best criticism. Most important, as you read more research on a topic, you will become more familiar with the questions being studied, the methods used to study the variables, the important theoretical issues being considered, and the problems that need to be addressed by future research. In short, you will find yourself generating your own research ideas and planning your own studies.

As you can see, previous research and thinking on a topic can be a critical source of ideas for a study. So, then, the next question is: How can you find previously published research?

EXPLORING PAST RESEARCH

For most of us, accessing information today has never been easier. Google alone searches hundreds of billions of web pages (How Search Works). Of course, having access to information is different from being able to assess its quality. Searching online for the answer to questions like "What has the impact of marijuana legalization been?" or "Is climate change real?" will generate lists of every conceivable answer, and probably some inconceivable ones, too! Anybody looking at such a list could cherry-pick the sources that they want, to tell the story that they want, and start writing—perhaps publishing what they write on a website and contributing to internet noise on a topic. So, how do you evaluate the quality of a source? How do you conduct a research project that is connected to other research?

Before conducting any research project, an investigator must have a thorough knowledge of previous research findings. Even if the researcher formulates the basic idea, a review of past studies will help the researcher clarify the idea and design of the study. Thus, it is important to know how to search the literature on a topic and how to read research reports in professional journals. In this section, we will discuss only the fundamentals of conducting library research; for further information, you should go to your college library and talk with a librarian (large libraries may have a librarian devoted to providing assistance in psychology and other behavioral sciences). Librarians have specialized training and a lot of practical experience in conducting library research.

Journals

There is an enormous number of scholarly journals in which researchers publish the results of their investigations. After a research project has been completed, the study is written as a report, which then may be submitted to the editor of an appropriate journal. The editor solicits reviews from other scientists in the same field and then decides whether the report is to be accepted for publication; this is the process of peer review, in which experts in the field assess the quality of the research. Because each journal has a limited amount of space and receives many more papers than it has room to publish, many papers are not accepted; rejection may be based on many factors, including overall study quality, an article's lack of potential to impact the field, a small or biased sample size, inappropriate analyses of results, or not the right fit for that particular journal. Papers that are accepted are published about a year later, although sometimes online editions are published more quickly.

Most journals specialize in one or two topic areas. Even so, the number of journals in many areas is so large that it is almost impossible for anyone to read them all. Some major journals in psychology lists some of the major journals in several areas of psychology; the table does not list any journals that are published only on the internet, and it does not include the many journals that publish in areas closely related to psychology or in highly specialized areas within psychology.

Some major journals in psychology

General	
*American Psychologist** (articles on a variety of topics)	*Psychological Methods**
	Advances in Methods and Practices in
*Psychological Science***	*Psychological Science***
*Psychological Bulletin** (literature reviews)	*Current Directions in Psychological Science***
*Psychological Review** (theoretical articles)	*Psychological Science in the Public Interest***
*Perspectives on Psychological Science***	*History of Psychology**
	*Qualitative Psychology**

Clinical and counseling psychology

*Journal of Psychopathology and Clinical Science**
*Journal of Consulting and Clinical Psychology**
*Clinical Psychological Science***
*Journal of Counseling Psychology**
*Behavior Analysis: Research and Practice**

*Professional Psychology: Research and Practice**

Experimental areas of psychology

Journal of Experimental Psychology:
   *General**
   *Applied**
   *Learning, Memory, and Cognition**
   *Human Perception and Performance**
   *Animal Learning and Cognition**
*Behavioral Neuroscience**
*Motivation Science**

Cognition
Cognitive Science
*Decision**
Journal of the Experimental Analysis of Behavior
*Neuropsychology**
*Emotion**
Canadian Journal of Experimental Psychology

Developmental psychology

*Developmental Psychology**
*Psychology and Aging**
Child Development

Journal of Applied Developmental Psychology

Personality and social psychology

*Journal of Personality and Social Psychology**
Personality and Social Psychology Bulletin
Journal of Experimental Social Psychology
Journal of Research in Personality
Personality and Social Psychology Review

*Personality Disorders**
Social Psychological and Personality Science
Basic and Applied Social Psychology
Journal of Social and Personal Relationships
Canadian Journal of Behavioural Science

Applied areas of psychology

*Journal of Applied Psychology**
*Journal of Educational Psychology**
*Health Psychology**
*Psychological Assessment**
*Psychology, Public Policy, and Law**
*Law and Human Behavior**
*Psychology of Violence**
*Psychology of Religion and Spirituality**

American Journal of Community Psychology
Evaluation and Program Planning
*Environment and Behavior Technology, Mind, and Behavior**
*Journal of Neuroscience, Psychology, and Economics**
*Journal of Family Psychology**

(continued)

(continued)

Ethnicity, gender, and cross-cultural psychology

Cultural Diversity and Ethnic Minority Psychology*	*Psychology of Sexual Orientation and Gender Diversity**
Journal of Latinx Psychology*	*Sex Roles*
Hispanic Journal of Behavioral Sciences	*Psychology of Women Quarterly*
Journal of Black Psychology	*Psychology of Men and Masculinities**
Journal of Cross-Cultural Psychology	*International Perspectives in Psychology: Research, Practice, Consultation**

* Published by the American Psychological Association. ** Published by the Association for Psychological Science.

Clearly, it would be difficult to read all of the journals listed, even if you restricted your reading to a single research area in psychology, such as learning and memory. If you were seeking research on a single specific topic, it would be impractical to look at every issue of every journal in which relevant research might be published. Fortunately, you do not have to.

Online Scholarly Research Databases

You are probably thinking that you should be able to find information on your topic with an internet search tool such as Google. Instead of looking through printed journals and books, you already have access to a very large database of information. Unfortunately, a search of websites may find some scholarly information but it will also likely access information that is not relevant and may even be inaccurate. In this section, we will explore search tools that specialize in access to databases of scholarly research in psychology and related fields. These include APA PsycInfo, Web of Science, and Scopus. We also describe a specialized Google search tool for scholarly information called Google Scholar.

APA PsycInfo   The American Psychological Association began the monthly publication of *Psychological Abstracts,* or *Psych Abstracts,* in 1927. The abstracts are brief summaries of articles in psychology and related disciplines, indexed by topic area. Today the abstracts are maintained in a digital database called **APA PsycInfo,** which is accessed via the internet and is updated weekly. The exact procedures you will use to search APA PsycInfo will depend on how your library has arranged to obtain access to the database. In all cases, you will obtain a list of abstracts that are related to your particular topic of interest. You can then find and read the articles in your library or, in many cases, link to full text that your library subscribes to. If an important article is not available in your library, ask a librarian about services to obtain articles from other libraries.

Conducting an APA PsycInfo Search

The exact look and feel of the system you will use to search APA PsycInfo will depend on your library website. Your most important task is to specify the search

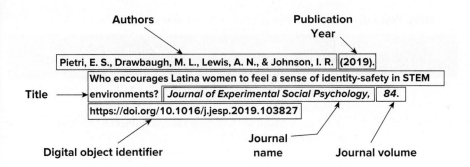

FIGURE 3
Anatomy of a standard reference

terms that you want the database to use. These are typed into a search box. How do you know what words to type in the search box? Most commonly, you will want to use standard psychological terms. The *Thesaurus of Psychological Index Terms* lists all the standard terms that are used to index the abstracts, and it can be accessed directly with most APA PsycInfo systems.

Suppose you are interested in the topic of preparing students for careers in STEM (Science, Technology, Engineering, Math) fields. One particular focus might be students who are underrepresented in these fields. A search on the terms *STEM* and *Gender* or *Ethnic* or *Race* will result in a listing of articles that used these terms. The reference citation for one of the articles (Pietri et al., 2019) is shown in Figure 3. Note that we have identified the elements of a reference in this figure. The reference citation provides everything you need to know about a given source.

Check Your Learning

Go to Check Your Learning: Practice Exercise #2 to see if you can identify the parts of a citation.

Below is the APA PsycInfo output for this article. The exact appearance of the output you receive will depend on your library's search system. The default output includes the citation information you will need, along with the abstract itself. Notice that the output is organized into "fields" of information. The full name of each field is included here; many systems allow abbreviations. You will almost always want to see the *title, author, source/publication title,* and *abstract.* Note that you also have fields such as publication type to briefly describe the article, and age group. When you do the search, some fields will appear as hyperlinks to lead you to other information in your library database or to other websites. Systems are continually being upgraded to enable users to more easily obtain full-text access to the articles and find other articles on similar topics. The *digital object identifier* (DOI) is particularly helpful in finding full-text sources of the article and is now provided with other publication information when journal articles are referenced.

APA PsycInfo output for Pietri et al. (2019) appears as follows:

Title:	**Who encourages Latina women to feel a sense of identity-safety in STEM environments?**

Authors:	Pietri, Evava S., Indiana University-Purdue University Indianapolis, IN, US, epietri@iupui.edu
	Drawbaugh, Montana L., Indiana University-Purdue University Indianapolis, IN, US
	Lewis, Arielle N., Indiana University-Purdue University Indianapolis, IN, US
	Johnson, India R., ORCID 0000-0001-9381-6364. Elon University, Elon, NC, US
Address:	Pietri, Evava S., Department of Psychology, LD 124, 402 N. Blackford Street, Indianapolis, IN, US, 46202, epietri@iupui.edu

Source:	Journal of Experimental Social Psychology, Vol 84, Sept. 2019. ArtID: 103827
Page Count:	7
Publisher:	Elsevier Science
ISSN:	0022-1031 (Print)
	1096-0465 (Electronic)
Language:	English
Keywords:	Gender, Group processes, STEM, Intersectionality, Identity-safe cues

Abstract:	Latinas are among the least represented groups in STEM and, thus, may have concerns about not belonging or feeling welcome in STEM environments. Identity-safe cues (i.e., scientists with shared identities) may address this issue and encourage Latinas' belonging and interest in STEM. To examine this possibility, in the first study we presented Latina women with a fictional STEM company and a scientist working at the company who was either Latino/a or a non-Latino/a White man or woman. We found that compared to those in the White man or woman scientist conditions, participants in the Latino/a scientist conditions believed the scientist had faced comparable adversity to themselves, identified more strongly with the scientist, and reported higher trust and belonging and attraction to the STEM company. Using the findings from Study 1 to inform a new intervention, in the second study we presented Latina high school students with a panel of Latina scientists. Relative to before the panel, the students reported enhanced feelings of trust and belonging in STEM after the panel. Exploratory analyses further revealed that among Latina students who did not already intend to pursue a career in STEM, the panel encouraged their interest in the sciences. Across both studies, we found that believing the scientists had past experiences with adversity related to stronger identification with the scientists, and identifying with scientists correlated with more trust and belonging and interest

in STEM environments. The current research has important implications for who acts as an identity-safe cue for Latinas in STEM. (APA PsycInfo Database Record © 2020 APA, all rights reserved)

Subjects:	*Ethnic Identity; *Scientists; *Social Identity; *Latinos/Latinas; *STEM; Business Organizations; Cues; Human Sex Differences; Students; Trust (Social Behavior); Belonging; Adversity
APA PsycInfo Classification:	Culture & Ethnology (2930)
Population:	Human Male Female
Location:	US
Age Group:	Adulthood (18 yrs & older)
Grant Sponsorship:	Sponsor: IUPUI, Office of Vice Chancellor for Research, US Sponsor: Spencer Foundation
Methodology:	Empirical Study; Quantitative Study
Tests & Measures:	Level of Identification With the Scientist Scale
Publication Type:	Journal; Peer Reviewed Journal
Document Type:	Journal Article
Copyright:	All rights reserved. Elsevier Inc. 2019
Digital Object Identifier:	https://doi.org/10.1016/j.jesp.2019.103827
Accession Number:	2019-49947-001
Database:	APA PsycInfo

When you do a simple search with a single word or a phrase, such as *STEM,* the default search yields articles that have that word or phrase anywhere in any of the fields listed. Often you will find that this produces too many articles, including articles that are not directly relevant to your interests. One way to narrow the search is to limit it to certain fields. Your APA PsycInfo search screen will allow you to limit the search to one field, such as the title of the article. You can also learn how to type a search that includes the field you want. For example, you could specify *STEM in TITLE* to limit your search to articles that have the term in the title of the article. Your search screen will also allow you to set limits on your search to specify, for instance, that the search should find only journal articles (not books or dissertations) or include participants from certain age groups.

Most APA PsycInfo systems have advanced search screens that enable you to use the Boolean operators AND, OR, and NOT. These can be typed as discussed below, but the advanced search screen uses prompts to help you design the search. Suppose you want to restrict the *STEM in TITLE* search to studies that also examined ethnicity. You can do this by asking for *(STEM in TITLE) AND (ethnicity)*. The AND forces both conditions to be true for an article to be included.

The parentheses are used to separate different parts of your search specification and are useful when your searches become increasingly complicated.

The OR operation is used to expand a search that is too narrow. Suppose you want to find articles that discuss romantic relationships on the internet. An APA PsycInfo search for *internet AND romance* in any field produces 252 articles; changing the specification to *internet AND (romance OR dating OR love OR relationship)* yields 12,377 articles. Articles that have the term *internet* and any of the other four terms specified were included in the second search. This number would be reduced to 6,693 by limiting the search to peer reviewed articles published since 2010.

The NOT operation will exclude sources based on a criterion you specify. The NOT operation is used when you anticipate that the search criteria will be met by some irrelevant abstracts. In the internet example, it is possible that the search will include articles on *child predators*. To exclude the term *child* from the results of the search, the following adjustment can be made: *internet AND (romance OR dating OR love OR relationship) NOT child*.

Another helpful search tool is the "wildcard" asterisk (*). The asterisk stands for any set of letters in a word, and so it can expand your search. Consider the word *romance* in the search above—by using *roman**, the search will expand to include both *romance* and *romantic*. The wildcard can be very useful with the term *child** to find *child, children, childhood,* and so on. You have to be careful when doing this, however; the *roman** search would also find *Romania* and *romanticism.* In this case, it might be more efficient to simply add *OR romantic* to the search. These and other search strategies are summarized in Figure 4.

It is a good idea to give careful thought to your search terms. Consider the case of a student who decided to do a paper on the topic of road rage. She wanted to know what might cause drivers to become so angry at other drivers that they become physically aggressive. A search on the term *road rage* led to a number of interesting articles. However, when looking at the output from the search, she noticed that the major keywords included *driving behavior* and *anger* but not *road rage.* When she asked about this, we realized that she had only found articles that included the term *road rage* in the title or abstract. This term has become popular, but it might not be used in many academic studies of the topic. She then expanded the search to include *driving AND anger.* The new search yielded many articles not found in the original search.

As you review the results of your search, you can print, save, or send information to your email address. Other options, such as printing a citation in APA style, may also be available.

Check Your Learning

Now, go to Check Your Learning: Practice Exercise #3 and do some of your searching in the literature.

General Strategies

- Use several databases—for example, both APA PsycInfo and Google Scholar. Become familiar with the databases available in your library to expand the range of information available to you.
- Record your search terms and repeat your searches to find updates.
- Do not restrict yourself to full-text articles, as this introduces a bias in your results.
- Try a variety of key words: *angry driving* and *road rage* generate two sets of results that do not completely overlap.
- Consider using the words *review* and *meta-analysis* in the title of an article to find literature reviews.
- Look for the perfect key article and then use that one to identify additional articles. Use the results that you do find to generate new results.
- Use the "times cited in this database" information from APA PsycInfo or the "related articles" information in Google Scholar.
- Use the "cited references" information provided by APA PsycInfo and Google Scholar.

APA PsycInfo Search Strategies

- Use fields such as the TITLE and AUTHOR. Example: Typing *divorce* in TITLE requires that the term appear in the title.
- Use AND, OR, and NOT. AND limits the search. Example: Typing *divorce AND child* requires both terms to be included.
- Use OR to expand search. Example: Typing *divorce OR breakup* includes either term.
- Use NOT to exclude search terms. Example: Typing *shyness NOT therapy* excludes any shyness articles that have the term *therapy*.
- Use the wildcard asterisk (*). Example: Typing *child** finds any word that begins with *child* (childhood, child's, etc.).
- Find the procedure for restricting the search to peer-reviewed articles.
- Review and use keywords that were selected by article authors (in APA PsycInfo, these are found in the more detailed result output).

Google Search Strategies

Use advanced search (http://www.google.com/advanced_search) to

- Search for a specific phrase
- Specify a set of "AND" words or phrases so that each of the results of your search will include all the words or phrases
- Specify a set of "OR" words or phrases to expand your search
- Specify a set of "NOT" words or phrases to limit your search

FIGURE 4
Some strategies for searching research databases

Web of Science & Scopus

Web of Science and Scopus are similar databases that allow searches of authors, titles, and psychological terms; in addition they let users perform searches for citations in a specific article. The most important feature of both resources is the ability to use the "key article" method. Here you need to first identify a key article on your topic that is particularly relevant to your interests. Choose an article that was published sufficiently long ago to allow time for subsequent related research to be conducted and reported. You can then search for the subsequent articles that cited the key article. This search will give you a bibliography of articles relevant to your topic. To provide an example of this process, we chose the following article:

> Krahé, B., & Möller, I. (2010). Longitudinal effects of media violence on aggression and empathy among German adolescents. *Journal of Applied Developmental Psychology, 31*(5), 401–409. https://doi.org/10.1016/j.appdev.2010.07.003

When we did an article search using Web of Science, we found 88 articles that had cited the Krahé and Möller paper since it was published in 2010. Here is one of them:

> Khurana, A., Bleakley, A., Ellithorpe, M. E., Hennessy, M., Jamieson, P. E., & Weitz, I. (2019). Media violence exposure and aggression in adolescents: A risk and resilience perspective. *Aggressive Behavior, 45*(1), 70–81. https://doi.org/10.1002/ab.21798

This article as well as the others on the list might then be retrieved. It may then turn out that one or more of the articles might become new key articles for further searches.

Other Electronic Search Resources

The American Psychological Association (APA) maintains several databases in addition to APA PsycInfo. These include APA PsycArticles, consisting of full-text scholarly articles, and APA PsycBooks, a database of full-text books and book chapters published by APA. Other major databases include Sociological Abstracts, PubMed, and ERIC (Educational Resources Information Center). In addition, services such as LexisNexis Academic and Factiva allow you to search general media resources such as newspapers. A reference librarian can help you use these and other resources available to you.

Internet Searches
The most widely available information resource is the wealth of material that is available on the internet and located using search services such as Google, Bing, and DuckDuckGo. The internet is a wonderful source of information; any given search may help you find websites devoted to your topic, articles that people have made available to others, book reviews, and even online discussions. Although it is incredibly easy to search, you can improve the quality

of your searches by learning (1) the differences in the way each service finds and stores information; (2) advanced search rules, including how to narrow your searches and how to find exact phrases; and (3) ways to critically evaluate the quality of the information that you find. You also need to make sure that you carefully record the search service and search terms you used, the dates of your search, and the exact location of any websites that you will be using in your research; this information will be useful as you provide documentation in the papers that you prepare.

Google Scholar   Google Scholar is a specialized scholarly search engine that can be accessed at https://scholar.google.com. When you do a search using Google Scholar, you find articles, theses, books, abstracts, and court opinions from a wide range of sources, including academic publishers, professional societies, online repositories, universities, and other websites. Both Google and Google Scholar rank the output of searches. In the case of Google Scholar, search output is ranked by the contents of the article (i.e., did the article contain the keywords that were used in the search?) along with an article's overall prominence based on author, journal, and how often it is cited in other articles.

Google Scholar operates like any other Google search. Access Google Scholar at https://scholar.google.com and type in a keyword as you would in a basic APA PsycInfo search. The key difference is that whereas the universe of content for APA PsycInfo comes from the published works in psychology and related sciences, the universe for Google Scholar includes the entire internet. This can be both a strength and a weakness. If your topic is broad—for example, if you are interested in doing a search for *depression* or *ADHD* or *color perception*—Google Scholar will generate many more hits than APA PsycInfo would, and many of those hits will not be from the scientific literature. On the other hand, if you have a narrow search (e.g., *adult ADHD treatment; color perception and reading speed*), then Google Scholar will generate a set of results more closely aligned with your intentions.

Google Scholar is powerful. It will be worth your while to explore its excellent documentation (https://scholar.google.com/intl/en/scholar/help.html) and learn about its more advanced features, including email alerts for searches and its reference management capabilities.

ENGAGING WITH RESEARCH: LAPTOPS IN CLASS

Ravizza et al. (2017) studied computer use in college classrooms by having students in an introductory psychology class log into a proxy server that monitored all online activity during class. They were specifically interested in the relationship between internet use and classroom performance.

First, search for the article in APA PsycINFO and acquire a full-text version. (Note: The article is available at https://journals.sagepub.com/doi/pdf/10.1177/0956797616677314.) Read the article:

Ravizza, S. M., Uitvlugt, M. G., & Fenn, K. M. (2017). Logged in and zoned out: How laptop internet use relates to classroom learning. *Psychological Science, 28*(2), 171–180. https://doi.org/10.1177/0956797616677314

After you have a full copy of the article, evaluate the study by answering these questions:

1. **What is the primary goal of this study? Description, Prediction, Determining Cause, or Explaining? Do the authors achieve their goals?**
   a. Summarize the authors' purpose for conducting the study; note that they will have supported their purpose by citing or discussing other studies.
   b. Identify the research question or questions that are being explored by this study. In some studies, research questions are clearly labeled as such.
   c. Identify the hypotheses that are being tested by this study. As with research questions, in some studies hypotheses are clearly labeled as such.
   d. How do they know that one thing caused another?

2. **What did these researchers do? What was the method?**

3. **What was measured?**
   a. How did they record the students' internet use?

4. **To what or whom can we generalize the results?**
   a. To whom can the results not be easily generalized? How many students did they invite to participate? How many participants did they collect data from? What was the breakdown of participant demographics?

5. **What did they find? What were the results?**
   a. How much time, on average, did their participants spend on non-class-related purposes during class?
   b. How did the authors measure class-related use versus non-class-related use of the internet?

6. **Have other researchers found similar results?**
   a. Are their findings similar to or different from the findings of others?

7. **What are the limitations of this study?**

8. **What are the ethical issues present in this study?**

BEING A SKILLED CONSUMER OF RESEARCH

Below are four examples of recent articles related to behavioral science in the popular press. For each article: (1) find the original published article—sometimes the articles are linked directly in the story, sometimes they are not (in those cases, use APA PsycInfo or Google Scholar), (2) read the article, and (3) compare and contrast what the published article says and the popular-media article says. What does the popular press get right about the original article? What does it miss?

1. Your Dog May Know If You've Done Something On Purpose, Or Just Screwed Up: https://www.npr.org/sections/health-shots/2021/09/01/1032841893/dog-human-mistake-study

2. Study unlocks the secrets to developing a regular workout habit: https://www.nbcnews.com/health/health-news/study-unlocks-secrets-developing-workout-habit-rcna8075

3. Social media is making you spend money: https://www.washingtonpost.com/us-policy/2019/02/19/your-friends-social-media-posts-are-making-you-spend-more-money-researchers-say/?noredirect=on

4. Study shows teaching teens about social, personality changes helps cope with stress: https://thedailytexan.com/2016/07/03/study-shows-teaching-teens-about-social-personality-changes-helps-cope-with-stress/

Check Your Learning: Practice Exercises

Practice Exercise #1

There are many common sayings or clichés about behavior, such as "Laughter is the best medicine" and "Beauty is only skin deep." For each of the two common sayings in this exercise, interpret the meaning, develop a hypothesis that is suggested by the saying, and form a research prediction that follows from the hypothesis.

Hypotheses and Predictions

Spare the rod, spoil the child

1. Interpret the saying:

2. Write a hypothesis:

3. Make a prediction:

Absence makes the heart grow fonder
1. Interpret the saying:
2. Write a hypothesis:
3. Make a prediction:
   Source: Based on Gardner, 1988.

Practice Exercise #2

Below are three articles published in 2019 in major journals. For each reference, identify:
1. The authors
2. The title of the article
3. The name of the journal
4. The pages in that journal that contain the article
5. The journal volume
6. The journal issue number
7. The digital object identifier (doi):
8. Then, find that article using APA PsycINFO or google scholar and list the first three words of the abstract

   O'Brien, E. (2019). Enjoy it again: Repeat experiences are less repetitive than people think. *Journal of Personality and Social Psychology, 116*(4), 519–540. https://doi.org/10.1037/pspa0000147

   Rodriguez-Seijas, C., Eaton, N. R., & Pachankis, J. E. (2019). Prevalence of psychiatric disorders at the intersection of race and sexual orientation: Results from the National Epidemiologic Survey of Alcohol and Related Conditions–III. *Journal of Consulting and Clinical Psychology, 87*(4), 321–331. https://doi.org/10.1037/ccp0000377

   Yechiam, E., Ashby, N. J. S., & Hochman, G. (2019). Are we attracted by losses? Boundary conditions for the approach and avoidance effects of losses. *Journal of Experimental Psychology: Learning, Memory, and Cognition, 45*(4), 591–605. https://doi.org/10.1037/xlm0000607

Practice Exercise #3

Conduct your own APA PsycInfo Search. There are so many articles, books, and book chapters that are indexed (collected, sorted, and identified) in databases like APA PsycInfo.
1. First, let's take a standard topic and just see how many things are published:
   a. In APA PsycInfo, search on the term "stress and college students." How many total hits in search results did you find? When we ran this search, we had 10,619 total hits.

    b. Now, specify that you'd like only articles that have been published since 2010. How many hits? Our search resulted in 4,717 articles.

    c. Now, specify articles that are peer reviewed. How many hits? Our search resulted in 3,741 hits.

    d. Now, limit the search to 2021. How many hits?

2. Now, search for whatever interests you. Start with some keywords (if you can't think of any, use the APA PsycInfo thesaurus, which indexes all keywords).

    a. Now do this process again, using Google Scholar—first using the terms "stress" and "college students," and then your own topic.

(Some answers are provided at the end of this chapter.)

CHAPTER REVIEW

Review Questions

1. What is a research question? What is a hypothesis? What is a prediction? What are the distinctions between a research question, a hypothesis, and a prediction?

2. What are the two primary functions of a theory?

3. Distinguish between literature reviews, meta-analyses, theory articles, and empirical research articles.

4. What are the components of a research article? What information does the researcher communicate in each of the sections of a research article?

5. How do you conduct an effective APA PsycInfo or Google Scholar search?

6. Describe the differences in the ways past research is found when you use APA PsycInfo versus the "key article" method of the Web of Science or Scopus.

Study Terms

APA PsycInfo (p. 38)

Hypothesis (p. 23)

Literature review (p. 30)

Meta-analysis (p. 31)

Prediction (p. 23)

Research questions (p. 23)

Theory (p. 27)

Check Your Learning: Answers

Practice Exercise #1

Spare the rod, spoil the child

- Interpret the idiom: Generally, a way of saying that children need to be disciplined when misbehaving. Otherwise, they will become spoiled and will always act out to get their own way. A more literal interpretation is that physical punishment (use of the "rod") is an effective way of changing behavior in children.
- Write a hypothesis: Parental use of physical punishment is related to less antisocial behavior in adolescence and adulthood.
- Make a prediction: Adolescents who indicate that their parents used higher amounts of punishment for misbehaving will be described by their teacher as less aggressive and disruptive in the classroom and when interacting with peers.

Absence makes the heart grow fonder

- Interpret the idiom: Physical separation enhances romantic emotional feelings.
- Write a hypothesis: Physical and psychological separation of romantic partners is related to romantic attraction.
- Make a prediction: Romantic partners who have been together for more than a year will report higher levels of romantic attraction when isolated from one another for one week.

Practice Exercise #2

1. The author(s): O'Brien, E
2. The title of the article: Enjoy it again: Repeat experiences are less repetitive than people think
3. The name of the journal: *Journal of Personality and Social Psychology*
4. The pages in that journal that contain the article: 519–540
5. The journal volume: 4
6. The journal issue number: 116
7. The digital object identifier (doi): https://doi.org/10.1037/pspa0000147
8. First three words of the abstract (the abstract may be found using the doi): What would it

Don Hammond/Design Pics

Ethics in Behavioral Research

LEARNING OBJECTIVES

- Summarize the ethical principles in the APA Ethics Code concerning research with human research participants.
- Provide examples of what is analyzed in a risk-benefit analysis.
- Describe the concept of informed consent and how to create a document to establish informed consent.
- Describe the function of an Institutional Review Board and understand the distinctions among exempt, expedited, limited, and full review.
- Analyze a study in terms of its risk and classify it as minimal risk or greater than minimal risk.
- Summarize the ethical issues concerning research with nonhuman animals
- Define and understand the concept of research fraud and its connection to ethics and the ethical code.
- Define and understand plagiarism (including word-for-word and paraphrasing) and describe how to avoid it.

ETHICAL PRACTICE IS FUNDAMENTAL TO THE CONCEPTUALIZA-
TION, PLANNING, EXECUTION, AND EVALUATION OF RESEARCH.
Researchers who do not consider the ethical implications of their projects risk
harming individuals, communities, and behavioral science. This chapter provides
a historical overview of ethics in behavioral research, reviews core ethical principles
for researchers, describes relevant institutional structures that protect research
participants, and concludes with a discussion of what it means to be an ethical
researcher.

MILGRAM'S OBEDIENCE EXPERIMENTS

Stanley Milgram conducted a series of experiments (1963, 1964, 1965) to study
obedience to authority. He placed an ad in the local newspaper in New Haven,
Connecticut, offering a small sum of money to men to participate in a "scientific
study of memory and learning" being conducted at Yale University. The volunteers
reported to Milgram's laboratory at Yale, where they met a scientist dressed in a
white lab coat and another volunteer in the study, a middle-aged man named
"Mr. Wallace." Mr. Wallace was actually a confederate (an accomplice) of the
experimenter, but the participants did not know this. The scientist explained that
the study would examine the effects of punishment on learning. One person would
be a "teacher" who would administer the punishment, and the other would be
the "learner." Mr. Wallace and the volunteer participant then drew slips of paper
to determine who would be the teacher and who would be the learner. The
drawing was rigged, however—Mr. Wallace was always the learner and the actual
volunteer was always the teacher.

The scientist attached electrodes to Mr. Wallace and then placed the "teacher"
in front of an impressive-looking shock machine that was located in an adjoining
room. The shock machine had a series of levers that, the individual was told, when
pressed would deliver shocks to Mr. Wallace. The first lever was labeled 15 volts,
the second 30 volts, the third 45 volts, and so on up to 450 volts. The levers were
also labeled "Slight Shock," "Moderate Shock," and so on up to "Danger: Severe
Shock," followed by red X's above 400 volts.

Mr. Wallace was instructed to learn a series of word pairs. Then he was
given a test to see if he could identify which words went together. Every time
Mr. Wallace made a mistake, the teacher was to deliver a shock as punishment.
The first mistake was supposed to be answered by a 15-volt shock, the second
by a 30-volt shock, and so on. Each time a mistake was made, the learner received
a greater shock.

The learner, Mr. Wallace, never actually received any shocks, but the participants in the study did not know that. In the experiment, Mr. Wallace made mistake
after mistake. When the teacher "shocked" him with about 120 volts, Mr. Wallace
began screaming in pain and eventually yelled that he wanted out. What if the
teacher wanted to quit? This happened—the volunteer participants became visibly
upset by the pain that Mr. Wallace seemed to be experiencing. The experimenter

told the teacher that he could quit but urged him to continue, using a series of verbal prods that stressed the importance of continuing the experiment.

To each volunteer, the study was purportedly an experiment on memory and learning, but Milgram really was interested in learning whether participants would continue to obey the experimenter by administering ever higher levels of shock to the learner. What happened? Approximately 65% of the participants continued to deliver shocks all the way to 450 volts.

Milgram went on to conduct several variations on this basic procedure with 856 subjects. The study received a great deal of publicity, and the results challenged many of our beliefs about our ability to resist authority. The Milgram study is important, and the results have implications for understanding obedience in real-life situations, such as the Holocaust in Nazi Germany and the Jonestown mass suicide (see Miller, 1986).

But the Milgram study is also an important example for discussing the problem of ethics in behavioral research. How should we make decisions about whether the Milgram study or any other study is ethical? The Milgram study was one of many that played an important role in the development of ethical standards that guide our ethical decision-making.

In this chapter, we work through some of these issues, and more. First, let us turn to an overview of the history of our current standards to help frame your understanding of ethics in research.

HISTORICAL CONTEXT OF CURRENT ETHICAL STANDARDS

Before we can delve into current ethical standards, it is useful to briefly talk about the origin of ethics codes related to behavioral research. Generally speaking, modern codes of ethics in behavioral and medical research have their origins in three important documents.

The Nuremberg Code, the Declaration of Helsinki, and the Belmont Report

Following World War II, the Nuremberg Trials were held to hear evidence against the Nazi doctors and scientists who had committed atrocities while forcing concentration camp inmates to be research subjects. The legal document that resulted from the trials contained what became known as the **Nuremberg Code:** a set of 10 rules of research conduct that would help prevent future research atrocities (see https://history.nih.gov/download/attachments/1016866/nuremberg.pdf).

The Nuremberg Code was a set of principles without any enforcement structure or endorsement by professional organizations. Moreover, it was rooted in the context of the Nazi experience and not generally seen as applicable to general research settings. Consequently, the World Medical Association developed a code that is known as the **Declaration of Helsinki.** This 1964 document is a broader application of the Nuremberg Code that was produced by the medical community and included a requirement that journal editors ensure that published research conform to the principles of the Declaration.

The Nuremberg Code and the Helsinki Declaration did not explicitly address behavioral research and were generally seen as applicable to medicine. In addition, by the early 1970s, news about numerous ethically questionable studies forced the scientific community to search for a better approach to protect human research subjects. Behavioral scientists were debating the ethics of the Milgram studies and the world was learning about the Tuskegee Syphilis Study, in which an effective treatment for syphilis was withheld from 399 African American men in Alabama in order to track the long-term effects of this disease (Reverby, 2000). This study, supported by the U.S. Public Health Service, took place from 1932 to 1972, when the details of the study were made public by journalists investigating the study. The outrage over the fact that this study was done at all and that the subjects were African Americans spurred scientists to overhaul ethical regulations in both medical and behavioral research. The fact that the Tuskegee study was not an isolated incident was brought to light in 2010 when documentation of another syphilis study done from 1946 to 1948 in Guatemala was discovered (Reverby, 2011). In this study (which was financed by the U.S. government), male prisoners were provided access to female sex workers who themselves had syphilis. Those prisoners who subsequently contracted syphilis were treated with penicillin, thereby testing its effectiveness in a natural setting. Reverby describes the study in detail and focuses on one doctor who was involved in both the Guatemala study and the Tuskegee study. In 1997, President Clinton formally apologized to the survivors and families of the study participants. Nevertheless, the study has contributed to general suspicions felt within the African American community toward the medical profession, including researchers and government scientists (Corbie-Smith et al., 1999). Most recently, these suspicions were associated with African Americans' high initial resistance to receiving COVID-19 vaccinations (Altman, 2020).

As a result of new public demand for action, a committee was formed that eventually produced the **Belmont Report,** the third critical document in the development of ethical standards in behavioral science. Current ethical guidelines for both behavioral and medical researchers have their origins in *The Belmont Report: Ethical Principles and Guidelines for the Protection of Human Subjects of Research* (National Commission for the Protection of Human Subjects of Biomedical and Behavioral Research, 1979). This report defined the principles and applications that have guided more detailed regulations developed by the American Psychological Association and other professional societies and U.S. federal regulations that apply to both medical and behavioral research investigations.

The three basic ethical principles of the Belmont Report are:

- **Principle of Beneficence:** Research should confer benefits, and risks must be minimal. The associated application is the necessity to conduct a risk-benefit analysis.

- **Principle of Respect for Persons (Autonomy):** Participants are treated as autonomous; they are capable of making deliberate decisions about whether to participate in research. The associated application is informed consent—potential participants in a research project should be provided with all information that might influence their decision on whether to participate.

- **Principle of Justice:** There must be fairness in receiving the benefits of research as well as bearing the burdens of accepting risks. This principle is applied in the selection of subjects for research.

APA ETHICS CODE

The American Psychological Association (APA) has provided leadership in formulating ethical principles and standards for behavioral research. The *Ethical Principles of Psychologists and Code of Conduct*—known as the **APA Ethics Code**—is amended periodically, and the current version is always available online at http://apa.org/ethics/code. The Ethics Code applies to psychologists in their many roles, including as teachers, researchers, and practitioners. The Ethics Code presents five general principles to guide the conduct of psychologists. These are followed by specific standards that apply to each of the major activities of psychologists, including research and publication (see APA Ethics Code: Standard 8).

The preamble to the APA Ethics Code states: "Psychologists are committed to increasing scientific and professional knowledge of behavior and people's understanding of themselves and others and to the use of such knowledge to improve the condition of individuals, organizations and society." Ethical principles support and nurture a healthy science.

APA Ethics Code: Five Principles

The APA Ethics Code includes five general ethical principles, many of which are echoes of the Belmont Report: beneficence and nonmaleficence, fidelity and responsibility, integrity, justice, and respect for rights and responsibilities. These principles and the associated standards help psychologists make ethical and responsible decisions and avoid prejudice and bias. Next, we will discuss the ways these principles relate to research practice.

Principle A: Beneficence and Nonmaleficence
As in the Belmont Report, the **principle of beneficence** refers to the need for research to maximize benefits and minimize any possible harmful effects of participation. The Ethics Code specifically states: "Psychologists strive to benefit those with whom they work and take care to do no harm. In their professional actions, psychologists seek to safeguard the welfare and rights of those with whom they interact professionally and other affected persons and the welfare of animal subjects of research."

Principle B: Fidelity and Responsibility   The **principle of fidelity and responsibility** states: "Psychologists establish relationships of trust with those with whom they work. They are aware of their professional and scientific responsibilities to society and to the specific communities in which they work." For researchers, such trust is primarily applicable to relationships with research participants.

Researchers make several implicit contracts with participants during the course of a study. For example, if participants agree to be present for a study at a specific time, the researcher should also be there. If researchers promise to send a summary of the results to participants, they should do so. If participants are to receive course credit for participation, the researcher must immediately let the instructor know that the person took part in the study. These may seem to be minor details, but they are very important in maintaining trust between participants and researchers.

Principle C: Integrity   The **principle of integrity** states: "Psychologists seek to promote accuracy, honesty and truthfulness in the science, teaching and practice of psychology. In these activities psychologists do not steal, cheat or engage in fraud, subterfuge or intentional misrepresentation of fact." Later in this chapter, we will cover the topic of integrity in the context of being an ethical researcher.

Principle D: Justice   As in the Belmont Report, the **principle of justice** refers to fairness and equity. Principle D states: "Psychologists recognize that fairness and justice entitle all persons to access to and benefit from the contributions of psychology and to equal quality in the processes, procedures and services being conducted by psychologists."

Consider the Tuskegee Syphilis study in which a cure for syphilis (i.e., penicillin) was withheld from participants. This is a violation of principle D of the APA Ethics Code and a violation of the Belmont Report's principle of justice.

Principle E: Respect for People's Rights and Dignity   The last of the five APA ethical principles builds upon the Belmont Report's **principle of respect for persons.** People are infinitely complex and diverse and must be treated without bias or prejudice. Principle E states: "Psychologists respect the dignity and worth of all people, and the rights of individuals to privacy, confidentiality, and self-determination. Psychologists are aware that special safeguards may be necessary to protect the rights and welfare of persons or communities whose vulnerabilities impair autonomous decision making. Psychologists are aware of and respect cultural, individual, and role differences, including those based on age, gender, gender identity, race, ethnicity, culture, national origin, religion, sexual orientation, disability, language, and socioeconomic status, and consider these factors when working with members of such groups. Psychologists try to eliminate the effect on their work of biases based on those factors, and they do not knowingly participate in or condone activities of others based upon such prejudices."

One of the ethical dilemmas in the Milgram obedience study was the fact that participants did not know that they were participating in a study of obedience. This limited participants' rights to self-determination. Later, we will explore this issue in depth.

With these principles in mind, we will consider the ways in which research subjects—humans and animals—are protected in behavioral research.

ASSESSMENT OF RISKS AND BENEFITS

The **principle of beneficence**—maximizing benefits and minimizing harms— leads us to examine potential risks and benefits that are likely to result from the research; this is called a **risk-benefit analysis.**

Potential risks to participants include factors like psychological or physical harm and loss of confidentiality; we will discuss these in detail. The benefits of a study include direct benefits to the participants, such as an educational benefit, acquisition of a new skill, or treatment for a psychological or medical problem. There may also be material benefits such as a monetary payment, some sort of gift, or even the possibility of winning a prize in a raffle. Other, less tangible benefits include the satisfaction gained through being part of a scientific investigation and the potential beneficial applications of the research findings (e.g., the knowledge gained through the research might improve future educational practices, psychotherapy, or social policy). As we will see when discussing the review boards that regulate research in universities and research centers, a risk-benefit analysis with a determination of the level of risk must be completed before research can be approved. We will discuss this later in this chapter.

Risks in Behavioral Research

Let's return to a consideration of Milgram's research. The risk of experiencing stress and psychological harm is obvious. It is not difficult to imagine the effect of delivering intense shocks to an obviously unwilling learner. A film that Milgram made shows participants protesting, sweating, and even laughing nervously while delivering the shocks. You might ask whether subjecting people to such a stressful experiment is justified, and you might wonder whether the experience had any long-range consequences for the volunteers. For example, did participants who obeyed the experimenter feel continuing remorse or begin to see themselves as cruel, inhumane people? Let's consider some common risks in behavioral research.

Physical Harm   Procedures that could conceivably cause physical harm to participants are rare but possible. Psychologists may take part in research on psychoactive substances such as alcohol, caffeine, marijuana, or nicotine. Other studies might expose subjects to physical stressors such as loud noise, extreme hot or cold temperatures, or deprivation of sleep for an extended period. The risks in such procedures require that great care be taken to make them ethically acceptable. Moreover, the research would have to offer clear benefits that would outweigh the potential risks.

Stress and Distress

More common than physical stress is psychological stress. The participants in the Milgram study were exposed to a high level of stress; they believed that they were delivering fatal doses of electricity to another person. Milgram described one of his participants:

> While continuing to read the word pairs with a show of outward strength, she mutters in a tone of helplessness to the experimenter, "Must I go on? Oh, I'm worried about him. Are we going all the way up there (pointing to the higher end of the generator)? Can't we stop? I'm shaking. I'm shaking. Do I have to go up there?" She regains her composure temporarily but then cannot prevent periodic outbursts of distress. (Milgram, 1974, p. 80)

There are other examples. For instance, participants might be told that they will receive some extremely intense electric shocks. They never actually receive the shocks; it is the fear or anxiety during the waiting period that is the variable of interest. Research by Schachter (1959) employing a procedure like this showed that the anxiety produced a desire to affiliate with others during the waiting period.

In another procedure that produces psychological stress, participants are given unfavorable feedback about their personalities or abilities. Researchers may administer a test that is described as a measure of social intelligence and then told that they scored very high or very low. The impact of this feedback can then be studied. Asking people about traumatic or unpleasant events in their lives might also cause stress for some participants. Thus, research that asks people to think about the deaths of a parent, spouse, or friend, or their memories of living through a disaster, could trigger a stressful reaction.

When using procedures that may create psychological distress, the researcher must ask whether all safeguards have been taken to help participants deal with the stress. Usually a debriefing session following the study is designed in part to address any potential problems that may arise during the research.

Confidentiality and Privacy

The loss of expected privacy and confidentiality is another important risk to consider. **Confidentiality** is an issue when the researcher has assured subjects that the collected data are accessible only to people who have permission to view them, generally only the researcher. This becomes particularly important when studying sensitive topics. For example, asking participants about sexual behavior, family history, or illegal activity ("Have you ever stolen something worth more than $50?") may leave them vulnerable if their answers became known to others. Or consider a study that obtained information about employees' managers. It is extremely important that responses to such questions be confidential; revealing their responses could result in real harm to the individual. In most cases, researchers will attempt to avoid confidentiality problems by making sure that the responses are completely anonymous—that there is no way to connect any person's identity with the data. This happens, for example, when questionnaires are administered to groups of people and no information is asked that could be used to identify an individual (such as name, taxpayer identification number, email address, or phone number). However, in other cases, such as a personal interview in which the identity of the person might be known, the researcher must carefully plan ways of coding data, storing data, and explaining the procedures to participants to ensure the confidentiality of responses.

Privacy becomes an issue when, without the subject's permission, the researcher collects information under circumstances that the subject ordinarily believes are private—free from unwanted observation by others. In some studies, researchers make observations of behavior in public places without informing the people being observed. Observing people as they are walking in a public space, stopped at a traffic light, or drinking in a bar does not seem to present any major ethical problems. However, what if a researcher wishes to observe behavior in more private settings or in ways that may violate individuals' privacy? For example, would it be ethical to rummage through people's trash or watch people in public restrooms like Laud Humphreys (1970) did in the 1960s or Borchgrevink et al. (2013) did to study hand-washing?

The internet has posed other issues of privacy. Every day, thousands of people post messages on websites. The messages can potentially be used as data to understand attitudes, disclosure of personal information, and expressions of emotion. Many messages are public postings, much like a letter sent to a newspaper or magazine. But consider websites devoted to psychological and physical problems that people seek out for information and support. Many of these sites require registration to post messages. Consider a researcher interested in using one of these sites for data. What ethical issues arise in this case? These and other ethical issues that arise when doing research using the internet are addressed by Buchanan and Williams (2010) and Roberts and Sipes (2018).

INFORMED CONSENT

Recall Principle E of the APA Ethics Code (**Respect for People's Rights and Dignity**)—research participants are to be treated as autonomous; they are capable of making deliberate decisions about whether to participate in research. The key idea here is **informed consent**—potential participants in a research project should be provided with all information that might influence their active decision of whether or not to participate in a study (see APA Ethics Code: Standard 8.02). Thus, research participants should be informed about the purposes of the study, the risks and benefits of participation, and their rights to refuse or terminate participation in the study. They can then freely consent or refuse to participate in the research.

Informed Consent Form

Participants are usually provided with some type of informed consent form that contains the information that participants need to make their decision. Most commonly, the form is presented for the participant to read and agree to. There are numerous examples of informed consent forms available on the internet. Your college may have developed examples through the research office. Figure 1 summarizes critical parts of the informed consent form in terms of both content and format. The content will typically cover (1) the purpose of the research, (2) procedures that will be used including time involved (remember that you do not need to tell participants exactly what is being studied), (3) risks and benefits, (4) any compensation, (5) confidentiality, (6) assurance of voluntary participation and permission to withdraw, and (7) contact information for questions.

Check to make sure the informed consent form is in the correct format and includes the necessary information:

Creating the Form

- Form is printed in no smaller than 11-point type (no "fine print").
- Form is free of technical jargon and written at sixth- to eighth-grade level.
- Form is not written in the first person (statements such as "I understand …" are discouraged).
- Contact information is provided for questions about the study (usually phone and email contacts for the researcher, faculty advisor, and the Institutional Review Board office).

Description of the Study

- Explanation of the purposes of the research in clear language.
- Expected duration of the subject's participation.
- Description of the procedures.

Description of the Risks and Benefits

- Description of any reasonably foreseeable risks or discomforts and safeguards to minimize the risks.
- Description of any benefits to the individual or to others that may reasonably be expected from the research.
- Description of the extent, if any, to which confidentiality or records identifying the individual will be maintained.
- If applicable, a disclosure of appropriate alternative procedures or courses of treatment, if any, that might be advantageous to the individual.

Request for Consent

- Statement that participants are being asked to participate in a research study.
- Statement that participation is voluntary; refusal to participate will involve no penalty or loss of benefits to which the subject is otherwise entitled, and the subject may discontinue participation at any time without penalty for loss of benefits to which the individual is otherwise entitled.
- If an incentive is offered, a description of the incentive and requirement to obtain it; also, a description of the impact of a decision to discontinue participation.

FIGURE 1
Creating the informed consent form: Format and content

The form must be written so that participants understand the information in the form. In some past cases, the form was so technical or loaded with legal terminology that it is very unlikely that the participants fully realized what they were signing. In general, consent forms should be written in simple and straightforward language that avoids jargon and technical terminology (generally at a sixth- to eighth-grade reading level; most word processors provide grade-level information with the Grammar Check feature). To make the form easier to understand, it should not be written in the first person. Instead, information should be provided as if the researcher were simply having a conversation with the participant. Thus, the form might say *Participation in this study is voluntary. You may decline to participate without penalty,* instead of *I understand that participation in this study is voluntary. I may decline to participate without penalty.* The first statement is providing information to the participant in a straightforward way using the second person ("you"), whereas the second statement has a legalistic tone that may be more difficult to understand. Finally, a participant cannot give informed consent if the consent form itself is not in a language the participant can read; researchers should provide each participant with a consent form in that participant's primary language.

Autonomy Issues

Informed consent seems simple enough; however, there are important issues to consider. The first concerns a lack of autonomy. What happens when the participants lack the ability to make a free and informed decision to voluntarily participate? Special populations such as minors, patients in psychiatric hospitals, or adults with cognitive impairments require special precautions. When minors are asked to participate, for example, a written consent form signed by a parent or guardian is generally required in addition to agreement by the minor; this agreement by a minor is formally called *assent*. The Society for Research on Child Development has established guidelines for ethical research with children (see http://www.srcd.org/about-us/ethical-standards-research).

Coercion is another threat to autonomy. Any procedure that limits an individual's freedom to consent is potentially coercive. For example, a supervisor who asks employees to fill out a survey during a staff meeting or a professor who requires students to participate in a specific study in order to pass the course is applying considerable pressure on potential participants. The employees may believe that the supervisor will somehow punish them if they do not participate; they also risk embarrassment if they refuse in front of co-workers. Sometimes the promise of benefits can also be coercive (see APA Ethics Code: Standard 8.06). Researchers often offer an incentive with the request to participate. Monetary incentives (actual money or gift cards) are usually small and must not be so great to induce people to discount any risks of participating in a study. Another incentive used is a chance to win a drawing for a larger prize. Again, the prize cannot be so valuable that potential subjects would fail to consider all the other risks and benefits of the research. Many institutions have specific guidelines for researchers to use when designing incentives.

Withholding Information and Deception

It may have occurred to you that providing all information about the study to participants might be unwise. Providing too much information could potentially invalidate the results of the study; for example, researchers usually will withhold information about the hypothesis of the study or the particular condition an individual is participating in (see Hertwig & Ortman, 2008; Kimmel et al., 2011; Sieber, 2009). Withholding information is sometimes described as a type of **deception** termed *passive deception*. It is generally acceptable to withhold information when the research is designated as minimal risk, the information would not affect the decision to participate, and the information will be provided later, usually in a debriefing session when the study is completed. Most people who volunteer for psychology research do not expect full disclosure about the study prior to participation. However, they do expect a thorough debriefing after they have completed the study. Debriefing will be described after we consider the more problematic issue of deception (see APA Ethics Code: Standard 8.07).

It may also have occurred to you that there are research procedures in which informed consent is not necessary or even possible. If you choose to observe the number of same-sex and mixed-sex study groups in your library, you probably do not need to announce your presence or obtain anyone's permission. If you study the content of the self-descriptions that people write for an online dating service, do you need to contact each person in order to include their information in your study? When planning research, it is important to make sure that you either acquire informed consent, or have very good reasons not to obtain informed consent.

In contrast to passive deception is *active deception* (Kimmel, 2001). Active deception is actively providing misinformation about the nature of a study. The Milgram experiment illustrates two types of active deception. First, participants were deceived about the purpose of the study. Participants in the Milgram experiment agreed to take part in a study of memory and learning, but they actually took part in a study on obedience. Who could imagine that a memory and learning experiment (that title does sound tame, after all) would involve delivering high-intensity, painful electric shocks to another person? Participants in the Milgram experiment did not know what they were letting themselves in for.

The Milgram study was conducted before it was routine to obtain informed consent; however, you can imagine that Milgram's consent form would deceptively have participants agree to be in a memory study. Is it possible that the informed consent procedure would affect the outcome of the study? If they had known that the research was designed to study obedience, participants likely would have behaved differently. Few of us like to think of ourselves as obedient, and we would probably go out of our way to prove that we are not.

The informed consent procedure for the Milgram study would include an assurance that the participant could withdraw from the experiment at any time without penalty. Research indicates that providing this assurance may bias participants' responses, at least in some research areas. For example, research on stressors such as noise or crowding has shown that a feeling of "control" over a stressor reduces its negative impact. If you know that you can terminate a loud, obnoxious noise, the noise produces less stress than when the noise is uncontrollable. Studies by Gardner (1978) and Dill et al. (1982) have demonstrated that informed consent procedures do increase perceptions of control in stress experiments and therefore can affect the conclusions drawn from the research.

It is also possible that the informed consent procedure may bias the sample. In the Milgram study, if participants had prior knowledge that they would be asked to give severe shocks to the other person, some might have declined to be in the experiment. Therefore, we might limit our ability to generalize the results only to those "types" who agreed to participate. If this were true, anyone could say that the obedient behavior seen in the Milgram experiment occurred simply because the people who agreed to participate were sadists in the first place!

The Milgram study also illustrates a second type of active deception in which participants become part of a series of events staged for the purposes of the study. A confederate of the experimenter played the part of another participant in the study (the "learner") who was attached to a shock machine operated by the actual participant. Milgram created a reality for the participant in which obedience to authority could be observed. In other research employing active deception, participants might be falsely informed that they failed a test or possessed an undesirable personality trait. Such deception has been most common in social psychology research; it is much less frequent in areas of experimental psychology such as human perception, learning, memory, and motor performance. Even in these areas, researchers may introduce some form of deception. For example, to make the experiment seem plausible and involving, participants may be told that they are reading actual newspaper stories for a study on readability when the true purpose is to examine memory errors or organizational schemes). In other memory research, the researchers may create a false memory about a video of a crime that participants had viewed.

Is deception a major ethical problem in behavioral research? In the decades since the Milgram experiments, researchers have become more sensitive to ethical issues when planning their studies. Moreover, ethics review committees at universities and colleges now carefully review proposed research; elaborate deception is likely to be approved only when the research is important and there are no alternative procedures available (ethics review boards are described later in this chapter.) Although both passive and active deceptions may be used, there are few instances of major problematic procedures (Korn, 1997; Sieber et al., 1995). Further, a case can be made that research participants do not find deception objectionable. Lasser et al. (2020) replicated a study done by Fisher & Fyrberg (1994) in which potential subjects read a description of a deception experiment. In one description, the participants heard a recording designed to influence their mood to feel happy or sad. In another, the subjects were deceived to think they had spilled coffee over a confederate's belongings. After reading about the experiments, all subjects believed that the benefits outweighed any costs to the participants and favored implementation of the study. This was true in the original study as well as the 2020 replication. Still, observers such as Hilbig et al. (2021) argue that researchers, journal editors, and institutional reviewers need to be vigilant about deception and try to adopt alternative procedures whenever possible.

THE IMPORTANCE OF DEBRIEFING

Debriefing occurs after the completion of a study, and includes an explanation of the purposes of the research that is given to participants following their participation (see APA Ethics Code: Standard 8.08). It is an opportunity for the researcher to deal with issues of withholding information, deception, and potential harmful effects of participation. Debriefing is one way that researchers can follow the guidelines in the APA Ethics Code, particularly Principles B (Fidelity and Responsibility), C (Integrity), and E (Respect for People's Rights and Dignity).

If participants were deceived in any way, the researcher needs to explain why the deception was necessary. If the research altered a participant's physical or psychological state in some way—as in a study that produces stress—the researcher must make sure that the participant has calmed down and is comfortable about having participated. If a participant needs to receive additional information or to speak with someone else about the study, the researcher should provide access to these resources. The participants should leave the experiment without any ill feelings toward the field of psychology, and they may even leave with some new insight into their own behavior or personality.

Debriefing also provides an opportunity for the researcher to explain the purpose of the study and tell participants what kinds of results are expected and perhaps discuss the practical implications of the results. In some cases, researchers may contact participants later to inform them of the actual results of the study. Thus, debriefing has both an educational and an ethical purpose.

The Milgram study can also teach us something about the importance of debriefing. Milgram described a very thorough debriefing. However, an examination of original records and interviews with subjects by Perry (2013) reveals that often the debriefing was little more than seeing that Mr. Wallace was indeed not harmed. Many subjects were rushed from the lab; some did not even learn that no shocks were actually administered but only found that out when Milgram mailed a report of his research findings to the subjects 6 months after data collection was completed (and some never received the letter). Today we would consider Milgram's less than thorough debriefing immediately following the experiment to be a real problem with his research procedure.

Despite all the problems of the stress of the procedure and the rather sloppy debriefing, most of the subjects in the Milgram studies were positive about their experience. The letter that Milgram sent with a detailed report of the study included a questionnaire to assess subjects' reactions to the experiment; 92% of the subjects returned the questionnaire. The responses showed that 84% were glad that they had participated, and 74% said they had benefited from the experience. Only 1% said they were sorry they had participated (Blass, 2004). Other researchers who have conducted further work on the ethics of the Milgram study reached the same conclusion (Ring et al., 1970).

More generally, research on the effectiveness of debriefing indicates that debriefing is an effective way of dealing with deception. Boynton et al. (2013) conducted an experiment in which college students were (a) provided with an inaccurate or accurate description of a task used in the study, and (b) given false feedback on how they performed on the task. Following debriefing, neither of these deceptive procedures had an impact on the participants' positive or negative emotions.

There is some evidence that at least in some circumstances, the debriefing needs to be thorough to be effective. In a recent study by Greenspan and Loftus (2021), participants watched a video of a theft; a woman in the video wore a gray jacket and the stolen item was a wallet. Subjects in a misinformation condition were asked misleading questions that might affect their memory ("Think about the woman in the red jacket..."). A control condition included a question without the misinformation. There was a strong misinformation effect with subjects later recalling the wrong color of the jacket and an incorrect stolen item. At the completion of the study, the subjects in the misinformation condition were debriefed; this included being told about the misinformation, the background of research on this topic, and why the deception was necessary. In a second session five days later, subjects received an email with a link to a questionnaire. Subjects in the misinformation condition responded that they thought they had learned a lot and felt positive about participating. However, they still reported that the jacket was red! Greenspan and Loftus then conducted the experiment with both the typical debriefing and a new "enhanced debriefing," which included more information about the effect and the connection to eyewitness memory errors. It also included a detailed description of the misleading information. The enhanced debriefing was associated with more positive ratings of the experience than the typical debriefing and elimination of the misinformation effect in the second session.

McFarland et al. (2007) reported a similar finding in an experiment in which subjects were given false feedback about their ability to accurately judge whether suicide notes were genuine; after making a judgment, they were told that they had succeeded or failed at the task. The researchers then gave different types of debriefing. A minimal debriefing only mentioned that the feedback they received was not based on their performance at all. A more thorough debriefing also included information that the suicide notes were not real. Participants with the additional information had a more accurate assessment of their ability than did subjects receiving the minimal debriefing procedure.

Debriefing is part of a researcher's obligation to treat participants with dignity and respect. Boynton et al. (2013) also pointed out that researchers have the same obligation throughout the entire study. Their debriefing study included a condition in which the experimenter fails to behave in a professional manner. The unprofessional experimenter spoke hurriedly, did not smile or have eye contact with the subject, and even sent a text while the subject waited. The professional experimenter was punctual, polite, smiled, and made eye contact. The unprofessional conduct had a strong negative effect on subjects. Researchers need to remember that they have a real human relationship when they interact with participants.

INSTITUTIONAL REVIEW BOARDS

Although the Belmont Report provided an outline for issues of research ethics, and the APA Ethics Code provides guidelines as well, the actual rules and regulations for the protection of human research participants were issued by the U.S. Department of Health and Human Services (HHS). Under these regulations (HHS, 2018), every institution that receives federal funds must have an **Institutional Review Board (IRB)** that is responsible for the review of research conducted within the institution (also see APA Ethics Code: Standard 8.01). IRBs are local review agencies composed of at least five individuals; at least one member of the IRB must be from outside the institution. Every college and university in the United States that receives federal funding has an IRB; in addition, most psychology departments have their own research review committee (Chastain & Landrum, 1999). All research conducted by faculty, students, and staff associated with the institution is reviewed in some way by the IRB. This includes research that may be conducted at another location such as a school, community agency, or hospital, or via the internet.

Federal regulations for IRB oversight of research require all researchers to complete specified educational requirements. Most colleges and universities now require faculty, students, and others conducting research to complete one or more online courses on research ethics to meet these requirements. A major provider of these courses is CITI (Collaborative IRB Training Initiative).

The HHS regulations also categorized research according to the amount of risk involved in the research. This concept of risk was later incorporated into the Ethics Code of the American Psychological Association.

Federal agencies that regulate IRBs define research as a "systematic investigation, including research development, testing, and evaluation designed to develop or contribute to generalizable knowledge" (HHS, 2018). There are two important parts of this definition:

- Systematic: The Belmont Report defined research as "an activity designed to test a hypothesis and permit conclusions to be drawn ... Research is usually described in a formal protocol that sets an objective and a sequence of procedures to reach that objective" (National Commission, 1979). This means that for a project or data collection to be considered research, it must be purposefully and intentionally designed.

- Generalizable knowledge: This means that for a project to be considered research, a person must have intent to create new knowledge with the results. For instance, a project wherein students watch parking behavior in a parking lot in order to learn how to measure parking behavior is not research, because the point of the data collection is not the creation of new knowledge. On the other hand, if a research team wanted to watch parking behavior in a parking lot to address a hypothesis about parking behavior, then it would be research. Finally, generalizable knowledge typically is created to share with others via presentation, publication, or another form of dissemination.

Researchers planning to conduct an investigation are required to submit an application to the IRB. The application requires a description of risks and benefits, procedures for minimizing risk, the exact wording of the informed consent form (in all languages in which the form will be used), how participants will be debriefed, and procedures for maintaining confidentiality. The IRB may specify procedures for continuing review. If it is a long-term project, it will be reviewed at least once each year. If there are any changes in procedures, researchers are required to obtain approval from the IRB.

Determining Type of IRB Review

For purposes of IRB review, research with human subjects is classified as either **minimal risk** or *greater than minimal risk*. Minimal risk means that the risks of harm to participants are no greater than risks encountered in daily life or in routine physical or psychological tests. If the research procedures are judged by the IRB as no greater than minimal risk, the study qualifies for one of three levels of review: exempt review, expedited review, or limited review. If a project is judged to be greater than minimal risk, then a full board review is required. Figure 2 shows this process.

Exempt Review of Minimal Risk Research   **Exempt review research** is exempt from the more rigorous review requirements of the federal regulations. Such research must fall into one of several exempt research categories. Examples of exempt research include:

- Research conducted in educational settings that does not have an adverse effect on learning opportunities. This includes research that focuses on comparisons of educational strategies, curriculum, and classroom management techniques.

- Research that only involves cognitive tests, surveys, interviews, or observation of public behavior. The identity of the subjects of such research cannot be ascertained. Research with children that only involves observation of public behavior with no contact with the researchers is included.

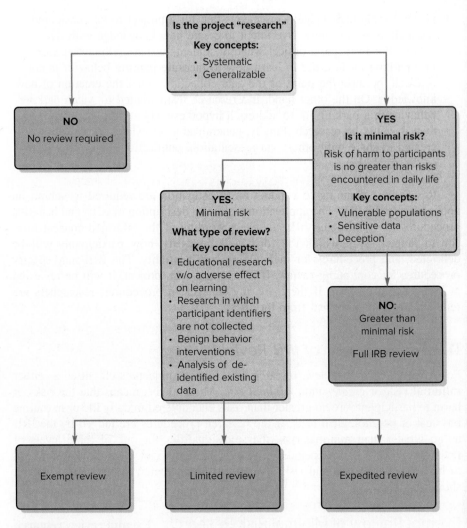

FIGURE 2
IRB decision tree. In order to determine which type of review is required, answer the questions in this decision tree

- Research using "benign behavior interventions" with adult participants who are able to provide their consent to participate. Examples of benign interventions include performing a cognitive or behavioral task and manipulation of the physical or social environment. The intervention must be brief in duration, harmless, and very unlikely to cause discomfort or embarrassment. Data collection is limited to self-report by the subjects themselves and observation of the subjects. Observation may not include wearing physical measurement devices but can involve audiovisual recording. Except as approved by the IRB, the data collected should be anonymous.

- Use of secondary data. Secondary data include information that already exists and was collected either for nonresearch purposes or as part of a research investigation in which informed consent was obtained. The data must be publicly available, and the identity of participants cannot be ascertained. An example of a secondary data source is the General Social Survey or GSS (https://www.norc.org), a series of surveys conducted regularly since 1972. Each survey covers a range of topics, such as attitudes, life satisfaction, health, religion, education, age, and marital status.

The IRB at each institution develops procedures to allow researchers to apply for exempt status and to evaluate whether the research is given the exemption. Researchers cannot decide by themselves that the research is exempt.

Expedited Review of Minimal Risk Research

Expedited review applies to research that is minimal-risk research but does not match the exempt research categories. Much expedited-review research is biological/medical (e.g., blood samples, collection of hair samples, or saliva); it also includes research procedures frequently used by behavioral researchers. These procedures include (HHS, 1998):

- Blood samples with limitations of the amount taken, frequency of taking samples, characteristics of participants.
- Taking "biological specimens" such as hair, saliva, sweat, and skin cells.
- Common physical measures made using healthy adults, such as heart rate, muscle tension, blood pressure. Further, participants may be asked to wear devices that record such measures.
- Data from voice, video, digital, or image recordings.
- "Research on individual or group characteristics or behavior (including, but not limited to, research on perception, cognition, motivation, identity, language, communication, cultural beliefs or practices, and social behavior) or research employing survey, interview, oral history, focus group, program evaluation, human factors evaluation, or quality assurance methodologies. (NOTE: Some research in this category may be exempt from the HHS regulations for the protection of human subjects. 45 CFR 46.101(b)(2) and (b)(3). This listing refers only to research that is not exempt.)"

The IRB develops a procedure for determining that proposed research should receive expedited review. The proposal will be reviewed by a subcommittee identified by the IRB. This review is less extensive and time-consuming than a full review, requiring meetings of the entire IRB.

Limited Review of Minimal Risk Research

The third category of IRB review for minimal risk research is called **limited review.** Studies that can be subject to limited review are those that include benign behavioral interventions for which sensitive data are collected from adult participants under the circumstance where participates would need to be identified.

Every IRB develops procedures for determining that proposed research should receive limited review. This review is less extensive and less time-consuming than full IRB review and does not require meetings of the entire IRB. Limited review is usually carried out by a member of the IRB. This person may approve the research as exempt or recommend further review.

Full Review of Greater Than Minimal Risk Research   Any research procedure that places participants at greater than minimal risk is subject to thorough full review by the IRB. Such review is more extensive and time-consuming than the exempt and expedited levels of review. The IRB will carefully consider the proposed informed consent procedure, the nature of the sample and plans for recruiting participants, potential risks, and whether there are alternative procedures available to the researcher. Changes in the methods may be required.

Check Your Learning

Now, head to Check Your Learning: Practice Exercise #1, to tests your skills in identifying the risks involved in research scenarios.

RESEARCH WITH NONHUMAN ANIMAL SUBJECTS

Although much of this chapter has been concerned with the ethics of research with humans, you are undoubtedly well aware that psychologists sometimes conduct research with animals (Akins et al., 2005). Psychologists and other behavioral researchers primarily work with rats and mice; they also study primates, birds, dogs, cats. They also study many other species, including fish, cockroaches and other insects, gerbils, hamsters, guinea pigs, horses, rabbits, arachnids, wolves, worms, and bears. Less than 10% of published empirical research in psychology uses nonhuman animals.

Animals are used in behavioral research for a variety of reasons. The key reason is that researchers can carefully control animals' environmental conditions, studying the same animals over a long period, sometimes even monitoring their behavior 24 hours a day if necessary. Another reason to use animals for behavioral research is that what motivates a mouse is less complex than what motivates a human: a mouse will stop exercising because it's tired, sick, or hurt, whereas a human will stop exercising because they want to check their resting heart rate. These advantages were clear in a recent study that used mice to focus on the question of what happens to the body if regular exercise takes place soon after waking or closer to the time of sleep onset (Sato et al., 2022). The researchers could control the amount and timing of exercise and perform complex measurements daily. They could control the lives of the mice in ways that would be much more difficult with humans because all sorts of things influence humans' sleep and exercise patterns!

Traditionally, much of the research with nonhuman animals focused on learning and conditioning. More recently, researchers have expanded beyond learning to focus on cognitive processes (see, for example, dogcognition.com and the journal *Animal Cognition*). In addition, more research is conducted to study the animals themselves—animal communication, migration, reproduction, and effects of climate change.

Animal research benefits humans and leads to many discoveries that would not have been possible otherwise (Bedwell, 2016; Carroll & Overmier, 2001; Miller, 1985). Surveys indicate that psychology professors and students also hold positive attitudes about research with animals (Plous, 1996a, 1996b). This research is indeed very important and will continue to be necessary.

Strict laws and ethical guidelines govern both research with animals and teaching procedures that involve using animals. Such regulations deal with providing the animals with proper housing, feeding, cleanliness, and health care. They specify that the research must avoid any cruelty in the form of unnecessary pain to the animal. In addition, institutions in which animal research is carried out must have an *Institutional Animal Care and Use Committee (IACUC)* composed of at least one scientist, one veterinarian, and a community member. An **IACUC** is an ethics review board that shares a lot of similarities with an IRB—the IACUC is charged with reviewing animal research procedures and ensuring that all regulations are adhered to (see Holden, 1987).

The APA Ethics Code (see APA Ethics Code: Standard 8.09) addresses the ethical responsibilities of researchers when studying nonhuman animals. APA has also developed a more detailed *Guidelines for Ethical Conduct in the Care and Use of Nonhuman Animals* (https://www.apa.org/science/leadership/care/guidelines.aspx). Four of the critical guidelines for the ethical treatment of animals in research settings are these:

- Research conducted with animals should have a clear scientific purpose

- Research conducted with animals should be significant enough to justify the use of nonhuman animals.

- An appropriate animal care committee (IACUC) must review all research on nonhuman animals to ensure that the methods are appropriate for the study and humane.

- Researchers using animals should carefully monitor their research subjects' welfare throughout any investigation.

BEING AN ETHICAL RESEARCHER: THE ISSUE OF MISREPRESENTATION

Principle C of the APA Ethics Code focuses on integrity—the promotion of accuracy, honesty, and truthfulness. The ethical researcher acts with integrity and in so doing does not engage in misrepresentation. Specifically, we will explore two specific types of misrepresentation: research fraud through fabrication of data (see APA Ethics Code: Standard 8.10) and plagiarism (see APA Ethics Code: Standard 8.11).

Fraud

Making up data, i.e., data fabrication, is **fraud.** Instances of fraud in the field of psychology are considered to be very serious (see, for instance, Hostetler, 1987; Riordan & Marlin, 1987), but fortunately, they are very rare (Murray, 2002). Perhaps the most famous case is that of Sir Cyril Burt, who reported that the IQ scores of identical twins reared apart were highly similar. The data were used to support the argument that genetic influences on IQ are extremely important. However, Kamin (1974) noted some irregularities in Burt's data. A number of correlations for different sets of twins were exactly the same to the third decimal place, virtually a mathematical impossibility. This observation led to the discovery that some of Burt's presumed co-workers had not in fact worked with him or had simply been fabricated. Ironically, though, Burt's "data" were close to what has been reported by other investigators who have studied the IQ scores of twins.

In most cases, fraud is detected when other scientists cannot replicate the results of a study. Suspicions of fabrication of research data by social psychologist Karen Ruggiero arose when other researchers had difficulty replicating her published findings. The researcher subsequently resigned from her academic position and retracted her research findings (Murray, 2002). Sometimes fraud is detected by a colleague or by students who worked with the researcher. For example, Stephen Breuning was guilty of faking data showing that stimulants could be used to reduce hyperactive and aggressive behavior in children (Byrne, 1988). In this case, another researcher who had worked closely with Breuning had suspicions about the data; he then informed the federal agency that had funded the research.

A case of extensive fraud that went undetected for years involves a social psychologist at Tilburg University in the Netherlands (Verfaellie & McGwin, 2011). Diederik Stapel not only created data that changed the outcome of studies that were conducted, he also reported results of studies that were never conducted at all. His studies were published in prestigious journals and often reported in popular news outlets because his research reported intriguing findings (e.g., that being in a messy, disorderly environment results in more stereotypical and discriminatory thoughts). Students eventually reported their suspicions to the university administration, but the fact that Stapel's misconduct continued for so long is certainly troublesome. According to a committee that investigated Stapel, one cause was the fact the professor was powerful, prestigious, and charismatic. He would work closely with students to design studies but then collect the data himself. He would invite a colleague to take his existing data set to analyze and write a report. These are highly unusual practices but his students and colleagues did not question him.

Fraud is not a major problem in science in part because researchers know that others will read their reports and conduct further studies, including replications. They know that their reputations and careers will be seriously damaged if other scientists conclude that the results are fraudulent. In addition, the likelihood of detection of fraud has increased in recent years as data accessibility has become more open: the adoption of Open Science standards by academic journals and funding agencies has led researchers to make their data accessible to other scientists (see APA Ethics Code: Standard 8.14).

Why, then, do researchers sometimes commit fraud? For one thing, scientists occasionally find themselves in jobs with extreme pressure to produce impressive results. This is not a sufficient explanation, of course, because many researchers maintain high ethical standards under such pressure. Another reason is that researchers who feel a need to produce fraudulent data have an exaggerated fear of failure, as well as a great need for success and the admiration that comes with it. Every report of scientific misconduct includes a discussion of motivations such as these.

One final point: Allegations of fraud should not be made lightly. If you disagree with someone's results on philosophical, political, religious, or other grounds, it does not mean that they are fraudulent. Even if you cannot replicate the results, the reason may lie in aspects of the methodology of the study rather than deliberate fraud. However, the fact that fraud could be a possible explanation of results stresses the importance of careful record keeping and documentation of the procedures and results.

Plagiarism

Plagiarism refers to misrepresenting another's work as your own. Writers must give proper citation of sources. Plagiarism can take the form of submitting an entire paper written by someone else; it can also mean including a paragraph or even a sentence that is copied without using quotation marks and a reference to the source of the quotation. Plagiarism also occurs when you present another person's ideas as your own rather than properly acknowledging the source of the ideas. Thus, even if you paraphrase the actual words used by a source, it is plagiarism if the source is not cited.

Although plagiarism is certainly not a new problem, access to internet resources and the ease of copying material from the internet may be increasing its prevalence. In fact, Szabo and Underwood (2004) report that more than 50% of a sample of British university students believe that using internet resources for academically dishonest activities is acceptable. It is little wonder that many schools are turning to computer-based mechanisms of detecting plagiarism.

Word-for-Word Plagiarism
It is useful to further distinguish between plagiarism that is "word for word" and plagiarism that is "paraphrased." A writer commits **word-for-word plagiarism** when he or she copies a section of another person's work word for word without placing those words within quotation marks to indicate that the segment was written by somebody else, and without citing the source of the information. As an example, consider the following paragraph from Burger (2009):

> Milgram's obedience studies have maintained a place in psychology classes and textbooks largely because of their implications for understanding the worst of human behaviors, such as atrocities, massacres, and genocide. (p. 10)

A writer who wrote the following in his or her work without attributing it to Burger (2009) would be committing word-for-word plagiarism:

> Since they were conducted in the 1960s, Milgram's obedience studies have maintained a place in psychology classes and textbooks largely because of their implications for understanding the worst of human behaviors, including atrocities, massacres, and genocide.

The highlighted text in this example is plagiarized. Note that adding a few words, or changing a few words, does not change the fact that much of the text is taken from another source, without attribution.

An ethical writer would put quotation marks around sentences that were directly taken from the original source and would include a citation. For instance:

> Burger (2009) concluded that since they were conducted in the 1960s "Milgram's obedience studies have maintained a place in psychology classes and textbooks largely because of their implications for understanding the worst of human behaviors, such as atrocities, massacres, and genocide" (p. 10).

Paraphrasing Plagiarism

When a writer expresses the meaning of a passage from a source text without using the actual words of that text, they are paraphrasing. In **paraphrasing plagiarism,** instead of the words being directly copied without attribution, the ideas are copied without attribution. Note that there is not a "number or percentage of words" that moves writing from paraphrasing to plagiarism, but instead it is the underlying idea.

Supplying an example of paraphrasing plagiarism is more difficult. Let us use the same passage:

> Milgram's obedience studies have maintained a place in psychology classes and textbooks largely because of their implications for understanding the worst of human behaviors, such as atrocities, massacres, and genocide (Burger, 2009, p. 10).

One example of paraphrasing plagiarism would be:

> Humans are capable of many vile and reprehensible acts. The reality is that Milgram's studies have remained important to psychology because they seem to explain these behaviors.

Here the basic idea presented is directly related to the passage in Burger (2009). In this case, ethical writing may be:

> Humans are capable of many vile and reprehensible acts. The reality is that Milgram's studies have remained important to psychology because they seem to explain these behaviors (Burger, 2009).

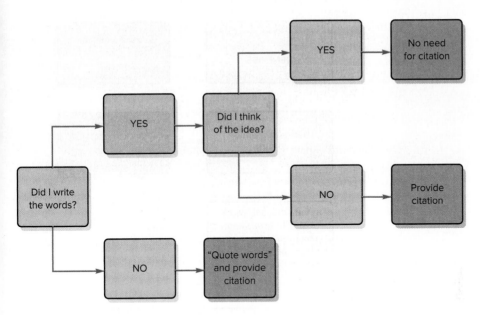

FIGURE 3
Guide for avoiding plagiarism in writing

The flowchart in Figure 3 can help you evaluate your own writing for plagiarism by using two key questions: Did I write the words? Did I think of the idea?

Plagiarism is wrong and can lead to many severe consequences, including academic sanctions such as a failing grade or expulsion from the school. Finally, it is interesting to note that some students believe that citing sources weakens their paper—that they are not being sufficiently original. But in fact, Harris (2002) notes that student papers are actually strengthened when sources are used and properly cited.

Check Your Learning

Visit Check Your Learning: Practice Exercises #2 and #3. Both are targeted on one of the most essential topics of the chapter: plagiarism.

CONCLUSION: RISKS AND BENEFITS REVISITED

You are now familiar with the ethical issues that confront researchers who study human and animal behavior. When you make decisions about research ethics, you need to consider the many factors associated with risk to the participants. Are there risks of psychological harm or loss of confidentiality? Who are the research participants? What types of deception, if any, are used in the procedure? How

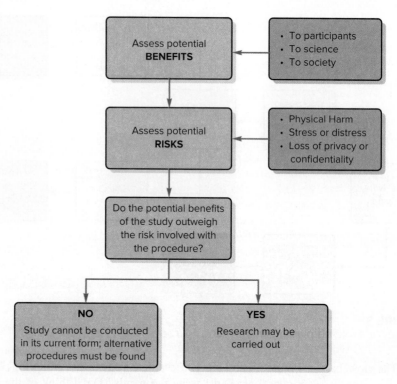

FIGURE 4
Analysis of risks and benefits

will informed consent be obtained? What debriefing procedures are being used? You also need to weigh the direct benefits of the research to the participants, as well as the scientific importance of the research and the educational benefits to the students who may be conducting the research for a class or degree requirement (see Figure 4).

These are not easy decisions. Consider a study in which a confederate posing as another subject insults the participant (Vasquez et al., 2013). The subject wrote an essay expressing attitudes on a controversial topic; subsequently, the subject heard the confederate evaluate the essay as unclear, unconvincing, and "one of the worst things I have read in a long time." The subject could then behave aggressively in choosing the amount of hot sauce that the other person would have to consume in another part of the experiment. The insult did lead to choosing more hot sauce, particularly if the subject was given an opportunity to ruminate about it rather than being distracted by other tasks. Instances of aggression following perceived insults are common so you can argue that this is an important topic. Do you believe that the potential benefits of the study to society and science outweigh the risks involved in the procedure?

Obviously, an IRB reviewing this study concluded that the researchers had sufficiently minimized risks to the participants such that the benefits outweighed the costs. If you ultimately decide that the costs outweigh the benefits, you must conclude that the study cannot be conducted in its current form. You may suggest alternative procedures that could make it acceptable. If the benefits outweigh the costs, you will likely decide that the research should be carried out. Your calculation might differ from another person's calculation, which is precisely why having ethics review boards is such a good idea. An appropriate review of research proposals makes it highly unlikely that unethical research will be approved.

Ethical guidelines and regulations evolve over time. The APA Ethics Code and federal, state, and local regulations may be revised periodically. Researchers need to always be aware of the most current policies and procedures. In the following chapters, we will discuss many specific procedures for studying behavior. As you read about these procedures and apply them to research you may be interested in, remember that ethical considerations are always paramount.

In the time when Stanley Milgram was conceptualizing his obedience experiments, there were no institutional review boards. If there had been, it might have been difficult to get his study approved. Participants were not informed of the purpose of the study (indeed, they were deceived into thinking that it was a study of learning), and they were also deceived into thinking that they were harming another person. The struggle is, of course, that if participants had known the true nature of the study, or that they were not really delivering electric shocks, the results would not have been as meaningful.

The Milgram study was partially replicated by Burger in 2009. That study is included as the Illustrative Article for this chapter.

ENGAGING WITH RESEARCH: REPLICATION OF MILGRAM

Burger (2009) conducted a partial replication of the classic Stanley Milgram obedience studies.

First, acquire and read the article (available at https://www.apa.org/pubs/journals/releases/amp-64-1-1.pdf):

Burger, J. M. (2009). Replicating Milgram: Would people still obey today? *American Psychologist, 64*(1), 1–11. https://doi.org/10.1037/a0010932

Then, after reading the article, consider the following:

1. **What is the primary goal of this study? Description, Prediction, Determining Cause, or Explaining? Do the authors achieve their goals?**

   a. How does Burger know that one thing caused another?

2. **What did these researchers do? What was the method?**

   a. How did Burger screen participants in the study? What was the purpose of the screening procedure?

3. **What was measured?**

4. **To what or whom can we generalize the results?**

5. **What did they find? What were the results?**

6. **Have other researchers found similar results?**

7. **What are the limitations of this study?**

8. **What are the ethical issues present in this study?**

   a. Conduct an informal risk-benefit analysis. What are the risks and benefits inherent in this study? Do you think that the study is ethically justifiable, given your analysis? Why or why not?

   b. Burger paid participants $50 for two 45-minute sessions. Could this be considered coercive? Why or why not?

   c. Burger uses deception in this study. Is it acceptable? Do you believe that the debriefing session described in the report adequately addresses the issues of deception?

BEING A SKILLED CONSUMER OF RESEARCH

1. What do you think about the ethics of the Milgram obedience study? Do you think that the study should have been allowed? Were the potential risks to Milgram's participants worth the knowledge gained by the outcomes? If you were a participant in the study, would you feel okay with having been deceived into thinking that you had harmed someone? What if the person you were "shocking" was a younger sibling? Or a grandparent? Would that make a difference? Why or why not?

2. A recent study showed that participants often don't read beyond the second paragraph of an informed consent document before signing (Douglas et al., 2021). Is this something researchers should be concerned about? Why? What might you do to increase the likelihood of reading more of the informed consent document?

3. Consider the following experiment, similar to one that was conducted by Smith et al. (1978). Each participant interacted for an hour with another person who was actually an accomplice of the researcher. After this interaction, both persons agreed to return one week later for another session together. When the real participants returned, they were informed that the person they had met the week before had died. The researchers then measured reactions to the death of the person.

   a. Discuss the ethical issues raised by the experiment in terms of the APA Ethics Code.

   b. What alternative methods for studying this problem (reactions to death) might you suggest?

c. Would your reactions to this study be different if the participants had played with an infant and then later been told that the infant had died? Would your analysis of the ethics of the study change? Why or why not?

4. Dr. Rodríguez conducted a study to examine various aspects of college students' drug use. The students filled out a questionnaire in a classroom on the campus; about 50 students were tested at a time. The questionnaire asked about prior experience with various illegal substances. If a student had experience with a drug, a number of other detailed questions were asked. However, if the student did not have any prior experience with a drug, they skipped the detailed questions and simply went on to answer another general question about drug use. What ethical issues arise when conducting research such as this? What problems might arise because of the "skip" procedure used in this study?

5. Find your college's code of student conduct online and review the section on plagiarism. How would you improve this section? What would you tell your professors to do to help students avoid plagiarism?

Check Your Learning: Practice Exercises

Practice Exercise #1

Levels of Risk for Research Scenarios

Scenario	No risk	Minimal risk	Greater than minimal risk
1. Researchers conducted a study with college students in which they manipulated the participants' emotions by having them recall and think about a very sad moment in their lives and measured their recall after watching a pre-recorded lecture.			
2. A group of researchers plans to measure differences in depth perception accuracy with and without perceptual cues. In one condition participants could use both eyes, and in another condition one eye was covered with an eye patch.			

Scenario	No risk	Minimal risk	Greater than minimal risk
3. Researchers conducted an anonymous survey on attitudes toward gun control among shoppers at a local mall.			
4. College students watched a 10-minute video presenting some news content. After the video played, participants completed a brief questionnaire to test their memory.			

Practice Exercise #2

Below is a direct passage from Burger (2009):

> "I cannot say with absolute certainty that the present participants would have continued to the end of the shock generator's range at a rate similar to Milgram's participants. Only a full replication of Milgram's procedure can provide such an unequivocal conclusion. However, numerous studies have demonstrated the effect of incrementally larger requests." (Burger, 2009, p. 9)

a. First—and hopefully the first and last time you are ever told to do this—commit word-for-word plagiarism of the passage above

b. Second—and hopefully this is the last time that you will ever do this—commit paraphrasing plagiarism of the passage above

c. Finally—and hopefully this is the beginning of a lifetime of ethical writing: paraphrase the passage and correctly cite the source

Practice Exercise #3

Indiana University created an excellent online resource called "How to Recognize Plagiarism." You can find it here: https://plagiarism.iu.edu.

This practice exercise is simple: First, complete their training program, then complete the test to earn a certificate.

(Some answers are provided at the end of this chapter.)

CHAPTER REVIEW

Review Questions

1. Discuss the major ethical issues in behavioral research, including risks, benefits, deception, debriefing, informed consent, and justice. How can researchers weigh the need to conduct research against the need for ethical procedures?

2. Why is informed consent an ethical principle? What are the potential problems with obtaining fully informed consent?

3. What alternatives to deception are described in the text?

4. Summarize the principles concerning research with human participants in the APA Ethics Code.

5. What is the difference between "no risk" and "minimal risk" research activities?

6. What is an Institutional Review Board?

7. Summarize the ethical procedures for research with animals.

8. What constitutes fraud, what are some reasons for its occurrence, and why does it not occur more frequently?

9. Describe how you would proceed to identify plagiarism in a writing assignment.

Study Terms

APA Ethics Code (p. 55)

Belmont Report (p. 54)

Confidentiality (p. 58)

Debriefing (p. 64)

Deception (p. 62)

Declaration of Helsinki (p. 53)

Exempt review research (p. 67)

Expedited review (p. 69)

Fraud (p. 72)

IACUC (p. 71)

Informed consent (p. 59)

Institutional Review Board (IRB) (p. 66)

Limited review (p. 69)

Minimal risk research (p. 67)

Nuremberg Code (p. 53)

Paraphrasing plagiarism (p. 74)

Plagiarism (p. 73)

Principle of Beneficence (Belmont Report) (p. 55)

Principle of Fidelity and Responsibility (p. 56)

Principle of Integrity (p. 56)

Principle of Justice (Belmont Report) (p. 56)

Principle of Respect for Persons (Autonomy) (Belmont Report) (p. 56)

Privacy (p. 59)

Risk (physical harm, stress and distress, confidentiality and privacy) (pp. 57–59)

Risk-benefit analysis (p. 57)

Word-for-word plagiarism (p. 73)

Check Your Learning: Answers

Practice Exercise 1

1. greater than minimal risk; 2. minimal risk; 3. no risk; 4. minimal risk

Practice Exercise 2

Example passages

a. I cannot say with absolute certainty that the present participants would have continued to the end of the shock generator's range at a rate similar to Milgram's participants. Only a full replication of Milgram's procedure can provide such an unequivocal conclusion. However, numerous studies have demonstrated the effect of incrementally larger requests.

b. Milgram study—that would require perfect replication.

c. Burger pointed out that it was unclear if the participants in his study would have gone as far as participants in the original Milgram study. Determining this would require perfect replication (Burger, 2009).

fstop123/Getty Images

Fundamental Research Issues

LEARNING OBJECTIVES

- Define construct validity, internal validity, external validity, and conclusion validity. Compare and contrast the four validities.
- Define what a variable is and be able to develop an operational definition of a variable.
- Identify the different relationships between variables: positive, negative, curvilinear, and no relationship.
- Compare and contrast nonexperimental and experimental research methods.
- Distinguish between an independent variable and a dependent variable.
- Summarize the strengths and limitations of laboratory experiments and the advantage of using multiple methods of research.

IN THIS CHAPTER, WE EXPLORE SOME OF THE KEY UNDERLYING ISSUES AND CONCEPTS THAT ARE NECESSARY FOR UNDERSTANDING THE SCIENTIFIC STUDY OF BEHAVIOR. We will focus on the nature of variables and the relationships between variables. We also examine general methods for studying these relationships. Most importantly, we introduce the concept of validity in research.

VALIDITY: AN INTRODUCTION

You are likely aware of the concept of validity, even if you cannot precisely define what it means. You use the term when asking whether the information that you found on a website is valid. A juror must decide whether the testimony given in a trial is valid. Someone on a diet may wonder if the weight shown on the bathroom scale is valid. Behavioral scientists use the term "validity" to refer to the extent to which, given everything that is known, a conclusion is reasonably accurate—that is, the extent to which it approaches what we would call truth. Should you conclude that the information on the website is true, given what you know about its source and the evidence used to support the claims made on the site? Does the testimony reflect what actually happened; are there sources of bias or error that lead you to doubt the validity of the testimony? Is the scale really showing your actual weight? In all these cases, someone is confronted with information and must draw a conclusion about the extent to which that information is accurate, true, or valid.

Scientists constantly evaluate the validity of their own research and of research conducted by others. Are the conclusions made on the basis of the research reasonable? Validity is a key concept in research methods. In fact, scientific research focuses on several aspects of validity. In this chapter, we introduce four types of validity:

- **Construct validity:** the extent to which the measurement or manipulation of a variable accurately represents the theoretical variable (construct) being studied.

- **Internal validity:** the accuracy of conclusions drawn about cause and effect.

- **External validity:** the extent to which a study's findings can accurately be generalized to other populations and settings.

- **Conclusion validity:** the accuracy of the conclusions drawn from the results of a research investigation (sometimes called *statistical conclusion validity* when the conclusions are drawn from statistical analyses).

These issues will be described in greater depth in this and subsequent chapters. Before exploring issues of validity, we need to have a fundamental understanding of variables and the operational definition of variables.

VARIABLES

A **variable** is something that changes. A variable can be a behavior, thought, feeling, situation, characteristic, or an event. Anything that varies and can be measured is a variable. Any variable must have two or more levels or values. Consider the following examples of variables that you might encounter in research and your own life. As you read a book, you encounter the variable of *word length,* with values defined by the number of letters of each word. You can take this one step further and think of the *average word length* used in paragraphs in the book. One book you read may use words of a longer average length than another book. When you think about yourself and your friends, you might categorize the people on a variable such as *extraversion.* Some people can be considered relatively low on the extraversion variable (or introverted); others are high on extraversion. You might volunteer at an assisted living facility and notice that the residents differ in their *subjective well-being:* Some of the people seem much more satisfied with their lives than others. When you are driving and the car in front of you brakes to slow down or stop, the period of time before you apply the brakes in your own car is called *response time.* You might wonder if response time varies depending on the driver's age or whether the driver is talking to someone using a cell phone. In your biology class, you are studying for a final exam that is very important and you notice that you are experiencing the variable of *test anxiety.* Because the test is important, everyone in your study group says that they are very anxious about it. You might remember that you never felt anxious when studying for quizzes earlier in the course. As you can see, we all encounter variables continuously in our lives even though we do not usually call them that. Researchers, however, systematically study variables.

Examples of variables a psychologist might study include cognitive task performance, depression, intelligence, reaction time, rate of forgetting, aggression, speaker credibility, attitude change, anger, stress, age, and self-esteem. For some variables, the values will have true numeric—quantitative—properties. Values for the number of free throws made, number of words correctly recalled, and the number of symptoms of major depression would all range from 0 to an actual value. The values of other variables are not numeric, but instead simply identify different categories. You might be asked to indicate your gender, eye color, major, or marital status. In all cases, your answer will be a category—for example, you might be a psychology major, and the person seated next to you might major in computer science. These majors are different, but they do not differ in amount or quantity.

OPERATIONAL DEFINITIONS OF VARIABLES

A variable such as *aggression, cognitive task performance, pain, gender bias, prejudice, self-esteem,* or even *word length* must be defined in terms of the specific method used to measure or manipulate it. The **operational definition** of a variable is the set of procedures used when you measure or manipulate the variable.

A variable must have an operational definition to be studied empirically. The variable *bowling skill* could be operationalized as a person's average bowling score over the past 20 games, or it could be operationalized as the number of pins that fall in a single roll. Such a variable is concrete and easily operationalized in terms of score or number of pins. But things become more complicated when studying behavior. For example, a variable such as *pain* is very general and more abstract. Pain is a subjective state that cannot be directly observed, but that does not mean that we cannot create measures to infer how much pain someone is experiencing. A common pain-measurement instrument in both clinical and research settings is the McGill Pain Questionnaire, which has both a long form and a short form (Melzack, 2005). The short form includes a 0-to-5 scale with descriptors *no pain, mild, discomforting, distressing, horrible, excruciating.* There is also a line with end points of *no pain* and *worst possible pain;* the person responds by making a mark at the appropriate place on the line. In addition, the questionnaire offers sensory descriptors such as *throbbing, shooting,* and *stabbing;* each of these descriptors has a rating of *none, mild, moderate,* or *severe.* This is a relatively complex set of questions and is targeted for use with adults.

When working with children over 3, a better measurement instrument would be the Wong-Baker FACES Pain Rating Scale (http://wongbakerfaces.org/). The FACES scale consists of a series of six faces with expressions described as ranging from "no hurt" to "hurts worst." To illustrate, the face indicating "no hurt" is similar to this:

Using the FACES scale, a researcher could ask a child, "How much pain do you feel? Point to how much it hurts." These examples illustrate that the same variable of pain can be studied using different operational definitions.

There are two important benefits in operationally defining a variable. First, the task of developing an operational definition of a variable forces scientists to discuss abstract concepts in concrete terms. The process can result in the realization that the variable is too vague to study. This realization does not necessarily indicate that the concept is meaningless; it might simply mean that systematic research is not possible until the concept can be operationally defined.

In addition, operational definitions help researchers communicate their ideas with others. If someone wishes to tell me about aggression, I need to know exactly what is meant by this term, because there are many ways of operationally defining it. For example, aggression could be defined as (1) the number and duration of shocks delivered to another person, (2) the number of times a child punches an inflated toy clown, (3) the number of times a child fights with other children during recess, (4) homicide statistics gathered from police records, (5) a score on a personality measure of aggressiveness, or even (6) the number of times a pitcher hits a batter with a pitch during baseball games. Communication with another person will be easier if we agree on exactly what we mean when we use the term *aggression* in the context of our research.

Of course, a very important question arises once a variable is operationally defined: How good is the operational definition? How well does it match up with reality? How well does my average bowling score really represent my skill?

Check Your Learning

Now do the Check Your Learning: Practice Exercise #1 that will test your skills at creating operational definitions.

Construct Validity

Construct validity refers to the accuracy of our operational definitions: Does the operational definition of a variable actually reflect the true theoretical meaning of the variable? If you wish to scientifically study the variable *extraversion,* you need some way to measure extraversion. Psychologists have developed measures that ask people whether they like to socialize with strangers or whether they prefer to avoid such situations. Do the answers on such a measure provide a good or "true" indication of the underlying variable of extraversion? If you are studying anger, will telling college students that judges have rated them unattractive create feelings of anger? Researchers are able to address these questions when they design their studies and examine the results.

RELATIONSHIPS BETWEEN VARIABLES

Many studies investigate the relationship between two variables: Do the levels of the two variables vary together? For example, does playing violent video games result in greater aggressiveness? Is a speaker's perceived credibility related to how fast they talk? As age increases, does well-being increase as well?

Recall that some variables have true numeric values, whereas the levels of other variables are simply different categories. Variables with levels that are non-numeric categories would include gender, major in college, and hair color. To describe relationships among variables, we will begin by discussing relationships in which both variables have true numeric properties.

When both variables have values along a numeric scale, many different "shapes" can describe their relationship. We begin by focusing on the four most common relationships found in research: the **positive linear relationship,** the **negative linear relationship,** the **curvilinear relationship,** and, of course, the situation in which there is *no relationship* between the variables. These relationships are best illustrated by line graphs that show the way changes in one variable are accompanied by changes in a second variable. The four graphs in Figure 1 show these four types of relationships.

FIGURE 1
Four types of
relationships
between
variables

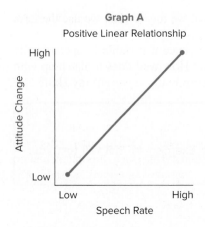

Graph A
Positive Linear Relationship

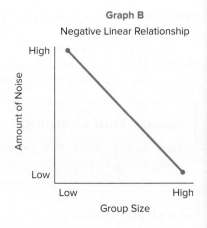

Graph B
Negative Linear Relationship

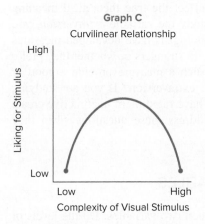

Graph C
Curvilinear Relationship

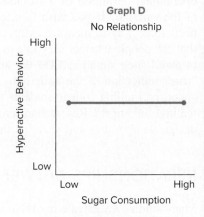

Graph D
No Relationship

Positive Linear Relationship

In a positive linear relationship, an increase in the value of one variable is accompanied by an increase in the value of the second variable. To illustrate, consider the variable of the rate of speech when delivering a persuasive message. Are "fast talkers" more persuasive? Research suggests that the answer is "yes" (Guyer et al., 2019; Smith & Shaffer, 1991). In the Smith and Shaffer study, students listened to a speech delivered at a slow (144 words per minute), intermediate (162 wpm), or fast (214 wpm) speech rate. The speaker advocated a position favoring legislation to raise the legal drinking age; the students initially disagreed with this position. Graph A in Figure 1 shows the positive linear relationship between speech rate and attitude change found in this study. That is, as the rate of speech increased, attitude change also increased. In a graph like this, we see horizontal and vertical axes, termed the *x-axis* and *y-axis,* respectively. Values of the first variable are placed on the horizontal axis, labeled from low to high.

Values of the second variable are placed on the vertical axis. Graph A shows that higher speech rates are associated with greater amounts of attitude change.

Negative Linear Relationship

Variables can also be negatively related. In a negative linear relationship, an *increase* in the value of one variable is accompanied by a *decrease* in the value of the other variable. Latané et al. (1979) were intrigued by reports that increasing the number of people working on a task may actually reduce group effort and productivity. The researchers designed an experiment to study this phenomenon, which they termed "social loafing" (which you may have observed in group projects!). The researchers asked participants to clap and shout to make as much noise as possible. They did this alone or in groups of two, four, or six people. Graph B in Figure 1 illustrates the negative relationship between the number of people in the group and the amount of noise each person makes. As the size of the group *increased,* the amount of noise made by each individual *decreased.* The two variables are systematically related, just as in a positive relationship; only the direction of the relationship is reversed.

Curvilinear Relationship

In a curvilinear relationship, increases in the values of one variable are accompanied by systematic increases and decreases in the values of the other variable. In other words, the direction of the relationship changes at least once. This type of relationship is sometimes referred to as a *nonmonotonic function* (as opposed to a *monotonic function* like a positive or negative relationship, a relationship that does not change direction).

Graph C in Figure 1 shows a curvilinear relationship. This particular relationship is called an *inverted-U*. Several inverted-U relationships are described by Grant and Schwartz (2011). Graph C depicts the relationship between the complexity of a visual stimulus and the liking of that stimulus. Having a complex visual stimulus—one with a lot of detail—is associated with more visual attractiveness, but only up to a point. With too many details, the relationship becomes negative as visual attractiveness diminishes. Of course, it is also possible to have a U-shaped relationship. Research on the relationship between age and happiness indicates that adults in their 40s are less happy than younger and older adults (Blanchflower & Oswald, 2008; Park et al., 2021). A U-shaped curve results when this relationship is graphed.

No Relationship

When there is no relationship between the two variables, the graph is simply a flat line. Graph D in Figure 1 illustrates the relationship between sugar consumption and hyperactivity in children. Many parents become convinced that their childs behavior becomes "hyper" after a sugar drink or a candy. However, many studies do not support the hypothesis that sugar causes an increase in such behavior (Milich et al., 1986; Wolraich et al., 1995). Unrelated variables vary independently of one another. Increases in one variable are not associated with any particular changes in the second variable; thus, a flat line describes the lack of relationship between the two variables.

You rarely hear about variables that are *not* related. In large-scale U.S. surveys such as the General Social Survey (http://gss.norc.org/), the size of the community in which a person lives is not associated with reported health problems or amount of internet use. Usually such findings are just not as interesting as results that do show a relationship, so there is little reason to focus on them (although research that does not support a widely assumed relationship may receive attention, as when a common medical procedure is found to be ineffective). We will examine "no relationship" findings in greater detail in the chapter "Understanding Research Results: Statistical Inference."

Remember that these are general patterns. Even if, in general, a positive linear relationship exists, it does not necessarily mean that everyone who scores high on one variable will also score high on the second variable. Individual deviations from the general pattern are likely. In addition to knowing the general type of relationship between two variables, it is also necessary to know the strength of the relationship. That is, we need to know the size of the correlation between the variables. Sometimes two variables are strongly related to each other and show little deviation from the general pattern. Other times the two variables are not highly correlated because many individuals deviate from the general pattern. A numerical index of the strength of the relationship between variables is called a **correlation coefficient.** Correlation coefficients are very important because we need to know how strongly variables are related to one another. Correlation coefficients are discussed in detail in the chapter "Understanding Research Results: Description and Correlation".

Check Your Learning

Check Your Learning: Practice Exercise #2 provides you with an opportunity to review types of relationships—for each example, identify the shape of the relationship as positive, negative, or curvilinear.

Relationships and Reduction of Uncertainty

When we detect a relationship between variables, we reduce uncertainty by increasing our understanding of the variables we are examining. The term *uncertainty* implies that there is randomness in events; scientists refer to this as *random variability* in events that occur. Research can reduce random variability by identifying systematic relationships between variables.

Identifying relationships between variables seems complex but is much easier to see in a simple example. For this example, the variables will have no quantitative properties—we will not describe *increases* in the values of variables but only differences in values—in this case, whether a person is an active user of Instagram. Suppose you have permission to ask 200 adults in your town whether they use Instagram. Before doing the research, your best estimate would be that 100 (50% or half) of the respondents would be users of the app. This is your best guess because you have no information other than that people will answer either "yes" or "no" to the Instagram question. Your estimate is derived from an assumption that variability in Instagram use is random.

This variability is called *random variability*. If you tried to guess if a town adult resident is a user of Instagram, you would have to make a random guess— you would be right about half the time and wrong half the time. However, if we could explain the variability, it would no longer be random. How can the random variability be reduced? The answer is to see if we can identify variables related to Instagram use.

Suppose you that have a hypothesis that Instagram use is related to age—that younger people will use Instagram more than older ones. To study this, you include a question on age that asks whether the person is 18–49 or 50 and over. Table 1 shows one possible outcome when examining the relationship between age and Instagram use. Note that 100 people are aged 18–49, and another 100 are over 50. The important thing, though, is that 60 of the younger participants in the study use Instagram compared to only 21 of those over 50.

Have we reduced the random variability? We clearly have. Before you had this information, there would be no way of predicting whether a given person would be an Instagram user. Now that you have the research finding, you can predict that any younger person would be an Instagram user and that any older person would not. For a younger person, you will be correct 60% of the time. And for an older person, you will make a correct prediction almost 80% of the time. This is a big increase from 50% when everything was random.

This discussion underscores once again that relationships between variables are rarely perfect: There are younger and older individuals who do not fit the general pattern. The relationship between the variables is stronger when there is less random variability—for example, if 90% of 18 to 49-year-olds and 10% of the people 50 and older were Instagram users, the relationship would be much stronger (with less uncertainty or randomness).

TABLE 1 Instagram use by age

		Age	
		18–49	**50+**
	Yes	60	21
Instagram user?	No	40	79
	Number of participants	100	100

Source: Based on Pew Research Center, Social Media Use in 2021.

Is there still random variability? The answer is clearly yes. You will be wrong about 40% of the time for younger people, and you do not know when you will be wrong. For unknown reasons, many younger residents will not use Instagram; also, there are older people who do use the app. Can you reduce this remaining uncertainty? The quest to do so motivates additional research. With further studies, you may be able to identify other variables that are also related to Instagram use. For example, variables such as income or extraversion may also be related to use of this app.

NONEXPERIMENTAL VERSUS EXPERIMENTAL METHODS

How can we determine whether variables are related? There are two general approaches to studying relationships among variables: the *nonexperimental method* and the *experimental method.* With the **nonexperimental method,** relationships are studied by observing variables of interest. This may be done by asking people to describe their behavior, directly observing behavior, recording physiological responses, or even examining various public records such as census data. In all these cases, variables are observed as they occur naturally. A relationship between variables is established when the two variables vary together. For example, the relationship between class attendance and course grades can be investigated by obtaining measures of these variables in college classes. A review of many studies that explored this relationship concluded that attendance is indeed related to grades (Credé et al., 2010), and Kim et al. (2020) found that the better grades earned by frequent attendees were related to higher class participation.

The second approach to studying relationships, the **experimental method,** involves direct manipulation and control of variables. The researcher manipulates the first variable of interest and then observes the response. For example, Ramirez and Beilock (2011) were interested in the anxiety produced by important "high-stakes" examinations. Because such anxiety may impair performance, it is important to find ways to reduce the anxiety. In their research, Ramirez and Beilock tested the hypothesis that writing about testing worries would improve performance on the exam. In their study, they used the experimental method. All students took a math test and were then given an opportunity to take the test again. To make this a high-stakes test, students were led to believe that the monetary payout to themselves and their partner was dependent on their performance. The writing variable was then manipulated. Some students spent 10 minutes before taking the test writing about what they thought and felt about the test. The other students constituted a control group; these students simply sat quietly for 10 minutes before taking the test. Next, the new, important test was then administered. The researchers found that students in the writing condition improved their scores; the control group's scores actually decreased. With the experimental method, the two variables do not merely vary together; one variable is introduced first to determine whether it affects the second variable.

Nonexperimental Method

Suppose a researcher is interested in the relationship between exercise and anxiety. How could this topic be studied? Using the nonexperimental method, the researcher would devise operational definitions to measure both the amount of exercise that people engage in and their level of anxiety. There are various ways of operationally defining either of these variables; for example, the researcher might simply ask people to provide self-reports of their exercise patterns and current anxiety level. Now suppose that the researcher collects data on exercise and anxiety from a number of people and finds that exercise is negatively related to anxiety—that is, the people who exercise more also have lower levels of anxiety. The two variables covary, or correlate, with each other: Observed differences in exercise are associated with the amount of anxiety. Because the nonexperimental method allows us to observe covariation between variables, another term that is frequently used to describe this procedure is the *correlational method*. With this method, we examine whether the variables correlate or vary together.

The nonexperimental method seems to be a reasonable approach to studying relationships between variables such as exercise and anxiety. A relationship is established by finding that the two variables vary together—the variables covary or correlate with each other. However, this method is not ideal when asking questions about cause and effect. We know the two variables are related, but what can we say about the causal impact of one variable on the other? There are two problems with making causal statements when the nonexperimental method is used: (1) It can be challenging to determine the direction of cause and effect, and (2) researchers face the third-variable problem—that is, extraneous variables may be causing an observed relationship. These problems are illustrated in Figure 2. The arrows linking variables depict the direction of causation.

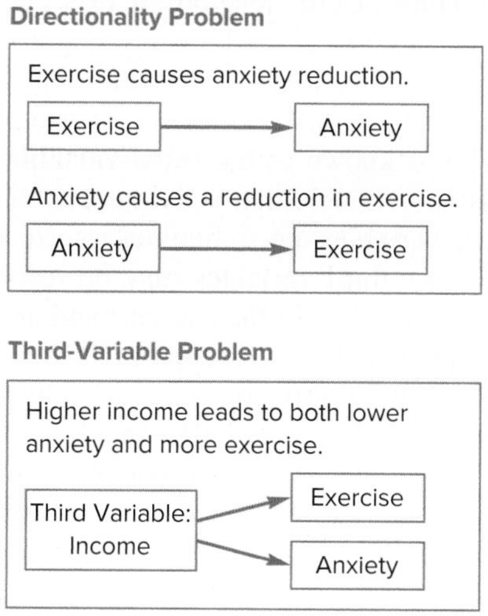

Directionality Problem

Exercise causes anxiety reduction.

Exercise ⟶ Anxiety

Anxiety causes a reduction in exercise.

Anxiety ⟶ Exercise

Third-Variable Problem

Higher income leads to both lower anxiety and more exercise.

Third Variable: Income ⟶ Exercise
⟶ Anxiety

FIGURE 2
Causal possibilities in a nonexperimental study

The Direction of Cause and Effect

The first problem involves the *direction of cause and effect*. With the nonexperimental method, it is difficult to determine which variable causes the other. In other words, it cannot really be said that exercise causes a reduction in anxiety. Although there are plausible reasons for this particular pattern of cause and effect, there are also reasons the opposite pattern might occur (both causal directions are shown in Figure 2). Perhaps high anxiety causes people to reduce exercise. The issue here is temporal precedence, which is very important in making causal inferences (see the chapter "Scientific Understanding of Behavior"). Knowledge of the correct direction of cause and effect, in turn, has implications for applications of research findings: If exercise reduces anxiety, then undertaking an exercise program would be a reasonable way to lower one's anxiety. However, if anxiety causes people to stop exercising, simply forcing someone to exercise is not likely to reduce the person's anxiety level.

The problem of the direction of cause and effect is not the most serious drawback to the nonexperimental method, however. Scientists have pointed out, for example, that astronomers can make accurate predictions even though they often cannot manipulate variables in an experiment. In addition, often the direction of cause and effect is not crucial, because for some pairs of variables the causal pattern may operate in both directions. For instance, there seem to be two causal patterns in the relationship between the variables of similarity and liking: (1) Similarity causes people to like each other, and (2) liking causes people to become more similar. In general, the third-variable problem is a much more serious fault of the nonexperimental method.

The Third-Variable Problem

When the nonexperimental method is used, there is the danger that no direct causal relationship exists between the two variables. Exercise might not influence anxiety, and anxiety might have no causal effect on exercise; this would be known as a spurious relationship. Instead, there may be a relationship between the two variables because some other variable causes both exercise *and* anxiety. This is known as the **third-variable problem.**

A **third variable** is any variable that is extraneous to the two variables being studied; this is why these variables are sometimes referred to as **extraneous variables.** Any number of other third variables may be responsible for an observed relationship between two variables. In the exercise and anxiety example, one such third variable could be income level. Perhaps high income allows people more free time to exercise (and the ability to afford a health club membership!) and also lowers anxiety. Income acting as a third variable is illustrated in Figure 2. If income is the determining variable, there is no direct cause-and-effect relationship between exercise and anxiety; the relationship was caused by the third variable, income level. The third variable is an alternative explanation for the observed relationship between the variables. Recall from the chapter "Scientific Understanding of Behavior" that the ability to rule out alternative explanations for the observed relationship between two variables is another important factor when we try to infer that one variable causes another.

The fact that third variables could be operating is a serious problem because third variables introduce alternative explanations that reduce the overall validity of a study. The fact that income could be related to exercise means that income level is an alternative explanation for an observed relationship between exercise and anxiety. The alternative explanation is that high income reduces anxiety levels, so exercise has nothing to do with it.

When we know that an uncontrolled third variable is operating, we can call the third variable a **confounding variable.** If two variables are confounded, they are intertwined, so you cannot determine which of the variables is operating in a given situation. If income is confounded with exercise, income level will be an alternative explanation whenever you study exercise. Fortunately, there is a solution to this problem: The experimental method provides us with a way of controlling for the effects of third variables.

As you can see, the direction of cause and effect and potential third variables are serious limitations of the nonexperimental method. Often they are not considered in media reports of research results. For instance, a newspaper may report the results of a nonexperimental study that found a positive relationship between the amount of coffee consumed and the likelihood of a heart attack. Obviously, there is not necessarily a cause-and-effect relationship between the two variables. Numerous third variables (e.g., occupation, personality, or genetic predisposition) could cause a person's coffee-drinking behavior and the likelihood of a heart attack. In sum, the results of such studies are ambiguous and should be viewed with skepticism.

Experimental Method

The experimental method reduces ambiguity, and thus uncertainty, in the interpretation of results. With the experimental method, one variable is manipulated and the other is then measured. The manipulated variable is called the **independent variable** and the variable that is measured is termed the **dependent variable.** If a researcher used the experimental method to study whether exercise reduces anxiety, exercise would be manipulated—perhaps by having one group of people exercise each day for a week and another group refrains from exercise for a week. Anxiety would then be measured. Suppose that people in the exercise group have less anxiety than the people in the no-exercise group. The researcher could now say something about the direction of cause and effect: In the experiment, exercise came first in the sequence of events. Thus, level of anxiety could not influence the amount of exercise that the people engaged in.

Another characteristic of the experimental method is that it attempts to eliminate the influence of all potential confounding third variables on the dependent variable. This is generally referred to as control of extraneous variables. Such control is usually achieved by making sure that every feature of the environment except the manipulated variable is held constant. Any variable that cannot be held constant is controlled by making sure that the effects of the variable are random. Through randomization, the influence of any extraneous variables is equal in the experimental conditions. Both procedures are used to ensure that any differences between the groups are due to the manipulated variable.

Experimental Control   In a perfect experiment, all extraneous variables are controlled by being held constant. This is called **experimental control.** If a variable is held constant—that is, the variable is not allowed to vary during the experiment—it cannot be responsible for the results of the experiment. In other words, any variable that is held constant cannot be a confounding variable. In the experiment on the effect of exercise, the researcher would want to make sure that the only difference between the exercise and no-exercise groups is the exercise. For example, because people in the exercise group are removed from their daily routine to engage in exercise, the people in the no-exercise group should be removed from their daily routine as well. Otherwise, the lower anxiety in the exercise condition could have resulted from the "rest" from the daily routine rather than from the exercise.

Experimental control is accomplished by treating participants in all groups in the experiment identically; the only difference between groups is the manipulated variable. In the Loftus (1979) experiment on memory (discussed in the chapter "Where to Start"), individuals in both groups witnessed the same accident, the same experimenter asked the same questions in both groups, the lighting and all other conditions were the same, and so on. When a difference occurred between the groups in reporting memory, researchers could be sure that the difference was the result of the method of questioning rather than of some other variable that was not held constant.

Randomization   The number of potential confounding variables is infinite, and sometimes it is difficult to keep a variable constant. The most obvious such variable is any personal characteristic of the participants. Consider an experiment in which half the research participants are in the exercise condition and the other half are in the no-exercise condition; the participants in the two conditions might be different on some extraneous, third variable such as income. This difference could cause an apparent relationship between exercise and anxiety. How can the researcher eliminate the influence of such extraneous variables in an experiment?

The experimental method eliminates the influence of such variables by **randomization.** Randomization ensures that an extraneous variable is just as likely to affect one experimental group as it is to affect the other group. To eliminate the influence of individual characteristics, the researcher assigns participants to the two groups in a random fashion. In actual practice, this means that assignment to groups is determined using a list of random numbers. To understand this, think of the participants in the experiment as forming a line. As each person comes to the front of the line, a random number is assigned, much like random numbers are drawn for a lottery. If the number is even, the individual is assigned to one group (e.g., exercise); if the number is odd, the subject is assigned to the other group (e.g., no exercise). By using a random assignment procedure, the researcher is confident that the characteristics of the participants in the two groups will be virtually identical. In this "lottery," for instance, people with low, medium, and high incomes will be distributed equally in the two groups. In fact, randomization ensures that the individual characteristic composition of the two groups will be virtually identical in every way. This ability to randomly assign research participants to the conditions in the experiment is an important difference between the experimental and nonexperimental methods.

To make the concept of random assignment more concrete, you might try an exercise like this one: Suppose you have a box full of old baseball cards. The box contains cards of 50 American League players and 50 National League players. The cards are thoroughly mixed up. Select 32 of the cards and assign them to "groups" using a sequence of random numbers obtained from a website that generates random numbers (www.randomizer.org). As each card is drawn, use the following decision rule: If the random number is even, the player is assigned to Group 1, and if the number is odd, the player is assigned to Group 2. Then check to see whether the two groups differ in terms of league representation. A likely outcome would be something like this: Group 1 has nine American League players and seven National League players, whereas Group 2 has an equal number of players from the two leagues. These two groups are virtually identical in terms of league representation!

Any other variable that cannot be held constant is also controlled by randomization. For instance, many experiments are conducted over a period of several days or weeks, with participants arriving for the experiment at various times during each day. In such cases, the researcher uses a random order for scheduling the sequence of the various experimental conditions. This procedure prevents a situation in which one condition is scheduled during the first days of the experiment whereas the other is studied during later days. Similarly, participants in one group will not be studied only during the morning and the others only in the afternoon.

Direct experimental control and randomization eliminate the influence of any extraneous variables (keeping variables constant across conditions). Thus, the experimental method allows a relatively unambiguous interpretation of the results. Any difference between groups on the observed variable can be attributed to the influence of the manipulated variable.

Internal Validity and the Experimental Method

Internal validity is the ability to draw conclusions about causal relationships from the results of a study. A study has high internal validity when strong inferences can be made that one variable caused changes in the other variable. We have seen that strong causal inferences can be made more easily when the experimental method is used.

Inferences of cause and effect require three elements. So, strong internal validity requires an analysis of these three elements:

- **Temporal precedence:** First, there must be temporal precedence: The causal variable should come first in the temporal order of events and be followed by the effect. The experimental method addresses temporal order by first manipulating the independent variable and then observing whether it has an effect on the dependent variable. In other situations, you may observe the temporal order or you may logically conclude that one order is more plausible than another.

- **Covariation of cause and effect:** Second, there must be covariation between the two variables. Covariation is demonstrated with the experimental method when participants in an experimental condition (e.g., an exercise condition) show the effect (e.g., a reduction in anxiety), whereas participants in a control condition (e.g., no exercise) do not show the effect.

- **Eliminate plausible alternative explanations:** Third, there is a need to eliminate plausible alternative explanations for the observed relationship. An alternative explanation is based on the possibility that some confounding third variable is responsible for the observed relationship. When designing research, a great deal of attention is paid to eliminating alternative explanations, because doing so brings us closer to truth. Indeed, eliminating alternative explanations is fundamental to internal validity. The experimental method begins by attempting to keep such variables constant through random assignment and experimental control.

Other issues of control will be discussed in later chapters. The main point here is that inferences about causal relationships are stronger when there are fewer alternative explanations for the observed relationships.

Independent and Dependent Variables

When researchers study the relationship between variables, the variables are usually conceptualized as having a cause-and-effect connection. That is, one variable is considered to be the cause and the other variable the effect. Thus, rate of speech is viewed as a cause of attitude change, and exercise is viewed as having an effect on anxiety. Researchers using both experimental and nonexperimental methods view the variables in this fashion, even though there is less ambiguity about the direction of cause and effect when the experimental method is used. As we have seen, researchers use the terms **independent variable** and **dependent variable** when referring to the variables being studied. The variable that is considered to be the cause is called the independent variable, and the variable that is the effect is called the dependent variable. It is often helpful to actually draw a relationship between the independent and dependent variables using an arrow as we did in Figure 2. The arrow always indicates your hypothesized causal sequence:

In an experiment, the manipulated variable is the independent variable. After manipulating the independent variable, the researchers measure a second variable, called the dependent variable. The basic idea is that the researchers make changes in the independent variable and then see if the dependent variable changes in response.

One way to remember the distinction between the independent and dependent variables is to relate the terms to what happens to participants in an experiment. First, the participants are exposed to a situation, such as watching a violent versus a nonviolent program or exercising versus not exercising. This is the manipulated variable. It is called the independent variable because the participant has nothing to do with its occurrence; the researchers vary it independently of any characteristics of the participant or situation.

In the next step of the experiment, the researchers want to see what effect the independent variable had on the participant; to find this out, they measure the dependent variable. In this step, the participant is responding to what happened to him or her; whatever the participant does or says, the researcher assumes must be caused by—or be dependent on—the effect of the independent (manipulated) variable. The independent variable, then, is the variable manipulated by the experimenter, and the dependent variable is the participant's measured behavior, which is assumed to be caused by the independent variable.

When the relationship between an independent and a dependent variable is plotted in a graph, the independent variable is always placed on the horizontal axis and the dependent variable is always placed on the vertical axis. If you look back to Figure 1, you will see that this graphing method was used to present the four relationships. In Graph B, for example, the independent variable, "Group Size," is placed on the horizontal axis; the dependent variable, "Amount of Noise," is placed on the vertical axis.

Note that some research focuses primarily on the independent variable, with the researcher studying the effect of a single independent variable on numerous behaviors. Other researchers may focus on a specific dependent variable and study how various independent variables affect that one behavior. To make this distinction more concrete, consider a study of the effect of jury size, the independent variable, on the outcome of a trial, the dependent variable. One researcher studying this issue might be interested in the effect of group size on a variety of behaviors, including jury decisions and risk taking among business managers. Another researcher, interested solely in jury decisions, might study the effects of many aspects of trials, such as jury size and the judge's instructions, on juror behavior. Both emphases lead to important research.

Check Your Learning

It is important to know the difference between a dependent and an independent variable. This can be challenging. To see if you understand these basic types of variables, complete the Check Your Learning: Practice Exercise #3.

EXPERIMENTAL METHODS: ADDITIONAL CONSIDERATIONS

The advantages of the experimental method for studying relationships between variables have been emphasized. You may be asking yourself, Why isn't every study an experiment? There *are* disadvantages to experiments and many good reasons for using methods other than experiments. Let's examine some of the issues that arise when choosing a method.

Experiments Are Tightly Controlled, Unlike the Real World

The **external validity** of a study is the extent to which the results can be generalized to other populations and settings. In thinking about external validity, several questions arise: Can the results of a study be replicated with other operational definitions of the variables? Can the results be replicated with different participants? Can the results be replicated in other settings?

The goal of designing a study that has high internal validity may require placing less importance on external validity. Consider a researcher interested in establishing that there is a causal relationship between variables is most interested in internal validity. An experiment would be designed in which the independent variable is manipulated and other variables are kept constant (experimental control).

This is most easily done in a laboratory setting, often with a highly restricted sample such as college students drawn from introductory psychology classes. This procedure permits relatively unambiguous inferences concerning cause and effect and reduces the possibility that extraneous variables could influence the results. These unambiguous inferences are another way of saying "strong internal validity." Laboratory experimentation is an extremely valuable way to study many problems. However, the high degree of control and the laboratory setting may sometimes create an artificial atmosphere that may limit the external validity of the results. So, although laboratory experiments often have strong internal validity, they may often have limited external validity. For this reason, researchers may decide to use a nonexperimental procedure to study relationships among variables.

Another alternative is to try to conduct an experiment in a field setting. In a **field experiment,** the independent variable is manipulated in a natural setting. As in any experiment, the researcher attempts to control extraneous variables via either randomization or experimental control. As an example of a field experiment, consider the Lee et al. (2010) study on the impact that public sneezing had on perceptions of risk resulting from flu. On a day when swine flu received broad media attention, students on a university campus were exposed to a confederate who either sneezed and coughed, or did not, as participants passed. Afterward, participants were asked to complete a measure of perceived risks in order to help on a "class project." The researchers then conducted similar studies at shopping malls and local businesses. In all cases, they found that participants who were exposed to sneezing and coughing reported feeling more risks to their health, including risks such as contracting a serious disease, having a heart attack prior to age 50, and dying from a crime or accident. It is not difficult to imagine that such responses would have been more dramatic during the coronavirus pandemic.

Other field experiments take place in public spaces such as street corners, retail stores, and parking lots. Researchers in one study sent Black and White "customers" to upscale stores to try on expensive sunglasses (Schreer et al., 2009). The customers asked a salesperson to remove the anti-theft device so the sunglasses could be better evaluated when looking in a mirror. The sales staff agreed to the customer's request for everyone. However, the Black customers were more likely to be stared at and followed when walking. These field experiment procedures are fairly complex. Using a simpler procedure, Weijers and de Koning (2021) placed signs next to a hand sanitizer station at the entrance to clothing stores in the Netherlands. The independent variable was manipulated by varying the information on the signs. A control sign simply stated "You can disinfect your hands here." A second sign added a "salience nudge"—three bright arrows pointing to the sanitizer. Another sign added additional information to encourage sanitizer use: "Disinfect your hands, to reduce the likelihood you or someone close to you becomes ill!" Sanitizer use was the same for all three signs, possibly because people had become accustomed to using sanitizer at home before going out.

The advantage of the field experiment is that the independent variable is investigated in a natural context. The disadvantage is that the researcher loses the ability to directly control many aspects of the situation. For instance, in the retail store, there are other shoppers in the area and possible interruptions and distractions. The laboratory experiment permits researchers to more easily keep extraneous variables constant, thereby eliminating their influence on the outcome of the experiment. Of course, it is precisely this control that leads to the artificiality of the laboratory investigation. Fortunately, when researchers have conducted experiments in both lab and field settings, the results of the experiments have been very similar (Anderson et al., 1999).

Some Variables Cannot Be—or Should Not Be—Manipulated

Sometimes the experimental method is not a feasible alternative because experimentation would be either unethical or impractical. Child-rearing practices would be impractical to manipulate with the experimental method, for example. Further, even if it were possible to randomly assign parents to two child-rearing conditions, such as using withdrawal of love versus physical types of punishment, the manipulation would be unethical. Similarly, we would not want to create conditions that harm people. Instead, we could do nonexperimental research. For example, Gutzviller et al. (2020) found that stress is related to poor mental health among young adult Hispanics; further, social support can help mitigate the effects of stress. Instead of manipulating variables such as child-rearing techniques or stress, researchers usually study them as they occur in natural settings. Many important research areas present similar problems—for example, studies of the effects of alcoholism, divorce and its consequences, or the impact of corporal punishment on children. Such problems need to be studied, and generally, the only techniques possible are nonexperimental.

When such variables are studied, people are often categorized into groups based on their experiences. When studying corporal punishment, for example, one group would consist of individuals who were spanked as children and another group would consist of people who were not. This is sometimes called an *ex post facto* design. Ex post facto means "after the fact"—the term was coined to describe research in which groups are formed on the basis of some actual difference rather than through random assignment as in an experiment. It is extremely important to study these differences. However, it is important to recognize that this is non-experimental research because there is no random assignment to the groups and no manipulation of an independent variable.

Participant variables (also called *subject variables* and *personal attributes*) are characteristics of individuals, such as age, gender, ethnic group, nationality, birth order, personality, or marital status. These variables are by definition non-experimental; they cannot be manipulated, they must only be measured. For example, to study a personality characteristic such as extraversion, you might have people complete a personality test that is designed to measure this variable. Such variables may be studied in experiments along with manipulated independent variables (see the chapter "Complex Experimental Designs").

Some Questions Are Not Answerable by an Experiment

A major goal of science is to provide an accurate description of events. Thus, the goal of much research is to describe behavior; in those cases, causal inferences are not relevant to the primary goals of the research. A classic example of descriptive research in psychology comes from the work of Jean Piaget, who carefully observed the behavior of his own children as they matured. He described in detail the changes in their ways of thinking about and responding to their environment (Piaget, 1952). Piaget's descriptions and his interpretations of his observations resulted in an important theory of cognitive development that greatly increased our understanding of this topic. Piaget's theory had a major impact on psychology that continues today (Flavell, 1996).

A more recent example of descriptive research in psychology is Meston and Buss's (2007) study on the motives for having sex. The purpose of the study was to describe the "multitude of reasons that people engage in sexual intercourse" (p. 496). In the study, 444 male and female college students were asked to list the reasons they had engaged in sexual intercourse in the past. The researchers combed through the answers and identified 237 reasons, including "I was attracted to the person," "I wanted to feel loved," "I wanted to make up after a fight," and "I wanted to defy my parents." The next step for the researchers was to categorize the reasons their participants reported for having sex, including physical reasons (such as attraction) and goal attainment reasons (such as revenge). In this case, as with some of Piaget's work, the primary goal was to describe behavior rather than to understand its causes.

In many real-life situations, a major concern is to make a successful prediction about a person's future behavior—for example, success in school, ability to learn a new job, or probable interest in various major fields in college. In such circumstances, there may be no need to be concerned about issues of cause and effect. It is possible to design measures that increase the accuracy of predicting future behavior. School counselors can give tests to decide whether students should be in "enriched" classroom programs, employers can test applicants to help determine whether they should be hired, and college students can take tests that help them decide on a major. These types of measures can lead to better decisions for many people. When researchers develop measures designed to predict future behavior, they must conduct research to demonstrate that the measure does, in fact, relate to the behavior in question. This research will be discussed in the chapter "Measurement Concepts."

Advantages of Multiple Methods

Perhaps most important, a complete understanding of any phenomenon requires study using multiple methods, both experimental and nonexperimental. No method is perfect, and no single study is definitive. To illustrate, consider the concept of meaning in life. What factors contribute to an individual's perception of meaning in life? Lambert et al. (2013) proposed that a "sense of belonging" in a set of secure and positive social relationships plays an important role in forming meaning in life. Their first study investigated whether a sense of belonging is related to meaning in life. Undergraduates completed a measure of sense of belonging consisting of five items such as "there are many people with whom I belong." At the same time, they completed a set of questions designed to assess a person's perception of meaning in life ("I understand my life's meaning"). The researchers found that sense of belonging was related to meaning in life in this study. Of course, this was a nonexperimental (correlational) study with inherent problems of inferring cause and effect.

Lambert et al. then conducted an experiment to further study this relationship. The researchers created conditions for student participants to be thinking about one of three kinds of social relationships. In a *belongingness* condition, participants were given guided instructions to "think about two people or groups or people with whom you really belong." They wrote down their names, described why they felt they belonged, and wrote a paragraph about a specific time when they felt a strong sense of belonging with the person or group. A second condition was similar, but the instructions focused on receiving *social support.* A third condition, termed *social value,* asked participants to think about receiving compliments from others that made them feel valued. Participants then completed a measure that asked them to indicate their current feelings of meaning in life. Higher meaning in life ratings were made in the belongingness condition than in the social support or social value conditions.

The important point here is that no study is a perfect test of a hypothesis. However, when multiple studies using multiple methods all lead to the same or a similar conclusion—as has been the case with research on belongingness (see, for example, Zhang et al., 2019)—our confidence in the findings and our understanding of the phenomenon are greatly increased.

EVALUATING RESEARCH: SUMMARY OF THE FOUR VALIDITIES

The key concept of validity was introduced at the outset of this chapter. *Validity* refers to the idea that, given everything that is known, a conclusion is reasonably accurate. Research can be described and evaluated in terms of four types of validity:

- **Construct validity:** the extent to which the measurement or manipulation of a variable accurately represents the theoretical variable (construct) being studied.

- **Internal validity:** the accuracy of conclusions drawn about cause and effect.

- **External validity:** the extent to which findings of a study can be accurately generalized to other populations and settings.

- **Conclusion validity:** the accuracy of the conclusions drawn from the results of a research investigation (sometimes called *statistical conclusion validity* when the conclusions are drawn from statistical analyses).

Each gives us a different perspective on any particular research investigation, and every research study should be evaluated on these aspects of validity.

At this point, you may be wondering how researchers select a methodology to study a problem. A variety of methods are available, each with advantages and disadvantages. Researchers select the method that best enables them to address the questions they wish to answer. No method is inherently superior to another. Rather, the choice of method is made after considering the problem under investigation, ethics, cost and time constraints, and issues associated with the four types of validity. In the remainder of this book, many specific methods will be discussed, all of which are useful under different circumstances. In fact, all are necessary to understand the wide variety of behaviors that are of interest to behavioral scientists. Complete understanding of any problem or issue requires research using a variety of methodological approaches.

ENGAGING WITH RESEARCH: STUDYING DISCRIMINATION

Discrimination is defined by differences in treatment toward individuals based on their membership in certain social groups. Discrimination is a persistent problem in just about every human context: families, peer groups, schools and universities, and the workplace.

Agerström et al. (2021) conducted a study of workplace discrimination using a "lost email" experiment wherein an email is sent to wrong recipients by "mistake." All of the emails said: "The other day you talked to my (boyfriend/girlfriend) [and said that] that I could contact you regarding a temporary job position. My (boyfriend/girlfriend) told me that you would check the details with your colleagues and get back to me. I am still very interested in the job! Unfortunately, I am unsure if I have the right contact information, but I hope I am writing to the right person." Each was signed by an Arab sender or a Swedish sender—this was accomplished by manipulating the sender's name (e.g., Fateme Mahmoodi versus Amanda Karlsson)—with a stereotypically male or female name. The email signaled the fake sender's sexual orientation by mentioning either a boyfriend or a girlfriend.

The researchers sent out 6,654 emails (which varied only in three ways: from a male or female, Swedish or Arab, and gay or heterosexual sender) to randomly selected university students and received 1,350 replies. The research team tracked the rate of responses to this "lost email" and measured how many of the randomly selected students replied to the "lost email."

First, acquire and read the article (available at https://doi.org/10.1027/1864-9335/a000464):

> Agerström, J., Carlsson, M., & Strinić, A. (2021). Intersected groups and discriminatory everyday behavior. *Social Psychology, 52*(6), 351–361. https://doi.org/10.1027/1864-9335/a000464

Then, after reading the article, consider the following:

1. **What is the primary goal of this study: Description, Prediction, Determining Cause, or Explaining? Do the authors achieve their goals?**
   a. On what basis did the authors conclude that they found "evidence of ethnic discrimination for our heterosexual senders" (p. 357)?
   b. How do they know that one thing caused another?
2. **What did these researchers do? What was the method?**
3. **What was measured?**
   a. What was measured? How did Agerström et al. (2021) operationally define "discrimination"? How did they operationally define "ethnic minority"?
4. **To what or whom can we generalize the results? Do you think that the researchers can generalize to all employers? All employers in Sweden?**
5. **What did they find? What were the results?**
6. **Have other researchers found similar results?**
7. **What are the limitations of this study?**
8. **What are the ethical issues present in this study?**

BEING A SKILLED CONSUMER OF RESEARCH

1. The dictionary definition of shy is "being reserved or having or showing nervousness or timidity in the company of other people." Create three different operational definitions of shyness and provide a critique of each one. Example: An operational definition of shyness could be the number of new people that a person reports meeting on a given day. Critique: What if an outgoing person has a job that requires them to meet very few people? They might (incorrectly) be considered shy by this operational definition.

2. Consider the hypothesis that stress at work causes family conflict at home.

   a. What type of relationship is proposed (e.g., positive linear, negative linear)?

   b. Graph the proposed relationship.

   c. Identify the independent variable and the dependent variable in the statement of the hypothesis.

   d. How might you investigate the hypothesis using the experimental method?

   e. How might you investigate the hypothesis using the nonexperimental method (recognizing the problems of determining cause and effect)?

   f. What factors might you consider in deciding whether to use the experimental or nonexperimental method to study the relationship between work stress and family conflict?

3. You observe that classmates who get good grades tend to sit toward the front of the classroom, and those who receive poorer grades tend to sit toward the back. What are three possible cause-and-effect relationships for this nonexperimental observation?

4. Identify the independent and dependent variables in the following descriptions of experiments:

   a. Students watched a cartoon either alone or with others and then rated how funny they found the cartoon to be.

   b. A comprehension test was given to students after they had studied textbook material either in silence or with the television on.

   c. Some elementary school teachers were told that a child's parents were college graduates, and other teachers were told that the child's parents had not finished high school; they then rated the child's academic potential.

   d. Workers at a company were assigned to one of two conditions: One group completed a stress management training program; another group of workers did not participate in the training. The number of sick days taken by these workers was examined for the two subsequent months.

5. A few years ago, newspapers reported a finding that Americans who have a glass of wine a day are healthier than those who have no wine (or who have a lot of wine or other alcohol). What are some plausible alternative explanations for this finding? That is, what variables other than wine could explain the finding? (Hint: What sorts of people in the United States are most likely to have a glass of wine with dinner?)

Check Your Learning: Practice Exercises

Practice Exercise #1

Identifying Variables

Think of five different variables. Then, describe two operational definitions for each variable.

Here are two examples:

Variable: age

- **Operational Definition 1:** What is your age (in years)? _____
- **Operational Definition 2:** What is your age? Check one: _____ 25 or younger; _____ 26 or older

Variable: happiness

- **Operational Definition 1:** Response to the question "How happy would you say you are" on a scale ranging from 1 (not at all happy) to 10 (very happy)
- **Operational Definition 2:** Count the number of positive and negative words in a 5-minute period after an interviewer asks a person to "tell me about yourself"

Practice Exercise #2

Identify the Type of Relationship

Read the following examples and identify the relationship by placing a check mark in the appropriate box.

	Positive	Negative	Curvilinear
1. Increased caloric intake is associated with increased body weight.			
2. As people gain experience speaking in public, their anxiety level decreases.			
3. Performance of basketball players increases as crowd noise increases from low to moderate levels, then decreases as crowd noise becomes extremely high.			
4. Increased partying behavior is associated with lower grades.			
5. A decrease in the number of headaches is associated with a decrease in the amount of sugar consumed per day.			
6. Higher amount of education is associated with higher income.			
7. Ratings of facial attractiveness are higher (more attractive) for people with medium-length eyelashes; ratings are lower when eyelashes are very short or long.			
8. The more you exercise your puppy, the less your puppy chews on things in your house.			

Practice Exercise #3

Types of Variables

Read the following and answer the questions below.

- Researchers conducted a study to examine the effect of music on exam scores.
- They predicted that scores would be higher when students listened to soft music compared to no music during the exam.
- One hundred (50 male, 50 female) students were randomly assigned to either the soft-music or no-music conditions.
- Students in the soft-music condition listened to music using headphones during the exam.
- Students in the no-music condition completed the exam as they normally would.
- As predicted, exam scores were significantly higher in the soft-music condition compared to the no-music condition.

1. The independent variable is : _____

2. The dependent variable is : _____

3. A potential confounding variable is : _____

(Some answers are provided at the end of this chapter.)

CHAPTER REVIEW

Review Questions _____

1. What is a variable?
2. Define "operational definition" of a variable.
3. Distinguish among positive linear, negative linear, and curvilinear relationships.
4. What is the difference between the nonexperimental method and the experimental method?
5. What is the difference between an independent variable and a dependent variable?
6. Distinguish between laboratory experiments and field experiments.
7. What is meant by the problem of direction of cause and effect and the third-variable problem?

8. How do direct experimental control and randomization influence the possible effects of extraneous variables?

9. What are some reasons for using the nonexperimental method to study relationships between variables?

Study Terms

Alternative explanation (p. 98)

Confounding variable (p. 95)

Conclusion validity (p. 84)

Construct validity (p. 87)

Correlation coefficient (p. 90)

Covariation of cause and effect (p. 98)

Curvilinear relationship (p. 87)

Dependent variable (p. 98)

Experimental control (p. 96)

Experimental method (p. 92)

External validity (p. 100)

Extraneous variable (p. 94)

Field experiment (p. 100)

Independent variable (p. 98)

Internal validity (p. 97)

Negative linear relationship (p. 87)

Nonexperimental method (correlational method) (p. 92)

Operational definition (p. 85)

Participant (subject) variable (p. 102)

Positive linear relationship (p. 87)

Randomization (p. 96)

Temporal precedence (p. 97)

Third variable (p. 94)

Third-variable problem (p. 94)

Variable (p. 85)

Check Your Learning: Answers

Practice Exercise #2

1. positive; 2. negative; 3. curvilinear; 4. negative; 5. positive; 6. positive; 7. curvilinear; 8. negative

Practice Exercise #3

1. Independent variable = music condition

2. Dependent variable = exam score

3. Potential confounding variables = use of headphones (headphones were worn only by participants in the soft-music condition)

Measurement Concepts

LEARNING OBJECTIVES

- Define reliability of a measure of behavior and describe the difference between test-retest, internal consistency, and interrater reliability.
- Define construct validity and discuss ways to establish construct validity.
- Compare face validity, content validity, predictive validity, concurrent validity, convergent validity, and discriminant validity.
- Describe the problem of reactivity of a measure of behavior and discuss ways to minimize reactivity.
- Describe the properties of the four scales of measurement: nominal, ordinal, interval, and ratio.

WE LEARN ABOUT BEHAVIOR THROUGH CAREFUL MEASUREMENT.
Behavior can be measured in many ways. Perhaps the most common measurement strategy is to ask people to tell you about themselves: How would you rate your overall happiness? How many times have you argued with your partner in the past week? How fair was the professor's grading system? Of course, you can also directly observe behaviors. You can count the number of errors someone makes on a task, whether or not people who you approach in a shopping mall give you change for a dollar, or how many times a person smiled during an interview. Physiological and neurological responses can be measured as well. How much did the subject's heart rate change while working on the problems? Did the subject's muscle tension increase during the interview? Did the part of the brain involved in emotion "light up" on the fMRI? There is an endless supply of fascinating variables that can be studied. We will describe many methods of measuring variables throughout this book. In this chapter we explore the technical aspects of measurement. We need to consider reliability, validity, and reactivity of measures. We will also consider scales of measurement.

RELIABILITY OF MEASURES

Reliability refers to the consistency or stability of a measure. Your everyday definition of reliability is quite close to the scientific definition. For example, you might say that Professor Fuentes is "reliable" because she begins class exactly at 10 a.m. each day; in contrast, Professor Fine might be called "unreliable" because, although she sometimes begins class exactly on the hour, on any given day she may appear anytime between 10:00 a.m. and 10:20 a.m.

Similarly, a reliable measure of a psychological variable like intelligence will yield the same result each time you administer the intelligence test to the same person. The test would be unreliable if it measured the same person as average one week, low the next, and bright the next. Put simply, a reliable measure does not fluctuate from one reading to the next. If the measure does fluctuate, there is error in the measurement device; it is, to some extent, unreliable.

An Intelligence Quotient (IQ) test is a measure of intelligence. Another way to think about the reliability of a measure is to think about the concepts of true score and measurement error. A **true score** is someone's real, "true" value on a given variable: true intelligence, true reaction time, true happiness, true memory. If we consider intelligence, a person's true score is the correct answer to the question: How smart are they? A true score cannot be directly measured; we cannot know a person's true intelligence, we can only know their score on an IQ test. But IQ tests are not perfect measures of intelligence any more than the thermostat in your bedroom is a perfect measure of temperature. The difference between a true score and a measured score is **measurement error.** You can think of measurement error as the distance between an unobservable true state (the true score) and a measured (observed) score. Here, then, is the connection between true scores, measurement error, and reliability. An unreliable measure of intelligence

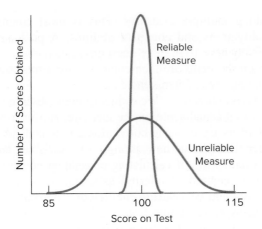

FIGURE 1
Comparing
data of a
reliable and
unreliable
measure

contains considerable measurement error. Thus, it cannot reflect an individual's true intelligence. In contrast, a reliable measure of intelligence—one that contains little measurement error—will yield an identical (or nearly identical) intelligence score each time the same individual is measured. Another way to think about reliability is that reliability is measurement that is free from measurement error.

To further illustrate the concept of reliability, imagine that you know someone whose true score for intelligence is 100. Now suppose that you administer an unreliable intelligence test to this person each week for a year. After the year, you calculate the person's average score on the test based on the 52 scores you obtained. Now suppose that you test another friend who also has a true intelligence score of 100; however, this time you administer a highly reliable test. Again, you calculate the average score. What might your data look like? Typical data are shown in Figure 1. In each case, the average score is 100. However, scores on the unreliable test range from 85 to 115, whereas scores on the reliable test range from 97 to 103. The *measurement error* in the unreliable test is revealed in the greater variability shown by the person to whom you administered the unreliable test.

When conducting research, you can measure each person only once; you cannot give the measure 50 or 100 times to discover a true score. Thus, it is very important that you use a reliable measure. Your single administration of the measure should closely reflect the person's true score.

The importance of reliability is obvious. An unreliable measure of length would be useless in building a table; an unreliable measure of a variable such as intelligence is equally useless in studying that variable. Researchers cannot use unreliable measures to systematically study variables or the relationships among variables. Trying to study behavior using unreliable measures is a waste of time because the results will be unstable and unable to be replicated.

Reliability is most likely to be achieved when researchers use careful measurement procedures. In some research areas this might involve carefully training observers to record behavior; in other areas it might mean paying close attention to the way questions are phrased or the way recording electrodes are placed on the body to measure physiological reactions. In many areas, reliability can be increased by making multiple measures. This is most commonly seen when assessing personality traits and cognitive abilities. A personality measure, for example, will typically have 10 or more questions (called *items*) designed to assess a trait. Responses on the items are then combined for a total score. Reliability is increased when the number of items increases.

How can we assess reliability? We cannot directly observe the true score and error components of an actual score on the measure. However, we can assess the statistical stability of measures using correlation coefficients. A correlation coefficient is a number that tells us how strongly two variables are related to each other. There are several ways of calculating correlation coefficients; the correlation coefficient most commonly referred to when discussing reliability is the **Pearson product-moment correlation coefficient.** The Pearson correlation coefficient (symbolized as r) can range from 0.00 to +1.00 and 0.00 to −1.00. A correlation of 0.00 tells us that the two variables are not related at all. The closer a correlation is to 1.00, either +1.00 or −1.00, the stronger is the relationship. The positive and negative signs provide information about the direction of the relationship. When the correlation coefficient is positive (a plus sign), there is a positive linear relationship—high scores on one variable are associated with high scores on the second variable. A negative linear relationship is indicated by a minus sign—high scores on one variable are associated with low scores on the second variable. The Pearson correlation coefficient is discussed further in the chapter "Understanding Research Results: Description and Correlation."

To assess the reliability of a measure, we will need to obtain at least two scores on the measure from many individuals. If the measure is reliable, the two scores should be very similar; a Pearson correlation coefficient that describes the relationship between the scores should be a high positive correlation. When you read about reliability, the correlation will usually be called a *reliability coefficient*. Let's examine specific methods of assessing reliability.

Test-Retest Reliability

Test-retest reliability is assessed by measuring the same individuals at two points in time. For example, the reliability of a test of intelligence could be assessed by giving the measure to a group of people on one day and again a week later. We would then have two scores for each person, and a correlation coefficient could be calculated to determine the relationship between the first test score and the retest score. Recall that high reliability is indicated by a high correlation coefficient showing that the two scores are very similar. If many people have very similar scores, we conclude that the measure reflects true scores rather than measurement error. It is difficult to say how high the correlation should be before we accept the measure as reliable, but for most measures the reliability coefficient should probably be at least .80.

Given that test-retest reliability requires administering the same test twice, the correlation might be artificially high because the individuals remember how they responded the first time. **Alternate forms reliability** is sometimes used to avoid this problem; it requires administering two different forms of the same test to the same individuals at two points in time. A drawback to this procedure is that creating a second equivalent measure may require considerable time and effort.

Intelligence is a variable that can be expected to stay relatively constant over time; thus, we expect the test-retest reliability for intelligence to be very high. However, some variables may be expected to change from one test period to the next. For example, a mood scale designed to measure a person's current mood state is a measure that might easily change from one test period to another, and so test-retest reliability might not be appropriate. On a more practical level, obtaining two measures from the same people at two points in time may sometimes be difficult. To address these issues, researchers have devised methods to assess reliability without two separate assessments.

Internal Consistency Reliability

It is possible to assess reliability by measuring individuals at only one point in time. We can do this because most psychological measures are made up of a number of different questions, called *items*. An intelligence test might have 100 items, a measure of extraversion might have 15 items, or a multiple-choice examination in a class might have 50 items. A person's test score would be based on the total of his or her responses on all items. In the class, an exam consists of a number of questions about the material, and the total score is the number of correct answers. An extraversion measure might ask people to agree or disagree with items such as "I enjoy lively parties." An individual's extraversion score is obtained by finding the total number of such items that are endorsed. Recall that reliability increases with increasing numbers of items.

Internal consistency reliability is the assessment of reliability using responses at only one point in time. Because all items measure the same variable, they should yield similar or consistent results.

One indicator of internal consistency is **split-half reliability;** this is the correlation of the total score on one half of the test with the total score on the other half. The two halves are created by randomly dividing the items into two parts. The actual calculation of a split-half reliability coefficient is a bit more complicated because the final measure will include items from both halves. Thus, the combined measure will have more items and will be more reliable than either half by itself. This fact must be taken into account when calculating the reliability coefficient; the corrected reliability is termed the *Spearman-Brown split-half reliability coefficient.*

Split-half reliability is relatively straightforward and easy to calculate, even without a computer. One drawback is that it is based on only one of many possible ways of dividing the measure into halves. The most commonly used indicator of reliability based on internal consistency, called **Cronbach's alpha,** provides us with the average of all possible split-half reliability coefficients. To actually perform the calculation, scores on each item are correlated with scores on every other item. A large number of correlation coefficients are produced; you would only want to do this with a computer! The value of Cronbach's alpha is based on the average of all the inter-item correlation coefficients and the number of items in the measure. Again, you should note that more items will be associated with higher reliability.

It is also possible to examine the correlation of each item score with the total score based on all items. Such **item-total correlations** are very informative because they provide information about each individual item. Items that do not correlate with the total score on the measure are actually measuring a different variable; they can be eliminated to increase internal consistency reliability. This information is also useful when it is necessary to construct a brief version of a measure. Even though reliability increases with longer measures, a shorter version can be more convenient to administer and still retain acceptable reliability.

Interrater Reliability

In some research, raters observe behaviors and make ratings or judgments. To do this, a rater uses instructions for making judgments about the behaviors—for example, by rating whether a child's behavior on a playground is aggressive and how aggressive the behavior is. You could have one rater make judgments about aggression, but the single observations of one rater might be unreliable. That is, one rater's scores may contain a lot of measurement error. The solution to this problem is to use at least two raters who observe the same behavior. **Interrater reliability** is the extent to which raters agree in their observations. Thus, if two raters are judging whether behaviors are aggressive, high interrater reliability is obtained when most of the observations result in the same judgment. A commonly used indicator of interrater reliability is called *Cohen's kappa*.

The methods of assessing reliability are summarized in Figure 2.

Test-Retest Reliability

• A measure is taken two times. The correlation of a score at time 1 with the score at time 2 represents *test-retest reliability*. The correlation between two versions of a measure is called *alternative forms reliability*.

Internal Consistency Reliability

• *Cronbach's Alpha:* Correlation of each item on the measure with every other item on the measure is the Cronbach's Alpha reliability coefficient.

• *Split-Half Reliability:* The correlation of total score on one half of a measure with the total score on the other half of the measure presents split-half reliability.

Interrater Reliability

• Evidence for reliability is present when multiple raters agree in their observations of the same thing. *Cohen's kappa* is a commonly used indicator of *interrater reliability*.

FIGURE 2
Three strategies for assessing reliability

Reliability and Accuracy of Measures

Reliability is clearly important when researchers develop measures of behavior. But reliability is not the only characteristic of a measure or the only thing that researchers worry about. Reliability tells us about measurement error, but it does not tell us whether we have a good measure of the variable of interest. To use a silly example, suppose you want to measure intelligence and the measure you develop looks remarkably like the device that is used to measure shoe size at your local shoe store. You ask your best friend to place one foot in the device, and you use the gauge to measure their intelligence. Numbers on the device provide a scale of intelligence so you can immediately assess a person's intelligence level. Will these numbers result in a reliable measure of intelligence? The answer is that they will! Consider what a test-retest reliability coefficient would be. If you administer the "foot intelligence scale" on Monday, it will be almost the same the following Monday; the test-retest reliability is high. But is this an accurate measure of intelligence? Obviously, the scores have nothing to do with intelligence; just because the device is labeled an intelligence test does not mean that it is a *good* measure of intelligence or that it is a measure of intelligence at all.

Let's consider a less silly example. Suppose your neighborhood gas station pump puts the same amount of gas in your car every time you purchase a gallon (or liter) of fuel; the gas pump gauge is reliable. However, the issue of accuracy is still open. The only way you can know about the accuracy of the pump is to compare the gallon (or liter) you receive with some standard measure. In fact, states have inspectors responsible for comparing an exact gallon measure with the amount that the pump says is a gallon. A pump with a gauge that does not deliver what it says it delivers must be repaired or replaced. This difference between the reliability and accuracy of measures leads us to a consideration of the validity of measures.

CONSTRUCT VALIDITY OF MEASURES

If something is valid, it is "true" in the sense that it is supported by available evidence. The amount of gasoline that the gauge indicates should match some standard measure of liquid volume; a measure of a personality characteristic such as shyness should be an accurate indicator of that trait. **Construct validity** refers to the adequacy of the operational definition of variables. To what extent does the operational definition of a variable actually reflect the true theoretical meaning of the variable? In terms of measurement, construct validity is a question of whether the measure that is employed actually measures the construct it is intended to measure. Applicants for some jobs are required to take a Clerical Ability Test; this measure is supposed to predict an individual's clerical ability. The validity of such a test is determined by whether it actually does measure this ability. A measure of shyness is an operational definition of the shyness variable; the validity of this measure is determined by whether it does measure this construct.

How do we know that a measure is valid? Evidence for construct validity takes many forms.

Indicators of Construct Validity

Face Validity   The simplest way to argue that a measure is valid is to suggest that the measure appears to assess the intended variable accurately. This is called **face validity**—the evidence for validity is that the measure seems "on the face of it" to measure what it is supposed to measure. Face validity is not very sophisticated; it involves only a judgment of whether, given the theoretical definition of the variable, the content of the measure appears to actually measure the variable. That is, do the procedures used to measure the variable appear to be an accurate operational definition of the theoretical variable? Thus, a measure of a variable such as shyness will usually appear to measure that variable. A measure of shyness called the Shy Q (Bortnik et al., 2002) includes items such as "I often feel insecure in social situations" but does not include an item such as "I learned to ride a bicycle at an early age"—the first item appears to be more closely related to shyness than does the second one. Note that the assessment of validity here is a very subjective, intuitive process. A way to improve the process somewhat is to systematically seek out experts in the field to make the face validity determination.

In either case, face validity is not sufficient to conclude that a measure is, in fact, valid. Appearance is not a very good indicator of accuracy. Some very poor measures may have face validity; for example, most personality measures that appear in popular magazines typically have several questions that look reasonable but often do not tell you anything meaningful. The interpretations of the scores may make fun reading, but there is no empirical evidence to support the conclusions drawn in the article. In addition, many good measures of variables do not have obvious face validity. For example, is it obvious that rapid eye movement during sleep is a measure of dreaming?

Content Validity   **Content validity** is based on comparing the content of the measure with the universe of content that defines the construct. For example, a measure of depression would have content that links to each of the symptoms that define the depression construct. Or consider a measure of "knowledge of psychology" that could be administered to graduating seniors at your college. In this case, the faculty would need to define a universe of content that constitutes this knowledge. The measure would then have to reflect that universe. Thus, if classical conditioning is one of the content areas that defines knowledge of psychology (it is!), then questions relating to this topic will be included in the measure.

Both face validity and content validity focus on assessing whether the content of a measure reflects the meaning of the construct being measured. Other indicators of validity rely on research that examines how scores on a measure relate to other measures of behavior. In validity research, the behavior is termed a *criterion*. These validity indicators are predictive validity, concurrent validity, convergent validity, and discriminant validity.

Predictive Validity   Sometimes we are interested in using a measure to predict some future behavior. A measure has **predictive validity** if research shows that scores on the measure do in fact predict the behavior or outcome it is intended to predict. Thus, with predictive validity, the criterion measure is a future behavior or outcome. The construct of "grit" is defined as a noncognitive individual difference variable characterized by passion and perseverance for long-term goals (Duckworth & Quinn, 2009). By definition, grit measured at one point in time will be related to goal completion at a later time. Eskreis-Winkler et al. (2014) used a measure of grit to predict successful completion of a difficult Army Special Forces selection course and the likelihood that a high school junior would graduate over a year later.

Predictive validity is important when studying measures that are designed to improve our ability to make predictions. Organizations may create a set of measures for prospective employees that are designed to select recruits who are likely to succeed in a training program or offer a work sample consistent with company expectations. Similarly, the Law School Admissions Test (LSAT) was developed to predict success in law school. The construct validity of such measures is demonstrated when scores on the measure predict the future behaviors. Predictive validity of the LSAT is demonstrated when research shows that people scoring high on the test do better in law school than people who score low on the test (i.e., when there is a positive relationship between the test score and grades in law school). The measure can be used to advise people on whether they are likely to succeed in law school or to select applicants for law school admission.

Concurrent Validity

Concurrent validity is demonstrated by research that examines the relationship between the measure and a criterion behavior at the same time (concurrently). Research using the concurrent validity approach can take many forms. A common method is to study whether two or more groups of people differ on the measure in expected ways. Suppose you have a measure of shyness. Your theory of shyness might lead you to expect that salespeople whose job requires making cold calls to potential customers would score lower on the shyness measure than salespeople in positions in which potential customers must make an effort to contact the company themselves.

Another approach to concurrent validity is to study how people who score either low or high on the measure behave in different situations. For example, you could compare a group of people who score high on the shyness score with another group consisting of low scorers. People in each group might be asked to describe themselves to a stranger while you measure their level of anxiety. Here you would expect that those who score high on the shyness scale would exhibit higher amounts of anxiety.

Convergent Validity

Any given measure is a particular operational definition of the variable being measured. Often there will be other operational definitions—other measures—of the same or similar constructs. **Convergent validity** is the extent to which scores on the measure in question are related to scores on other measures of the same construct or similar constructs. Measures of similar constructs should converge—for example, one measure of shyness should correlate highly with another shyness measure or a measure of a similar construct such as social anxiety. In actual research on a shyness scale, the convergent validity of a measure of shyness called the Shy Q was demonstrated by showing that Shy Q scores were highly correlated (.77) with a scale called the Fear of Negative Evaluation (Bortnik et al., 2002). Because the constructs of shyness and fear of negative evaluation have many similarities (such fear is thought to be a component of shyness), the high correlation is expected and increases our confidence in the construct validity of the Shy Q measure.

Discriminant Validity   When the measure is *not* related to variables with which it should not be related, **discriminant validity** is demonstrated. The measure should discriminate between the construct being measured and other unrelated constructs. In other words, evidence for construct validity can be found when a measure is unrelated to other variables and constructs that it should be unrelated to. In research on the discriminant validity of their shyness measure, Bortnik et al. (2002) found no relationship between Shy Q scores and several conceptually unrelated interpersonal values such as being forceful with others.

Ways in which we can assess validity are summarized in Table 1.

TABLE 1   Indicators of construct validity of a measure

Validity	Definition	Example
Face validity	The content of the measure appears to reflect the construct being measured.	If the new measure of depression includes items like "I feel sad" or "I feel down" or "I cry a lot," this would be evidence that the measure has face validity.
Content validity	The content of the measure is linked to the universe of content that defines the construct.	Depression is defined by a mood and by cognitive and physiological symptoms. If the new measure of depression has content validity, it will include items from each domain.
Predictive validity	Scores on the measure predict behavior on a criterion measured at a future time.	If the measure of depression predicts a future diagnosis of depression, this is evidence that the measure has predictive validity.
Concurrent validity	Scores on the measure are related to a criterion measured at the same time (concurrently).	If two groups of participants were given the measures, and they differed in predictable ways (e.g., if those in therapy for depression scored higher than those in treatment for an anxiety disorder), this would be evidence for concurrent validity.
Convergent validity	Scores on the measure are related to other measures of the same construct.	If scores from the new measure, collected at the same time as other measures of depression (e.g., Beck Depression Inventory or Duke Anxiety-Depression Scale), were related to scores from those other measures, then it could be said to have evidence for convergent validity.
Discriminant validity	Scores on the measure are not related to other measures that are theoretically different.	If the new measure, collected at the same time as other measures of anxiety (e.g., state/trait anxiety), was unrelated to those measures, then it could be said to have evidence for discriminant validity because it would indicate that what was being measured was *not* anxiety.

Check Your Learning

Now do the Check Your Learning: Practice Exercise #1 to help solidify your understanding of indicators of construct validity.

Measurement Validity: For Whom

Construct validity is of critical importance to behavioral research. When conducting research to assess the construct validity, a sample of individuals with particular characteristics will be recruited. As we will discuss in the chapter Generalization, much of the early work in psychology and other behavioral sciences was conducted by White men studying White male research participants. There are few more critical consequences of this fact than in measurement. Many measures have been validated with samples consisting primarily of White, college-educated people—this has been true for a long time. Consequently, we do not know if the measure will have validity when used to study diverse samples of people from other cultures, ages, and educational backgrounds. That has begun to change as researchers become more sensitive to this issue, though perhaps not fast enough (Han et al., 2019).

To illustrate, consider a hypothetical situation—a gay, young adult man born, raised, and living in a West African country and a straight young adult man, born, raised, and living in the U.S. Midwest where he currently attends college, complete the same measure of life stress in their native languages. If their scores on the measures are the same, should you be comfortable assuming similar levels of life stress? If their scores were radically different, would you believe you understood those differences? Valid measurement across groups is possible. Han et al. (2019) concluded that researchers need to study and assess how well behavioral measures truly measure constructs among diverse groups. Today, many studies are conducted to evaluate the validity of measures across groups. For example, Avila et al. (2020) studied neuropsychological measures of cognitive aging by race, ethnicity, sex, and gender groups, while Bertola et al. (2020) assessed neuropsychological tests among different sociodemographic groups in Brazil.

Construct validity is the critical guiding concept. If we measure a construct, is the measure valid (and reliable!) across sub-groups. Does a measure of life stress consider that life stress varies by culture?

REACTIVITY OF MEASURES

Besides group differences, another potential problem when measuring behavior is **reactivity.** A measure is said to be reactive if awareness of being measured changes an individual's behavior. A reactive measure describes what the person is like when they are aware of being observed, but it does not describe how the person would behave under natural circumstances. Simply having various devices such as electrodes and blood pressure cuffs attached to your body may change the physiological responses being recorded. Knowing that a researcher is observing you or recording your behavior on tape might change how you behave. Measures of behavior vary in terms of their potential reactivity. There are also ways to minimize reactivity, such as allowing time for individuals to become used to the observer's presence or the recording equipment.

A book by Webb et al. (1981) has drawn attention to a number of measures that are called *nonreactive* or *unobtrusive.* Many such measures involve clever ways of indirectly recording a variable. For example, an unobtrusive measure of preferences for paintings in an art museum is the frequency with which floor tiles near each painting must be replaced—the most popular paintings are the ones with the most tile wear. Levine (1990, 1997) measured the pace of life in cities, using indirect measures such as the accuracy of bank clocks and the speed of processing standard requests at post offices. Some of the measures described by Webb et al. (1981) are simply humorous. For instance, in 1872 Sir Francis Galton studied the efficacy of prayer in producing long life. Galton wondered whether British royalty, who were frequently the recipients of prayers by the populace, lived longer than other people. He checked death records and found that members of royal families actually led shorter lives than other people, such as "men of literature and science." The book by Webb and his colleagues is a rich source of such nonreactive measures. More importantly, it draws attention to the problem of reactivity and sensitizes researchers to the need to reduce reactivity whenever possible. We will return to this issue at several points in this book.

VARIABLES AND MEASUREMENT SCALES

Every variable that is studied must be operationally defined. The operational definition is the specific method used to manipulate or measure the variable. There must be at least two values or levels of the variable. The values may be quantitatively different or they may reflect categorical differences. In actuality, the world is a bit more complex. The levels can be conceptualized as a scale that uses one of four kinds of measurement scales: nominal, ordinal, interval, and ratio.

Nominal Scales

Nominal scales have no numerical or quantitative properties. Instead, categories or groups simply differ from one another (sometimes nominal variables are called "categorical" variables). An obvious example is the variable of handedness. A person is classified as either left-handed, right-handed, or ambidextrous. Being right-handed does not imply a greater amount of "handedness" than being left-handed or ambidextrous; the three levels are merely different. This is called a nominal scale because we simply assign names to different categories. Another example is the classification of undergraduates according to major. A psychology major would not be entitled to a higher number than a history major, for instance. Even if you were to assign numbers to the different categories, the numbers would be meaningless, except for identification.

In an experiment, the independent variable is often a nominal or categorical variable. For example, Hölzel et al. (2011) studied the effect of meditation on brain structures using magnetic resonant imaging (MRI). They found that after participants underwent an 8-week mindfulness meditation-based stress-reduction program, there was an increase in the density of gray matter in specific areas of their brains, as compared with other participants who did not take part in the program. The independent variable in this case (participating in the program or not) was clearly nominal because the two levels are merely different; participants either did, or did not, participate in the stress reduction program.

Ordinal Scales

Ordinal scales allow us to rank order the levels of the variable being studied. Instead of having categories that are simply different, as in a nominal scale, the categories can be ordered from first to last. Letter grades are a good example of an ordinal scale. Another example of an ordinal scale is provided by the movie rating system used on a movie review website, where movies are given one to four stars, based on these descriptions:

★ ★ ★ ★   Great! New or old, a classic

★ ★ ★   Good! First rate

★ ★   Flawed, but may have some good moments

★   Poor! Desperation time

The rating system is not a nominal scale, because the number of stars is meaningful in terms of a continuum of quality. However, the stars allow us only to rank order the movies. A four-star movie is better than a three-star movie; a three-star movie is better than a two-star movie; and so on. Although we have this quantitative information about the movies, we cannot say that the difference between a one-star and a two-star movie is always the same or that it is equal to the difference between a two-star and a three-star movie. No particular value is attached to the intervals between the numbers used in the rating scale.

Interval and Ratio Scales

One problem with ordinal scales is that while they provide rank-ordered categories, they do not provide any information about the distance between the categories. All four-star movies are equally good, all one-star movies are equally bad. In an **interval scale,** the difference between the numbers on the scale is meaningful. Specifically, the intervals between the numbers are equal in size. The difference between 1 and 2 on the scale, for example, is the same as the difference between 2 and 3. Interval scales generally have five or more quantitative levels.

A household thermometer (Fahrenheit or Celsius) measures temperature on an interval scale. The difference in temperature between 40° and 50° is equal to the difference between 70° and 80°. However, there is no absolute zero on the scale that would indicate the *absence* of temperature. The zero on an interval scale is only an arbitrary reference point. (Note that the zero point on the Celsius scale was chosen to reflect the temperature at which water freezes; this is the same as 32° on the Fahrenheit scale. The zero on both scales is arbitrary, and there are even negative numbers on the scale.) Without an absolute zero point on interval scales, we cannot form ratios of the numbers. That is, we cannot say that one number on the scale represents twice as much (or three times as much, and so forth) temperature as another number. You cannot say, for example, that 60° is twice as warm as 30°.

An example of an interval scale in the behavioral sciences might be a personality measure of a trait such as extraversion. If the measurement is an interval scale, we cannot validly claim that "the person who scored 20 is twice as extraverted as the person who scored 10," because there is no absolute zero point that indicates an absence of the trait being measured.

Ratio scales do have an absolute zero point that indicates the absence of the variable being measured. Examples include many physical measures, such as length, weight, or time. With a ratio scale, it is possible to make true claims such as "a person who weighs 220 pounds weighs twice as much as a person who weighs 110 pounds" or "participants in the experimental group responded twice as fast as participants in the control group."

Ratio scales are used in the behavioral sciences when variables that involve physical measures are being studied—particularly time measures such as reaction time, rate of responding, and duration of response. However, many variables in the behavioral sciences are less precise and therefore use nominal, ordinal, or interval scale measures. It should also be noted that the statistical tests for interval and ratio scales are the same. Table 2 summarizes the four kinds of measurement scales.

TABLE 2   Scales of measurement

Scale	Description	Examples	Distinction
Nominal	▪ Categories with no numeric scales	▪ Left-handed/right-handed ▪ Eye color ▪ College major	▪ Impossible to define any quantitative values and/or differences between/across categories
Ordinal	▪ Rank ordering Numeric values limited	▪ Two-, three-, and four-star restaurants ▪ Ranking TV programs by popularity	▪ Intervals between items not known
Interval	▪ Numeric properties are literal ▪ Assume equal interval between values	▪ A measure of intelligence ▪ Aptitude test score ▪ Temperature (Fahrenheit or Celsius)	▪ No true zero
Ratio	▪ Zero indicates absence of variable measured	▪ Reaction time ▪ Age ▪ Frequencies of behaviors	▪ Can form ratios (one person weighs twice as much as another person)

The Importance of the Measurement Scales

When you read about the operational definitions of variables, you will recognize the levels of the variable in terms of these types of scales. The conclusions one draws about the meaning of a particular score on a variable depend on which type of scale was used. With interval and ratio scales, you can make quantitative distinctions that allow you to talk about amounts of the variable. With nominal scales, there is no quantitative information. To illustrate, suppose that after reading a review of the research on math anxiety by Chang and Beilock (2016), you decide to do your own research on math anxiety and performance on a statistics test. For your study, you will need a measure of math anxiety. You might ask participants to report how anxious they are about math. You could use a nominal scale such as:

_____ Not Anxious About Math   _____ Anxious About Math

These scale values allow participants to state whether they are anxious about math, but does not allow you to know about the amount of anxiety. As an alternative, you could use a scale that asks participants to rate their anxiety when thinking about doing math problems:

Very Anxious _____ _____ _____ _____ _____ Not at All Anxious

This rating scale provides you with quantitative information about anxiety levels because you can assign numeric values to each of the response options on the scale; in this case, the values would range from 1 to 5.

The scale that is used also determines the types of statistics that are appropriate when the results of a study are analyzed. For now, we do not need to worry about statistical analysis. However, we will return to this point in the chapter "Understanding Research Results: Description and Correlation."

Check Your Learning

Now do the Check Your Learning: Practice Exercise #2 to help solidify your understanding of scales of measurement.

We are now ready to consider methods for measuring behavior. A variety of observational methods are described in the chapter "Observational Methods." We focus on questionnaires and interviews in the chapter "Asking People About Themselves: Survey Research."

ENGAGING WITH RESEARCH: MEASUREMENT CONCEPTS

Every term, millions of students complete student evaluation of teaching (SET) forms in an effort to assess the quality and performance of their instructors. The specific measurement instrument can vary from campus to campus, but the overall goal is the same. Course evaluations are used to inform hiring decisions, promotion decisions, and classroom instruction decisions, and they are also used by individual instructors to improve the courses they teach. However, they are also biased against female instructors, who are evaluated more negatively than male instructors.

Peterson et al. (2019) were interested in reducing bias in SET ratings by using language intended to reduce that bias. Using four college classes with large enrollments, and two male instructors and two female instructors, students were randomly assigned the standard SET form or a form that had been modified to reduce bias. They found that students who completed a form with anti-bias language rated female instructors higher than students who were given the standard form; no differences were found in ratings of the male instructors.

For this exercise, acquire and read the following article (available at https://doi.org/10.1371/journal.pone.0216241):

Peterson, D. A. M., Biederman, L. A., Andersen, D., Ditonto, T. M., & Roe, K. (2019). Mitigating gender bias in student evaluations of teaching. *PLoS ONE, 14*(5), e0216241. https://doi.org/10.1371/journal.pone.0216241

After reading the article, consider the following:

1. **What is the primary goal of this study: Description, Prediction, Determining Cause, or Explaining? Do the authors achieve their goals? Can you think of any other explanation of their results?**

2. **What did these researchers do? What was the method?**

3. **What was measured?**

   a. The authors don't report any evidence for reliability or validity. How would you test their measure for reliability? How would you test it for validity?

   b. Do you think that SET measures teaching quality at all? That is, even if we are able to reduce bias, do you think that we are still measuring good teaching with instruments like the one that Peterson et al. (2019) used?

4. **To what or whom can we generalize the results?**

   a. Do you think that their findings would be the same if they studied SET ratings for courses in psychology? Or in mathematics? Why or why not?

b. Do you think that their findings would be generalizable to all college courses, including courses that are offered online? Why or why not?

c. What do you think would happen if this intervention were used widely at your college? Do you think that bias would be decreased? Why or why not?

5. **What did they find? What were the results?**

6. **Have other researchers found similar results? Are the findings of this study similar to the findings of other studies on the same topic?**

7. **What are the limitations of this study?**

8. **What are the ethical issues present in this study?**

BEING A SKILLED CONSUMER OF RESEARCH

1. Take a personality test on the internet (you can find such tests by searching the internet). Based on the information provided, what can you conclude about the test's reliability, construct validity, and reactivity?

2. The "five-factor" or "Big 5" model of personality describes five fundamental personality traits: Extraversion, Agreeableness, Conscientiousness, Emotional stability (Neuroticism), and Openness to experience. You can assess yourself on the Big 5 using this link: https://projects.fivethirtyeight.com/personality-quiz/#personality. For this exercise, choose one of the Big 5 factors and then:

a. provide a definition,

b. describe how you might measure the personality trait, and

c. describe a method that you might use to assess construct validity.

3. Few concepts are more important to behavioral science—or to any science!—than measurement. Consider the following three broad categories of behavioral research and the ways in which measurement impacts what we understand. For each, consider: (1) How reliable would each of your strategies be? (2) How might the measurement strategy be biased (i.e., how valid would your strategy be)?

a. Emotional experience. Few things are more important to humans than our emotions. Of course, emotions are difficult to measure. For this exercise, think of two ways you could measure a specific emotion. For example, you could measure grief by interviewing people at a funeral (consider the ethical implications of this strategy before you implement it!).

b. Parenting practice. Parenting practices can be difficult to directly measure because when you are a parent you are always parenting! (Likewise, when you are a child, you are always being parented.) Think of two ways you could measure a specific parenting practice. For example, you could ask teenagers about their parents' parenting practices related to curfew.

c. Racism. A microaggression is an act of casually degrading any marginalized group (Sue et al., 2007). For example, asking a co-worker who appears to be Asian or Latinx where they are from is a microaggression because it implies that they are "not from here." For this exercise, think of two ways you could measure occurrences of microaggressions in a workplace (for example, you could conduct face-to-face interviews with employees and ask them if they have observed microaggressions).

Check Your Learning: Practice Exercises

Practice Exercise #1

Dr. Williams has created a new measure of social anxiety for teens. The measure has 10 items that present social scenarios, such as "going to a party with 10 people, none of whom you know" and "having dinner with a friend and the friend's parents," and asks how "appealing" each scenario is on a scale of 1 (highly unappealing) to 10 (highly appealing). For each of the following, identify the correct type of validity.

1. Dr. Williams administers the new measure and the obsessive-compulsive inventory; the two measures are not highly related.

2. Dr. Williams administers the new measure and the Beck Anxiety Inventory to groups of research participants. The two measures are related.

3. Dr. Williams's new measure is predictive of a diagnosis of social anxiety disorder.

4. The new measure uses only ratings of "unappealing – appealing" as indicators of social anxiety about each situation. A suggestion was made to include other indicators (e.g., ratings of "not anxious – anxious").

5. After reviewing all of the questions in the new measure of social anxiety for teens, Dr. Ling, an expert on social anxiety, finds the measure valid.

6. Dr. Williams administers the new measure and the Wilson Social Anxiety Inventory to groups of research participants; the measures are related.

Practice Exercise #2

Scales of Measurement

For each of the following, identify whether the scale being used is nominal, ordinal, interval, or ratio:

1. The type of programming on each radio station in your city (e.g., KPSY plays jazz, KSOC is talk radio).

2. The number of hours you spent studying each day during the past week.

3. Ethnic group categories of people in a neighborhood.

4. Your friend's score on an intelligence test.

5. The temperatures in various U.S. cities that are listed in most U.S. newspapers.

6. The number of votes received by each of the candidates for Congress in your district in the last election.

7. The cell phone listed as third best on an online electronics review website.

8. The birth weights of babies who were born at Wilshire General Hospital last week.

9. Georgia's listing as the number one team in a poll of sportswriters, with Kansas listed number two.

10. Yellow walls in your office and white walls in your boss's office.

11. The amount of the tip left after each meal at a restaurant during a 3-hour period.

(Answers are provided at the end of this chapter.)

CHAPTER REVIEW

Review Questions

1. What is meant by the reliability of a measure? Distinguish between true score and measurement error.

2. Describe the methods of determining the reliability of a measure.

3. Discuss the concept of construct validity. Distinguish among the indicators of construct validity.

4. Why isn't face validity sufficient to establish the validity of a measure?

5. What is a reactive measure?

6. Distinguish between nominal, ordinal, interval, and ratio scales.

Study Terms

Alternate forms reliability (p. 114)

Concurrent validity (p. 119)

Construct validity (p. 117)

Content validity (p. 118)

Convergent validity (p. 119)

Cronbach's alpha (p. 115)

Discriminant validity (p. 120)

Face validity (p. 118)

Internal consistency reliability (p. 115)

Interrater reliability (p. 116)

Interval scale (p. 123)

Item-total correlation (p. 116)

Measurement error (p. 112)

Nominal scale (p. 122)

Ordinal scale (p. 123)

Pearson product-moment correlation coefficient (p. 114)

Predictive validity (p. 118)

Ratio scale (p. 124)

Reactivity (p. 121)

Reliability (p. 112)

Split-half reliability (p. 115)

Test-retest reliability (p. 114)

True score (p. 112)

Check Your Learning: Answers

Practice Exercise #1

1. discriminant; 2. concurrent; 3. predictive; 4. content; 5. face; 6. convergent

Practice Exercise #2

1. nominal; 2. ratio; 3. nominal; 4. interval; 5. interval; 6. ratio; 7. ordinal; 8. ratio; 9. ordinal; 10. nominal; 11. ratio

Rawpixel.com/Shutterstock

6

Observational Methods

LEARNING OBJECTIVES

- Compare and contrast quantitative and qualitative methods of studying behavior.
- Describe naturalistic observation and discuss methodological issues, such as participation and concealment, and the limitations of the approach.
- Describe systematic observation and discuss methodological issues, such as the use of equipment, reactivity, reliability, and sampling.
- Summarize the features of a case study.
- Define archival research and describe the different sources of archival data—statistical records, survey archives, and written records—and how they can be used to answer research questions.

ALL SCIENTIFIC RESEARCH REQUIRES CAREFUL OBSERVATION. In this chapter we will explore a variety of observational methods, including naturalistic observation, systematic observation, case studies, and archival research. Because so much research involves surveys using questionnaires or interviews, we cover the topic of survey research in the chapter "Asking People About Themselves: Survey Research." Before we describe these methods in detail, it will be helpful to understand the distinction between quantitative and qualitative methods of describing behavior.

QUANTITATIVE AND QUALITATIVE APPROACHES

Approaches to research based on observational methods can be broadly classified as primarily quantitative or qualitative. Quantitative research focuses on variables that can be quantified (e.g., counted). Quantitative investigations often have large samples, and results are expressed in numerical terms using statistical descriptions. Quantitative researchers typically investigate research questions using experiments, surveys, structured interviews, and systematic observations.

Creswell (2013) defined qualitative research as follows:

> Qualitative research begins with assumptions and the use of interpretive/ theoretical frameworks that inform the study of research problems addressing the meaning individuals or groups ascribe to a social or human problem. To study this problem, qualitative researchers use an emerging qualitative approach to inquiry, the collection of data in a natural setting sensitive to the people and places under study, and data analysis that is both inductive and deductive and establishes patterns or themes. The final written report or presentation includes the voices of participants, the reflexivity of the researcher, a complex description and interpretation of the problem, and its contribution to the literature or a call for change. (p. 44)

Just as there are many types of quantitative approaches to answering research questions, there are many approaches to qualitative inquiry. Creswell and Poth (2018) described five broad approaches: Narrative Research, Phenomenological Research, Grounded Theory Research, Ethnographic Research, and Case Study Research. While a detailed description of these strategies falls outside of the scope of this book, it is essential to understand that qualitative research approaches can be used to give different and highly valuable perspectives to research questions.

To more concretely understand the distinction, imagine that you are interested in describing how teenagers' lives are affected when they have a paying job. You might take a quantitative approach by developing a questionnaire that you would ask a sample of teenagers to complete. You could ask about the number of hours they work, the type of work they do, their levels of stress, their school grades, and their involvement with various school, community, and social activities. After assigning numerical values to the responses, you could look at the answers from the entire sample: you could subject the data to quantitative, statistical analysis. A quantitative description of the results would perhaps focus on the percentage of teenagers who work and how this percentage varies by age. There might also be an examination of whether the number of work hours is related to school grades, use of drugs and alcohol, and sleep patterns.

Suppose, instead, that you take a qualitative approach to describe the situation, setting, or behavior. You might conduct a series of focus groups, each consisting of 8–10 teenagers, and engage them in a discussion about their perceptions and experiences with the world of work. You would ask them to tell you about the topic using their own words and their own ways of thinking about the world. You might use a video or audio recorder to record the group discussions and have a transcript prepared later. You might have observers take detailed notes during the discussions. A qualitative description of the findings would focus on the themes that emerged from the discussions and how the teenagers conceptualized the issues. Such description is qualitative because it is expressed in non-numeric, narrative terms.

It is also possible to conduct mixed-methods research that uses both quantitative and qualitative methodologies to collect data. Goodrum et al. (2021) used a mixed-methods research design to study what happens after mothers diagnosed with HIV disclose their HIV status to their children. The sample for the quantitative element of the study consisted of 174 mother-child pairs; a majority of children in the study were Black (58%), and 35% were Latinx. The mothers and children completed measures of parental stress, children's behaviors, children's depression, and family conflict at the beginning of the study and again after 3, 9, and 15 months. At the beginning of the study, none of the mothers had disclosed their HIV status to their children. After the first session, the researchers asked the mothers if they had disclosed their HIV status to the child and categorized them into groups: no disclosure, partial disclosure, and full disclosure. The researchers examined potential changes after a mother had fully disclosed HIV status to the child and found that full disclosure was associated with some positive changes in the mother-child relationship.

The qualitative portion of the study focused on families in which full disclosure had occurred. Goodrum et al. recruited 17 of the mothers and 16 children. The qualitative investigation aimed to obtain in-depth information about HIV disclosure and how it affected the child and the family. Mothers and children were interviewed separately. The interview content was organized with three themes: (1) Children's reaction to the disclosure; (2) Mothers' experiences of the disclosure; (3) Family changes after HIV disclosure. The mothers' experiences include a positive feeling about the disclosure being appropriate and relief after having a conversation that was approached with some anxiety. Family relationships were improved by more and deeper conversations and children taking more responsibility for household chores and monitoring things like taking pills. The qualitative report provides a clearer representation of what happened after the HIV disclosure, thereby giving meaning and depth to the quantitative conclusions.

NATURALISTIC OBSERVATION

Naturalistic observation is sometimes called *field work, field observation,* or *ethnography* (see Lofland et al., 2006). In a study using **naturalistic observation,** the researcher makes observations of individuals in their natural environments (the field). This research approach has roots in anthropology and the study of animal behavior and is currently widely used in the social sciences to study many phenomena in all types of social and organizational settings. Thus, you may encounter naturalistic observation studies that focus on employees in a business organization, members of a sports team, patrons of a bar, students and teachers in a school, or prairie dogs in a colony in Arizona.

Sylvia Scribner's (1997) research on "practical thinking" is a good example of naturalistic observation research in psychology. Scribner studied ways people in a variety of occupations make decisions and solve problems. She describes the process of this research: "My colleagues and I have driven around on a 3 a.m. milk route, helped cashiers total their receipts and watched machine operators logging in their production for the day. ... We made detailed records of how people were going about performing their jobs. We collected copies of all written materials they read or produced—everything from notes scribbled on brown paper bags to computer printouts. We photographed devices in their working environment that required them to process other types of symbolic information—thermometers, gauges, scales, measurement instruments of all kinds" (Scribner, 1997, p. 223). One aspect of thinking that Scribner studied was how workers made mathematical calculations. She found that milk truck drivers and other workers made complex calculations that depended on their acquired knowledge. For example, a delivery invoice might have required the driver to multiply 32 quarts of milk by $.68 per quart. To arrive at the answer, drivers used knowledge acquired on the job about how many quarts were in a case and the cost of a case; thus, they multiplied 2 cases of milk by $10.88 per case. In general, the workers whom Scribner observed employed complex but very efficient strategies to solve problems at work. More important, the strategies used could often not be predicted from formal models of problem solving. Scribner's research had a particular emphasis on people making decisions in their everyday environments. Scribner has since expanded her research to several more occupations and many types of decisions.

Other naturalistic research may examine a narrower range of behaviors. For example, Graham and her colleagues observed instances of aggression that occurred in bars in a large city late on weekend nights (Graham, et al., 2006). The Scribner study and the Graham study are both instances of naturalistic research because the observations were made in natural settings and the researchers did not attempt to influence what occurred in the settings.

Description and Interpretation of Data

The goal of naturalistic observation is to provide a complete and accurate picture of what occurred in the setting, rather than to test hypotheses formed prior to the study. To achieve this goal, the researcher must keep detailed field notes—that is, write or dictate on a regular basis (at least once each day) everything that has happened. Field researchers rely on a variety of techniques to gather information, depending on the particular setting. In the Graham et al. (2006) study in bars, the observers were alert to any behaviors that might lead to an incident of aggression. They carefully watched and listened to what happened. They immediately made notes on what they observed; these were later given to a research coordinator. In other studies, the observers might interview key "informants" to provide inside information about the setting, talk to people about their lives, and examine documents produced in the setting, such as newspapers, newsletters, or memos. In addition to taking detailed field notes, researchers conducting naturalistic observation usually use audio or video recordings.

The researcher's first goal is to describe the setting, events, and persons observed. The second, equally important goal is to analyze what was observed. The researcher must interpret what occurred, essentially generating hypotheses that help explain the data and make them understandable. Such an analysis is done by building a coherent structure to describe the observations. The final report, although sensitive to the chronological order of events, is usually organized around the structure developed by the researcher. Specific examples of events that occurred during observation are used to support the researcher's interpretations.

A good naturalistic observation report will support the analysis by using multiple confirmations. For example, similar events may occur several times, similar information may be reported by two or more people, and several different events may occur that all support the same conclusion.

The data in naturalistic observation studies are primarily *qualitative* in nature; that is, they are the descriptions of the observations themselves rather than *quantitative* statistical summaries. Such qualitative descriptions are often richer and closer to the phenomenon being studied than are statistical representations. However, it is often useful to also gather quantitative data. Depending on the setting, data might be gathered on income, family size, education levels, age, or sex of individuals in the setting. Such data can be reported and interpreted along with qualitative data gathered from interviews and direct observations.

Participation and Concealment

Two related issues facing the researcher are whether to be a participant or non-participant in the social setting and whether to conceal their purposes from the other people in the setting. Recall the discussion related to reactivity of a measure from the chapter "Measurement Concepts" and ask yourself: Do you become an active participant in the group, or do you observe from the outside? Do you conceal your purposes or even your presence, or do you openly let people know what you are doing?

A nonparticipant observer is an outsider who does not become an active part of the setting. In contrast, a participant observer assumes an active, insider role. By using **participant observation** the researcher may be able to experience events in the same way as natural participants. Friendships and other experiences of the participant observer may yield valuable data. A potential problem with participant observation, however, is that the observer may lose the objectivity necessary to conduct scientific observation. Remaining objective may be especially difficult when the researcher already belongs to the group being studied or is a dissatisfied former member of the group. Remember that naturalistic observation requires accurate description and objective interpretation with no prior hypotheses. If a researcher has some prior reason to either criticize people in the setting or give a glowing report of a particular group, the observations will likely be biased and the conclusions will lack objectivity.

Should the researcher remain concealed or be open about the purposes of the research? Concealed observation may be preferable because the presence of the observer may influence and alter the behavior of those being observed. Imagine how a nonconcealed observer might alter the behavior of high school students in many situations at a school. Thus, concealed observation is less reactive than nonconcealed observation because people are not aware that their behaviors are being observed and recorded. Still, nonconcealed observation may be preferable from an ethical viewpoint: Consider the invasion of privacy when researchers hid under beds in dormitory rooms to discover what college students talk about (Henle & Hubbell, 1938)! Also, people often quickly become accustomed to the observer and behave naturally in the observer's presence. This fact allows documentary filmmakers to record very private aspects of people's lives, as was done in the 2009 British documentary *Love, Life, and Death in a Day*. For the death segments, the filmmaker, Sue Bourne, contacted funeral homes to find families willing to be filmed throughout their grieving over the death of a loved one.

The decision of whether to conceal one's purpose or presence depends on both ethical concerns and the nature of the particular group and setting being studied. Sometimes a participant observer is nonconcealed to certain members of the group, who give the researcher permission to be part of the group as a concealed observer. Often a concealed observer decides to say nothing directly about his or her purposes but will completely disclose the goals of the research if asked by anyone. Nonparticipant observers are also not concealed when they gain permission to "hang out" in a setting or use interview techniques to gather information. In actuality, then, there are degrees of participation and concealment: A nonparticipant observer might not become a member of the group, for example, but might over time become accepted as a friend or simply part of the ongoing activities of the group. In sum, researchers who use naturalistic observation to study behavior must carefully determine what their role in the setting will be.

You may be wondering about informed consent in naturalistic observation. Recall from the chapter "Ethics in Behavioral Research" that observation in public places when anonymity is not threatened may be considered exempt research—informed consent might not be necessary. Moreover, in nonconcealed observation, informed consent may be given verbally or in written form. Nevertheless, researchers must be sensitive to ethical issues when conducting naturalistic observation. Of particular interest is whether the observations are made in a public place with no clear expectations that behaviors are private. For example, should a neighborhood bar be considered public or private?

Limits of Naturalistic Observation

Naturalistic observation obviously cannot be used to study all issues or phenomena. The approach is most useful when investigating complex social settings in order to both understand the settings and develop theories based on the observations. It is less useful for studying well-defined hypotheses under precisely specified conditions or phenomena that are not directly observable by a researcher in a natural setting (e.g., color perception, mood, response time on a cognitive task).

Field research is also very difficult to do. Unlike a typical laboratory experiment, field research data collection cannot always be scheduled at a convenient time and place. In fact, field research can be extremely time-consuming, often placing the researcher in an unfamiliar setting for extended periods. In the Graham et al. (2006) investigation of aggression in bars, observers spent more than 1,300 nights in 118 different bars (74 pairs of observers were required to accomplish this feat).

Also, in more carefully controlled settings, such as laboratory research, the procedures are well defined and the same for each participant and the data analysis is planned in advance. In naturalistic observation research, however, there is an ever-changing pattern of events, some important and some unimportant; the researcher must record them all and remain flexible in order to adjust to them as research progresses. Finally, the process of analysis that follows the completion of the research is not simple (imagine the task of sorting through the field notes of every incident of aggression that occurred on more than 1,300 nights). The researcher must repeatedly sort through the data to develop hypotheses to explain the data, and then make sure all data are consistent with the hypotheses. Although naturalistic observation research is a difficult and challenging scientific procedure, it yields invaluable knowledge when done well.

SYSTEMATIC OBSERVATION

Systematic observation refers to the careful observation of one or more specific behaviors in a particular setting. This research approach is much less global than naturalistic observation research. The researcher is interested in only a few very specific behaviors, the observations are quantifiable, and often the researcher has developed prior hypotheses about the behaviors. We will focus on systematic observation in naturalistic settings; these techniques may also be applied in laboratory settings.

Bakeman and Brownlee (1980; also see Bakeman, 2000), for instance, were interested in the social behavior of young children. Three-year-olds were videotaped in a room in a "free play" situation. Each child was taped for 100 minutes;

observers viewed the videotapes and coded each child's behavior every 15 seconds, using the following coding system:

Unoccupied: Child is not doing anything in particular or is simply watching other children.

Solitary play: Child plays alone with toys but is not interested in or affected by the activities of other children.

Together: Child is with other children but is not occupied with any particular activity.

Parallel play: Child plays beside other children with similar toys but does not play with the others.

Group play: Child plays with other children, including sharing toys or participating in organized play activities as part of a group of children.

Bakeman and Brownlee were particularly interested in the sequence or order in which the different behaviors were engaged in by the children. They found, for example, that the children rarely went from being unoccupied to engaging in parallel play. However, they frequently went from parallel to group play, indicating that parallel play is a transition state in which children decide whether to interact in a group situation.

Coding Systems

Numerous behaviors can be studied using systematic observation. The researcher must decide which behaviors are of interest, choose a setting in which the behaviors can be observed, and most importantly, develop a **coding system,** such as the one described above, to measure the behaviors. In another example, Rhoades and Stocker (2006) describe the use of the Marital Interaction Video Coding System. Couples are recorded for 10 minutes as they discuss an area of conflict; they then discuss a positive aspect of their relationship for 5 minutes. The video is later coded for hostility and affection displayed during every 5 minutes of the interaction. To code hostility, the observers rated the frequency of behaviors such as "blames other" and "provokes partner." Affection behaviors that were coded included "expresses concern" and "agrees with partner."

Methodological Issues

We should briefly mention several methodological issues in systematic observation.

Equipment   The first issue concerns equipment. You can directly observe behavior and code it at the same time; for example, you could use paper-and-pencil measures to directly observe and record the behavior of children in a classroom or couples interacting on campus. However, it is becoming more common to use video and audio recording equipment to make such observations because they provide a permanent record of the behavior observed that can be coded later.

An interesting method for audio recording is called the Electronically Activated Recorder (EAR), which was used to compare sociability behaviors of Americans and Mexicans (Ramírez-Esparza et al., 2009). The EAR is a small audio recorder that a subject wears throughout the day. It is set to turn on periodically to record sounds in the subject's environment (Mehl, 2017). The study examined frequency of sociable behaviors. Previous research had found that Americans score higher than Mexicans on self-report measures of sociability, contradicting stereotypes that Mexicans are generally more sociable. Coders applied the *Social Environment of Sound Inventory* to code the recorded sounds as: alone, talking with others in a public environment, or on the phone. When sociability was measured this way, the Mexican subjects were in fact more sociable than the American subjects.

Reactivity

A second issue is **reactivity**—the possibility that the presence of the observer will affect people's behaviors (see the chapter "Measurement Concepts"). Reactivity can be reduced by concealed observation. Using small cameras and microphones can make the observation unobtrusive, even in situations in which the participant has been informed of the recording. Also, reactivity can be reduced by allowing time for people to become accustomed to the observer and equipment.

Reliability

Recall from the chapter "Measurement Concepts" that reliability refers to the degree to which a measurement reflects a true score rather than measurement error. Reliable measures are stable, consistent, and precise. When conducting systematic observation, two or more raters are usually used to code behavior. Reliability is indicated by a high agreement among the raters. Very high levels of agreement (generally 80% agreement or higher) are reported in virtually all published research using systematic observation. For some large-scale research programs in which many observers will be employed over a period of years, observers are first trained using videotapes, and their observations during training are checked for agreement with results from previous observers.

Sampling Behaviors and Experiences

For many research questions, samples of behavior taken over an extended period provide more accurate and useful data than single, short observations. Traditionally, this was most easily done by making observations at random times of people or animals in a specific setting. For example, staff and elderly people in a residential assisted living facility could be observed in 3 minute segments during the lunch hour; random assignment would determine the individuals observed during each segment (Stabell et al., 2004). With the ability to easily make audio and video recordings of such situations, researchers can avoid having observers present. Instead, they can later randomly take selections from the recordings for analysis.

More recently, technology enables researcher to sample individuals' behaviors as people are living their lives in real time in everyday situations. The Electronically Activated Recorder (EAR) that was described earlier samples sounds when it is activated (Mehl, 2017). A method called Lifelogging uses wearable cameras that can be activated to take photos of the person's current environment (Brown et al., 2017). These have proven useful but are limited to audio and video data.

The **experience sampling method (ESM)** is used to alert participants to complete a data collection procedure at that moment in time (Larson & Csikszentmihalyi, 2014). Therefore, it can be used to study many different types of behaviors, moods, and situations. Participants may be asked their setting (home, work, school, etc.), activities (studying, television, exercising, socializing, dining), mood (anxious, relaxed, depressed), and current feelings of wellbeing. The alert usually comes via a text message on the participant's cellphone (when ESM was first used, participants were given a pager that received the alert!). The text alert can include a link that opens an online questionnaire containing rating scales and other types of questions; it can also contain spaces for written responses. Most ESM studies require about a week of daily attention to the incoming alerts although sometimes a longer time frame may be used with fewer alerts each day. Instead of responding online, a paper measure may be used and later returned to the researcher. A note on terminology: ESM is sometimes called Ecological Momentary Assessment (EMA); searches for research that uses ESM may benefit by including that alternative term in the search.

The **day reconstruction method (DRM)** is another method of obtaining self-reports of daily activities, moods, and emotions (Khaneman et al., 2004). The DRM asks participants to think about the previous day and write about distinct episodes that occurred. They may be asked to provide details of three or more episodes: duration, location, mood, interactions with others, and activities that took place. Because the data collection occurs only once each day, DRM is somewhat easier for participants to complete.

Han et al. (2019) used ESM and DRM in a study of mood and creative activities in a sample of 31 corporate employees over a 15-day period. The ESM alerts were made three times per day during work hours in mid-morning, early afternoon, and late afternoon. The DRM asked participants to provide details of three episodes dealing with their most impressive events during the day. The DRM alert was at 11 p.m. with a request to complete it by 8 a.m. The ESM rating scales asked about creativity during the last 30 minutes along with positive and negative mood states. As you might expect, creativity was associated with more positive moods. In addition, similar conclusions were drawn for both data collection methods.

CASE STUDIES

A **case study** is an observational method that provides a detailed description of an individual; or a group of people who constitute a family, a workgroup, a school, or a neighborhood; or even a situation, such as a business that failed or a school that succeeded. Here, the key idea is that it is a "case." A naturalistic observation study is sometimes called a case study, and in fact, the naturalistic observation and case study approaches sometimes overlap. We have included case studies as a separate category in this chapter because case studies do not necessarily involve naturalistic observation. Instead, the case study may be a description of a client's history, symptoms, and therapeutic intervention by a clinical psychologist.

Depending on the purpose of the investigation, the case study may present the individual's history, symptoms, characteristic behaviors, reactions to situations, or responses to treatment. Typically a case study is done when an individual possesses a particularly rare, unusual, or noteworthy condition. One famous case study involved a man with an amazing ability to recall information (Luria, 1968). The man, called "S.," could remember long lists and passages with ease, apparently using mental imagery for his memory abilities. Luria also described some of the drawbacks of S.'s ability. For example, he frequently had difficulty concentrating because mental images would spontaneously appear and interfere with his thinking.

Individuals with particular types of brain damage can allow researchers to test hypotheses. For example, Stone et al. (2002) studied an individual, R.M., who had extensive damage to the limbic system. The researchers were interested in studying people's ability to detect cheaters in social exchange relationships. Social exchange is at the core of our relationships: One person provides goods or services for another person in exchange for some other resource. Stone et al. were seeking evidence that social exchange can evolve in a species only when there is a biological mechanism for detecting cheaters—that is, those who do not reciprocate by fulfilling their end of the bargain. R.M. completed two types of reasoning problems. One type involved detecting violations of social exchange rules (e.g., you must fulfill a requirement if you receive a particular benefit); the other type focused on nonsocial precautionary action rules (e.g., you must take this precaution if you engage in a particular hazardous behavior). Individuals with no brain injury do equally well on both types of measures. However, R.M. performed very poorly on the social exchange problems but did well on the precautionary problems, as well as other general measures of cognitive ability. This finding supports the hypothesis that our ability to engage in social exchange relationships is grounded in the development of a biological mechanism—specifically, one related to the limbic system—that differs from general cognitive abilities.

Most case studies do not draw the attention of the public through general interest books. Instead, they provide valuable information for professional psychologists who have specialties related to the case study topic. For example, Halstead et al. (2021) published a case study of a client with post-traumatic stress disorder (PTSD) as a result of racial discrimination and sexual abuse during childhood. The PTSD symptoms were treatment-resistant. In addition to psychotherapy, the client received ketamine doses over a 13-day period. The outcome of this treatment demonstrated that ketamine can be successfully used in conjunction with traditional therapy for clients with treatment-resistant PTSD.

A **psychobiography** is a type of case study in which a researcher applies psychological theory to explain the life of an individual, usually an important historical figure (Schultz, 2005; Mayer, 2019). Thus, case studies may use such techniques as library research and telephone interviews with persons familiar with the case but no direct observation at all (Yin, 2018).

Case studies can also be used to provide unique descriptions of events in a particular setting that may prove useful to others. A case study related to research practices was published by Stout et al. (2020) after they had recruited Black and Non-Hispanic White older adults to volunteer for a research investigation on Alzheimer's disease. Two recruitment methods were used: Traditional (a newspaper article in the major daily newspaper and advertising in a community paper) and Social Media (Twitter, Facebook, NextDoor, and other online sources). Later, the researchers were able to determine how volunteers who responded had heard about the study. They found that social media was more effective for recruiting Non-Hispanic White research participants, while newspaper advertising was more successful in recruiting Black participants. This information may prove useful for other community health researchers.

Case studies are valuable sources of information regarding conditions that are rare or unusual, and they can provide unique data about some psychological phenomena, such as memory, language, or social exchange. Insights gained through a case study may also lead to the development of hypotheses that can be tested using other methods.

ARCHIVAL RESEARCH

Archival research involves using previously compiled information to answer research questions. In an archival research project, the researcher does not actually collect the original data (thus, it may be referred to as secondary research data). Instead, the researcher analyzes existing data, such as statistics that are part of publicly accessible records (e.g., the number of texting-related traffic accidents; the number of children born in a given state or county), reports of anthropologists, the content of letters to the editor, or information contained in databases (e.g., tweets, Facebook or Instagram posts, census data), or original data made available from prior research studies (see the "Open Science" box).

Next, we will describe three general types of archival research.

Statistical Records

Statistical records are collected by many public and private organizations. The U.S. Census Bureau maintains the most extensive set of statistical records available, but state and local agencies also maintain such records. The National Longitudinal Mortality Study (NLMS), for instance, is a database that researchers can use to study the effects of demographic and socioeconomic characteristics on mortality rates. In one such study, Aram et al. (2020) studied 438,739 records from the NLMS to examine the associations between employment status and occupation on deaths due to drug overdose, and found higher overdose mortality among people who were disabled, unemployed, or retired. They also reported higher risk among people who worked in service, construction, management, installation, and administrative occupations compared to professional occupations. In a study using public

Open Science and Data Accessibility

The U.S. Office of Science and Technology Policy (2013) published a memorandum about data accessibility. The memorandum, titled "Expanding Public Access to the Results of Federally Funded Research," further energized the open science movement by declaring that "the direct results of federally funded scientific research are made available to and useful for the public, industry, and the scientific community."

One of the organizations at the forefront of the open science movement is the Center for Open Science (https://cos.io/), a nonprofit group dedicated to "increasing the openness, integrity and reproducibility of scientific research." We will come back to the idea of reproducibility in the chapter "Generalization." Here, we will focus on the idea of openness and accessibility as it relates to archival research.

The Center for Open Science envisions a "future scholarly community in which the process, content, and outcomes of research are openly accessible by default." One of the things this would mean is that data would be accessible to other researchers as well as consumers of research. If a researcher publishes a paper in the context of Open Science, a data set is made available so that others can evaluate a project or use the data in their own projects (e.g., a **meta-analysis**). As you can imagine, this will create a lot of opportunities for archival research now and in the future.

records, Bushman et al. (2005) examined the relationship between temperature and aggression. They used temperature data in Minneapolis that had been recorded in 3-hour periods in 1987 and 1988; data on assaults were available through police records. They found that higher temperature is related to more aggression; however, this effect was limited to data recorded between 9:00 p.m. and 3:00 a.m. The relationship between temperature and aggression has been found in so many studies that Anderson and DeLisi (2011) predicted that a future of increasing global warming will lead to higher levels of violence across many societies.

There are also numerous less-obvious sources of statistical records, including public health statistics, test score records kept by testing organizations such as the Educational Testing Service, and even sports organizations. Major league sports organizations and dedicated fans keep extensive records on many aspects of team and individual performance. Wanic et al. (2019) took advantage of this fact to investigate the notion that National Basketball League (NBA) players who were traded perform better in games played against their old teams. The dataset was drawn from multiple sources: Player trade data is kept on a Wikipedia page and the NBA website was used to calculate game performance data. They specifically compared player performance against their old team with performance immediately before and after that game. Using these archival data, they found that traded players performed better when playing against their former team in their old arena. Wanic et al. concluded that players might be highly motivated to "show them" when playing against their old fans, teammates, and team management.

Survey Archives

Survey archives consist of data from surveys that are stored digitally and available to researchers who wish to analyze them. Major polling organizations make many of their surveys available. Also, many universities are part of the Inter-university Consortium for Political and Social Research (ICPSR; http://www.icpsr.umich.edu/), which makes survey archive data available. One very useful data set is the General Social Survey (GSS; https://www.norc.org), a series of surveys of the U.S. population conducted since 1972; GSS surveys are now conducted in 60 countries. Each survey includes over 200 questions covering a range of topics such as attitudes, life satisfaction, health, religion, education, age, gender, and race.

Survey archives are now available online at sites that enable researchers to analyze the data online. GSS online analysis tools are available at https://www.norc.org and https://sda.berkeley.edu (which also includes a variety of other surveys in its archive, including Racial Attitudes and Prejudice, American National Election Studies, and Survey of Consumer Finances). Survey archives are extremely important because most researchers do not have the financial resources to conduct surveys of randomly selected national samples; the archives allow them to access such samples to test their ideas and examine trends in attitudes and behaviors over time. Twenge et al. (2017) looked at the frequency of sexual activity among U.S. adults during five-year intervals from 1989 to 2014 using the GSS. The total sample size was 26,620. The study's primary conclusion was widely publicized: Frequency of sex decreased over time. The researchers looked for differences by sub-groups and they found similar decreases regardless of gender, race, region, educational level, and work status. Tenge et al. attributed the decrease in sex frequency to two factors. First, married and cohabiting individuals are reporting less frequent sex in 2014 than in 1989. Second, with people now delaying marriage, there are more individuals living without a regular sexual partner. This contributes to a lower overall average frequency of sex in 2014.

Written, Audio, and Video Records

We can also conduct archival research using previously written, audio, and video records, including diaries and letters that historical societies have preserved, books, ethnographies of other cultures written by anthropologists, speeches by politicians, tweets, Instagram or Facebook posts, magazine articles, movies, podcasts, television programs, newspapers, and blog posts.

Researchers have begun to analyze Twitter: Golder and Macy (2011) studied 509 million tweets from 2.4 million individuals from all over the world, classifying each tweet as having positive affect (e.g., enthusiasm, delight, activeness, and alertness) or negative affect (distress, fear, anger, guilt, and disgust). They found that people worldwide generally wake up in a good mood but that their moods get worse over the day. They also found, unsurprisingly, that on weekends people tweeted happier tweets. Using a similar strategy, Kruspe et al. (2020) analyzed Twitter messages (tweets) during the first months of the COVID-19 pandemic in Europe to describe the impact on people's moods. They found—you will be shocked to read—those lockdown announcements were related to worsening mood. Mood recovered, however, after a short time. And on a smaller scale, Corbett and Savarimuthu (2022) analyzed 6,528 Twitter messages for 27 electricity utilities in the United States over 5 months to understand people's feelings about sustainable energy. They hope to provide a roadmap for future researchers interested in understanding social acceptance (and thus policy) on sustainable energy programs.

Internet search trends are another potential source for archival research. Trivedi et al. (2021) wanted to evaluate the public interest in suicide prevention using Google-search trends. They found that in September (when National Suicide Prevention Week is celebrated), there was an increase in the number of people searching for "Suicide Prevention," whereas in the other months, searches for "suicide prevention" fluctuated at a very low level. The researchers believed that National Suicide prevention week was having an impact on population interest—that it was effective in getting people to think about preventing suicide.

Content analysis is the systematic analysis of existing documents. Like systematic observation, content analysis requires researchers to devise coding systems that raters can use to quantify the information in the documents. Sometimes the coding is quite simple; for example, it is easy to code whether the addresses of the applicants on marriage license applications are the same or different. More often, the researcher must define categories to code the information. In a study of 487 anti-smoking ads conducted by Rhodes et al. (2009), the researchers defined categories to describe the ads—for example, attacks tobacco companies or causes cancer. Similar procedures would be used in studies examining archival documents such as speeches, magazine articles, television shows, and reader comments on articles published on the internet. And Lewis et al. (2020) conducted a content analysis of 247 popular books for young children to detect and quantify gender biases. Their analysis—using humans and machine-learning techniques to detect patterns of gender content—was that children's books might indeed be an early source of gendered language and stereotypes.

The use of archival data allows researchers to study interesting questions, some of which could not be studied in any other way. Archival data are a valuable supplement to more traditional data collection methods. However, there are at least two significant problems with the use of archival data. First, the desired records may be difficult to obtain: they might have been placed in long-forgotten storage places, or they may have been destroyed. Second, we can never be entirely sure of the accuracy of the information collected by someone else.

Check Your Learning

Visit Check Your Learning: Practice Exercise #1 and see if you can distinguish among various observational methods.

This chapter has provided a great deal of information about important qualitative and quantitative observational methods that can be used to study a variety of questions about behavior. In the chapter "Asking People About Themselves: Survey Research" we will explore a very common way of finding out about human behavior—simply asking people to tell us about themselves.

ENGAGING WITH RESEARCH: OBSERVATIONAL METHODS

Childhood obesity in the United States is a serious problem that puts children and adolescents at high risk for long-term poor health outcomes—19.3% of U.S. children and adolescents (14.4 million) were classified as obese in 2017–2018, up from 5.2% in 1971–1974. The problem is more prevalent among Mexican American children, 24.9% of whom are classified as obese (Fryar et al., 2020).

Penilla et al. (2022) conducted an observational study aimed at preventing obesity among Mexican American children by exploring the style of meal service and environment, parental feeding practices, and child's eating behaviors at evening family mealtime by using electronically activated recorders and coding the recordings.

First, acquire and read this article (available at https://www.sciencedirect.com/science/article/pii/S0195666321007583):

Penilla, C., Tschann, J. M., Pasch, L. A., Flores, E., Deardorff, J., Martinez, S. M., Butte, N. F., & Greenspan, L. C. (2022). Style of meal service and feeding practices among Mexican American fathers and mothers: An analysis of video-recorded children's evening mealtime at home. *Appetite, 169.* https://doi.org/10.1016/j.appet.2021.105851

Then, after reading the article, consider the following:

1. **What is the primary goal of this study: Description, Prediction, Determining Cause, or Explaining? Do the authors achieve their goals?**

    a. The introduction to this study begins by stating a problem: the rates of childhood obesity. Why do the authors conduct a study of meal service and feeding practices to address this problem?

    b. Do you think that this study included any confounding variables that may have impacted this study? Provide examples.

    c. Does this study suffer from the problem involving the direction of causation? How so?

2. **What did these researchers do? What was the method?**

    a. Is the basic approach in this study qualitative or quantitative?

    b. Is this study an example of concealed or nonconcealed observation?

3. **What was measured?**

   a. How did the researchers operationally define Mealtime Environment, Child Eating Behavior, and Parental Feeding Practices? What do you think about the quality of these operational definitions?

   b. Do you think participants would be reactive to this data collection method?

   c. How reliable were the coders? Did the authors assess their reliability?

4. **To what or whom can we generalize the results? Do you think this study would generalize across cultures, age groups, or other demographic variables? Why or why not?**

5. **What did they find? What were the results?**

6. **Have other researchers found similar results? Do the results of this study line up with other studies on the same topic?**

7. **What are the limitations of this study?**

8. **What are the ethical issues present in this study?**

BEING A SKILLED CONSUMER OF RESEARCH

1. Briefly describe your ideas for four studies on the following topics, using each of the four observational research strategies described in this chapter: (1) naturalistic observation, (2) systematic observation, (3) case study, and (4) archival research.

   a. Taking an exam in college: exam speed and performance

   b. Shopping for groceries: factors that influence healthy food choices

   c. Discrimination in housing: finding a place to rent or buying a home

2. Design a simple coding system that would be used in a systematic observation study that included video recordings:

   a. Taking an exam in college: the class is recorded taking an exam

   b. Shopping for groceries: video recording equipment is set up in the produce section of a grocery store

   c. Discrimination in housing: video recording equipment is set up in the lobby of an apartment complex

3. Describe how data would be collected using an experience sampling strategy in a study for each of the following topics:

   a. Stress among college students over a semester

   b. Alcohol use among college students over a semester

   c. Roommate conflicts among college students over a semester

4. The NORC General Social Survey website has a Data Exploration feature that allows you to examine GSS "Key Trends" over time. Go to https://gssdataexplorer.norc.org/trends. Select a topic area from the categories shown (Gender & Marriage, Current Affairs, Civil Liberties, Politics, Religion & Spirituality) — for example, Life Satisfaction. Explore the data over time (by default, you are shown the percentage of respondents saying they are "very happy"). Describe any observed trend and how you might explain any change over time; you can also look at breakdowns by other variables such as health or marital status.

Check Your Learning: Practice Exercise

Practice Exercise #1

Read each scenario below and determine whether the research method was case study, naturalistic observation, systematic observation, or archival research.

1. Researchers conducted in-depth interviews with front-line healthcare workers at a community hospital during the fourth month of the COVID-19 pandemic to draw conclusions about the psychological impact of working in pandemic conditions.

2. Researchers recorded the time it took drivers in parking lots to back out of a parking stall. They also recorded the gender and approximate age of the drivers, and whether another car was waiting for the space.

3. A researcher spent more than a year meeting with and interviewing a refugee in order to describe their lives in detail in order to construct a psychobiography.

4. Researchers examined unemployment rates and the incidence of domestic-violence police calls in six cities.

5. A group of researchers studied recycling behavior at three local parks over a 6-month period. They concealed their presence and kept detailed field notes.

(Answers are provided at the end of this chapter.)

CHAPTER REVIEW

Review Questions _____

1. What are the differences between qualitative and quantitative approaches to studying behavior?

2. What is naturalistic observation? How does a researcher collect data when conducting naturalistic observation research?

3. Why are the data in naturalistic observation research primarily qualitative?

4. Distinguish between participant and nonparticipant observation; and between concealed and nonconcealed observation.

5. What is systematic observation? Why are the data from systematic observation primarily quantitative?

6. What is a coding system? What are some important considerations when developing a coding system?

7. What is a case study? When are case studies used? What is a psychobiography?

8. What is archival research? What are the major sources of archival data?

9. What is content analysis?

Study Terms

Archival research (p. 142)

Case study (p. 140)

Coding system (p. 138)

Content analysis (p. 145)

day reconstruction method (DRM) (p. 140)

experience sampling method (ESM) (p. 140)

Naturalistic observation (p. 134)

Participant observation (p. 135)

Psychobiography (p. 141)

Reactivity (p. 139)

Systematic observation (p. 137)

Check Your Learning: Answers

Practice Exercise #1

1. case study; 2. systematic observation; 3. case study; 4. archival research; 5. naturalistic observation

Customer Satisfaction

On the scale of 1 to 4 how would you rate your satisfaction?

	Excellent	Good	Average	Poor
1. Overall quality		✓		
2. Products value			✓	
3. Purchase experience			✓	
4. After purchase service	✓			
5. Customer serv...				

7

Rawpixel.com/Shutterstock

Asking People About Themselves: Survey Research

LEARNING OBJECTIVES

- Discuss the reasons for conducting survey research.
- Identify factors to consider when writing questions for interviews and questionnaires: simplicity, double-barreled questions, loaded questions, and negative wording.
- Describe different ways to construct questionnaire responses, including closed-ended questions, open-ended questions, and rating scales.
- Compare the two ways to administer surveys: written questionnaires and interviews.
- Distinguish between probability and nonprobability sampling techniques, including simple random sampling, stratified random sampling, and cluster sampling; convenience (or haphazard) sampling, purposive sampling, and quota sampling.
- Describe how samples are evaluated for potential bias, including sampling frame and response rate.

SURVEY RESEARCH INVOLVES USING QUESTIONNAIRES AND INTER-VIEWS TO ASK PEOPLE TO PROVIDE INFORMATION ABOUT THEMSELVES—THEIR ATTITUDES AND BELIEFS, DEMOGRAPHICS (AGE, GENDER, INCOME, MARITAL STATUS, AND SO ON), AND PAST OR INTENDED FUTURE BEHAVIORS. In this chapter we will explore methods of designing and conducting surveys. We will also introduce sampling techniques.

WHY CONDUCT SURVEYS?

Surveys are a way to collect data directly from research participants by asking them questions. Surveys have become extremely important as society demands data about people's behavior and what people think about issues.

Surveys are being conducted all the time. Just look at your daily newspaper, local TV news broadcast, your email, or the internet. From the Centers for Disease Control and Prevention comes a report on a survey of new mothers asking about breastfeeding. A college survey center reports the results of a telephone survey asking about political attitudes. If you look around your campus, you will find academic departments conducting surveys of seniors or recent graduates. If you make a significant purchase, you will likely receive a request to complete a survey that asks about your satisfaction. Each year since 2007, the American Psychological Association has conducted an online survey that focuses on topics related to stress. You can download the *Stress in America* reports from their website at https://www.apa.org/news/press/releases/stress.

Clearly, surveys are a common and important method of studying behavior. Every university needs data from graduates to help determine changes that should be made to the curriculum and student services. Auto companies want data from buyers to assess and improve product quality and customer satisfaction. Without collecting such data, we are totally dependent upon stories we might hear or letters that a graduate or customer might write. Other surveys can be crucial to lawmakers and public agencies when making public policy decisions. In research, many important variables—including attitudes, current emotional states, and self-reports of behaviors—are most easily studied using questionnaires or interviews.

We often think of survey data as providing a snapshot of how people think and behave at a given time. However, the survey method is also an important way for researchers to study relationships among variables and ways that attitudes and behaviors change over time. For example, the *Monitoring the Future* project (https://www.drugabuse.gov/drug-topics/trends-statistics/monitoring-future) has been conducted every year since 1975—its purpose is to monitor the behaviors, attitudes, and values of American high school and college students. Each year, 50,000 8eighth-, tenth-, and twelfth-grade students participate in the survey. Figure 1 shows a typical finding: Each line on the graph represents the percentage of survey respondents who reported using marijuana in the past 12 months. Note the trend that shows the peak of marijuana popularity occurring in the late 1970s and the least reported use in the early 1990s. After some increases in the late 1990s, use has been relatively stable: 20% to 25% of twelfth-grade students, 15%

FIGURE 1
Percentage
of survey
respondents
who reported
using
marijuana
in the past
12 months,
over time

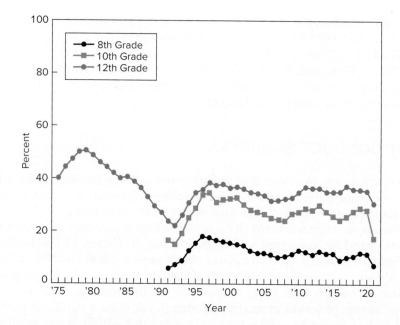

to 20% of tenth-grade students, and 5% to 10% of eighth-grade students report using marijuana in the past year. In 2021 the percentage of students who reported using marijuana within the past year decreased significantly for eighth-, tenth-, and twelfth-grade students.

Survey research is often important as a complement to experimental research findings. Recall from the chapter "Where to Start" that Winograd and Soloway (1986) conducted experiments on the conditions that lead to forgetting where we place something. To study this topic using survey methods, Brown and Rahhal (1994) asked both younger and older adults about their actual experiences when they hid something and later forgot its location. They reported that older adults take longer than younger adults to find the object and that older adults hide objects from potential thieves, whereas younger people hide things from friends and relatives. Interestingly, most lost objects are eventually found, usually by accident, in a location that had been searched previously. This research illustrates a key point: Multiple methods are needed to fully understand any behavior.

An assumption that underlies questionnaires and interviews is that people are willing and able to provide truthful and accurate answers. Researchers have addressed this issue by studying possible biases in the way people respond. A **response set** is a tendency to respond to all questions from a particular perspective rather than to provide answers that are directly related to the questions. Thus, response sets can affect the usefulness of data obtained from self-reports. Response sets include a tendency to express agreement or disagreement with anything asked. But the most common response set is called **social desirability,** or "faking good." The social desirability response set leads the individual to answer in the most socially acceptable way—the way that person perceives "most people" to respond or the way that would reflect most favorably on the person. Thus, a social desirability response set might lead a person to underreport undesirable behaviors (e.g., alcohol or drug use, fighting with partners, cheating) and overreport positive behaviors such as the amount of exercise, vegetable intake, amount of time spent studying for an upcoming exam (Krumpal, 2013). However, it should not be assumed that people consistently misrepresent themselves. If the researcher openly and honestly communicates the purposes and uses of the research, promises to provide feedback about the results, and ensures confidentiality, then the participants can reasonably be expected to give honest responses.

We turn now to three primary considerations when designing a survey research project or conducting survey research: constructing the questions that are asked, choosing the methods for presenting the questions, and sampling the individuals taking part in the research.

CONSTRUCTING QUESTIONS TO ASK

A great deal of thought must be given to writing questions for questionnaires and interviews. This section describes some of the most important factors to consider when constructing questions.

Defining the Research Objectives

When constructing questions for a survey, the researcher must first explicitly determine the research objectives: What do they want to know? The survey questions must be tied to the research questions being addressed. Too often, surveys get out of hand—researchers begin to ask any question that comes to mind about a topic without considering precisely what useful information will be gained by doing so. This process will usually require the researcher to decide on the type of questions to ask. Generally, survey questions look for information in three major areas: (1) facts and demographics, (2) behaviors, and (3) attitudes and beliefs (Maruyama & Ryan, 2014).

Facts and Demographics   Factual questions ask people to indicate things they know about themselves and their situation. In most studies, asking for some demographic information is necessary to describe your sample adequately; thus, questions about age, gender, and ethnicity are typically asked. Depending on the topic of the study, questions on marital status, employment status, and the number of children living in the household might be included. Obviously, if you are interested in characteristics of groups that differ by income, such as people with annual incomes under $50,000 compared to people with annual incomes over $50,000, you must ask the relevant information about income. You may also need such information to describe the sample adequately. However, you should not ask questions for which you have no legitimate reason to collect the information.

Other factual information you might ask will depend on the topic of your survey. For example, factual questions about illnesses, medical history, and other medical information would be asked in a survey of health and quality of life.

Behaviors   Other survey questions can focus on past behaviors or intended future behaviors: How many days last week did you exercise for 20 minutes or longer? How many children do you plan to have? Have you ever been so depressed that you called in sick to work?

Attitudes and Beliefs   Questions about attitudes and beliefs focus on the ways people evaluate and think about issues. Should more money be spent on mental health services? Are you satisfied with how our customer representative responded to your call? How do you evaluate this instructor? Next, we look at question-wording generally and bias in question-wording.

Question-Wording

A great deal of care is necessary to write the very best questions for a survey. After all, the validity of a study based on a survey depends on the quality of the questions on the survey. Cognitive psychologists have identified several potential problems with question-wording (see Graesser et al., 1999). Many of the issues stem from a difficulty with understanding the question. Problematic aspects of how questions are phrased include (a) unfamiliar technical terms, (b) vague or imprecise terms, (c) ungrammatical sentence structure, (d) phrasing that overloads working memory, and (e) embedding the question with misleading information. Here is a question that illustrates some of the problems identified by Graesser et al.:

> Did your mother, father, full-blooded sisters, full-blooded brothers, daughters, or sons ever have a heart attack or myocardial infarction?

This example has many problems. First, this is an example of memory over-load because of the length of the question and the need to keep track of all those relatives while reading the question. The respondent must also worry about two different diagnoses with regard to each relative. Further, the term *myocardial infarction* may be unfamiliar to most people.

So, how do you write questions to avoid such problems? The following items are important to consider when you are writing questions.

Simplicity   The questions asked in a survey should be relatively simple and straightforward. People should be able to understand and respond to the questions easily. Avoid jargon and technical terms that most people will not understand. Sometimes, however, you have to make the question a bit more complex—or longer—to make it easier to understand. Usually this occurs when you need to define a term or describe an issue before asking the question. Thus, before asking whether someone approves or disapproves of "Ballot Proposition A" in the November election, you will probably want to provide a brief description of the content of this ballot measure. Likewise, if you want to know about the frequency of alcohol use in a population, then asking, "Have you had a drink of alcohol in the past 30 days?" may generate a slightly different answer than "One drink of alcohol is one full can of beer, one shot of liquor, or one glass of wine. Have you had a drink of alcohol in the past 30 days?" The latter question would probably elicit answers that are closer to what you would be interested in knowing.

Double-Barreled Questions

Avoid double-barreled questions that ask two things at once. A question such as "Should senior citizens be given more money for recreation centers and food assistance programs?" is difficult to answer because it taps two potentially very different attitudes. If you are interested in both issues, ask two questions.

Loaded Questions

A loaded question is written to lead people to respond in one way. For example, the questions "Do you favor eliminating the wasteful excesses in the public school budget?" and "Do you favor reducing the public school budget?" will likely elicit different answers. Or consider that respondents are less likely to say they have been raped than to say that they have been forced to have unwanted sex (Donde et al., 2018; Hamby & Koss, 2003; Hammond et al., 2017). Questions that include emotionally charged words—such as *rape, waste, immoral, ungodly,* or *dangerous*—influence how people respond and thus lead to biased responses; more neutral, behavior-based terminology is preferable.

Negative Wording

Avoid phrasing questions with negatives. This question is phrased negatively: "Do you feel that the city should not approve the proposed shelter for people who are unhoused?" Agreement with this question means disagreement with the proposal. This phrasing can confuse people and result in inaccurate answers. A better format would be: "Do you believe that the city should approve the proposed shelter for people who are unhoused?"

"Yea-Saying" and "Nay-Saying"

When you ask several questions about a topic, a respondent may employ a response set to agree or disagree with all the questions. The tendency to agree consistently is referred to as **yea-saying** (also called *acquiescence* response set). The tendency to disagree consistently is termed **nay-saying.** The problem here is that the respondent may, in fact, be expressing true agreement, but alternatively, may simply be agreeing with anything you say. One way to detect this response set is to word the questions so that consistent agreement is unlikely. For example, a study of family communication patterns might ask people how much they agree with the following statements: "The members of my family spend a lot of time together" and "I spend most of my weekends with friends." Similarly, a measure of loneliness could phrase some questions so that agreement means the respondent is lonely ("I feel isolated from others") and others with the meaning reversed so that disagreement indicates loneliness (e.g., "I feel part of a group of friends"). Although it is possible that someone could legitimately agree with both items, consistently agreeing or disagreeing with a set of related questions phrased in both standard and reversed formats is an indicator that the individual is "yea-saying" or "nay-saying."

> **Check Your Learning**
>
> You can test your analysis of question-wording using the examples in Check Your Learning: Practice Exercise #1.

RESPONSES TO QUESTIONS

You have undoubtedly completed (or at least started) many surveys and observed many different types of questions on those surveys. Next, we will consider the many varieties of responses to questions.

Closed-Ended Versus Open-Ended Questions

First, questions may be either closed-ended or open-ended. With **closed-ended questions,** a limited number of response alternatives are given; with **open-ended questions,** respondents are free to answer in any way they like. Thus, you could ask a person, "What is the most important thing children should learn to prepare them for life?" followed by a list of answers to choose from (a closed-ended question), or you could leave this question open-ended for the person to provide the answer.

Closed-ended questions provide a more structured approach; they make it easier to assign values to responses because the response alternatives are the same for everyone. Open-ended questions require time to categorize and code the responses, and are therefore this sort of survey is more costly to conduct and more difficult to interpret. Sometimes a respondent's response cannot be categorized at all because the response does not make sense or the person could not think of an answer. Still, an open-ended question can yield valuable insights. Open-ended questions are most useful when the researcher needs to know what people are thinking and how they naturally view their world; closed-ended questions are more likely to be used when the dimensions of the variables are well defined.

Schwarz (1999) points out that the two approaches can sometimes lead to different conclusions. He cites the results of a survey question about preparing children for life. When "To think for themselves" was one alternative in a closed-ended list, 62% chose this option; however, only 5% gave this answer when the open-ended format was used. This finding points to the need to have a good understanding of the topic when asking closed-ended questions.

Number of Response Alternatives

With closed-ended questions, there is a fixed number of response alternatives. In public opinion surveys, a simple "yes or no" or "agree or disagree" dichotomy is often sufficient. In other research, it is often preferable to provide more quantitative distinctions—for example, a 5- or 7-point scale ranging from *strongly agree* to *strongly disagree* or *very positive* to *very negative*. Such a 7-point scale might appear as follows:

Strongly agree ____ ____ ____ ____ ____ ____ ____ Strongly disagree

Rating Scales

Rating scales such as the one shown above are very common in many areas of research. Rating scales ask people to provide "how much" judgments on any number of dimensions—amount of agreement, liking, or confidence, for example. Rating scales can have many different formats. The format that is used depends on various factors, such as the topic being investigated. Perhaps the best way to gain an understanding of the variety of formats is simply to look at a few examples. The simplest and most direct scale presents people with five or seven response alternatives with the endpoints on the scale labeled to define the extremes. The response choices might be lines to mark on a paper questionnaire, check boxes, or option buttons in an online survey form. Here are two examples:

Students at the university should be required to pass a comprehensive examination to graduate.

Strongly agree ☐ ☐ ☐ ☐ ☐ ☐ ☐ Strongly disagree

How confident are you that the defendant is guilty of attempted murder?

Not at all confident ☐ ☐ ☐ ☐ ☐ Very confident

Graphic Rating Scale

A **graphic rating scale** requires a mark along a continuous 100-millimeter line that is anchored with descriptions at each end.

How would you rate the movie you just saw?

Not very enjoyable _____ Very enjoyable

A ruler is then placed on the line to obtain the score on a scale that ranges from 0 to 100.

Semantic Differential Scale

The **semantic differential scale** is a measure of the meaning of concepts that was developed by Osgood and his associates (Osgood et al., 1957). Respondents are asked to rate any concept—persons, objects, behaviors, ideas—on a series of bipolar adjectives using 7-point scales, as follows:

Smoking cigarettes

Good ____ ____ ____ ____ ____ ____ ____ Bad

Strong ____ ____ ____ ____ ____ ____ ____ Weak

Active ____ ____ ____ ____ ____ ____ ____ Passive

Research on the semantic differential shows that virtually anything can be measured using this technique. Ratings of specific things (marijuana), places (the student center), people (the governor, accountants), ideas (death penalty, marriage equality), and behaviors (attending church, using public transit) can be obtained. A large body of research shows that the concepts are rated along three basic dimensions: the first and most important is *evaluation* (e.g., adjectives such as good–bad, wise–foolish, kind–cruel); the second is *activity* (active–passive, slow–fast, excitable–calm); and the third is *potency* (weak–strong, hard–soft, large–small).

Pictorial Scales   When studying young children, adults with problems understanding verbal instructions, or even adults who are amused by emojis, researchers will often use response scales that use pictorial representations. The most common such scales are sometimes referred to as "Smiley Face" rating scales. That describes exactly what they are: A series of 5 to 7 "smiley faces" drawn to express a range of expressions of happiness, sadness, anger, pain, or other moods and emotions. The simplest ones use the faces you probably find on your smartphone. Others may use professional drawings. Often each face is associated with a number and/or a verbal caption such as "1 – Very Happy." Emojis are also used as a substitute for the common 5- or 7-point rating scales with end points of *Strongly Disagree* and *Strongly Agree*.

An internet search will identify smiley face and other pictorial rating scales developed for behavioral research, classrooms, and even those customer satisfaction ratings following a call to a company's customer service representative. Massey (2021) found that such a scale could be used to study children's attitude toward mathematics, a more complex topic than is normally associated with such measures. Hall et al. (2016) obtained data with children that suggest that a 5-point scale using only happy faces (*VERY Happy* to *Happy* with no neutral or unhappy faces) may provide more accurate ratings than the standard happy to unhappy faces.

Lewis and Sauro (2020) studied adults filling out a customer satisfaction survey, e.g., "This product is easy to use" rated on a scale with end points labeled *Strongly disagree* and *Strongly agree*. The response scale consisted of either numbers 1 through 5 or five smiley faces. The results for the two formats were exactly the same; they did not measure other data such as how long the subjects took to complete the form.

In addition to measures of attitudes and emotional states, pictorial measures of personality traits have been developed for children. For example, Maćkiewicz and Cieciuch (2016) describe a children's measure of Big 5 personality traits using choices of drawings of various situations (e.g., choosing whether a picture of a child playing alone or with other children best describes them).

Labeling Response Alternatives

The examples thus far have labeled only the endpoints on the rating scale. Respondents decide the meaning of the response alternatives that are not labeled. This is a reasonable approach, and people are usually able to use such scales without difficulty. Sometimes researchers need to provide labels to more clearly define the meaning of each alternative. Here is a fairly standard alternative to the *agree-disagree* scale shown above:

○ ○ ○ ○ ○

Strongly agree Agree Undecided Disagree Strongly disagree

This type of scale assumes that the middle alternative is a "neutral" point halfway between the endpoints. Sometimes, however, a perfectly balanced scale may not be possible or desirable. Consider a scale asking a college professor to rate a student for a job or graduate program. This particular scale asks for comparative ratings of students:

In comparison with other graduates, how would you rate this student's potential for success?

○ ○ ○ ○ ○

Lower 50% Upper 50% Upper 25% Upper 10% Upper 5%

Notice that more of the alternatives ask people to make a rating within the top 25% of students. This is done because students who apply for such programs tend to be very bright and motivated, and so professors rate them favorably. The wording of the alternatives attempts to force the raters to make finer distinctions among generally very good students.

Labeling alternatives is particularly interesting when asking about the frequency of a behavior. For example, you might ask, "How often do you exercise for at least 20 minutes?" What kind of scale should you use to let people answer this question? You could list (1) never, (2) rarely, (3) sometimes, (4) frequently. These terms convey your meaning but they are vague. Here is another set of alternatives with greater specificity (Schwarz et al., 2008):

○ less than twice a week

○ about twice a week

○ about four times a week

○ about six times a week

○ at least once each day

A different scale might be:

○ less than once per month

○ about once a month

○ about once every 2 weeks

○ about once a week

○ more than once per week

Schwarz et al. (2008) call the first scale a *high-frequency scale* because most alternatives indicate a high frequency of exercise. The other scale is referred to as low frequency. Schwarz et al. point out that the labels should be chosen carefully because people may interpret the meaning of the scale differently, depending on the labels used. If you were actually asking the exercise question, you might decide on alternatives different from the ones described here. Moreover, your choice should be influenced by factors such as the population you are studying. If you are studying people who generally exercise a lot, you will be more likely to use a higher-frequency scale than you would if you were studying people who generally do not exercise a great deal.

FINALIZING THE SURVEY INSTRUMENT

Once questions are written, and responses to questions are finalized, it is time to make final adjustments to the survey. Formatting, question sequence, and survey pilot-testing are critical steps before submitting your survey project to an Institutional Review Board. Once you have approval from the IRB, you can administer the survey to a sample of research participants.

Formatting

A questionnaire is the set of questions in a survey designed to be administered using a printed or a web-based instrument (in contrast to questions posed in a face-to-face or telephone interview). The questionnaire should appear attractive and professional. It should be neatly designed and free of spelling errors. Respondents should find it easy to identify the questions and the response alternatives to the questions. Leave enough space between questions, so people do not become confused when reading the questionnaire. If you have a particular scale format, such as a 5-point rating scale, use it consistently. For example, do not change from 5- to 4- to 7-point scales.

Sequence of Questions

It is also a good idea to carefully consider the sequence in which you will ask your questions—survey respondents' answers can be influenced by question order. Multiple researchers have found that questions related to "overall satisfaction" such as *Overall, how satisfied were you with the restaurant?* should come after questions about specific attributes, such as *How satisfied were you with the appetizer?* (Auh et al., 2003; Kaplan et al., 2013; Thau et al., 2021).

It is best to ask the most interesting and important questions first to capture your respondents' attention and motivate them to complete the survey. Roberson and Sundstrom (1990) obtained the highest return rates in an employee attitude survey when important questions were presented first, and demographic questions were asked last.

In addition, it is a good idea to group questions together when they address a similar theme or topic. Doing so will make your survey appear more professional, and your respondents will be more likely to take it seriously. The critical point is that question order can matter in multiple ways.

Refining Questions: Pilot Testing the Survey

Before actually administering a survey, it is good to give the questions to a small group of people and have them think aloud while answering them. The participants might be chosen from the population being studied, or they could be friends or colleagues who can give reasonable responses to the questions. For the think-aloud procedure, you will need to ask the individuals to tell you how they interpret each question and how they respond to the response alternatives. This procedure can provide valuable information that can make it easier to identify and correct problems like negative wording, overly complex language, and double-barreled or loaded questions. (The importance of pilot studies such as this is discussed further in the chapter "Conducting Experiments.")

ADMINISTERING SURVEYS

There are two ways to administer surveys. One is to use a written questionnaire, either printed or online, wherein respondents read the questions and indicate their responses on a form. The other way is to use an interview format. An interviewer asks the questions and records the responses in a personal verbal interaction. Both questionnaires and interviews can be presented to respondents in several ways. Let's examine the various methods of administering surveys.

Questionnaires

With questionnaires, the questions are presented in written (or the digital equivalent) format and respondents write their answers. There are several benefits to using questionnaires. First, they generally cost less than interviews, as questionnaires can be administered in-person to groups or individuals, through the mail, on the internet, and with other technologies. Second, they also allow the respondent to be completely anonymous as long as no identifying information (e.g., name, Social Security number, or driver's license number) is asked for. However, questionnaires require that the respondents be able to read and understand the questions. In addition, many people find it boring to sit by themselves reading questions and providing answers; thus, a problem of motivation may arise.

Administration to Groups or Individuals Often researchers are able to distribute questionnaires to groups of individuals. This might be a college class, parents attending a school meeting, people attending a new employee orientation, students waiting for an appointment with an advisor, and so on. An advantage of this approach is that you have a captive audience of individuals who are likely to complete the questionnaire once they start it. Also, the researcher is present, so people can ask questions if necessary.

Mail Surveys   A mail survey can be mailed to individuals at a home or business address. This is a very inexpensive way of contacting the people who were selected for the sample. However, the mail format is a drawback because of potentially low response rates (**response rate** is the percentage of people who are asked to complete a survey who actually complete a survey). The recipients can easily put the questionnaire aside and forget it, given all the other tasks people must attend to at home and work. Even if people start to fill out the questionnaire, something may happen to distract them, or they may become bored and simply throw the survey in the trash. Some of the methods for increasing response rates are described later in this chapter. Another drawback is that no one is present to help if the person doesn't understand some of the questions.

Online Surveys   Online surveys are increasingly being used by academic researchers (Sue & Ritter, 2012; Toepoel, 2016). There are many benefits to conducting survey research online. It is very easy to design a questionnaire for online administration using one of several online survey software services. Both open- and closed-ended questions can be included. After users complete the questionnaire, their responses are immediately available to the researcher. Also, there is some evidence that online surveys result in higher response rates than paper-and-pencil surveys for some types of research questions (Patrick et al., 2021). However, whether a mail or online survey will have a better response rate will depend on characteristics of the sample, the topic of the survey, and how the survey is presented to prospective respondents.

The major survey research organizations that conduct surveys of large randomly selected samples are also moving to online surveys. For example, the Pew Research Center created a research panel called the *American Trends Panel*. A research panel consists of individuals who agree to complete surveys when requested. The American Trends Panel has over 10,000 adults randomly selected from the entire United States. Almost all complete surveys online; those without internet access complete the surveys using specially equipped tablets that were provided to them. With so many individuals in the panel, any survey that is conducted can be completed with a smaller subset selected using probability sampling methods. For more information on the American Trends Panel methodology, see https://www.pewresearch.org/our-methods/u-s-surveys/the-american-trends-panel/ and https://www.pewresearch.org/our-methods/u-s-surveys/u-s-survey-methodology/.

As researchers increasingly use online research strategies, it is important to consider ethical implications. The ethical issues of internet research are described in detail by Buchanan and Williams (2010), Hoerger and Currell (2012), and Roberts and Sipes (2018).

Interviews

The fact that an interview requires an interaction between people has important implications. First, people are often more likely to agree to answer questions for a real person than to answer a mailed questionnaire. Good interviewers become quite skilled in convincing people to participate. Thus, response rates tend to be higher when interviews are used. The interviewer and respondent often establish a rapport that helps motivate the person to answer all the questions and complete the survey. People are more likely to leave questions unanswered on a written questionnaire than in an interview. An important advantage of an interview is that the interviewer can clarify any problems the person might have in understanding questions. Further, an interviewer can ask follow-up questions if needed to help clarify answers.

One potential problem in interviews is **interviewer bias** (also called interviewer effects). This term describes all of the biases that can arise from the fact that the interviewer is a unique human being interacting with another human being. One potential problem is that the interviewer could subtly bias the respondent's answers by inadvertently showing approval or disapproval of certain answers—they can even influence participation in future studies (Liu, 2019). Also, interviewer characteristics such as ethnicity, race, sex, gender identity, or age can influence responses (Kühne et al., 2021). This is especially likely when asking about sensitive topics like health behaviors (Davis et al., 2010), political preferences (Finkel et al., 1991), gender and gender attitudes (Kane & Macauley, 1993), and racial or ethnic identity (An & Winship, 2017; Krysan & Couper, 2003).

Another problem is that interviewers may have expectations that could lead them to "see what they are looking for" in the respondents' answers. Such expectations could bias their interpretations of responses or lead them to probe further for an answer from certain respondents but not from others. Careful screening and training of interviewers help to limit such biases.

We can now examine three methods of conducting interviews: face-to-face, telephone, and focus groups.

Face-to-Face Interviews

Face-to-face interviews require that the interviewer and respondent meet to conduct the interview. Usually the interviewer travels to the person's home or office, although sometimes the respondent goes to the interviewer's office. Such interviews tend to be quite expensive and time-consuming. Therefore, they are most likely to be used when the sample size is fairly small and there are clear benefits to a face-to-face interaction.

Telephone Interviews

Almost all interviews for large-scale research projects are done via telephone. *Telephone interviews* are less expensive than face-to-face interviews, and they allow efficient data collection because many respondents can be contacted quickly with no need for travel. There are two forms of telephone interviews. The first is a live interview in which an interviewer asks questions and records responses. This is usually conducted using a *computer-assisted telephone interview* (CATI) system—the interviewer's questions are prompted on the computer screen, and the data are entered directly into the computer for analysis. *Interactive voice response* (IVR) technology has been adapted for survey data collection. With IVR, respondents listen to the pre-recorded questions and respond via the telephone keypad or a speech recognition system. There are cost advantages of IVR technology. However, the surveys should be relatively brief or include optional time-out periods, the questions need to be easily understood, the keypad or voice responses should not produce annoying errors, and there should be a way for respondents to stop the survey to reach a live representative. IVR surveys may be particularly useful when asking sensitive questions about sensitive topics (Midanik & Greenfield, 2008). It is also possible to combine the methods—the interviewer can switch to IVR for a portion of the interview.

Focus Group Interviews   An interview strategy that is often used by businesses is the focus group interview. A **focus group** is an interview with a group of about 6 to 10 individuals brought together for a period of usually 2–3 hours. Virtually any topic can be explored in a focus group. Often the group members are selected because they have a particular knowledge of or interest in the topic. Focus groups are traditionally held in-person at a central location; the wide availability of live group meeting software has made online focus groups much more feasible.

The questions in a focus group tend to be open-ended, and they are asked of the whole group. An advantage here is that group interaction is possible: People can respond to one another, and one comment can trigger a variety of responses. The interviewer must be skilled in working with groups both to facilitate communication and to deal with problems that may arise, such as one or two persons trying to dominate the discussion or hostility between group members.

The group discussion is usually recorded and may be transcribed. The recordings and transcripts are then analyzed to find themes and areas of group consensus and disagreement. Sometimes the transcripts are analyzed with a computer program to search for certain words and phrases. Researchers usually prefer to conduct multiple discussion groups on a given topic to make sure that the information gathered is not unique to one group of people. However, because each focus group is time-consuming and costly and provides a great deal of information, researchers do not conduct very many such groups on any one topic.

SURVEY DESIGNS TO STUDY CHANGES OVER TIME

Surveys most frequently study people at one point in time. Often, however, researchers wish to make comparisons over time. For example, local newspapers often hire firms to conduct an annual random survey of county residents. Because the questions are the same each year, it is possible to track changes over time in such variables as satisfaction with the area, attitudes toward the school system, and perceived major problems facing the county. Similarly, a large number of first-year students are surveyed each year at colleges throughout the United States to study changes in the composition, attitudes, and aspirations of this group (Eagan et al., 2016; Stolzenberg et al., 2020).

First-year college students today, for instance, come from more diverse backgrounds than those in the 1970s: In the fall of 2019, 50% of first-time college students identify as White, and 33% identify as Asian, Black, or Latino/a/x; fully 16% chose to identify themselves using two or more racial or ethnic categories. In 1971, 90% of first-time college students identified as White. In 1966, men constituted 53.0% of all first-time college students; by 2015, 54.7% of full-time students identified as female. Political attitudes have also shifted over time among this group: Trends in opinions about taxes, the legalization of marijuana, and abortion rights can be seen. And the percentage of new students who think that their "emotional health" is above average or in the "top 10%" has decreased considerably from 1985 to 2019. For men, that percentage decreased from 68.1% to 50.4%; the percentage of women reporting that their emotional health is high went from 59.3% to 34.0%. Research is needed to identify the causes of such changes. Most important, colleges are alerted to the need to provide more student mental health services.

Another way to study changes over time is to conduct a longitudinal **panel study** in which the same people are surveyed at two or more points in time. A research panel consists of a set of individuals who have volunteered to be research participants for multiple studies over time. In a two-wave panel study, the same people in the research panel are surveyed at two points in time; in a three-wave panel study, three surveys are conducted; and so on. Panel studies are particularly important when the research question addresses the relationship between one variable at "time 1" and another variable at some later "time 2." For example, McBride et al. (2021) studied the impact of concerns about climate change on psychological well-being in a large national panel of 13,453 New Zealanders. They found that concern about climate change in 2017 predicted an increase in psychological distress, but not in life satisfaction, one year later.

SAMPLING FROM A POPULATION

Most research projects involve selecting a **sample** of participants from a population of interest. The **population** is composed of all individuals of interest to the researcher. One population of interest in a large public opinion poll, for instance, might be all eligible voters in the United States. This implies that the population of interest does not include people under the age of 18, people who are incarcerated, visitors from other countries, and anyone else not eligible to vote. You might conduct a survey in which your population consists of all students at your college or university. With enough time and money, a survey researcher could conceivably contact everyone in the population. The United States attempts to do this every ten years with an official census of the entire population. With a relatively small population, however, you might find it relatively easy to study the whole population.

Let's use another example. What if you asked every single student at your college or university to tell you whether they prefer to study at home or at school, and you found that 64% preferred studying at home. In this case, you would be very certain of the answer to your question—after all, you asked everybody. That, of course, would be quite costly; you would likely have to hire a team of research assistants to track down every student. But suppose you are not independently wealthy (or you have better uses for your wealth). In that case, you could randomly select a subgroup of students at your university and ask them the question. With proper sampling, we can use information obtained from the participants (or "respondents") who were sampled to estimate the characteristics of the population as a whole. Statistical theory allows us to use data obtained from a sample to estimate what the entire population is like.

Confidence Intervals

When researchers make inferences about a population from a sample, they do so with a certain degree of confidence. Here is a statement that you might see when you read the survey results based on a sample of a population: "The results from the survey are accurate within ±3 percentage points, using a 95% level of confidence." What does this tell you?

To extend our example above, suppose you asked a small sample of students at your college to tell you whether they prefer to study at home or school, and in that case the survey results from the sample indicate that 61% prefer to study at home. Using the same degree of confidence, you would now know that the actual population value is probably between 58% (61% − 3%) and 64% (61% + 3%). This is called a **confidence interval**—you can have 95% confidence that the true population value lies within this interval around the obtained sample result. Indeed, in our example we know the population value (64%). Your best estimate of the population value is the sample value. However, because you have only a sample and not the entire population, your result may be in error. The confidence interval gives you information about the likely amount of the error. The formal term for this error is **sampling error,** although you are probably more familiar with the term *margin of error.* Recall the concept of measurement error discussed in the chapter "Measurement Concepts." When measuring a single individual on a variable, the obtained score may deviate from the true score because of measurement error. Similarly, when you study one sample, the obtained result may deviate from the true population value because of sampling error.

The surveys you often read about in newspapers and the previous example deal with percentages. What about questions that ask for more quantitative information? The logic in this instance is very much the same. For example, if you also ask students to report how many hours and minutes they studied during the previous day, you might find that the average amount of time was 76 minutes. A confidence interval could then be calculated based on the size of the sample; for example, the 95% confidence interval is 76 minutes plus or minus 10 minutes. It is highly likely that the true population value lies within the interval of 66 to 86 minutes.

Sample Size

It is important to note that a larger sample size will reduce the size of the confidence interval—the closer you get to receiving responses from every member of a population, the more accurate the estimate of that answer can be! Although several factors determine the size of a confidence interval, the most important is the sample size. Larger samples are more likely to yield data that accurately reflect the true population value. This statement should make intuitive sense to you; a sample of 200 people from your school should yield more accurate data about your school than a sample of 25 people.

How large should the sample be? The sample size can be determined using a mathematical formula that takes into account the size of the confidence interval and the size of the population you are studying. Table 1 shows the sample size needed for a sample percentage to be accurate within plus or minus 3%, 5%, and 10%, given a 95% level of confidence. Note first that you need a larger sample size for increased accuracy. With a population size of 10,000, you need a sample of 370 for accuracy within ±5%; the needed sample size increases to 964 for accuracy within ±3%. Note that sample size is *not* a constant percentage of the population size. Many people believe that proper sampling requires a certain percentage of the population; these people often complain about survey results when they discover that a survey of an entire state was done with "only" 700 or 1,000 people. However, you can see in the table that the needed sample size does not change much, even as the population size increases from 5,000 to 100,000 or more. As Fowler (2014) notes, "A sample of 150 people will describe a population of 1,500 or 15 million with virtually the same degree of accuracy" (p. 38).

TABLE 1 Sample size and precision of population estimates (95% confidence level)

Size of population	Precision of estimate		
	±3%	±5%	±10%
2,000	696	322	92
5,000	879	357	94
10,000	964	370	95
50,000	1,045	381	96
100,000	1,055	383	96
Over 100,000	1,067	384	96

Note: The sample sizes were calculated using conservative assumptions about the nature of the true population values.

SAMPLING TECHNIQUES

There are two broad categories of techniques for sampling individuals from a population: probability sampling and nonprobability sampling.

- **Probability sampling:** Each member of the population has a specifiable probability (chance) of being chosen.
- **Nonprobability sampling:** The probability (chance) of any particular member of the population being chosen is unknown.

Probability sampling is required when you want to make precise statements about a specific population on the basis of the results of your survey. Although nonprobability sampling is not as sophisticated as probability sampling, we shall see that nonprobability sampling is quite common and useful in many circumstances.

Probability Sampling

Simple Random Sampling   With **simple random sampling,** every member of the population has an equal probability of being selected for the sample. If the population has 1,000 members, each member of the population has one chance out of a thousand of being selected. Suppose you want to sample students who attend your school. A list of all students would be needed; from that list, students would be chosen at random to form the sample.

When conducting telephone interviews, researchers commonly have a computer generate phone numbers used in the area of the sample. This will produce a random sample of the population of people with phones (but not necessarily of the population of people, because some people do not have phones).

Stratified Random Sampling   A somewhat more complicated probability sampling procedure is called **stratified random sampling.** In stratified random sampling, the population is divided into subgroups (also known as *strata*), and random sampling techniques are then used to select sample members from each stratum. Any number of dimensions could be used to divide the population, but the dimension (or dimensions) chosen should be relevant to the problem under study. For instance, a survey of political attitudes might stratify on the basis of age, gender, political affiliation, and amount of education, because these factors are related to political attitudes. Stratification on the basis of hair color would be ridiculous for this survey, as these variables are likely to be unrelated to a survey of political attitudes.

Stratified random sampling has the advantage of a built-in assurance that the sample will accurately reflect the numerical composition of the various subgroups. This kind of accuracy is particularly important when some important subgroups represent very small percentages of the population. Suppose you conduct a survey on student attitudes about food services on your 10,000-student campus. The attitudes of vegetarians are important, but you have evidence that vegetarians make up only 5% of the student body. A simple random sample of 100 students might not include any vegetarians; a stratified random sample would include five vegetarians chosen randomly from the population of vegetarians. In practice, when it is important to represent a small group within a population, researchers will "over-sample" that group to ensure that a representative sample is surveyed; a large enough sample must be obtained to make inferences about the population. For the campus food survey, to compare attitudes of vegetarians and non-vegetarians, you will need to sample a large percentage of the vegetarian students and only a small percentage of the non-vegetarian students to obtain a reasonable number of respondents from each group.

Cluster Sampling   It might have occurred to you that obtaining a list of all members of a population might be difficult. What if officials at your school decide that you cannot have access to a list of all students? What if you want to study a population that has no list of members, such as people who work in county health care agencies? In such situations, a technique called **cluster sampling** can be used to create a probability sample. Rather than randomly sampling from a list of individuals, the researcher can identify "clusters" of individuals and then sample from these clusters. After the clusters are chosen, all individuals in each cluster are included in the sample. For example, you might use cluster sampling to conduct the survey of students by identifying all classes being taught—the classes are the clusters of students. You could then randomly sample from this list of classes and have all members of the chosen classes complete your survey (making sure, of course, that no one completes the survey twice).

Most often, the use of cluster sampling requires a series of samples from larger to smaller clusters—a multistage approach. For example, a researcher interested in studying county health care agencies might first randomly determine a number of states to sample and then randomly sample counties from each state chosen. The researcher would then go to the health care agencies in each of these counties and study the people who work in them. Note that the main advantage of cluster sampling is that the researcher does not have to sample from lists of individuals to obtain a truly random sample of individuals.

Nonprobability Sampling

In contrast to probability sampling, in which the probability of a member of the population being selected is knowable, in nonprobability sampling the probability of being selected is not known. Nonprobability sampling techniques can be quite arbitrary. A population might be defined, but little effort is expended to ensure that the sample accurately represents the population. However, nonprobability samples are inexpensive and convenient. We will primarily discuss three types of nonprobability sampling: convenience sampling, purposive sampling, and quota sampling.

Convenience Sampling   One common form of nonprobability sampling is **convenience sampling,** also called "haphazard" sampling. Convenience sampling could be called a "take-them-where-you-find-them" method of obtaining participants. Thus, you would select a sample of students from your school in any way that is convenient. You might stand in front of the student union at 9 a.m. and interview passersby, ask people who sit around you in your classes to participate, or visit a couple of fraternity and sorority residences. Unfortunately, such procedures are likely to introduce biases into the sample so that the sample may not be an accurate representation of the population of all students. If you selected your sample from students walking by the student union at 9 a.m., your sample excludes students who do not frequent this location. It may also eliminate afternoon and evening students. At many colleges this sample would differ from the population of all students by being younger, working fewer hours, and being more likely to belong to a fraternity or sorority. Sample biases such as these limit your ability to use your sample data to estimate the actual population values. Your results might not generalize to your intended population but instead might describe only the biased sample you obtained.

Convenience samples are increasingly obtained through online participant recruitment services such as Amazon Mechanical Turk (MTurk, https://www.mturk.com). MTurk provides a way for "requesters" (e.g., researchers) to recruit "workers" (also known as "turkers") who are paid to complete a task—to participate in a research investigation. The turkers constitute the sampling frame from which researchers obtain samples of volunteers for their studies. The sample is clearly a convenience sample, but the MTurk samples are more diverse than a college student sample in age and other characteristics, although most of them are young and have extensive familiarity with computer applications. Still, there is a growing literature that many established research findings are replicated using MTurk samples (Buhrmester et al., 2018; Gerlich et al., 2018). For more information on using MTurk, see Buhrmeister's MTurk Guide at https://michaelbuhrmester.wordpress.com/mechanical-turk-guide/ and the MTurk faqs at https://www.mturk.com/help.

Unfortunately, there has been a documented decrease in the quality of data provided through use of MTurk (Chmielewski & Kucker, 2020) as result of bots and "server farms" that access ongoing research and provide unusable data. Researchers are following recommendations to implement procedures to identify and remove inappropriate data (Chmielewski & Kucker, 2020; Kennedy et al., 2020; Peer et al., 2021). Also, Prolific (https://www.prolific.co) is similar to MTurk but was developed specifically to address the needs of academic researchers. In a comparison of Prolific and MTurk, Peer et al. (2017) concluded that research findings are the same for both and that Prolific samples are more diverse and have more participants from outside the United States.

There are several newer platforms for recruiting research participants, including Qualtrics Research Panels, CloudResearch, and Survey Monkey Audience. Researchers request samples based on their research questions and desired population, and these services offer to deliver a representative online sample. Felix et al. (2022), for example, used a Qualtrics Panel that included a fairly diverse sample of 342 teenagers to study how initial emotional reactions, threat perception, and core beliefs influence the relationship between media exposure to mass shootings and anxiety and depression. These services can be expensive, but they can also create efficient paths to collect data.

Purposive and Snowball Sampling

Purposive sampling is a nonprobability sampling procedure in which the researcher makes a judgment regarding selection of an individual for the sample. The *purpose* is to obtain a sample of people who meet some predetermined criterion. Sometimes at a large movie complex, you may see researchers asking customers to fill out a questionnaire about one or more movies. They are always doing purposive sampling. Instead of sampling anyone walking toward the theater, they take a look at each person to make sure that they fit some criterion—under the age of 30 or an adult with one or more children, for example. This is a good way to limit the sample to a certain group of people. However, it is not a probability sample, because selection was determined by convenience.

Purposive sampling relies on judgments by the researcher. **Snowball sampling** is a nonprobability sampling procedure in which one or more current research participants recruit others to become part of the sample. This method relies on the participants to identify others who possess attributes needed for the sample. They may provide a method for the researcher to make contact or ask people to participate by contacting the researcher. Snowball sampling is most often used when the research participant knows individuals with a desired characteristic who the researcher may not be able to identify or access. A study of sex workers might begin with one individual who has agreed to participate and can contact other sex workers who are friends or acquaintances.

Quota Sampling

Another form of nonprobability sampling is **quota sampling.** A researcher who uses this technique chooses a sample that reflects the numerical composition of various subgroups in the population. Thus, quota sampling is similar to the stratified sampling procedure previously described; however, random sampling does not occur when you use quota sampling. To illustrate, suppose you want to ensure that your sample of students includes 19% first-year students, 23% sophomores, 26% juniors, 22% seniors, and 10% graduate students because these are the percentages of the classes in the total population. A quota sampling technique would make sure you have these percentages, but you would still collect your data using convenience techniques. If you did not get enough graduate students in front of the student union, perhaps you could go to a graduate class to complete the sample. Although quota sampling is a bit more sophisticated than convenience sampling, the problem remains that no restrictions are placed on how individuals in the various subgroups are chosen. The sample does reflect the numerical composition of the whole population of interest, but respondents within each subgroup are selected in a haphazard manner. These techniques are summarized in Table 2.

TABLE 2   Advantages and disadvantages of sampling techniques

Sample technique	Example	Advantages	Disadvantages
Probability sampling techniques			
Simple random sampling	A computer program randomly chooses 100 students from a list of all 10,000 students at College X.	Representative of population.	May cost more. May be difficult to get a full list of all members of any population of interest.
Stratified random sampling	The names of all 10,000 College X students are sorted by major, and a computer program randomly chooses 50 students from each major.	Representative of population.	May cost more. May be difficult to get full list of all members of any population of interest.
Cluster sampling	Two hundred clusters of psychology majors are identified at schools all over the United States. Out of these 200 clusters, 10 clusters are chosen randomly, and every psychology major in each cluster is sampled.	Researcher does not have to sample from lists of individuals in order to get a full, random sample.	May cost more. May be difficult to get full list of all members of any randomly chosen cluster.
Nonprobability sampling techniques			
Convenience sampling	Ask students around you at lunch or in class to participate.	Inexpensive, efficient, convenient.	Likely to introduce bias into the sample; results may not generalize to intended population.
Purposive sampling	In an otherwise haphazard sample, the researcher selects individuals who meet a criterion (e.g., an age group).	Sample includes only types of individuals you are interested in.	Likely to introduce bias into the sample; results may not generalize to intended population.
Snowball sampling	Research participants recruit others with known. characteristics to become participants	Same as purposive.	Same as purposive.
Quota sampling	Collect specific proportions of data representative of percentages of groups within population, then use haphazard techniques.	Inexpensive, efficient, convenient.	Likely to introduce bias into the sample; results may not generalize to intended population; no method for choosing individuals in subgroups.

Check Your Learning

Now, try organizing your own nonprobability sampling technique in Check Your Learning: Practice Exercise #2.

EVALUATING SAMPLES

Samples should be representative of the population from which they are drawn. A completely unbiased sample is one that is highly representative of the population. How do you create a completely unbiased sample? First, you would use a probability sampling technique and randomly sample from a population that contains *all* individuals in the population. Second, you would contact and obtain completed responses from *all* individuals selected to be in the sample. Unfortunately, such standards are rarely achieved. Even if random sampling is used, bias can be introduced from two sources: the sampling frame used and poor response rates. Moreover, even though nonprobability samples have more potential sources of bias than probability samples, they are used for many reasons (summarized in Table 2) and should be evaluated positively.

Sampling Frame

The **sampling frame** is the *actual* population of individuals (or clusters) from which a random sample will be drawn. Rarely will this perfectly coincide with the population of interest—some biases will be introduced. Suppose you want to know what doctors think about a new state law that impacts patient rights. A reasonable sampling frame would be all doctors listed in your telephone directory. Immediately you can see that you have limited your sample to a particular geographical area. More important, you have also limited the sample to doctors who have private practices—doctors who work only in clinics and hospitals have been excluded. At this point, you may want to find out if the state medical board lists doctors by name and address—this might produce a better sampling frame. When evaluating the results of the survey, you need to consider how well the sampling frame matches the population of interest. Often the biases introduced are quite minor; however, they could be consequential to the results of a study.

Response Rate

The **response rate** in a survey is simply the percentage of people who were selected in the sample who actually completed the survey. Suppose you send 1,000 email requests with links to a questionnaire to a random sample of undergraduates at your school. Subsequently, 500 questionnaires are completed; the response rate is 50%.

Response rate is important because it indicates how much bias there might be in the final sample of respondents. Nonrespondents may differ from respondents in any number of ways, including age, income, marital status, and education. The lower the response rate, the greater the likelihood that such biases may distort the findings and in turn limit the ability to generalize the findings to the population of interest (i.e., reduce the external validity of the results).

In general, mail surveys have lower response rates than telephone surveys. With both methods, however, steps can be taken to maximize response rates. With mail surveys, an explanatory postcard or letter can be sent a week or so prior to mailing the survey. Follow-up reminders and even second mailings of the questionnaire are often effective in increasing response rates. It often helps to have a personally stamped return envelope rather than a business reply envelope. Even the look of the cover page of the questionnaire can be important (Dillman et al., 2014; Guiding Principles for Mail and Internet Surveys, 2012).

With telephone surveys, respondents who are not home can be called again, and people who cannot be interviewed today can be scheduled for a call at a more convenient time. Sometimes an incentive may be necessary to increase response rates. Such incentives can include cash, a gift, or a gift certificate for agreeing to participate. A crisp dollar bill "thank you" can be included with a mailed questionnaire—monetary incentives have been shown to positively impact response rates (Stanley et al., 2021). People who participate in paid online surveys are also sensitive to the amount of monetary incentive (Stanley et al., 2020). Other incentives include a chance to win a prize drawing or a promise to contribute money to a charity. Finally, researchers should attempt to convince people that the survey's purposes are important and their participation will be a valuable contribution.

REASONS FOR USING CONVENIENCE SAMPLES

Much of the research in psychology uses nonprobability sampling techniques to obtain participants for either surveys or experiments. The advantage of these techniques is that the investigator can obtain research participants without spending a great deal of money or time on selecting—or collecting data from—the sample. For example, it is common practice to select participants from students in introductory psychology classes. Often these students are asked to participate in studies being conducted by faculty and their students; the introductory psychology students can choose which studies they wish to participate in.

Even in studies that do not use college students, the sample is often based on convenience rather than concern for obtaining a random sample. One of our colleagues studies children, but they are almost always from one particular elementary school. You can guess that this is because our colleague has established a good relationship with the teachers and administrators; thus, obtaining permission to conduct the research is fairly easy. Even though the sample is biased because it includes only children from one neighborhood that has certain social and economic characteristics, the advantages outweigh the sample concerns for the researcher.

Why aren't researchers more worried about obtaining random samples from the "general population" for their research? Most psychological research is focused on studying the relationships between variables even though the sample may be biased (e.g., the sample will have more college students, be younger, etc., than the general U.S. population). But to put this in perspective, remember that even a random sample of the general population of U.S. residents tells us nothing about citizens of other countries. So our research findings provide important information even though the data cannot be strictly generalized beyond the population defined by the sample that was used. For example, the findings of Brown and Rahhal (1994) regarding experiences of younger and older adults when they hid an object but later forgot the location are meaningful even though the actual sample consisted of current students (younger adults) and alumni (older adults) of a particular university who received a mailed questionnaire.

In the chapter "Generalization" we will emphasize that generalization in science is dependent upon replicating the results. We do not need better samples of younger and older adults; instead, we should look for replications of the findings using multiple samples and multiple methods. The results of many studies can then be synthesized to gain greater insight into the findings (cf. Albright & Malloy, 2000).

These issues will be explored further in the chapter "Generalization." For now, it is also important to recognize that some nonprobability samples are more representative than others. Introductory psychology students, for instance, are fairly representative of college students in general, and most college student samples are fairly representative of young adults. So there are not many obvious biases, particularly if you are studying basic psychological processes.

On the other hand, other samples might be much less representative of an intended population. When local news programs, 24-hour news channels, or websites ask viewers to vote on a topic, the resulting samples are not representative of the population to which they are often trying to generalize. First, their viewers may be different from the U.S. population in meaningful ways (e.g., more Fox News viewers are conservative, more MSNBC viewers are liberal). Second, these programs and websites often ask about hot-button topics, things that people care passionately about, because that is what drives viewers and visitors to tune in. Questions about abortion, taxes, and wars tend to drive certain types of viewers to these informal "polls." The results, whatever they may be, are biased because the sample consists primarily of people who have chosen to watch the program or visit the website, and they have chosen to vote because they are deeply interested in a topic.

You now have a great deal of information about methods for asking people about themselves. If you engage in this type of research, you will often need to design your own questions by following the guidelines described in this chapter and consulting sources such as Groves et al. (2009), Fowler (2014), and Stern et al. (2014). However, you can also adapt questions and entire questionnaires that have been used in previous research. Consider using previously developed questions, particularly if they have proven useful in other studies (make sure you do not violate any copyrights, however). A variety of measures of social, political, and occupational attitudes developed by others have been compiled by Robinson and his colleagues (Robinson et al., 1991, 1999).

ENGAGING WITH RESEARCH: SURVEY RESEARCH

The COVID-19 pandemic affected every aspect of our lives. In March 2020, colleges and universities pivoted to remote teaching—and in many places in the United States and around the world, "stay-at-home" orders were put in place. The experience was isolating. Behavioral researchers were interested in many aspects of life during the pandemic. Son et al. (2020) conducted interviews with 195 college students from a large public university in the United States in an effort to understand the effects of the COVID-19 pandemic on mental health and well-being.

First, acquire and read the following article (available at https://www.jmir.org/2020/9/e21279):

> Son, C., Hegde, S., Smith, A., Wang, X., & Sasangohar, F. (2020). Effects of COVID-19 on college students' mental health in the United States: Interview survey study. *Journal of Medical Internet Research, 22*(9), e21279. https://doi.org/10.2196/21279

Then, after reading the article, consider the following:

1. **What is the primary goal of this study? Description, Prediction, Determining Cause, or Explaining? Do the authors achieve their goals?**

2. **What did these researchers do? What was the method? How did Son et al. (2020) sample students? What sampling strategies did they use?**

3. **What was measured? These researchers set out to understand the impact of the pandemic on mental health. How did they measure mental health?**

4. **To what or whom can we generalize the results?**

   a. Where was this study conducted? Do you think that the results of this study would be generalizable to other states? Why or why not? Do you think that they would be generalizable to other countries? Why or why not?

   b. See Table 1: Do you think that this distribution of survey participants by major is representative of all students? Why or why not?

   c. Do you think that the results of this study would be generalizable to noncollege populations? Why or why not?

   d. Son et al. (2020) did not report the ethnic/racial makeup of their sample, nor gender-identity beyond male/female. What are the implications for this lack of data?

5. **What did they find? What were the results?**

6. **Have other researchers found similar results?**

7. **What are the limitations of this study?**

8. **What are the ethical issues present in this study?**

BEING A SKILLED CONSUMER OF RESEARCH

1. As we noted at the beginning of this chapter, surveys are being conducted all the time. Many survey reports are not published in peer-reviewed journals. Identify a survey report of interest to you and answer the questions below. Survey reports can be found on the internet. Here are some examples: Youth Risk Behavior Survey Surveillance: https://www.cdc.gov/healthyyouth/data/yrbs/index.htm; Pew Religious Landscape Study: https://www.pewforum.org/religious-landscape-study/; National Crime Victimization Survey (NCVS): https://www.bjs.ojp.gov/programs/ncvs; Behavioral Risk Factor Surveillance System: https://cdc.gov/brfss/.

   a. What kinds of questions were included in the survey? Identify examples of each.

   b. How were the questions developed?

   c. How and when was the survey administered?

   d. What was the nature of the sampling strategy? What was the final sample size?

   e. What was the response rate for the survey?

   f. What was the confidence interval for the survey findings?

   g. Describe at least one survey finding that you found particularly interesting or surprising.

2. Suppose you want to study the relationships between ratings of family satisfaction, job satisfaction, and life satisfaction. Describe how you might conduct an online survey of adults to obtain your data. What would be the reason to conduct a two-wave panel study rather than a one-wave-only procedure?

3. Graesser et al. (2006) developed an application called QUAID (Question Understanding Aid) that analyzes question-wording. Write three survey questions you might ask on a topic of interest to you and go to the QUAID website (https://quaid.cohmetrix.com/) for feedback. What did you find?

4. Corbie-Smith et al. (1999) conducted a focus group with 33 Black adults at an urban public hospital to better understand barriers to the participation of Black people in medical research. They found that the participants in this study were distrustful of the medical community, which was a prominent barrier to their participation in research. Cain et al. (2016) conducted a survey of 304 African-American participants from the Washington, D.C., metropolitan area on a similar topic. Compare and contrast the findings. Identify the strengths and weaknesses of each research approach.

5. Professional polling operations that conduct polls to describe political opinions of a population use the survey research methods described in this chapter. Political polls are often reported by news media; however, people seldom explore where the data come from. Given what you know now about survey research, educate yourself on a few different political polling operations and ask yourself what effect those methods might have on the answers people give or the nature of the samples that polling operations have access to. Here are a few examples: https://www.surveyusa.net/methodology/; https://www.gallup.com/224855/gallup-poll-work.aspx; https://poll.qu.edu/methodology/.

Check Your Learning: Practice Exercises

Practice Exercise #1

Question Wording: What Is the Problem?

Read each of the following questions and identify the problems for each.

	Negative wording	Simplicity	Double-barreled	Loaded
1. Professors should not be required to take daily attendance. 1 = (Strongly Disagree) and 5 = (Strongly Agree)				
2. I enjoy studying and spending time with friends on weekends.				
3. Do you support the legislation that would unfairly tax hardworking farmers?				
4. I would describe myself as funny and intelligent.				
5. Do you believe the relationship between cell phone behavior and consumption of fast food is orthogonal?				
6. Restaurants should not have to be inspected each month.				
7. Are you in favor of the boss's whim to cut lunchtime to 30 minutes?				

Practice Exercise #2:

Suppose you want to know how many books in your local bookstore have only male authors, only female authors, or male and female co-authors. Because there are thousands of books in the store, you decide to study a sample of the books rather than examine every book there. Describe a possible sampling procedure using a nonprobability sampling technique. Then describe how you might sample books using a probability sampling technique. Now speculate on how the outcomes of your research might differ using the two techniques. You might think about an additional complication: What if you want to conduct your study with a sample of books available from an online bookseller?

(Some answers are provided at the end of this chapter.)

CHAPTER REVIEW

Review Questions

1. What is a survey? Describe some research questions you might address with a survey.

2. What are some factors to take into consideration when constructing questions for surveys (including both questions and response alternatives)?

3. What are the advantages and disadvantages of using questionnaires versus interviews in a survey?

4. Compare the different questionnaire, interview, and internet survey administration methods.

5. Define interviewer bias.

6. What is a social desirability response set?

7. How does sample size affect the interpretation of survey results?

8. Distinguish between probability and nonprobability sampling techniques. What are the implications of each?

9. Distinguish between simple random, stratified random, and cluster sampling.

10. Distinguish between convenience (haphazard) sampling and quota sampling.

11. Why don't researchers who want to test hypotheses about the relationships between variables worry a great deal about random sampling?

Study Terms _____

Closed-ended questions (p. 156) Quota sampling (p. 171)
Cluster sampling (p. 169) Rating scale (p. 157)
Confidence interval (p. 166) Response rate (p. 173)
Convenience sampling (p. 170) Response set (p. 152)
Focus group (p. 164) Sample (p. 165)
Graphic rating scale (p. 157) Sampling error (p. 166)
Interviewer bias (p. 163) Sampling frame (p. 173)
Nay-saying (p. 155) Semantic differential scale (p. 157)
Nonprobability sampling (p. 168) Simple random sampling (p. 168)
Open-ended questions (p. 156) Snowball sampling (p. 171)
Panel study (p. 165) Social desirability (p. 152)
Population (p. 165) Stratified random sampling (p. 168)
Probability sampling (p. 168) Survey research (p. 151)
Purposive sampling (p. 171) Yea-saying (p. 155)

Check Your Learning: Answers

1. negative wording; 2. double-barreled; 3. loaded; 4. double-barreled;
5. simplicity; 6. negative wording; 7. loaded

Klaus Vedfelt/Getty Images

8

Experimental Design

LEARNING OBJECTIVES

- Define what a confounding variable is and describe how confounding variables are related to internal validity.
- Describe the posttest-only design and the pretest-posttest design, including the advantages and disadvantages of each design.
- Compare and contrast an independent groups (between-subjects) design with a repeated measures (within-subjects) design.
- Summarize the advantages and disadvantages of using a repeated measures design.
- Explain how counterbalancing provides a way of addressing the order effects problem.
- Describe a matched pairs design, including reasons to use this design.

IN THE EXPERIMENTAL METHOD, THE RESEARCHER ATTEMPTS TO CONTROL ALL EXTRANEOUS VARIABLES. Suppose you want to test the hypothesis that exercise affects mood. To do this, you might put one group of people through a 1-hour aerobics workout and put another group in a room where they are asked to watch a video of people exercising for an hour. All participants would then complete the same mood assessment. Now suppose that the people in the aerobics class rate themselves as happier than those in the video-viewing condition. Can the difference in mood be attributed to the difference in the exercise? Yes, *if* there is no other difference between the groups. However, what if the aerobics group was given the mood assessment in a room with windows but the video-only group was tested in a room without windows? In that case, it would be impossible to know whether the better mood of the participants in the aerobics group was due to the exercise or to the presence of windows.

CONFOUNDING VARIABLES AND INTERNAL VALIDITY

Recall from the chapter "Fundamental Research Issues" that the experimental method has the advantage of allowing a relatively unambiguous interpretation of results. To conduct a true experiment, the researcher manipulates the independent variable to create groups (an experimental group and a comparison or control group). All other variables are kept constant, either through *experimental control* or through *randomization,* including random assignment to groups. The groups are then compared on the dependent variable. If the groups differ on the dependent variable, the researcher can conclude that the independent variable caused the results because the only difference between the groups is the manipulated independent variable.

Although the task of designing an experiment is logically elegant and exquisitely simple, you should be aware of possible pitfalls. In the hypothetical exercise experiment just described, the variables of exercise and window presence are confounded. The window variable was not kept constant. A **confounding variable** is a variable that varies along with the independent variable. Confounding occurs when the effects of the independent variable and an uncontrolled variable are intertwined so that you cannot determine which of the variables is responsible for the observed effect on the dependent variable. If the window variable had been held constant, the exercise condition and the video condition would have taken place in identical rooms. That way, the effect of windows would not be a factor to consider when interpreting the difference between the groups.

In short, both rooms in the exercise experiment should have had windows, or both should have been windowless. Because one room had windows and one room did not, any difference in the dependent variable (mood) cannot be attributed solely to the independent variable (exercise). An alternative explanation can be offered: The difference in mood may have been caused, at least in part, by the window variable.

Good experimental design requires eliminating all possible confounding variables that could result in alternative explanations. A claim that the independent variable caused the results can be justified only when competing, alternative explanations have been eliminated. When the results of an experiment can confidently be attributed to the effect of the independent variable, the experiment is said to have **internal validity.** (Remember that internal validity refers to the accuracy of conclusions drawn about cause and effect; see the chapter "Fundamental Research Issues.") To achieve a high degree of internal validity, the researcher must design and conduct the experiment so that only the independent variable can be the cause of the results (Campbell & Stanley, 1966; Shadish et al., 2002). This chapter will focus on true experimental designs, which provide the highest degree of internal validity.

BASIC EXPERIMENTS

The simplest possible experimental design has two variables: the independent variable and the dependent variable. The independent variable has a minimum of two levels, an experimental group and a control group. Researchers must make every effort to ensure that the only difference between the two groups is the manipulated (independent) variable.

Remember, the experimental method requires maintaining control over extraneous variables, through either keeping such variables constant (experimental control) or using randomization to make sure that any extraneous variables will affect both groups equally. The basic, simple experimental design can take one of two forms: a posttest-only design or a pretest-posttest design.

Posttest-Only Design

A researcher using a **posttest-only design** must (1) obtain two equivalent groups of participants, (2) manipulate the independent variable, and (3) measure the effect of the independent variable on the dependent variable. The posttest-only design looks like this:

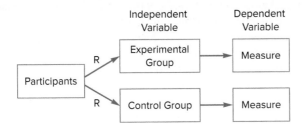

Thus, the first step is to choose the participants and assign them to the two groups. The procedures used must achieve equivalent groups to eliminate any potential **selection differences:** The people selected to be in the conditions cannot differ in any systematic way. For example, you cannot select high-income individuals to participate in one condition and low-income individuals for the other. The groups can be made equivalent by randomly assigning participants to the two conditions or by having the same participants participate in both conditions. Recall from the chapter "Fundamental Research Issues" that random assignment is done in such a way that each participant is assigned to a condition randomly without regard to any personal characteristics. The R in the diagram means that participants were randomly assigned to the two groups.

Next, the researcher must choose two levels of the independent variable, such as an experimental group that receives a treatment and a control group that does not. Thus, a researcher might study the effect of reward on motivation by offering a reward to one group of children before they play a game and offering no reward to children in the control group. A study testing the effect of a treatment method for reducing smoking could compare a group that receives the treatment with a control group that does not. Another approach would be to use two different amounts of the independent variable—that is, to use more reward in one group than the other or to compare the effects of different amounts of relaxation training designed to help people quit smoking (e.g., 1 hour of training compared with 10 hours). Another approach would be to include two qualitatively different conditions; for example, prior to taking a test, one group of test-anxious students might write about their anxiety and the other group could participate in a meditation exercise. All of these approaches would provide a basis for comparison of the two groups. (Of course, experiments may include more than two groups; for example, we might compare two different smoking cessation treatments along with a no-treatment control group—these types of experimental designs will be described in the chapter "Complex Experimental Designs.")

Finally, the effect of the independent variable is measured. The same measurement procedure is used for both groups, so that comparison of the two groups is possible. Because the groups were equivalent prior to the introduction of the independent variable and there were no confounding variables, any difference between the groups on the dependent variable must be attributed to the effect of the independent variable. This elegant experimental design has a high degree of internal validity. That is, we can confidently conclude that the independent variable caused the dependent variable. In actuality, a statistical significance test would be used to assess the difference between the groups. However, we do not need to be concerned with statistics at this point. An experiment must be well designed, and confounding variables must be eliminated before we can draw conclusions from statistical analyses.

Pretest-Posttest Design

The only difference between the posttest-only design and the **pretest-posttest design** is that in the latter a pretest is given before the experimental manipulation is introduced:

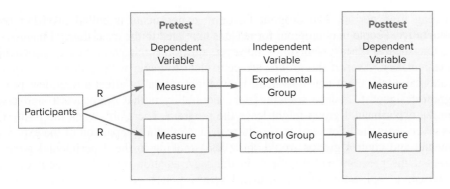

This design makes it possible to ascertain that the groups were, in fact, equivalent at the beginning of the experiment. However, this precaution is usually not necessary if participants have been randomly assigned to the two groups. With a sufficiently large sample of participants, random assignment will produce groups that are virtually identical in all respects.

You are probably wondering how many participants are needed in each group to make sure that random assignment has made the groups equivalent. The larger the sample, the less likelihood there is that the groups will differ in any systematic way prior to the manipulation of the independent variable. In addition, as sample size increases, so does the likelihood that any difference between the groups on the dependent variable is due to the effect of the independent variable. There are formal procedures for determining the sample size needed to detect a statistically significant effect, but as a rule of thumb you will probably need a minimum of 50 participants per condition (Simmons et al., 2013). In some areas of research, many more participants may be necessary. However, fewer participants may be appropriate when conducting exploratory research. Further issues in determining the number of participants needed for an experiment are described in the chapter "Understanding Research Results: Statistical Inference."

Comparing Posttest-Only and Pretest-Posttest Designs

Each of these two experimental designs has advantages and disadvantages that influence the decision whether to include or omit a pretest. The first decision concerns the equivalence of the groups in the experiment. Although randomization is likely to produce equivalent groups, it is possible that, with small sample sizes, the groups will not be equal. Thus, a pretest enables the researcher to tell whether the groups are in fact equivalent to begin with.

The pretest-posttest design immediately makes us focus on the *change* from pretest to posttest. This emphasis on change is incorporated into the analysis of the group differences. Also, the extent of change in each individual can be examined. If a smoking reduction program appears to be effective for some individuals but not others, attempts can be made to find out why.

A pretest is also useful whenever there is a possibility that participants will drop out of the experiment; this is most likely to occur in a study that lasts over a long time period. The dropout factor in experiments is called **attrition** or **mortality.** People may drop out for reasons unrelated to the experimental manipulation, such as illness; sometimes, however, attrition is related to the experimental manipulation. Even if the groups are equivalent to begin with, different attrition rates can make them nonequivalent. How might mortality affect a treatment program designed to reduce smoking? One possibility is that the heaviest smokers in the experimental group might leave the program. Therefore, when the posttest is given, only the light smokers would remain, so that a comparison of the experimental and control groups would show less smoking in the experimental group even if the program had no effect. In this way, attrition (mortality) becomes an alternative explanation for the results. Use of a pretest enables you to assess the effects of attrition; you can look at the pretest scores of the dropouts and know whether their scores differed from the scores of the individuals completing the study. Thus, with the pretest, it is possible to examine whether attrition is a plausible alternative explanation—an advantage in the experimental design.

One disadvantage of a pretest, however, is that it may be time-consuming and awkward to administer in the context of the particular experimental procedures being used. Perhaps most important, a pretest can sensitize participants to what you are studying, enabling them to figure out what is being studied and (potentially) why. They may then react differently to the manipulation than they would have without the pretest. When a pretest affects the way participants react to the manipulation, it is very difficult to generalize the results to people who have not received a pretest. That is, the independent variable may not have an effect in the real world, where pretests are rarely given. We will examine this issue more fully in the chapter "Generalization."

However, if awareness of the pretest is a problem, the pretest can be disguised. One way to do this is by administering it in a completely different situation with a different experimenter. Another approach is to embed the pretest in a set of irrelevant measures so it is not obvious that the researcher is interested in a particular topic.

It is also possible to assess the impact of the pretest directly with a combination of both the posttest-only and the pretest-posttest design. In this design, half the participants receive only the posttest, and the other half receive both the pretest and the posttest (see Figure 1). This is formally called a **Solomon four-group design.**

If there is no impact of the pretest, the posttest scores will be the same in the two control groups (with and without the pretest) and in the two experimental groups. Rew et al. (2022) employed a Solomon four-group design to study the effect of an intervention to promote responsible substance use, safe sex, and other positive behaviors in a diverse sample of 18–24-year-olds experiencing homelessness. Two possible outcomes of this study are shown in Figure 2. The top graph illustrates an outcome in which the pretest has no impact on the outcome of the study: The intervention resulted in more safe sex behavior in both the posttest-only and the pretest-posttest conditions. This is one of the things that Rew and her colleagues found in their study. The lower graph shows an outcome in which taking the pretest does affect the results of the study. There is a difference between the treatment and control groups when there is a pretest, but there is no group difference when the pretest is absent.

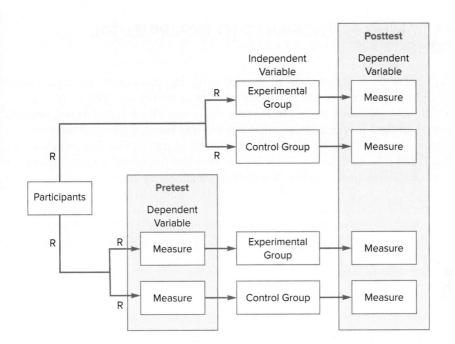

FIGURE 1
Solomon
four-group
design

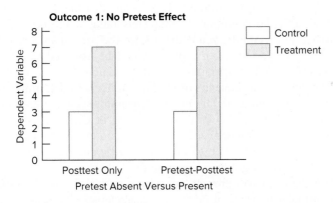

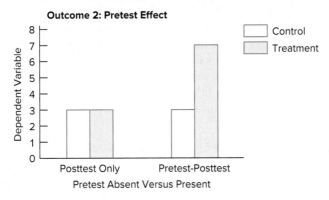

FIGURE 2
Examples of
outcomes
of Solomon
four-group
design

ASSIGNING PARTICIPANTS TO EXPERIMENTAL CONDITIONS

Recall that there are two basic ways of assigning participants to experimental conditions. In one procedure, participants are randomly assigned to the various conditions so that each participates in only one group. This is called an **independent groups design.** It is also commonly known as a **between-subjects design** because comparisons are made between different groups of participants (you may also see this called a *between-persons design*). In the other procedure, all participants are in all conditions. In an experiment with two conditions, for example, each participant is assigned to both levels of the independent variable. This is called a **repeated measures design,** because each participant is measured after receiving each level of the independent variable. You will also see this called a **within-subjects design** or a *within-person design;* in this design, comparisons are made within the same participants (subjects, persons). In the next two sections, we will examine each of these designs in detail.

Independent Groups Design

In an independent groups design, different participants are assigned to each of the conditions using **random assignment.** This means that the decision to assign an individual to a particular condition is completely random and beyond the control of the researcher. For example, you could ask for the participant's month of birth; individuals born in odd-numbered months would be assigned to one group and those born in even-numbered months would be assigned to the other group. In practice, researchers use a sequence of random numbers to determine assignment. Such numbers come from a random number generator such as Research Randomizer, available online at http://www.randomizer.org or QuickCalcs at http://www.graphpad.com/quickcalcs/randomize1.cfm. Excel can also generate random numbers. This procedure enables you to randomly determine the assignment of each participant to the various groups in your study.

Random assignment will prevent any systematic biases, and the groups can be considered equivalent in terms of participant characteristics such as income, intelligence, age, personality, and political attitudes. In this way, participant differences cannot be an explanation for results of the experiment. Thus, in our experiment on the effects of exercise on mood, more positive mood levels in the exercise group than in the no-exercise group cannot be explained by saying that people in the groups somehow differ in characteristics such as income, education, or personality.

An alternative procedure is to have the *same* individuals participate in all of the groups. This is called a repeated measures experimental design.

Repeated Measures Design

Consider an experiment investigating the relationship between the meaningfulness of material and the learning of that material. In an independent groups design, one group of participants is given highly meaningful material to learn and another group receives less meaningful material. Meaningfulness refers to the ease with which new material can be related to something that is already known. For example, new material might be more meaningful if it is connected to a story about a familiar real-life event. In a repeated measures design, the same individuals participate in both conditions. Thus, participants might first read low-meaningful material and take a recall test to measure learning; the same participants would then read high-meaningful material and take the recall test. You can see why this is called a repeated measures design; participants are repeatedly measured on the dependent variable after being in each condition of the experiment.

Advantages and Disadvantages of Repeated Measures Design
The repeated measures design has several advantages. An obvious one is that fewer research participants are needed, because each individual participates in all conditions. When participants are scarce or when it is costly to run each individual in the experiment, a repeated measures design may be preferred. In much research on perception, for instance, extensive training of participants is necessary before the actual experiment can begin. Such research often involves only a few individuals, who participate in all conditions of the experiment.

An additional advantage of repeated measures designs is that they are extremely sensitive to finding statistically significant differences between groups. This is because we have data from the same people in both conditions. To illustrate why this is important, consider possible data from the recall experiment. Using an independent groups design, the first three participants in the high-meaningful condition had scores of 68, 81, and 92. The first three participants in the low-meaningful condition had scores of 64, 78, and 85. If you calculated an average score for each condition, you would find that the average recall was a bit higher when the material was more meaningful. However, there is a lot of variability in the scores in both groups. You certainly are not finding that everyone in the high-meaningful condition has high recall and everyone in the other condition has low recall. The reason for this variability is that people differ—there are individual differences in recall abilities, so there is a range of scores in both conditions. This is part of "random error" in the scores that we cannot explain.

However, if the same scores were obtained from the first three participants in a repeated measures design, the conclusions would be much different. Let's line up the recall scores for the two conditions:

	High meaning	Low meaning	Difference
Participant 1	68	64	+4
Participant 2	81	78	+3
Participant 3	92	85	+7

With a repeated measures design, the individual differences can be seen and explained. It is true that some people score higher than others because of individual differences in recall abilities, but now you can much more clearly see the effect of the independent variable on recall scores. It is much easier to separate the systematic individual differences from the effect of the independent variable: Scores are higher for every participant in the high-meaningful condition. As a result, we are much more likely to detect an effect of the independent variable on the dependent variable.

The major problem with a repeated measures design stems from the fact that the different conditions must be presented in a particular sequence. For instance, suppose that there is greater recall in the high-meaningful condition. Although this result could be caused by the manipulation of the meaningfulness variable, the result could also simply be an **order effect**—the order of presenting the treatments affects the dependent variable. Thus, greater recall in the high-meaningful condition could be attributed to the fact that the high-meaningful task came second in the order of presentation of the conditions.

There are a variety of types of order effects. For instance, performance on the second task might improve merely because of the practice gained on the first task. This improvement is in fact called a **practice effect,** or learning effect. It is also possible that a **fatigue effect** could result in a deterioration in performance from the first to the second condition as the research participant becomes tired, bored, or distracted. It is also possible for the effect of the first treatment to carry over to influence the response to the second treatment—this is known as a **carryover effect.** Suppose the independent variable is severity of a crime. After reading about the less severe crime, the more severe one might seem much worse to participants than it normally would. In addition, reading about the severe crime might subsequently cause participants to view the less severe crime as much milder than they normally would. In both cases, the experience with one condition carried over to affect the response to the second condition. In this example, the carryover effect was a psychological effect of the way that the two situations contrasted with one another.

A carryover effect may also occur when the first condition produces a change that is still influencing the person when the second condition is introduced. Suppose the first condition involves experiencing failure at an important task. This may result in a temporary increase in stress responses. How long does it take before the person returns to a normal state? If the second condition is introduced too soon, the stress may still be affecting the participant.

There are two approaches to dealing with order effects. The first is to employ counterbalancing techniques. The second is to devise a procedure in which the interval between conditions is long enough to minimize the influence of the first condition on the second.

Counterbalancing

Because of the problem that order-effects present, in a repeated measures design it is very important to counterbalance the order of the conditions.

Complete Counterbalancing With complete **counterbalancing,** all possible orders of presentation are included in the experiment. In the example of a study on learning high- and low-meaningful material, half of the participants would be randomly assigned to the low-high order, and the other half would be assigned to the high-low order. This design is illustrated below:

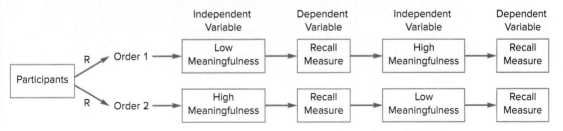

By counterbalancing the order of conditions, it is possible to determine the extent to which order is influencing the results. In the hypothetical memory study, you would know whether the greater recall in the high-meaningful condition is consistent for both orders; you would also know the extent to which a practice effect is responsible for the results.

Counterbalancing principles can be extended to experiments with three or more groups. With three groups, there are 6 possible orders ($3! = 3 \times 2 \times 1 = 6$). With four groups, the number of possible orders increases to 24 ($4! = 4 \times 3 \times 2 \times 1 = 24$); you would need a minimum of 24 participants to represent each order, and you would need 48 participants to have only two participants per order. Imagine the number of orders possible in an experiment by Shepard and Metzler (1971). In their basic experimental paradigm, each participant is shown a three-dimensional object along with the same figure rotated at 1 of 10 different angles ranging from 0 degrees to 180 degrees (see the sample objects illustrated in Figure 3). Each time, the participant presses a button when it is determined that the two figures are the same or different. The dependent variable is reaction time—the amount of time it takes to decide whether the figures are the same or different. The results show that reaction time becomes longer as the angle of rotation increases away from the original. In this experiment with 10 conditions, there are 3,628,800 possible orders! Fortunately, there are alternatives to complete counterbalancing that still allow researchers to draw valid conclusions about the effect of the independent variable without running some 3.6 million tests.

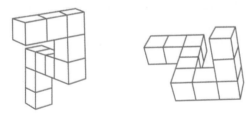

FIGURE 3
Example of the three-dimensional figures used by Shepard and Metzler (1971)

Order of Conditions

	1	2	3	4
Row 1	A (60)	B (0)	D (120)	C (180)
Row 2	B (0)	C (180)	A (60)	D (120)
Row 3	C (180)	D (120)	B (0)	A (60)
Row 4	D (120)	A (60)	C (180)	B (0)

FIGURE 4
A Latin square with four conditions
Note: The four conditions were randomly given letter designations. A = 60 degrees, B = 0 degrees, C = 180 degrees, and D = 120 degrees. Each row represents a different order of running the conditions.

Latin Squares   A technique to control for order effects without having all possible orders is to construct a **Latin square:** a limited set of orders constructed to ensure that (1) each condition appears at each ordinal position and (2) each condition precedes and follows each condition one time. Using a Latin square to determine order controls for most order effects without having to include all possible orders. Suppose you replicated the Shepard and Metzler (1971) study using only 4 of the 10 rotations: 0, 60, 120, and 180 degrees. A Latin square for these four conditions is shown in Figure 4. Each row in the square is one of the orders of the conditions (the conditions are labeled A, B, C, and D). The number of orders in a Latin square is equal to the number of conditions; thus, if there are four conditions, there are four orders. When you conduct your study using the Latin square to determine order, you need at least one participant per row. Usually, you will have two or more participants per row; the number of participants tested in each order must be equal.

Check Your Learning

Now, design your own repeated measures by completing Check Your Learning: Practice Exercise #1.

Time Interval Between Treatments   In addition to counterbalancing the order of treatments, researchers need to carefully determine the time interval between presentation of treatments and possible activities between them. A rest period may counteract a fatigue effect; attending to an unrelated task between treatments may reduce the possibility that participants will contrast the first treatment with the second. If the treatment is the administration of a drug that takes time to wear off, the interval between treatments may have to be a day or more. Lane et al., (2005) used a repeated measures design to study the effect of marijuana on risk taking. The subjects came to the lab in the morning and passed a drug test. They were then given one of three marijuana doses. The dependent variable was a measure of risk taking. Subjects were tested in this way for each dosage. Because of the time necessary for the effects of the drug to wear off, the three conditions were run on separate days at least 5 days apart. A similarly long time interval would be needed with procedures that produce emotional changes, such as heightened anxiety or anger. You may have noted that introduction of an extended time interval may create a separate problem: Participants will have to commit to the experiment for a longer period of time. This can make it more difficult to recruit volunteers, and if the study extends over 2 or more days, some participants may drop out of the experiment altogether. And for the record, increased marijuana doses did result in making riskier decisions.

Choosing Between Independent Groups and Repeated Measures Designs

Repeated measures designs have two major advantages over independent groups designs: (1) a reduction in the number of participants required to complete the experiment and (2) greater control over participant differences and thus greater ability to detect an effect of the independent variable. As noted previously, in certain areas of research, these advantages are very important. However, the disadvantages of repeated measures designs and the precautions required to deal with them are usually sufficient reasons for researchers to use independent groups designs.

A very different consideration in whether to use a repeated measures design concerns generalization to conditions in the "real world." Greenwald (1976) has pointed out that in actual everyday situations, we sometimes encounter independent variables in an independent groups fashion: We encounter only one condition without a contrasting comparison. However, some independent variables are most frequently encountered in a repeated measures fashion: Both conditions appear, and our responses occur in the context of exposure to both levels of the independent variable. Thus, for example, if you are interested in how a defendant's characteristics affects jurors, an independent groups design may be most appropriate because actual jurors focus on a single defendant in a trial. However, if you are interested in the effects of a job applicant's characteristics on employers, a repeated measures design would be reasonable because employers typically consider several applicants at once. Whether to use an independent groups or repeated measures design may be partially determined by these generalization issues.

Finally, any experimental procedure that produces a relatively permanent change in an individual cannot be used in a repeated measures design. Examples include a psychotherapy treatment or a surgical procedure such as the removal of brain tissue.

Matched Pairs Design

A somewhat more complicated method of assigning participants to conditions in an experiment is called a **matched pairs design:** Instead of simply randomly assigning participants to groups, the goal is to first match people on a participant variable such as age or a personality trait. The matching variable will be either the dependent measure or a variable that is strongly related to the dependent variable. For example, in a learning experiment, participants might be matched on the basis of scores on a cognitive ability measure or even grade point average. If cognitive ability is not related to the dependent measure, however, matching would be a waste of time. The goal is to achieve the same equivalency of groups that is achieved with a repeated measures design without the necessity of having the same participants in both conditions. The design is shown below:

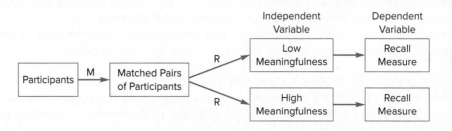

When using a matched pairs design, the first step is to obtain a measure of the matching variable from each individual. The participants are then rank ordered from highest to lowest based on their scores on the matching variable. Now the researcher can form matched pairs that are approximately equal on the characteristic (the highest two participants form the first pair, the next two form the second pair, and so on). Finally, the members of each pair are randomly assigned to the conditions in the experiment. (Note that there are methods of matching pairs of individuals on the basis of scores derived from multiple variables; these methods are described briefly in the chapter "Single-Case, Quasi-Experimental, and Developmental Research.")

A matched pairs design ensures that the groups are equivalent (on the matching variable) prior to introduction of the independent variable manipulation. This assurance could be particularly important with small sample sizes because random assignment procedures are more likely to produce equivalent groups as the sample size increases. Matching, then, is most likely to be used when only a few participants are available or when it is very costly to run large numbers of individuals in the experiment—as long as there is a strong relationship between a dependent measure and the matching variable. The result is a greater ability to detect a statistically significant effect of the independent variable because it is possible to account for individual differences in responses to the independent variable, just as we saw with a repeated measures design. (The issues of variability and statistical significance are discussed further in the chapter "Understanding Research Results: Statistical Inference" and in Appendix C.)

Check Your Learning

Assess your understanding of the designs discussed in this chapter by completing the Check Your Learning: Practice Exercise #2.

However useful they are, matching procedures can be costly and time-consuming, because they require measuring participants on the matching variable prior to the experiment. Such efforts are worthwhile only when the matching variable is strongly related to the dependent measure and you know that the relationship exists prior to conducting your study. For these reasons, matched pairs is not a commonly used experimental design. However, we will discuss matching again in the chapter "Single-Case, Quasi-Experimental, and Developmental Research" when describing quasi-experimental designs that do not have random assignment to conditions. You now have a fundamental understanding of the design of experiments. In the chapter "Conducting Experiments" we will consider issues that arise when you decide how to actually conduct an experiment.

ENGAGING WITH RESEARCH: EXPERIMENTAL DESIGN

Education reform is often focused on STEM education (i.e., education in science, technology, engineering, and math) in an effort to support future citizens and the workforce. Educational Robotics is a new educational approach that requires students to design, assemble, and program robots through play. Researchers have shown positive impacts of Educational Robotics learning on a wide range of developmental important variables: cognitive and learning processes, social communication, and STEM learning and attitudes. Recent studies have shown that education using Educational Robotics may affect cognitive development by improving critical reasoning and planning skills. Di Lieto et al. (2020) conducted a study to see if Educational Robotics training could impact children's cognitive executive functions in a sample of 187 neurotypical 5- and 6-year-old children.

For this exercise, acquire and read the following article (available at https://doi.org/10.3389/fpsyg.2019.03084):

> Di Lieto, M. C., Pecini, C., Castro, E., Inguaggiato, E., Cecchi, F., Dario, P., Cioni, G., & Sgandurra, G. (2020). Empowering executive functions in 5- and 6-year-old typically developing children through educational robotics: An RCT study. *Frontiers in Psychology, 10.* https://doi.org/10.3389/fpsyg.2019.03084

After reading the article, answer the following questions:

1. **What is the primary goal of this study? Description, Prediction, Determining Cause, or Explaining? Do the authors achieve their goals?**
2. **What did these researchers do? What was the method?**
   a. What was the independent variable? How many levels did the independent variable have? How were research participants assigned to groups?
   b. Was this study a independent groups design or a repeated measures design?

3. **What was measured? How was visuospatial memory measured?**
4. **To what or whom can we generalize the results?**
   a. Where did the participants from this study come from?
   b. Did the authors include information about the demographics of their sample?
5. **What did they find? What were the results?**
6. **Have other researchers found similar results?**
7. **What are the limitations of this study?**
8. **What are the ethical issues present in this study?**

BEING A SKILLED CONSUMER OF RESEARCH

1. Professor Foley conducted a cola taste test. Each participant in the experiment first tasted 2 ounces of Coca-Cola, then 2 ounces of Pepsi, and finally 2 ounces of Sam's Choice Cola. A rating of the cola's flavor was made after each taste. What are the potential problems with this experimental design and the procedures used? Revise the design and procedures to address these problems. Consider several alternatives and think about the advantages and disadvantages of each.

2. Dr. Kim wanted to study the impact of different volumes of music on dart-throwing performance. She hypothesized that distraction would affect dart-throwing skills. She decided to design a repeated measures experiment with three conditions: no music, soft music, and loud music. Answer these two questions:
   a. Why would she choose a repeated measures design?
   b. Her participants threw darts in a room with music volume set to none, soft, or loud. All subjects started in the no-music room, and then proceeded to the soft-music room and finally to the loud-music room. How could her study results be affected by these three order effects—practice, fatigue, carryover? How could Dr. Kim address these problems?

Check Your Learning: Practice Exercises

Practice Exercise #1

Design a repeated measures experiment that investigates the effect of report presentation style on the grade received for the report. Use two levels of the independent variable: a "professional style" presentation (correct spelling and grammar) and a "nonprofessional style" (spelling and grammar mistakes). Discuss the necessity for using counterbalancing. Create a table illustrating the experimental design.

Practice Exercise #2

Match the design on the left with the definition on the right

Design	Definition
1. Posttest-Only Design	A. A method of assigning subjects to groups in which pairs of subjects are first matched on some characteristic and then individually assigned randomly to groups.
2. Pretest-Posttest Design	B. An experiment in which different subjects are assigned to each group. Also called independent groups design.
3. Solomon Four-Group Design	C. A true experimental design in which the dependent variable (posttest) is measured only once, after manipulation of the independent variable.
4. Between-Subjects Design	D. An experiment in which the same subjects are assigned to each group.
5. Within-Subjects Design (also known as Repeated Measures Design)	E. A true experimental design in which the dependent variable is measured both before (pretest) and after (posttest) manipulation of the independent variable.
6. Matched Pairs Design	F. Experimental design in which the experimental and control groups are studied with and without a pretest.

(Some answers are provided at the end of this chapter.)

CHAPTER REVIEW

Review Questions

1. What is a confounding variable?
2. What is meant by the internal validity of an experiment?
3. How do the two true experimental designs eliminate the problem of selection differences?
4. Distinguish between the posttest-only design and the pretest-posttest design. What are the advantages and disadvantages of each?
5. What is a repeated measures design? What are the advantages of using a repeated measures design? What are the disadvantages?
6. What are ways of dealing with the problems of a repeated measures design, including counterbalancing?
7. When would a researcher decide to use the matched pairs design? What would be the advantages of this design?
8. The procedure used to obtain your sample (i.e., random or nonrandom sampling) is not the same as the procedure for assigning participants to conditions; distinguish between random sampling and random assignment.

Study Terms

Attrition (also mortality) (p. 186)

Between-subjects design (also independent groups design) (p. 188)

Carryover effect (p. 190)

Confounding variable (p. 182)

Counterbalancing (p. 191)

Fatigue effect (p. 190)

Independent groups design (also between-subjects design) (p. 188)

Internal validity (p. 183)

Latin square (p. 192)

Matched pairs design (p. 193)

Mortality (also attrition) (p. 186)

Order effect (p. 190)

Posttest-only design (p. 183)

Practice effect (also learning effect) (p. 190)

Pretest-posttest design (p. 184)

Random assignment (p. 188)

Repeated measures design (also within-subjects design) (p. 188)

Selection differences (p. 184)

Solomon four-group design (p. 186)

Within-subjects design (also repeated measures design) (p. 188)

Check Your Learning: Answers

Practice Exercise #2

1. C; 2. E; 3. F; 4. B; 5. D; 6. A

LeoPatrizi/Getty Images

9

Conducting Experiments

LEARNING OBJECTIVES

- Explain the differences between straightforward and staged manipulations of an independent variable.
- Distinguish among the three types of dependent variables: self-report, behavioral, and physiological.
- Discuss sensitivity of a dependent variable, contrasting floor effects and ceiling effects.
- Describe ways to control participant expectations and experimenter expectations.
- Summarize the reasons for conducting pilot studies.
- Describe the advantages of including a manipulation check in an experiment.

THE PREVIOUS CHAPTERS HAVE LAID THE FOUNDATION FOR PLANNING A RESEARCH INVESTIGATION. In this chapter, we will focus on some very practical aspects of conducting research: How do you select the research participants? What should you consider when deciding how to manipulate an independent variable? What should you worry about when you measure a variable? What do you do when the study is completed?

SELECTING RESEARCH PARTICIPANTS

The focus of your study may be children, college students, elderly adults, employees, rats, pigeons, or even cockroaches or flatworms; in all cases, the participants or subjects must somehow be selected. The method used to select participants can have a profound impact on the external validity of your study. Remember that external validity is defined as the extent to which results from a study can be generalized to other populations and settings.

Most research projects involve sampling research participants from a population of interest. The population is composed of all of the individuals of interest to the researcher. Samples may be drawn from the population using probability sampling or nonprobability sampling techniques. When it is important to accurately describe the population, you must use probability sampling. This is why probability sampling is so crucial when conducting scientific polls. Much research, on the other hand, is more interested in testing hypotheses about behavior: attempting to detect whether X causes Y rather than describing a population. Here, the study focuses on the relationships between the variables being studied and tests of predictions derived from theories of behavior. In such cases, the participants may be found in the easiest way possible using nonprobability sampling methods such as convenience sampling. You might ask students in introductory psychology classes to participate, obtain permission to distribute questionnaires to employees during their break time, or recruit participants using an online crowdsourcing platform such as Prolific or MTurk (Buhrmester et al., 2018; Chandler, 2017; Palan & Schitter, 2018). Nothing is wrong with such methods as long as you recognize that they affect the ability to generalize your results to some larger population. In chapter "Generalization," we examine the issues of generalizing from the rather atypical samples of college students and other conveniently obtained research participants.

Researchers also need to determine sample size. How many participants will they need in their study? In general, increasing the sample size increases the likelihood that your results will be statistically significant, because larger samples provide more accurate estimates of population values (see the chapter "Asking People About Themselves: Survey Research," Table 2). A more formal approach to determine sample size, called power analysis, is discussed in the chapter "Understanding Research Results: Description and Correlation."

MANIPULATING THE INDEPENDENT VARIABLE

To manipulate an independent variable, you have to construct an operational definition of the variable. That is, you must turn a conceptual variable into a set of operations—specific instructions, events, and stimuli to be presented to the research participants. The manipulation of the independent variable, then, is when a researcher changes the conditions to which participants are exposed. In addition, the independent and dependent variables must be introduced within the context of the total experimental setting. This has been called *setting the stage* (Wilson et al., 2010).

Setting the Stage

In setting the stage, you usually have to supply the participants with the information necessary for them to provide their informed consent to participate (informed consent is covered in the chapter "Ethics in Behavioral Research"). This generally includes information about the underlying rationale of the study. Sometimes the rationale given is completely truthful, although only rarely will you want to tell participants the actual hypothesis. For example, you might say that you are conducting an experiment on memory, when in fact you are studying a specific aspect of memory (your independent variable). If participants know what you are studying, they may try to confirm (or even deny) the hypothesis, or they may try to look good by behaving in the most socially acceptable way. If you find that deception is necessary, you have a special obligation to address the deception when you debrief the participants at the conclusion of the experiment.

There are no clear-cut rules for setting the stage, except that the experimental setting must seem plausible to the participants. Nor are there any clear-cut rules for translating conceptual variables into specific operations. Exactly how the variable is manipulated depends on the variable and the cost, practicality, and ethics of the procedures being considered.

Types of Manipulations

Straightforward Manipulations   Researchers are usually able to manipulate an independent variable with relative simplicity by presenting written, verbal, or visual material to the participants. Such **straightforward manipulations** manipulate variables with instructions and stimulus presentations. Stimuli may be presented verbally, in written form, via videotape, or with a computer. Let's look at a few examples.

Goldstein et al. (2008) were interested in the influence of signs that hotels leave in their bathrooms encouraging guests to reuse their towels. In their research, they simply printed signs that were hooked on towel shelves in the rooms of single guests staying at least two nights. In a standard message, the sign read "HELP SAVE THE ENVIRONMENT. You can show your respect for nature and help save the environment by reusing towels during your stay." In this case, 35% of the guests reused their towels on the second day. Another condition invoked a social norm that other people are reusing towels: "JOIN YOUR FELLOW GUESTS IN HELPING TO SAVE THE ENVIRONMENT. Almost 75% of guests who are asked to participate in our new resource savings program do help by using their towels more than once. You can join your fellow guests in this program to save the environment by reusing your towels during your stay." This sign resulted in 44% reusing their towels. As you might expect, the researchers have extended this research to study ways to make the sign even more effective in increasing conservation.

Most research on memory and cognition relies on straightforward manipulations. For example, Cushing and Bodner (2022) were interested in factors that might improve proofreading accuracy. Participants read eight brief, typed texts that contained errors; some errors were "noncontextual" (typos) and others were "contextual" (grammar, word choice). The independent variable was the reading situation: the material was read aloud or in silence. Participants in the read-aloud condition detected more errors of both types.

Studies involving the impact of education programs most often use straightforward manipulations. Pawlenko et al. (2013) examined the effectiveness of three educational training programs designed to improve jurors' ability to evaluate eyewitness testimony. Subjects viewed one of three 15-minute slide presentations on a computer screen. The Interview-Identification-Eyewitness training focused on three steps to analyze eyewitness evidence: Ask if the eyewitness interviews were done properly, ask if identification methods were proper, and evaluate if the conditions of the crime scene allowed for an accurate identification. A second presentation, *Biggers* Training, was a presentation of five eyewitness factors that the U.S. Supreme Court determined should be used (developed in a case called *Neil v. Biggers*). The Jury Duty presentation was a summary of standard information provided to jurors, such as the need to be fair and impartial and the importance of hearing all evidence before reaching a verdict. After viewing the presentations, subjects read a trial transcript that included problems with the eyewitness identification procedures. The subjects in the Interview-Identification-Eyewitness conditions were most likely to use these problems in reaching a verdict.

Or, consider the research conducted by De Groot et al. (2015) that studied reactions of student participants to a series of 16 tweets posted by a female professor. One professor posted professional content in her tweets (e.g., "Students considering careers in SM need to remember that your storytelling/writing skills are as important as knowledge of the SM platforms"). The other professor posted personal content focused on her personal life (e.g., "Just reserved my spot in a kickboxing class tonight. I've heard it's challenging but fun"). All of the subjects were experienced twitter users — the instructor posting the professional tweets was rated as more credible and competent than the instructor who posted personal information. You might wonder if TikTok videos posted by instructors would elicit the same reactions.

Finally, it may be possible to obtain existing stimulus materials that may be used in other investigations. Such materials may be available online in archives maintained by the author of a particular published investigation or by a third party developer of the materials. For example, the Bank of Standardized Stimuli (BOSS) consists of a large number of photos that have been rated on dimensions such as familiarity and visual complexity (Brodeur et al., 2014). Hies and Lewis (2022) used a face database to obtain stimuli for a study on perceptions of people wearing masks during the COVID pandemic. The Chicago Face Database is a set of frontal faces of 85 Black and 73 White individuals, photographed under identical circumstances wearing a neutral t-shirt and shown against a plain white background (Ma et al., 2015). The faces have been rated on attractiveness and other dimensions. Heis and Lewis used male faces as stimuli; faces were shown to female subjects with no mask, a medical mask, and a patterned cloth "kerchief" mask. The medical mask faces were rated more attractive than the cloth mask and both were more attractive than the no mask faces. It should be noted that the study was conducted seven months after mask mandates had been in effect during the COVID pandemic.

You will find that most manipulations of independent variables in all areas of research are straightforward. Researchers vary in a straightforward manner the difficulty of material to be learned, the way questions are asked, characteristics of people to be judged, and a variety of other factors.

Staged Manipulations

Other manipulations are less straightforward. Sometimes it is necessary to stage events during the experiment in order to manipulate the independent variable successfully. When this occurs, the manipulation is called a **staged manipulation** or *event manipulation*.

Staged manipulations are most frequently used for one of two reasons. First, the researcher may be trying to create some psychological state in the participants, such as frustration, anger, or a temporary lowering or raising of self-esteem. For example, Zitek and her colleagues studied what is termed a *sense of entitlement* that occurs when a person has been unfairly treated (Zitek et al., 2010). The sense of entitlement leads to behaving more selfishly with others. In their study, all participants played a computer game. The researchers programmed the game so that some participants would lose when the game crashed. This is an unfair outcome because the participants lost for no good reason. Participants in the other condition also lost, but they thought it was because the game itself was very difficult. The participants experiencing the broken game did in fact behave more selfishly after the game; they later allocated themselves more money than deserved when competing with another participant.

Second, a staged manipulation may be necessary in order to simulate some situation that occurs in the real world. In the Milgram obedience study, an elaborate procedure—ostensibly to study learning—was constructed to actually study obedience to an authority (see the chapter "Ethics in Behavioral Research"). Or consider a study on computer multitasking conducted by Bowman et al. (2010), wherein students read academic material presented on a computer screen. In one condition, the participants received and responded to instant messages while they were reading. Other participants did not receive any messages. Student performance on a test was equal in the two conditions. However, students in the instant message condition took longer to read the material (after the time spent on the message was subtracted from the total time working on the computer).

Staged manipulations frequently employ a **confederate** (sometimes termed an "accomplice"). Usually the confederate appears to be another participant in an experiment but is actually part of the manipulation. A confederate may be useful to create a particular social situation. For example, Forrin et al. (2021) studied how the behavior of one student in a learning situation might affect the behavior of another. They proposed that inattention (or attention) to learning could spread, a phenomenon called "attention contagion." In an experiment, pairs of undergraduate students watched a recorded lecture. One student was a confederate who was seated in front of the actual participant. An attentive confederate leaned forward to pay close attention throughout the video, and took notes during the lecture. The inattentive confederate was distracted by glancing at the clock during the lecture, slouching in the chair, and failing to take notes. The confederate's behavior did in fact affect the actual student with students in the attentive confederate condition taking more notes and demonstrating better memory of the lecture.

The classic Asch (1956) conformity experiment provides another example of how confederates may be used. Asch gathered people into groups and asked them to respond to a line judgment task such as the one in Figure 1. Which of the three test lines matches the standard? Although this appears to be a simple task, Asch made it more interesting by having several confederates announce the same incorrect judgment prior to asking the actual participant; this procedure was repeated over a number of trials with different line judgments. Asch was able to demonstrate how easy it is to produce conformity—participants conformed to the unanimous majority on many of the trials even though the correct answer was clear.

Finally, confederates may be used in field experiments as well as laboratory research. Finally, confederates may be used in field experiments as well as laboratory research. Randall et al. (2017) investigated weight discrimination in a field experiment conducted on a college campus. Male and female confederates approached students walking toward the entrance of the student center and asked them to help out by signing a petition. The confederates wore their regular size M clothing appropriate for the campus or they put on a prosthetic to add apparent weight with size XXL clothing. The subjects in this study were less likely to sign the petitions

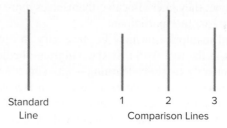

Standard
Line

1   2   3
Comparison Lines

FIGURE 1
Example of the Asch line judgment task

presented by the heavy-weight female confederates. However, they were equally likely to sign the petitions of the male confederates, regardless of weight.

As you can see, staged manipulations demand a great deal of creativity and ingenuity, and even some acting ability. They are used to involve the participants in an ongoing social situation that the individuals perceive not as an experiment but as a real experience. Researchers assume that the result will be natural behavior that truly reflects the feelings and intentions of the participants. However, such procedures allow for a great deal of subtle interpersonal communication that is hard to put into words; this may make it difficult for other researchers to replicate the experiment. Also, a complex manipulation is difficult to interpret. If many things happened during the experiment, what *one* thing was responsible for the results? In general, it is easier to interpret results when the manipulation is relatively straightforward. However, the nature of the variable you are studying sometimes demands complicated procedures.

Check Your Learning

Now, test your understanding of staged versus straightforward manipulation by completing Check Your Learning: Practice Exercise #1 at the end of the chapter.

Strength of the Manipulation

The simplest experimental design has two levels of the independent variable. In planning the experiment, the researcher has to choose these levels. A general principle to follow is to make the manipulation as strong as possible; the **strength of manipulation** matters. A strong manipulation maximizes the differences between the two groups and increases the chances that the independent variable will have a statistically significant effect on the dependent variable.

To illustrate, suppose you think that there is a positive linear relationship between attitude similarity and liking ("birds of a feather flock together"). In conducting the experiment, you could arrange for participants to encounter a person who is a confederate. In one group, the confederate and the participant would share similar attitudes; in the other group, the confederate and the participant would have dissimilar attitudes. Similarity, then, is the independent variable, and liking is the dependent variable. Now you have to decide on the amount of similarity. Figure 2 shows the hypothesized relationship between attitude similarity and liking at 10 different levels of similarity. Level 1 represents the least amount of similarity, with no common attitudes, and level 10 the greatest amount of similarity (all attitudes are similar). To achieve the strongest manipulation, the participants in one group would encounter a confederate of level 1 similarity; those in the other group would encounter a confederate of level 10 similarity. This would result in the greatest difference in the liking means—a 9-point difference. A weaker manipulation—using levels 4 and 7, for example—would result in a smaller mean difference.

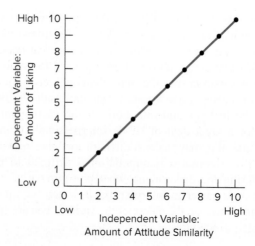

FIGURE 2
Relationship between attitude similarity and liking

A strong manipulation is particularly important in the early stages of research, when the researcher is most interested in demonstrating that a relationship does, in fact, exist. If the early experiments reveal a relationship between the variables, subsequent research can systematically manipulate the other levels of the independent variable to provide a more detailed picture of the relationship.

The principle of using the strongest manipulation possible should be tempered by at least two considerations. The first concerns the external validity of a study: The strongest possible manipulation may entail a situation that rarely, if ever, occurs in the real world. For example, an extremely strong crowding manipulation might involve placing so many people in a room that no one could move—a manipulation that might significantly affect a variety of behaviors. However, we would not know if the results were similar to those occurring in more common, less crowded situations, such as many classrooms or offices.

A second consideration is ethics: A manipulation should be as strong as possible within the bounds of ethics. A strong manipulation of fear or anxiety, for example, might not be possible because of the potential physical and psychological harm to participants.

Cost of the Manipulation

Cost is another factor in the decision about how to manipulate the independent variable. Researchers with limited monetary resources may not be able to afford expensive equipment, salaries for confederates, or payments to participants in long-term experiments. Also, a manipulation in which participants must be run individually requires more of the researcher's time than a manipulation that allows running many individuals in a single setting. In this respect, a manipulation that uses straightforward presentation of written or verbal material is less costly than a complex, staged experimental manipulation. Some government and private agencies offer grants for research; because much research is costly, continued public support of these agencies is very important.

MEASURING THE DEPENDENT VARIABLE

In previous chapters we have discussed various aspects of measuring variables, including reliability, validity, and reactivity of measures; observational methods; and the development of self-report measures for questionnaires and interviews. In this section, we will focus on measurement considerations that are particularly relevant to experimental research.

Types of Measures

The dependent variable in most experiments is one of three general types: self-report, behavioral, or physiological.

Self-Report Measures

Self-reports can be used to measure attitudes, liking for someone, judgments about someone's personality characteristics, intended behaviors, emotional states, attributions about why someone performed well or poorly on a task, confidence in one's judgments, and many other aspects of human thought and behavior. The most commonly used rating scales are those with descriptive anchors (endpoints). For example, Funk and Todorov (2013) studied the impact of a facial tattoo on impressions of a man accused of assault. The man, Jack, had punched another man in a bar following a dispute over a spilled drink. A description of the incident included a photo of Jack with or without a facial tattoo. After viewing the photo and reading the description, subjects responded to several questions on a 7-point scale that included the following:

How likely is it that Jack is guilty?

Very unlikely ☐ ☐ ☐ ☐ ☐ ☐ ☐ Very likely

Behavioral Measures

Behavioral measures are direct observations of behaviors. As with self-reports, it is possible to measure an almost endless number of behaviors. Sometimes the researcher might record whether a given behavior occurs—for example, whether an individual responds to a request for help, makes an error on a test, or chooses to engage in one activity rather than another. Often the researcher needs to quantify observed behaviors:

- Rate of a behavior—how many times the behavior occurs in a given time period
- Reaction time—how quickly a response occurs after a stimulus (e.g., a sound, a light, a word)
- Duration—how long a behavior persists

The decision about which aspect of behavior to measure depends on which aspect is most theoretically relevant for the study of a particular problem or which measure logically follows from the independent variable manipulation.

As an example, consider a study on eating behavior while viewing either a food-related or a nature television program (Bodenlos & Wormuth, 2013). Participants had access to chocolate-covered candies, cheese curls, and carrots; all snacks were weighed before and after the session. More candy was consumed during the food-related program; there were no differences for the other two foods.

Sometimes the behavioral measure is not an actual behavior but a behavioral intention or choice. In a study on aggression after being provoked by another subject, participants decided how much hot sauce the other subject would have to consume later in the study (Vasquez et al., 2013). They did not actually pour the hot sauce, but they did commit to an action rather than simply indicate their feelings about the other subject.

Physiological Measures   **Physiological measures** are recordings of responses of the body. Many such measurements are available; examples include the **galvanic skin response (GSR), electromyogram (EMG),** and **electroencephalogram (EEG).** The GSR is a measure of general emotional arousal and anxiety; it measures the electrical conductance of the skin, which changes when sweating occurs. The EMG measures muscle tension and is frequently used as a measure of tension or stress. The EEG is a measure of electrical activity of brain cells. It can be used to record general brain arousal as a response to different situations, such as activity in certain parts of the brain as learning occurs or brain activity during different stages of sleep.

The GSR, EMG, and EEG have long been used as physiological indicators of important psychological variables. Measures are available for many other physiological variables, including temperature, heart rate, and analysis of blood or urine (see Cacioppo & Cacioppo, 2020; Cacioppo & Tassinary, 1990). In recent years, **MRI (magnetic resonance imagery)** has become an increasingly important tool for researchers in behavioral neuroscience. An MRI provides an image of an individual's brain structure. It allows scientists to compare the brain structure of individuals with a particular condition (e.g., a cognitive impairment, schizophrenia, attention deficit hyperactivity disorder) with the brain structure of people without the condition. In addition, a **functional MRI (fMRI)** allows researchers to scan areas of the brain while a research participant performs a physical or cognitive task, or experiences something new in the environment. The data provide evidence for what brain processes are involved in these situations. The nucleus accumbens (NAcc) is an area of the brain that has drawn increasing attention of neuroscientists because of its role in human emotions and motivation — pleasures, rewards, and satisfaction (Salgado & Kaplitt, 2015). Researchers have used fMRI to study how NAcc is involved with the intense emotion of love. In one study, the fMRI of research participants who were romantically involved showed a different NAcc response when they anticipated seeing a positive facial expression by their partner compared to someone unfamiliar (Ueda and Abe, 2021).

Advances in technology are opening many new doors in measurement. Wang et al. (2021) used a technology called the Contain Intelligent Facial Expression Recognition System (CIFERS) to explore real-time emotions (joy and anxiety) of college students. This facial recognition software was employed while the students' faces were broadcast from remote locations via an online meeting application (Zoom). Eye-tracking devices are used to provide information on eye fixation and movements. They may use a computer screen that displays stimuli or special glasses or a head monitor that will allow eye-tracking in the subject's natural or even virtual reality environment. They have become less expensive and easier to use in recent years. Eye-tracking has been used to study topics ranging from marketing (Wedel, 2015), to processing of written text (Olkoniemi & Kaakinen, 2021), autism (Andreou & Raxioni, 2022; Mastergeorge et al., 2021), and other attention processes (e.g., Günther et al., 2021). This research is relatively new so researchers should be aware of issues such as validity when interpreting data (Orquin & Holmqvist, 2018).

Check Your Learning

Now test your understanding of the three basic types of dependent measures by completing Check Your Learning: Practice Exercise #2 at the end of the chapter.

Multiple Measures

Although it is convenient to describe single dependent variables, most studies include more than one dependent measure. One reason to use multiple measures stems from the fact that a variable can be measured in a variety of concrete ways (recall the discussion of operational definitions in the chapter "Fundamental Research Issues"). In a study on the effects of an employee wellness program on health, the researchers might measure self-reported fatigue, stress, physical activity, and eating habits along with physical measures of blood pressure, blood sugar, cholesterol, and weight (see Clark et al., 2011). If the independent variable has the same effect on several measures of the same dependent variable, our confidence in the results is increased. It is also useful to know whether the same independent variable affects some measures but not others. For example, an independent variable designed to affect liking might have an effect on some measures of liking (e.g., desirability as a person to work with) but not others (e.g., desirability as a dating partner). Researchers may also be interested in studying the effects of an independent variable on several different behaviors. For example, an experiment on the effects of a new classroom management technique might examine academic performance, interaction rates among classmates, and teacher satisfaction.

When you have more than one dependent measure, the question of *order* arises. Does it matter which measures are made first? Is it possible that the results for a particular measure will be different if the measure comes earlier rather than later? The issue is similar to the order effects that were discussed in the chapter "Experimental Design" in the context of repeated measures designs. Perhaps responding to the first measures will somehow affect responses on the later measures, or perhaps the participants attend more closely to first measures than to later measures. There are two possible ways of responding to this issue. If it appears that the problem is serious, the order of presenting the measures can be counterbalanced using the techniques described in the chapter "Experimental Design." Often there are no indications from previous research that order is a serious problem. In this case, the prudent response is to present the most important measures first and the less important ones later. With this approach, order will not be a problem in interpreting the results on the most important dependent variables. Even though order may be a potential problem for some of the measures, the overall impact on the study is minimized.

Making multiple measurements in a single experiment is valuable when it is feasible to do so. However, it may be necessary to conduct a separate series of experiments to explore the effects of an independent variable on various behaviors.

Sensitivity of the Dependent Variable

The dependent variable should be sensitive enough to detect differences between groups. A measure of liking that asks "Do you like this person?" with only a simple "yes" or "no" response alternative is less sensitive than one that asks "How much do you like this person?" on a 5- or 7-point scale. With the first measure, people may tend to be nice and say yes even if they have some negative feelings about the person. The second measure allows for a gradation of liking; such a scale would make it easier to detect differences in amount of liking.

The issue of **sensitivity** is particularly important when measuring human performance. Memory can be measured using recall, recognition, or reaction time; cognitive task performance might be measured by examining speed or number of errors during a proofreading task; physical performance can be measured through various motor tasks. Such tasks vary in their difficulty. Sometimes a task is so easy that everyone does well regardless of the conditions that are manipulated by the independent variable. This results in what is called a **ceiling effect**—the independent variable appears to have no effect on the dependent measure only because participants quickly reach the maximum performance level. The opposite problem occurs when a task is so difficult that hardly anyone can perform well; this is called a **floor effect.**

The need to consider sensitivity of measures is nicely illustrated by a study examining the effect of crowding on various measures of cognitive task performance (Freedman et al., 1971). In the study, crowding did not impair performance. You could conclude that crowding has no effect on performance; however, it is also possible that the measures were either too easy or too difficult to detect an effect of crowding. In fact, subsequent research showed that the tasks may have been too easy; when subjects perform complex cognitive tasks in laboratory or natural settings, crowding does result in lower performance (Bruins & Barber, 2000; Paulus et al., 1976).

Cost of Measures

Another consideration is cost—some measures may be more costly than others. Paper-and-pencil self-report measures are generally inexpensive; measures that require trained observers or elaborate equipment can become quite costly. A researcher studying nonverbal behavior, for example, might have to use a video camera to record each participant's behaviors in a situation. Two or more observers would then have to view the tapes to code behaviors such as eye contact, smiling, or self-touching (two observers are needed to ensure that the observations are reliable). Thus, there would be expenses for both equipment and personnel. Physiological recording devices are also expensive. Researchers need resources from the university or outside agencies to carry out such research.

ADDITIONAL CONTROLS

The basic experimental design has two groups: in the simplest case, an experimental group that receives the treatment and a control group that does not. Use of a control group makes it possible to eliminate a variety of alternative explanations for the results, thus improving internal validity. Sometimes additional control procedures may be necessary to address other types of alternative explanations. Two general control issues concern participant expectations and experimenter expectations.

Controlling for Participant Expectations

Demand Characteristics   We noted previously that experimenters generally do not wish to inform participants about the specific hypotheses being studied or the exact purpose of the research. The reason for this lies in the problem of **demand characteristics** (Orne, 1962), which is any feature of an experiment that might inform participants of the purpose of the study. The concern is that when participants form expectations about the hypothesis of the study, they will then do whatever is necessary to confirm the hypothesis. For a research subject, there can be many sources of cues about the study's hypothesis. The title of the study could be a cue. Something the experimenter emphasizes when reading instructions could be a cue. Participants can also draw inferences based on the study's procedures. For example, consider a study where, after being shown 20 photos of nature scenes, subjects rate their current mood (e.g., happy–sad, calm–excited). It is easy to imagine that subjects would guess that "these kinds of photos are supposed to make people feel more calm and relaxed." Agreeable subjects might describe themselves as more relaxed because of this conclusion about the purpose of the study.

One way to control for demand characteristics is to use deception—to make participants think that the experiment is studying one thing when actually it is studying something else. The experimenter may devise elaborate cover stories to explain the purpose of the study and to disguise what is really being studied. The researcher may also attempt to disguise the dependent variable by using an unobtrusive measure or by placing the measure among a set of unrelated **filler items** on a questionnaire. Another approach is simply to assess whether demand characteristics are a problem by asking participants about their perceptions of the purpose of the research. It may be that participants do not have an accurate view of the purpose of the study; or if some individuals do guess the hypotheses of the study, their data may be analyzed separately.

Demand characteristics may be eliminated when people are not aware that an experiment is taking place or that their behavior is being observed. Thus, experiments conducted in field settings and observational research in which the observer is concealed or unobtrusive measures are used minimize the problem of demand characteristics.

Placebo Groups

A special kind of participant expectation arises in research on the effects of drugs. Consider an experiment that is investigating whether a drug such as Prozac reduces depression. One group of people diagnosed as depressive receives the drug and the other group receives nothing. Now suppose that the drug group shows an improvement. We do not know whether the improvement was caused by the properties of the drug or by the participants' expectations about the effect of the drug—what is called a *placebo effect*. In other words, just administering a pill or an injection may be sufficient to cause an observed improvement in behavior. To control for this possibility, a **placebo group** can be added. Participants in the placebo group receive a pill or injection containing an inert, harmless substance; they do not receive the drug given to members of the experimental group. If the improvement results from the active properties of the drug, the participants in the experimental group should show greater improvement than those in the placebo group. If the placebo group improves as much as the experimental group, all improvement could be caused by a placebo effect.

Sometimes participants' expectations are the primary focus of an investigation. For example, De Vita et al. (2021) conducted research to examine the pain-reducing effects of cannabidiol (CBD) and determine the degree to which observed pain reduction is due to the effects of CBD as opposed to the psychological expectancies associated with this substance. The experimental design to examine these effects had four groups: (1) expect an inactive placebo—receive a placebo; (2) expect an inactive placebo—receive CBD; (3) expect CBD—receive the placebo; and (4) expect CBD—receive CBD. This design is called a *balanced placebo design* (Marlatt and Rohsenow, 1980). De Vita et al. reported that the three conditions in which the cannabidiol was expected or given (Groups 2, 3, and 4) produced lowered pain reports. The highest reported pain level was experienced by subjects expecting and receiving a placebo (Group 1).

In some areas of research, the use of placebo control groups has ethical implications. Suppose you are studying a treatment that does have a positive effect on people (for example, by reducing migraine headaches or alleviating symptoms of depression). It is important to use careful experimental procedures to make sure that the treatment does have an impact and that alternative explanations for the effect, including a placebo effect, are eliminated. However, it is also important to help those people who are in the control conditions; this aligns with the concept of beneficence that was covered in the chapter "Ethics in Behavioral Research."

Placebo effects are real and must receive serious study in many areas of research. A great deal of current research and debate focuses on the extent to which any beneficial effects of antidepressant medications, such as Prozac, are due to placebo effects (e.g., Kirsch, 2010; Wampold et al., 2005).

Controlling for Experimenter Expectations

Experimenters are usually aware of the purpose of the study and thus may develop expectations about how participants should respond. These expectations can in turn bias the results. This general problem is called **expectancy effects** or *experimenter bias* (Rosenthal, 1966, 1967, 1969).

Expectancy effects may occur whenever the experimenter knows which condition the participants are in. There are two potential sources of experimenter bias. First, the experimenter might unintentionally treat participants differently in the various conditions of the study. For example, certain words might be emphasized when reading instructions to one group but not the other, or the experimenter might smile more when interacting with people in one of the conditions. The second source of bias can occur when experimenters record the behaviors of the participants; there may be subtle differences in the way the experimenter interprets and records the behaviors.

Research on Expectancy Effects   Expectancy effects have been studied in a variety of ways. Perhaps the earliest demonstration of the problem is the case of Clever Hans, a horse with alleged mathematical and other abilities that attracted the attention of Europeans in the early 20th century (Rosenthal, 1967). The owner of the horse posed questions to Hans, who in turn would provide answers by tapping his hoof (e.g., the question "What is two times five?" would be followed by 10 taps). Pfungst (1911) later showed that Hans was actually responding to barely detectable cues provided by the person asking the question. The person would look at the hoof as Hans started to tap and then changed to look at Hans as the correct answer was about to be given. Hans was responding to these head and eye movements that went undetected by observers.

If a clever horse can respond to subtle cues, it is reasonable to suppose that clever humans can too. In fact, research has shown that experimenter expectancies can be communicated to humans by both verbal and nonverbal means (Duncan et al., 1969; Jones & Cooper, 1971). An example of more systematic research on expectancy effects is a study by Rosenthal (1966). In this experiment, graduate students trained rats that were described as coming from either "maze bright" or "maze dull" genetic strains. The animals actually came from the same strain and had been randomly assigned to the bright and dull categories; however, the "bright" rats *did* perform better than the "dull" rats! Subtle differences in the ways the students treated the rats or recorded their behavior must have caused this result. A generalization of this particular finding is called "teacher expectancy."

Research has shown that telling a teacher that a pupil will bloom intellectually over the next year results in an increase in the pupil's IQ score (Rosenthal & Jacobson, 1968). In short, teachers' expectations can influence students' performance. More recently, Jacoby-Senghor et al. (2016) conducted an experiment and found that instructors' implicit bias predicted Black participants' test performance, suggesting that underperformance by minoritized individuals in academic domains could be affected by educators' implicit racial biases.

The problem of expectations influencing ratings of behavior is nicely illustrated in an experiment by Langer and Abelson (1974). Clinical psychologists were shown a videotape of an interview in which the person interviewed was described as either an applicant for a job or a patient; in reality, all saw the same tape. The psychologists later rated the person as more "disturbed" when they thought the person was a patient than when the person was described as a job applicant. More recently, Sodos et al. (2018) found an "examiner" expectancy effect with 41 cannabis users and 20 non-users. Before testing the research participants, examiners privately rated whether they believed the examinee was a cannabis user or not. Next, examiners administered a battery of neuropsychological tests, including the California Verbal Learning Test, the National Adult Reading Test, and the Word Memory Test. Sodos et al. found that participants who were judged as cannabis users scored lower than those who were judged as non-users. That is, examiners' judgments of cannabis user status predicted scores on neuropsychological test performance—examiner's judgments seemed to influence performance.

Solutions to the Expectancy Problem
Clearly, experimenter expectations can influence the outcomes of research investigations. How can this problem be solved? Fortunately, there are a number of ways to minimize expectancy effects. First, experimenters should be well trained and should practice behaving consistently with all participants. The benefit of training was illustrated in the Langer and Abelson (1974) study with clinical psychologists. The bias of rating the "patient" as disturbed was much less among behavior-oriented therapists than among traditional ones. Presumably, the training of the behavior-oriented therapists led them to focus more on the actual behavior of the person, so they were less influenced by expectations stemming from the label "patient."

Another solution is to run all conditions simultaneously so that the experimenter's behavior is the same for all participants. However, this solution is feasible only under certain circumstances, such as when the study can be carried out with the use of printed materials or the experimenter's instructions to participants are the same for everyone.

Expectancy effects are also minimized when the procedures are automated. As noted earlier in this chapter, it may be possible to manipulate independent variables and record responses using computers; with automated procedures, the experimenter's expectations are less likely to influence the results.

A final solution is to use experimenters who are unaware of the hypothesis being investigated. In these cases, the person conducting the study or making observations is blind regarding what is being studied or which condition the participant is in. This procedure originated in drug research using placebo groups. In a **single-blind experiment,** the participant is unaware of whether a placebo or the actual drug is being administered; in a **double-blind experiment,** neither the participant nor the experimenter knows whether the placebo or actual treatment is being given. To use a procedure in which the experimenter or observer is unaware of either the hypothesis or the group the participant is in, you must hire other people to conduct the experiment and make observations.

Because researchers are aware of the problem of expectancy effects, solutions such as the ones just described are usually incorporated into the procedures of the study. The procedures used in scientific research must be precisely defined so they can be replicated by others. This allows other researchers to build on previous research. If a study does have a potential problem of expectancy effects, researchers are bound to notice and will attempt to replicate the experiment with procedures that control for them. It is also a self-correcting mechanism that ensures that methodological flaws will be discovered. The importance of replication will be discussed further in the chapter "Generalization."

FINAL PLANNING CONSIDERATIONS

So far we have discussed several of the factors that a researcher considers when planning a study. Actually conducting the study and analyzing the results are time-consuming processes. Before beginning the research, the investigator wants to be as sure as possible that everything will be done right. And once the study has been designed, there are some additional procedures that will improve it.

Research Proposals

After putting considerable thought into planning the study, the researcher writes a research proposal. The proposal will include a literature review that provides a background for the study. The intent is to clearly explain why the research is being done—what questions the research is designed to answer. The details of the procedures that will be used to test the idea are then given. The plans for analysis of the data are also provided. A research proposal is very similar to the introduction and method sections of a journal article. Such proposals must be included in applications for research grants; ethics review committees require some type of proposal as well (see the chapter "Ethics in Behavioral Research" for more information on Institutional Review Boards).

When planning any research project, it is a good idea to prepare a proposal, because simply putting your thoughts on paper will help you organize and systematize your ideas. In addition, you can show the proposal to friends, colleagues, professors, and other interested parties who can provide useful feedback about the adequacy of your procedures. They may see problems that you did not recognize, or they may offer ways of improving the study.

Pilot Studies

When the researcher has finally decided on all the specific aspects of the procedure, it is possible to conduct a **pilot study** in which the researcher does a trial
run with a small number of participants. The pilot study will reveal whether
participants understand the instructions, whether the total experimental setting
seems plausible, whether any confusing questions are being asked, and so on.

Sometimes participants in the pilot study are questioned in detail about the
experience following the experiment. Another method is to use the think-aloud
protocol, in which the participants in the pilot study are instructed to verbalize
their thoughts about everything that is happening during the study. Such procedures provide the researcher with an opportunity to make any necessary changes
in the procedure before doing the entire study. Also, a pilot study allows the
experimenters who are collecting the data to become comfortable with their roles
and to standardize their procedures.

Manipulation Checks

A **manipulation check** is an attempt to directly measure whether the independent
variable manipulation has the intended effect on the participants. Manipulation
checks provide evidence for the construct validity of the manipulation. If you are
manipulating anxiety, for example, a manipulation check will tell you whether
participants in the high-anxiety group really were more anxious than those in the
low-anxiety condition. The manipulation check might involve a self-report of anxiety, a behavioral measure (such as number of arm and hand movements), or a
physiological measure. All manipulation checks, then, ask whether the manipulation of the independent variable was in fact a successful operationalization of the
conceptual variable being studied. Consider, for example, a manipulation of physical attractiveness as an independent variable. In an experiment, participants
respond to someone who is supposed to be perceived as attractive or unattractive.
The manipulation check in this case would determine whether participants do rate
the highly attractive person as more physically attractive.

There is some debate about the use of manipulation checks (Ejelöv and Luke,
2020; Hauser et al., 2018). One concern is that the manipulation check might
serve as a demand characteristic, alerting subjects to the purpose of the study. As
a precaution, it is usually wise to position the administration of the manipulation
check measure near the end of the experiment; in most cases, this would be after
measuring the dependent variables and prior to the debriefing session. The problem here is that the effect of the independent variable may have weakened over
time. The preferred use of a manipulation check may be in the pilot study (Hauser
et al., 2018). In the pilot study, the manipulation check can become a focus, perhaps using several measurement methods including interviewing subjects. If the
pilot study feedback leads to a conclusion that the independent variable manipulation is not effective, the procedures can be changed prior to investing time and
effort into the larger experiment.

A manipulation check has two advantages. First, if the check shows that your manipulation was not effective, you have saved the expense of running the actual experiment. You can turn your attention to changing the manipulation to make it more effective. For instance, if the manipulation check shows that neither the low-nor the high-anxiety group was very anxious, you could change your procedures to increase the anxiety in the high-anxiety condition.

Second, a manipulation check is advantageous if you get nonsignificant results—that is, if the results indicate that no relationship exists between the independent and dependent variables. A manipulation check can identify whether the nonsignificant results are due to a problem in manipulating the independent variable. If your manipulation is not successful, it is only reasonable that you will obtain nonsignificant results. If both groups are equally anxious after you manipulate anxiety, anxiety cannot have any effect on the dependent measure. What if the check shows that the manipulation was successful, but you still get nonsignificant results? Then you know at least that the results were not due to a problem with the manipulation; the reason for not finding a relationship lies elsewhere. Perhaps you had a poor dependent measure, or perhaps there really is no relationship between the variables.

Debriefing

After all the data are collected, a debriefing session is usually held. This is an opportunity for the researcher to interact with the participants to discuss the ethical and educational implications of the study. The debriefing session can also provide an opportunity to learn more about what participants were thinking during the experiment. Researchers can ask participants what they believed to be the purpose of the experiment, how they interpreted the independent variable manipulation, and what they were thinking when they responded to the dependent measures. Such information can prove useful in interpreting the results and planning future studies.

Finally, researchers may ask the participants to refrain from discussing the study with others. Such requests are typically made when more people will be participating and they may talk with one another in classes or residence halls. People who have already participated are aware of the general purposes and procedures; it is important that these individuals not provide expectancies about the study to potential future participants.

Open Science and Preregistration

As you have been reading research articles, you may have come across a statement like this, from Sommet et al. (2022): "We conducted four preregistered studies to test this idea)" along with statements like "In Study 1, we aimed to test the following preregistered hypotheses: Income inequality is a positive predictor of perceived competitiveness (Hypothesis 1A) and a negative predictor of perceived cooperativeness (Hypothesis 1B)" (see "Preregistration (PISA) 2018.pdf" on https://osf.io/mz3tn/).

What is preregistration?

The Open Science movement emerged as a response to threats to the integrity of modern science. As we noted in the chapter "Observational Methods" in the Open Science and Data Accessibility section, the Center for Open Science (https://cos.io/) is dedicated to "increasing the openness, integrity, and reproducibility of scientific research." We will come back to the idea of reproducibility—one of the most important topics in science—in the chapter "Generalization." Here, we will focus briefly on the concept of preregistration, the process by which researchers identify and articulate their research questions, hypotheses, and analysis plan for their studies before they collect and analyze data.

Science is a process; when that process works, over time, uncertainty is reduced. As we study a phenomenon, we understand it better. The integrity of the process directly influences the quality of those outcomes. In the chapter "Where to Start," we defined the fundamental concepts of a research question, hypothesis, and prediction. One of the underpinnings of science is that we make predictions that are confirmed or not confirmed by the results of our research.

Suppose you are part of a research team that has designed an app to help improve sleep quality. Before proceeding, you need to design a study that will test the hypothesis that using the app will improve sleep. If you "preregister" the study with an independent registry (e.g., https://osf.io/), the plan is preserved and accessible to all. In the preregistration process, your research team would describe the planned research methods and data analysis. This commits you and your team to "define the research questions and analysis plan before observing any outcomes to the study" (Nosek et al., 2018). The preregistration is a public disclosure of how your study will be conducted and how the data will be analyzed; because this disclosure occurs before you begin, other scientists and ultimately the public may be more confident in the results. Without preregistration, you could continue to refine the study design until the data supports your hypothesis. Or, you could keep analyzing the data until it shows "what you want." Preregistration is an attempt to manage this problem. As Nosek et al. (2018) noted, "With preregistration, prediction is achieved because selection of tests is not influenced by the observed data, and all conducted tests are knowable. The analysis plan provides constraint to specify how the data will be used to confront the research questions."

So your final planning consideration would be to preregister your study and analysis plan in an open-access archive. It is to commit an act of open science.

ANALYZING AND INTERPRETING RESULTS

After the data have been collected, the next step is to analyze them. Statistical analyses of the data are carried out to allow the researcher to examine and interpret the pattern of results obtained in the study. The statistical analysis helps the researcher decide whether there really is a relationship between the independent and dependent variables. The logic underlying the use of statistical tests is discussed in the chapter "Understanding Research Results: Statistical Inference."

It is not the purpose of this book to teach statistical methods; however, the calculations involved in several statistical tests are provided in Appendix C.

COMMUNICATING RESEARCH TO OTHERS

The final step is to write a report that details why you conducted the research, how you obtained the participants, what procedures you used, and what you found. A description of how to write such reports is included in Appendix A. After you have written the report, what do you do with it? How do you communicate the findings to others? Research findings are most often submitted as journal articles or as papers to be read at scientific meetings. In either case, the submitted paper is evaluated by two or more knowledgeable reviewers who decide whether the paper is accepted for publication or presentation at the meeting.

Professional Meetings

Meetings sponsored by professional associations are important opportunities for researchers to present their findings to other researchers and the public. National and regional professional associations such as the American Psychological Association (APA) and the Association for Psychological Science (APS) hold annual meetings at which psychologists and students present their own research and learn about the latest research being done by their colleagues. Some findings are reported in verbal presentations delivered to an audience. However, poster sessions are more common; here, researchers display posters that summarize the research and the researchers are available to discuss the research with others.

Journal Articles

As we noted in the chapter "Where to Start," many journals publish research papers. Nevertheless, the number of journals is small compared to the number of reports written; thus, it is not easy to publish research. When a researcher submits a paper to a journal, two or more reviewers read the paper and recommend acceptance (often with the stipulation that revisions be made) or rejection. This process is called *peer review* and it is very important in making sure that research has careful external review before it is published. As many as 90% of papers submitted to the more prestigious journals are rejected. Many rejected papers are submitted to other journals and eventually accepted for publication, but much research is never published. This is not necessarily bad; it simply means that selection processes separate high-quality research from that of lesser quality.

Many of the decisions that must be made when planning an experiment were described in this chapter. The discussion focused on experiments that use the simplest experimental design with a single independent variable. In the chapter "Complex Experimental Designs," more complex experimental designs are described.

ENGAGING WITH RESEARCH: CONDUCTING EXPERIMENTS

Social media is ubiquitous—you were probably on social media right before you read this sentence! In the United States, more than 70% of respondents in a national sample reported using social media; the rate among 18- to 29-year-olds was 84% (Faverio, 2022). The social media industrial complex is fueled by advertising and on some platforms, advertising is driven by influencers. Advertising for some products, such as tobacco, requires more regulation in order to protect public health; this is why there are no ads for beer on shows for kids. Klein et al. (2020) conducted a study of Instagram influencer posts using eye-tracking technology to see how specific tags on posts (#ad versus #sponsored) would impact people's visual attention to those ads.

First, acquire and read the following article (available here: https://doi.org/10.1080/10810730.2020.1849464):

> Klein, E. G., Czaplicki, L., Berman, M., Emery, S., & Schillo, B. (2020). Visual attention to the use of #ad versus #sponsored on e-cigarette influencer posts on social media: A randomized experiment. *Journal of Health Communication, 25*(12), 925–930. https://doi.org/10.1080/10810730.2020.1849464

Then, answer the following question from our set of Being a Skilled Consumer of Research questions.

1. **What is the primary goal of this study? Description, Prediction, Determining Cause, or Explaining? Do the authors achieve their goals?**

2. **What did these researchers do? What was the method?**

   a. How did they measure visual attention?

   b. What did they manipulate?

   c. What was the independent variable? How many levels did the independent variable have? How were research participants assigned to groups?

3. **What was measured? How was Visuospatial Memory measured?**

4. **To what or whom can we generalize the results?**

   a. Who were the people in the sample?

   b. What sampling strategy did they use and what are the implications of that strategy?

   c. Where did the participants from this study come from?

   d. Did the authors include information about the demographics of their sample?

5. **What did they find? What were the results?**

6. **Have other researchers found similar results?**
7. **What are the limitations of this study?**
8. **What are the ethical issues present in this study?**

BEING A SKILLED CONSUMER OF RESEARCH

1. Dr. García has decided to conduct an experiment to see if moods impact political attitudes. She is planning on manipulating positive mood and measuring the strength of people's attitudes toward polarizing political topics (e.g., how strongly a person holds an attitude that climate change is a serious problem). She believes that people who are in a positive mood state will show weaker attitudes; they will care less about divisive issues if they are happy. First, she needs to consider the independent variable.

   a. Should she choose a straightforward manipulation or a staged manipulation? Why or why not?

   b. Identify two examples of manipulations that she could make (e.g., she could show a funny video).

   c. How should she test the strength of the manipulation?

2. Next, Dr. García needs to consider her dependent variable:

   a. Identify examples of self-report and behavioral measures to recommend to Dr. García.

   b. Should she include multiple DVs? Why or why not?

   c. Given the examples that you identified, describe the sensitivity of each measure. Is there potential for a floor effect? Or a ceiling effect?

3. Then, Dr. García has to consider experimental controls:

   a. What additional controls should Dr. García include in the experiment to control for demand characteristics?

   b. What additional controls should Dr. García include in the experiment to control for experimenter expectancies?

4. Finally, Dr. García decides to conduct a pilot study and finds no significant difference between the experimental conditions. Should she continue with the experiment? Why or why not? What should she do next? Explain your recommendations.

Check Your Learning: Practice Exercises

Practice Exercise #1
Read each statement and then mark it as T (true) or F (false).

	T	F
1. Staged manipulations are designed to involve participants in a situation that becomes a real experience.		
2. A staged experiment may be difficult to replicate by other researchers.		
3. Presenting participants with one of three versions of a written confession to a crime is an example of an event manipulation.		
4. In some staged manipulations, a confederate appears to be another participant in an experiment but is actually part of the manipulation.		
5. To study helping behavior, a confederate of the experimenter drops a stack of papers in front of one individual or a group of five people. The amount of time it takes for the confederate to receive help picking up the papers is the dependent variable. The manipulation employed in this experiment would be an example of a straightforward manipulation.		

Practice Exercise #2
For the following five variables, place a checkmark to indicate the general type of dependent measure:

	Self-Report	Behavioral	Physiological
1. Rating of current mood (e.g., "How happy are you?" on a scale of 1–10).			
2. Number of positive and negative words used during a couple's 10-minute interaction.			
3. Heart rate during and after giving a speech.			

	Self-Report	Behavioral	Physiological
4. Number of eye-blinks in a 5-second span.			
5. Number of errors on a spelling test.			

(Some answers are provided at the end of this chapter.)

CHAPTER REVIEW

Review Questions

1. What is the difference between straightforward and staged manipulations of an independent variable?
2. What are the three general types of dependent variables?
3. What is meant by the sensitivity of a dependent measure? What are ceiling effects and floor effects?
4. What are demand characteristics? Describe ways to minimize demand characteristics.
5. What is the reason for having a placebo group?
6. What are experimenter expectancy effects? What are some solutions to the experimenter bias problem?
7. What is a pilot study?
8. What is a manipulation check? How does it help the researcher interpret the results of an experiment?
9. Describe the value of a debriefing following the study.
10. What does a researcher do with the findings after completing a research project?

Study Terms

Behavioral measure (p. 207)

Ceiling effect (p. 210)

Confederate (p. 204)

Demand characteristics (p. 211)

Double-blind experiment (p. 215)

Electroencephalogram (EEG) (p. 208)

Electromyogram (EMG) (p. 208)

Expectancy effects (experimenter bias) (p. 213)

Filler items (p. 212)

Floor effect (p. 210)

Functional magnetic resonance imagery (fMRI) (p. 208)

Galvanic skin response (GSR) (p. 208)

Manipulation check (p. 216)

MRI (Magnetic resonance imagery) (p. 208)

Physiological measure (p. 208)

Pilot study (p. 216)

Placebo group (p. 212)

Self-report (p. 207)

Sensitivity (p. 210)

Single-blind experiment (p. 215)

Staged manipulation (p. 203)

Straightforward manipulation (p. 201)

Strength of manipulation (p. 205)

Check Your Learning: Answers

Practice Exercise #1

1. T; 2. T; 3. F; 4. T; 5. F

Practice Exercise #2

1. self-report; 2. behavioral; 3. physiological; 4. physiological; 5. behavioral

shironosov/Getty Images

10

Complex Experimental Designs

LEARNING OBJECTIVES

- Define *factorial design* and discuss reasons a researcher would use this design.
- Describe the information provided by main effects and interaction effects in a factorial design.
- Discuss the role of simple main effects in interpreting interactions.
- Compare the assignment of participants in an independent groups design, a repeated measures design, and a mixed factorial design.

THUS FAR WE HAVE FOCUSED PRIMARILY ON THE SIMPLEST EXPERIMENTAL DESIGN, IN WHICH ONE INDEPENDENT VARIABLE IS MANIPULATED AND ONE DEPENDENT VARIABLE IS MEASURED. However, researchers often investigate problems that demand more complicated designs. These complex experimental designs are the subject of this chapter.

We begin by discussing the idea of increasing the number of levels of an independent variable in an experiment. Then we describe experiments that expand the number and types of independent variables. These changes impact the complexity of an experiment.

INCREASING THE NUMBER OF LEVELS OF AN INDEPENDENT VARIABLE

In the simplest experimental design, there are only two levels of the independent variable (IV). However, a researcher might want to design an experiment with three or more levels for several reasons. First, a design with only two levels of one independent variable cannot provide very much information about the exact form of the relationship between the independent and dependent variables. For example, Figure 1 is based on the outcome of an experiment on the relationship between amount of "mental practice" and performance on a motor task: dart-throwing score (Kremer et al., 2009). In this study, mental practice consisted of imagining practice throws prior to an actual dart-throwing task. So, did mental practice improve dart performance? The solid line describes the results when only two levels were used—no mental practice throws and 100 mental practice throws. Because there are only two levels, the relationship can be described only with a

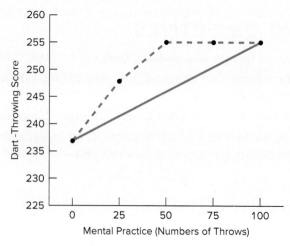

FIGURE 1
Linear versus positive monotonic functions
Source: Experiment conducted by Kremer et al. (2009).

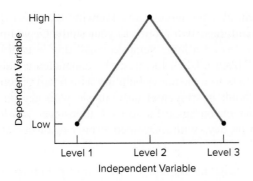

FIGURE 2
Curvilinear relationship
Note: At least three levels of the independent variable are required to show curvilinear relationships.

straight line. We do not know what the relationship would be if other practice amounts were included as separate levels of the independent variable. The broken line in Figure 1 shows the results when 25, 50, and 75 mental practice throws are also included. This result is a more accurate description of the relationship between amount of mental practice and performance. The amount of practice is very effective in increasing performance up to a point, after which further practice is not helpful. This type of relationship is termed a *positive monotonic relationship;* there is a positive relationship between the variables, but it is not a strictly positive linear relationship. An experiment with only two levels cannot yield such exact information.

Recall from the chapter "Fundamental Research Issues" that variables are sometimes related in a curvilinear or nonmonotonic fashion; that is, the direction of relationship changes. Figure 2 shows an example of a curvilinear relationship; this particular form is called an *inverted-U* because the wide range of levels of the independent variable produces an inverted U shape (recall our discussion of inverted-U relationships in the chapter "Fundamental Research Issues"). An experimental design with only two levels of the independent variable cannot detect curvilinear relationships between variables. If a curvilinear relationship is predicted, at least three levels must be used. As Figure 2 shows, if only levels 1 and 3 of the independent variable had been used, no relationship between the variables would have been detected. Many such curvilinear relationships exist in psychology. The relationship between fear arousal and attitude change is one example—we can be scared into changing an attitude, but if we think that a message is "over the top," attitude change does not occur. In other words, increasing the amount of fear aroused by a persuasive message increases attitude change up to a moderate level of fear; further increases in fear arousal actually reduce attitude change.

Finally, researchers frequently are interested in comparing more than two groups. Suppose you want to know whether playing with an animal has beneficial effects on nursing home residents. You could have two conditions, such as a no-animal control group and a group in which a dog is brought in for play each day.

However, you might also be interested in knowing the effect of a cat and a bird, and so you could add these two groups to your study. Or you might be interested in comparing the effect of a large versus a small dog in addition to a no-animal control condition. Niven (2015), for example, conducted a field experiment with three groups of callers to a customer helpline who heard different types of music while waiting on hold: instrumental only, music with neutral lyrics, and music with prosocial lyrics encouraging kindness. Caller anger was lower on days with neutral lyrics than on days with instrumental only or prosocial lyrics.

INCREASING THE NUMBER OF INDEPENDENT VARIABLES: FACTORIAL DESIGNS

Researchers recognize that in any given situation a number of variables are operating to affect behavior. So, researchers often manipulate more than one independent variable in a single experiment. Typically, two or three independent variables are operating simultaneously. This type of experimental design is a closer approximation of real-world conditions, in which independent variables do not exist by themselves.

In the chapter "Experimental Design" we described a hypothetical experiment in which exercise was the independent variable and mood was the dependent variable. An actual experiment on the relationship between exercise and depression was conducted by Dunn et al. (2005). In this study, participants were randomly assigned to one of two exercise conditions—a low amount or a high amount, with energy expenditure of either 7.0 or 17.5 kcal per kilogram body weight per week. The dependent variable was the score on a standard depression measure after 12 weeks of exercise. You might be wondering how often the participants exercised each week. Indeed, the researchers did wonder if frequency of exercising would be important, so they scheduled some subjects to exercise 3 days per week and others to exercise 5 days per week. Thus, the researchers designed an experiment with two independent variables—in this case, (1) amount of exercise and (2) frequency of exercise.

Factorial designs are experimental designs with more than one independent variable (or *factor*). In a factorial design, all levels of each independent variable are combined with all levels of the other independent variables. The simplest factorial design—known as a 2 × 2 (two by two) factorial design—has two independent variables, each having two levels.

An experiment by Hermans et al. (2009) illustrates a 2 × 2 factorial design. Hermans et al. studied modeling of food intake when someone is with another person who is eating. What influences whether you will model the other person's eating? In the experiment, a subject was paired with a confederate to view and rate movie trailers. They were seated in a comfortable living room environment with a bowl of M&Ms within easy reach on a coffee table. After 10 minutes of viewing, there was a break period. Two independent variables were manipulated: (1) confederate sociability and (2) confederate food intake. The sociable

Independent variable B: Confederate food intake	Independent variable A: Confederate sociability	
	Sociable	Unsociable
Low	Sociable/ low food intake	Unsociable/ low food intake
High	Sociable/ high food intake	Unsociable/ high food intake

FIGURE 3
2 × 2 factorial design: Setup of food intake modeling experiment

confederate initiated a conversation; the unsociable confederate did not initiate a conversation, responded with only brief answers if the subject said something, and avoided eye contact. The confederate also was first to reach for the M&Ms. One piece was taken in the low food intake condition; a total of 6 pieces were taken during the break. In the high food intake condition, 4 pieces were taken immediately; a total of 24 pieces were eaten by the confederate in this condition. During the break period (lasting 15 minutes), the subject could ignore the bowl of M&Ms or eat as many as desired.

This 2 × 2 design results in four experimental conditions: (1) sociable confederate—low food intake, (2) unsociable confederate—low food intake, (3) sociable confederate—high food intake, (4) unsociable confederate—high food intake. A 2 × 2 design always has four groups. Figure 3 shows how these experimental conditions are created.

The general format for describing factorial designs is

Number of levels of × Number of levels of × Number of levels of
first IV   second IV   third IV

and so on. A design with two independent variables, one having two levels and the other having three levels, is a 2 × 3 factorial design; there are six conditions in the experiment. A 3 × 3 design has nine conditions.

Interpretation of Factorial Designs

Factorial designs yield two kinds of information. The first is information about the effect of each independent variable taken by itself: This is called the **main effect** of an independent variable. In a design with two independent variables, there are two main effects—one for each independent variable.

The second type of information is called an **interaction** (sometimes you will see researchers refer to variables in an interaction as moderating or moderator variables). If there is an interaction between two independent variables, the effect of one independent variable depends on the particular level of the other variable. In other words, the effect that an independent variable has on the dependent variable depends on the level of the other independent variable. Interactions are a new

TABLE 1   2 × 2 factorial design: Results of the food intake modeling

Confederate food intake (independent variable B)	Confederate sociability (independent variable A)		Overall means (main effect of B)
	Sociable	Unsociable	
Low	6.58	2.14	4.36
High	5.68	10.63	8.16
Overall means (main effect of A)	6.13	6.39	

Data based on results of Hermans et al. (2009).

Source: Hermans, Roel C. J., Rutger C. M. E. Engels, Junilla K. Larsen, and C. Peter Herman. "Modeling of Palatable Food Intake: The Influence of Quality of Social Interaction." *Appetite 52,* no. 3 (July 2009): 801–04. https://doi.org/10.1016/j.appet.2009.03.008

source of information that cannot be obtained in a simple experimental design in which only one independent variable is manipulated.

To illustrate main effects and interactions, we can look at the results of the Hermans et al. (2009) study on food intake modeling. Table 1 illustrates a common method of presenting outcomes for the various groups in a factorial design. The number in each cell represents the mean number of M&Ms consumed by the subjects in the four conditions.

Main Effects   A main effect is the effect each variable has by itself. The main effect of independent variable A, confederate sociability, is the overall effect of the variable on the dependent measure. Similarly, the main effect of independent variable B, confederate food intake, is the effect of number of M&Ms that the confederate ate on the number of M&Ms consumed by the subject.

The main effect of each independent variable is the overall relationship between that independent variable and the dependent variable. For independent variable A, is there a relationship between sociability and food intake? We can find out by looking at the overall means in the sociable and unsociable confederate conditions. These overall main effect means are obtained by averaging across all participants in each group, irrespective of confederate food intake (low or high). The main effect means are shown in the rightmost column and bottom row (called the margins of the table) of Table 1. The average number of M&Ms consumed by participants in the sociable confederate condition is 6.13, and the number eaten in the unsociable condition is 6.39. Note that the overall mean of 6.13 in the sociable confederate condition is the average of 6.58 in the sociable—low food intake group and 5.68 in the sociable—high food intake group (this calculation assumes equal numbers of participants in each group). You can see that, overall, somewhat more M&Ms are eaten when the confederate is unsociable. Statistical tests would enable us to determine whether this is a significant main effect.

The main effect for independent variable B (confederate food intake) is the overall relationship between that independent variable, by itself, and the dependent variable. You can see in Table 1 that the average number of candies consumed by subjects in the low food intake condition is 4.36, and the overall number eaten in the high food intake condition is 8.16. Thus, in general, more M&Ms are eaten by subjects when they were with a confederate who had consumed a high number of M&Ms (this is a modeling effect).

Interactions   The mean for each main effect tell us that, overall, subjects eat (1) slightly more M&Ms when the confederate is unsociable and (2) considerably more when the confederate eats a large amount of candy. There is also the possibility that an interaction exists; if so, the main effects of the independent variables must be qualified. This is because an interaction between independent variables indicates that the effect of one independent variable is different at different levels of the other independent variable. That is, an interaction tells us that the effect of one independent variable depends on the particular level of the other.

We can see an interaction in the results of the Hermans et al. (2009) study. The effect of confederate food intake is different depending on whether the confederate is sociable or unsociable. When the confederate is unsociable, subjects consume many more M&Ms when the confederate food intake is high (10.68 in the unsociable condition versus 2.14 in the sociable condition). However, when the confederate is sociable, confederate food intake has little effect and in fact is the opposite of what would be expected based on modeling (6.58 in the low food intake condition and 5.68 in the high food intake condition). Thus, the relationship between confederate food intake and subject food intake is best understood by considering both independent variables: We must consider the food intake of the confederate *and* whether the confederate is sociable or unsociable.

Interactions can be seen easily when the means for all conditions are presented in a graph. Figure 4 shows a bar graph of the results of the Hermans et al. (2009) food intake modeling experiment. Note that all four means have been graphed. Two bars compare low versus high confederate food intake in the sociable confederate condition; the same comparison is shown for the unsociable confederate. You can see that confederate food intake has a small effect on the participants' modeling of M&Ms consumed when the confederate is sociable; however, when the confederate is unsociable, the participants do model the food intake of the confederate. Hermans et al. noted that they expected to observe

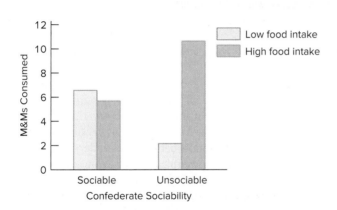

FIGURE 4
Interaction between confederate sociability and food intake

the modeling effect primarily when the confederate is sociable. Why do you think someone might actually model the food intake of the unsociable confederate instead?

The concept of interaction is a relatively simple one that you probably use all the time. When we say "it depends," we are usually indicating that some sort of interaction is operating—it depends on some other variable. Suppose, for example, that a friend has asked you if you want to go to a movie. Whether you want to go may reflect an interaction between two variables: (1) Is an exam coming up? and (2) Who stars in the movie? If there is an exam coming up, you will not go under any circumstance (obviously). If you do not have an exam to worry about, your decision will depend on whether you like the actors in the movie; that is, you will be much more likely to go if a favorite actor is in the movie.

You might try graphing the movie example in the same way we graphed the food intake example in Figure 4. The dependent variable (likelihood of going to the movie) is always placed on the vertical axis. One independent variable is placed on the horizontal axis. Bars are then drawn to represent each of the levels of the other independent variable. Graphing the results in this manner is a useful method of visualizing interactions in a factorial design.

It is also possible to include a participant variable (i.e., a subject variable) in a factorial design. This usually occurs when there is interest in a subject variable that might interact with one of the independent variables in the study. You might have two or even three age groups, personality categories such as low and high on agreeableness, extraversion or conscientiousness, or a background characteristic such as growing up in a rural or urban environment. For example, you might anticipate that students who studied in a quiet environment would perform better on a test than students who studied in a room with a distraction such as a television with volume at a level of normal conversation. As you plan an experiment to test this idea, you might think, "Would this be true for both introverts and extraverts?" At this point, you could add the extraversion variable to create a 2 × 2 factorial design. The presence of an interaction effect would tell you that the nature of the relationship between distraction and test performance depends on whether the person is extraverted or introverted. Remember, though, that extraversion and other participant variables are not manipulated here, so it would be difficult to draw cause-and-effect inferences.

OUTCOMES OF A 2 × 2 FACTORIAL DESIGN

A 2 × 2 factorial design has two independent variables, each with two levels. When analyzing the results, researchers deal with several possibilities: (1) There may or may not be a significant main effect for independent variable A, (2) there may or may not be a significant main effect for independent variable B, and (3) there may or may not be a significant interaction between the independent variables.

Figure 5 illustrates the eight possible outcomes in a 2 × 2 factorial design. The independent and dependent variables in Figure 5 do not have variable labels,

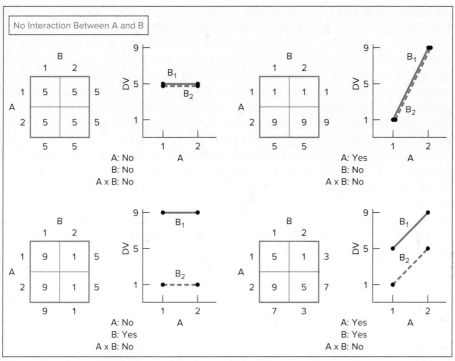

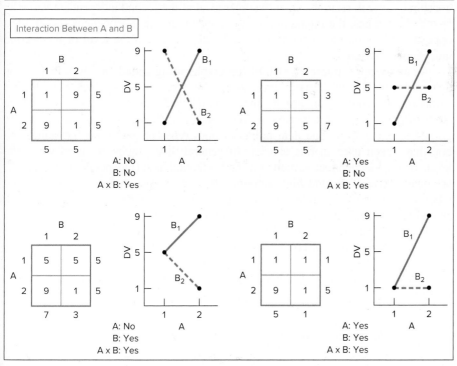

FIGURE 5
Outcomes
of a factorial
design
with two
independent
variables

the independent variables are labeled A and B, the dependent variable is labeled DV. For each outcome, the means are given and then graphed. In addition, for each graph, the presence of a main effect for each variable (A, B) is indicated by a Yes (indicating the presence of a main effect) or No (no main effect). Similarly, the A × B interaction is either present ("Yes" on the figure) or not present ("No" on the figure). The means that are given in the figure are idealized examples; such perfect outcomes rarely occur in actual research. Nevertheless, you should study the graphs to determine for yourself why, in each case, there is or is not a main effect for A, a main effect for B, and an A × B interaction.

It may help you to think of concrete variables to represent the two independent variables and the dependent variable. Consider how the amount (A) and frequency (B) of exercise impacts depression. Suppose that independent variable A is amount of exercise per week (A_1 is low exercise per week; A_2 is high exercise per week) and independent variable B is the frequency of exercise (B_1 is 3 times per week and B_2 is 5 times per week). The dependent variable (DV) is the score on a depression measure, with higher numbers indicating greater depression.

The top four graphs illustrate outcomes in which there is no A × B interaction, and the bottom four graphs depict outcomes in which there is an A × B interaction. When there is a statistically significant interaction, you need to carefully examine the means to understand why the interaction occurred. In some cases, there is a strong relationship between the first independent variable and the dependent variable at one level of the second independent variable, but no relationship or a weak relationship at the other level of the second independent variable. In other outcomes, the interaction may indicate that one independent variable has opposite effects on the dependent variable, depending on the level of the second independent variable.

As an exercise, interpret each of the graphs using actual variables from three different hypothetical experiments, using the scenarios suggested below. This works best if you draw the graphs, including labels for the variables, on a separate sheet of paper for each experiment. You can try depicting the data as either line graphs or bar graphs. The data points in both types of graph are the same, and both have been used in this chapter. In general, line graphs are used when the levels of the independent variable on the horizontal axis (independent variable A) are quantitative—low and high amounts. Bar graphs are more likely to be used when the levels of the independent variable represent different categories, such as one type of therapy compared with another type.

Hypothetical experiment 1: Effect of music (versus quiet) and type room color (warm colors versus cool colors) on mood.

Independent variable A: Music—music versus no music (quiet)

Independent variable B: Room color—cool color (blue) versus warm color (yellow)

Dependent variable: Mood (range from 1 to 9)

Using the example above, the results for two of the eight possible outcomes (there are four possible "no interaction" outcomes and four possible "interaction present" outcomes) would be:

- A: yes, B: no, A × B: no—Music impacted mood (quiet increased mood), room color did not impact mood, and there was no interaction between music and room color that affected mood.
- A: no, B: yes, A × B: yes—Music did not impact mood, room color affected mood (warm colors increased mood), and there was an interaction between music and room color (in the room with music, blue improved mood; in the quiet room, yellow improved mood).

For the next hypothetical experiment, describe what each of the eight possible outcomes would mean.

Hypothetical experiment 2: Effect of age and viewing violent ad content on recall of advertising. Participants (those aged 13–18 years old versus those aged 19–25) viewed a video that was either violent or not violent. They were then asked to read print ads for eight different products over the next 3 minutes. The dependent variable was the number of ads correctly recalled.

Independent variable A: Exposure to violence—nonviolent versus violent video

Independent variable B: Participant age—being 13–18 years old or being 19–25 years old

Dependent variable: Number of ads recalled (range from 1 to 9)

Finally, for hypothetical experiment 3, devise your own experiment with two independent variables and one dependent variable, and then describe what each of the eight possible outcomes would mean.

Interactions and Simple Main Effects

A statistical procedure called *analysis of variance* is used to assess the statistical significance of the main effects and the interaction in a factorial design. When a significant interaction occurs, the researcher must statistically evaluate the individual means. If you take a look at Table 1 and Figure 4 once again, you see a clear interaction. When there is a significant interaction, the next step is to look at the **simple main effects.** A simple main effect analysis examines mean differences at *each level* of the independent variable. Recall that the main effect of an independent variable averages across the levels of the other independent variable; with simple main effects, the results are analyzed as if we had separate experiments at each level of the other independent variable.

Simple Main Effect of Confederate Food Intake

In Figure 4, we can look at the simple main effect of confederate food intake. This will tell us whether the difference between the low and high confederate food intake is significant when the confederate is (1) sociable and (2) unsociable. In this case, the simple main effect of confederate food intake is significant when the confederate is unsociable (means of 2.14 versus 10.63), but the simple main effect of confederate food intake is not significant when the confederate is sociable (means of 6.58 and 5.68).

Simple Main Effect of Sociability

We could also examine the simple main effect of confederate sociability; here we would compare the sociable versus unsociable conditions when the food intake is low and then when food intake is high. The simple main effect that you will be most interested in will depend on the predictions that you made when you designed the study. The exact statistical procedures do not concern us; the point here is that the pattern of results with all the means must be examined when there is a significant interaction in a factorial design.

ASSIGNMENT PROCEDURES AND FACTORIAL DESIGNS

Methods of assigning participants to conditions were discussed in the chapter "Experimental Design." There are two basic ways of assigning participants to conditions: (1) In an independent groups design, different participants are assigned to each of the conditions in the study; and (2) in a repeated measures design, the *same* individuals participate in all conditions in the study. These two types of assignment procedures have implications for the number of participants necessary to complete the experiment. We can illustrate this fact by looking at a 2 × 2 factorial design. The design can be completely independent groups, completely repeated measures, or a mixed factorial design—that is, a combination of the two.

Independent Groups (between-subjects) Design

In a 2 × 2 factorial design, there are four conditions. If we want a completely **independent groups (between-subjects) design,** a different group of participants will be assigned to each of the four conditions. The food intake modeling study illustrates a factorial design with different individuals in each of the conditions. Suppose that you have planned a 2 × 2 design and want to have 10 participants in each condition; you will need a total of 40 *different* participants, as shown in the first table in Figure 6.

Repeated Measures (within-subjects) Design

In a completely **repeated measures (within-subjects) design,** the same individuals will participate in *all* conditions. Suppose you have planned a study on the effects of marijuana: One factor is marijuana (marijuana treatment versus placebo control) and the other factor is task difficulty (easy versus difficult). In a 2 × 2 completely

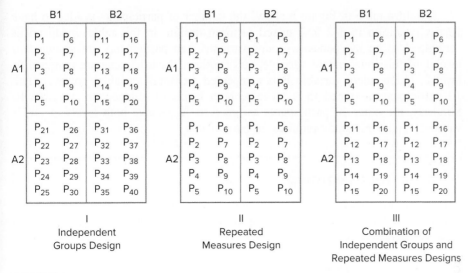

FIGURE 6
Number of participants (P) required to have 10 observations in each condition

repeated measures design, each individual would participate in all of the conditions by completing both easy and difficult tasks under both marijuana treatment conditions. If you wanted 10 participants in each condition, a total of 10 subjects would be needed, as illustrated in the Repeated Measures Design table in Figure 6. This design offers considerable savings in the number of participants required. In deciding whether to use a completely repeated measures assignment procedure, however, the researcher would have to consider the potential disadvantages of repeated measures designs.

Mixed Factorial Design Using Combined Assignment

Some studies use both independent groups and repeated measures procedures in a **mixed factorial design.** Pan et al. (2020), for example, were interested in identifying factors that might help college students pay attention to the material presented in a recorded lecture. Specifically, they used a mixed factorial design to look at whether giving a "pretest quiz" on the material before the lecture would reduce mind wandering during the lecture and thus enhance learning. In their study, undergraduate students first completed an ungraded pretest quiz or an algebra problem-solving activity (this was the between-subjects, independent groups, factor) and then viewed a recorded lecture. The pretest quiz covered a portion of the material in the lecture; the actual lecture also included new material not covered by pretest questions. The within-subjects (repeated measures) factor was the type of question on the test given after the lecture. All students completed a test that consisted of both (a) questions that were on the pretest quiz and (b) questions on new material in the lecture. Incidentally, Pan et al. found that students who first completed a pretest quiz showed less mind wandering and better test performance.

The third table in Figure 6 shows the number of participants needed to have 10 per condition in a 2 × 2 mixed factorial design. In this table, independent variable A is an independent groups variable. Ten participants are assigned to level 1 of this independent variable, and another 10 participants are assigned to level 2. Independent variable B is a repeated measures variable, however. The 10 participants assigned to A_1 receive both levels of independent variable B. Similarly, the other 10 participants assigned to A_2 receive both levels of the B variable. Thus, this study requires 20 participants.

Check Your Learning

Now complete Check Your Learning: Practice Exercise #1 to test your understanding of more complex assignment strategies.

FROM 2 × 2 TO N × N FACTORIAL DESIGNS

The 2 × 2 is the simplest factorial design. With this basic design, the researcher can arrange experiments that are more and more complex. One way to increase complexity is to increase the number of levels of one or more of the independent variables. A 2 × 3 design, for example, contains two independent variables: Independent variable A has two levels, and independent variable B has three levels. Thus, the 2 × 3 design has six conditions.

Table 2 shows a 2 × 3 factorial design with the independent variables of task difficulty (easy, hard) and anxiety level (low, moderate, high). The dependent variable is performance on the task. The numbers in each of the six cells of the design indicate the mean performance score of the group. The overall means in the margins (rightmost column and bottom row) show the main effects of each of the independent variables. The results in Table 2 indicate a main effect of task difficulty because the *overall* performance score in the easy-task group is higher than the hard-task mean. However, there is no main effect of anxiety because the mean performance score is the same in each of the three anxiety groups. Is there an interaction between task difficulty and anxiety? Note that increasing the amount of anxiety has the effect of increasing performance on the easy task but *decreasing*

TABLE 2 2 × 3 factorial design

Task difficulty	Anxiety level			Overall means (main effect)
	Low	Moderate	High	
Easy	4.0	7.0	10.0	7.0
Hard	7.0	4.0	1.0	4.0
Overall means (main effect)	5.5	5.5	5.5	

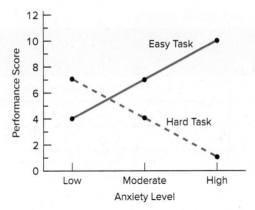

FIGURE 7
Line graph of data from 2 (task difficulty) × 3 (anxiety level) factorial design

performance on the hard task. The effect of anxiety is different, depending on whether the task is easy or hard; thus, there is an interaction.

This interaction can be easily seen in a graph. Figure 7 is a line graph in which one line shows the effect of anxiety for the easy task and a second line represents the effect of anxiety for the difficult task. As noted previously, line graphs are used when the independent variable represented on the horizontal axis is quantitative—that is, the levels of the independent variable are increasing amounts of that variable (not differences in category).

FACTORIAL DESIGNS WITH THREE OR MORE INDEPENDENT VARIABLES

We can also increase the number of variables in the design. A 2 × 2 × 2 factorial design contains three variables, each with two levels. Thus, there are 8 conditions in this design. In a 2 × 2 × 3 design, there are 12 conditions; in a 2 × 2 × 2 × 2 design, there are 16. The rule for constructing factorial designs remains the same throughout.

A 2 × 2 × 2 factorial design is constructed in Table 3. The independent variables are (1) instruction method (lecture, discussion), (2) class size (10, 40), and (3) class time (noon, 7:00 p.m.). If participants are randomly assigned, this would be a completely between-subjects design because all three variables would be manipulated. The dependent variable is performance on a standard test.

Notice that the 2 × 2 × 2 design can be seen as two 2 × 2 designs, one for the classes held at noon and another for classes held at 7:00 p.m. The design yields main effects for each of the three independent variables. For example, the overall mean for the lecture method is obtained by considering all participants who experience the lecture method, irrespective of class size or class time. Similarly, the discussion method mean is derived from all participants in this condition. The *two* means are then compared to see whether there is a significant main effect: Is one of these methods superior to the other *overall?*

TABLE 3 2 × 2 × 2 factorial design

	Class size	
Instruction method	**10**	**40**
	Class held at noon	
Lecture		
Discussion		
	Class held at 7:00 p.m.	
Lecture		
Discussion		

The design also allows us to look at interactions. In the 2 × 2 × 2 design, we can look at the interaction between (1) method and class size, (2) method and class time, and (3) class size and class time. We can also look at a three-way interaction that involves all three independent variables. Here, we want to determine whether the nature of the interaction between two of the variables differs depending on the particular level of the other variable. Three-way interactions are rather complicated; fortunately, you will not encounter too many of these in your explorations of behavioral science research.

Sometimes students are tempted to include in a study as many independent variables as they can think of. A problem with this is that the design may become needlessly complex and require enormous numbers of participants. The design previously discussed had 8 groups; a 2 × 2 × 2 × 2 design has 16 groups; adding yet another independent variable with two levels means that 32 groups would be required. Also, when there are more than three or four independent variables, many of the particular conditions that are produced by the combination of so many variables do not make sense or could not occur under natural circumstances. Finally, as the number of independent variables grows, the results become more difficult to interpret. We just saw that describing a significant three-way interaction is complicated. Interactions with more independent variables are much more difficult to describe or understand.

The designs described thus far all use the same logic for determining whether the independent variable did in fact cause a change on the dependent variable measure. In the chapter "Single-Case, Quasi-Experimental, and Developmental Research" we consider alternative designs that use somewhat different procedures for examining the relationship between independent and dependent variables.

Check Your Learning

Now complete Check Your Learning: Practice Exercise #2 at the end of the chapter to test your understanding of more complex experiments.

ENGAGING WITH RESEARCH: COMPLEX EXPERIMENTAL DESIGNS

Instagram, which launched its first app in 2010, has more than one billion monthly users. Social media platforms like Instagram have been studied since their inception. Because of Instagram's focus on sharing photos, researchers have studied the impact of viewing photos on Instagram on a variety of mental health outcomes. Wallace and Buil (2020) conducted an experiment with 280 Instagram users in the United States to test whether hiding "likes" would affect the users' mood and loneliness. That is, they wondered how "likes" affected users.

First, acquire and read the article (available at https://doi.org/10.1016/j.paid.2020.110509)

> Wallace, E., & Buil, I. (2020). Hiding Instagram likes: Effects on negative affect and loneliness. *Personality and Individual Differences*. https://doi.org/10.1016/j.paid.2020.110509

Then, after reading the article, answer the following questions:

1. **What is the primary goal of this study? Description, Prediction, Determining Cause, or Explaining? Do the authors achieve their goals?**
2. **What did these researchers do? What was the method?**
   a. How many independent variables were there? How many levels did each IV have?
   b. How were participants assigned to groups? Was this a repeated measures design or an independent groups design?
   c. How was the IV manipulated? Was the manipulation staged or straightforward?
   d. How did they conduct a manipulation check?
3. **What was measured?**
4. **To what or whom can we generalize the results?**
   a. Who were the participants, was the population diverse?
   b. Do you think that asking participants to "imagine a scenario where you have posted on your Instagram feed an image about climate change" would be the same as asking participants to "imagine a scenario where you have posted on your Instagram feed an image about a party that you attended"?
5. **What did they find? What were the results?**
   a. Describe the interaction depicted in figure 1.
6. **Have other researchers found similar results?**
7. **What are the limitations of this study?**
8. **What are the ethical issues present in this study?**
   a. How were research participants compensated?

BEING A SKILLED CONSUMER OF RESEARCH

1. Participants were randomly assigned to conditions in a 2 × 2 between-subjects (independent groups) experiment exploring the potential impact of distraction on reaction time. In this study, two variables were manipulated: (1) a confederate in the room reading a book, either aloud or to themselves, and (2) popular music playing on a speaker (present, absent). One variable was measured: time in seconds taken to complete a Sudoku puzzle.

   a. Describe what you think the results would be if there was a main effect for reading.

   b. Describe what you think the results would be if there was also a main effect for music.

   c. Describe what you think the results would be if there was an interaction between reading and music.

   d. What assignment procedures would you recommend—completely independent groups, completely repeated measures, or a mixed factorial design? Why?

2. Research participants were randomly assigned to read one of four "resumés," which were identical except for being described as written by a 25-year-old high school graduate, a 25-year-old college graduate, a 35-year-old high school graduate, or a 35-year-old college graduate. After reviewing the resumé, participants rated the resumé for overall job qualification. The results (higher numbers indicate more qualification) showed: 25-year-old high school graduate (2.02), 25-year-old college graduate (2.05), 35-year-old high school graduate (3.82), and 35-year-old college graduate (4.90).

   a. Identify the design of this experiment.

   b. Identify the independent variable(s) and dependent variable(s).

   c. How many conditions are in the experiment?

   d. Is there a participant variable in this experiment? If so, identify it. If not, can you suggest a participant variable that might be included?

   e. Given the results, do you think that there could be any main effects, or an interaction?

Check Your Learning: Practice Exercises

Practice Exercise #1

In a series of studies designed to assess the impact of lunch nutrients and caffeine on nursing home patients' sleepiness, participants were assigned to levels of the independent variables using different strategies. For each of the strategies listed below, describe the study design and identify the assignment procedures (e.g., completely independent groups, completely repeated measures, or mixed factorial design). In all three cases, the dependent measure was the score on the Stanford Sleepiness Scale 1 hour after lunch.

1. Study 1: Over the course of 2 days, participants are assigned to one of two different conditions in one variable (extra protein at lunch in the form of protein powder in the soup: yes, no), and to both conditions of another variable (caffeine with lunch: cola on day 1, caffeine-free cola on day 2).

2. Study 2: On a single day, participants are assigned to one of two levels of one variable (extra protein with lunch: yes, no), and to one of the conditions of another variable (caffeine with lunch: yes, no).

3. Study 3: Over the course of 4 days, participants are assigned to both levels of one variable (extra protein with lunch: yes, no), and to both of the conditions of another variable (caffeine with lunch: yes, no). Day 1: extra-protein/caffeine, Day 2: extra-protein/no caffeine, Day 3: no extra-protein/caffeine, Day 4: no extra-protein/no caffeine.

Practice Exercise #2

Scenario	Number of independent variables	Number of experimental conditions	Number of possible main effects	Number of possible interactions
1. Participants were randomly assigned to read a short story printed in either 12-point or 14-point font in one of three font style conditions: Courier, Times Roman, or Arial. Afterward they answered several questions designed to measure memory recall.				
2. Researchers conducted an experiment to examine age and weight biases in juror behavior. Participants were randomly assigned to read a scenario describing a crime committed by either a younger (25-year-old) or older (55-year-old) person who was described as overweight or average weight.				

(Answers are provided at the end of this chapter.)

CHAPTER REVIEW

Review Questions

1. Why would a researcher have more than two levels of the independent variable in an experiment?
2. What is a factorial design? Why would a researcher use a factorial design?
3. What are main effects in a factorial design? What is an interaction?
4. Identify the number of conditions in a factorial design on the basis of knowing the number of independent variables and the number of levels of each independent variable.
5. Describe 2 × 2 factorial designs in which (a) both independent variables are independent groups (between-subjects), (b) both independent variables are repeated measures (within-subjects), and (c) the design is mixed, so that one independent variable is independent groups and the other is repeated measures.

Study Terms

Factorial design (p. 228)

Independent groups design (between-subjects design) (p. 236)

Interaction (p. 229)

Main effect (p. 229)

Mixed factorial design (p. 237)

Repeated measures design (within-subjects design) (p. 236)

Simple main effect (p. 235)

Check Your Learning: Answers

Practice Exercise #1

1. 2 (extra protein: yes, no) × 2 (caffeine: yes, no) mixed factorial design with repeated measures on caffeine.
2. 2 (extra protein: yes, no) × 2 (caffeine: yes, no) factorial design with completely independent groups.
3. 2 (extra protein: yes, no) × 2 (caffeine: yes, no) factorial design with completely repeated measures.

Practice Exercise #2

1. 2 IVs (font size and font style); 6 conditions; 2 possible main effects; 1 possible interaction
2. 3 IVs (gender, attractiveness, weight level); 8 conditions; 3 possible main effects; 4 possible interactions (3 two-way interactions and 1 three-way interaction)

FatCamera/Getty Images

11

Single-Case, Quasi-Experimental, and Developmental Research

LEARNING OBJECTIVES

- Describe single-case experimental designs and discuss reasons to use this design.
- Explain the one-group posttest-only design, and describe the situations where it would be useful.
- Describe the one-group pretest-posttest design and the associated threats to internal validity that may occur: history, maturation, testing, instrument decay, and regression toward the mean.
- Compare and contrast the nonequivalent control group design and nonequivalent control group pretest-posttest design; discuss the advantages of having a control group.
- Distinguish between the interrupted time series design and control series design.
- Describe cross-sectional, longitudinal, and sequential research designs, including the advantages and disadvantages of each design.
- Explain what a cohort effect is.

IN THE CLASSIC POSTTEST-ONLY EXPERIMENTAL DESIGN, PARTICI-
PANTS ARE RANDOMLY ASSIGNED TO THE INDEPENDENT VARIABLE
CONDITIONS, AND A DEPENDENT VARIABLE IS MEASURED. The
responses on the dependent measure are then compared to determine whether
the independent variable had an effect. Because all other variables are held constant,
differences on the dependent variable must be due to the effect of the independent
variable. This design has high internal validity—we are very confident that the
independent variable caused the observed responses on the dependent variable. You
will often encounter this experimental design when you explore research in the
behavioral sciences. However, other research designs have been devised to address
special research problems.

This chapter focuses on three of these research designs. First we will look
at the instance in which the effect of an independent variable must be inferred
from an experiment with only one participant: single-case experimental designs.
Second, we will describe pre-experimental and quasi-experimental designs that
may be considered if it is not possible to use one of the true experimental
designs. Third, we consider research designs for studying changes that occur
with age.

SINGLE-CASE EXPERIMENTAL DESIGNS

Single-case experimental designs have traditionally been called *single-subject*
designs; an equivalent term you may see is *small-N* designs. Much of the early
interest in single-case designs in psychology came from research on operant conditioning pioneered by B. F. Skinner (e.g., Skinner, 1953). Today, research using
single-case designs is often seen in applied behavior analysis in which operant
conditioning techniques are used in clinical, counseling, educational, medical, and
other applied settings (Kazdin, 2013, 2021a, 2021b).

Single-case experiments were developed from a need to determine whether
an experimental manipulation had an effect on a single research participant. In a
single-case design, the subject's behavior is measured over time during a **baseline**
control period. A treatment period follows in which the experimental manipulation
is introduced, and the subject's behavior continues to be observed. A change
in the subject's behavior from baseline to treatment periods is evidence for the
effectiveness of the manipulation. The problem, however, is that there could
be many explanations for the change other than the experimental treatment (i.e.,
alternative explanations). For example, some other event may have coincided with
the introduction of the treatment. The single-case designs described in the following
sections address this problem.

Reversal Designs

As noted, the basic issue in single-case experiments is how to determine that
the manipulation of the independent variable had an effect. One method is to

demonstrate the reversibility of the manipulation. A simple **reversal design** takes the following form:

A (baseline period) → B (treatment period) → A (baseline period)

This basic reversal design is called an ABA design; it requires observation of behavior during the baseline control (A) period, again during the treatment (B) period, and also during a second baseline (A) period after the experimental treatment has been removed. (Sometimes this is called a *withdrawal design,* in recognition of the fact that the treatment is removed or withdrawn.) For example, the effect of a reinforcement procedure on a child's academic performance could be assessed with an ABA design. The number of correct homework problems could be measured each day during the baseline. A reinforcement treatment procedure would then be introduced in which the child received stars for correct problems; the stars could be accumulated and exchanged for toys or candies. Later, this treatment would be discontinued during the second baseline (A) period. Hypothetical data from such an experiment are shown in Figure 1. The fact that behavior changed when the treatment was introduced and reversed when the treatment was withdrawn is evidence for its effectiveness.

Figure 1 depicts a treatment that had a relatively dramatic impact on behavior. Some treatments do produce an immediate change in behavior, but many other variables may require a longer time to show an impact.

The ABA design can be greatly improved by extending it to an ABAB design, in which the experimental treatment is introduced a second time, or even to an ABABAB design that allows the effect of the treatment to be tested a third time. This is done to address two problems with the ABA reversal design. First, a single reversal is not extremely powerful evidence for the effectiveness of the treatment. The observed reversal might have been due to a random fluctuation in the child's

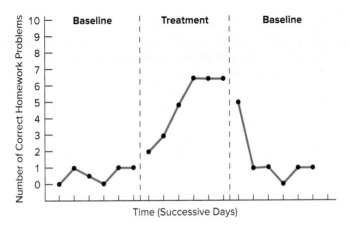

FIGURE 1
Hypothetical data from ABA reversal design

behavior; perhaps the treatment happened to coincide with some other event, such as the child's upcoming birthday, that caused the change (and the post-birthday reversal). These possibilities are much less likely if the treatment has been shown to have an effect two or more times; random or coincidental events are unlikely to be responsible for both reversals. The second problem is related to ethics. As Barlow et al. (2009) point out, it does not seem right to end the design with the withdrawal of a treatment that may be very beneficial for the participant. Using an ABAB design provides the opportunity to observe a second reversal when the treatment is introduced again. The sequence ends with the treatment rather than the withdrawal of the treatment.

The logic of the reversal design can also be applied to behaviors observed in a single setting. For example, Kazbour and Bailey (2010) examined the effectiveness of a procedure designed to increase the use of designated drivers in a bar. The percentage of bar patrons either serving as or being with a designated driver was recorded over a baseline period of 2 weeks. A procedure to increase the use of designated drivers was then implemented during the treatment phase. Designated drivers received a $5 gas card, and the driver and passengers received free pizza on their way out of the bar. The pizza and gas incentive was discontinued during the final phase of the study. The percentage of bar patrons engaged in designated driver arrangements increased substantially during the treatment phase but returned to baseline levels when the incentive was withdrawn.

Multiple Baseline Designs

It may have occurred to you that a reversal of some behaviors may be impossible or unethical. For example, it would be unethical to reverse treatment that reduces dangerous or illegal behaviors, such as indecent exposure or alcoholism, even if the possibility exists that a second introduction of the treatment might be effective. Other treatments might produce a long-lasting change in behavior that is not reversible. In such cases, multiple measures over time can be made before and after the manipulation. If the manipulation is effective, a change in behavior will be immediately observed, and the change will continue to be reflected in further measures of the behavior. In a **multiple baseline design,** the effectiveness of the treatment is demonstrated when a behavior changes only after the manipulation is introduced. To demonstrate the effectiveness of the treatment, such a change must be observed under *multiple* circumstances to rule out the possibility that other events were responsible.

There are several variations of the multiple baseline design (Barlow et al., 2009). In the multiple baseline *across subjects,* the behavior of several subjects is measured over time; for each subject, though, the manipulation is introduced at a different point in time. Figure 2 shows data from a hypothetical smoking-reduction experiment with three subjects. Note that introduction of the manipulation was followed by a change in behavior for each subject. However, because this change occurred across all individuals and the manipulation was introduced at a different time for each subject, we can rule out explanations based on chance, historical events, and so on.

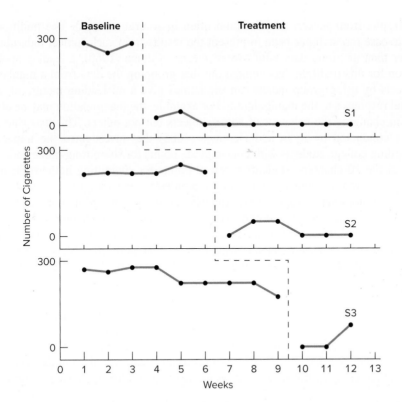

FIGURE 2
Hypothetical data from multiple baseline design across three subjects
(S1, S2, and S3)

In a multiple baseline *across behaviors,* several different behaviors of a single subject are measured over time. At different times, the same manipulation is applied to each of the behaviors. For example, a reward system could be instituted to increase the socializing, grooming, and reading behaviors of a psychiatric patient. The reward system would be applied to each of these behaviors at different times. Demonstrating that each behavior increased when the reward system was applied would be evidence for the effectiveness of the manipulation.

The third variation is the multiple baseline *across situations,* in which the same behavior is measured in different settings, such as at home and at work. Again, a manipulation is introduced at a different time in each setting, with the expectation that a change in the behavior in each situation will occur only after the manipulation.

Replications in Single-Case Designs

The procedures for use with a single subject can, of course, be replicated with other subjects, greatly enhancing the generalizability of the results. Usually, reports of research that employs single-case experimental procedures do present the results from several subjects (and often in several settings). The tradition in single-case research has been to present the results from each subject individually rather than as group data with overall means. Sidman (1960), a leading spokesperson for this tradition, has pointed out that grouping the data from a number of subjects by using group means can sometimes give a misleading picture of individual responses to the manipulation. For example, the manipulation may be effective in changing the behavior of some subjects but not others. This was true in a study conducted by Ryan and Hemmes (2005) that investigated the impact of rewarding college students with course grade points for submitting homework. For half of the 10 chapters, students received points for submitting homework; however, there were no points given if they submitted homework for the other chapters (to control for chapter topic, some students had points for odd-numbered chapters only and others received points for the even-numbered chapters). Ryan and Hemmes found that, on average, students submitted more homework assignments and performed better on chapter-based quizzes that were directly associated with point rewards. However, some individual participants performed about the same regardless of condition. Because the emphasis of the study was on the individual subject, this pattern of results was quickly revealed.

Single-case designs are useful for studying many research problems and should be considered a powerful alternative to more traditional research designs. They can be especially valuable for someone who is applying some change technique in a natural environment—for example, a teacher who is trying a new technique in the classroom. In addition, complex statistical analyses are not required for single-case designs.

Check Your Learning

Now complete Check Your Learning: Practice Exercise #1 to assess your understanding of single-case experimental designs.

QUASI-EXPERIMENTAL DESIGNS

Quasi-experimental designs address the need to study the effect of an independent variable in settings in which the control features of true experimental designs cannot be achieved. Thus, a quasi-experimental design allows us to examine the impact of an independent variable on a dependent variable, but causal inference is much more difficult because quasi-experiments lack important features of true experiments such as random assignment to conditions. In this section, we will examine several quasi-experimental designs that might be used in situations in which a true experiment is not possible. This is most likely to occur in applied settings when an independent variable is manipulated in a natural setting such as a school, business, hospital, or an entire city or state.

There are many types of quasi-experimental designs—see Campbell (1968, 1969), Campbell and Stanley (1966), Cook and Campbell (1979), and Shadish et al. (2002). Only six designs will be described here. As you read about each design, compare the design features and problems with the randomized true experimental designs described in the chapter "Experimental Design." We start out with the simplest and most problematic of the designs. In fact, the first three designs we describe are sometimes called "pre-experimental" to distinguish them from other quasi-experimental designs. This is because of the problems associated with these designs. Nevertheless, all may be used in different circumstances, and it is important to recognize the internal validity issues raised by each design.

One-Group Posttest-Only Design

Suppose you want to investigate whether sitting close to a stranger will cause the stranger to move away. You might try sitting next to a number of strangers and measure the number of seconds that elapse before they leave. Your design would look like this:

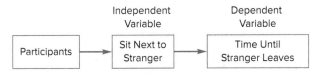

Now suppose that the average amount of time before the people leave is 9.6 seconds. Unfortunately, this finding is not interpretable. You do not know whether they would have stayed longer if you had not sat down or whether they would have stayed for 9.6 seconds anyway. It is even possible that they would have left sooner if you had not sat down—perhaps they liked you!

This **one-group posttest-only design**—called a "one-shot case study" by Campbell and Stanley (1966)—lacks a crucial element of a true experiment: a control or comparison group. There must be some sort of comparison condition to enable you to interpret your results. The one-group posttest-only design with its missing comparison group has serious deficiencies in the context of designing an internally valid experiment that will allow us to draw causal inferences about the effect of an independent variable on a dependent variable.

You might wonder whether this design is ever used. In fact, you may see this type of design used as evidence for the effectiveness of a program. For example, employees in a company might participate in a 4-hour information session on emergency procedures. At the conclusion of the program, they complete a knowledge test on which their average score is 90%. This result is then used to conclude that the program is successfully educating employees. Such studies lack internal validity—our ability to conclude that the independent variable had an effect on the dependent variable. With this design, we do not even know if the score on the dependent variable would have been equal, lower, or even higher without the program. The reason such results are sometimes accepted is that we may have an implicit idea of how a control group would perform. Unfortunately, we need that comparison data.

One-Group Pretest-Posttest Design

One way to obtain a comparison is to measure participants before the manipulation (a pretest) and again afterward (a posttest). An index of change from the pretest to the posttest could then be computed. Although this **one-group pretest-posttest design** sounds fine, there are some major problems with it.

To illustrate, suppose you want to test the hypothesis that a relaxation training program will result in a reduction in cigarette smoking. Using the one-group pretest-posttest design, you would select a group of people who smoke, administer a measure of smoking, have them go through relaxation training, and then re-administer the smoking measure. Your design would look like this:

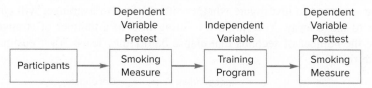

If you did find a reduction in smoking, you could not assume that the result was due to the relaxation training program. This design has failed to take into account several alternative explanations. These alternative explanations are threats to the internal validity of studies using this design and include history, maturation, testing, instrument decay, and regression toward the mean.

History

History refers to any event that occurs between the first and second measurements but is not part of the manipulation. Any such event is confounded with the manipulation. For example, suppose that a famous person dies of lung cancer during the time between the first and second measures. This event, and not the relaxation training, could be responsible for a reduction in smoking. Admittedly, the celebrity death example is dramatic and perhaps unlikely. However, **history effects** can be caused by virtually any confounding event that occurs at the same time as the experimental manipulation.

Maturation

People change over time. In a brief period they become bored, fatigued, perhaps wiser, and certainly hungrier; over a longer period, children become more coordinated and analytical; and so on. Any changes that occur systematically over time are called **maturation effects.** Maturation could be a problem in the smoking reduction example if people generally become more concerned about health as they get older. Any such time-related factor might result in a change from the pretest to the posttest. If this happens, you might mistakenly attribute the change to the treatment rather than to maturation.

Testing

Testing becomes a problem if simply taking the pretest changes the participant's behavior. This is the problem of **testing effects.** For example, the smoking measure might require people to keep a diary in which they note every cigarette smoked during the day. Simply keeping track of smoking might be sufficient to cause a reduction in the number of cigarettes a person smokes. Thus, the reduction found on the posttest could be the result of taking the pretest rather than of the program itself. In other contexts, taking a pretest may sensitize people to the purpose of the experiment or make them more adept at a skill being tested. Again, the experiment would not have internal validity.

Instrument Decay   Sometimes, the basic characteristics of the measuring instrument change over time; this is called **instrument decay.** Consider sources of instrument decay when human observers are used to measure behavior: Over time, an observer may gain skill, become fatigued, or change the standards on which observations are based. In our example on smoking, participants might be highly motivated to record all cigarettes smoked during the pretest when the task is new and interesting, but by the time the posttest is given they may be tired of the task and sometimes forget to record a cigarette. Such instrument decay would lead to an apparent reduction in cigarette smoking.

Regression Toward the Mean   Sometimes called *statistical regression,* **regression toward the mean** is likely to occur whenever participants are selected because they score extremely high or low on some variable. When they are tested again, their scores tend to change in the direction of the mean. Extremely high scores are likely to become lower (closer to the mean), and extremely low scores are likely to become higher (again, closer to the mean).

Regression toward the mean would be a problem in the smoking experiment if participants were selected because they were initially found to be extremely heavy smokers. By choosing people for the program who scored highest on the pretest, the researcher may have selected many participants who were, for what-ever reason, smoking much more than usual at the particular time the measure was administered. Those people who were smoking much more than usual will likely be smoking less when their smoking is measured again. If we then compare the overall amount of smoking before and after the program, it will appear that people are smoking less. The alternative explanation is that the smoking reduction is due to statistical regression rather than the effect of the program.

Regression toward the mean will occur whenever you gather a set of extreme scores taken at one time and compare them with scores taken at another point in time. The problem is actually rooted in the reliability of the measure. Recall from the chapter "Measurement Concepts" that any given measure reflects a true score plus measurement error. If there is perfect reliability, the two measures will be the same (if nothing happens to lower or raise the scores). If the measure of smoking is perfectly reliable, a person who reports smoking 20 cigarettes today will report smoking 20 cigarettes 2 weeks from now. However, if the two measures are not perfectly reliable and there is measurement error, most scores will be close to the true score but some will be higher and some will be lower. Thus, one smoker with a true score of 20 cigarettes per day might sometimes smoke 5 and sometimes 35; however, most of the time the number is closer to 20 than to the extremes. Another smoker might have a true score of 35 but on occasion smokes as few as 20 and as many as 50; again, most of the time the number is closer to the true score than to the extremes. Now suppose that you select two people who said they smoked 35 cigarettes on the previous day, and that both of these people are included in the group—you picked the first person on a very unusual day and the second person on a very ordinary day. When you measure these people 2 weeks later, the first person is probably going to report smoking close to 20 cigarettes and the second person close to 35. If you average the two, it will appear that there is an overall reduction in smoking.

What if the measure were perfectly reliable? In this case, the person with a true score of 20 cigarettes would always report this amount and therefore would not be included in the heavy smoker (35+ cigarettes) group at all. Only people with true scores of 35 or more would be in the group, and any reduction in smoking would be due to the treatment program. The point here is that regression toward the mean is a problem if there is measurement error.

Statistical regression occurs when we try to explain events in the "real world" as well. Sports columnists often refer to the hex that awaits an athlete who appears on the cover of *Sports Illustrated.* The performances of a number of athletes have dropped considerably after they were the subjects of *Sports Illustrated* cover stories. Although these cover stories might cause the lower performance (perhaps the notoriety results in nervousness and reduced concentration), statistical regression is also a likely explanation. An athlete is selected for the cover of the magazine because they are performing at an exceptionally high level; the principle of regression toward the mean states that very high performance is likely to deteriorate. We would know this for sure if *Sports Illustrated* also did cover stories on athletes who were in a slump and this became a good omen for them!

All these problems can be eliminated by the use of an appropriate control group. A group that does not receive the experimental treatment provides an adequate control for the effects of history, statistical regression, and so on. For example, outside historical events would have the same effect on both the experimental group and the control group. If the experimental group differs from the control group on the dependent measure administered after the manipulation, the difference between the two groups can be attributed to the effect of the experimental manipulation.

Given these problems, is the one-group pretest-posttest design ever used? This design may in fact be used in many applied settings. Recall the example of the evaluation of a program to teach emergency procedures to employees. With a one-group pretest-posttest design, the knowledge test would be given before and after the training session. The ability to observe a change from the pretest to the posttest does represent an improvement over the posttest-only design, even with the threats to internal validity that we identified. In addition, the ability to use data from this design can be enhanced if the study is replicated at other times with other participants. However, formation of a control group is always the best way to strengthen this design.

In any control group, the participants in the experimental condition and the control condition must be equivalent. If participants in the two groups differ *before* the manipulation, they will probably differ *after* the manipulation as well. The next design illustrates this problem.

Check Your Learning

Now complete Check Your Learning: Practice Exercise #2 to test your understanding of threats to internal validity using one-group pretest-posttest designs.

Nonequivalent Control Group Design

The **nonequivalent control group design** employs a separate control group, but the participants in the two conditions—the experimental group and the control group—are not equivalent. In other words, the two groups are not the result of random assignment. The differences become a confounding variable that provides an alternative explanation for the results. This problem, called **selection differences** or *selection bias,* usually occurs when participants who form the two groups in the experiment are chosen from existing natural groups. If the relaxation training program is studied with the nonequivalent control group design, the design will look like this:

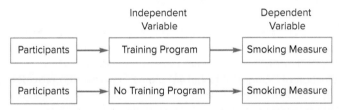

This design may be confused with one in which the participants themselves are selected based on known individual differences—subject variables (sometimes termed participant variables). For example, after participants have completed a Big 5 Personality Inventory, they might be divided into high and low scorers on the extraversion scale. This is clearly a nonexperimental design; there was no random assignment or manipulation of an independent variable.

Another similar design is the ex-post-facto (after the fact) design, in which participants are placed into groups based on some prior experience. For instance, while a researcher could not ethically (or easily!) randomly assign children to live in smokers' or non-smokers' homes to test the effects on their development, they could find individuals to form after-the-fact groups. This design looks like an experiment, but the lack of random assignment means this is not a true experimental design.

It is important to note that the problem of selection differences arises in this design even when the researcher apparently has successfully manipulated the independent variable using two similar groups. For example, a researcher might have all smokers in the engineering division of a company participate in the relaxation training program and smokers who work in the marketing division serve as a control group. The problem here, of course, is that the smokers in the two divisions may have differed in smoking patterns *prior* to the relaxation program.

Nonequivalent Control Group Pretest-Posttest Design

The nonequivalent control group posttest-only design can be greatly improved if a pretest is given. When this is done, we have a **nonequivalent control group pretest-posttest design,** one of the most useful quasi-experimental designs. It can be diagrammed as follows:

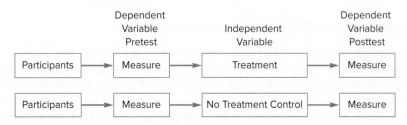

This design is similar to the pretest-posttest design described in the chapter "Experimental Design." However, this is not a true experimental design because assignment to groups is not random; the two groups might not be equivalent. We have the advantage, however, of knowing the pretest scores. Thus, we can see whether the groups were the same on the pretest. Even if the groups are not equivalent, we can look at *changes* in scores from the pretest to the posttest. If the independent variable has an effect, the experimental group should show a greater change than the control group (see Kenny, 1979).

An evaluation of National Alcohol Screening Day (NASD) provides an example of the use of a nonequivalent control group pretest-posttest design (Aseltine et al., 2008). NASD is a community-based program that provides free access to alcohol screening, a private meeting with a health professional to review the results, educational materials, and referral information if necessary. For the evaluation, NASD attendees at five community locations completed a baseline (pretest) measure of their recent alcohol consumption. This measure was administered as a posttest 3 months later. A control group was formed 1 week following NASD at the same locations using displays that invited people to take part in a health survey. These individuals completed the same pretest measure and were contacted in 3 months for the posttest. The data analysis focused on participants identified as at-risk drinkers; the NASD participants showed a significant decrease in alcohol consumption from pretest to posttest when compared with similar individuals in the control group.

An interesting variation of this design was employed by Rathje et al. (2021). In their study, research participants watched a play. It was hypothesized that watching the play would increase empathy. The play centered on the plight of auto workers in Detroit following the 2008 financial crisis; there were 30 performances of the show. Recruitment flyers asking people to participate in the study were placed in the play program. Half the shows had a flyer inviting audience members to take a survey prior to the show, using their phone or a paper questionnaire. The other shows had flyers asking audience members to complete the survey after the show. Audience members who took the survey after seeing the play did show a greater expression of empathy for the factory workers than did the audiences who were measured only before the play; the individuals who took the survey after the play were also more supportive of efforts to help workers (e.g., by reducing income inequality and racial discrimination). This design has one group completing the pretest but not the posttest; the other group does complete the posttest after seeing the play but did not provide pretest data.

Propensity Score Matching of Nonequivalent Treatment and Control Groups

The nonequivalent control group designs lack random assignment to conditions, and so the groups may in fact differ in important ways. For example, people who decide to attend an alcohol-screening event may differ from those who are interested in a health screening. Perhaps the people at the health screening are in fact healthier than the alcohol-screening participants.

One approach to making the groups equivalent on a variable such as health is to match participants in the conditions on a measure of health (this is similar to matched pairs designs, covered in the chapter "Experimental Design"). The health measure can be administered to everyone in the treatment condition and all individuals who are included in the control condition. Each person in the treatment condition would be matched with a control individual who possesses an identical or highly similar health score. Once this has been done, the analysis of the dependent measure can take place. This procedure is most effective when the measure used for the matching is highly reliable and the individuals in the two conditions are known to be very similar. Nonetheless, it is still possible that the two groups are different on other variables that were not measured.

Advances in statistical methods have made it possible to simultaneously match individuals on multiple variables. Instead of matching on just one variable, such as health, the researcher can obtain measures of other variables thought to be important when comparing the groups. The scores on these variables are combined to produce what is called a *propensity score* (the statistical procedure is beyond the scope of the book). Individuals in the treatment and control groups can then be matched on propensity scores—this process is called **propensity score matching** (Guo & Fraser, 2010; Shadish et al., 2002).

Interrupted Time Series Design and Control Series Design

Campbell (1969) discusses at length the evaluation of one specific legal reform: the 1955 crackdown on speeding in Connecticut. Although seemingly an event in the distant past, the example is still a good illustration of an important methodological issue. The crackdown was instituted after a record high number of traffic fatalities occurred in 1955. The easiest way to evaluate this reform is to compare the number of traffic fatalities in 1955 (before the crackdown) with the number of fatalities in 1956 (after the crackdown). Indeed, the number of traffic deaths fell from 324 in 1955 to 284 in 1956. This single comparison is really a one-group pretest-posttest design with all of that design's problems of internal validity; there are many other reasons traffic deaths might have declined. One alternative is to

FIGURE 3
Connecticut
traffic fatalities,
1951–1959

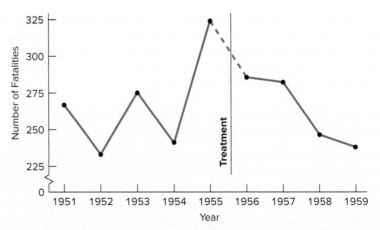

use an **interrupted time series design** that would examine the traffic fatality rates over an extended period of time, both before and after the reform was instituted. Figure 3 shows this information for the years 1951–1959. Campbell (1969) argues that the drop from 1955 to 1956 does not look particularly impressive, given the great fluctuations in previous years, but there is a steady downward trend in fatalities after the crackdown. Even here, however, Campbell sees a problem in interpretation. The drop could be due to statistical regression: Because 1955 was a record high year, the probability is that there would have been a drop anyway. Still, the data for the years extending before and after the crackdown allow for a less ambiguous interpretation than would be possible with data for only 1955 and 1956.

One way to improve the interrupted time series design is to find some kind of control group—a **control series design.** In the Connecticut speeding crackdown, this was possible because other states had not instituted the reform. Figure 4 shows the same data on traffic fatalities in Connecticut plus the fatality figures of four comparable states during the same years. The fact that the fatality rates in the

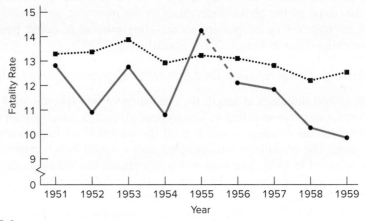

FIGURE 4
Control series design comparing Connecticut traffic fatality rate (solid color line) with the fatality rate of four comparable states (dotted black line)

control states remained relatively constant while those in Connecticut consistently declined led Campbell to conclude that the crackdown did indeed have some effect.

Check Your Learning

Now complete Check Your Learning: Practice Exercise #3 to test your understanding of quasi-experimental design.

DEVELOPMENTAL RESEARCH DESIGNS

Developmental psychologists often study the ways individuals change as a function of age. A researcher might test a theory concerning changes in reasoning ability as children grow older, the age at which self-awareness develops in young children, or the global values people have as they move from adolescence through old age. In all cases, the major variable is age. Developmental researchers face an interesting choice in designing their studies, because there are two general methods for studying individuals of different ages: the cross-sectional method and the longitudinal method. You will see that the cross-sectional method shares similarities with the independent groups design whereas the longitudinal method is similar to the repeated measures design. We will also examine a hybrid approach called the sequential method. The three approaches are illustrated in Figure 5.

Cross-Sectional Method

	Year of Birth (cohort)	Time 1: 2010
Group 1:	1955	55 years old
Group 2:	1950	60 years old
Group 3:	1945	65 years old

Longitudinal Method

	Year of Birth (cohort)	Time 1: 2010	Time 2: 2015	Time 3: 2020
Group 1:	1955	55 years old ⟶	60 years old ⟶	65 years old

Sequential Method

	Year of Birth (cohort)	Time 1: 2010	Time 2: 2015	Time 3: 2020
Group 1:	1955	55 years old ⟶	60 years old ⟶	65 years old
Group 2:	1945	65 years old ⟶	70 years old ⟶	75 years old

FIGURE 5
Three designs for developmental research

Cross-Sectional Method

In a study using the **cross-sectional method,** persons of different ages are studied at only one point in time. Suppose you are interested in examining how the ability to learn a computer application changes as people grow older. Using the cross-sectional method, you might study people who are currently 20, 30, 40, and 50 years of age. The participants in your study would be given the same computer learning task, and you would compare the groups on their performance.

In a study by Tymula et al. (2013) using this method, subjects in four age groups (12–17, 21–25, 30–50, 65–90) completed the same financial decision-making task. The task involved choosing among options with varying levels of risk and reward that led to an expected financial outcome for each subject. Individuals in the oldest age group made the poorest financial decisions with more inconsistent decisions and lower financial outcomes.

Longitudinal Method

In the **longitudinal method,** the same group of people is observed at different points in time as they grow older. Perhaps the most famous longitudinal study is the Terman Life Cycle Study, which was begun by Stanford psychologist Lewis Terman in 1921. Terman studied 1,528 California schoolchildren who had intelligence test scores of at least 135. The participants, who called themselves "Termites," were initially measured on numerous aspects of their cognitive and social development in 1921 and 1922. Terman and his colleagues continued studying the Termites from childhood through adulthood (see Terman, 1925; Terman & Oden, 1947, 1959).

Terman's successors at Stanford have continued to track the Termites. The study has provided a rich description of the lives of highly intelligent individuals and disconfirmed many negative stereotypes of high intelligence—for example, the Termites were very well adjusted both socially and emotionally. The data have now been archived for use by other researchers, such as Friedman and Martin (2011), who used the Terman data to study whether personality and other factors are related to health and longevity. To complete their investigations, Friedman and Martin obtained death certificates of Terman participants to have precise data on both how long they lived and the causes of death. One strong pattern that emerged was that the personality dimension of "conscientiousness" (being self-disciplined, organized) that was measured in childhood was related to longevity. Of interest is that changes in personality qualities also affected longevity. Participants who had become less conscientious as adults had a reduction in longevity; those who became more conscientious as adults experienced longer lives. Another interesting finding concerned interacting with pets. Questions about animals were asked when participants were in their sixties; contrary to common beliefs, having or playing with pets was not related to longevity.

A unique longitudinal study on aging and Alzheimer's disease called the Nun Study illustrates a different approach (Snowden, 1997). In 1991, all members of a particular religious order born prior to 1917 were asked to participate by providing access to their archived records as well as various annual medical and psychological measures taken over the course of the study. The sample consisted of 678 women with a mean age of 83. One fascinating finding from this study was based on autobiographies that all sisters wrote in 1930 (Danner et al., 2001). The researchers devised a coding system to measure positive emotional content in the autobiographies. Greater positive emotions were strongly related to actual survival rate during the course of the study. Other longitudinal studies may study individuals over only a few years. For example, a 9-year study of U.S. children found a variety of impacts—positive and negative—of early nonmaternal child care (NICHD Early Child Care Research Network, 2005).

Comparison of Longitudinal and Cross-Sectional Methods

The cross-sectional method is much more common than the longitudinal method, primarily because it is less expensive and yields results immediately. Note that with a longitudinal design, it would take 30 years to study the same group of individuals from age 20 to age 50, but with a cross-sectional design, comparisons of different age groups can be obtained relatively quickly.

There are some disadvantages to cross-sectional designs, however. Most important, the researcher must infer that differences among age groups are due to the developmental variable of age. The developmental change is not observed directly among the same group of people, but instead is based on comparisons among different cohorts of individuals. You can think of a **cohort** as a group of people born at about the same time, exposed to the same events in a society, and influenced by the same demographic trends such as divorce rates and family size. If you think about the hairstyles of people you know who are in their 30s, 40s, 50s, and 60s, you will immediately recognize the importance of **cohort effects!** More crucially, differences among cohorts reflect different economic and political conditions in society, different music and arts, different educational systems, and different child-rearing practices. In a cross-sectional study, a difference among groups of different ages may reflect developmental age changes; however, the differences may result from cohort effects (Schaie, 1986).

To illustrate this issue, let's return to our hypothetical study on learning to use a computer application. Suppose you found that age is associated with a decrease in ability, such that the people in the 50-year-old group score lower on the learning measure than the 40-year-olds, and so on. Should you conclude that the ability to learn to use a computer application decreases with age? That may be an accurate conclusion; alternatively, the differences could be due to a cohort effect: The older people had less experience with computers while growing up. The key point here is that the cross-sectional method confounds age and cohort effects. (Review the discussion of confounding and internal validity at the beginning of the chapter "Experimental Design.") Finally, you should note that cohort effects are most likely to be a problem when the researcher is examining age effects across a wide range of ages (e.g., adolescents through older adults).

The only way to conclusively study changes that occur as people grow older is to use a longitudinal design. Also, longitudinal research is the best way to study how scores on a variable at one age are related to another variable at a later age. For example, the National Longitudinal Survey of Youth (NLSY79) is a longitudinal project that follows the lives of a sample of American youth who were born between 1957 and 1964. This study focused on educational experiences, family background, government program participation, family life, health issues, and economic factors like work, wealth, and income. The original sample included 12,686 respondents who were ages 14–22 when first interviewed in 1979. Today, 9,964 respondents remain in the study. Longitudinal studies are both valuable and expensive to conduct—there are many projects around the world (see CLOSER in the United Kingdom; the Health and Aging Study in Africa: A Longitudinal Study of an INDEPTH Community in South Africa (HAALSI); and the Longitudinal Aging Study in India (LASI) for examples). The alternative, in this case, would be to study samples of children of various ages and ask them or their parents about the earlier home environment; this *retrospective* approach has its own problems when one considers the difficulty of remembering events in the distant past.

Thus, the longitudinal approach, despite being expensive and difficult, has definite advantages. However, there is another major problem: Over the course of a longitudinal study, people may move, die, or lose interest in the study. Researchers who conduct longitudinal studies become adept at convincing people to continue, often travel anywhere to collect more data, and compare test scores of people who drop out with those who stay, to provide better analyses of their results. In sum, a researcher should not embark on a longitudinal study without considerable resources and a great deal of patience and energy!

Sequential Method

A compromise between the longitudinal and cross-sectional methods is to use the **sequential method.** This method, along with the cross-sectional and longitudinal methods, is illustrated in Figure 5, where the goal of the study is to minimally compare 55- and 65-year-olds. The first phase of the sequential method begins with the cross-sectional method; for example, you could study groups of 55- and 65-year-olds. These individuals are then studied using the longitudinal method with each individual tested at least one more time.

Orth et al. (2010) studied the development of self-esteem over time using just such a sequential method. Using data from the Americans' Changing Lives study, Orth and his colleagues identified six different age cohorts (25–34, 35–44, 45–54, 55–64, 65–74, and 75+) and examined their self-esteem ratings from 1986, 1989, 1994, and 2002. Thus, they were interested in changes in self-esteem for participants at various ages, over time. Their findings provide an interesting picture of how self-esteem changes over time: They found that self-esteem gradually increases from age 25 to around age 60 and then declines in later years. Imagine how many years it would take if this were conducted as a full longitudinal study!

Clearly, this method takes fewer years and less effort to complete than a longitudinal study, and the researcher reaps immediate rewards because data on the different age groups are available in the first year of the study. On the other hand, the participants are not followed over the entire time span as they would be in a full longitudinal investigation; that is, no one in the Orth study was followed from age 25 to 100.

We have now described most of the major approaches to designing research. In the chapters "Understanding Research Results: Description and Correlation" and "Understanding Research Results: Statistical Inference" we consider methods of analyzing research data.

Check Your Learning

Now complete Check Your Learning: Practice Exercise #4 to test your understanding of developmental research designs.

ENGAGING WITH RESEARCH: DEVELOPMENTAL RESEARCH

Food security is defined as the availability of nutritious food and people's access to it. Nutrition is critical to children's positive development. Sub-Saharan Africa has a large number of children experiencing food insecurity.

Aurino et al. (2020) conducted a longitudinal study of children in Ghana, in sub-Saharan Africa. They noted, "To the best of our knowledge, this is the first study that examines longitudinal associations between food insecurity and early childhood development across multiple developmental domains in a LMIC [low- or middle-income country], a remarkable knowledge gap." The data, a part of the Quality Preschool for Ghana project, were collected in 2015, 2017, and 2018. Aurino et al. investigated the consequences of food insecurity on five outcome variables: literacy skills, numeracy (math) skills, short-term memory, socio-emotional development, and self-regulation.

First, acquire and read the article (available at https://doi.org/10.1371/journal.pone.0230965/):

Aurino, E., Wolf, S., & Tsinigo, E. (2020). Household food insecurity and early childhood development: Longitudinal evidence from Ghana. *PLoS ONE, 15*(4). https://doi.org/10.1371/journal.pone.0230965

Then, after reading the article, consider the following:

1. **What is the primary goal of this study? Description, Prediction, Determining Cause, or Explaining? Do the authors achieve their goals?**
2. **What did these researchers do? What was the method?**
   a. Where, how, and by whom were the data collected?
3. **What was measured?**
   a. How was each of the five outcome variables measured?

4. **To what or whom can we generalize the results?**

   a. Do you think we can generalize these results to other sub-Saharan African countries? Other countries in Africa? Other places in the world? Why or why not?

5. **What did they find? What were the results?**

6. **Have other researchers found similar results?**

   a. How do these results compare with or contrast with studies that have been conducted in India? What about studies that have been conducted in the United States?

7. **What are the limitations of this study?**

8. **What are the ethical issues present in this study?**

BEING A SKILLED CONSUMER OF RESEARCH

1. Go to CLOSER (https://www.closer.ac.uk)—a research center housed in the University College London's Social Research Institute—and explore their datasets. From their homepage, click on *Search Our Data* and then *Explore* (on the right side). Then, choose a topic of interest (e.g., Life Events, Mental Health, Family & Social Networks), and explore answers to survey questions. Or, from the homepage, click on *Search Our Data* and then *CLOSER Discovery* and pick a study (e.g., The Millennium Cohort Study) and find out about the cohort, or the methodologies used to collect the data. Keep the key-questions for being a skilled consumer of research in mind as your explore their data:

   a. What is the primary goal of this study? Description, Prediction, Determining Cause, or Explaining? Do the authors achieve their goals?

   b. What did these researchers do? What was the method?

   c. What was measured?

   d. To what or whom can we generalize the results?

   e. What did they find? What were the results?

   f. Have other researchers found similar results?

   g. What are the limitations of this study?

   h. What are the ethical issues present in this study?

2. You leave your dog alone at home while you are at work. When you are away, your dog engages in destructive activities like chewing on

your shoes, pulling down curtains, strewing wastebasket contents all over the floor. You decide that playing a radio while you are gone might help. How might you determine whether this "treatment" is effective?

3. Your best friend frequently suffers from severe headaches. You have noticed that your friend consumes a great deal of diet cola, and so you consider the hypothesis that the artificial sweetener in the cola is responsible for the headaches. Devise a way to test your hypothesis using a single-case design. What do you expect to find if your hypothesis is correct? If you obtain the expected results, what do you conclude about the effect of the artificial sweetener on headaches?

4. Gilovich (1991) described an incident he had read about during a visit to Israel. A very large number of deaths had occurred during a brief time period in one region of the country. A group of rabbis attributed the deaths to a recent change in religious practice that allowed women to attend funerals. Women were immediately forbidden to attend funerals in that region, and the number of deaths subsequently decreased. How would you explain this phenomenon?

5. The captain of each precinct of a metropolitan police department selected two officers to participate in a program designed to reduce prejudice by increasing sensitivity to racial and ethnic group differences and community issues. The training program took place every Friday morning for 3 months. At the first and last meetings, the officers completed a measure of prejudice. To assess the effectiveness of the program, the average prejudice score at the first meeting was compared with the average score at the last meeting; it was found that the average score was in fact lower (indicating less prejudice) following the training program. What type of design is this? What specific problems arise if you try to conclude that the training program was responsible for the reduction in prejudice?

6. Many elementary schools have implemented a daily "sustained silent reading" period during which students, faculty, and staff spend 15–20 minutes silently reading a book of their choice. Advocates of this policy claim that the activity encourages pleasure reading outside the required silent reading time. Design a nonequivalent control group pretest-posttest quasi-experiment to test this claim. Include a well-reasoned dependent measure as well. Discuss the advantages and disadvantages of using a quasi-experimental design in contrast to conducting a true experiment.

Check Your Learning: Practice Exercises

Practice Exercise #1

A youth soccer/football coach has three children who volunteered to play goalie. Coach normally spends 20 minutes each week having the three children practice being goalie and records the number of goals saved and scored during that time. The coach has just read an article on how to improve goalie performance; it requires the coach to spend 3 hours with a child outside of regular practice. All of the goalies receive the new goalie training—1 hour per week for 6 weeks; the coach starts the first goalie in week 1, the second goalie in week 2, and the last goalie in week 3. Meanwhile, all the goalies continued to practice for 20 minutes during regular practice sessions. Which of the following designs best fits this scenario? Explain your answer:

a. reversal design

b. multiple baseline across subjects

c. multiple baseline across behaviors

d. time series

Practice Exercise #2

In the third week of the fall term, some first-year college students were given a measure of overall adjustment to college life. A week later, the students were trained on meditation/mindfulness techniques designed to help people cope with stress. Then, in the fifth week, the participants were asked again to complete the measures adjustment to college life. Results showed that the intervention improved self-reported adjustment and stress.

What is the design of this study?

Describe how each of the threats to internal validity listed below could influence the results of this study:

a. history

b. maturation

c. testing

d. regression toward the mean (statistical regression)

Practice Exercise #3

In 2009 a donor provided the State of Colorado with funding to provide no-cost Long-Acting Reversible Contraception (LARC) devices at clinics through-out the state. LARC contraception methods include IUDs and implants. The funding lasted from 2009 to 2015. Researchers have now presented data supporting the effectiveness of the program. For example, the unintended pregnancy rate for 15- to 19-year-olds in 2007 and 2008, prior to the program, was 38 pregnancies per 1,000 females. The rates in subsequent years were 35 in 2009, 34 in 2010, 29 in 2011, 26 in 2012, 24 in 2013, and 21 in 2014. There were also decreases in number of abortions, births to mothers with less than high school education, and other measures (see https://www.colorado.gov/pacific/sites/default/files/PSD_TitleX3_CFPI-Report.pdf). Which of the following designs best fits this scenario? Explain your answer:

a. reversal design

b. interrupted time-series design

c. control series design

d. one group posttest-only design

Practice Exercise #4

A community weekly newspaper in Southern California in 1975 published the names of the parents of all children born in the community's three hospitals during the previous week. For one year, a team of university researchers contacted the parents about participating in a study. If the parents agreed, they would provide data about themselves and the child once each year until 2015. Which of the following designs best fits this scenario? Explain your answer:

a. longitudinal

b. cross-sectional

CHAPTER REVIEW

Review Questions

1. What is a reversal design? Why is an ABAB design superior to an ABA design?

2. What is meant by *baseline* in a single-case design?

3. What is a multiple baseline design? Why is it used? Distinguish between multiple baseline designs across subjects, across behaviors, and across situations.

4. Why might a researcher use a quasi-experimental design rather than a true experimental design?

5. Why does the use of a control group eliminate the problems associated with the one-group pretest-posttest design?

6. Describe the threats to internal validity discussed in the text: history, maturation, testing, instrument decay, regression toward the mean, and selection differences.

7. Describe the nonequivalent control group pretest-posttest design. Why is this a quasi-experimental design rather than a true experiment?
8. Describe the interrupted time series and the control series designs. What are the strengths of the control series design as compared with the interrupted time series design?
9. Distinguish between longitudinal, cross-sectional, and sequential methods.
10. What is a cohort effect?

Study Terms

Baseline (p. 246)

Cohort (p. 261)

Cohort effects (p. 261)

Control series design (p. 258)

Cross-sectional method (p. 260)

History effects (p. 252)

Instrument decay (p. 253)

Interrupted time series design (p. 258)

Longitudinal method (p. 260)

Maturation effects (p. 252)

Multiple baseline design (p. 248)

Nonequivalent control group design (p. 255)

Nonequivalent control group pretest-posttest design (p. 256)

One-group posttest-only design (p. 251)

One-group pretest-posttest design (p. 252)

Propensity score matching (p. 257)

Quasi-experimental design (p. 250)

Regression toward the mean (statistical regression) (p. 253)

Reversal design (p. 247)

Selection differences (p. 255)

Sequential method (p. 262)

Single-case experimental design (p. 246)

Testing effects (p. 252)

Check Your Learning: Answers

Practice Exercise #1

b. Multiple baseline across subjects. The behavior of several subjects is measured over time. For each subject, the manipulation is introduced at a different point in time.

Practice Exercise #2

The design of this study is a one group pre-test/post-test.

a. It's possible that, instead of the intervention, a major event (e.g., a speaker who focuses on life in college, a crime on campus, an event at the national level) could have changed students' perceptions of their adjustment.

b. Students change over time. It's possible that, as first-year students experience increasingly more of college life, their scores change naturally, and not as the result of the intervention.

c. The adjustment scale was given twice in a 3-week period. It's possible that the first administration could affect the second. For instance, after the students were first asked about their adjustment, they might have begun to think more deeply about their adjustment and then changed as a result of the measure, rather than as a result of the intervention.

d. Regression toward the mean is possible if many of the participants scored particularly low on the pretest adjustment measure (lower than their true score) because of random error. When measured later on the posttest, we would expect these individuals to score closer to their true score. Therefore, they would show an improvement in adjustment with no effect of the meditation training.

Practice Exercise #3

a. Interrupted time-series design. Measurements are made over time, both before and after the "treatment" (in this case, the LARC funding) is in place.

Practice Exercise #4

a. Longitudinal. Research participants are followed over time.

Adam Hester/Getty Images

Understanding Research Results: Description and Correlation

LEARNING OBJECTIVES

- Compare and contrast the three ways of describing results: comparing group percentages, correlating scores, and comparing group means.
- Describe a frequency distribution, including the various ways to display a frequency distribution.
- Compare and contrast the three measures of central tendency
- Describe how to determine how much variability exists in a set of scores.
- Define what a correlation coefficient is.
- Explain what an effect size is.
- Describe how researchers use regression equations to predict behavior.
- Distinguish between mediation and moderation as ways to explore more complex relationships among variables.
- Explain the purpose of more advanced statistical techniques like structural equation modeling.

IN THE CHAPTER "FUNDAMENTAL RESEARCH ISSUES" WE IDENTIFIED FOUR TYPES OF VALIDITY: *CONSTRUCT VALIDITY, INTERNAL VALIDITY, EXTERNAL VALIDITY,* AND *CONCLUSION VALIDITY.* Statistical conclusion validity was defined as the accuracy of the statistical conclusions drawn from results that are based on statistical analyses. This chapter and the chapter "Understanding Research Results: Statistical Inference" are critical in understanding statistical conclusion validity.

There are two ways in which statistics help us understand data collected in research investigations. First, statistics are used to describe the data. Second, statistics are used to make inferences and draw conclusions about a population on the basis of sample data. This chapter will focus on the underlying logic and general procedures for making statistical decisions. We examine descriptive statistics and correlation in this chapter. Inferential statistics are discussed in the chapter "Understanding Research Results: Statistical Inference," and specific calculations for a variety of statistics are provided in Appendix B. These chapters will also provide an introduction to the statistical techniques that you will see presented in published studies. While some of these techniques are quite advanced, to be a skilled consumer of research you must have some knowledge of them.

SCALES OF MEASUREMENT: A REVIEW

Before looking at any statistics, we need to review the concept of scales of measurement. Whenever a variable is studied, the researcher must create an operational definition of the variable and devise two or more levels of the variable. Recall from the chapter "Measurement Concepts" that the levels of the variable can be described using one of four scales of measurement: nominal, ordinal, interval, and ratio. The scale used determines the types of statistics that are appropriate when analyzing data. Also recall that the meaning of a particular score on a variable depends on which type of scale was used when the variable was measured or manipulated.

The levels of **nominal scale** variables have no numerical, quantitative properties. The levels are simply different categories or groups. Most independent variables in experiments are nominal—for example, as in an experiment that compares behavioral and cognitive therapies for depression. Variables such as eye color, hand dominance, college major, and marital status are nominal scale variables; left-handed and right-handed people differ from each other, but not in a quantitative way.

Variables with **ordinal scale** levels exhibit minimal quantitative distinctions. We can rank order the levels of the variable being studied from lowest to highest. The clearest example of an ordinal scale is one that asks people to make rank-ordered judgments. For example, you might ask people to rank the most important problems facing your state today. If education is ranked first, health care second, and crime third, you know the order but you do not know how strongly people feel about each problem: Education and health care may be deemed very close together in seriousness, with crime a distant third. With an ordinal scale, the intervals between items probably are not equal.

Interval scale and ratio scale variables have much more detailed quantitative properties. With an **interval scale** variable, the intervals between the levels are equal in size. The difference between 1 and 2 on the scale, for example, is the same as the difference between 2 and 3. Interval scales generally have five or more quantitative levels. You might ask people to rate their mood on a 7-point scale ranging from a "very negative" to a "very positive" mood. There is no absolute zero point that indicates an "absence" of mood.

In the behavioral sciences, it can be difficult to know precisely whether an ordinal or an interval scale is being used. However, it is often useful to assume that the variable is being measured on an interval scale, because interval scales allow for more sophisticated statistical treatments than do ordinal scales. Of course, if the measure is a rank ordering (for example, a rank ordering of professors on the basis of popularity), an ordinal scale clearly is being used.

Ratio scale variables have both equal intervals and an absolute zero point that indicates the absence of the variable being measured. Time, weight, length, and other physical measures are the best examples of ratio scales. Interval and ratio scale variables are conceptually different; however, the statistical procedures used to analyze data with such variables are identical. An important implication of interval and ratio scales is that data can be summarized using the mean, or arithmetic average. It is possible to provide a number that reflects the mean amount of a variable—for example, "the average mood of people who won a contest was 5.16" or "the mean weight of the men completing the weight loss program was 187.7 pounds."

DESCRIBING RESULTS

Scales of measurement have important implications for the way the results of research investigations are described and analyzed. Most research focuses on the study of relationships between variables. Depending on the way the variables are studied, there are three basic ways of describing the results: (1) comparing group percentages, (2) correlating scores of individuals on two variables, and (3) comparing group means.

Comparing Group Percentages

This first way of describing results is useful when a key variable is measured on a nominal scale. Suppose you notice that two speakers have been scheduled on the same evening on your campus—one will speak on climate change, and the other will speak on adolescents' mental health. You would like to know if the audiences for the talks differ in some ways. You prepare a survey questionnaire that can be completed using a smartphone and ask people to complete it as they enter the lecture halls. One question asks the attendees if they used public transportation in the last month (yes/no, a nominal variable). To describe your results, you will need to calculate the percentage of climate change attendees who have used public transportation in the past month and compare this with the percentage of the mental health audience who have. Suppose you tested 50 people attending each lecture and found that 40 of the climate audience and 30 of the mental health attendees indicated that they used public transportation in the past month. In describing your findings, you would report that 80% of those attending a climate change lecture used public transportation, in comparison with 60% of the mental health audience. Thus, you have identified a difference in the two groups. Note that we are focusing on percentages because the using public transportation variable is nominal: one either has, or has not, used public transportation in the past month.

After describing your data, the next step would be to perform a statistical analysis to determine whether there is a statistically significant difference between the two groups of lecture attendees, or if the differences in the sample are due to chance. Statistical significance is discussed in the chapter "Understanding Research Results: Statistical Inference"; statistical analysis procedures are described in Appendix B.

Correlating Individual Scores

A second type of analysis is needed when you have an interval or ratio scale of measurement. In this circumstance, individuals are measured on two variables, and each variable has a range of numerical values. For example, we will consider an analysis of data on the relationship between location in a classroom and grades in the class: Do people who sit near the front receive higher grades?

Comparing Group Means

Much research is designed to compare the mean responses of participants in two or more groups. For example, in an experiment designed to study the effect of exposure to an aggressive adult, one group might be children who observe an adult "model" behaving aggressively and the control group might be children who do not. Each child then plays alone for 10 minutes in a room containing a number of toys, while observers record the number of times the child behaves aggressively during play. Aggression is a ratio scale variable because there are equal intervals and a true zero on the scale.

In this case, you would be interested in comparing the mean number of aggressive acts by children in the two conditions to determine whether the children who observed the model were more aggressive than the children in the control condition. Hypothetical data from such an experiment in which there were 10 children in each condition are shown in Table 1; the scores in the table represent the number of aggressive acts by each child. In this case, the mean aggression score in the model group is 5.20 and the mean score in the no-model condition is 3.10.

For all types of data, it is important to understand your results by carefully describing the data collected. We begin by constructing frequency distributions.

TABLE 1   Scores on aggression measure in a hypothetical experiment on modeling and aggression

Model group	No-model group
3	1
4	2
5	2
5	3
5	3
5	3
6	4
6	4
6	4
7	5
$\Sigma X = 52$	$\Sigma X = 31$
$\overline{X} = 5.20$	$\overline{X} = 3.10$
$s^2 = 1.29$	$s^2 = 1.43$
$s = 1.14$	$s = 1.20$
$n = 10$	$n = 10$

FREQUENCY DISTRIBUTIONS

When analyzing results, researchers often start by constructing a frequency distribution of the data. A **frequency distribution** indicates the number of individuals who receive each possible score on a variable. Frequency distributions of exam scores are familiar to most college students—they tell how many students received a given score on the exam. Along with the number of individuals associated with each response or score, it is useful to examine the percentage associated with this number.

Graphing Frequency Distributions

It is often useful to graphically depict frequency distributions. Let's examine several types of graphs: pie chart, bar graph, frequency polygon, and histogram.

Pie Charts   **Pie charts** divide a whole circle, or "pie," into "slices" that represent relative percentages. Figure 1 shows a pie chart depicting a frequency distribution in which 70% of people like to travel and 30% dislike travel. Because there are two pieces of information to graph, there are two slices in this pie. Pie charts are particularly useful when representing nominal scale information. In the figure, the number of people who chose each response has been converted to a percentage—the simple number could have been displayed instead, of course. Pie charts are most commonly used to depict simple descriptions of categories

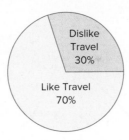

FIGURE 1
Pie chart

for a single variable. They are useful in applied research reports and articles written for the general public. Articles in scientific journals require more complex information displays.

Bar Graphs   **Bar graphs** use a separate and distinct bar for each piece of information. Figure 2 represents the same information about travel using a bar graph. In this graph, the *x* or horizontal axis shows the two possible responses. The *y* or vertical axis shows the number of people who chose each response, and so the height of each bar represents the number of people who responded to the "like" and "dislike" options.

Frequency Polygons   **Frequency polygons** use a line to represent the distribution of frequencies of scores. This is most useful when the data represent interval or ratio scales, as in the modeling and aggression data shown in Table 1. Here we have a clear numeric scale of the number of aggressive acts during the observation period. Figure 3 graphs the data from the hypothetical experiment using two frequency polygons—one for each group. The solid line represents the no-model group, and the dotted line stands for the model group.

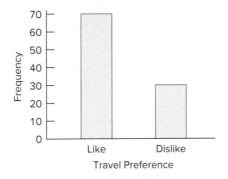

FIGURE 2
Bar graph displaying data obtained in two groups

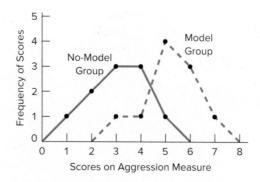

FIGURE 3
Frequency polygons illustrating the distributions of scores in Table 1

Note: Each frequency polygon is anchored at scores that were not obtained by anyone (0 and 6 in the no-model group; 2 and 8 in the model group).

Histograms   A **histogram** uses bars to display a frequency distribution for a quantitative variable. In this case, the scale values are continuous and show increasing amounts on a variable such as age, blood pressure, or stress. Because the values are continuous, the bars are drawn next to each other. A histogram is shown in Figure 4 using data from the model group in Table 1.

What can you discover by examining frequency distributions? First, you can directly observe how your participants responded. You can see what scores are most frequent, and you can look at the shape of the distribution of scores. You can tell whether there are any outliers—scores that are unusual, unexpected, or very different from the scores of other participants. In an experiment, you can compare the distribution of scores in the groups.

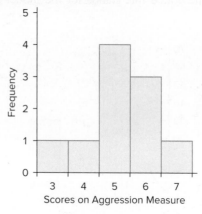

FIGURE 4
Histogram showing frequency of responses in the model group

DESCRIPTIVE STATISTICS

In addition to examining the distribution of scores, you can calculate descriptive statistics. **Descriptive statistics** allow researchers to make precise statements about the data. Two statistics are needed to describe the data. A single number can be used to describe the central tendency, or how participants scored overall. Another number describes the variability, or how widely the distribution of scores is spread. These two numbers summarize the information contained in a frequency distribution.

Central Tendency

A **central tendency** statistic tells us what the sample as a whole, or on the average, is like. There are three measures of central tendency—the mean, the median, and the mode.

The **mean** of a set of scores is obtained by adding all the scores and dividing by the number of scores. It is symbolized as $\overline{X}$; in scientific reports, it is abbreviated as *M*. The mean is an appropriate indicator of central tendency only when scores are measured on an interval or ratio scale, because the actual values of the numbers are used in calculating the statistic. In Table 1, the mean score for the no-model group is 3.10 and for the model group is 5.20. Note that the Greek letter Σ (sigma) in Table 1 is a statistical notation for summing a set of numbers. Thus, ΣX is shorthand for "sum of the values in a set of scores."

The **median** is the score that divides the group in half (with 50% scoring below and 50% scoring above the median). In scientific reports, the median is abbreviated as *Mdn*. The median is appropriate when scores are on an ordinal scale, because it takes into account only the rank order of the scores. It is also useful with interval and ratio scale variables, however. The median for the no-model group is 3 and for the model group is 5.

The **mode** is the most frequent score. The mode is the only measure of central tendency that is appropriate if a nominal scale is used. The mode does not use the actual values on the scale, but simply indicates the most frequently occurring value. There are two modal values for the no-model group—3 and 4 occur equally frequently. The mode for the model group is 5.

The median or mode can be a better indicator of central tendency than the mean if a few unusual scores bias the mean. For example, the median family income of a county or state is usually a better measure of central tendency than the mean family income. Because a relatively small number of individuals have extremely high incomes, using the mean would make it appear that the "average" person makes more money than is actually the case.

Variability

We can also determine how much **variability** exists in a set of scores. A measure of variability is a number that characterizes the amount of spread in a distribution of scores. One such measure is the **standard deviation,** symbolized as *s*, which indicates the average deviation of scores from the mean. Income is a good example.

The Census Bureau reports that the median U.S. household income in 2020 was $67,521 (https://www.census.gov/library/publications/2021/demo/p60-273.html). Suppose that you live in a community that matches the U.S. median and there is very little variation around that median (i.e., every household earns something close to $67,521); your community would have a smaller standard deviation in household income compared to another community in which the median income is the same but there is a lot more variation (e.g., where many people earn $15,000 per year and others $5 million per year). It is possible for measures of central tendency in two communities to be close with the variability differing substantially.

In scientific reports, the standard deviation is abbreviated as *SD*. It is derived by first calculating the **variance,** symbolized as s^2 (the standard deviation is the square root of the variance). The standard deviation of a set of scores is small when most people have similar scores close to the mean. The standard deviation becomes larger as more people have scores that lie farther from the mean value. For the model group, the standard deviation is 1.14, which tells us that most scores in that condition lie 1.14 units above and below the mean—that is, between 4.06 and 6.34. Thus, the mean and the standard deviation provide a great deal of information about the distribution. Note that, as with the mean, the calculation of the standard deviation uses the actual values of the scores; thus, the standard deviation is appropriate only for interval and ratio scale variables.

Another measure of variability is the **range,** which is simply the difference between the highest score and the lowest score. The range for both the model and no-model groups is 4.

Check Your Learning

Now, go to Check Your Learning: Practice Exercise #1 to work on your own descriptive statistics and figures.

GRAPHING RELATIONSHIPS

Graphing relationships between variables was discussed briefly in the chapter "Fundamental Research Issues." A common way to graph relationships between variables is to use a bar graph or a line graph. Figure 5 is a bar graph depicting

FIGURE 5
Graph of the results of the modeling experiment showing mean aggression scores

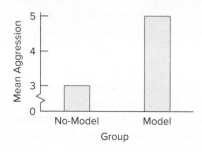

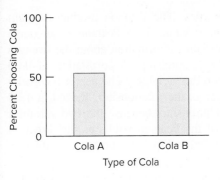 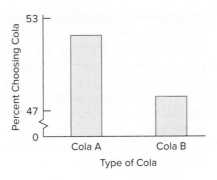

FIGURE 6
Two ways to graph the same data

the means for the no-model and model groups. The levels of the independent variable (no-model and model) are represented on the horizontal *x-axis*, and the dependent variable values are shown on the vertical *y-axis*. For each group, a point is placed along the *y-axis* that represents the mean for the groups, and a bar is drawn to visually represent the mean value. Bar graphs are used when the values on the *x-axis* are nominal categories (e.g., a no-model and a model condition). Line graphs are used when the values on the *x-axis* are numeric (e.g., marijuana use over time, as shown in the chapter "Asking People About Themselves," Figure 1). In line graphs, a line is drawn to connect the data points to represent the relationship between the variables.

Choosing the scale for a bar graph allows a common manipulation that is sometimes used by scientists and all too commonly used by advertisers. The trick is to exaggerate the distance between points on the measurement scale to make the results appear more dramatic than they really are. Suppose, for example, that a cola company (cola A) conducts a taste test that shows 52% of the participants prefer cola A and 48% prefer cola B. How should the cola company present these results? The two bar graphs in Figure 6 show the most honest method, as well as a truncated bar graph. Viewers of a truncated bar graph that shows only a portion of the possible values on the Y-axis conclude that the difference is much larger (Yang et al., 2021). It is always wise to look carefully at the numbers on the scales depicted in graphs.

CORRELATION COEFFICIENTS: DESCRIBING THE STRENGTH OF RELATIONSHIPS

It is important to know whether a relationship between variables is relatively weak or strong. A **correlation coefficient** is a statistic that describes how strongly variables are related to one another. You are probably most familiar with the **Pearson product-moment correlation coefficient,** which is used when both variables have interval or ratio scale properties. The Pearson product-moment correlation coefficient is called the Pearson *r*. Values of a Pearson *r* can range from 0.00 to ± 1.00. Thus, the Pearson *r* provides information about the strength of the relationship and the direction of the relationship. A correlation of 0.00 indicates that there is no relationship between the variables. The nearer a correlation is to 1.00 (plus or minus), the stronger is the relationship. Indeed, a 1.00 correlation is sometimes called a perfect relationship, because the two variables go together in a perfect fashion. The sign of the Pearson *r* tells us the direction of the relationship—that is, whether the relationship between the variables is positive or negative.

Data from studies examining similarities of intelligence test scores among siblings illustrate the connection between the magnitude of a correlation coefficient and the strength of a relationship. The relationship between scores of monozygotic (identical) twins reared together is .86 and the correlation for monozygotic twins reared apart is .74, demonstrating a strong similarity of test scores in these pairs of individuals. The correlation for dizygotic (fraternal) twins reared together is less strong, with a correlation of .59. The correlation among nontwin siblings raised together is .46, and the correlation among nontwin siblings reared apart is .24. Data such as these are important in ongoing research on the relative influence of heredity and environment on intelligence (Devlin et al., 1997; Gustavson et al., 2022; Kaplan, 2012).

There are several different types of correlation coefficients. Each coefficient is calculated somewhat differently depending on the measurement scale that applies to the two variables. As noted, the Pearson *r* correlation coefficient is appropriate when the values of both variables are on an interval or ratio scale. We will now focus on the details of the Pearson product-moment correlation coefficient.

Pearson r Correlation Coefficient

To calculate a correlation coefficient, we need to obtain pairs of observations from each subject. Thus, each individual has two scores, one on each of the variables. Table 2 shows fictitious data for 10 students measured on the variables of classroom seating pattern and exam grade. Students in the first row receive a seating score of 1, those in the second row receive a 2, and so on. Once we have made our observations, we can see whether the two variables are related. Are the variables associated in a systematic fashion?

The Pearson *r* provides two types of information about the relationship between the variables. The first is the strength of the relationship; the second is the direction of the relationship. As noted previously, the values of *r* can range from 0.00 to ±1.00. The absolute size of *r* is the coefficient that indicates the strength of the relationship irrespective of whether the coefficient is positive or negative. A value of 0.00 indicates that there is no relationship. The nearer *r* is to 1.00 (plus or minus), the stronger is the relationship. The plus and minus signs indicate whether there is a positive linear or negative linear relationship between the two variables. It is important to remember that it is the size of the correlation

TABLE 2 Pairs of scores for 10 participants on seating pattern and exam scores (fictitious data)

Subject identification number	Seating	Exam score
01	2	95
02	5	50
03	1	85
04	4	75
05	3	75
06	5	60
07	2	80
08	3	70
09	1	90
10	4	70

coefficient, not the sign, that indicates the strength of the relationship. Thus, a correlation coefficient of −.54 indicates a stronger relationship than does a coefficient of +.45.

Scatterplots   The data in Table 2 can be visualized in a **scatterplot** in which each pair of scores is plotted as a single point in a diagram. Figure 7 shows two scatterplots. The values of the first variable are depicted on the *x-axis,* and the values of the second variable are shown on the *y-axis*. These scatterplots show a perfect positive relationship (+1.00) and a perfect negative relationship (−1.00). You can easily see why these are perfect relationships: The scores on the two variables fall on a straight line that is on the diagonal of the diagram. Each person's score on one variable correlates precisely with their score on the other variable. If we know an individual's score on one of the variables, we can predict exactly what the person's score will be on the other variable. Such "perfect" relationships are rarely observed in reality.

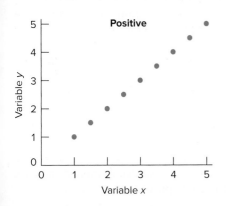
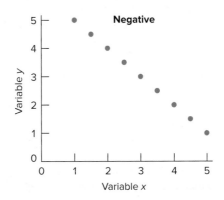

FIGURE 7
Scatterplots of perfect (±1.00) relationships

FIGURE 8
Scatterplots
depicting
patterns of
correlation

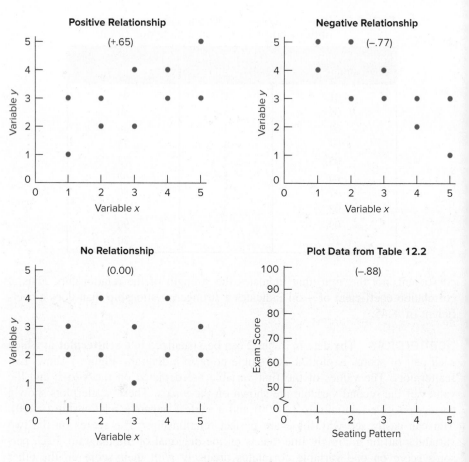

The scatterplots in Figure 8 show patterns of correlation you are more likely to encounter in exploring research findings. The first diagram shows pairs of scores with a positive correlation of +.65; the second diagram shows a negative relationship, −.77. The data points in these two scatterplots reveal a general pattern of either a positive or negative relationship, but the relationships are not perfect. You can make a general prediction in the first diagram—for instance, that the higher the score on one variable, the higher the score on the second variable. However, even if you know a person's score on the first variable, you cannot perfectly predict what that person's score will be on the second variable. To confirm this, take a look at value 1 on variable *x* (the horizontal axis) in the positive scatterplot. Looking along the vertical *y-axis,* you will see that two individuals had a score of 1. One of these had a score of 1 on variable *y,* and the other had a score of 3. The data points do not fall on the perfect diagonal shown in Figure 7. Instead, there is a variation (scatter) from the perfect diagonal line.

The third diagram shows a scatterplot in which there is absolutely no correlation (*r* = 0.00). The points fall all over the diagram in a completely random pattern. Thus, scores on variable *x* are not related to scores on variable *y.*

The fourth diagram has been left blank so that you can plot the scores from the data in Table 2. The x (horizontal) axis has been labeled for the seating pattern variable, and the y (vertical) axis for the exam score variable. To complete the scatterplot, you will need to plot the 10 pairs of scores. For each individual in the sample, find the score on the seating pattern variable; then go up from that point until you are level with that person's exam score on the *y-axis*. A point placed there will describe the score on both variables. There will be 10 points on the finished scatterplot.

The correlation coefficient calculated from these data shows a negative relationship between the variables ($r = -.88$). In other words, as the seating distance from the front of the class increases, the exam score decreases. Although these data are fictitious, a (much smaller) negative relationship has been reported in research on this topic (Benedict & Hoag, 2004; Brooks & Rebata, 1991; Will et al., 2020).

Important Considerations

Correlation coefficients are a useful way to understand the relationship between two variables. That said, there are two important factors to consider when thinking about correlations: restriction of range and the fact that the two variables could have a nonlinear relationship.

Restriction of Range
It is important that the researcher sample from the full range of possible values of both variables. If the range of possible values is restricted, the magnitude of the correlation coefficient is reduced. For example, if the range of seating pattern scores is restricted to the first two rows, you will not get an accurate picture of the relationship between seating pattern and exam score. In fact, when only scores of students sitting in the first two rows are considered, the correlation between the two variables is exactly 0.00. With a restricted range comes restricted variability in the scores and thus less variability that can be explained. Figure 9 illustrates a scatterplot with the entire

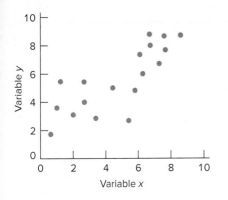 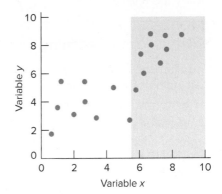

FIGURE 9
Left scatterplot—positive correlation with entire range of values. Right scatterplot—no correlation with restricted range of values

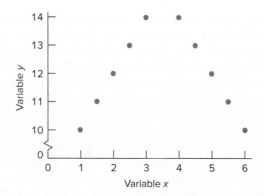

FIGURE 10
Scatterplot of a curvilinear relationship (Pearson product-moment correlation coefficient = 0.00)

range of X values represented and with a portion of those values missing because of restriction of range.

The problem of **restriction of range** occurs when the individuals in your sample are very similar on the variable you are studying. If you are studying age as a variable, for instance, testing only 6- and 7-year-olds will reduce your chances of finding age effects. Likewise, trying to study the correlates of intelligence will be almost impossible if everyone in your sample is very similar in intelligence (e.g., the senior class of a prestigious college).

Curvilinear Relationship

The Pearson product-moment correlation coefficient (r) is designed to detect only linear relationships. If the relationship is curvilinear, as in the scatterplot shown in Figure 10, the correlation coefficient will not indicate the existence of a relationship. The Pearson r correlation coefficient calculated from these data is exactly 0.00, even though the two variables clearly are related.

Check Your Learning

Go to Check Your Learning: Practice Exercise #2 to check your understanding of these important aspects of correlation coefficients.

Because a relationship may be curvilinear, it is important to construct a scatterplot in addition to looking at the magnitude of the correlation coefficient. The scatterplot is valuable because it gives a visual indication of the shape of the relationship. Computer programs for statistical analysis will usually display scatterplots and can show you how well the data fit to a linear or curvilinear relationship. When the relationship is curvilinear, another type of correlation coefficient must be used to determine the strength of the relationship.

EFFECT SIZE

We have presented the Pearson r correlation coefficient as the appropriate way to describe the relationship between two variables with interval or ratio scale properties. Researchers also want to describe the strength of relationships between variables in all studies. **Effect size** refers to the strength of association between variables. The Pearson r correlation coefficient is one indicator of effect size; it indicates the strength of the linear association between two variables. In an experiment with two or more treatment conditions, other types of correlation coefficients can be calculated to indicate the magnitude of the effect of the independent variable on the dependent variable. For example, in our experiment on the effects of witnessing an aggressive model on children's aggressive behavior, we compared the means of two groups. In addition to knowing the means, it is valuable to know the effect size. An effect size correlation coefficient can be calculated for the modeling and aggression experiment. In this case, the effect size correlation value is .69. As with all correlation coefficients, the values of this effect size correlation can range from 0.00 to 1.00 (we do not need to worry about the direction of relationship, so plus and minus values are not used).

The advantage of reporting effect size is that it provides us with a scale of values that is consistent across all types of studies. The values range from 0.00 to 1.00, irrespective of the variables used, the particular research design selected, or the number of participants studied. You might be wondering what correlation coefficients should be considered indicative of small, medium, and large effects. A general guide is that correlations around .10 are considered small, those near .30 are medium/moderate, and correlations near .50 and above are large (see Cohen, 1992, 2016).

It is sometimes preferable to report the squared value of a correlation coefficient; instead of r, you will see r^2. Thus, if the obtained $r = .50$, the reported $r^2 = .25$. Why transform the value of r? This reason is that the transformation changes the obtained r to a percentage. The percentage value represents the percent of variance in one variable that is accounted for by the second variable. The range of r^2 values can range from 0.00 (0%) to 1.00 (100%).

The r^2 value is sometimes referred to as the *percent of shared variance between the two variables*. What does this mean, exactly? Recall the concept of variability in a set of scores: If you measured the weight of a random sample of American adults, you would observe variability in that weights would range from relatively low weights to relatively high weights. If you are studying factors that contribute to people's weight, you would want to examine the relationship between weights and scores on the contributing variable. One such variable might be sex: In actuality, the correlation between sex and weight is about .70 (with, for instance, males weighing more than females). That means that 49% (squaring .70) of the variability in weight is accounted for by variability in sex. You have therefore explained 49% of the variability in the weights, but there is still 51% of the variability that is not accounted for. This variability might be accounted for by other variables, such as the weights of the biological mother and father, prenatal stress, diet, and exercise. In an ideal world, you could account for 100% of the variability in weights if you had enough information on all other variables that contribute to people's weights: Each variable would make an incremental contribution until all the variability is accounted for.

REGRESSION EQUATIONS

A correlation coefficient r is the strength of the linear relationship between two variables. The correlation between classroom seating and exam score using our example was −.88. **Regression equations** are calculations used to predict a person's score on one variable when that person's score on another variable (or set of variables) is already known. They are essentially "prediction equations" that are based on known information about the relationship between the two variables. For example, after discovering that seating pattern and exam score are related, a regression equation may be calculated that predicts anyone's exam score based only on information about where the person sits in the class. The general form of a regression equation is:

$$Y = a + bX$$

where Y is the score we wish to predict, X is the known score, a is a constant, and b is a weighting adjustment factor that is multiplied by X (it is the slope of the line created with this equation). In our seating–exam score example, the following regression equation is calculated from the data:

$$Y = 99 + (-8)X$$

Thus, if we know a person's score on X (seating), we can insert that into the equation and predict what that person's exam score (Y) will be. If the person's X score is 2 (by sitting in the second row), we can predict that $Y = 99 + (-16)$, or that the person's exam score will be 83.

The regression equation can be used to produce a graph showing the straight line describing the linear relationship. Figure 11 shows the data and the line generated by the regression equation. Note that when the seating is in row 1 ($X = 1$), the line shows a predicted score of 91. When the seating is row 5, the predicted score is 59.

When researchers are interested in predicting some future behavior (called the **criterion variable**) on the basis of a person's score on some other variable (called the **predictor variable**), it is first necessary to demonstrate that there is a reasonably high correlation between the criterion variable and predictor variable. The regression equation then provides the method for making predictions on the basis of the predictor variable score only.

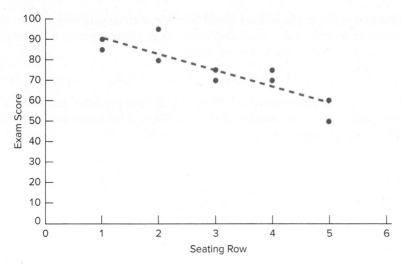

FIGURE 11
Regression line for hypothetical data: Classroom seating and exam score

MULTIPLE CORRELATION AND REGRESSION

In this chapter, we have thus far focused on the relationship between two variables at a time. Researchers recognize that a number of different variables may be related to a given behavior (this is the same point noted above in the discussion of factors that contribute to weight). A technique called **multiple regression** is used to analyze the relationship between a criterion variable and more than one predictor variable.

A **multiple correlation** (symbolized as *R* to distinguish it from the simple *r*) is the correlation between a combined set of two or more predictor variables and a single criterion variable. Taking all of the predictor variables into account usually permits greater accuracy of prediction than if any single predictor is considered alone. For example, applicants to graduate school in psychology could be evaluated on a combined set of predictor variables using multiple correlation. The predictor variables might be (1) quality of personal statement, (2) favorability of letters of recommendation, (3) college grades, and (4) scores on the Graduate Record Exam (GRE) General Test. (Many graduate programs in psychology stopped using GRE scores as admission criteria, or made it optional, after studies questioned the validity and fairness of the test (see Newman et al. 2022); such programs are working to become more reflective of human diversity.) No one of these factors is a perfect predictor of success in graduate school, but this combination of variables can yield a more accurate prediction. The multiple correlation is usually higher than the correlation between any one of the predictor variables and the criterion or outcome variable.

In actual practice, predictions would be made with an extension of the regression equation technique discussed previously. A multiple regression equation can be calculated that takes the following form:

$$Y = a + b_1X_1 + b_2X_2 + \ldots + b_nX_n$$

Where Y is the criterion variable, X1 to Xn are the predictor variables, a is a constant, and b_1 to b_n are weights that are multiplied by scores on the predictor variables. For example, a regression equation for graduate school admissions would be:

Predicted grade point average $= a + b_1$ (quality of personal statement)

$+ b_2$ (favorability of recommendation letters)

$+ b_3$ (college grades)

$+ b_4$ (score on GRE General Test)

You will also find multiple regression used in basic research on models that specify complex relationships among variables. For example, Ajzen (1991, 2011) developed a model called the Theory of Planned Behavior that uses multiple regression to predict specific behavioral intentions (e.g., to attend church on Sunday, buy a particular product, or join an alcohol recovery program) based on three predictor variables: (1) attitude toward the behavior, (2) perceived normative pressure to engage in the behavior, termed the subjective social norm, and (3) perceived behavioral control, a person's estimation of their ability to actually engage in the behavior. Attitude is one's own evaluation of the behavior, subjective normative pressure comes from other people such as parents and friends, and perceived behavioral control relies on overcoming potential barriers to achieving a behavior. In one study, Magid et al. (2021) used this theory to understand college students' intentions to use CPR in an emergency. They found that the multiple correlation (R) between college students' intention to perform CPR and the combined predictors of attitude, subjective social norm, and perceived behavioral control was .71 ($R^2 = .51$). The regression equation was as follows:

Intention = .38(Attitude) + .30(Norm) + .17(Behavioral Control)

This equation is somewhat different from those described previously. In much research, you are not interested in predicting an exact score (such as an exam score or GPA), so the mathematical calculations can assume that all variables are measured on the same scale. The coefficients in the equation are termed standardized beta weights. Two things are important when you interpret these beta weights. First, the beta weights are similar to correlation coefficients; the weighting factor reflects the magnitude of the correlation between the criterion variable and each predictor variable. Second, the beta weights are independent; they reflect the amount of variability accounted for by each variable in the equation after statistically controlling for the other predictor variables. In the CPR study, the weights for the attitude and subjective norm predictors are higher than for perceived behavioral control; all were significant predictors of intention to administer CPR though. The researchers noted that training designed to provide potential rescuers with the knowledge and skills to successfully administer CPR should also incorporate the three factors from the Theory of Planned Behavior. For example, training programs can include a focus on positive outcomes of performing CPR (attitude) and awareness of supportive social norms.

It is also possible to visualize the regression equation. In the CPR example, the relationships among variables could be diagrammed as follows:

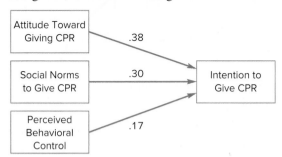

You should note that the squared multiple correlation coefficient (R^2) is interpreted much the same way as the squared correlation coefficient (r^2). That is, R^2 tells you the percentage of variability in the criterion variable that is accounted for by the combined set of predictor variables. Again, this value will be higher than any of the single predictors by themselves.

MEDIATING AND MODERATING VARIABLES

Behavior and mental processes, of course, are often more complex than one variable predicted by a set of other variables. This fact, along with the development of more advanced multiple regression techniques, has led to the exploration of a more complex view of the dynamics of human behavior. Mediating and moderating variables are examples of regression techniques that have been applied (Jose, 2013).

In its most basic form, a relationship between variables (we'll name them variable X and variable Y) can be conceptualized as:

This conceptualization holds for experimental research in which it is hypothesized that independent variable X causes changes in a dependent variable Y; similarly, with nonexperimental research, predictor variable X predicts criterion variable Y. Of course, other variables may also be important, and for now we can name any of those variables M.

Mediation

The word *mediation* means that something is coming between two forces, as in coming between two sides in a conflict. In research, a mediating variable is hypothesized to be intervening between variable X and variable Y. A researcher might propose that variable X is related to variable Y by means of an intervening, mediator variable M (Baron & Kenny, 1986; Kenny, 2021). A mediating model with three variables would take the following form:

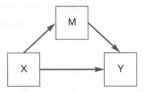

In a mediation model, the independent or predictor variable affects a mediating variable. The mediating variable then affects the dependent or criterion variable. As an example, you might propose that adolescents who are bullied subsequently experience depression (M), which in turn is related to misuse of alcohol and marijuana (Luk et al., 2010). This relationship may be diagrammed as:

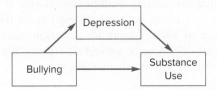

The arrows should be read as "influences" or "leads to"—thus, the model specifies that depression mediates the relationship between bullying and substance use. Note that there is also an arrow from bullying to substance use; this shows the direct influence of bullying that may be mediated by other variables specified in other research investigations. The statistical analyses of data generated to examine a mediation model can get complicated and are beyond the scope of this book. Published research that tests a mediation model will usually include coefficients that indicate the strength of each relationship in the model. There may or may not be a direct relationship between the predictor and criterion variables.

It is very tempting to use causation language when describing the relationships in this kind of model. Much of the research that examines a mediation model uses nonexperimental methods to collect data; strong causal statements are not warranted. Researchers will usually address this issue in the discussion section of their paper.

Moderation

Moderation implies restraint or change. In research, a moderating variable changes or limits the relationship between variable X and variable Y. Specifically, the relationship depends on the level of the moderator variable *M*. At one level of *M*, there may be a positive relationship between *X* and *Y;* at the other level of *M*, there may be no relationship between the *X* variable and the *Y* variable. That statement may sound familiar to you—it describes an interaction effect. We can diagram a moderation effect as a relationship between *X* and *Y* that is impacted by the moderating variable:

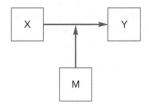

A study by Rahman et al. (2022) is a good example of a moderation hypothesis. Young Hispanic adults often encounter ethnic discrimination that is associated with psychological stress. Rahman et al. hypothesized that optimism might act as a moderator of this relationship—that optimism might be a variable that "impacts" the relationship between discrimination and stress. And, they did find that an optimistic worldview weakens the relationship between experiencing discrimination and stress in this population.

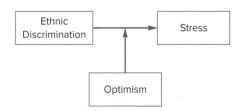

The two terms, *moderation* and *interaction,* developed from different research traditions, but they mean essentially the same thing when interpreting research findings.

Third Variables

The topic of the third-variable problem has been discussed in several chapters. Researchers face the third-variable problem in nonexperimental research when some uncontrolled third variable may be responsible for the relationship between the two variables of interest. The third variable (we can call it variable *Z*) effect can be diagrammed as:

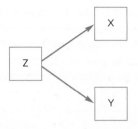

In this diagram, the third variable is responsible for an apparent relationship between variable X and variable Y, and X and Y are, in fact, not related at all when the effect of the third variable is taken into account. For an example, suppose that a researcher finds that people who exercise more (variable X) have lower anxiety levels (variable Y) than people who exercise less; this could be due to a third variable, such as income (variable Z). High income might cause greater exercise and lower levels of anxiety.

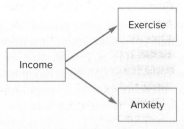

When experimental research is properly designed, there is no third-variable problem—because all extraneous variables are controlled, either by keeping the variables constant or by using randomization.

Multiple regression can be used to statistically control for the effects of third variables. In our example, a researcher would need to have measures of exercise, anxiety, and income. A statistical adjustment can be made to "control" for income. This is done with a multiple regression analysis that includes exercise along with income as predictors, and anxiety as the criterion variable. The beta weights will tell you if exercise is still related to anxiety after controlling for income. You may find that the relationship still exists, but it is smaller once income is removed in the regression analysis.

There could, of course, be other third variables that could be responsible for the relationship, The researcher could also measure age and education in addition to income. All those variables would be included in the multiple regression that predicts anxiety. The results would indicate whether exercise and anxiety are still related even after statistically removing the possible third variables of income, age, and education.

ADVANCED STATISTICAL ANALYSES

Our ability to analyze quantitative data has taken many steps forward in the past few decades—the result of the ubiquity of programmable statistical software raw computing power, and vibrant scholarship on data analysis.

You may have come across research articles that include some of these analytic strategies. While this chapter is about understanding research results, the deeper details of these techniques are beyond the scope of this book. Know, however, that some of these techniques are extensions of those that we've already presented. For example, when you are trying to predict a dichotomous outcome variable—such as "Do you exercise regularly, yes or no?"—you are dealing with logistic regression.

Structural equation modeling (SEM) is a family of related statistical analysis techniques that includes (among others) confirmatory factor analysis, path analysis, and latent growth modeling, in which researchers examine models that specify a set of relationships among variables. See Klein (2016) for a complete and accessible overview.

You will likely encounter some research findings that use SEM, so it is worthwhile to provide an overview. A model is an expected pattern of relationships among a set of variables. The proposed model is based on a theory of how the variables are causally related to one another. After data have been collected, statistical methods can be applied to examine how closely the proposed model actually "fits" the obtained data.

Researchers typically present diagrams to visually represent the models being tested. Such diagrams show the theoretical causal paths among the variables. The multiple regression diagram derived from a study on predicting intention to give CPR in an emergency was one such diagram. In another study that used SEM, Plotnikoff et al. (2011) studied physical exercise in a large sample of Canadian adolescents. They measured attitudes with questions about enjoying physical activity. The subjective norm that was measured included items like: "Most people important to me think I should take part in regular physical activity." They measured perceived control with questions about barriers to physical activity. They also measured intention to exercise and actual physical activity (behavior).

The theory of planned behavior predicts that behavioral beliefs, normative beliefs, and perceived behavioral control will each predict the intention to exercise. Intention will, in turn, predict actual exercise behavior. The researchers used structural equation modeling techniques to study this model. It is easiest to visualize the results using the path diagram shown in Figure 12. In the diagram, arrows leading from one variable to another depict the paths that relate the variables in the model. The arrows indicate a proposed causal sequence. Note that the model specifies that behavioral beliefs, subjective beliefs, and control beliefs are related to intention, and that intention, in turn, predicts actual behavior. The statistical analysis provides path coefficients similar to the standardized weights derived in the regression equations described previously. They indicate the strength of a relationship on our familiar −1.00 to +1.00 scale.

In Figure 12, you can see that attitude, subjective norm, and perceived behavioral control were significant predictors of intention to exercise, and that intention to exercise was related to actual behavior. Note also that behavioral control had a direct path to behavior; this indicates that difficulty in exercising is directly related to actual exercise.

Besides illustrating how variables are related, a final application of SEM in the Plotnikoff et al. (2011) study was to evaluate how closely the obtained data fit the specified model. The researchers concluded that the model did in fact

FIGURE 12
Structural
model based
on data from
Plotnikoff
et al. (2011)

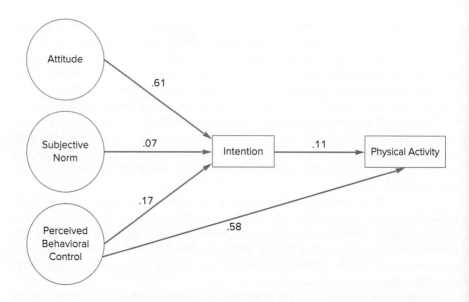

closely fit the data. They also explore other variables and their roles in the model. There are many other applications of SEM. More advanced data analysis using SEM and other techniques leads to a better understanding of the complex networks of relationships among variables.

In the chapter "Understanding Research Results: Statistical Inference" we turn from description of data to making decisions about statistical significance. These two topics are of course related. The topic of effect size that was described in this chapter is also very important when evaluating statistical significance.

BEING A SKILLED CONSUMER OF RESEARCH

1. Ask 20 students on campus how many units (credits) they are taking, as well as how many hours per week they work in paid employment. Create a frequency distribution and find the mean for each data set. Construct a scatterplot showing the relationship between class load and hours per week employed. Does there appear to be a relationship between the variables? (Note: There might be a restriction of range problem on your campus if few students work or most students take about the same number of units. If so, ask different questions, such as the number of hours spent studying and watching videos each week.)

2. Think of three variables that use a nominal scale, three variables that use an ordinal scale, three variables that use an interval scale, and three variables that use a ratio scale. What would be the best way to describe each of your examples statistically and graphically?

Check Your Learning: Practice Exercises

Practice Exercise #1

1. Review the income and poverty 2020 report from the U.S. Census Bureau (https://www.census.gov/library/publications/2021/demo/p60-273.html). Download Table A-1 and answer the following questions:

   a. How did the median income of all households change from 2019 to 2020?

   b. What was the 2020 median household income for households headed by a person with some college education?

   c. What does the median value tell you about income?

Practice Exercise #2

1. This exercise has two steps. First refer to the figure below, then select the correct answer to questions a, b, and c.

−1.00	← Stronger Relationship Negative Relationship (−)	0.00	Stronger Relationship → Positive Relationship (+)	+1.00

The size (value) of the coefficient indicates the strength of the relationship.
The sign (plus or minus) of the coefficient indicates the direction of the linear relationship.

   a. Which one of the following numbers could *not* be a correlation coefficient?

   −.99 +.71 +1.02 +.01 +.38

   b. Which one of the following correlation coefficients indicates the strongest relationship?

   +.23 −.89 −.10 −.91 +.77

   c. Which of the following correlation coefficients indicates the weakest negative relationship?

   −.28. +.08 −.42 +.01 −.29

2. Second, use the axes below to draw a scatterplot depicting (a) a positive linear relationship, (b) a negative linear relationship, and (c) no linear relationship.

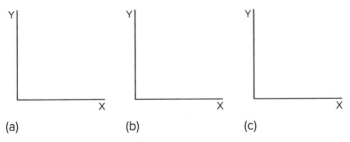

(a)   (b)   (c)

(Answers are provided at the end of this chapter.)

CHAPTER REVIEW

Review Questions

1. What are the differences between the three ways of describing results: comparing percentages, comparing means, and correlating scores?
2. What is a frequency distribution?
3. Distinguish between a pie chart, bar graph, frequency polygon, and histogram. Construct one of each.
4. What is a measure of central tendency? Distinguish between the mean, median, and mode.
5. What is a measure of variability? Distinguish between the standard deviation and the range.
6. What is a correlation coefficient? What do the size and sign of the correlation coefficient tell us about the relationship between variables?
7. What is a scatterplot?
8. What happens when a scatterplot shows the relationship to be curvilinear?
9. What is a regression equation? How might an employer use a regression equation?
10. How does multiple correlation increase the accuracy of prediction?
11. What is the purpose of partial correlation?
12. Provide an example of a mediation hypothesis.
13. Describe how a variable might moderate the relationship between two other variables.
14. What is the purpose of more advanced statistical techniques like structural equation modeling?
15. When a path diagram is shown, what information is conveyed by the arrows leading from one variable to another?

Study Terms

Bar graph (p. 275)	Frequency distribution (p. 274)
Central tendency (p. 277)	Frequency polygons (p. 275)
Correlation coefficient (p. 279)	Histogram (p. 276)
Criterion variable (p. 286)	Interval scales (p. 272)
Descriptive statistics (p. 277)	Mean (p. 277)
Effect size (p. 285)	Median (p. 277)

Mode (p. 277)

Multiple correlation (p. 287)

Multiple regression (p. 287)

Nominal scales (p. 271)

Ordinal scales (p. 271)

Pearson product-moment correlation coefficient (p. 279)

Pie chart (p. 274)

Predictor variable (p. 286)

Range (p. 278)

Ratio scales (p. 272)

Regression equations (p. 286)

Restriction of range (p. 284)

Scatterplot (p. 281)

Standard deviation (p. 277)

Structural equation modeling (SEM) (p. 293)

Variability (p. 277)

Variance (p. 278)

Check Your Learning: Answers

Practice Exercise #1

1a. Median income of all households rose 2.9%; b. $63,653; c. half of house-holders earned less than the median, and half earned more than the median

Practice Exercise #2

1. a. +1.02; b. −.91; c. −.28

2.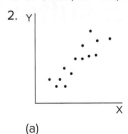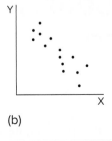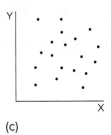

(a)   (b)   (c)

golero/E+/Getty Images

13

Understanding Research Results: Statistical Inference

LEARNING OBJECTIVES

- Explain how researchers use inferential statistics to evaluate sample data.
- Distinguish between the null hypothesis and the research hypothesis.
- Discuss probability in statistical inference, including the meaning of statistical significance.
- Describe the *t* test and explain the difference between one-tailed and two-tailed tests.
- Describe the *F* test, including systematic variance and error variance.
- Describe what a confidence interval tells you about your data.
- Distinguish between Type I and Type II errors and discuss the factors that influence the probability of a Type II error.
- Discuss the reasons a researcher might obtain nonsignificant results.
- Define power of a statistical test and describe how power influences research.
- Demonstrate skills in selecting an appropriate statistical test.

IN THE CHAPTER "UNDERSTANDING RESEARCH RESULTS: DESCRIP-
TION AND CORRELATION" WE EXAMINED WAYS OF DESCRIBING
THE RESULTS OF A STUDY USING DESCRIPTIVE STATISTICS AND A
VARIETY OF GRAPHING TECHNIQUES. In addition to using descriptive
statistics to describe the data, researchers use inferential statistics to draw more
general conclusions about their data. In short, inferential statistics allow researchers to (a) assess just how confident they are that their results reflect what is true
in the larger population and (b) assess the likelihood that their findings would
still occur if their study was repeated over and over. In this chapter, we examine
inferential statistics.

In order to determine whether a study is accurate, true, or valid, we must
understand and trust its statistical methodology. Recall from the chapter "Fundamental Research Issues" the four types of validity: construct validity, internal
validity, external validity, and statistical validity. This chapter and the chapter
"Understanding Research Results: Description and Correlation" are meant to
introduce the concept of statistical validity, support your thinking about this kind
of validity, and help you evaluate existing studies in the literature in terms of their
statistical validity. These chapters are also meant to help you design the analysis
for your own study.

SAMPLES AND POPULATIONS

Inferential statistics are necessary because the results of a given study are based
only on data obtained from a single sample of research participants. Researchers
rarely, if ever, study entire populations; their findings are based on sample data.
In addition to describing the sample data, we want to make statements about
populations. Would the results hold up if the experiment were conducted repeatedly,
each time with a new sample?

In the hypothetical experiment described in the chapter "Understanding
Research Results: Description and Correlation," aggression scores were obtained
in model and no-model conditions. Results from this hypothetical study are shown
in Table 1. The mean aggression score in the model condition was 5.20, and the
mean aggression score in the no-model group mean was 3.10. These means are
different: Children who observe an aggressive model subsequently behave more
aggressively than children who do not see an aggressive model. **Inferential
statistics** are used to determine whether the results match what would happen if
we were to conduct the experiment again and again with multiple samples. In
essence, we are asking whether we can infer that the difference in the *sample
means* shown in Table 1 reflects a true difference in the *population means*.

You may recognize the issue of samples and populations from presentations
of survey results. A news story might report that a sample of people in your state
found that 55% support a measure that will increase education funding in your
state; 45% oppose the measure. The report then says that these results are accurate
to within 3 percentage points, with a 95% confidence level. This means that the

TABLE 1 Aggression score data from a hypothetical experiment on modeling and aggression

	Model group	No-model group
Mean ($\overline{X}$)	5.20	3.10
Standard deviation (s)	1.14	1.20
Variance (s^2)	1.29	1.43
n	10	10

researchers are very (95%) confident that, if they were able to study the entire population rather than a sample, the actual percentage who support the education measure would be between 58% and 52% and the percentage opposing the measure would be between 48% and 42%. In this case the researcher could predict with a great deal of certainty that the state's citizens support the measure, because there is no overlap in the projected population values. Note, however, that even when we are very (in this case, 95%) sure, we still have a 5% chance of being wrong.

Inferential statistics allow us to arrive at such conclusions on the basis of sample data. In our study with the model and no-model conditions, are we confident that the means are sufficiently different to infer that the difference would be obtained in an entire population?

INFERENTIAL STATISTICS

Much of the previous discussion of experimental design centered on the importance of ensuring that the groups are equivalent in every way except for the manipulation of the independent variable. Equivalence of groups is achieved by experimentally controlling all other variables or by randomization. The assumption is that if the groups are equivalent, any differences in the dependent variable must be due to the effect of the independent variable.

This assumption is usually valid. However, it is also true that the difference between any two groups will almost never be zero. In other words, there will be some difference in the sample means, even when all of the principles of experimental design are rigorously followed. This happens because we are dealing with samples, rather than populations. Random or chance error will be responsible for some difference in the means, even if the independent variable had no effect on the dependent variable.

So, differences in sample means reflect actual difference in the population means (i.e., the effect of the independent variable), but they also reflect some random error. Inferential statistics allow researchers to make inferences about the true difference in the population on the basis of the sample data. Specifically, inferential statistics give the probability that the difference between means reflects random error rather than a real difference.

NULL AND RESEARCH HYPOTHESES

Statistical inference begins with a statement of the null hypothesis and a research (or alternative) hypothesis. The **null hypothesis** is simply that the population means are equal—the observed difference is due to random error. The **research hypothesis** is that the population means are, in fact, not equal. The null hypothesis states that the independent variable had no effect; the research hypothesis states that the independent variable did have an effect. In the aggression modeling experiment, the null and research hypotheses are:

H_0 (null hypothesis): The population mean of the no-model group is equal to the population mean of the model group.

H_1 (research hypothesis): The population mean of the no-model group is not equal to the population mean of the model group.

The logic of the null hypothesis is this: If we can determine that the null hypothesis is incorrect, then we accept the research hypothesis as correct. Acceptance of the research hypothesis means that the independent variable had an effect on the dependent variable.

The null hypothesis is used because it is a very precise statement—the population means are exactly equal. This permits us to know precisely the probability of obtaining our results if the null hypothesis is correct. Such precision is not possible with the research hypothesis, so we infer that the research hypothesis is correct only by rejecting the null hypothesis. We reject the null hypothesis when we find a very low probability that the obtained results could be due to random error. This is what is meant by **statistical significance:** A significant result is one that has a very low probability of occurring if the population means are equal. More simply, significance indicates that there is a low probability that the difference between the obtained sample means was due to random error. Significance, then, is a matter of probability.

PROBABILITY AND SAMPLING DISTRIBUTIONS

Probability is the likelihood of the occurrence of some event or outcome. We all use probabilities frequently in everyday life. For example, if you say that there is a high probability that you will get an A in this course, you mean that this outcome is likely to occur. Your probability statement is based on specific information, such as your grades on examinations. The weather forecaster says there is a 10% chance of rain today; this means that the likelihood of rain is very low. A gambler gauges the probability that a particular horse will win a race on the basis of the past records of that horse.

Probability in statistical inference is used in much the same way. We want to specify the probability that an event (in this case, a difference between means in the sample) will occur if there is no difference in the population. The question is: What is the probability of obtaining this result if only random error is operating? If this probability is very low, we reject the possibility that only random or chance error is responsible for the obtained difference in means.

Probability: The Case of ESP

The use of probability in statistical inference can be understood intuitively from a simple example. Suppose that a friend claims to have ESP (extrasensory perception) ability. You decide to test your friend with a set of five cards commonly used in ESP research; a different symbol is presented on each card. In the ESP test, you look at each card and think about the symbol, and your friend tells you which symbol you are thinking about. In your actual experiment, you have 10 trials; each of the five cards is presented two times in a random order. Your task is to know whether your friend's answers reflect random error (guessing) or whether they indicate that something more than random error is occurring. The null hypothesis in your study is that only random error is operating. In this case, the research hypothesis is that the number of correct answers shows more than random or chance guessing. (Note, however, that accepting the research hypothesis could mean that your friend has ESP ability, but it could also mean that the cards were marked, that you had somehow cued your friend when thinking about the symbols, and so on.)

You can easily determine the number of correct answers to expect if the null hypothesis is correct. Just by guessing, 1 out of 5 answers (20%) should be correct. On 10 trials, 2 correct answers are expected under the null hypothesis. If, in the actual test, more (or less) than 2 correct answers are obtained, would you conclude that the obtained data reflect random error or something more than merely random guessing?

Suppose that your friend gets 3 correct. Then you would probably conclude that only guessing is involved, because you would recognize that there is a high probability that there would be 3 correct answers *even though only 2 correct are expected under the null hypothesis.* You expect that exactly 2 answers in 10 trials would be correct in the long run, if you conducted this experiment with this subject over and over again. However, small deviations away from the expected 2 are highly likely in a sample of 10 trials.

Suppose, though, that your friend gets 7 correct. You might conclude that the results indicate more than random error in this one sample of 10 observations. This conclusion would be based on your intuitive judgment that an outcome of 70% correct when only 20% is expected is very unlikely. At this point, you would decide to reject the null hypothesis and state that the result is significant. A significant result is one that is very unlikely if the null hypothesis is correct.

A key question then becomes: How unlikely does a result have to be before we decide it is significant? A decision rule is determined prior to collecting the data. The probability required for significance is called the **alpha level.** The most common alpha-level probability used is .05. The outcome of the study is considered significant when there is a .05 or less probability of obtaining the results; that is, there are only 5 chances out of 100 that the results were due to random error in one sample from the population. If it is very unlikely that random error is responsible for the obtained results, the null hypothesis is rejected.

Sampling Distributions

You may have been able to judge intuitively that obtaining 7 correct on the 10 trials is very unlikely. Fortunately, we do not have to rely on intuition to determine the probabilities of different outcomes. Table 2 shows the probability of actually obtaining each of the possible outcomes in the ESP experiment with 10 trials and a null hypothesis expectation of 20% correct. An outcome of 2 correct answers has the highest probability of occurrence. Also, as intuition would suggest, an outcome of 3 correct is highly probable, but an outcome of 7 correct is highly unlikely.

The probabilities shown in Table 2 were derived from a probability distribution called the *binomial distribution;* all statistical significance decisions are based on probability distributions such as this one. Such distributions are called **sampling distributions.** The sampling distribution is based on the assumption that the null hypothesis is true; in the ESP example, the null hypothesis is that the person is only guessing and should therefore get 20% correct. Such a distribution assumes that if you were to conduct the study with the same number of observations over and over again, the most frequent finding would be 20%. However, because of the random error possible in each sample, there is a certain probability associated with other outcomes. Outcomes that are close to the expected null hypothesis value of 20% are very likely. However, outcomes farther from the expected result are less and less likely if the null hypothesis is correct. When your obtained results are highly unlikely if you are, in fact, sampling from the distribution specified by the null hypothesis, you conclude that the null hypothesis is incorrect. Instead of concluding that your sample results reflect a random deviation from

TABLE 2   Exact probability of each possible outcome of the ESP experiment
with 10 trials

Number of correct answers	Probability
10	.00000+
9	.00000+
8	.00007
7	.00079
6	.00551
5	.02642
4	.08808
3	.20133
2	.30199
1	.26844
0	.10737

the long-run expectation of 20%, you decide that the null hypothesis is incorrect. That is, you conclude that you have not sampled from the sampling distribution specified by the null hypothesis. Instead, in the case of the ESP example, you decide that your data are from a different sampling distribution in which, if you were to test the person repeatedly, most of the outcomes would be near your obtained result of 7 correct answers.

All statistical tests rely on sampling distributions to determine the probability that the results are consistent with the null hypothesis. When the obtained data are very unlikely according to null hypothesis expectations (usually a .05 probability or less), the researcher decides to reject the null hypothesis and therefore to accept the research hypothesis.

Sample Size

The ESP example also illustrates the impact of sample size—the total number of observations—on determinations of statistical significance. Suppose you had tested your friend on 100 trials instead of 10 and had observed 30 correct answers. Just as you had expected 2 correct answers in 10 trials, you would now expect 20 of 100 answers to be correct. However, 30 out of 100 has a much lower likelihood of occurrence than 3 out of 10. This is because, with more observations sampled, you are more likely to obtain an accurate estimate of the true population value. Thus, as the size of your sample increases, you are more confident that your outcome is actually different from the null hypothesis expectation.

GROUP DIFFERENCES: THE *t* AND *F* TESTS

Different statistical tests allow us to use probability to decide whether to reject the null hypothesis. In this section, we will examine the *t* test and the *F* test. The *t* **test** is commonly used to examine whether two groups are significantly different from each other. In the hypothetical experiment on the effect of a model on aggression, a *t* test is appropriate because we are asking whether the mean of the no-model group differs from the mean of the model group. The *F* test is a more general statistical test that can be used to ask whether there is a difference among three or more groups or to evaluate the results of factorial designs (discussed in the chapter "Complex Experimental Designs").

To use a statistical test, you must first specify the null hypothesis and the research hypothesis that you are evaluating. The null and research hypotheses for the modeling experiment were described previously. You must also specify the significance level that you will use to decide whether to reject the null hypothesis; this is the alpha level. As noted, researchers generally use a significance level of .05.

t Test

The sampling distribution of all possible values of *t* is shown in Figure 1. (This particular distribution is for the sample size we used in the hypothetical experiment on modeling and aggression; the sample size was 20 with 10 participants in each group.) This sampling distribution has a mean of 0 and a standard deviation of 1. It reflects all the possible outcomes we could expect if we compare the means of two groups *and* the null hypothesis is correct.

To use this distribution to evaluate our data, we need to calculate a value of *t* from the obtained data and evaluate the obtained *t* in terms of the sampling distribution of *t* that is based on the null hypothesis. If the obtained *t* has a low probability of occurrence (.05 or less), then the null hypothesis is rejected.

The *t* value is a ratio of two aspects of the data, the difference between the group means and the variability within groups. The ratio may be described as follows:

$$t = \frac{\text{group difference}}{\text{within-group variability}}$$

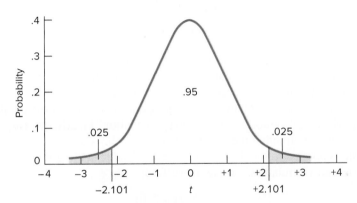

Critical Value for Two-Tailed Test with .05 Significance Level

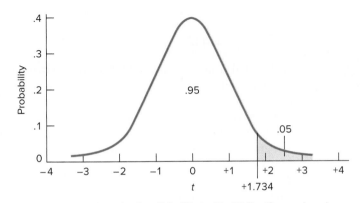

Critical Value for One-Tailed Test with .05 Significance Level

FIGURE 1
Sampling distributions of *t* values with 18 degrees of freedom

The group difference is simply the difference between your obtained means; under the null hypothesis, you expect this difference to be zero. The value of t increases as the difference between your obtained sample means increases. Note that the sampling distribution of t assumes that there is no difference in the population means; thus, the expected value of t under the null hypothesis is zero. The within-group variability is the amount of variability of scores about the mean. The denominator of the t formula is essentially an indicator of the amount of random error in your sample. Recall from the chapter "Understanding Research Results: Description and Correlation" that s, the standard deviation, and s^2, the variance, are indicators of how much scores deviate from the group mean.

A concrete example of a calculation of a t test should help clarify these concepts. The formula for the t test for two groups with equal numbers of participants in each group is:

$$t = \frac{\overline{X}_1 - \overline{X}_2}{\sqrt{\frac{s_1^2}{n_1} + \frac{s_2^2}{n_2}}}$$

The numerator of the formula is simply the difference between the means of the two groups. In the denominator, we first divide the variance (s_1^2 and s_2^2) of each group by the number of subjects in that group (n_1 and n_2) and add these together. We then find the square root of the result; this converts the number from a squared score (the variance) to a standard deviation. Finally, we calculate our obtained t value by dividing the mean difference by this standard deviation. When the formula is applied to the data in the chapter "Understanding Research Results: Description and Correlation," Table 1, we find:

$$t = \frac{5.20 - 3.10}{\sqrt{\frac{1.29}{10} + \frac{1.43}{10}}}$$

$$= \frac{2.1}{\sqrt{.1289 + .1433}}$$

$$= 4.02$$

Thus, the t value calculated from the data is 4.02. Is this a significant result? A computer program analyzing the results would immediately tell you the probability of obtaining a t value of this size with a total sample size of 20. Without such a program, there are internet resources to find a table of "critical values" of t (http://davidmlane.com/hyperstat/t_table.html) or to calculate the probability for you (http://vassarstats.net/tabs.html). Before going any farther, you should know that the obtained result is significant. Using a significance level of .05, the critical value from the sampling distribution of t is 2.101. Any t value greater than or equal to 2.101 has a .05 or less probability of occurring under the assumptions of the null hypothesis. Because our obtained value is larger than the critical value, we can reject the null hypothesis and conclude that the difference in means obtained in the sample reflects a true difference in the population.

Degrees of Freedom

You are probably wondering how the critical value was selected from the table. To use the table, you must first determine the **degrees of freedom** for the test (the term *degrees of freedom* is abbreviated *df*). When comparing two means, you assume that the degrees of freedom are equal to $n_1 + n_2 - 2$, or the total number of participants in the groups minus the number of groups. In our experiment, the degrees of freedom would be $10 + 10 - 2 = 18$. The degrees of freedom are the number of scores free to vary once the means are known. For example, if the mean of a group is 6.0 and there are five scores in the group, there are 4 degrees of freedom; once you have any four scores, the fifth score is known because the mean must remain 6.0.

One-Tailed Versus Two-Tailed Tests

In the table, you must choose a critical *t* for the situation in which your research hypothesis either (1) specified a direction of difference between the groups (e.g., "group 1 will be greater than group 2") or (2) did not specify a predicted direction of difference (e.g., "group 1 will differ from group 2"). Somewhat different critical values of *t* are used in the two situations: The first situation is called a one-tailed test, and the second situation is called a two-tailed test.

The issue can be visualized by looking at the sampling distribution of *t* values for 18 degrees of freedom, as shown in Figure 1. As you can see, a value of 0.00 is expected most frequently. Values greater than or less than zero are less likely to occur. The first distribution shows the logic of a two-tailed test. We used the value of 2.101 for the critical value of *t* with a .05 significance level because a direction of difference was not predicted. This critical value is the point beyond which 2.5% of the positive values and 2.5% of the negative values of *t* lie (hence, a total probability of .05 combined from the two "tails" of the sampling distribution). The second distribution illustrates a one-tailed test. If a directional difference had been predicted, the critical value would have been 1.734. This is the value beyond which 5% of the values lie in only one "tail" of the distribution. Whether to specify a one-tailed or two-tailed test will depend on whether you originally designed your study to test a directional hypothesis.

F Test

The **analysis of variance,** or **F test,** is an extension of the *t* test. The analysis of variance is a more general statistical procedure than the *t* test. When a study has only one independent variable with *two* groups, *F* and *t* are virtually identical—the value of *F* equals t^2 in this situation. However, analysis of variance is also used when there are more than two levels of an independent variable and when a factorial design with two or more independent variables has been used. Thus, the *F* test is appropriate for the simplest experimental design, as well as for the more complex designs discussed in the chapter "Complex Experimental Designs."

The *t* test was presented first because the formula allows us to demonstrate easily the relationship of the group difference and the within-group variability to the outcome of the statistical test. However, in practice, analysis of variance is the more common procedure. The calculations necessary to conduct an *F* test are provided in Appendix B.

The *F* statistic is a ratio of two types of variance: systematic variance and error variance (hence the term *analysis of variance*). **Systematic variance** is the deviation of the group means from the grand mean, or the mean score of all individuals in all groups. Systematic variance is small when the difference between group means is small and increases as the group mean differences increase. **Error variance** is the deviation of the individual scores in each group from their respective group means. Terms that you may see in research instead of systematic and error variance are *between-group variance* and *within-group variance*. Systematic variance is the variability of scores between groups, and error variance is the variability of scores within groups. The larger the *F* ratio is, the more likely it is that the results are significant.

Calculating Effect Size

The concept of effect size was discussed in the chapter "Understanding Research Results: Description and Correlation." After determining that there was a statistically significant effect of the independent variable, researchers will want to know the magnitude of the effect. Therefore, we want to calculate an estimate of effect size. For a *t* test, the calculation is

$$\text{effect size } r = \sqrt{\frac{t^2}{t^2 + df}}$$

where *df* is the degrees of freedom. Thus, using the obtained value of *t*, 4.02, and 18 degrees of freedom, we find:

$$\text{effect size } r = \sqrt{\frac{(4.02)^2}{(4.02)^2 + 18}} = \sqrt{\frac{16.201}{34.201}} = .69$$

This value is a type of correlation coefficient that can range from 0.00 to 1.00; as mentioned in the chapter "Understanding Research Results: Description and Correlation," .69 is considered a large effect size. For additional information on effect size calculation, see Fritz et al. (2012). The same distinction between *r* and r^2 that was made in the chapter "Understanding Research Results: Description and Correlation" applies here as well.

Another effect size estimate used when comparing two means is called Cohen's *d* (websites to calculate Cohen's *d* and convert to effect size *r* are available; see, e.g., https://www.uccs.edu/lbecker/). Cohen's *d* expresses effect size in terms of standard deviation units. A *d* value of 1.0 tells you that the means are 1 standard deviation apart; a *d* of .2 indicates that the means are separated by .2 standard deviation.

TABLE 3   Guidelines For Effect Size Descriptions

Strength of effect size	Effect size *r*	Cohen's *d*
Small	0.10	0.20
Moderate/medium	0.30	0.50
Large	0.50	0.80

You can calculate the value of Cohen's *d* using the means (*M*) and standard deviations (*SD*) of the two groups:

$$d = \frac{M_1 - M_2}{\sqrt{\frac{(SD_1^2 + SD_2^2)}{2}}}$$

Note that the formula uses *M* and *SD* instead of $\overline{X}$ and *s*. These abbreviations are used in APA style (see Appendix A).

The value of *d* is larger than the corresponding value of *r*, but it is easy to convert *d* to a value of *r*. Both statistics provide information on the size of the relationship between the variables studied. You might note that both effect size estimates have a value of 0.00 when there is no relationship. The value of *r* has a maximum value of 1.00, but *d* has no maximum value. You may also be wondering what should be considered a small or large effect size. Table 3 expands on the guidelines presented in the chapter "Understanding Research Results: Description and Correlation."

Confidence Intervals and Statistical Significance

Confidence intervals were described in the chapter "Asking People About Themselves: Survey Research." After obtaining a sample value, we can calculate a confidence interval. An interval of values defines the most likely range of actual population values. The interval has an associated confidence interval: A 95% confidence interval indicates that we are 95% sure that the population value lies within the range; a 99% interval would provide greater certainty but the range of values would be larger.

A confidence interval can be obtained for each of the means in the aggression experiment. The 95% confidence intervals for the two conditions are shown in Table 4.

TABLE 4   Confidence intervals for model and no-model groups

	Obtained sample value	Low population value	High population value
Model group	5.20	4.39	6.01
No-model group	3.10	2.24	3.96

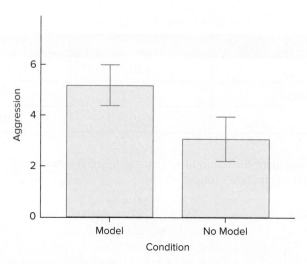

FIGURE 2
Mean aggression scores from the hypothetical modeling experiment including the 95% confidence intervals

A bar graph that includes a visual depiction of the confidence interval can be very useful. The means from the aggression experiment are shown in Figure 2. The shaded bars represent the mean aggression scores in the two conditions. The confidence interval for each group is shown with a vertical I-shaped line that is bounded by the upper and lower limits of the 95% confidence interval. It is important to examine confidence intervals to obtain a greater understanding of the meaning of your obtained data. Although the obtained sample means provide the best estimate of the population values, you are able to see the likely range of possible values. The size of the interval is related to both the size of the sample and the confidence level. As the sample size increases, the confidence interval narrows. This is because sample means obtained with larger sample sizes are more likely to reflect the population mean. Second, higher confidence is associated with a larger interval. If you want to be almost certain that the interval contains the true population mean (e.g., a 99% confidence interval), you will need to include more possibilities. Note that the 95% confidence intervals for the two means do not overlap. This should be a clue to you that the difference is statistically significant. Indeed, examining confidence intervals is an alternative way of thinking about statistical significance. The null hypothesis is that the difference in population means is 0.00. However, if you were to subtract all the means in the 95% confidence interval for the no-model condition from all the means in the model condition, none of these differences would include the value of 0.00. We can be very confident that the null hypothesis should be rejected.

Statistical Significance: An Overview

The logic underlying the use of statistical tests rests on statistical theory. There are some general concepts, however, that should help you understand what you are doing when you conduct a statistical test. First, the goal of the test is to allow you to make a decision about whether your obtained results are reliable; you want to be confident that you would obtain similar results if you conducted the study over and over again. Second, the significance level (alpha level) you choose indicates how confident you wish to be when making the decision. A .05 significance level says that you are 95% sure of the reliability of your findings; however, there is a 5% chance that you could be wrong. There are few certainties in life! Third, you are most likely to obtain significant results when you have a large sample size because larger sample sizes provide better estimates of true population values. Finally, you are most likely to obtain significant results when the effect size is large—that is, when differences between groups are large and variability of scores within groups is small.

In the remainder of this chapter, we will expand on these issues. We will examine the implications of making a decision about whether results are significant, the way to determine a significance level, and the way to interpret nonsignificant results. We will then provide some guidelines for selecting the appropriate statistical test in various research designs.

TYPE I AND TYPE II ERRORS

The decision to reject the null hypothesis is based on probabilities rather than on certainties. That is, the decision is made without direct knowledge of the true state of affairs in the population. Thus, the decision might not be correct; errors may result from the use of inferential statistics.

A decision matrix is shown in Figure 3. Notice that there are two possible decisions: (1) Reject the null hypothesis or (2) accept the null hypothesis. There are also two possible truths about the population: (1) The null hypothesis is true or (2) the null hypothesis is false. In sum, as the decision matrix shows, there are two kinds of correct decisions and two kinds of errors.

	True State in Population	
	Null Hypothesis Is True	Null Hypothesis Is False
Reject the Null Hypothesis	Type I Error (α)	Correct Decision $(1 - \beta)$
Accept the Null Hypothesis	Correct Decision $(1 - \alpha)$	Type II Error (β)

FIGURE 3
Decision matrix for Type I and Type II errors

Correct Decisions

One correct decision occurs when we reject the null hypothesis and the research hypothesis is true in the population. Here, our decision is that the population means are not equal, and in fact, this is true in the population. This is the decision you hope to make when you begin your study.

The other correct decision is to accept the null hypothesis, and the null hypothesis is true in the population: The population means are in fact equal.

Type I Errors

A **Type I error** is made when we reject the null hypothesis but the null hypothesis is actually true. Our decision is that the population means are not equal when they actually are equal. Type I errors occur when, simply by chance, we obtain a large value of t or F. For example, even though a t value of 4.025 is highly improbable if the population means are indeed equal (less than 5 chances out of 100), this *can* happen. When we do obtain such a large t value by chance, we *incorrectly* decide that the independent variable had an effect.

The probability of making a Type I error is determined by the choice of significance or alpha level (alpha may be shown as the Greek letter alpha, α). When the significance level for deciding whether to reject the null hypothesis is .05, the probability of a Type I error (alpha) is .05. If the null hypothesis is rejected, there are 5 chances out of 100 that the decision is wrong. The probability of making a Type I error can be changed by either decreasing or increasing the significance level. If we use a lower alpha level of .01, for example, there is less chance of making a Type I error. With a .01 significance level, the null hypothesis is rejected only when the probability of obtaining the results is .01 or less if the null hypothesis is correct.

Type II Errors

A **Type II error** occurs when the null hypothesis is accepted although in the population the research hypothesis is true. The population means are not equal, but the results of the experiment do not lead to a decision to reject the null hypothesis.

Research should be designed so that the probability of a Type II error (this probability is called beta, often designated by the Greek letter β) is relatively low. The probability of making a Type II error is related to three factors. The first is the significance (alpha) level. If we set a very low significance level to decrease the chances of a Type I error, we increase the chances of a Type II error. In other words, if we make it very difficult to reject the null hypothesis, the probability of incorrectly accepting the null hypothesis increases. The second factor is sample size. True differences are more likely to be detected if the sample size is large. The third factor is effect size. If the effect size is large, a Type II error is unlikely. However, a small effect size may not be significant with a small sample.

The Everyday Context of Type I and Type II Errors

The decision matrix used in statistical analyses can be applied to the kinds of decisions people frequently must make in everyday life. For example, consider the decision made by a juror in a criminal trial. As is the case with statistics, a decision must be made on the basis of evidence: Is the defendant innocent or guilty? However, the decision rests with individual jurors and does not necessarily reflect the true state of affairs: that the person really is innocent or guilty.

The juror's decision matrix is illustrated in Figure 4. To continue the parallel to the statistical decision, assume that the null hypothesis is the defendant is innocent (i.e., the dictum that a person is innocent until proven guilty). Thus, rejection of the null hypothesis means deciding that the defendant is guilty, and acceptance of the null hypothesis means deciding that the defendant is innocent. The decision matrix also shows that the null hypothesis may actually be true or false. There are two kinds of correct decisions and two kinds of errors like those described in statistical decisions. A Type I error is finding the defendant guilty when the person really is innocent; a Type II error is finding the defendant innocent when the person actually is guilty. In our society, Type I errors by jurors generally are considered to be more serious than Type II errors. Thus, before finding someone guilty, the juror is asked to make sure that the person is guilty "beyond a reasonable doubt" or to consider that "it is better to have a hundred guilty persons go free than to find one innocent person guilty."

The decision that a doctor makes to operate or not operate on a patient provides another illustration of how a decision matrix works. The matrix is shown in Figure 5. Here, the null hypothesis is that no operation is necessary. The decision is whether to reject the null hypothesis and perform the operation or to accept the null hypothesis and not perform surgery. In reality, the surgeon is faced with two possibilities: Either the surgery is unnecessary (the null hypothesis is true) or the patient will die without the operation (a dramatic case of the null hypothesis being false). Which error is more serious in this case? Most doctors would believe that not operating on a patient who really needs the operation—making a Type II error—is more serious than making the Type I error of performing surgery on someone who does not really need it.

	True State	
	Null Is True (Innocent)	Null Is False (Guilty)
Reject Null (Find Guilty)	Type I Error	Correct Decision
Accept Null (Find Innocent)	Correct Decision	Type II Error

(Decision)

FIGURE 4
Decision matrix for a juror

FIGURE 5
Decision
matrix for a
doctor

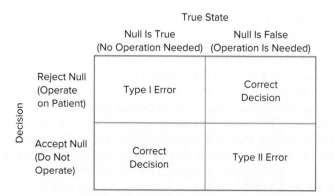

One final illustration of the use of a decision matrix involves the important decision to marry someone. If the null hypothesis is that the person is "wrong" for you, and the true state is that the person is either "wrong" or "right," you must decide whether to go ahead and marry the person. You might try to construct a decision matrix for this particular problem. Which error is more costly: a Type I error or a Type II error?

CHOOSING A SIGNIFICANCE LEVEL

Researchers traditionally have used either a .05 or a .01 significance level in the decision to reject the null hypothesis. If there is less than a .05 or a .01 probability that the results occurred because of random error, the results are said to be significant. However, there is nothing magical about a .05 or a .01 significance level. The significance level chosen merely specifies the probability of a Type I error if the null hypothesis is rejected. The significance level chosen by the researcher usually is dependent on the consequences of making a Type I versus a Type II error. As previously noted, for a juror a Type I error is more serious than a Type II error; for a doctor, however, a Type II error may be more serious.

Researchers generally believe that the consequences of making a Type I error are more serious than those associated with a Type II error. If the null hypothesis is rejected, the researcher might publish the results in a journal, and the results might be reported by others in textbooks or in newspaper or magazine articles. Researchers do not want to mislead people or risk damaging their reputations by publishing results that are not reliable and so cannot be replicated. Thus, they want to guard against the possibility of making a Type I error by using a very low significance level (.05 or .01). In contrast to the consequences of publishing false results, the consequences of a Type II error are not seen as being very serious.

Thus, researchers want to be very careful to avoid Type I errors when their results may be published. However, in certain circumstances, a Type I error is not serious. For example, if you were engaged in pilot or exploratory research, your results would be used primarily to decide whether your research ideas were worth pursuing. In this situation, it would be a mistake to overlook potentially important data by using a very conservative significance level. In exploratory research, a significance level of .25 may be more appropriate for deciding whether to do more research. Remember that the significance level chosen and the consequences of a Type I or a Type II error are determined by what the results will be used for.

INTERPRETING NONSIGNIFICANT RESULTS

Although "accepting the null hypothesis" is convenient terminology, it is important to recognize that researchers are not generally interested in accepting the null hypothesis. Research is designed to show that a relationship between variables does exist, not to demonstrate that variables are unrelated.

More important, a decision to accept the null hypothesis when a single study does not show significant results is problematic, because negative or nonsignificant results are difficult to interpret. For this reason, researchers often say that they simply "fail to reject" or "do not reject" the null hypothesis. The results of a single study might be nonsignificant even when a relationship between the variables in the population does in fact exist. This is a Type II error. Sometimes, the reasons for a Type II error lie in the procedures used in the experiment. For example, a researcher might obtain nonsignificant results by providing incomprehensible instructions to the participants, by having a very weak manipulation of the independent variable, or by using a dependent measure that is unreliable and insensitive. Rather than concluding that the variables are not related, researchers may decide that a more carefully conducted study would find that the variables are related.

We should also consider the statistical reasons for a Type II error. Recall that the probability of a Type II error is influenced by the significance (alpha) level, sample size, and effect size. Thus, nonsignificant results are more likely to be found if the researcher is very cautious in choosing the alpha level. If the researcher uses a significance level of .001 rather than .05, it is more difficult to reject the null hypothesis (there is not much chance of a Type I error). However, that also means that there is a greater chance of accepting an incorrect null hypothesis (i.e., a Type II error is more likely). In other words, a meaningful result is more likely to be overlooked when the significance level is very low.

A Type II error may also result from a sample size that is too small to detect a real relationship between variables. A general principle is that the larger the sample size is, the greater the likelihood of obtaining a significant result. This is because large sample sizes give more accurate estimates of the actual population than do small sample sizes. In any given study, the sample size may be too small to permit detection of a significant result.

A third reason for a nonsignificant finding is that the effect size is small. Very small effects are difficult to detect without a large sample size. In general, the sample size should be large enough to find a real effect, even if it is a small one.

The fact that it is possible for a very small effect to be statistically significant raises another issue. A very large sample size might enable the researcher to find a significant difference between means; however, this difference, even though statistically significant, might have very little *practical* significance. For example, if an expensive new psychiatric treatment technique significantly reduces the average hospital stay from 60 to 59 days, it might not be practical to use the technique despite the evidence for its effectiveness. The additional day of hospitalization costs less than the treatment. There are other circumstances, however, in which a treatment with a very small effect size has considerable practical significance. Usually this occurs when a very large population is affected by a fairly inexpensive treatment. Suppose a simple flextime policy for employees reduces employee turnover by 1% per year. This does not sound like a large effect. However, if a company normally has a turnover of 2,000 employees each year and the cost of training a new employee is $10,000, the company saves $200,000 per year with the new procedure. This amount may have practical significance for the company.

The key point here is that you should not accept the null hypothesis just because the results are nonsignificant. Nonsignificant results do not necessarily indicate that the null hypothesis is correct. However, there must be circumstances in which we can accept the null hypothesis and conclude that two variables are, in fact, not related. Frick (1995) describes several criteria that can be used in a decision to accept the null hypothesis. For example, we should look for well-designed studies with sensitive dependent measures and evidence from a manipulation check that the independent variable manipulation had its intended effect. In addition, the research should have a reasonably large sample to rule out the possibility that the sample was too small. Further, evidence that the variables are not related should come from multiple studies. Under such circumstances, you are justified in concluding that there is in fact no relationship.

Check Your Learning

Next, head to Check Your Learning: Practice Exercise #1 to try your own null hypothesis testing.

CHOOSING A SAMPLE SIZE: POWER ANALYSIS

You will also need to determine your sample size. How many participants will you need in your study? In general, increasing your sample size increases the likelihood that your results will be statistically significant, because larger samples provide more accurate estimates of population values (see the chapter "Asking People About Themselves: Survey Research," Table 2). Most researchers take note of the sample sizes in the research area being studied and select a sample size that is typical for studies in the area. A more formal approach is to select a sample size on the basis of a desired probability of correctly rejecting the null hypothesis. This probability is called the **power** of the statistical test. It is obviously related to the probability of a Type II error:

$$\text{Power} = 1 - p \text{ (Type II error)}$$

TABLE 5 Total sample size needed to detect a significant difference for a *t* test

Effect size r	Power = .80	Power = .90
.10	789	1052
.20	200	266
.30	88	116
.40	52	68
.50	26	36

Note: Effect sizes are correlations, based on two-tailed tests.

We previously indicated that the probability of a Type II error is related to significance level (alpha), sample size, and effect size. Statisticians such as Cohen (1988) have developed procedures for determining sample size based on these factors—and software, including the commonly used G*Power (Faul et al. 2007, Faul et al. 2009), can make quick work of the calculations for many different statistical tests. Table 5 shows the total sample size needed for an experiment with two groups and a significance level of .05. The effect sizes range from .10 to .50, and the desired power is shown at .80 and .90. Smaller effect sizes require larger samples to be significant at the .05 level. Higher desired power demands a greater sample size; this is because you want a more certain "guarantee" that your results will be statistically significant. Researchers usually use a power between .70 and .90 when using this method to determine sample size. Several computer programs have been developed to allow researchers to easily make the calculations necessary to determine sample size based on effect size estimates, significance level, and desired power.

If a researcher is studying a relationship with an effect size correlation of .20, a fairly large sample size is needed for statistical significance at the .05 level. An inappropriately low sample size in this situation is likely to produce a nonsignificant finding.

THE IMPORTANCE OF REPLICATIONS

Throughout this discussion of statistical analysis, the focus has been on the results of a single research investigation. What were the means and standard deviations? Was the mean difference statistically significant? If the results are significant, you conclude that they would likely be obtained over and over again if the study were repeated. We now have a framework for understanding the results of the study. Be aware, however, that scientists do not attach too much importance to the results of a single study. A rich understanding of any phenomenon comes from the results of numerous studies investigating the same variables. Instead of inferring population values on the basis of a single investigation, we can look at the results of several studies that replicate previous investigations (see Cohen, 1994). The importance of replications is a central concept in the chapter "Generalization."

SIGNIFICANCE OF A PEARSON *r* CORRELATION COEFFICIENT

Recall from the chapter "Understanding Research Results: Description and Correlation" that the Pearson *r* correlation coefficient is used to describe the strength of the relationship between two variables when both variables have interval or ratio scale properties. However, there remains the issue of whether the correlation is statistically significant. The null hypothesis in this case is that the true population correlation is 0.00—that is, the two variables are not related. What if you obtain a correlation of .27 (plus or minus)? A statistical significance test will allow you to decide whether to reject the null hypothesis and conclude that the true population correlation is, in fact, greater than 0.00. The technical way to do this is to perform a *t* test that compares the obtained coefficient with the null hypothesis correlation of 0.00. The procedures for calculating a Pearson *r* and determining significance are provided in Appendix B.

STATISTICAL ANALYSIS SOFTWARE

Although you can calculate statistics with a calculator using the formulas provided in the chapter "Understanding Research Results: Description and Correlation" and Appendix B, most data analysis is carried out via specially designed statistical software. Sophisticated statistical analysis software packages make it easy to calculate statistics for any data set. Descriptive and inferential statistics are obtained quickly, the calculations are accurate, and information on statistical significance is provided in the output. Statistical software also facilitates graphic displays of data.

Some of the major statistical programs include SPSS, SAS, SYSTAT, and freely available R. Other programs may be used on your campus. Many people do most of their simple statistical analyses using a spreadsheet program such as Microsoft Excel. You will need to learn the specific details of the computer system used at your college or university. No one program is better than another; they all differ in the appearance of the output and the specific procedures needed to input data and have the program perform the test. However, the general procedures for doing analyses are quite similar in all of the statistics programs.

The first step in doing the analysis is to input the data. Suppose you want to input the data from the chapter "Understanding Research Results: Description and Correlation," Table 1, the modeling and aggression experiment. Data are entered into columns. It is easiest to think of data analysis as a matrix with rows and columns. Data for each research participant are the rows of the matrix. The columns contain each participant's scores on one or more measures, and an additional column may be needed to indicate a code to identify which condition the individual was in (e.g., Group 1 or Group 2). A data matrix in SPSS for Windows is shown in Figure 6. The numbers in the "group" column indicate whether the individual is in Group 1 (model) or Group 2 (no model), and the numbers in the "aggscore" column are the aggression scores from the chapter "Understanding Research Results: Description and Correlation," Table 1.

	group	aggscore
1	1	3
2	1	4
3	1	5
4	1	5
5	1	5
6	2	1
7	2	2
8	2	2
9	2	3
10	2	3
11	1	5
12	1	6
13	2	3
14	2	4
15	2	4

Data Matrix in SPSS for Windows

	A	B
1	Model	No Model
2	3	1
3	4	2
4	5	2
5	5	3
6	5	3
7	5	3
8	6	4
9	6	4
10	6	4
11	7	5
12		
13		

Excel Method of Data Input

t Test: Two-Sample Assuming Equal Variances

	Model	No Model
Mean	5.200	3.100
Variance	1.289	1.433
Observations	10.000	10.000
Pooled Variance	1.361	
Hypothesized Mean Difference	0.000	
df	18.000	
t Stat	4.025	
P(T<=t) one-tail	0.000	
t Critical one-tail	1.734	
P(T<=t) two-tail	0.001	
t Critical two-tail	2.101	

Output for a *t* test using Excel

FIGURE 6
Sample input and output using data from the chapter "Understanding Research Results: Description and Correlation," Figure 1 (modeling experiment)

Other programs may require somewhat different methods of data input. For example, in Excel, it is usually easiest to set up a separate column for each group, as shown in Figure 6.

The next step is to provide instructions for the statistical analysis. Again, each program uses somewhat different steps to perform the analysis; most require you to choose from various menu options. When the analysis is completed, you are provided with the output that shows the results of the statistical procedure you performed. You will need to learn how to interpret the output. Figure 6 shows the output for a *t* test using Excel.

When you are first learning to use a statistical analysis program, it is a good idea to practice with some data from a statistics text to make sure that you get the same results. This will ensure that you know how to properly input the data and request the statistical analysis.

The appropriate statistical tests are shown as the output in Figure 6.

SELECTING THE APPROPRIATE STATISTICAL TEST

We have covered several types of designs, and the variables that we study may have nominal, ordinal, interval, or ratio scale properties. How do you choose the appropriate statistical test for analyzing your data? Fortunately, there are a number of online guides and tutorials, such as https://wise.cgu.edu/wise-tutorials/tutorial-choosing-the-correct-statistical-test/; SPSS even has its own Statistics Coach to help with the decision: https://www.ibm.com/docs/en/spss-statistics/25.0.0?topic=coach-statistics.

We cannot cover every possible analysis. Our focus will be on variables that have either (1) nominal scale properties—two or more discrete values, such as vegetarian and not vegetarian—or (2) interval/ratio scale properties with many values such as reaction time or rating scales (also called continuous variables). We will not address variables with ordinal scale values.

Research Studying Two Variables (Bivariate Research)

In these cases, the researcher is studying whether two variables are related. In general we would refer to the first variable as the independent variable (IV) and the second variable as the dependent variable (DV). However, because it does not matter whether we are doing experimental or nonexperimental research, we could just as easily refer to the two variables as Variable X and Variable Y or Variable A and Variable B (Table 6).

Research with Multiple Independent Variables

There are more-complex research designs that include two or more independent variables that are studied with a single outcome or dependent variable (see Table 7).

These research design situations have been described in previous chapters. There are, of course, many other types of designs. Designs with multiple variables

TABLE 6 Statistical tests for different combinations of IV and DV

IV	DV	Statistical test
Nominal *Right-handed; left-handed*	Nominal *Vegetarian—yes/no*	Chi-square
Nominal (2 groups) *Right-handed; left-handed*	Interval/ratio *Grade point average*	*t* test
Nominal (3 groups) *Study time (low, medium, high)*	Interval/ratio *Test score*	One-way analysis of variance
Interval/ratio *Optimism score*	Interval/ratio *Sick days last year*	Pearson correlation

TABLE 7 Statistical Tests for research designs with multiple independent variables

IV	DV	Statistical test
Nominal (2 or more variables)	Interval/ratio	Analysis of variance (factorial design)
Interval/ratio (2 or more variables)	Interval/ratio	Multiple regression

(multivariate statistics) are described in detail by Tabachnick and Fidell (2019). Procedures for research using ordinal level measurement may be found in books by Siegel and Castellan (1988) and Corder and Foreman (2014).

Check Your Learning

Next, go to Check Your Learning: Practice Exercise #2 and match the independent/dependent variable combination to the correct statistical test.

BEING A SKILLED CONSUMER OF RESEARCH

1. In an experiment, one group of research participants is given 10 pages of material to proofread for errors. Another group proofreads the same material on a computer screen. The dependent variable is the number of errors detected in a 5-minute period. A .05 significance (alpha) level is used to evaluate the results.

   a. What statistical test would you use?

   b. What is the null hypothesis? The research hypothesis?

    c. Given the hypothesis, what is the Type I error? The Type II error?

    d. What is the probability of making a Type I error?

    e. When Professor Rodríguez conducted the proofreading study, the average number of errors detected in the print and computer conditions was 38.4 and 13.2, respectively; this difference was not statistically significant. When Professor Seuss conducted the same experiment, the means of the two groups were 21.1 and 14.7, but the difference was statistically significant. Explain how this could happen.

2. A researcher investigated attitudes toward individuals in wheelchairs. The question was: Would people react differently to a person they perceived as being temporarily confined to the wheelchair than to a person they perceived as having a permanent disability? Participants were randomly assigned to two groups. Individuals in one group each worked on various tasks with a confederate in a wheelchair; members of the other group worked with the same confederate in a wheelchair, but this time the confederate wore a leg cast. After the session was over, participants filled out a questionnaire regarding their reactions to the study. One question asked, "Would you be willing to work with your test partner in the future on a class assignment?" with "yes" and "no" as the only response alternatives. What would be the appropriate significance test for this experiment? Can you offer a critique of the dependent variable? If you changed the dependent variable, would it affect your choice of significance tests? If yes, how?

Check Your Learning: Practice Exercises

Practice Exercise #1

A simple random sample of the inhabitants of the Island of Broccoli was selected. There are 5,000 inhabitants, and the sample was 100 inhabitants. Everyone who was identified in the sample agreed to be studied (Broccolivians are very agreeable people). Two pieces of data were collected from each person in the sample: the presence or absence of the "Broccoli gene" (https://www.livescience.com/39578-why-some-hate-broccoli.html), which determines whether broccoli tastes bitter to the person (Lipchock et al., 2013), and general evaluation of broccoli on a scale of 1 to 10.

1. First, answer these questions:

    a. How many members are in the population?

    b. How many members are in the sample?

2. Next, given the hypothesis—people without the "broccoli gene" will like broccoli more than people with the gene—answer the following questions:

   a. What statistical test should be used to test the hypothesis? Why?

   b. Given the hypothesis, should we use a one-tailed or two-tailed test? Why?

3. Now, answer these questions related to statistical significance and error:

   a. You conduct the statistical test (alpha = .05) and conclude there is a significant difference in broccoli preference between those with and without the gene. Describe what the Type I error would be in this case.

   b. You conduct the statistical test (alpha = .05) and conclude there is not a significant difference in broccoli preference between those with and without the gene. Describe what the Type II error would be in this case.

Practice Exercise #2

For each of the independent variable–dependent variable combinations below, indicate the appropriate statistical test procedure: 1. F test (analysis of variance). 2. t test. 3. Chi-square test. 4. Pearson correlation coefficient. 5. Multiple regression.

Independent variable(s)	Dependent variable(s)	Statistical test procedure
Age (under 21; over 21)	Number of alcoholic beverages in past 2 weeks	
Age in years	Number of alcoholic beverages in past 2 weeks	
Age in years; Exercise hours per week	Number of alcoholic beverages in past 2 weeks	
Enrollment in college (yes; no)	Any alcohol use in past month (yes; no)	
Age (under 21; over 21); Enrollment in college (yes; no)	Number of alcoholic beverages in past 2 weeks	

(Answers are provided at the end of this chapter.)

CHAPTER REVIEW

Review Questions _____

1. Distinguish between the null hypothesis and the research hypothesis. When does the researcher decide to reject the null hypothesis?
2. What is meant by statistical significance?
3. What factors are most important in determining whether obtained results will be significant?
4. Distinguish between a Type I and a Type II error. Why is your significance level the probability of making a Type I error?
5. What factors are involved in choosing a significance level?
6. What influences the probability of a Type II error?
7. What is the difference between statistical significance and practical significance?
8. Discuss the reasons a researcher might obtain nonsignificant results.

Study Terms _____

Alpha level (p. 302)

Analysis of variance (*F* test) (p. 307)

Confidence interval (p. 309)

Degrees of freedom (p. 307)

Error variance (p. 308)

F test (p. 307)

Inferential statistics (p. 299)

Null hypothesis (p. 301)

Power (p. 316)

Probability (p. 301)

Research hypothesis (p. 301)

Sampling distribution (p. 303)

Statistical significance (p. 301)

Systematic variance (p. 308)

t test (p. 304)

Type I error (p. 312)

Type II error (p. 312)

Check Your Learning: Answers

Practice Exercise #1

1a. 5,000; b. 100; 2a. *t* test, the dependent variable is an interval scale; b. One-tailed, the hypothesis states a direction—that the average broccoli score would be higher as opposed to just 'different'; 3a. When there is no difference in the population, a Type I error would be incorrectly concluding that the difference observed in the sample is true in the population; 3b. When there is a difference in the population, a Type II error would be incorrectly concluding that there is no difference in the population.

Practice Exercise #2

Independent variable(s)	Dependent variable(s)	Statistical test procedure
Age (under 21; over 21)	Number of alcoholic beverages in past 2 weeks	2. t test
Age in years	Number of alcoholic beverages in past 2 weeks	4. Pearson correlation coefficient
Age in years; Exercise hours per week	Number of alcoholic beverages in past 2 weeks	5. Multiple regression
Enrollment in college (yes; no)	Any alcohol use in past month (yes; no)	3. Chi-square
Age (under 21; over 21) Enrollment in college (yes; no)	Number of alcoholic beverages in past 2 weeks	1. F test

Pekic/E+/Getty Images

Generalization

LEARNING OBJECTIVES

- Define external validity.
- Discuss how our ability to generalize research findings to broader populations is affected by sex and gender, race and ethnicity, and culture.
- Describe threats to external validity related to using college students and volunteers as participants, the location where a student takes place, and the use of online samples.
- Describe the issues surrounding external validity when researchers study nonhuman animals.
- Describe how laboratory settings, the use of a pretest, and the characteristics of the research team may impact external validity.
- Define and discuss the importance of replications; distinguish between exact replications and conceptual replications.
- Describe what a literature review and meta-analysis are. Compare and contrast their role in providing evidence for external validity.

IN THIS CHAPTER, WE WILL CONSIDER THE ISSUE OF THE GENER-
ALIZATION OF RESEARCH FINDINGS. When a single study is conducted
with a particular sample and procedure, can the results be generalized to other
populations of research participants, or to other ways of manipulating or measuring
the variables? Recall from the chapter "Fundamental Research Issues" that **external
validity** is the extent to which findings may be generalized to other populations
and settings. In this chapter, we will first discuss the issues around generalization
across populations.

GENERALIZING ACROSS PEOPLE

Researchers may randomly assign participants to experimental conditions, yet
rarely are participants randomly selected from the general population. Individuals
who participate in psychological research are usually selected because they are
available. For academic researchers, the most readily-available population of
potential participants is college students. Most commonly, the students are in their
first or second year and enrolled in an introductory psychology course to satisfy
a general education requirement. So, are research findings limited to these types
of research participants, or can we generalize our findings across populations?
Humans are a very diverse species; can we generalize across all humanity?

People have multiple identities, and those identities can impact how participants react, respond, and engage with research projects. Common salient identities are
sex, gender, sexual orientation, race, and ethnicity. These identities can be the focus
of research or simply descriptive characteristics that help us understand the makeup of
a specific sample. They are also important when we evaluate the external validity
of research projects. One of our eight key questions for being a skillful consumer of
research is: To whom can we generalize the results?

Sex and Gender Identity

Our collective understanding of sex and gender has evolved rapidly, as has the
language around these topics. Although the terms *sex* and *gender* are frequently
used interchangeably, it is critical to remember that *sex* generally refers to biological classification, typically assigned at birth based on the external appearance of
specific genitalia, and denoted most often with the terms *male* and *female*. Sex
differences, then, refer to physiological differences.

Gender is a sociocultural classification shaped by cultural and historical forces
and often denoted with the terms *man* and *woman*. Thus, gender involves social
roles, groups, and identities associated with a person's sex in a given culture.

The term *gender identity* refers to a person's personal and psychological experience of gender. There is significant diversity in gender identity. The term
cisgender refers to people whose biological sex matches their gender identity. People
whose gender identity does not match their sex assigned at birth may identify as
transgender. Transgender identities may be binary—for example, an individual

assigned male at birth may identify as a woman. However, other forms of gender identity reject the notion of two discrete genders and include other identifications (e.g., nonbinary, agender). Here, the key is understanding that sex, gender, and gender identity are interrelated and complex.

What does the complexity of sex and gender identity mean for research?

Much research in the recent past ignored gender—all too frequently, only males were included in the sample without explanation, the number of men and women in the study was not reported, and analysis of possible gender differences were either not done or not reported. Today it is more common for researchers to report that an analysis of the data did not reveal a gender difference—or, if there was a difference, to report it. One of the central themes of this book—and of behavioral science research—is external validity. To be a skillful consumer of research, it is essential always to review the gender makeup of a sample and consider who the results might apply to.

And what does the complexity of sex and gender mean for researchers today? First and foremost, it is important to note that real gender gaps remain in the behavioral sciences, and representation among researchers is critical to the success of the science (Chrisler et al., 2013; Gruber et al., 2021). Second, researchers should not exclude sex or gender categories when recruiting or studying participants if they have a research question for which they would like to generalize the findings to all humans. In that case, they need to make sure that their samples represent all humans, including people of varied sexes, genders, and gender identities. To build a behavioral science of humanity, studies must be built from samples that represent humanity. That said, it can also be essential to study subgroups: studying almost any topic in samples of people who identify as men, women, or transgender may reveal something important, and understanding the unique needs of a particular subpopulation for treatment can lead to better treatments and better outcomes.

Racial and Ethnic Identity

Race is the social categorization of humans based on skin color and other physical characteristics. It is one of our fundamental social identities and has played a harrowing role throughout human history: colonization, genocide, enslavement, and subjugation can all be tied to race. No science of human behavior can be complete without considering this critical identity.

As you might expect, classifying people by race is very complicated. When race was considered only a biological feature of humans, as few as two or three categories were used (see Teo, 2009, for a deeper dive into racial classifications). The U.S. Census is required by law to have five categories for a race question: White, Black or African American, American Indian or Alaska Native, Asian, and Native Hawaiian or Other Pacific Islander. Many people objected that these categories do not reflect the diversity of racial self-identification. In 2010 the U.S. Census experimented with a new question that identified 15 categories: White; Black, African American, or Negro; American Indian or Alaska Native; Asian Indian; Japanese; Chinese; Filipino; Korean; Vietnamese; Native Hawaiian;

Samoan; Guamanian or Chamorro; Other Pacific Islander; Other Asian. It also allowed respondents to choose as many categories as they liked. The new question is much closer to the categories people use as they describe themselves in a way that may include some combination of race, ethnicity, and nationality and may include multiracial self-identification. One positive consequence of the new system is that more respondents complete the race question. The more important consequence is that we have a more accurate view of the racial makeup of the United States. Still, the 2020 strategy excluded categories for people identified as American Arab, Middle Eastern, or North African (AMENA), and the Census Bureau itself reported an undercount of "Black or African American population, the American Indian or Alaska Native population living on a reservation, the Hispanic or Latino population, and people who reported being of Some Other Race" and an overcount of White and Asian people (U.S. Census Bureau, 2022).

The construct of race is related to but different from ethnicity. Ethnicity is how a person belongs—or is thought to belong—to a population or subpopulation made up of people who share a common cultural background or descent. Ethnicity, too, is a complex variable to measure. The 2010 U.S. Census asked if respondents identify as "Hispanic, Latino, or Spanish origin." People who responded yes were asked to select a specific Hispanic, Latino, or Spanish ethnic group: Mexican, Mexican American, or Chicano; Puerto Rican; Cuban; another Hispanic Latino, or Spanish origin category such as Argentinian, Colombian, Dominican. A new question was proposed for the 2020 Census—one that would include a category for people with roots in the Middle East or North Africa—but it was not implemented (Wang, 2018). Asking about race and ethnicity is very important in the Census and in surveys in which the data will be used for making policy decisions for such things as housing and education.

Race and ethnicity are related to many critical psychological processes and outcomes. For example, a wealth of information points to serious disparities in access to and use of health care across ethnic and racial groups. But let's not only look at deficits; there is also ample research that shows different patterns of interactions and behaviors across ethnic and racial groups (for instance, in ways of parenting). Race and ethnicity are critical to understanding human behavior, and measuring race and ethnicity can be complex. Consider the research that you have been reading. What are the racial and ethnic characteristics of samples in those studies? The history of psychology is full of examples of systematic exclusion of entire groups of people in research, in which only people who are White were studied (Guthrie, 2004). The ability for scientists to generalize research from one population to another—regardless of whether they are studying emotion, memory, development, social relations, mental health, or motivation—has been and continues to be limited by samples that do not represent the diversity of race and ethnicity. What can we learn from a study of emotion that excludes more than a billion people? What can we say about memory, motivation, emotion, or depression if whole racial or ethnic groups are excluded from research? Much of the research you have been reading, much of the research conducted, has not had a range of research participants that represents the whole of humanity.

And what does this mean for your current or future research projects? The answer is simple, but the path forward is not. First, when designing a research project, don't overlook the impact that race and ethnicity may have on your variables of interest. Make sure to explore the literature on your topic to capture the work of scholars who have incorporated race and ethnicity into their studies. And incorporate their findings into your design—consider how race and ethnicity interact with and influence your research project. Second, collect data from diverse samples and report your results accordingly: Are there important and meaningful differences among the subgroups? Or were subgroups similar? Both answers move research questions forward.

Culture

Culture is the set of behaviors, customs, values, beliefs, knowledge, language, and expressions of a social group; culture is passed from generation to generation and is often, but not always, associated with a specific time or place (Mio et al., 2019). Whether theories and research findings generalize across cultures is also a critically important issue. Some observers of current psychological research have been critical, noting that theories have been developed on findings from behavioral research that lacked diversity in their samples.

Arnett (2008) estimated that a majority of research was conducted with research participants that represented only 5% of the globe's population; they concluded that behavioral science is built on the study of WEIRD (Western, Educated, Industrialized, Rich, Democratic) persons. More than a decade later, Thalmayer et al. (2021) found that although things had improved, they had not improved very much. Dominant cultures have been studied more extensively than nondominant cultures, which may bias our understanding of humanity. Henrich et al. (2010) examined the results of experimental research from very varied areas, including visual perception, cooperation, spatial reasoning, moral reasoning, self-concept, and the heritability of IQ, and found important differences across cultural groups. That is, they found that the WEIRD samples differed from the rest of the world in meaningful ways and concluded that behavioral scientists "need to be less cavalier in addressing questions of human nature on the basis of data drawn from this particularly thin, and rather unusual, slice of humanity" (p. 61).

In many cases, research samples consist primarily of college students from the United States, other English-speaking countries, and Europe. Ultimately, researchers wish to discover aspects of human behavior that have universal applications, but in fact they cannot generalize beyond their limited samples. At its heart, this is a critique of the external validity of behavioral research: Does our human behavioral research generalize to all humans?

How does culture impact research and our understanding of research results? And how does our understanding of culture influence researchers?

If psychologists want to understand human behavior, they must understand human behavior across and among cultures (Henrich et al., 2010; Miller, 1999). Miller described research on self-concept by Kitayama et al. (1997) to illustrate the benefits of incorporating culture into psychological theory. Traditional theories of self-concept are grounded in the United States and Western Europe; the "self" is an individualistic concept where people are independent of others, and self-enhancement comes from individual achievements. Kitayama and his colleagues take a broader cultural perspective: In contrast to the U.S. meaning of self, in some other cultures the "self" is a collective concept in which self-esteem is derived from relationships with others. Often, people from Japan engage in self-criticism, which can be seen as relationship-maintaining. In contrast, Americans work to maintain and enhance self-esteem. Thus, very different activities contribute to a positive self-concept in the two cultures (Kitayama et al., 1997). This common theme in research incorporates culture in psychological processes: "The significance of self-esteem, however, may be much more specific to a culture than has typically been supposed in the literature" (p. 1262).

Much of the research on culture centers on identifying similarities and differences in personality and other psychological characteristics and how individuals from different cultures respond to the same environments (Matsumoto, 1994). Research by Kim et al. (2008) provides another example of the limits of external validity across cultural groups. This research focused on how people from different cultures use social support to cope with stress. In reviewing the research on the topic, they concluded that Asians and Asian Americans might benefit from other styles of social support than those that are better suited to European Americans. For example, Asian Americans are more likely to benefit from support that does not involve intense disclosure of personal stressful events and feelings, which is the hallmark of support in many White American groups. Instead, they suggest that Asians and Asian Americans may benefit more from the support that comes with the comforts of proximity (being with close friends) rather than sharing.

Finally, we should emphasize that behavioral research across the globe has increased dramatically, and researchers everywhere now have more direct access to this literature. To illustrate, the APA PsycInfo database now includes almost 3,000 journals published in multiple countries and languages, with new journals added regularly (https://www.apa.org/pubs/databases/psycinfo/coverage).

Threats to External Validity

The use of college-student volunteers from a specific location (or online!) is common in behavioral research. Each of those characteristics can threaten our ability to generalize a study to all humans.

College Students College students have been oversampled. Smart (1966) found that college students were studied in over 70% of the articles published between 1962 and 1964 in the *Journal of Experimental Psychology* and the *Journal of Abnormal and Social Psychology*. Later, Sears (1986) reported finding similar percentages in 1980 and 1985 in various social psychology journals, and Arnett (2008) found that 67% of the articles in the 2007 volume of

The Journal of Personality and Social Psychology used college student samples. Nearly 15 years later, Thalmayer et al. (2021) found that the number had grown to 80%! Because research using college students is research on a highly restricted population—generally first- and second-year students taking the introductory psychology class—the subjects tend to be young and to possess the characteristics of emerging adults: a sense of self-identity that is still developing, social and political attitudes that are in a state of flux, a high need for peer approval, and peer relationships that often change.

Furthermore, they are college students and possess characteristics associated with academic success (e.g., cognitive abilities, test-wiseness). Moreover, Peterson (2001) found that students, as a group, are more homogeneous than nonstudent samples. That is, students are more similar to each other than adults are similar to other adults in the general population. So, what we learn from such studies might apply only to a highly select and unusual group and not to "people in general."

Research by Henry (2008) illustrates how the use of college students may affect the external validity of research on prejudice. In a sample of articles from 1990 to 2005, an increasing percentage of studies used college students as participants. Further, looking at the actual results of studies on prejudice that compared college students with adults, he reported differences between adults and college students.

It is easy to criticize research based on participant characteristics, yet criticism by itself does not mean that results cannot be generalized. Although we need to be concerned about the potential problems of generalizing from unique populations such as college students (Sears, 1986), we should also keep several things in mind when thinking about this issue. First, while college student populations are increasingly diverse and increasingly representative of society (although college students will always be characterized by having the ability and motivation to pursue a college degree), there will always be ways in which they are not. Still, just because a study is not generalizable to "all people" doesn't mean that it has no value, it only means that the study's findings can't be generalized outside of the group of people who participated. Second, replication of research studies provides a safeguard against the limited external validity of a single study. Studies are replicated at other colleges using different mixes of students. Many findings first established with college students are later found to apply to other populations, such as children, aging adults, and people in other countries. It is also worth noting that internet samples are increasingly used in many studies. Although such studies raise their own issues of external validity, they frequently complement studies based on college student samples.

Volunteers   Researchers often ask people to volunteer to participate in their research. At many colleges, introductory psychology students are required to volunteer for research or complete an alternative project. Suppose you are studying populations other than college students. In that case, you are even more dependent on volunteers—for example, asking people living in an apartment complex to participate in a study of neighborliness or conducting research on the internet in which people must go to your website and then agree to participate in the study, or conducting a telephone survey of county residents to determine health-care needs. In all these cases, the external validity of the findings may be limited because the data from volunteers may be different from what would be obtained with a more general sample.

Research indicates that volunteers differ in various ways from nonvolunteers. In their comprehensive study on the topic, Rosenthal and Rosnow (1975) reported that volunteers tend to be more highly educated, of a higher socioeconomic status, more in need of approval, and more social.

Finally, it seems that different kinds of people volunteer for different types of experiments. Often, there are many studies running at the same time, and potential participants choose which one to participate in. People who are drawn to a study titled "Problem Solving" might be significantly different from people who are drawn to a study titled "Interaction in Small Groups" or one titled "Feeling Anxious?" Available evidence indicates that the title on a call for participants influences who signs up (Hood & Back, 1971; Silverman & Margulis, 1973).

Location   The location where participants are recruited can also impact a study's external validity. Participants in one locale may differ from participants in another locale. For example, students at the University of California, Los Angeles, may vary from students at a nearby state university, who may differ from students at a community college. People in rural Iowa may vary from people in New York City. Thus, a finding obtained from the students in one type of educational setting or one geographic region may not generalize to people in other locations or areas. In fact, studies have explored how personality traits like extraversion and openness to new experiences vary across geographic regions. Rentfrow et al. (2008) looked at geographic differences in personality traits among citizens of various U.S. states and found extraversion to vary by state. People in midwestern states tended to be more extraverted than people in northeastern states, and people in western states tended to be more open to new experiences. Thus, a study conducted in one location may not generalize well to another, mainly if the variables in question somehow relate to place.

Online Research Participants   Another important consideration arises when asking participants to volunteer for online surveys and experiments. Researchers can find potential participants through online survey design services. Psychologists are increasingly using crowdsourcing research recruitment sites such as MTurk (https://www.mturk.com; Buhrmester et al., 2011; Chandler, 2017; Jacquet, 2011) or Prolific (https://www.prolific.co/). This sort of sampling strategy has important implications for external validity. Although online samples can be more diverse than the typical college student sample, they are still not representative and so there are still generalization issues—internet users represent a unique demographic. It is estimated that 90% of U.S. adults use the internet, and the share of Americans who say that they own a smartphone has increased from 35% in

2011 to 85% in 2021 (Pew Research Center, 2021). The Pew data also indicate that internet use is associated with living in an urban/suburban area, being a high school graduate or higher, being under 65 years of age, and having a higher income. Thus, by recruiting a sample of internet users, researchers introduce some biases that need to be recognized when interpreting the results.

Nonhuman Animals

In the chapter "Ethics in Behavioral Research," we noted that about 7% of psychological research is conducted with nonhuman animals. Almost all of this research is conducted with rats, mice, and birds. Most research with other species is undertaken to study the behavior of those animals directly to gather the information that may help with the survival of endangered species and increase our understanding of our bonds with nonhuman animals such as dogs, cats, and horses (https://www.apa-hai.org).

The basic research that psychologists conduct with nonhuman animals is usually conducted with the expectation that the findings can be generalized to humans. This is not always an easy connection to make. For instance, there is a very long history of studying depression using animal subjects (particularly rats; McKinney & Bunney, 1969), and the connections to human depression are still discussed today (Harro, 2019). Bird and Parlee (2000) tackle the issue of generalization and suggest that researchers should state their reasons for selecting a particular animal to study and describe how well that animal generalizes to humans.

Research with nonhuman animals is useful because some research questions are more difficult to answer with humans. Take, for instance, studies that require long-term observation: it would be difficult to recruit human subjects to participate in such a study. Beyond that, there are studies related to biological bases of memory, food preferences, sexual behavior, choice behavior, and drug addictions that are only possible using nonhuman animals as subjects.

The American Psychological Association's brochure on animal research is available at https://www.apa.org/research/responsible/research-animals.pdf.

GENERALIZING ACROSS SITUATIONS

The generalization of a study from its participants to the population is a critical aspect of external validity. Generalizing the results of one study to others across situations is also essential. For instance, if we measure the relationship between altruism and helping behavior in three different ways, do we get similar results from all three methods of measuring? There are three crucial aspects of a study's methodology that need to be considered, when thinking about external validity: the influences of the people conducting the study, the effects of a pretest, and the differences between a field study and a laboratory study.

First, research conducted in a laboratory setting allows the experimenter to study the impact of independent variables under highly controlled conditions. In this sort of highly controlled environment, the internal validity of the research is the primary consideration. But does the artificiality of the laboratory setting limit the ability to generalize laboratory observations to real-life settings? Consider, for instance, a carefully controlled laboratory study of college-student learning, in which participants are invited into a room, shown a "lecture" on a screen, and then asked to recall different facts from the lecture. This sort of experiment may provide an opportunity to manipulate variables to test their impact on "learning," but it is what we would call a simulated classroom rather than the actual lived experience of students in a classroom—with real grades on the line, an interactive lecturer, several students talking to each other, and another distractingly watching YouTube! On the other hand, it would be challenging to run a study with clear and clean findings tying an independent variable to a dependent variable, given the "noise" of the live classroom.

A field experiment is a "real-life" alternative to the artificiality of a laboratory. Recall from the chapter "Fundamental Research Issues" that in a field experiment, the researcher manipulates the independent variable in a natural setting—such as a store, a school, a street corner. Thus, a learning experiment originally conducted in a lab setting could be adapted for study in a simulated classroom or even a corporate training exercise.

Second, the use of a pretest—which was covered in the chapter "Experimental Design"—can also create external validity problems. Intuitively, pretesting seems to be a good idea: a researcher can ensure that the groups are equivalent on the pretest. It is often more satisfying to see that individuals changed their scores than to look only at group means on a posttest. Pretesting, however, may limit the ability to generalize to populations that did not receive a pretest (see Lana, 1969). That is, simply taking the pretest may cause subjects to behave differently than they would without the pretest. Do posttest scores on the dependent variable differ depending on whether the pretest was given? Sometimes researchers conduct two studies in these circumstances: first study with the pretest, the second without.

Finally, Does et al. (2018) point out that the characteristics of the individuals conducting research can impact the external validity of the results. In most laboratory research, only one experimenter is used, and rarely is much attention paid to the personal characteristics of the experimenter (McGuigan, 1963). The main goal is to ensure that any influence the experimenter has on subjects is constant throughout the experiment. However, there is always the possibility that the results are generalizable only to certain types of experimenters. Kintz and his colleagues (1965) discussed some of the important characteristics of experimenters: the experimenter's personality, gender identity, and amount of practice in the role of the experimenter. A warm, friendly experimenter will almost certainly produce different results than a cold, unfriendly experimenter. Does et al. (2018) discuss demographic characteristics of the researcher: Do they match or differ from the characteristics of the participants? Participants also may behave differently with experimenters based on visible differences in gender, race, ethnicity, or disability status.

REPLICATIONS

It may seem as if no research can possibly be generalizable! In some ways, this is true. **Replication** of research is a way of overcoming any problems of generalization that occur in a single study. There are two types of replications to consider: exact replications and conceptual replications.

Exact Replications

An **exact replication** is an attempt to precisely replicate the procedures of a study to see whether the same results are obtained. A researcher who obtains an unexpected finding will frequently attempt a replication to make sure that the finding is reliable. If you are starting your own work on a problem, you may try to replicate a crucial study to make sure that you understand the procedures and can obtain the same results. Exact replications often occur when a researcher builds on the findings of a prior study. For example, suppose you are intrigued by the research in Singh et al. (2010) on waist-to-hip ratio that was mentioned previously. Singh reports that males rate females with a ratio of .70 as most attractive. In your research, you might replicate the procedures used in the original study and expand on the original research. For example, you might study this phenomenon with males similar to those in the original sample as well as males from different cultures or age groups. When you replicate the original research findings using very similar procedures, your confidence in the external validity of the original findings is increased.

The "Mozart effect" provides us with an interesting example of the importance of replications. In the original study by Rauscher et al. (1993), college students listened to 10 minutes of a Mozart sonata. These students then showed better performance on a spatial-reasoning measure drawn from the Stanford-Binet Intelligence Scale than students exposed to a relaxation tape or simple silence. This finding received a great deal of media attention as people quickly generalized it to the possibility of increasing children's intelligence by having them listen to Mozart sonatas. In fact, one state governor began producing Mozart CDs to distribute in maternity wards, and entrepreneurs began selling Mozart kits to parents over the internet. Over the next few years, however, there were many failures to replicate the Mozart effect (see Steele et al., 1999). We noted above that failures to replicate may occur because the exact conditions for producing the effect were not used. In this case, Rauscher and Shaw (1998) responded to the many replication failures by precisely describing the conditions necessary to produce the Mozart effect. However, Steele et al. (1999) and McCutcheon (2000) were unable to obtain the effect even though they followed the recommendations of Rauscher and Shaw. Research on the Mozart effect continues. Some recent findings suggest that the effect is limited to music that also increases arousal, and that it is this arousal that can cause better performance following exposure to the music (Thompson et al., 2001). Bangerter and Heath (2004) present a detailed analysis of the development of the research on the Mozart effect, and a meta-analysis by Pietschnig et al. (2010) concludes that there is little evidence for the effect.

A single failure to replicate does not reveal much, though; it is unrealistic to assume, on the basis of a single failure to replicate, that the previous research is necessarily invalid. Failures to replicate share the same problems as nonsignificant results, discussed in the chapter "Understanding Research Results: Statistical Inference." A failure to replicate could mean that the original results are invalid, but it could also mean that the replication attempt was flawed. For example, if the replication is based on the procedure as reported in a journal article, it is possible that the article omitted an important aspect of the procedure. For this reason, it is usually a good idea to write to the researcher to obtain detailed information on all of the materials that were used in the study.

Several scientific societies are encouraging systematic replications of important scientific findings. The journal *Perspectives on Psychological Science* (published by the Association for Psychological Science) is sponsoring the publication of Registered Research Replications (https://www.psychologicalscience.org/publications/replication). Multiple groups of researchers will undertake replications of important studies using procedures that are made public before initiating the research. When completed, all of the replications will be described in a single report. In addition to the Psychological Science initiative, the online journal *PLOS ONE* (*Public Library of Science*) has developed the Reproducibility Initiative to encourage independent replication of research in the clinical sciences (Pattinson, 2012). Such developments should lead to greater understanding of the generalizability of research findings.

Conceptual Replications

A **conceptual replication** is the use of different procedures to replicate a research finding. In a conceptual replication, researchers attempt to understand the relationships among abstract conceptual variables by using new, or different, operational definitions of those variables. Conceptual replications are even more important than exact replications in furthering our understanding of behavior.

In most research, a key goal is to discover whether there exists a relationship between conceptual variables. In the original Mozart effect study, researchers examined the effect of *exposure to classical music* on *spatial reasoning*. These are conceptual variables; in the actual study, specific operational definitions of the variables were used. *Exposure to classical music* was operationalized as 10 minutes of exposure to the Mozart Sonata for Two Pianos in D Major. *Spatial reasoning* was operationalized as performance on a particular spatial reasoning measure.

In a conceptual replication, the same independent variable is operationalized in a different way, and the dependent variable may be measured in a different way, too. Conceptual replications are extremely important in the social sciences because the variables used are complex and can be operationalized in many ways. Complete understanding of any variable involves studying the variable using a variety of operational definitions. A crucial generalization question is whether the relationship holds when other ways of manipulating or measuring the variables are studied.

Sometimes the conceptual replication may involve an alternative stimulus (e.g., a different Mozart sonata, or a selection by a different composer) or an alternative dependent measure (e.g., a different spatial reasoning task). Or as we previously noted, the same variables are sometimes studied in both laboratory and field settings. When conceptual replications produce similar results, our confidence in the generalizability of relationships between variables is greatly increased.

This discussion should also alert you to an important way of thinking about research findings. The findings represent relationships between conceptual variables but are grounded in specific operations. You may read about the specific methods employed in a study conducted 20 years ago and question whether the study could be replicated today. You might also speculate that the methods used in a study are so unusual that they could never generalize to other situations. These concerns are not as serious when placed within the context of conceptual replications, because although operational definitions can change over time, the underlying conceptual variable often remains more consistent. Admittedly, a specific method from a study conducted at one time might not be effective today, given changes in today's political and cultural climate. A conceptual replication of the manipulation, however, might demonstrate that the relationship between the conceptual theoretical variables is still present. Similarly, the narrow focus of a particular study is less problematic if the general finding is replicated with different procedures.

Open Science and Replication

In 2012 the Open Science Collaboration launched an effort to understand the replicability of behavioral research. "Reproducibility," they noted, "is a defining feature of science." To study reproducibility, the leaders of the Open Science Collaboration initiated a large-scale project to conduct replications of 100 studies published in three psychology journals. Researchers from around the globe joined in to complete the studies. The results were published with the title "Estimating the Reproducibility of Psychological Science" (Open Science Collaboration, 2015). The results were disappointing: Depending on the criteria used to define a successful replication, 36% to 47% of the replications projects were successful. That is, when other scientists tried to replicate studies from the past, less than half were successful. As you can imagine, this attracted a great deal of media attention with newspaper and Web-based features describing the "replication crisis" facing psychology.

How should this result be interpreted? As with any failure to replicate, there are numerous possible explanations. One is that too many journal articles in psychology are reporting results that cannot be replicated—a Type I error. We should note that the replication study included articles primarily in social or cognitive psychology published in just three journals. We should also note that the cognitive psychology articles were more likely to be replicated than were the social psychology articles. Of course, even before the report from the Open Science group there had been concerns about problems replicating many recent studies on unconscious priming that were being published in social psychology journals (Kahneman, 2012). There are other explanations. Gilbert et al. (2016) noted, along with Kahneman (2014), that replications are most likely to be successful when the original author is involved. Some of the Open Science replications were given prior approval by the original researcher, and these had more successful replications (Gilbert et al., 2016). In addition, original research results with greater effect sizes were more often replicated. It may be that statistically significant findings with small effect sizes need replication research with large sample sizes and attention paid to the smallest details of methodology. Finally, the Open Science replications attempted exact replications—it may be that the unsuccessful replications were particularly tied to the context of the subject populations, the independent variable manipulation, or the dependent measures (Gilbert et al., 2016; Open Science Collaboration, 2015).

We hope, along with Anderson et al. (2016), that the reproducibility project motivates researchers to attempt to replicate more studies and discover the factors that lead to reproducible research findings. Moreover, *you* can help resolve this "crisis" by doing good science. By conducting well-designed research and writing detailed, well-written research reports, you can play a critical role in addressing the crisis. When research reports are sufficiently detailed so as to make studies easy to replicate—and much of what we have described in this book is related to you learning how to do just that—findings can be replicated. You can participate in the open science movement. By making data sets publicly accessible, and publishing in journals that have wide access, you support replications. In science, answers to questions and problems are found in the data.

The Collaborative Replications and Education Project (CREP) (https://osf.io/wfc6u/) is a project designed to support undergraduate students and their mentors in the completion of replication projects. It is housed within the Open Science Framework, which is a free and open-source software project designed to facilitate open collaboration in science. As an example of CREP's work, seven teams of researchers conducted replications of a study by Forest and Wood (2012). Leighton et al. (2018) published the summary and analysis of those replications.

How can you get involved? CREP has a straightforward process to select the study, plan your replication, execute your replication, and submit a report: https://osf.io/wfc6u/wiki/home/

ASSESSING EXTERNAL VALIDITY VIA LITERATURE REVIEWS AND META-ANALYSES

Researchers have traditionally drawn conclusions about the external validity of research findings by conducting literature reviews. In a **literature review,** a reviewer reads a number of studies that address a particular topic and then writes a paper that summarizes and evaluates the literature. The literature review provides information that (1) summarizes what has been found, (2) tells the reader which findings are strongly supported and which are only weakly supported in the literature, (3) points out inconsistent findings and areas in which research is lacking, and (4) discusses future directions for research.

Sometimes a review will be a narrative in which the author provides descriptions of research findings and draws conclusions about the literature. The conclusions in a narrative literature review are based on the reviewer's subjective impressions. Another technique for comparing a large number of studies in an area is **meta-analysis** (Borenstein et al., 2009). In a meta-analysis, the researcher combines the actual results of a number of studies. The analysis consists of a set of statistical procedures that employ effect sizes to compare a given finding across many different studies. Instead of relying on judgments obtained in a narrative literature review, you can draw statistical conclusions from this material. The statistical procedures need not concern you. They involve examining several features of the results of studies, including the effect sizes and significance levels obtained. The important point here is that meta-analysis is a method for determining the reliability of a finding by examining the results from many different studies.

Stewart and Chambless (2009) conducted a meta-analysis of research on the effectiveness of cognitive behavioral therapy (CBT) for anxiety disorders. Both a traditional literature review and a meta-analysis begin with a body of previous research on a topic; in this case, Stewart and Chambless located 56 studies using CBT with adults diagnosed with an anxiety disorder (including panic disorder, social anxiety, post-traumatic stress disorder, generalized anxiety disorder, and obsessive-compulsive disorder). Studies that included an additional medication treatment were excluded. The researchers performed a statistical analysis of the results of these studies and concluded that CBT was effective in treating all of the types of anxiety disorders. In a traditional literature review it can be difficult to provide the type of general conclusion that was reached with the meta-analysis, because it is necessary to integrate information from many studies with different experimental designs, disorders, and measures of anxiety.

One of the most important reasons a meta-analysis can lead to clear conclusions is that meta-analytic studies focus on effect size (recall that an effect size indicates the strength of the relationship between two or more variables.). A typical table in a meta-analysis will show the effect size obtained in a number of studies, along with a summary of the average effect size across the studies. More importantly, the analysis allows comparisons of the effect sizes in different types of studies to allow tests of hypotheses. For example, Venturo-Conerly et al. (2022) analyzed the results of 37 articles that examined the effectiveness of psychotherapy delivered remotely for children and adolescents. Table 1 shows a few of the findings. The effect size averaged across all studies was .47—that is, remote

TABLE 1 Some meta-analysis findings for effectiveness of remotely delivered therapy

Variable	Effect size r
Overall relationship	.47
Target Problem	
ADHD	−.03
Anxiety	.62
Conduct Disorder	.78
Depression	.09
Therapeutic Provider Contact	
Yes	.64
No	.22

Source: Venturo-Conerly et al. (2022).

treatment was found to be moderately effective (in fact, as effective as in-person treatment). Several variables moderated this relationship: the effect was larger—therapy was more effective—for remote psychotherapies that included contact with a therapist (.64) compared to those that were more self-administered (.22). There was also stronger effectiveness for the treatment of anxiety (.62) and conduct problems (.78), compared to ADHD (−.03) and depression (.09).

A study by Bushman and Wells (2001) points to an interesting way in which knowledge of meta-analysis can improve how we interpret information for literature reviews.

The reviewers in their study were undergraduates who were provided with the titles of 20 studies and information about the studies' findings dealing with the effect of attitude similarity on attraction. Sometimes the titles were salient with respect to the findings ("Birds of a Feather Flock Together") and others were nonsalient ("Research Studies Who Likes Whom"). Salient titles are obviously easier to remember. When asked to draw conclusions about the findings, naive reviewers with no knowledge of meta-analysis overestimated the size of the relationship between similarity and attraction when provided with salient titles. Other reviewers were given brief training in meta-analysis; these reviewers drew accurate conclusions about the actual findings. That is, they were not influenced by the article title. Thus, even without conducting a meta-analysis, a background in meta-analysis can be beneficial when reviewing research findings.

Both narrative reviews and meta-analyses provide valuable information and in fact are often complementary. A meta-analysis allows statistical, quantitative conclusions, whereas a narrative review identifies trends in the literature and directions for future study—a more qualitative approach.

Check Your Learning

Now, test your knowledge of meta-analyses with Check Your Learning: Practice Exercise #1.

USING RESEARCH TO IMPROVE LIVES

The behavioral sciences are not very old. Most historians identify the establishment of Wilhelm Wundt's lab at the University of Leipzig in 1879 as the start of a formalized science of behavior (Woody et al., 2017). This is not to say that people have not been thinking about human behavior before that; people have been thinking about human behavior for as long as there have been humans! Indeed, culture and cultural artifacts like political systems and religions potentially emerged as ways to regulate human behavior based on how they understood human nature.

Many "early" psychologists—such as Wilhelm Wundt, William James, Edward Thorndike, John B. Watson, Sigmund Freud, and B. F. Skinner—were White men. That is not to say that psychology did not benefit from contributions by women or people from nondominant cultures. Indeed, the essential and often unrecognized contributions of Mary Whiton Calkins, Francis Cecil Sumner, Helen Bradford Thompson, Mamie Phipps Clark, Eleanor J. Gibson, and Kenneth Clark (among many others) are now being foregrounded in textbooks and courses on the history of the discipline. Still, much of the early work in the behavioral sciences was conducted by White men on White male research participants. It is a central fact that psychology is a scientific discipline built on a single, segmented view of humanity.

Over time, psychology and other behavioral sciences have become more diverse in perspectives and practices. We are seeing research conducted by a worldwide cohort of scientists studying subject populations from many cultures. The behavioral sciences have started to move toward an inclusive and diverse science of humanity rather than what Arnett (2008) described as a WEIRD science.

In an address to the American Psychological Association (APA), Dr. Martin Luther King Jr.(1967) implored social scientists to use their methods to address racism, "We know we haven't found the answers to all forms of social change. We know, however, that we did find some answers. We have achieved and we are confident. We also know we are confronted now with far greater complexities and we have not yet discovered all the theory we need." In a presidential address to APA just two years later, George Miller (1969) described the role of psychology as a "means of promoting human welfare" and spoke of "giving psychology away." Miller addressed the broadest issue of generalization: taking what we know about human behavior and allowing it to be applied by many people in all areas of everyday life as a way of improving lives. Taken together, Drs. Miller and King were urging psychologists to apply their theories and research to enable people to make positive changes in society.

Zimbardo (2004) described psychology's continuing commitment to giving psychology away. The impact of psychological research can be seen in areas such as health (programs to promote health-related behaviors related to stress, heart disease, and sexually transmitted diseases), education (providing methods for encouraging academic performance), and work environments (providing workers with more control and improving how people interact with computers and other machines in the workplace). In addition, psychologists are using the internet to provide the public with information on parenting, education, mental health, and many other topics—examples are the websites of the American Psychological Association and the Association for Psychological Science (https://www.apa.org; https://www.psychologicalscience.org), national mental health resource websites (https://www.mentalhealth.gov and https://www.samhsa.gov), and many individual psychologists who are sharing their expertise with the public.

The APA itself has made significant contributions. *Multicultural Guidelines* (American Psychological Association, 2017) is a comprehensive framework for all psychologists, including clinicians, researchers, consultants, and educators; it is a step forward for our discipline as it works to develop an "appreciation for, understanding of, and willingness to learn about" human differences (p. 7). The APA report *Equity, Diversity, and Inclusion Framework* (American Psychological Association, 2021) noted that APA strives for "an accessible, equitable, and inclusive psychology that promotes human rights, fairness, and dignity for all" (p. 6). The field has made great progress and is improving human lives. For an optimistic review of psychology's response to these challenges, see Pettigrew (2018). Still, there is work to do: Buchanan et al. (2021) called for embracing new "strategies to change how science is conducted, reviewed, reported, and disseminated."

Science is a process, not a destination. There is a lot of work left to do, and we hope that you feel more prepared to do it. The behavioral sciences can be a "means of promoting human welfare" only insofar as we understand, acknowledge, and value that there is a vast diversity of human beings. Indeed, a healthy, flourishing science depends on it.

ENGAGING WITH RESEARCH: GENERALIZING RESULTS

The tools in the behavioral researcher's toolbox can be used for many tasks. In this chapter, we discussed how a study's design and sample can impact our ability to generalize the findings across people and methods.

In their study, Haskett et al. (2022) sought to understand the challenges and positive experiences of economically disadvantaged mothers during the COVID-19 pandemic. They measured COVID-19 stress and asked an open-ended question about potential positive experiences during the pandemic: "We have talked about ways in which COVID-19 has been stressful, but you may have experienced some positive changes as well. Please tell me what has been going well for you and your family since coronavirus has begun to affect everyday lives."

For this exercise, acquire and read the article (available at https://onlinelibrary.wiley.com/doi/10.1111/fare.12684):

Haskett, M. E., Hall, J. K., Finster, H. P., Owens, C., & Buccelli, A. R. (2022). "It brought my family more together": Mixed-methods study of low-income U.S. mothers during the pandemic. *Family Relations, 71*(3), 1–16. https://doi.org/10.1111/fare.12684

After reading the article, consider the following:

1. **What is the primary goal of this study? Description, Prediction, Determining Cause, or Explaining? Do the authors achieve their goals?**

2. **What did these researchers do? What was the method?**

   a. The authors described the study as mixed-methods. What did they mean?

3. **What was measured?**

   a. How did they measure COVID-19-related stress?

   b. How did they measure the positive experiences that they may have experienced during the pandemic?

   c. How did the researchers operationalize "low-income"?

4. **To what or whom can we generalize the results?**

   a. Should we generalize the results of this study to a sample of economically disadvantaged mothers from Alaska? Or Syria? Or Bangladesh?

   b. If another research with the same research question used a different method, how do you think the results would differ?

   c. What was the racial and ethnic breakdown of the participants?

   d. How did the participants identify their gender?

5. **What did they find? What were the results?**

6. **Have other researchers found similar results?**

7. **What are the limitations of this study?**

8. **What are the ethical issues present in this study?**

BEING A SKILLED CONSUMER OF RESEARCH

If you conducted a study using a sample of participants from your college or university, in what ways do you think the sample would:

   a. differ from the population of the city that your college/university is in?

   b. differ from the population of the state? or the population of the country?

   c. differ from the population of another country?

   d. differ from other college student samples by gender, race, and/or ethnicity?

   e. differ from other college student samples by other factors (e.g., regional, cultural, social class)?

Check Your Learning: Practice Exercises

Practice Exercise #1

Fraundorf et al. (2019) conducted a meta-analysis of 232 previously conducted studies on aging and recognition memory (i.e., recognizing something that has been previously encountered: words, faces, pictures). They concluded that younger adults showed superior performance on recognition tasks compared with older adults. The article title was "Aging and Recognition Memory: A Meta-analysis." Now address the following:

1. What does it mean that Fraundorf et al. (2019) conducted a meta-analysis; in other words, what do you know about this article just from the title and our brief description?

2. What conclusions were drawn from the meta-analysis?

3. In what ways is your confidence in a conclusion about a finding different when based on a meta-analysis instead of based on the results of a single investigation?

(Answers are provided at the end of this chapter.)

CHAPTER REVIEW

Review Questions

1. What is external validity?

2. Why should a researcher be concerned about generalizing to other populations?

3. How can the fact that most studies are conducted with college students, volunteers, and individuals from a limited location and culture potentially impact external validity?

4. How does the use of the internet to recruit subjects and collect data impact external validity?

5. What is the source of the problem of generalizing to other experimenters? How can this problem be solved?

6. Why is it important to pretest a problem for generalization? Discuss why including a pretest *may* affect the ability to generalize results.

7. Distinguish between an exact replication and a conceptual replication. What is the value of a conceptual replication?

8. What is a meta-analysis?

Study Terms

Conceptual replication (p. 337)

Exact replication (p. 336)

External validity (p. 327)

Literature review (p. 340)

Meta-analysis (p. 340)

Replication (p. 336)

Check Your Learning: Answers

Practice Exercise #1

1. It means that they combined the actual results from many published studies to generate their conclusions.

2. They found that older adults, compared to younger adults, were less effective at recognizing stimuli such as words, faces, or pictures to which they had been previously exposed.

3. Because meta-analysis combines the results from many studies, a conclusion that is drawn from the meta-analysis should be stronger than a conclusion based on a single study. You should be more confident that the result will be able to be replicated.

Appendix A

Reporting Research

INTRODUCTION

Communicating science is one of the most important jobs of the scientist. This is accomplished primarily by researchers writing detailed research reports and attending scientific conferences to give talks and present posters describing their results. This appendix focuses on writing research reports, but we will also summarize guidelines for preparing a poster or a talk for a professional meeting. This appendix also includes a sample paper, which illustrates the stylistic features of a research report, and a set of useful APA Style Resources to guide your writing in APA style and serve as accessible references.

We will consider the specific rules that should be followed in organizing and presenting research results. These rules are a great convenience for both the writer and the reader. They provide structure for the report and a uniform method of presentation, making it easier for the reader to understand and evaluate the report. Specific rules vary from one discipline to another. A rule for presenting research results in psychology may not apply to the same situation in, for example, sociology research. Also, the rules may vary depending on whether you are preparing the report for a class, a thesis, or submission to a journal. Fortunately, the variation is usually minor, and the general rules of presentation are much the same across disciplines and situations.

The format presented here for writing research reports is drawn from the seventh edition of the *Publication Manual of the American Psychological Association* (APA, 2020b). APA style is used in many journals in psychology, child development, family relations, and education. If you are concerned about specific rules for a particular journal, consult a recent issue of that journal. The APA has also published a book titled *Concise Guide to APA Style* (APA, 2020a). You may purchase the *Publication Manual* through your college bookstore, at retail bookstores, or directly from the American Psychological Association. Useful online resources for APA style include https://www.apastyle.org, Purdue's Online Writing Lab at https://owl.english.purdue.edu/owl/resource/560/01/, and the Owl APA Formatting and Style Guide at https://owl.purdue.edu/owl/research_and_citation/apa_style/apa_style_introduction.html. Other recommended sources for preparing papers are Gernsbacher (2018), Landrum (2020), and Schwartz et al. (2020).

The APA manual identifies types of articles that students and professionals might prepare:

- Five types of empirical studies—qualitative articles, quantitative articles, mixed-methods articles, replication articles, and meta-analyses. Three of these are described in the chapter "Where to Start."
- Literature reviews describe past research in a specific area of psychology. These reports integrate research findings, evaluate the current status of research on the topic, and point to new directions for research.
- Theoretical articles emphasize the status of existing theory and may propose changes in a theory or development of a new theory.
- Methodological articles focus on methods of conducting research and analyzing data.

In this appendix, we will describe only procedures for reporting empirical studies. Further, we will simplify the discussion by focusing primarily on articles that present the results of a single study rather than multiple studies.

WRITING YOUR REPORT

Writing well is important. A poorly written report that is difficult to understand is of no value (and almost certainly will bring you a poor grade!). Also, a good paper will not contain typos, misspellings, or grammatical errors. In this section, we will cover some fundamentals of good writing and will include solutions to some of the key issues that students face when writing their first scientific paper.

Clarity

Clarity in writing is essential. Be precise and clear in presenting ideas, and think about your intended audience. It is helpful to write your paper as if it were addressed to an audience that is unfamiliar with your general topic and the methods you used to study the topic. Eliminate jargon that most readers will not comprehend. Sometimes a researcher will develop an abbreviated notation for referring to a specific variable or procedure. Such abbreviations may be convenient when communicating with others who are directly involved in the research project, but they are confusing to the general reader. However, you should assume that the reader has a general familiarity with statistics and hypothesis testing. Statistical outcomes can usually be presented without defining terms such as the *mean, standard deviation,* or *significance.* These are only general guidelines, however. Rosnow and Rosnow (2012) point out that when your intended audience is your instructor, you should pay close attention to what they have to say about expectations for the paper!

The entire report should have a coherent structure. Ideas should be presented in an orderly, logical progression to facilitate understanding. If you write your report as if it were addressed to someone who is being introduced to your ideas and research findings for the first time, you will be more likely to communicate clearly with the reader.

One method of producing a more organized report is to use an outline. Many writers plan a paper by putting their thoughts and ideas into outline form. The outline then serves as a writing guide. This method forces writers to develop a logical structure before writing the paper. Other writers prefer to use a less structured approach for the first draft. They then try to outline what has been written. If the paper does not produce a coherent outline, the organization needs to be improved. Word-processing programs usually have an outline feature to help you organize your paper; find this feature using the program's help menu.

Paragraphs should be well organized. It is a good idea for a paragraph to contain a topic sentence. Other sentences within a paragraph should be related to the topic sentence and develop the idea in this sentence by elaborating, expanding, explaining, or supporting the idea in the topic sentence. Also, avoid one-sentence paragraphs. If you find such paragraphs in your paper, expand the paragraph, move the idea to another paragraph, or simply delete the sentence.

After completing the first draft of your paper, let it sit for a day or so before you reread it. Carefully proofread the paper, paying attention to grammar and spelling. Some grammatical considerations are described here; your document-editing app may include a spell checker, and you can download a grammar app to help as you write your report. After you make changes and corrections, you may want to get feedback from others. Find one or more persons who will read your report critically and suggest improvements. Students may have access to advice from a university writing center. Professionals often benefit from hiring a copyeditor. Be prepared to write several drafts before you have a satisfactory finished product.

Acknowledging the Work of Others

It is extremely important to clearly separate your own words and ideas from those obtained from other sources. Recall our discussion of plagiarism in the chapter "Ethics in Behavioral Research." If you use a passage drawn from an article or book, make sure the passage is presented as a direct quotation. There is nothing wrong with quoting another author as long as you acknowledge your source. Never present another person's idea as your own. This is plagiarism and is inexcusable. You should cite your sources even if you are not using direct quotations. Indicating that your paper draws on the works of others actually strengthens your paper.

Sometimes writers are tempted to fill a paper with quotes from other sources or to quote another paper at great length (e.g., several paragraphs or more). This practice is distracting and counterproductive. Be direct and use your own descriptions and interpretations while acknowledging your sources. If you have any questions about how to properly include material from source articles in your own paper, consult your instructor.

Active Versus Passive Voice

Many writers rely too much on the passive voice in their reports, perhaps because they believe that the passive voice makes their writing seem more "scientific." Consider the following sentences:

> It was found by Alcalá et al. (2021) that children's household contributions . . .
>
> Participants were administered the test after a 10-minute rest period.
>
> Participants were read the instructions by the experimenter.

Now try writing those sentences in a more active voice. For example:

> Alcalá et al. (2021) found that children's household contributions . . .
>
> Participants took the test after a 10-minute rest period.
>
> I read the instructions to the participants.

Prose written in passive voice can seem stilted. Prose written in active voice is much more direct and sounds more natural.

Although APA style allows the author to use "I" (or "we" when there are multiple authors), many authors are still uncomfortable with the use of the first-person pronoun and instead refer to themselves in the third person. They might say "The experimenter distributed the questionnaires" instead of "I distributed the questionnaires," or "This researcher contacted the head administrators at five community mental health centers" instead of "I contacted the head administrators at five community mental health centers." Thus, when reading research papers, you should not be surprised to see this form of wording.

Avoiding Biased Language

The APA publication manual describes several ways of reducing bias, and in 2021 the APA published Inclusive Language Guidelines (APA, 2021b) that includes a glossary of terms related to equity and power, the use of person-first and identity-first language, identity-related terms, and a section on avoiding microaggressions in conversation.

First, it is essential to be specific and inclusive when describing the participants in your study. The APA manual allows the use of either *participants* or *subjects* when describing humans who take part in psychological research. In addition, it is appropriate to describe participants as *respondents* in survey research. You may also use specific descriptors such as *children*, *patients*, *clients*, and so on if these terms more accurately describe the participants in your study. Moreover, you should make sure to provide specific information about your participants. Descriptors such as *toddlers* or *teenagers* or *young adults* are not sufficiently specific; you should also provide exact age ranges.

Second, be sensitive to labels. You must also be sensitive to the possibility that your writing might convey a bias, however unintentional, regarding gender, sexual orientation, or ethnic or racial group. As a general principle, be as specific as possible when referring to groups of people. For example, referring to the participants in your study as "Korean Americans and Vietnamese Americans" is more specific and accurate than describing them as "Asians." Also, be sensitive to the use of labels that might be offensive to members of certain groups. In practice, this means that you refer to people using the terms that these people prefer.

The APA manual has numerous examples of ways of being sensitive to many identities: age, disability status, gender, racial and ethnic identity, and socioeconomic status (and the intersections of these identities). The term *gender* refers to social roles and identities associated with being male and female. Thus, *gender* is the proper term to use in a phrase such as "gender difference in average salary." The term *sex* refers to biological classification. Take care when using gender pronouns. Do not use *he, his, man, man's,* and so on when referring to multiple genders or gender identities. Sentences can usually be rephrased or specific pronouns deleted to avoid linguistic biases. For example, "The worker is paid according to his productivity" can be changed to "The worker is paid according to productivity" or "Workers are paid according to their productivity." In the first case, *his* was simply deleted; in the second case, the subject of the sentence was changed to plural. Do *not* try to avoid sexist language by simply substituting *s/he* whenever that might appear convenient.

Care should also be taken when referring to racial and ethnic groups. In APA style, the names of these groups are capitalized and never hyphenated—for example, Black, White, African American, Latino or Latinx, Asian, Asian American. The manual also reminds us that the terms that members of racial and ethnic groups use to describe themselves may change over time, and there may be a lack of consensus about a preferred term. Currently, for example, both *Black* and *African American* are generally acceptable. Depending on a number of factors, participants may prefer to be called Hispanic, Latino/Latina, Latinx, Latine, Chicano/Chicana, Mexican American, or Puerto Rican. You are urged to use the term most preferred by your participants.

The APA publication manual includes a great deal of information and numerous examples to encourage sensitivity in writing reports. The best advice is to review your papers for possible problems at least once prior to writing your final draft—consider a review specifically for sensitivity. If you have any questions about appropriate language, consult the manual and colleagues whose opinions you respect.

Some Grammatical Considerations

Transition Words and Phrases
One way to produce a clearly written research report is to pay attention to how you connect sentences within a paragraph and connect paragraphs within a section. The transitions between sentences and paragraphs should be smooth and consistent with the line of reasoning. Some commonly used transition words and phrases and their functions are described in this section.

Adverbs   Adverbs can be used as introductory words in sentences. However, you must use them to convey their implied meanings.

Adverb	*Implied meaning*
(Un)fortunately	It is (un)fortunate that . . .
Similarly	In a similar manner . . .
Certainly	It is certain that . . .
Clearly	It is clear that . . .

One adverb that is frequently misused as an introductory or transition word is *hopefully*. *Hopefully* means "in a hopeful manner," *not* "it is hoped that . . ."

> *Incorrect:* Hopefully, this is not the case.

> *Correct:* I hope this is not the case.

Words Suggesting Contrast   Some words and phrases suggest a contrast or contradiction between what was written immediately before and what is now being written:

Between sentences	*Within sentences*
By contrast,	whereas
On the other hand,	although
However,	but

The words in the left list refer to the previous sentence. The words in the right list connect phrases within a sentence; that is, they refer to another point in the same sentence.

Words Suggesting a Series of Ideas   The following words and phrases suggest that information after the transition word is related or similar to information in the sentence:

First	In addition	Last	Further
Second	Additionally	Finally	Moreover
Third	Then	Also	Another

Words Suggesting Implication   These words and phrases indicate that the information following the transition word is implied by or follows from the previous information:

Therefore	If . . . then
It follows that	Thus
In conclusion	Then

When you use transition words, be sure that they convey the meaning you intend. Sprinkling them around to begin sentences leads to confusion on the reader's part and defeats your purpose.

Troublesome Words and Phrases

"That" Versus "Which"   *That* and *which* are relative pronouns that introduce subordinate clauses and reflect the relationship of the subordinate clause to the main clause. *That* clauses are called restrictive clauses and are essential to the meaning of the sentence; *which* clauses are nonrestrictive and simply add more information. Note the different meanings of the same sentence using *that* and *which:*

> The mice that performed well in the first trial were used in the second trial.

> The mice, which performed well in the first trial, were used in the second trial.

The first sentence states that only mice that performed well in the first trial were used in the second. The second sentence states that all the mice were used in the second trial and they also happened to perform well in the first trial.

"While" Versus "Since"   *While* and *since* are subordinate conjunctions that also introduce subordinate clauses. To increase clarity in scientific writing, the APA manual suggests that *while* and *since* should be used only to refer to time. *While* is used to describe simultaneous events, and *since* is used to refer to a subsequent event:

> The participants waited together while their personality tests were scored.

> Since the paper by Steele (1997), many studies have been published on this topic.

The APA manual suggests other conjunctions to use when linking phrases that do not describe temporal events. *Although, whereas,* and *but* can be used in place of *while,* and *because* should be substituted for *since.*

> *Incorrect:* While the study was well designed, the report was poorly written.

> *Correct:* Although the study was well designed, the report was poorly written.

"Effect" Versus "Affect"   A common error in student reports is incorrect use of *effect* and *affect. Effect* is a noun that is used in scientific reports to mean "what is produced by a cause," as in the sentence: "The movie had a strong effect on me." *Affect* can be a noun or a verb. As a noun it means emotion, as in "The patient seemed depressed but she displayed very little affect." As a verb it means "to have an influence on," as in "The listeners' responses were affected by the music they heard."

> *Incorrect:* The independent variable effected their responses.

> *Correct:* The independent variable affected their responses.

> *Incorrect:* The independent variable had only a weak affect on the participants' behavior.

> *Correct:* The independent variable had only a weak effect on the participants' behavior.

Singular and Plural The following words are often misused. The left list shows singular nouns requiring singular verb forms. The right list contains plural nouns that must be used with plural verbs.

Singular	*Plural*
datum	data
stimulus	stimuli
analysis	analyses
phenomenon	phenomena
medium	media
hypothesis	hypotheses
schema	schemas
appendix	appendices
criterion	criteria

Probably the most frequently misused word is *data.*

Incorrect: The data *was* coded for computer analysis.

Correct: The data *were* coded for computer analysis.

Some Spelling Considerations Here are the currently accepted spelling and capitalization for some of the words that are frequently used in behavioral science papers:

questionnaire
database
email
URL
internet
website
webpage
the web
home page
smartphone
username
ebook
Wi-Fi

FORMATTING YOUR REPORT

You will eventually have to prepare a printed copy of your paper. In APA style, the paper should be *entirely double-spaced.* The margins for text should be set to 1 inch on all four sides of the page. APA style also dictates that text should not be "justified" on the right-hand margin. That is, text should be left-aligned with justification turned off—this is sometimes referred to as "ragged right" formatting.

Page headers—the information that appears at the top of each page, including the page number—are set approximately 0.5 inch from the top of the page. All pages are numbered. Paragraphs are indented 0.5 inch (use the tab function or paragraph-specific formatting, not the space bar). Make sure that hyphenation is turned off: There should not be hyphenated word breaks at the end of a line.

Be sure to take advantage of the features of your word-processing application, including double-spacing text, centering, and spell-check. Use the tabs and table functions to format text correctly; do not use the space bar to format text or tables.

You will need to place a page header and/or page number at the top of each page. Don't type this yourself at the top of every page—instead, use the header/footer feature of your word-processing application.

Use the same font throughout your paper. You may select a serif font or sans serif font. Serif fonts have short lines at the ends of the strokes that form the letters; sans serif literally means "without serif" and so does not have serif lines. Here are examples:

This is Times New Roman serif text.

`This is Arial sans serif text.`

Serif fonts recommended in the APA publication manual include 12-point Times New Roman, 11-point Georgia, or 10-point Computer Modern. San serif fonts include 11-point Arial, 11-point Calibri, or 10-point Lucinda Sans Unicode.

There should be one space following a period or a colon. If you find yourself inserting two spaces, you can always perform a "search and replace" when you have completed the paper. Search for two spaces and replace with a single space. In some cases there should not be a space following a period, as in U.S. (for United States) and initials used to identify an individual (such as H.M.).

You will need to use italic and boldface fonts correctly. Use the italics feature of your word processor to create italics for (a) titles and volume numbers of periodicals, (b) titles of books, (c) some headings in your paper, (d) most statistical terms, (e) anchors of a scale, such as 1 (*strongly disagree*) to 5 (*strongly agree*), (f) emphasis of a particular word or phrase when first mentioned in the paper, and (g) words used as words, as in "Authors now routinely use the word *participants.*" Pay attention to the use of italics in the examples used throughout this appendix. Boldface font is used for some of the headings of your paper (examples are shown below).

APA style uses a "hanging indent" for the reference list at the end of your paper. Here is an example:

> Li, Y., Luan, S., Li, Y., Wu, J., Li, W., & Hertwig, R. (2022). Does risk perception motivate preventive behavior during a pandemic? A longitudinal study in the United States and China. *American Psychologist, 77*(1), 111—123. https://doi.org/10.1037/amp0000885

Note that the first line of a reference begins flush with the left margin, but subsequent lines are indented 0.5 inch (you might want to think of the old "hangman" game to remember why this is called a hanging indent). Do not try to create a hanging indent using the space bar. This takes time and can cause problems when printing. Use the hanging indent feature of your word processor for correct, reliable formatting. It is very easy to learn how to do this through your Help menu or a search on your browser.

Professional and Student Paper Formats

The APA *Publication Manual* (2020b) makes a distinction between professional and student papers. Professional papers are prepared for submission to a journal for possible publication. Student papers are prepared for submission to an instructor for a course requirement. A thesis or dissertation is also a student paper in that it may have a set of special preparation rules even though it may use the general format of APA style. Student papers for a class may be a report of a research study, a review of the literature on a specific topic, an annotated bibliography, or any number of other assigned writing projects.

The differences between professional and student papers are minimal. We will provide information on both types when they differ. When you are getting ready to prepare your own report, be sure to check the particular requirements of your instructor.

TABLE 1 APA Style Resource: Basic page formatting

Level	Example
Margins	1 in. (2.54 cm) on all sides.
Font	Recommended Serif: 12-point Times New Roman, 11-point Georgia, or 10-point Computer Modern. Recommended Sans Serif: 11-point Arial, 11-point Calibri, or 10-point Lucinda Sans Unicode.
Spacing	Double-space all paragraphs.
Paragraph style	Indent first line by 0.5 in. No additional spaces between paragraphs. Format flush left and ragged right.

ORGANIZATION OF THE REPORT

As you start to prepare your own research report, you are probably already familiar with the major parts of a paper prepared using APA style. A paper prepared using APA style has several major parts (see Fig. 1):

- Title page (formatted for a professional or student paper)
- Abstract (required for professional papers; not required for student papers unless assigned by instructor)
- Body of the paper, including Introduction, Method, Results, and Discussion
- References
- Footnotes (if any)
- Tables and figures
- Appendix (if necessary)

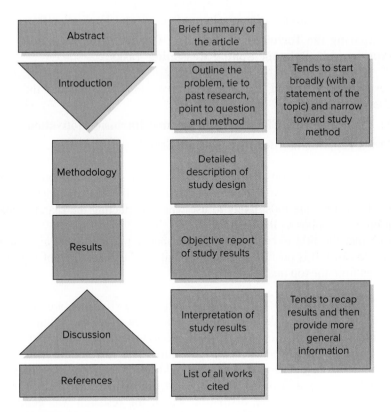

FIGURE 1
Major sections of a research article

We will consider the parts of the paper in the order prescribed by APA style. Recall from the chapter "Where to Start" the figure that depicts the structure of a standard empirical article.

Refer to the Sample Paper at the end of this appendix as you read the material that follows.

Title Page

Title   The first page of the paper is the title page. It is a separate page and is numbered page 1. There is no prescribed limit on the number of words for the title; however, it should be succinct and should inform the reader of the nature of your research. A good way to do this is to include the names of your variables in the title. For example, the following titles are both short and informative:

Effect of Anxiety on Mathematical Problem Solving

Memory for Faces Among Elderly and Young Adults

Sometimes a subtitle, following a colon, will help convey the nature of your research or even add a bit of "flair" to your title, as in

Cognitive Responses in Persuasion: Affective and Evaluative Determinants

Comparing the Tortoise and the Hare: Gender Differences and Experience in Dynamic Spatial Reasoning Tasks

Another method of titling a paper is to pose the question that the research addresses. For example,

Do Rewards in the Classroom Undermine Intrinsic Motivation?

Does Occupational Stereotyping Still Exist?

One further consideration in the choice of a title is that computer literature searches are most likely to include your article if the title includes words and phrases that people are most likely to use when conducting the search. This consideration also applies to the abstract.

Note that the title is centered, boldface, and typed in upper- and lowercase (called title case). It is positioned in the top half of the page, three of four double-space lines from the top margin of the page.

Author and Affiliation   The author's name and affiliation are provided two double-space lines below the title. This is sometimes called the byline. The name usually includes the full first name, middle initial, and last name. Some people adopt a professional name that has a first initial and full middle name. Do not use your initials only. The author name should not include any other descriptive information such as professional title (e.g., Dr.) or degree (e.g., PhD, MA).

The author's institutional affiliation where the research was conducted is typed below the byline. The affiliation will list the name of your department (or major) and the name of your college or university. Use the complete name of your college without abbreviations or shortened names. If in doubt, check how the college or university name is presented on its official website. If there are two or more authors, the order is determined by the relative contribution of each author to the research.

Following are examples of bylines with affiliation, first for one author:

Amanda S. Jackson

Department of Psychology, New Mexico State University

Here is an example when there are two authors:

Jorge Orozco and Wei Li

School of Communications, University of Houston–Clear Lake

The APA manual also includes examples for other authorship possibilities with three or more authors, authors with multiple affiliations, and authors with no affiliation.

Additional Information on Student Title Page

This section summarizes the elements of the student paper title page described in the APA manual. There is no running head. You will need to include the following information. Remember that your entire paper will be double-spaced. Refer to the example in Figure 2.

- Page numbering that continues on all pages
- Title of your paper (bold)
- Your name
- Department and Affiliation (usually your college/university)
- Course number and name
- Instructor name (check if instructor has a preferred form such as Dr. Kenneth Mio or Professor May)
- Assignment due date in format used in your location (e.g., December 5, 2022, or 30 March 2023)

Page Number—Student Papers

Student papers should have a page number on every page, located in the upper right area of the page. Most word-processing applications will have a page number feature. Use it to specify the location of the number; indicate that the first page is numbered "1" if needed. The page number is placed in the header area of the page.

When the title page is complete, insert a page break to begin the second page. Do not simply press the Enter key multiple times, or your page numbers may be incorrect.

1

Memory for Text and Text + Image Advertisements

Samuel B. Fuller

Department of Psychology, Darwin College

PSYC 200: Research Methods

Dr. Rosa Aguire

May 9, 2022

FIGURE 2a.
Example title page for APA-style student paper.

TABLE 2 APA Style Resource: Title page

Student paper	Professional paper
Page formatting	
1 in. margins on all sides	1 in. margins on all sides
Title centered, bold	Title centered, bold
Page elements	
Page number, top of the page, flush right	Page number, top of the page, flush right
	RUNNING HEAD: all caps, flush left on each page in the header section
Author(s): First name and last name	Authors: First name and last name
Authors' affiliation(s)	Authors' affiliation(s)
Course	
Professor's name	
Due Date	
	Author note

Title Page—Professional Papers   This section summarizes the elements of the professional paper title page described in the APA manual. Refer to the professional paper example in Figure 2b.

- Page numbering that continues on all pages
- Running head that continues on all pages
- Title of your paper (bold)
- Your name and names of co-authors, each with a footnote to indicate affiliation and department
- Affiliation and department
- Author note

Running Head and Page Number—Professional Papers

Professional papers require a running head and a page number in the header area of every page. This should be done when typing the title page. The header is located between the page edge and the top margin, and the information that you type there will be printed at the top of the page. Use your word processor's Help feature or an internet search to learn how to create a header; do not manually type

SELF-HELP FOR COLLEGE STUDENT MENTAL HEALTH   1

**Evaluating Acceptance and Commitment Therapy and Mindfulness-Based
Stress Reduction Self-Help Books for College Student Mental Health**

Michael E. Levin[1], Woolee An[1], Carter Davis[1], and Michael P. Twohig[1]

[1]Department of Psychology, Utah State University

Author Note

We have no known conflict of interest to disclose.

Correspondence regarding this article should be addressed to Michael E. Levin,

Department of Psychology, Utah State University, Logan, UT 55555, United States. Email:

levin@college.edu

FIGURE 2b.
Example title page for APA-style professional paper.

the information at the top of each page of your paper. Your word processor may have a Header/Footer menu choice to facilitate this.

First you must decide on the wording of the running head, which should be a brief summary (up to 50 characters, including spaces) of your title. Thus, a title such as "Aging and Memory for Pictures of Faces" might use MEMORY FOR FACES as the running head. It will be printed on each page of your paper. In a published paper, it is printed at the top (or head) of the pages. It helps the reader identify your paper.

The running head is typed in all capital letters against the left margin and will look like this:

MEMORY FOR FACES

The APA manual's guidelines for student papers do not require a running head. You will need to have a page number, however. Again, check your instructor requirements.

You need to activate the automatic page-numbering feature of your word-processing application. Move your cursor to the right margin of the header and insert the automatic page number command that will cause page numbers to appear throughout your paper.

When the title page is complete, insert a page break to begin the second page. Do not simply press the Enter key multiple times; this can cause unanticipated errors later.

Author Note in Professional Papers

The author note is included in professional papers. It is typed in the lower half of the title page, provides information on contacting the author, acknowledges the assistance of others, and specifies any funding sources that supported the research. Student research papers, theses, and dissertations will probably not require an author note; the Sample Paper in this appendix therefore does not include one.

Begin the author note by typing "Author Note" in bold and centered several lines below the last author affiliation. The first paragraph (with first line indented) gives detailed department affiliations of the authors. Here you specify that an author is in the Department of Psychology, the Department of Human Development, or a special research laboratory or institute.

A second paragraph provides information on changes of affiliation of any authors, if this is needed. Most commonly, an author publishing a master's thesis from one institution may describe a new affiliation in this paragraph.

The next paragraph contains acknowledgments and any special information that the author wishes to include with the paper. This would include sources of grant support, names of colleagues who assisted with the study in some way, and any details about authorship (e.g., that authors are listed alphabetically because their contributions were equal).

A final paragraph begins with "Correspondence concerning this article should be addressed to . . ." followed by the mailing address of the person designated for that purpose. The email address for correspondence is included as well.

Abstract

An abstract is required for APA professional papers. The abstract is not included in APA student papers. However, your instructor may require an abstract in your class. An abstract page follows the title page in professional papers and in student papers if required.

The abstract is a brief summary of the research report and is usually 150 to 250 words in length, depending on the rules specified by the publication or your college. The purpose of the abstract is to introduce the article, allowing readers to decide whether the article appears relevant to their own interests. The abstract should provide enough information to enable the reader to decide whether to read the entire report, and it should make the report easier to comprehend when it is read.

Although the abstract appears at the beginning of your report, it is easiest to write the abstract last. Read a few abstracts and you will get some good ideas for how to condense a full-length research report down to 8–10 information-packed sentences. An informative exercise is to write an abstract for a published article and then compare your abstract to the one written by the original authors.

Abstracts generally include a sentence or two about each of the four main sections in the body of the article. First, from the Introduction section, state the problem under study and the primary hypotheses. Second, from the Method section, include information on the characteristics of the participants (e.g., number, age, sex, and any special characteristics) and a brief summary of the procedure (e.g., self-report questionnaires, direct observation, repeated measurements on several occasions). Third, from the Results section, describe the pattern of findings for major variables. This is typically done by reporting the direction of differences without relying on numerical values. Finally, the abstract will include implications of the study taken from the Discussion section. Informative comments about the findings are preferred to general statements such as "the implications of the study are addressed" (Kazdin, 1995).

The abstract is typed on a separate page and is numbered page 2. The word "Abstract" is centered at the top of the page in boldface type.

The abstract is always typed as a single paragraph with no paragraph indentation.

When you have completed the abstract page, insert a page break to take you to page 3 of your paper.

Some journals require, in addition to an abstract, a more focused statement that provides a different perspective for readers. The most common statements are titled *Impact Statement*, *Public Significance Statement*, or *Public Policy Relevance Statement*.

Keywords on the Abstract Page

Keywords associated with the article are also included on the abstract page. Keywords help other researchers find your article when conducting searches. Provide three to five words that you might use to search for an article on your topic using APA PsycInfo.

Insert a double-spaced line below the abstract; indent for a new paragraph. Type "Keywords:" in italic and then list your keywords, all in lowercase with no period.

Keywords: word1, word2, word3

Body of the Paper

Begin page 3 by typing the complete title of your paper, centered on the first line. Do not include your name or affiliation (this allows a masked review in which the reader cannot identify the author). You are now ready to type the body of your paper. For most research reports, the body of the paper will have four sections: Introduction, Method, Results, and Discussion. These are organized through the use of headings.

Introduction   The Introduction section begins after the boldface title at the top of the page. It is not labeled "Introduction"—instead, you (and your readers) understand that the first part of the body of the paper is the Introduction. The Introduction has three components, although formal subsections introduced by headings are rarely used. The components are (1) the problem under study, (2) the literature review, and (3) the rationale and hypotheses of the study. After reading the Introduction, the reader should know why you decided to do the research and how you decided to go about doing it. In general, the Introduction progresses from broad theories and research findings to specific details and expectations of the current research.

Gernsbacher (2018) notes that the Introduction should begin with a hook that will grab the attention of the reader as you describe the problem under study. In one or two paragraphs, give the reader an appreciation of the broad context and significance of the topic being studied. The hook may start with something familiar to the reader, such as an incident from the news or a common situation in everyday life, that then leads to the purpose of the study. Stating what problem is being investigated is worthwhile; it helps readers, even those who are unfamiliar with the topic, understand and appreciate why the topic was studied in the first place.

Following the opening statement, the Introduction provides a description of past research and theory. This is called the *literature review.* An exhaustive review of past theory and research is not necessary. (If there are major literature reviews of the topic, you would of course refer the reader to the reviews.) Rather, you want to describe only the research and theoretical issues that are clearly related to your study. State explicitly how this previous work is logically connected to your research problem. This tells the reader why your research was conducted and shows the connection to prior research.

The final part of the Introduction tells the reader the rationale of the current study. Here you state what variables you are studying and what results you expect. The links between the research hypotheses, prior research, and the current research design are shown by explaining why the hypotheses are being examined by the study.

Method   As noted above, the body of the paper is organized using headings. The Method section begins immediately after you have completed the Introduction (on the same page, if space permits). The heading for this section is the word "Method," centered on the line using boldface type, as follows:

Method

The Method section provides the reader with detailed information about how your study was conducted. Ideally, there should be enough information in the Method section to allow a reader to replicate your study.

The Method section is typically divided into a number of subsections. Both the order of the subsections and the number of subsections vary in published articles. Decisions about which subsections to include are guided by the complexity of the investigation. The Method section in the sample paper in this appendix uses two subsections: *Participants* and *Materials and Procedures.* Some of the most commonly used subsections are discussed next.

Overview   If the experimental design and procedures used in the research are complex, a brief overview of the method should be presented to help the reader understand the information that follows.

Participants   A subsection on the participants (or subjects or respondents) is always necessary. The number and nature of the participants should be described. Age, sex, ethnicity, and any other relevant characteristics should be described. Special characteristics of participants are described, such as firstborn children, adolescent children of alcoholics, student teachers, or police officers. State explicitly how participants were recruited and what incentives for participation, if any, were used. The number of individuals in each experimental condition also can be included here. Finally, you should state that the procedures were approved by your IRB.

Apparatus, Materials, or Measures   A subsection labeled as Apparatus or Materials or Measures may be necessary to describe special equipment or materials used in the experiment. The apparatus, materials, or measures should be described in sufficient detail to allow other researchers to replicate the study. For example, if your project used the CESD-R (Center for Epidemiological Studies Depression Scale, Revised; https://cesd-r.com/) to measure depression, provide a citation, describe the number of items, and provide evidence of reliability and validity.

Procedure   The Procedure subsection tells the reader what instructions were given to the participants, how the independent variables were manipulated, and how the dependent variables were measured. The methods used to control extraneous variables also should be described. These include randomization procedures, counterbalancing, and special means that were used to keep a variable constant across all conditions. Finally, the method of debriefing should be described. If your study used a nonexperimental method, you would still provide details on exactly how you conducted the study and the measurement techniques you used.

It is up to you to decide how much detail to include here. Use your own judgment to determine the importance of a specific aspect of the procedure and the amount of detail that is necessary for the reader to clearly understand what was done in the study. Include any detail that might be important in a replication of the study.

Other Subsections   Include other subsections if they are needed for clear presentation of the method. For example, a subsection on testing materials might be necessary instead of an Apparatus subsection. Other sections are customized by the authors to suit their study. If you glance through a recent issue of a journal, you will find that some studies have only two subsections and others have many more subsections. This reflects the varying complexity of the studies and the particular writing styles of the researchers.

Results   In the Results section, present the results as clearly as possible. The Results section is a straightforward description of your analyses. Although it is tempting to explain your findings in the Results section, save that discussion for the next section of the paper.

Be sure to state the alpha (probability) level that you used in making decisions about statistical significance: This will usually be .05 or .01 and requires only a simple sentence such as "An alpha level of .05 was used for statistical analyses."

Present your results in the same order in which your predictions are stated in the Introduction section of the paper. If a manipulation check was made, present it before you describe the major results.

The content of your Results section will vary according to the type of statistical test performed and the number of analyses you conducted. However, every Results section includes some basic elements. If applicable, describe any scoring or coding procedures performed on the data to prepare them for analysis. This is particularly important when coding qualitative data. (Sometimes data transformations are included in a subsection of the Method section.) State which statistical test was performed on the data (t test, F test, correlation, etc.). Justify the selection of a particular statistical comparison to address your hypothesis. Be sure to summarize each finding in words as well as to include the results of statistical tests in the form of statistical phrases. The APA manual includes guidelines for reporting statistics that were recommended by an APA Task Force on Statistical Inference (Wilkinson et al., 1999). One major recommendation is to report exact probability values that are routinely provided by computer programs used to perform statistical analyses. In the past, most researchers reported probabilities as "less than" the standard probabilities shown in statistical tables, for example, $p < .10$, $p < .05$, or $p < .01$. It is now possible to report exact probabilities of the null hypothesis being correct, for example, $p = .09$, $p = .03$, or $p = .02$. This change allows readers to apply their own standards of statistical significance when evaluating the study.

Another recommendation is to report effect size. The manual recognizes that there are currently many indicators of effect size associated with different statistical procedures; the primary concern is to have an effect size in the published article (see the chapter "Understanding Research Results: Description and Correlation" for a review of effect size).

A related APA guideline is to report statistical values (e.g., mean, standard deviation, t, F, or chi-square) using two decimal places. When you are reporting statistical significance, probabilities are rounded to two or three decimals (e.g., $p = .03$ or $p = .034$). If you are consistently using two decimals, any value less than .01 should be reported as $p < .01$. For three decimals, values less than .001 are reported as $p < .001$. Your instructor may specify a decimal place rule for your papers.

The results should be stated in simple sentences. For example, the results of the modeling and aggression experiment described in the chapter "Understanding Research Results: Description and Correlation" might be expressed as follows:

> As predicted, children who viewed the aggressive model were significantly more aggressive than children in the no-model condition, $t(18) = 4.03$, $p < .01$. The mean aggression score in the model group was 5.20 ($SD = 1.14$) and the no-model mean was 3.10 ($SD = 1.20$). The effect size r associated with this finding was .69.

These brief sentences inform the reader of the general patterns of the results, the obtained means, statistical significance, and effect size. You should note the wording of the phrase that includes the symbol for the t test, degrees of freedom, and significance level (probability).

If the results are relatively straightforward, they can be presented entirely in sentence form. If the study involved a complex design, tables and figures may be needed to clarify presentation of the results.

Tables and Figures   Tables are generally used to present large arrays of data. For example, a table might be useful in a design with several dependent measures; the means of the different groups for all dependent measures would be presented in the table. Tables are also convenient when a factorial design has been used. For example, in a $2 \times 2 \times 3$ factorial design, a table could be used to present all 12 means.

Figures are used when a visual display of the results would help the reader understand the outcome of the study. Figures may be used to illustrate a significant interaction or show trends over time. When preparing a figure, you will need to decide whether to present the information as a pie chart, a bar graph, or a line graph. Pie charts are used when showing percentages or proportions. The entire pie represents 100% and is divided into slices. In this way, the whole is divided into separate groups or responses. Bar graphs are used when describing the responses of two or more groups— for example, the mean aggression score of a model and a no-model group in an experiment. Line graphs are used when both the independent and dependent variables have quantitative properties—for example, the average response time of two groups on days 1, 2, 3, 4, and 5 of an experiment. Nicol and Pexman (2010a, 2010b) provide detailed information on creating figures, tables, and other visual displays of data.

In APA style, tables and figures are not presented in the main body of the manuscript. Instead they are placed at the end of the paper. Each table and figure appears on a separate page. A table or figure is noted in the text by referring to a table or figure number and describing the content of the table or figure. Never make a reference to the placement of the figure because the placement is determined by the typesetter. In the Results section, make a statement such as "As shown in Figure 2, the model group . . ." or "Table 1 presents the demographic characteristics of the survey respondents." Describe the important features of the table or figure; don't rely on mere cross-references, such as "See Figure 3."

Do not repeat the same data in more than one place. An informative table or figure supplements, and does not duplicate, the text. Using tables and figures does not diminish your responsibility to clearly state the nature of the results in the text of your report.

Your instructor may have a different requirement for placement of tables and figures. Theses and dissertations may have their own rules. Because rules about the placement of tables and figures may vary, check on the proper format before writing your report.

Discussion of the Results   It is usually *not* appropriate to discuss the implications of the results in the Results section. However, the Results and Discussion sections may be combined if the discussion is brief and greater clarity is achieved by the combination.

Discussion   The Discussion section is the proper place to discuss the implications of the results. One way to organize the Discussion is to begin by summarizing the original purpose and expectations of the study, then to state whether the results were consistent with your expectations. If the results do support your original ideas, you should discuss how your findings contribute to knowledge of the problem you investigated. You will want to consider the relationship between your results and past research and theory. If you did not obtain the expected results, discuss possible explanations. The explanations would be quite different, of course, depending on whether you obtained results that were the opposite of what you expected or the results were not significant.

It is often a good idea to include your own criticisms of the study. Many published articles include limitations of the study. Try to anticipate what a reader might find wrong with your methodology. For example, if you used a nonexperimental research design, you might point out problems of cause and effect and possible extraneous variables that might be operating. Sometimes there may be major or minor flaws that could be corrected in a subsequent study (if you had the time, money, and so on). You can describe such flaws and suggest corrections. If there are potential problems in generalizing your results, state the problems and give reasons why you think the results would or would not generalize.

The results will probably have implications for future research. If so, you should discuss the direction that research might take. It is also possible that the results have practical implications—for example, for childrearing or improving learning in the classroom. Discussion of these larger issues is usually placed at the end of the Discussion section. Finally, you will probably wish to have a brief concluding paragraph that provides "closure" to the entire paper.

References

The list of references begins on a new page with the word "References" in bold and centered at the top. The list of references must contain complete citations for all sources mentioned in your report. Do not omit any sources from the list of references; also, do not include any sources that are not mentioned in your report. The exact procedures for citing sources within the body of your report and in your list of references are described later in this appendix in the section "Citing and Referencing Sources." Follow the examples in recent publications.

TABLE 3 APA Style Resource: Reference list formatting rules

Section formatting
The title (**"References"**) is bold and centered.
All references are double-spaced.
The first line of each reference, flush-left, and subsequent lines indented 0.5 in. (called a "hanging indent")
Citation formatting
Alphabetized by first author's last name. Use one space after a period.
The journal title and volume number are *italicized*. The issue number is not italicized.
Use one space after a period.
A period is placed after the page numbers. Then one space and begin typing the DOI.
No period at the end of the DOI.
Sources with multiple authors
The last author's last name is preceded by an ampersand (&)
For sources with 1–20 authors, include all authors, with the last author preceded by an ampersand (&).
For sources with more than 20 authors include the first 19 authors, then an ellipsis (without an ampersand), and then the last author.

References

Agerström, J., Carlsson, M., & Strinić, A. (2021). Intersected groups and discriminatory everyday behavior. *Social Psychology, 52*(6), 351–361. https://doi.org/10.1027/1864-9335/a000464

Aurino, E., Wolf, S., & Tsinigo, E. (2020). Household food insecurity and early childhood development: Longitudinal evidence from Ghana. *PLoS ONE, 15*(4). https://doi.org/10.1371/journal.pone.0230965

Burger, J. M. (2009). Replicating Milgram: Would people still obey today? *American Psychologist, 64*(1), 1–11. https://doi.org/10.1037/a0010932

Corona, K., Senft, N., Campos, B., Chen, C., Shiota, M., & Chentsova-Dutton, Y. (2020). Ethnic variation in gratitude and well-being. *Emotion, 20*(3), 518–524. http://dx.doi.org/10.1037/emo0000582

Di Lieto, M. C., Pecini, C., Castro, E., Inguaggiato, E., Cecchi, F., Dario, P., Cioni, G., & Sgandurra, G. (2020). Empowering executive functions in 5- and 6-year-old typically developing children through educational robotics: An RCT study. *Frontiers in Psychology, 10.* https://doi.org/10.3389/fpsyg.2019.03084

Haskett, M. E., Hall, J. K., Finster, H. P., Owens, C., & Buccelli, A. R. (2022). "It brought my family more together": Mixed-methods study of low-income U.S. mothers during the pandemic. *Family Relations,* 1–16. https://doi.org/10.1111/fare.12684

Klein, E. G., Czaplicki, L., Berman, M., Emery, S., & Schillo, B. (2020). Visual attention to the use of #ad versus #sponsored on e-cigarette influencer posts on social media: A randomized experiment. *Journal of Health Communication, 25*(12), 925–930. https://doi.org/10.1080/10810730.2020.1849464

Penilla, C., Tschann, J. M., Pasch, L. A., Flores, E., Deardorff, J., Martinez, S. M., Butte, N. F., & Greenspan, L. C. (2022). Style of meal service and feeding practices among Mexican American fathers and mothers: An analysis of video-recorded children's evening mealtime at home. *Appetite, 169.* https://doi.org/10.1016/j.appet.2021.105851

Peterson, D. A. M., Biederman, L. A., Andersen, D., Ditonto, T. M., & Roe, K. (2019). Mitigating gender bias in student evaluations of teaching. *PLoS ONE, 14*(5), e0216241. https://doi.org/10.1371/journal.pone.0216241

Ravizza, S. M., Uitvlugt, M. G., & Fenn, K. M. (2017). Logged in and zoned out: How laptop internet use relates to classroom learning. *Psychological Science, 28*(2), 171–180. https://doi.org/10.1177/0956797616677314

Son, C., Hegde, S., Smith, A., Wang, X., & Sasangohar, F. (2020). Effects of COVID-19 on college students' mental health in the United States: Interview survey study. *Journal of Medical Internet Research, 22*(9), e21279. https://doi.org/10.2196/21279

Wallace, E., & Buil, I. (2020). Hiding Instagram likes: Effects on negative affect and loneliness. *Personality and Individual Differences, 170,* e110509. https://doi.org/10.1016/j.paid.2020.110509

FIGURE 3
APA style reference list

Tables

Each table should be on a separate page. APA style requires placement of the table at the end of the paper, but for a class or thesis you may be asked to place your tables on separate pages within the body of the paper. In preparing your table, allow enough space so that the table does not appear cramped on a small portion of the page. Define areas of the table using typed horizontal lines (do not use vertical lines). Give some thought to the title so that it accurately and clearly describes the content of the table. You may wish to use an explanatory note in the table to show significance levels or the range of possible values on a variable. The body of the table (including table headings) may be single-spaced, one-and-a-half-spaced, or double-spaced—consider how the spacing will appear to the reader and a general rule to fit the table on one page whenever possible.

Before you make up your own tables, examine the tables in a recent issue of one of the journals published by the American Psychological Association as well as the examples in the *Publication Manual* and in Nicol and Pexman (2010b), and the sample paper in this appendix. Formats are provided for many types of tables—for example, tables of means, correlation coefficients, multiple regression analyses, and so on. For example, here is a table of correlations. Note that the table number is bold and the title of the table is italic. Also, the areas of the table are separated by horizontal lines. Never use vertical lines.

Table 1

Correlations Between Measures

Measure	1	2	3	4
1. Attractiveness	–	.52	.35	.29
2. Extraversion		–	.11	.23
3. Conscientiousness			–	.49
4. Starting salary				–

Figures

Figures consist of graphic displays of information, including results depicted in graphs (e.g., a line graph or bar graph), drawings, or photographs. In APA style for professional papers, figures are placed after any tables in your paper. However, when preparing a student report or thesis, you may be asked to include figures within the body of the paper, usually on a separate page following the first time the table or figure is mentioned in the paper.

Although it is sometimes tempting to draw a graph by hand, you will find it much easier to use a computer program such as Excel to create graphs. Most spreadsheet, word-processing, and statistical analysis programs have graphing features. Independent and predictor variables are placed on the horizontal axis; dependent and criterion variables are placed on the vertical axis. The horizontal axis and the vertical axis must both be labeled. Figures should be easy to read and should fit on

Figure 1

Average Minutes Spent During One Day by U.S. Males and Females Age 25–34

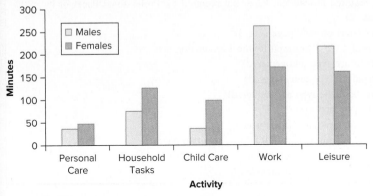

Note. A figure note (double-spaced) may appear beneath the figure. It provides additional information needed to understand the figure. Data shown represent selected data derived from 2018 U.S. Bureau of Labor Statistics American Time Use Survey (ATUS). Personal care does not include sleep. Leisure does not include exercise.

the page along with the figure caption. Select a sans serif font for figures; font sizes should be no larger than 14 point and no smaller than 8 point. The figure number and figure caption start at the top left margin of the page.

The figure below shows a column bar graph. The figure number is typed in bold at the top of the page. The figure caption is typed one double-space line below using italics and title case. A note may be included below the figure to provide additional information that a reader might find helpful. Refer to the *APA Publication Manual* and Nicol and Pexman (2010a) for examples of many type of designs for figures.

Remember that the purpose of a figure is to increase comprehension of results by having a graphic display of data. If the graph is cluttered with information, it will confuse the reader and will not serve its purpose. Plan your graphs carefully to make sure that you are accurately and clearly informing the reader. If you become interested in the topic of how to display information in graphs and charts, Tufte's (1983, 1990, 1997, 2006) books are recommended. Tufte explores a variety of ways of presenting data, factors that lead to data clarity, and ways that graphs can deceive the reader.

Appendix and Supplemental Materials

An appendix is not common in published research reports. However, an appendix can be appropriate when material that may be helpful to a reader would be distracting in the main body of the report. The appendix might include the entire questionnaire that was used, a new test that was developed, exact stimulus materials, or other materials employed in the study. An appendix (or several appendices) is much more appropriate for a student research project or a thesis. Check with your instructor concerning the appropriateness of an appendix for your paper. If an appendix is provided, it begins on a new page with the word "Appendix" centered at the top. It is the last item in the research report.

TABLE 4 APA Style Resource: Order of pages

1. Title page, formatted as a Student Paper or Professional Paper (page 1)
2. Abstract, not required for Student Paper but required for Professional Paper or by instructor (page 2)
3. Body of paper (start on new page 2 or 3)
a. Title at top of page 3 followed by the Introduction text
b. Method (boldface type and centered)
c. Results (boldface type and centered)
d. Discussion (boldface type and centered)
4. References (start on new page)
5. Footnotes (start on new page if included)
6. Tables, with table captions (each table on a separate page)
7. Figures, with figure captions (each figure on a separate page)
8. Appendix (start on new page if included)

The appendix is included in the printed report. Supplemental Materials are useful materials that are stored online and available for download. Such materials are very rare in student papers but are becoming more common with the advent of inexpensive data storage. Examples include audio and video files, photos and graphic images, computer code, tables that are too large for publication, and raw data files.

You should now have a general idea of how to structure and write your report. The remainder of this appendix focuses on some of the technical rules that may be useful as you prepare your own research report.

THE USE OF HEADINGS

The body of the paper in APA style is organized through the use of headings. There are five levels of heading. Most commonly, you will use the first three levels. The five levels of heading are shown below:

TABLE 5 APA Style Resource: Section headings

	Descriptions	Example
Level 1	Bold, centered, title case. Text begins with a new paragraph.	**Title of Paper**
Level 2	Bold, flush left, title case. Text begins with a new paragraph.	**Procedure**
Level 3	Bold, italic, flush left, title case. Text begins with a new paragraph.	***Dependent Measures***
Level 4	Indented, bold, title case, ends with a period. Text begins on the same line.	**Depression.** Text begins here...
Level 5	Indented, bold, italic, title case, ends with a period. Text begins on the same line.	***Depression Inventory.*** Text begins here...

The paper title is used as the heading for the introduction section. The headings for the other main sections of the paper—Method, Results, Discussion—are centered using boldface type; these are Level 1 headings. Each of these sections can be further divided into subsections using Level 2 headings. If needed, Level 3 headings allow you to provide an organizational structure for any subsections. Figure 4 shows an example of the use of headings in the body of your paper.

CITING SOURCES AND CREATING A REFERENCE LIST

Researchers often use citation management software like Zotero (open source software available at https://www.zotero.org) to collect, store, and organize references. If you integrate your citation management software with a popular word-processing application, it will also help you cite an article in-text and create an APA-styled bibliography.

Citation Style

Whenever you refer to information reported by other researchers, you *must* accurately identify the sources. APA journals use the author–date citation method: The author name(s) and year of publication are inserted at appropriate points. The citation style depends on whether the author names are part of the narrative or are in parentheses.

One Author   When the author's name is part of the narrative, include the publication date in parentheses immediately after the name:

> Papp (2017) studied marital conflicts among "empty nest" marital partners.

When the author's name is not part of the narrative, the name and date are cited in parentheses at the end of an introductory phrase or at the end of the sentence:

> In one study (Papp, 2017), married couples completed diary entries describing . . .

> Problems of communication, chores, and habits are the most frequent reasons for conflict (Papp, 2017).

Two Authors   When the work has two authors, both names are included in each reference citation. The difference between narrative and parenthetical citations is in the use of the conjunction "and" and the ampersand "&" to connect authors' names. When the names are part of a sentence, use the word "and" to join the names of two authors. When the complete citation is in parentheses, use the "&" symbol:

> Sana and Yan (2022) studied the benefits of interleaving questions about different concepts in a quiz.

> Students who complete a quiz with interleaved questions perform better on a final test (Sana & Yan, 2022).

Title of Paper

The title is a Level 1 Heading. The text for the Introduction section begins after the title. Your first paragraphs introduce your research. You may or may not wish to organize the Introduction using subsections.

Level 2 Heading for a Subsection

Text would continue here.

Level 2 Heading for Another Subsection

Text begins here for the second subsection.

Method

Begin the Method, Results, and Discussion sections with a centered and boldface Level 1 heading. Further subsections will have Level 2 and Level 3 headings as shown below.

Participants

Describe your participants and sampling procedures here.

Procedure

This is your description of how the study was conducted. Level 3 paragraph headings may be useful. These are only examples.

Stimuli

Here you might describe the stimuli that participants were given in various conditions. Note that this is a Level 3 heading.

Dependent Measures

Describe the measures that were made after participants were presented with the stimuli. This is another Level 3 heading.

Results

An introduction to the results would go here.

Perceived Competence (Example of a Level 2 Heading)

This subsection would be a description of results for the first dependent measure.

Perceived Attractiveness (Example of a Level 2 Heading)

Here you would present the results for the second dependent variable.

Discussion

You may wish to divide the discussion into subsections. Begin with a discussion of the ways that your results supported or did not support your predictions. Explain what you found and relate your findings to past research. You may include additional subsections. The following are only examples.

Limitations

Future Research

Possible Applications

FIGURE 4
Example of Level 1, 2, and 3 headings in the body of a paper

Three or More Authors When a report has three or more authors, cite the first author's surname followed by the abbreviation et al. ("and others") along with the publication date. The abbreviation may be used in narrative and parenthetical citations:

> Sewall et al. (2022) examined whether social media use by young adults predicts depression.
>
> Social media use has a very small relationship to depression (Sewall et al., 2022).

Another question about subsequent citations is whether to include the publication date each time an article is referenced. Within a paragraph, you do *not* need to include the year in subsequent citations as long as the study cannot be confused with other studies cited in your report.

Citation within a paragraph

> In a study of reaction times, Yokoi and Jones (2006) reported . . .
>
> Yokoi and Jones also reported that . . .

When subsequent citations are in another paragraph or in another section of the report, the publication date should be included.

Multiple Works within the Same Parentheses A convenient way to cite several studies on the same topic or several studies with similar findings is to reference them as a series within the same parentheses. When two or more works are by the same author(s), report them in order of year of publication, using commas to separate citations:

> Mio and Willis (2003, 2005) found . . .
>
> Past research (Mio & Willis, 2003, 2005) indicates . . .

When two or more works by different authors are cited within the same parentheses, arrange them in alphabetical order and separate citations with semicolons:

> Investigations of families in economic distress consistently report that girls react with internalization problems whereas boys respond with externalization problems (Conger et al., 1994; Flanagan & Eccles, 1993; Lempers et al., 1989).

TABLE 6 APA Style Resource: Conventions for citing authors in APA style

	Narrative citation	Parenthetical citation
One author	Gupta (2021)	(Gupta, 2021)
Two authors	Gupta and Smith (2020)	(Gupta & Smith, 2020)
Three or more authors	Gupta et al. (2022)	(Gupta et al., 2022)

TABLE 7   APA Style Resource: Additional rules for parenthetical citations

Rule	Example
Separate names with semicolons.	(Alonzo, 2021; Kim, 2019; Whitman, 1991)
Always alphabetize by first author's last name.	(Alonzo, 2021; Kim, 2019; Whitman, 1991)
Use standard conventions for citing authors (above).	(Alonzo, 2021; Jackson et al., 2020; Zhang & Potter, 2008)
Authors with multiple papers may be identified with an "a," "b," et cetera.	(Alonzo, 2021a; Jackson et al., 2020; Zhang & Potter, 2008)

Reference List Style

The APA *Publication Manual* (2020b) provides reference formatting guidelines for more than 100 different sources including journal articles, books, book chapters, conference presentations, Wikipedia entries, YouTube videos, tweets, song lyrics, and webpages, among many others. Only a few of these are presented here. When in doubt about how to construct a reference, consult the APA manual. The general format for a reference list is as follows:

- The references are listed in alphabetical order by the first author's last name. Do not categorize references by type (i.e., books, journal articles, and so on). Note that commas and periods are followed by one space in APA style.
- Elements of a reference (authors' names, article title, publication data) are separated by periods.
- The first line of each reference is typed flush to the left margin; subsequent lines are indented. This is called a "hanging indent":

  Bushman, B. (2006). Effects of warning and information labels on attraction to television violence in viewers of different ages. *Journal of Applied Social Psychology, 36*(9), 2073–2078. https://doi.org/10.1111/j.0021-9029.2006.00094.x

Each reference begins on a new line (think of each reference as a separate paragraph). Most word-processing applications will allow you to easily format the paragraph with a hanging indent so you do not have to manually insert spaces on the second and subsequent lines. Using Microsoft Word, for example, set the paragraph style for your references using the hanging indent option; you can also manually create a hanging indent with Ctrl-t.

Page Numbers
APA recommends using the en-dash symbol between page numbers in the references rather than a simple hyphen. To type an en dash in Microsoft Word for Windows, choose Symbol from the Insert menu, click the Special Characters tab, highlight En Dash, and click Insert. Tip to save time and

effort: Type your references using the hyphen for page numbers; when done, type Ctrl-H to Find (type a hyphen) and Replace (click Special and select en-dash). Tip 2 alternative: Because you will be using the en dash often, create a shortcut key (such as Alt-1) for quick insertion of en dashes.

To type an en dash on an Apple device, press Option-hyphen (not the hyphen on the numeric keypad). Check with your instructor to determine if using an en dash is necessary in your papers (the alternative use of a hyphen may be acceptable).

Inclusion of a DOI or URL

The seventh edition of the *Publication Manual* has incorporated changes that reflect the fact that we usually access sources using websites and library or publisher databases. It is therefore often necessary to provide readers with additional information on the source that you used.

The DOI (Digital Object Identifier) was devised by publishers to provide a unique and consistent method of identifying and locating electronic sources of information. The APA *Publication Manual,* seventh edition, no longer accepts DOI citations in the form "doi:10.xxxx/xxxxxxxxx"—instead, DOI cites must now have this form: https://doi.org/xxxx/xxxxxxxxx. What follows after ".org/" is a "prefix" that identifies the publishing organization, a slash, and then a "suffix" that the publisher assigns to the article.

You will see the DOI when you access research articles using databases such as APA PsycInfo. The DOI also appears on the first page of the full-text version of the article, no matter where it appears (e.g., a printed journal article or a downloaded version that might be available in either PDF or HTML format). The *APA Publication Manual* now requires including the DOI in the reference for all sources that have a DOI.

The URL is used when your source was a website. This is the full website address of the location and file name of the document as it appears in your web browser. Examples will be provided below. An important rule about typing the URL (location) of the document you are citing concerns insertion of line breaks. It is acceptable to have the URL carry over to a second line if it will not fit on a single line. However, never insert a hyphen, because this is not part of the address. Instead, let your word processor wrap the URL to the next line by its own line-break rules.

Format for Journal Articles

Most journals are organized by volume and year of publication (e.g., volume 74 of *American Psychologist* consists of journal issues published in 2022). A common confusion is whether to include the journal issue number in addition to the volume number. The rule is simple: If the issues in a volume are paginated consecutively throughout the volume, *do not* include the journal issue number. If each issue in a volume begins with page 1, the issue number should be included.

In the reference list, both the name of the journal and the volume number are italicized. Also, only the first letter of the first word in article titles is capitalized (except for proper nouns and the first word after a colon or question mark).

Following are examples:

One author—issue number provided, DOI provided
Bilali, R. (2022). Fighting violent extremism with narrative intervention: Evidence from a field experiment in West Africa. *Psychological Science, 33*(2), 184–195. https://doi.org/10.1177/09567976211031895

One author—issue number provided, no DOI provided
Newby, T. J. (1991). Classroom motivation strategies: Strategies of first-year teachers. *Journal of Educational Psychology, 83*(2), 195–200.

Two authors—issue number provided, DOI provided
Garcia-Rada, X., & Kim, T. (2021). Shared time scarcity and the pursuit of extraordinary experiences. *Psychological Science, 32*(12), 1871–1883. https://doi.org/10.1177/09567976211026981

Three to twenty authors—DOI provided
Hammen, C., Brennan, P. A., & Le Brocque, R. (2011). Youth depression and early childrearing: Stress generation and intergenerational transmission of depression. *Journal of Consulting and Clinical Psychology, 79*(3), 353–363. https://doi.org/10.1037/a0023536

21 or more authors—DOI provided

For sources with 2 to 20 authors, include all authors, with the last author preceded by an ampersand (&). For sources with more than 20 authors include the first 19 authors, then an ellipsis (without an ampersand), and then the last author.

Anders, A., Bitter, B., Cape, C., Deal, D., Egan, E., Forest, F., Gordan, G., Haley, H., Itin, I., Jade, J., King, K., Lash, L., Moore, M., Noone, N., Ortiz, O., Pan, P., Quick, Q., Rami, R., Song, S., . . . Zappa, Z. (2019). Some articles have many authors. *Journal of Popular Psychology, 12*(1), 34–45. https://doi.org/10.1000/a0000001

Format for Books
When a book is cited, the title of the book is italicized. Capitalize only the first word of the title, proper nouns, and the first word after a colon or question mark. Include the name of the publisher (location of publisher is no longer required).

One-author book
Levine, R. (1997). *A geography of time: The temporal misadventures of a social psychologist, or how every culture keeps time just a little bit differently.* Basic Books.

Book retrieved from a website
James, W. (1929). *The varieties of religious experience: A study in human nature.* Modern Library. https://www.google.com/books/edition/The_Varieties_of_Religious_Experience/Qi4XAAAAIAAJ?gbpv=1

One-author book—second or later edition
Regan, P. C. (2008). *The mating game: A primer on love, sex, and marriage* (2nd ed.). Sage.

Edited book
Dass-Brailsford, P. (Ed.). (2010). *Crisis and disaster counseling: Lessons learned from Hurricane Katrina and other disasters.* Sage.

Format for Articles/Chapters in Edited Books
For edited books, the reference begins with the names of the authors of the article, not the book. The title of the article follows. The name(s) of the book editor(s), the book title, the inclusive page numbers for the article, and the publisher of the book follow, in that order. Only the book title is italicized, and only the first letters of the article and book titles are capitalized. Here are some examples:

One editor
Goldstein, N. J., & Cialdini, R. B. (2009). Normative influences on consumption and conservation behaviors. In M. Wänke (Ed.), *Social psychology of consumer behavior* (pp. 273–296). Psychology Press.

Two editors
Bartlett, A. (2010). Gender, crime, and violence. In A. Bartlett & G. McGauley (Eds.), *Forensic mental health: Concepts, systems, and practice* (pp. 53–65). Oxford University Press.

Chapter from book in multivolume series
Stors, T. J. (2006). Stressful experience and learning across the lifespan. In S. T. Fiske, A. E. Kazdin, & D. L. Schachter (Eds.), *Annual review of psychology: Vol. 57* (pp. 55–85). Annual Reviews, Inc. https://doi.org/10.1146/annurev.psych.57.102904.190205

Format for "Popular" Articles
The reference styles shown below should be used for articles from popular magazines and newspapers appearing in print or on websites. As a general rule, popular press articles are used sparingly (e.g., when no scientific articles on a topic can be found, or to provide an example of an event that is related to your topic).

Magazine—continuous pages
Begley, S. (1995, March 27). Gray matters. *Newsweek, 125,* 48–54.

Magazine—retrieved from website
Cullen, L. T. (2006, Jan. 6). How to get smarter, one breath at a time. *Time.* http://www.time.com/time/magazine/article/0,9171,1147167-2,00.html

Newspaper—retrieved from website
Parker-Pope, T. (2010, May 10). The science of a happy marriage. *The New York Times.* https://archive.nytimes.com/well.blogs.nytimes.com/2010/05/10/tracking-the-science-of-commitment/

Newspaper—discontinuous pages
Cole, K. C. (1995, May 1). Way the brain works may play role in bias, experts say. *Los Angeles Times,* pp. Al, A18.

Format for Papers and Posters Presented at Conferences
Occasionally you may need to cite a presentation made at a professional meeting, including a poster, paper, or address. The general format is to provide: Names of

authors, year and dates of the professional meeting, title in italics plus type of presentation in brackets, and the name and location of the meeting. Sometimes the speaker will provide a URL to access a written manuscript or the slides used in the presentation; that URL should be provided also.

Conference poster presentation
Beitia, K., McGlowan, T., & Caldwell-Harris, C. (2022, March 3–5). *Special interests in women with autism* [Poster presentation]. Eastern Psychological Association Annual Meeting, New York City, NY, United States.

Conference paper presentation
Tran, S. (2022, June 17–19). *Drawing compared to writing in a diary enhances recall* [Paper presentation]. 83rd Canadian Psychological Association Annual National Convention, Calgary, Alberta, Canada.

Secondary Sources

Sometimes you need to cite an article, book, or book chapter that you read about through a textbook, an abstract, or a book review. Although it is always preferable to read primary sources, sometimes you may have to cite a secondary source when the primary source cannot be found in a timely manner (with internet searches, this is becoming less likely!).

Suppose you wish to cite an article that you read about in a book. When you refer to the article in your paper, you need to say that it was cited in the book. In the following example, a paper by Conway and Pleydell-Pearce is the secondary source:

Conway and Pleydell-Pearce (as cited in Woll, 2002) suggested that autobiographical memory . . .

In the reference list at the end of the paper, simply provide the reference for the primary source you used (in this case, the 2002 book by Woll).

Sometimes you may need to cite the abstract of an article that you found in a search of APA PsycInfo or another database. Although it is preferable to find the original article, the original article may not be available online or at any nearby libraries or might be published in a foreign language with only the abstract available in English. Here is an example:

King, Y., & Parker, D. (2008). Driving violations, aggression and perceived consensus. *European Review of Applied Psychology, 58*(1), 43–49. Abstract retrieved from APA PsycInfo database. (Accession No. 2007-19875-005)

In this example, the complete reference is given. However, you also provide the crucial information that you have only examined the abstract of the article and you found the abstract through a search of the APA PsycInfo database. The accession number is provided with the abstract.

Citing Specific Web Documents/Pages

Many webpages were written just for the web and should not be considered journal articles *or* books. For example, a document prepared by David Kenny provides information on mediating variables. Here you would cite the title of the document and retrieval information. To cite this document, your text might read as follows:

> Kenny (2018) describes a procedure for using multiple regression to examine causal models that include mediating variables.

This document's entry in the reference list would be:

> Kenny, D. A. (2018). *Mediation.* http://davidakenny.net/cm/mediate.htm

Note that the reference includes the author, a date that was provided in the document, and a title. Some web documents do not include a date; in this case, simply substitute "n.d." in parentheses to indicate that there is no date. You might need to cite an internet document that may be changed or deleted in the future. If you suspect this may happen with the document you wish to cite, you should include the date that you accessed the website. This will make it clear to others that you may have accessed a different version than the one that is currently available. To do this, simply add this wording: Retrieved [provide date] from https://website. It would also be a good idea to take a screenshot of the material so that you can document the changed or deleted content.

Citing All the Other Sources
The seventh edition of the APA Publication Manual (APA, 2020b) provides guidance for citing many types of sources. Obviously, journal articles, books, and chapters in books constitute a large portion of the citations in research reports. Most of these have actual authors listed but some may simply show the name of the sponsoring organization. Other sources are considered as well: Technical reports, documents of government agencies, personal communications, written documents on the internet including blogs, posts on Twitter or Facebook, and online publications, videos, podcasts, films, television shows, and other media sources. For example, you might need to cite a video from YouTube. Here is a rule for this and an example that you can easily find on the internet:

> Name of person or organization providing the video. Date of publication. *Title of video.* Website name. URL of the video
>
> OWLPurdue. (2020, November 11). *APA 7th edition: In-text citations.* Youtube. https://www.youtube.com/watch?v=-yi6GXPhybs

It is relatively easy to find the rule for any type of source by searching at https://www.apastyle.org, the Purdue Online Writing Lab (OWL) at https://owl.purdue.edu/, or one of the major web search services.

TABLE 8   APA Style Resource: Citing works, nature of the source

Nature of the Source	Example
Journal article without page numbers	Aurino, E., Wolf, S., & Tsinigo, E. (2020). Household food insecurity and early childhood development: Longitudinal evidence from Ghana. *PLoS ONE, 15*(4). https://doi.org/10.1371/journal.pone.0230965
Journal articles with page numbers	Agerström, J., Carlsson, M., & Strinić, A. (2021). Intersected groups and discriminatory everyday behavior. *Social Psychology, 52*(6), 351–361. https://doi.org/10.1027/1864-9335/a000464
Book	Kenrick, D. T., & Lundberg-Kenrick, D. E. (2022). *Solving modern problems with a stone-age brain: Human evolution and the seven fundamental motives.* American Psychological Association.
Edited book	McClintock, S. M., & Choi, J. (Eds.) (2022). *Neuropsychology of depression.* Guilford Press.
Edited book chapter	Kaser, M., & Sahakian, B. J. (2022). Executive functions in depression. In S. M. McClintock & J. Choi (Eds.), *Neuropsychology of depression.* (pp. 144–161). Guilford Press.
Newspaper article	Span, P. (2021, August 23). Seeking early signals of dementia in driving and credit scores. *The New York Times.* https://www.nytimes.com/2021/08/23/health/dementia-behavior-alzheimers.html

ABBREVIATIONS

Abbreviations are not used extensively in APA-style papers. They can be distracting because the reader must constantly try to translate the abbreviation into its full meaning. However, APA style does allow for the use of abbreviations that are accepted as words in the dictionary (specifically, Webster's *Collegiate Dictionary*). These include IQ, REM, ESP, and AIDS.

Certain well-known terms may be abbreviated when it would make reading easier, but the full meaning should be given when first used in the paper. Examples of commonly used abbreviations are:

MMPI   Minnesota Multiphasic Personality Inventory

STM   short-term memory

CS	conditioned stimulus
RT	reaction time
CVC	consonant-vowel-consonant
ANOVA	analysis of variance

Statistical terms are sometimes used in their abbreviated or symbol form. These are always italicized in a manuscript. For example,

M	mean
SD	standard deviation
Mdn	median
df	degrees of freedom
n	number of individuals in a group or experimental condition
N	total number of participants or respondents
p	probability (significance) level
SS	sum of squares
MS	mean square
F	value of F in analysis of variance
r	Pearson correlation coefficient
R	multiple correlation coefficient

The following scientific abbreviations for various measurement units are frequently used. Note that periods are not used—with the exception of "in." (inches) to avoid confusion of the inch abbreviation with the word *in* ("in a second").

cm	centimeter
g	gram
hr	hour
in.	inch
kg	kilogram
km	kilometer
m	meter
mg	milligram
min	minute
ml	milliliter
mm	millimeter
ms	millisecond
s	second

Finally, certain abbreviations of Latin and Middle English terms are regularly used in papers, although the APA manual states that they should be used only in parenthetical material. Some of these abbreviations and their meanings are given below:

cf.	compare	(from Latin *confer*)
e.g.,	for example,	(from Latin *exempli gratia*)
etc.	and so forth	(from Latin *et cetera*)
i.e.,	that is,	(from Latin *id est*)
viz.,	namely,	
vs.	versus	

REPORTING NUMBERS AND STATISTICS

Virtually all research papers report numbers: number of participants, number of groups, the values of statistics such as t, F, or r. Should you use numbers (e.g., *43*), or should you use words (e.g., *forty-three*)? The general rule is to use words when expressing the numbers zero through nine but to use numbers for 10 and above. There are some important qualifications, however.

If you start a sentence with a number, you should use words even if the number is 10 or larger (e.g., *Eighty-five student teachers participated in the study*). Starting a sentence with a number is often awkward, especially with large numbers. Therefore, you should try to revise the sentence to avoid the problem (e.g., *The participants were 85 students enrolled in teaching-credential classes*).

When numbers both above and below 10 are being compared in the same sentence, use numerals for both (e.g., *Participants read either 8 or 16 paragraphs*). However, this sentence contains an appropriate mix of numbers and words: *Participants read eight paragraphs and then answered 20 multiple-choice questions.* The sentence is correct because the paragraphs and the questions are different entities and so are not being compared.

When reporting a percentage, always use numerals followed by a percent sign except when beginning a sentence. This is true regardless of whether the number is less than 10 (e.g., *Only 6% of the computer games appealed to younger students.*) or greater than 10 (e.g., *When using this technique, 85% of the participants improved their performance*).

Always use numbers when describing ages (e.g., *5-year-olds*), points on a scale (e.g., *a 3 on a 5-point scale*), units of measurement (e.g., *the children stood 2 m from the target*), sample size (e.g., *6 girls and 6 boys were assigned to each study condition*), and statistics (e.g., *the mean score in the no-model group was 3.10*). An odd but sensible exception to the word–number rule occurs when two different types of numbers must appear together. An example is: *Teachers identified fifteen 7-year-olds as the most aggressive.* This sentence avoids an awkward juxtaposition of two numbers.

For a multiplication sign, use either a lowercase x or the multiplication symbol used by your word processor. This is true whether you are describing a mathematical operation or a factorial design (e.g., *a 2 × 2 design*). For a minus sign, go to Symbol and select the minus sign (note that the Symbol menu shows both an en dash and a minus sign—they are not the same). More generally, Word has an easy way to insert mathematical symbols: Insert > Equation brings up an equation input box and a set of symbols including addition, subtraction, multiplication, and division. You can choose to use a single symbol or type an entire equation. You should also use the multiplication symbol when describing a factorial design (e.g., *a 2 × 3 design*).

Finally, you need to know about presenting statistical results within your paper. As noted previously, statistical terms are abbreviated and typed with italics (e.g., *M*, *r*, *t*, *F*). In addition, when reporting the results of a statistical significance test, provide the name of the test, the degrees of freedom, the value of the test statistic, and the probability level. Here are two examples of sentences that describe statistical results:

> As predicted, participants in the high-anxiety condition took longer to recognize the words ($M = 2.63$, $SD = .42$) than did the individuals in the low-anxiety condition ($M = 1.42$, $SD = .36$), $t(20) = 2.54$, $p = .02$.

> Job satisfaction scores were significantly correlated with marital satisfaction, $r(50) = .48$, $p < .001$.

Recall that exact probabilities are reported using two or three decimal places. However, the computer printout may not indicate very small probabilities so you should use the < (less than) symbol for probabilities less than .01, as follows: $p < .01$. Many researchers prefer to report probabilities using three decimal places (e.g., $p = .037$) because the major statistical software applications provide that level of precision. In that case, use $p < .001$ with very small probabilities.

Pay attention to the way statistics are described in the articles you read. You will find that you can vary your descriptions of results to best fit your data and presentation, as well as vary your sentence constructions.

PAPER AND POSTER PRESENTATIONS

Students present their research findings in many different ways: in class, at regional and national meetings of psychology organizations, and at conferences specifically designed to highlight student research. Advice on preparing paper and poster presentations is available in books (e.g., Nicol & Pexman, 2010a) and on a variety of websites, such as:

- http://colinpurrington.com/tips/academic/posterdesign
- http://www.apa.org/science/about/psa/2010/04/presentation.aspx
- http://www.apa.org/convention/poster-instructions.pdf
- http://www.psychologicalscience.org/index.php/members/apssc/undergraduate_update/fall-2010/standing-in-front-of-your-poster-a-guide-for-new-presenters

Remember: (1) Prepare your presentation in advance to allow time for practice, (2) time is limited, and (3) have handouts available with a summary of your research and contact information including email address. Your presentation may take the form of a talk to an audience or a poster presentation in which individuals may read the poster and engage in conversation with you.

Oral Presentations

Paper presentations are only about 10 to 12 minutes long, and people in attendance receive lots of information in many sessions of the meeting. The major thing to remember, then, is that you should attempt to convey only a few major ideas about why and how you conducted your research. You can avoid describing the details of past research findings, discussing exactly how you did your data analysis, or listing every step in your procedure. Remember that your audience wants the "big picture," so make sure that you do not use technical jargon. Instead, use clear language to convey the reason you conducted the research, the general methods used, and the major results. You should try to provide a summary at the end, along with the conclusions you have reached about the meaning of the results.

It is a good idea to write the presentation in advance but not to read it to your actual audience. You can use the written version for practice and timing. Remember that many people in the audience would like a written summary to which they can refer later. Therefore, bring copies of a summary that includes your name, the title of the presentation, when and where it was presented, and how you can be contacted.

Posters

A poster session consists of a fairly large number of presenters who are provided with space to display poster material. During the poster session, members of the audience may stop to read the poster, and some may have questions or comments. The chance to have conversations about your research with people who find your work interesting is the most valuable feature of a poster session.

The conference organizers will provide information on the amount of space available for each poster. Typical dimensions are 4 feet high (1.22m) and 6 to 8 feet wide (1.83–2.44m); the poster itself is typically 30 to 36 inches high (76–91cm) and 40 to 48 inches wide (102–123cm). The poster materials will usually be divided up into areas of (1) title, name, affiliation, (2) abstract, (3) introduction information, (4) method, (5) results, along with tables and figures, and (6) conclusions. Examples of poster layouts are provided in Figures 5 and 6. The actual construction of the poster may consist of a series of separate pages or a single professionally printed poster using large-format printing technology.

Your college may have template files for constructing posters. A template is already formatted for a title, author, text, tables, and figures; it is ready for

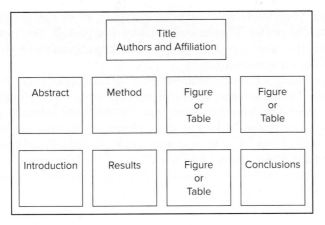

FIGURE 6
A sample poster

Title of Poster Presentation

University Name
or Logo

Student Name, *University Name* | Student or faculty, *University Name*

I. Introduction

Lor min eum facestiat. Voluptur rem ius quatis molorum hicimus apicim quate re dem aut es qui nimus sunt utaspellab idererum quatus.

pliquis doluptasi ne se sim evel ius quid quunt volupta tiundistrume atibus vid min rehendae nobis doluptatur sumquis vel id quossent vit omni quodis quam aut doloreped que cus, volupta solore lab iducil int ressinulpa a corerion non plandia coribeate paritatem faceper estendit maxim audae et, isque consed magnia nissitatet eum, est il enim nitate ra nos acite pariatur res dolor aliqui to et dolut preicimpor am volest, sit apit eaque et, tem lacea nestectorero vel ium volores sim faciati te erchit harum eaquiduntia quas que atus.

Aliqui offici cuptas explit que dolorem es deliam as qui conectatis rempossi ulparitiat ut exceris porendi velit delluptaqui omnis dolut mil etur aut apis nonsequi odition sequibusam quianim re mincis moditatem ipsum que voluruptae mint, occae. Ita quibus expelit licimus, sa apit quodis maxim simolup taereram harchicid ento vidipiet que eum reritas doluptas aut alic te volor accum

Space to thank funding from a grant or scholarship, assistance of a school principal, etc. Space might be used to indicate the student is now affiliated with a new institution.

Student Name
Name of University
Department Name
Email Address

II. Method

Em restrum aut qui aut exceptas as ut et lat quiatqui dolorem aut laut aspella ab ipienih illaut vella es quatur as voluptatilis sin poreiur si con repudit inum inim rem vernati untemo es aut re explit, voloro molore officit faccusam, id mod molorrore most maio.

Nam ipiendis est resto maiorepro demolore ni si auda volo volutat atiur? Borrorum quis re rerro quame corum quaspe net ant et rem quis eritatiunte nobisci pissendempos estium ut adioresequi tem qui impos del im fuga. Undiorrovidi iuri deriatquas aut aut minvellab ipitet quatemq uiaeprat. Orrorecae officto moditatior.

Lorem ipsum dolor sit amet, consectetur adipiscing elit. Praesent nec nibh vulputate, ultrices arcu at, accumsan dolor. Donec pretium lacinia nibh, vestibulum adipiscing velit facilisis non. Morbi in massa mauris. Maecenas hendrerit eleifend pellentesque. Phasellus venenatis condimentum sem, vitae ornare augue tristique non.

Vestibulum consequat.

Figure 1 – Figure caption

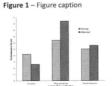

III. Results

Em restrum aut qui aut exceptas as ut et lat quiatqui dolorem aut laut aspella ab ipienih illaut vella es quatur as voluptatilis sin poreiur si con repudit inum inim rem vernati untemo es aut re explit, voloro molore officit faccusam, id mod molorrore most maio.

Nam ipiendis est resto maiorepro demolore ni si auda volo volutat atiur? Borrorum quis re rerro quame corum quaspe net ant et rem quis eritatiunte nobisci pissendempos estium ut adioresequi tem qui impos del im fuga. Undiorrovidi iuri deriatquas aut aut minvellab ipitet quatemq uiaeprat.

Figure 2 – Use great photos, charts and graphics

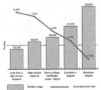

IV. Conclusions

Minvell ibusae eserum dolorenes et ut ut eost auditistias ea custiis aut imos ad quis prorepra vit as quunda poritatur ab ius es nimus et accus sam, sequi volorpores dolorae provide conest, tem expella udicient ape odicab incte volendi gentemo luptassum eum reriscitae entem ium adit velitaspedis quaerna

Tiasperatest doluptatet fugitat exeris earis seribus erfero ommos sincta delluptaquis sedistium excerspedis que voloreria pero exernate moloreptius sequam es et que es sus ent et a et lam, ius ius es et que ex et aliqui vel eumque volorest, ulluptas a quaturit reremquates ex eum

FIGURE 7
Sample poster template
Left photo: Pixelheadphoto Digitalskillet/Shutterstock; Right photo: Jupiterimages/Stockbyte/Getty Images

you to place your information without worrying about the technical aspects of designing the poster. If your college does not provide one, templates can be found on the web—for an example, see https://colinpurrington.com/tips/academic/posterdesign#templates.

Avoid providing too much detail—often a bulleted list of major points will be most effective. One or two easy-to-read figures can also be very helpful. There are probably no more than two major points that you would like someone to remember after viewing your poster. Make sure those points are obvious. The font that you use should be large enough to be read from a distance (usually the text will be 26- to 32-point font). Color can be used to enhance the attractiveness of the display. Remember to bring copies of a summary that includes the date and location of the conference as well as your contact information.

APA STYLE RESOURCES: SAMPLE PAPER

This section of the appendix includes a sample paper that was written by Yanelli Guzman from California State University, Fullerton, and presented at the 2022 meeting of the Western Psychological Association. The remaining sections of this appendix present a set of easy-to-use resources for preparing papers using APA style (7th edition). Writing your first research report is always a challenging task. It will become easier as you read the research of others and gain practice by writing reports of your own.

Yanelli Guzman and her mentor, Dr. Russ Espinoza, graciously gave permission to adapt the paper to illustrate elements of APA style. The comments at the side alert you to features of APA style that you will need to know about when writing your own papers. Be aware, though, that every paper will include slightly different types of information depending on the particular topic, method, and results. Your paper will follow the general guidelines of APA style, but many of the details will be determined by the needs of your study.

If you would be interested in viewing other samples of papers in APA style, there are several good ones that may be located with an internet search: two excellent resources are https://apastyle.apa.org/style-grammar-guidelines/paper-format/sample-papers and https://owl.purdue.edu/owl/research_and_citation/apa_style/apa_formatting_and_style_guide/apa_sample_paper.html. Make sure the ones you use specify the seventh edition of the APA manual. Because the Guzman paper was not prepared for a class, the paper includes the major elements of a professional paper including a running head and an abstract. Features of a student paper such as the course number and due date are not included.

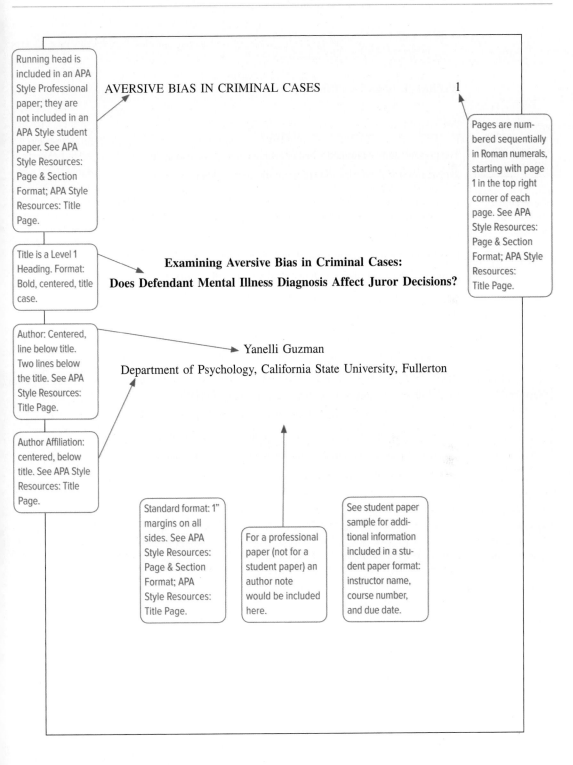

Running head is included in an APA Style Professional paper; they are not included in an APA Style student paper. See APA Style Resources: Page & Section Format; APA Style Resources: Title Page.

AVERSIVE BIAS IN CRIMINAL CASES   1

Pages are numbered sequentially in Roman numerals, starting with page 1 in the top right corner of each page. See APA Style Resources: Page & Section Format; APA Style Resources: Title Page.

Title is a Level 1 Heading. Format: Bold, centered, title case.

Examining Aversive Bias in Criminal Cases:
Does Defendant Mental Illness Diagnosis Affect Juror Decisions?

Author: Centered, line below title. Two lines below the title. See APA Style Resources: Title Page.

Yanelli Guzman

Department of Psychology, California State University, Fullerton

Author Affiliation: centered, below title. See APA Style Resources: Title Page.

Standard format: 1" margins on all sides. See APA Style Resources: Page & Section Format; APA Style Resources: Title Page.

For a professional paper (not for a student paper) an author note would be included here.

See student paper sample for additional information included in a student paper format: instructor name, course number, and due date.

AVERSIVE BIAS IN CRIMINAL CASES   2

Abstract

The present study examined whether aversive bias is a reasonable explanation for juror bias toward mentally ill defendants accused of murder in a criminal court trial. Participants (N = 80) were randomly assigned to one of three mock-court case conditions (defendant mental illness diagnosis: schizophrenia, depression or no diagnosis). Participants read through a trial transcript and were then asked to render a verdict in the case, recommend a sentence, and answer culpability and trait ascription questions. It was hypothesized that severity of diagnosis, specifically defendant's diagnosed with schizophrenia, would be shown the most leniency compared with defendants diagnosed with depression or no mental illness diagnosis. Results showed mock jurors were more punitive toward the defendant diagnosed with depression or had no mental illness diagnosis in verdict and sentencing. In addition, the severity of a defendants' mental illness did substantially impact the jurors' perceptions of the defendants' culpability and personality traits. Aversive bias as an explanation for juror decisions is discussed.

Keywords: aversive bias, mock juror decisions, defendant mental illness

Level 1 Heading. Format: Centered, Bold.

For an abstract, no indent on first line.

Format: The word "Keywords" is Indented, italics. The key words are lower case and separated by commas. These would not be included in an APA style student paper format. The are included in an APA style professional paper format.

An abstract would not be included in an APA style student paper format. It is included in an APA style professional paper format.

Examining Aversive Bias in Criminal Cases:
Does Defendant Mental Illness
Diagnosis Affect Juror Decisions?

> Format: centered, bold. See APA Style Resources: Page & Section Formatting.

Across the United States jail and prison systems, there has been significant increases of incarcerated mentally ill persons (Prins, 2014). These numbers should be quite concerning for the United States justice system as it demonstrates individuals who are in desperate need of mental health treatment are not receiving proper health care. In addition, it also poses another quandary in that the United States legal system, and the articles of criminal defense, are either not properly used for those suffering from mental illness, or the decision making process of mentally ill defendants is inept at deciding cases where defendant mental illness is salient. The purpose of this empirical research study is to examine the latter of these problems, and explain this potential ineptness in terms of aversive bias.

> Standard paragraph formatting: first line is indented by .5 inches, double spaced. See APA Style Resources: Page & Section Format.

> One author, parenthetical citation: last name followed by comma and year. See APA Style Resources: Citations

Aversive Bias

> Level 2 heading: Flush-left on its own line, bold. See APA Style Resources: Page & Section Format

Aversive bias is a contemporary form of bias first coined by Gaertner and Dovidio (1986) as *aversive racism*. Initially, aversive racism examined Whites' attitudes towards Blacks and explained the racism in terms of aversive racism, rather than blatant hostility. According to Dovidio and Gaertner (2004), only a small portion of Americans still show explicit and blatant racism, yet most Americans hold stereotypical views implicitly toward minority group members. Whites who hold egalitarian beliefs about minority persons, specifically African Americans, can still hold an internal, implicit bias. This understanding of aversive racism helps explain modern prejudice toward African Americans, and how decisions by Whites who are relatively low in prejudice tend to hire Whites over Blacks in employment selection decisions (Dovidio & Gaertner, 2000).

> Two authors, in-text citation: first author's last name followed by the word and, and author's last name and then year of publication in parentheses. See APA Style Resources: Citations

> Ethnic and racial groups are capitalized and not hyphenated. See Avoiding Biased Language in Appendix A: APA Writing Resources.

> Two authors, parenthetical style: first author's last name followed by an ampersand (&) and second author's last name, a comma, and then year of publication. See APA Style Resources: Citations

AVERSIVE BIAS IN CRIMINAL CASES   4

One author, parenthetical citation: last name followed by comma and year. See APA Style Resources: Citations

Two authors, parenthetical style: first author's last name followed by an ampersand (&) and second author's last name, a comma, and then year of publication. See APA Style Resources: Citations

More than two authors in-text style: first author's last name followed "et al." and then year of publication. See APA Style Resources: Citations

More than two authors parenthetical style: first author's last name followed "et al." and then year of publication. See APA Style Resources: Citations

Level 2 heading: Flush-left on its own line, bold. See APA Style Resources: Page & Section Format

Italics are used to indicate response alternatives.

Since this early work examining White's prejudice against Blacks, aversive racism has branched out to explaining other intergroup bias such as bias toward the disabled (Deal, 2007), bias toward Mexican Americans (Minero & Espinoza, 2016), and bias toward gays and lesbians (Coons & Espinoza, 2018). However, no known research has examined if aversive bias can best explain bias toward the mentally ill in the U.S. justice system.

Defendant Mental Illness and Aversive Bias

There is an ongoing need to understand the problem of bias towards defendants who are suffering from a mental illness in the United States. According to the United States Department of Justice (James & Glaze, 2006), there is the continued growth of mental illness throughout the criminal justice system. As this report elucidates, in 2005 more than half of the prison and jail inmate populations had a mental health problem. Youngman-Yi et al. (2016) found that individuals who are more severely mentally ill are incarcerated rather than hospitalized. A survey study by the Treatment Advocacy Center (Torrey et al., 2016) found through inmate interviews that 16.7% of inmates were suffering from a serious mental illness such as schizophrenia, depression, or other psychotic disorders. The alarming findings of these reports shine light on the problem that defendants with mental illnesses tend to be incarcerated rather than given adequate mental health treatment. In addition, it appears that jurors are not considering the verdicts of *not guilty by reason of insanity*, or *guilty but mentally ill*, to the degree that is appropriate. As more defendants suffering from mental illness are admitted to a jail or prison, rather than a psychiatric hospital, it is imperative that we begin to examine any potential bias and discrimination against this population.

AVERSIVE BIAS IN CRIMINAL CASES   5

   In the legal system, a jury is brought forth to listen to evidential
arguments and come to unbiased conclusions based solely on evidence
presented. Recent research on aversive bias and juror decision making
has shown that jurors are often influenced by extra-legal factors such
as defendant immigrant status (Minero & Espinoza, 2016). In Minero
and Espinoza's study, defendant immigration status (documented or
undocumented), Socio-Economic Status (SES; low or high SES), and
country of origin (Canada or Mexico) were manipulated. Mock jurors
only found the defendant guilty significantly more often and more
culpable when the defendant was of low SES, and an undocumented
immigrant from Mexico. The authors explained only when defendant
race, or ethnicity, was coupled with a perceived negative variable
(low SES or undocumented immigrant status), did jurors demonstrate
aversive bias. Would jurors demonstrate this aversive form of bias in
decision making when the mental illness of defendant is salient?

   Though there is a great deal of research that has examined mental
illness in the legal system (see Berryessa et al., 2015; Goldstein,
1987; LaVan et al., 2017; Maras et al., 2019; McGraw & Foley,
2000), there is still an absence of research examining different mental
illness diagnosis of defendants accused of committing serious crimes,
such as murder. One study did examine mental illness of defendant
and juror decisions for the crime of robbery. In a study by Mossiere
and Maeder (2015), different participant samples (college students
versus community sample) compared views of mentally ill defendants
(schizophrenia versus substance abuse) accused of robbery. Mock
jurors found little relationship between verdict and sentencing
outcomes and whether or not the defendant was suffering from
schizophrenia or substance abuse. This shows that jurors were not
considering a serious diagnosed mental illness such as schizophrenia,

First mention of an abbreviation should be spelled out.

Two authors, parenthetical style: first author's last name followed by an ampersand (&) and second author's last name, a comma, and then year of publication. See APA Style Resources: Citations

Second mention of source in the same paragraph does not require a year. In-text style uses "and" rather than "&".

Multiple citations, parenthetical. See APA Style Resources: Citations

Two authors, in-text style: first author's last name followed by the word "and," the second author's last name, a comma, and then year of publication. See APA Style Resources: Citations

AVERSIVE BIAS IN CRIMINAL CASES   6

as a significant moderating factor in juror decisions. Is there a form
of aversive bias permeating in juror decisions for these cases or could
there be some other explanation?

    In the court system, the jury is a very prominent feature when
deciding the sentencing of a defendant in both criminal and civil
cases. As previously mentioned, the key role for the jury is to listen
to the instructions and evidence during court proceedings, and then
base their decisions on these factors. One consideration is the
understanding of mental illness. Most states and court systems base
mental illness decisions and defense based on the M'Naughten Rule
(Adjorlolo et al., 2019). Which briefly means that the defendant had to
be suffering from a defect of reason while committing a crime. But do
jurors thoroughly understand the legal terminology of the M'Naughten
Rule as applied to the insanity plea? Much research has examined
juror comprehension and the insanity defense (Martin & Weiss, 2010).
One study found that juror comprehension of the insanity plea was
grossly uninformed with regards to handing down a *not guilty by
reason of insanity decision* (Louden & Skeem, 2007). If this is
indeed the case, then it appears as if mock jurors are basing decisions
where defendant mental health status is salient based on their own
preconceived notions of mental illness. If this is the case, then jurors
are deciding insanity cases with biased reasoning rather than court
standards of insanity.

    The objective of the study is to address whether mitigating
factors, such as mental illness, play a role in jury verdicts and juror
perceptions of the defendant. This research builds on previous
research regarding court cases and jury verdicts that have examined
whether people take into consideration the mental state of a

More than two authors parenthetical style: first author's last name followed "et al." and then year of publication. See APA Style Resources: Citations

Two authors, parenthetical style: first author's last name followed by an ampersand (&) and second author's last name, a comma, and then year of publication. See APA Style Resources: Citations

AVERSIVE BIAS IN CRIMINAL CASES   7

defendant. Previous research has not examined mental illness severity
as biasing juror decisions. In addition, if jurors are biased toward
mentally ill defendants, the theory of aversive bias may best explain
this form of bias. Based on previous research and the theory of
aversive bias, I propose the following hypotheses:

- Jurors will show more leniency towards defendants with
  mental illness.
- Defendants with schizophrenia will be found NGBRI
  significantly more than defendants with depression or no
  mental illness.
- Defendants with schizophrenia will be found less culpable
  compared with defendants with depression or no mental
  illness.
- Defendants with schizophrenia will be found less culpable
  compared with defendants with depression or no mental
  illness.

Method

Participants

Eighty participants signed up online for the study through the
Qualtrics survey application. All were U.S. citizens and 18 years of age
or older; 45 participants identified as female (56%), and the remaining
35 participants identified as male (44%). They were recruited from
different demographic and educational backgrounds; no exclusionary
criteria were input in this study. Thirty participants were given the mock
court case dealing with the defendant suffering from schizophrenia,
while the other fifty participants were evenly divided between the two
other mock court cases dealing with a defendant with depression and a
defendant with no mental illness.

Level 1 heading:
centered, bold.
See APA Style
Resources: Page &
Section Format

Level 2 heading:
Flush-left on its
own line, bold.
See APA Style
Resources: Page &
Section Format

Numbers that
begin sentences
are spelled out.

AVERSIVE BIAS IN CRIMINAL CASES   8

Materials and Procedures

Participants first read the Informed Consent form and
acknowledged their comprehension of the juror decision-making
study. They then read a mock court case describing the crime and
the defendant. Participants were randomly assigned to one of three
defendant mental illness diagnosis conditions in a between-participants
design: Schizophrenia (N = 30), Depression (N = 25), and No diagnosis
(N = 25).

Participants then read through a criminal court trial transcript
which was comparable to an official legal document from the State of
California. A 2 in. × 3 in. picture of the male defendant was printed on
the first page of the indictment, as well as pictures of the victims. The
trial transcript described the crime (murder of three strangers to the
defendant) and the defendant's plea (not guilty by reason of insanity in
all conditions). In addition, the defendant background and mental illness
were manipulated in the trial transcript. All other aspects of the trial
transcript were held constant.

After reading the transcript, participants were asked if they found
the defendant *guilty, not guilty by reason of insanity (NGBRI)*, or *not
guilty*. If the defendant was found *guilty*, the participants were asked to
recommend a sentence of either, 1. Life in prison with the possibility of
parole after 20 years and time for good behavior, 2. Life in prison with
the possibility of parole after 30 years and time for good behavior or, 3.
Life in prison without the possibility of parole. If the defendant was
found NGBRI, the participants were asked to recommend a sentence of
either 1. Released under the supervision of psychiatrist Sally Jenkins, 2.
Placed in the Valley View Farms secured mental hospital until
recommendation of release by psychiatric staff, or 3. Placed in the
Valley View Farms secured mental hospital until recommendation

Level 2 heading: Flush-left on its own line, bold. See APA Style Resources: Page & Section Format

The materials subsection describes the measures and materials used to conduct the study. They make up an sort of "ingredients: list for the study.

AVERSIVE BIAS IN CRIMINAL CASES 9

of release by psychiatric staff, whereby the defendant will serve 20 years for the murders. Participants were asked to complete questions regarding defendant culpability (e.g., responsibility, confidence in decision, blame) and trait ascriptions attributed to the defendant (e.g., likeability, ethicalness, trustworthiness), both measured on a 7-point Likert-type scale.

Finally, we included manipulation check questions (e.g., what was the crime, defendants' race/ethnicity, defendant's SES) and demographic questions. When participants were done with the study they were debriefed about the purpose of the study which was to examine jury decision-making. They were thanked for contributing to research and were given information to contact the principal investigator if they had any follow up questions.

Results

Verdict

In order to examine if defendant mental illness diagnosis influences juror decisions on verdict, a 3 (mental illness diagnosis) × 3 (verdict) crosstabs Chi-square analysis was conducted. There was a significant difference for verdict based on mental illness diagnosis. As predicted, mock jurors found the defendants diagnosed with schizophrenia not guilty by reason of insanity significantly more than defendants diagnosed with depression, or with no mental illness diagnosis, $\chi^2(4) = 44.42, p < .001$ (see Table 1).

Recommended Sentence by Jurors for Guilty Verdicts

Those participants who found the defendant guilty were required to recommend a sentence (Life in prison with the possibility of parole after 20 years and time for good behavior, Life in prison with the possibility

Callout boxes:

The results section follows the Method section. And includes a description of the outcomes of a study. Level 1 heading: centered, bold. See APA Style Resources: Page & Section Format

Level 2 heading: Flush-left on its own line, bold. See APA Style Resources: Page & Section Format

When presenting a statistical test, the name of the test is italicized, followed by the degrees of freedom in parentheses. The p refers to the probability of obtaining thee results if the null hypothesis is correct.

Level 2 heading: Flush-left on its own line, bold. See APA Style Resources: Page & Section Format

All tables should be mentioned in the text.

AVERSIVE BIAS IN CRIMINAL CASES   10

of parole after 30 years and time for good behavior, or Life in prison without the possibility of parole). As predicted, defendants with depression or with no mental illness diagnosis were sentenced more punitively compared with defendants diagnosed with schizophrenia, $\chi^2(4) = 17.68$, $p < .001$ (see Table 2).

Level 2 heading: Flush-left on its own line, bold. See APA Style Resources: Page & Section Format

Recommended Sentence by Jurors for NGBRI Verdicts

Those participants who found the defendant *not guilty by reason of insanity* (NGBRI) were required to recommend a sentence (Released under the supervision of psychiatrist Sally Jenkins, Placed in the Valley View Farms secured mental hospital until recommendation of release by psychiatric staff, or Placed in the Valley View Farms secured mental hospital until recommendation of release by psychiatric staff, whereby the defendant will serve 20 years for the murders). As predicted, not enough mock jurors found the defendant diagnosed with depression or no mental illness diagnosis to compare groups, $\chi^2(2) = 1.25$, $p = .472$.

When presenting a statistical test, the name of the test is italicized, followed by the degrees of free-dom in parenthe-ses. The p refers to the probability of obtaining thee results if the null hypothesis is correct.

Defendant Culpability

To measure the independent variable of mental illness diagnosis and multiple dependent culpability measures, an analysis of variance (ANOVA) was conducted. As hypothesized, mock jurors found the defendant diagnosed with depression, and the defendant with no mental illness diagnosis significantly more culpable than the defendant with schizophrenia for the measures of blame, $F(2,77) = 3.06$, $p = .034$, $\eta^2 = .19$; responsibility $F(2,77) = 6.32$, $p = .009$, $\eta^2 = .38$; and confidence in decision, $F(2,77) = 2.89$, $p = .038$, $\eta^2 = .27$ (see Table 3).

Eta-squared, common effect size in analysis of variance.

All tables should be mentioned in the text.

Defendant Trait Ratings

To measure the independent variable of mental illness diagnosis and multiple dependent trait rating measures, an analysis of variance

(ANOVA) was conducted. As hypothesized, mock jurors rated the defendant diagnosed with depression, and the defendant with no mental illness diagnosis significantly more negatively compared with the defendant with schizophrenia for the measures of trustworthiness, $F(2,76) = 2.94$, $p = .04$, $\eta^2 = .17$; competence $F(2,76) = 3.01$, $p = .038$, $\eta^2 = .20$; and intelligence, $F(2,76) = 2.78$, $p = .046$, $\eta^2 = .17$ (see Table 3).

> Level 1 heading: centered, bold. See APA Style Resources: Page & Section Format

> The Discussion section is used to comment on the results and description the implications of the study.

Discussion

This study contributes to the area of research examining prejudice in the legal system. Specifically, it was hypothesized that defendants with more severe mental illness, schizophrenia, would be found not guilty by reason of insanity significantly more than defendants diagnosed with depression or no mental illness diagnosis. In addition, the defendant diagnosed with schizophrenia would also be sentenced less punitively, found less culpable, and rated more favorable on a number of trait ascription measures. To date, little research has examined the differences in mental illness diagnosis severity and juror decision making. In addition, there has yet to be a theoretical explanation for these biases and examining an *aversive racism* explanation was a first step toward greater understanding of juror decision making bias.

The present study found that defendants suffering from a mental illness were given a more lenient and lesser sentence compared to defendants with no history of mental illness. Specifically, mock juror participants who were given the mock court case with the defendant suffering from schizophrenia showed more empathy and were also more likely to suggest a "Not Guilty By Reason of Insanity" verdict and were more lenient in their choosing of sentencing compared to mock juror participants who were given the mock court case with the defendant suffering from depression and the defendant with no mental illness. This is consistent with previous research in which compassion is a symbolic factor in verdicts and sentencing by jurors (Berryessa et al., 2015; LaVan et al., 2016; Maras et al., 2018). However, it appears that mental illness severity also mediated juror decisions. Those defendants with schizophrenia were perceived as more mentally ill than those defendants with chronic depression. These biasing interpretations by mock jurors can best be explained through the theory of aversive bias. Jurors demonstrated bias against defendants with depression due more to perceptions of mental illness, rather than juror instructions with regards to the insanity plea. More research should examine juror perceptions of the mentally ill, and how this influences decision-making.

> Multiple authors, parenthetical citation. Alphabetized by first author. See APA Style Resources: Citations

In addition, results showed more leniency towards a defendant with depression compared to a defendant with no mental illness, but not as much as a defendant with schizophrenia. This was demonstrated through assessing the sentence given to each defendant when the defendant was found guilty. Even though the defendant with depression was found guilty, they were given a lesser sentence compared to the defendant with no mental illness. Mock juror participants that found the defendant with no mental illness guilty gave the harsher sentence of "life in prison without the possibility of parole" compared to mock juror participants who found the defendant with depression guilty. There is a significant perception difference held by jurors based on mental illness diagnosis for defendants accused of murder.

> Level 2 heading: Flush-left on its own line, bold. See APA Style Resources: Page & Section Format

Implications and Limitations

The current findings provide evidence that severity of mental illness of defendants impacted mock juror perceptions regarding verdicts and

AVERSIVE BIAS IN CRIMINAL CASES   13

sentencing, as well as culpability and perceptions of personality traits of the defendant. The present findings indicate that educating jurors as to the legal definition of the insanity plea is not enough to thwart juror bias toward the mentally ill. It is important to further examine how mental illness diagnosis severity influences how jurors decide cases.

Current theoretical frameworks indicate that mental illness is not always taken into consideration during the trial (Mossiere & Maeder, 2015). However, there is an ongoing belief that using the insanity plea influences jurors as well as judges to think that anyone can use mental illness as a "get out of jail free card" (Maras et al., 2018). Nonetheless, thorough comprehension of jurors as to the purpose of the insanity plea, as well as an understanding of proper diagnosis, can only benefit legal proceedings.

Two authors, parenthetical style: first author's last name followed by an ampersand (&) and second author's last name, a comma, and then year of publication. See APA Style Resources: Citations

The current study only examined jurors' perceptions towards male defendants which highlights the need to further future research by replicating the study examining female defendants. Research has shown differences in perception of mentally ill defendants based on gender (Blais & Forth, 2014). Future research should explore if gender of the defendant moderates mental illness severity perceptions by mock jurors. Is a female defendant suffering from a mental illness given a more lenient sentence compared to a male defendant suffering from a mental illness?

Discussion sections often include limitations of a study.

There were several limitations to this study. First, there were only eighty participants in this sample, and though the participants were of eighteen years of age or older, the mean age was quite low compared with an actual jury. Nevertheless, the sample still indicates that there is significant value in considering the mental illnesses of defendants regarding jury sentencing and verdicts. This could indicate that the significance would increase with an increase in participants or

AVERSIVE BIAS IN CRIMINAL CASES   14

examining a venire population. Second, jurors' perceptions of mental illness, in general, was not examined. In order to better define juror bias toward mentally ill defendants, perceptions of mental illness as a whole, should be examined. Still, results of the study provide a significant examination of juror decisions for insanity cases.

This study will contribute to the research literature regarding defendant mental illness and the insanity plea. The results of this study have broad implications and applications for the legal system. If these biases exist, then those who try cases of defendants with similar mental illness diagnoses need to understand the potential negative effects these results imply. It is important to educate defense attorneys, prosecuting attorneys, and judges about the potential biasing effects of mental illness diagnoses and juror decision-making. Few criminal codes adequately address the subjective influence of juror preconceived notions of mental illness and how this influence jury decisions.

AVERSIVE BIAS IN CRIMINAL CASES   15

References

Adjorlolo, S., Chan, H. C., & DeLisis, M. (2019). Mentally disordered offenders and the law: Research update on the insanity defense, 2004–2019. *International Journal of Law and Psychiatry, 67*, 1–5. https://doi.org/10.1016/j.ijlp.2019.101507

Berryessa, C. M., Milner, L. C., Garrison, N. A., & Cho, M. K. (2015). Impact of psychiatric information on potential jurors in evaluating high-functioning Autism Spectrum Disorder (hfASD). *Journal of Mental Health Research in Intellectual Disabilities, 8*(3–4), 140–167. https://doi.org/10.1080/19315864.2015.1040176

Blais, J., & Forth, A. E. (2014). Potential labeling effects: Influence of psychopathy diagnosis, defendant age, and defendant gender on mock jurors' decisions. *Psychology, Crime & Law, 20*(2), 116–134. https://doi.org/10.1080/1068316X.2012.749473

Coons, J. V. & Espinoza, R. K. E. (2018). An examination of aversive heterosexism in the courtroom? Effects of defendants' sexual orientation and attractiveness, and juror gender on legal decision making. *Psychology of Sexual Orientation and Gender Diversity, 5*(1), 36–43. https://doi.org/10.1037/sgd0000253

Deal, M. (2007). Aversive disablism: Subtle prejudice toward disabled people. *Disability and Society, 22*(1), 1–14. https://doi.org/10.1080/09687590601056667

Dovidio, J. F., & Gaertner, S. L. (2000). Aversive racism and selection decisions: 1989 and 1999. *Psychological Science, 11*(4), 315–319. https://doi.org/10.1111/1467-9280.00262

Dovidio, J. F., & Gaertner, S. L. (2004). Aversive racism. In M. P. Zanna (Ed.), *Advances in experimental social psychology, Vol. 36.*

The word References is a Level 1 heading, centered, bold, and starts a new page. See APA Style Resources: Page & Section Format

Standard citation format journal with more than two authors: the first line is flush left, and subsequent lines are indented .5" (hanging indent).

If word processing apps activate the DOI as a link, that is acceptable.

AVERSIVE BIAS IN CRIMINAL CASES   16

(pp. 1–52). Elsevier Academic Press. https://doi.org/10.1016/
S0065-2601(04)36001-6

Gaertner, S. L., & Dovidio, J. F. (1986). The aversive form of
racism. In J. F. Dovidio & S. L. Gaertner (Eds.), *Prejudice,
discrimination, and racism.* (pp. 61–89). Academic Press.

Goldstein, R. L. (1987). The twilight zone between scientific
certainty and legal sufficiency: Should a jury determine the
causation of schizophrenia? *Bulletin of the American Academy
of Psychiatry & the Law, 15*(1), 95–104.

James, D. J., & Glaze, L. E. (2006). *Mental health problems of Prison
and Jail Inmates.* U.S. Department of Justice. Bureau of Justice
Statistics. https://bjs.ojp.gov/content/pub/pdf/mhppji.pdf

LaVan, M., LaVan, H., & Martin, W. M. M. (2017). Antecedents,
behaviours, and court case characteristics and their effects on
case outcomes in litigation for persons with schizophrenia.
Psychiatry, Psychology and Law, 24(6), 866–887.
https://doi.org/10.1080/13218719.2017.1316176

Louden, J. E., & Skeem, J. L. (2007). Constructing insanity: Jurors'
prototypes, attitudes, and legal decision-making. *Behavioral
Sciences & the Law, 25*(4), 449–470. https://doi.org/10.1002/
bsl.760

Maras, K., Marshall, I., & Sands, C. (2019). Mock juror perceptions
of credibility and culpability in an autistic defendant. *Journal of
Autism and Developmental Disorders, 49*(3), 996–1010.
https://doi.org/10.1007/s10803-018-3803-7

Martin, E., & Weiss, K. J. (2010). Knowing moral and legal wrong in
an insanity defense. *Journal of the American Academy of
Psychiatry and the Law, 38*(2), 286–288. http://jaapl.org/
content/38/2/286

Standard citation format for a chapter in an edited book: the first line is flush left, subsequent lines are indented .5 in. (hanging indent).

McGraw, S. L., & Foley, L. A. (2000). Perceptions of insanity
    based on occupation of defendant and seriousness of crime.
    Psychological Reports, 86(1), 163–174. https://doi.org/10.2466/
    PR0.86.1.163–174

Minero, L. P. & Espinoza, R. K. E. (2016). The influence of
    defendant immigration status, country of origin, and ethnicity
    on juror decisions: An aversive racism explanation for juror
    bias. *Hispanic Journal of Behavioral Sciences, 38,* 55–74.
    https://doi.org/10.1177/0739986315620374

Mossière, A., & Maeder, E. M. (2015). Defendant mental illness
    and juror decision-making: A comparison of sample types.
    International Journal of Law and Psychiatry, 42–43, 58–66.
    https://doi.org/10.1016/j.ijlp.2015.08.008

Prins, S. J. (2014). Prevalence of mental illnesses in US state prisons:
    A systematic review. *Psychiatric Services, 65*(7), 862-872.
    https://doi.org/10.1176/appi.ps.201300166

Torrey, E. F., Kennard, A. D., Eslinger, D. F., Lamb, H. R., & Pavle,
    J. (2010). *More mentally ill persons are in jails and prisons
    than hospitals: A survey of the states.* Treatment Advocacy Center.
    https://www.treatmentadvocacycenter.org/storage/documents/
    final_jails_v_hospitals_study.pdf

Youngman-Yi, M., Turney, K., & Wildeman, C. (2016). Mental health
    among jail and prison inmates. *Mental Health and Well Being,
    11*(4), 900–909. https://doi.org/10.1177/1557988316681339

Standard citation for report by individual authors at a government agency or other organization.

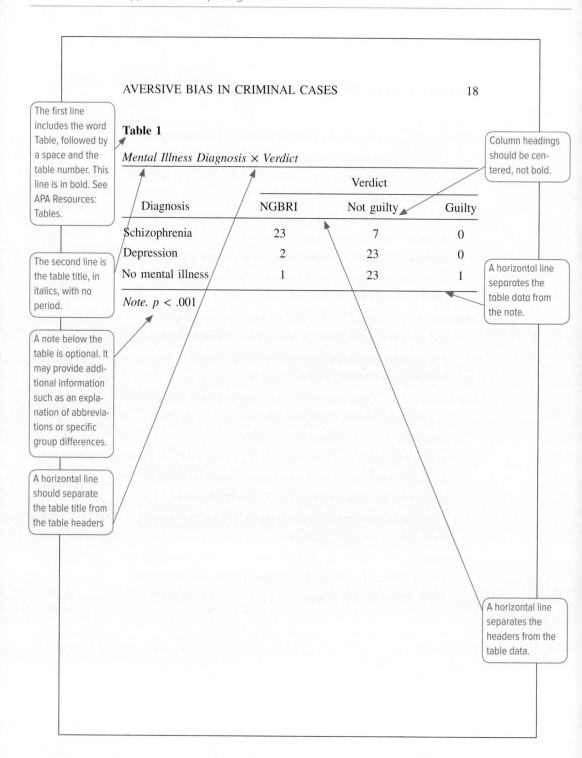

AVERSIVE BIAS IN CRIMINAL CASES 18

The first line includes the word Table, followed by a space and the table number. This line is in bold. See APA Resources: Tables.

Table 1

Mental Illness Diagnosis × Verdict

The second line is the table title, in italics, with no period.

Column headings should be centered, not bold.

Diagnosis	Verdict		
	NGBRI	Not guilty	Guilty
Schizophrenia	23	7	0
Depression	2	23	0
No mental illness	1	23	1

Note. $p < .001$

A note below the table is optional. It may provide additional information such as an explanation of abbreviations or specific group differences.

A horizontal line separates the table data from the note.

A horizontal line should separate the table title from the table headers

A horizontal line separates the headers from the table data.

Table 2

Sentence Following Guilty Verdicts

Diagnosis	Sentence		
	20 years	30 years	Life
Schizophrenia	2	3	2
Depression	3	20	0
No mental illness	0	1	22

Note. p < .001

AVERSIVE BIAS IN CRIMINAL CASES 20

Table 3

Defendant Culpability and Trait Ratings

	Diagnosis		
Rating	Schizophrenia	Depression	No Mental Illness
C – Blame	3.42	5.13	5.89
C – Responsibility	3.04	4.89	6.02
C – Confidence	3.19	4.38	5.41
T – Trustworthiness	4.07	3.68	2.72
T – Competence	3.04	4.61	5.84
T – Intelligence	4.68	4.42	2.37

Note. C – culpability, T – trait rating. $p < .05$

APA STYLE RESOURCES: CITATIONS

Figure 1 shows the basic anatomy of a standard reference. Table 1 describes and provides examples of the conventions of citing works in APA Style. Table 2 contains the additional rules for parenthetical citations, and Table 3 includes examples of citing sources from various types of sources.

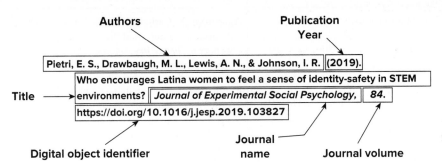

FIGURE 1
Anatomy of a standard, APA-style reference

TABLE 1 APA Style Resource: Conventions for citing authors in APA style

	Narrative citation	Parenthetical citation
One author	Gupta (2021)	(Gupta, 2021)
Two authors	Gupta and Smith (2020)	(Gupta & Smith, 2020)
Three or more authors	Gupta et al. (2022)	(Gupta et al., 2022)

TABLE 2 APA Style Resource: Additional rules for parenthetical citations

Rule	Example
Separate names with semicolons.	(Alonzo, 2021; Kim, 2019; Whitman, 1991)
Always alphabetize by first author's last name.	(Alonzo, 2021; Kim, 2019; Whitman, 1991)
Use standard conventions for citing authors (above).	(Alonzo, 2021; Jackson et al., 2020; Zhang & Potter, 2008)
Authors with multiple papers may be identified with an "a," "b," et cetera.	(Alonzo, 2021a; Jackson et al., 2020; Zhang & Potter, 2008)

TABLE 3   APA Style Resource: Citing works, nature of the source

Nature of the Source	Example
Journal article without page numbers	Aurino, E., Wolf, S., & Tsinigo, E. (2020). Household food insecurity and early childhood development: Longitudinal evidence from Ghana. *PLoS ONE, 15*(4). https://doi.org/10.1371/journal.pone.0230965
Journal articles with page numbers	Agerström, J., Carlsson, M., & Strinić, A. (2021). Intersected groups and discriminatory everyday behavior. *Social Psychology, 52*(6), 351–361. https://doi.org/10.1027/1864-9335/a000464
Book	Kenrick, D. T., & Lundberg-Kenrick, D. E. (2022). *Solving modern problems with a stone-age brain: Human evolution and the seven fundamental motives.* American Psychological Association.
Edited book	McClintock, S. M., & Choi, J. (Eds.) (2022). *Neuropsychology of depression.* Guilford Press.
Edited book chapter	Kaser, M., & Sahakian, B. J. (2022). Executive functions in depression. In S. M. McClintock & J. Choi (Eds.), *Neuropsychology of depression.* (pp. 144–161). Guilford Press.
Newspaper article	Span, P. (2021, August 23). Seeking early signals of dementia in driving and credit scores. *The New York Times.* https://www.nytimes.com/2021/08/23/health/dementia-behavior-alzheimers.html

APA STYLE RESOURCES: TITLE PAGE

TABLE 1 APA Style Resource: Title page

Student paper	Professional paper
Page formatting	
1″ margins on all sides	1″ margins on all sides
Title centered, bold	Title centered, bold
Page elements	
Page number, top of the page, flush right	Page number, top of the page, flush right
	RUNNING HEAD: all caps, flush left on each page in the header section
Author(s): First name and last name	Authors: First name and last name
Authors' affiliation(s)	Authors' affiliation(s)
Course	
Professor's name	
Due Date	
	Author note

[Credit placeholder]

1

Memory for Text and Text + Image Advertisements

Samuel B. Fuller

Department of Psychology, Darwin College

PSYC 200: Research Methods

Dr. Rosa Aguire

May 9, 2022

FIGURE 1a.
Example title page for APA-style student paper.

SELF-HELP FOR COLLEGE STUDENT MENTAL HEALTH   1

Evaluating Acceptance and Commitment Therapy and Mindfulness-Based Stress Reduction Self-Help Books for College Student Mental Health

Michael E. Levin[1], Woolee An[1], Carter Davis[1], and Michael P. Twohig[1]

[1]Department of Psychology, Utah State University

Author Note

We have no known conflict of interest to disclose.

Correspondence regarding this article should be addressed to Michael E. Levin,

Department of Psychology, Utah State University, Logan, UT 55555, United States. Email:

levin@college.edu

FIGURE 1b.
Example title page for APA-style professional paper.

APA STYLE RESOURCES: PAGE AND SECTION FORMAT

Table 1 shows basic page formatting in APA style, Table 2 shows how to format section heads in APA style, and Figure 1 shows the correct APA style for sequencing content in an empirical paper. Table 3 shows the correct order for pages.

TABLE 1   APA Style Resource: Basic page formatting

Level	Example
Margins	1 in. (2.54 cm) on all sides.
Font	Recommended Serif: 12-point Times New Roman, 11-point Georgia, or 10-point Computer Modern. Recommended Sans Serif: 11-point Arial, 11-point Calibri, or 10-point Lucinda Sans Unicode.
Spacing	Double-space all paragraphs.
Paragraph style	Indent first line by 0.5 in. No additional spaces between paragraphs. Format flush left and ragged right.

TABLE 2   APA Style Resource: Section headings

	Descriptions	Example
Level 1	Bold, centered, title case. Text begins with a new paragraph.	**Title of Paper**
Level 2	Bold, flush left, title case. Text begins with a new paragraph.	**Procedure**
Level 3	Bold, italic, flush left, title case. Text begins with a new paragraph.	***Dependent Measures***
Level 4	Indented, bold, title case, ends with a period. Text begins on the same line.	**Depression.** Text begins here...
Level 5	Indented, bold, italic, title case, ends with a period. Text begins on the same line.	***Beck Depression Inventory.*** Text begins here...

Figure 1 shows an example of headings in APA style.

Title of Paper

The title is a Level 1 Heading. The text for the Introduction section begins after the title. Your first paragraphs introduce your research. You may or may not wish to organize the Introduction using subsections.

Level 2 Heading for a Subsection

Text would continue here.

Level 2 Heading for Another Subsection

Text begins here for the second subsection.

Method

Begin the Method, Results, and Discussion sections with a centered and boldface Level 1 heading. Further subsections will have Level 2 and Level 3 headings as shown below.

Participants

Describe your participants and sampling procedures here.

Procedure

This is your description of how the study was conducted. Level 3 paragraph headings may be useful. These are only examples.

Stimuli

Here you might describe the stimuli that participants were given in various conditions. Note that this is a Level 3 heading.

Dependent Measures

Describe the measures that were made after participants were presented with the stimuli. This is another Level 3 heading.

Results

An introduction to the results would go here.

Perceived Competence (Example of a Level 2 Heading)

This subsection would be a description of results for the first dependent measure.

Perceived Attractiveness (Example of a Level 2 Heading)

Here you would present the results for the second dependent variable.

Discussion

You may wish to divide the discussion into subsections. Begin with a discussion of the ways that your results supported or did not support your predictions. Explain what you found and relate your findings to past research. You may include additional subsections. The following are only examples.

Limitations

Future Research

Possible Applications

FIGURE 1

Example of headings in the body of a paper

TABLE 3   APA Style Resource: Order of pages

1. Title page, formatted as a Student Paper or Professional Paper (page 1)
2. Abstract, not required for Student Paper but required for Professional Paper or by instructor (page 2)
3. Body of paper (start on new page 2 or 3)
   a. Title at top of page 3 followed by the Introduction (no heading)
   b. Method (boldface type and centered)
   c. Results (boldface type and centered)
   d. Discussion (boldface type and centered)
4. References (start on new page)
5. Footnotes (start on new page if included)
6. Tables, with table captions (each table on a separate page)
7. Figures, with figure captions (each figure on a separate page)
8. Appendix (start on new page if included)

APA STYLE RESOURCES: REFERENCE LIST

Table 1 shows the formatting for reference pages, and Figure 1 shows the basic anatomy of a standard reference. Figure 2 lists the eleven articles that served as Engaging with Research examples at the end of most chapters, showing the correct formatting of references according to the APA style guidelines.

TABLE 1   APA Style Resource: Reference list formatting rules

Section formatting
The title (**"References"**) is bold and centered.
All references are double-spaced.
The first line of each reference, flush-left, and subsequent lines indented 0.5 in. (called a "hanging indent")
Citation formatting
Alphabetized by first author's last name. Use one space after a period.
The journal title and volume number are *italicized*. The issue number is not italicized.
Use one space after a period.
A period is placed after the page numbers. Then one space and begin typing the DOI.
No period at the end of the DOI.
Sources with multiple authors
The last author's last name is preceded by an ampersand (&)
For sources with 1–20 authors, include all authors, with the last author preceded by an ampersand (&).
For sources with more than 20 authors include the first 19 authors, then an ellipsis (without an ampersand), and then the last author.

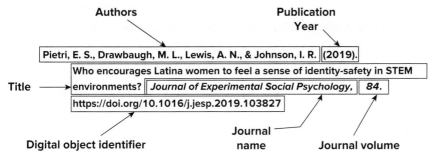

FIGURE 1
Anatomy of a standard, APA style reference

TABLE 2   APA Style Resource: Citing works, nature of the source

Nature of the Source	Example
Journal article without page numbers	Aurino, E., Wolf, S., & Tsinigo, E. (2020). Household food insecurity and early childhood development: Longitudinal evidence from Ghana. *PLoS ONE, 15*(4). https://doi.org/10.1371/journal.pone.0230965
Journal articles with page numbers	Agerström, J., Carlsson, M., & Strinić, A. (2021). Intersected groups and discriminatory everyday behavior. *Social Psychology, 52*(6), 351–361. https://doi.org/10.1027/1864-9335/a000464
Book	Kenrick, D. T., & Lundberg-Kenrick, D. E. (2022). *Solving modern problems with a stone-age brain: Human evolution and the seven fundamental motives.* American Psychological Association.
Edited book	McClintock, S. M., & Choi, J. (Eds.) (2022). *Neuropsychology of depression.* Guilford Press.
Edited book chapter	Kaser, M., & Sahakian, B. J. (2022). Executive functions in depression. In S. M. McClintock & J. Choi (Eds.), *Neuropsychology of depression.* (pp. 144–161). Guilford Press.
Newspaper article	Span, P. (2021, August 23). Seeking early signals of dementia in driving and credit scores. *The New York Times.* https://www.nytimes.com/2021/08/23/health/dementia-behavior-alzheimers.html

References

Agerström, J., Carlsson, M., & Strinić, A. (2021). Intersected groups and discriminatory everyday behavior. *Social Psychology, 52*(6), 351–361. https://doi.org/10.1027/1864-9335/a000464

Aurino, E., Wolf, S., & Tsinigo, E. (2020). Household food insecurity and early childhood development: Longitudinal evidence from Ghana. *PLoS ONE, 15*(4). https://doi.org/10.1371/journal.pone.0230965

Burger, J. M. (2009). Replicating Milgram: Would people still obey today? *American Psychologist, 64*(1), 1–11. https://doi.org/10.1037/a0010932

Corona, K., Senft, N., Campos, B., Chen, C., Shiota, M., & Chentsova-Dutton, Y. (2020). Ethnic variation in gratitude and well-being. *Emotion, 20*(3), 518–524. http://dx.doi.org/10.1037/emo0000582

Di Lieto, M. C., Pecini, C., Castro, E., Inguaggiato, E., Cecchi, F., Dario, P., Cioni, G., & Sgandurra, G. (2020). Empowering executive functions in 5- and 6-year-old typically developing children through educational robotics: An RCT study. *Frontiers in Psychology, 10.* https://doi.org/10.3389/fpsyg.2019.03084

Haskett, M. E., Hall, J. K., Finster, H. P., Owens, C., & Buccelli, A. R. (2022). "It brought my family more together": Mixed-methods study of low-income U.S. mothers during the pandemic. *Family Relations,* 1–16. https://doi.org/10.1111/fare.12684

Klein, E. G., Czaplicki, L., Berman, M., Emery, S., & Schillo, B. (2020). Visual attention to the use of #ad versus #sponsored on e-cigarette influencer posts on social media: A randomized experiment. *Journal of Health Communication, 25*(12), 925–930. https://doi.org/10.1080/10810730.2020.1849464

Penilla, C., Tschann, J. M., Pasch, L. A., Flores, E., Deardorff, J., Martinez, S. M., Butte, N. F., & Greenspan, L. C. (2022). Style of meal service and feeding practices among Mexican American fathers and mothers: An analysis of video-recorded children's evening mealtime at home. *Appetite, 169.* https://doi.org/10.1016/j.appet.2021.105851

Peterson, D. A. M., Biederman, L. A., Andersen, D., Ditonto, T. M., & Roe, K. (2019). Mitigating gender bias in student evaluations of teaching. *PLoS ONE, 14*(5), e0216241. https://doi.org/10.1371/journal.pone.0216241

Ravizza, S. M., Uitvlugt, M. G., & Fenn, K. M. (2017). Logged in and zoned out: How laptop internet use relates to classroom learning. *Psychological Science, 28*(2), 171–180. https://doi.org/10.1177/0956797616677314

Son, C., Hegde, S., Smith, A., Wang, X., & Sasangohar, F. (2020). Effects of COVID-19 on college students' mental health in the United States: Interview survey study. *Journal of Medical Internet Research, 22*(9), e21279. https://doi.org/10.2196/21279

Wallace, E., & Buil, I. (2020). Hiding Instagram likes: Effects on negative affect and loneliness. *Personality and Individual Differences. Differences, 170,* e110509. https://doi.org/10.1016/j.paid.2020.110509

FIGURE 2
APA style reference list

Appendix B

Statistical Tests

The purpose of this appendix is to provide the formulas and calculational procedures for analysis of data. Not all possible statistical tests are included, but a variety of tests are given that should be appropriate for many of the research designs you might use.

We will examine both descriptive and inferential statistics. Before you study the statistics, however, you should review the properties of measurement scales described in the chapter "Measurement Concepts." Remember that there are four types of measurement scales: nominal, ordinal, interval, and ratio. Nominal scales have no numerical properties, ordinal scales provide rank-order information only, and interval and ratio scales have equal intervals between the points on the scale. In addition, ratio scales have a true zero point. You will also recall from the chapter "Understanding Research Results: Statistical Inference" that the appropriate statistical analysis is determined by the type of design and by the measurement scale that was used in the study. As we proceed, the discussion of the various statistical tests will draw to your attention the relevant measurement scale restrictions that apply.

The examples here use small and simple data sets, so the calculations can be easily done by hand using a calculator. You will probably use a computer program (such as SPSS, SAS, R, SYSTAT/MYSTAT, or Excel). You might also use a no-cost statistical analysis app such as JASP (https://jasp-stats.org/) or VassarStats (http://vassarstats.net/). However, a review of the underlying calculations will help you understand the output from these computer programs.

DESCRIPTIVE STATISTICS

With a knowledge of the types of measurement scales, we can turn to a consideration of statistical techniques. We can start with two ways of describing a set of scores: central tendency and variability.

Measures of Central Tendency

A measure of central tendency gives a single number that describes how an entire group scores as a whole, or on the average. Three different central tendency measures are available: the mode, the median, and the mean.

TABLE 1 Descriptive statistics for a set of scores

Score	Descriptive statistic
1	Mode = 5
2	Median = 5
4	
4	
5	$\bar{X} = \dfrac{\sum X}{N} = 4.5$
5	
5	
6	Range = 6
6	
7	$S^2 = \dfrac{\sum (X - \bar{X})^2}{N - 1} = \dfrac{\sum X^2 - N\bar{X}^2}{N - 1} = \dfrac{233 - 202.5}{9} = 3.388$
$\sum X = 45$	
$\sum X^2 = 233$	$S = \sqrt{S^2} = 1.84$
$N = 10$	

The Mode The mode is the most frequently occurring score. Table 1 shows a set of scores and the descriptive statistics that are discussed in this section. The most frequently occurring score in these data is 5. No calculations are necessary to find the mode. The mode can be used with any of the four types of measurement scales. However, it is the only measure of central tendency that can be used with nominal scale data. If your variable is measured using non-numeric categories (e.g., major; method used for traveling to campus today), the mode will be the most frequently selected category (e.g., psychology; automobile).

The Median The median is the score that divides the group in half: 50% of the scores are below the median and 50% are above the median. When the scores have been ordered from lowest to highest (as in Table 1), the median is easily found. If there is an odd number of scores, you simply find the middle score. (For example, if there are 11 scores, the sixth score is the median, because there are 5 lower and 5 higher scores.) If there is an even number of scores, the median is the midpoint between the two middle scores. In the data in Table 1, there are 10 scores, so the fifth and sixth scores are the two middle scores. To find the median, we add the two middle scores and divide by 2. Thus, in Table 1, the median is

$$\frac{5 + 5}{2} = 5$$

The median can be used with ordinal, interval, or ratio scale data. It is most likely to be used with ordinal data, however. This is because calculation of the median considers only the rank ordering of scores and not the actual size of the scores.

The Mean

The mean is based on more information about the scores than either the mode or the median. However, it is appropriate only for interval or ratio scale data.

The mean is the sum of the scores in a group divided by the number of scores. The calculational formula for the mean can be expressed as

$$\overline{X} = \frac{\Sigma X}{N}$$

where $\overline{X}$ is the symbol for the mean. In this formula, X represents a score obtained by an individual, and the Σ symbol indicates that scores are to be summed or added. The symbol ΣX can be read as "sum of the Xs" and simply is an indication that the scores are to be added. Thus, ΣX in the data from Table 1 is

$$1 + 2 + 4 + 4 + 5 + 5 + 5 + 6 + 6 + 7 = 45$$

The N in the formula symbolizes the number of scores in the group. In our example, $N = 10$. Thus, we can now calculate the mean:

$$\overline{X} = \frac{\Sigma X}{N} = \frac{45}{10} = 4.5$$

Measures of Variability

In addition to describing the central tendency of the set of scores, we want to describe how much the scores vary. That is, how much spread is there in the set of scores?

The Range

The range is the highest score minus the lowest score. In our example, the range is 6. The range is not a very useful statistic, however, because it is based on only two scores in the distribution. It does not take into account all of the information that is available in the entire set of scores.

The Variance and Standard Deviation

The variance and a related statistic called the standard deviation use all the scores to yield a measure of variability. The variance indicates the degree to which scores vary about the group mean. The formula for the variance (symbolized as s^2) is

$$s^2 = \frac{\Sigma (X - \overline{X})^2}{N - 1}$$

where $(X - \overline{X})^2$ is an individual score, X, minus the mean, $\overline{X}$, and then squared. Thus $(X - \overline{X})^2$ is the squared deviation of each score from the mean. The Σ sign indicates that these squared deviation scores are to be summed. Finally, dividing by $N - 1$ gives the mean of the squared deviations. The variance, then, is the mean of the squared deviations from the group mean. (Squared deviations are used because simple deviations would add up to zero. $N - 1$ is used in most cases for statistical purposes because the scores represent a sample and not an entire population. As the sample size becomes larger, it makes little difference whether N or $N - 1$ is used.)

The data in Table 1 can be used to illustrate calculation of the variance. $\sum (X - \overline{X})^2$ is equal to

$$(1 - 4.5)^2 + (2 - 4.5)^2 + (4 - 4.5)^2 + (4 - 4.5)^2 + (5 - 4.5)^2 + (5 - 4.5)^2$$
$$+ (5 - 4.5)^2 + (6 - 4.5)^2 + (6 - 4.5)^2 + (7 - 4.5)^2 = 30.50$$

The next step is to divide $\sum (X - \overline{X})^2$ by $N - 1$. The calculation for the variance, then, is

$$s^2 = \frac{\sum (X - \overline{X})^2}{N - 1} = \frac{30.50}{9} = 3.388$$

A simpler, and equivalent, calculational formula for the variance is

$$s^2 = \frac{\sum X^2 - N\overline{X}^2}{N - 1}$$

where $\sum X^2$ is the sum of the squared individual scores, and $\overline{X}^2$ is the mean squared. You can confirm that the two formulas are identical by computing the variance using this simpler formula. (Remember that $\sum X^2$ tells you to square each score and then sum the squared scores.)

The standard deviation is the square root of the variance. Because the variance uses squared scores, the variance does not describe the amount of variability in the same units of measurement as the original scale. The standard deviation (s) corrects this problem. Thus, the standard deviation is the average deviation of scores from the mean.

STATISTICAL SIGNIFICANCE AND EFFECT SIZE

This section describes several statistical significance tests. These tests are used to determine the probability that the outcome of the research was due to chance. All use the logic of the null hypothesis discussed in the chapter "Understanding Research Results: Statistical Inference." We will consider two significance tests in this section: the chi-square test and the analysis of variance or F test.

Chi-Square (χ^2)

The chi-square (Greek letter chi, squared) test is used when dealing with nominal scale data. It is used when the data consist of frequencies—the number of subjects who fall into each of several categories.

Chi-square can be used with either experimental or nonexperimental data. The major requirement is that both variables are studied using nominal scales.

Example   Suppose you want to know whether there is a relationship between optimism and preferences for easy or difficult goals. To answer this question, you ask people to describe themselves as either an "optimist" or "pessimist" – your sample is composed of 50 optimists and 50 pessimists. Each participant receives the same description of three potential tasks: (1) an easy task with a $1 prize for successful completion, (2) a moderately difficult task with a $10 prize, and (3) a very difficult task with an associated $20 prize. The participant then makes their choice of preferred task and the study is complete.

Fictitious data for such a study are presented in Table 2. The frequencies labeled as "O" in each of the six cells in the table refer to the *observed* number of pessimist and optimist subjects who chose each of the three tasks. The frequencies labeled "E" refer to frequencies that are *expected* if the null hypothesis is correct. It is important that each subject falls into only one of the cells when using chi-square (that is, no subject can be counted as both optimist and pessimist or choosing more than one task.

TABLE 2   Data for hypothetical study on optimism—pessimism: Chi-square test

Task Difficulty	Optimism Category		Row totals
	Pessimists	Optimists	
Easy—$1	$O_1 = 20$ $E_1 = 12.5$	$O_2 = 5$ $E_2 = 12.5$	25
Moderate—$10	$O_3 = 10$ $E_3 = 22.5$	$O_4 = 35$ $E_4 = 22.5$	45
Difficult—$20	$O_5 = 20$ $E_5 = 15$	$O_6 = 10$ $E_6 = 15$	30
Column totals	50	50	$N = 100$

Computations:	Cell number	$\dfrac{(O - E)^2}{E}$
	1	4.50
	2	4.50
	3	6.94
	4	6.94
	5	1.67
	6	1.67
		$\Sigma = 26.22 = \chi^2$

The chi-square test examines the extent to which the frequencies that are actually observed in the study differ from the frequencies that are expected if the null hypothesis is correct. The null hypothesis states that there is no relationship between optimism and task preference: Optimists and pessimists have the same preferences when making their choice.

The formula for computing chi-square is

$$\chi^2 = \Sigma \frac{(O - E)^2}{E}$$

where O is the *observed* frequency in each cell, E is the *expected* frequency in each cell, and the symbol Σ refers to summing over all cells. The steps in calculating the value of χ^2 are these:

Step 1: Arrange the observed frequencies in a table such as Table 2. Note that in addition to the observed frequencies in each cell, the table presents row totals, column totals, and the total number of observations (N).

Step 2: Calculate the expected frequencies for each of the cells in the table. The expected frequency formula is

$$E = \frac{\text{row total} \times \text{column total}}{N}$$

where the row total refers to the row total for the cell, and the column total refers to the column total for the cell. Thus, the expected frequency for cell 1 (easy task-difficulty for pessimists) is

$$E_1 = \frac{50 \times 25}{100} = 12.50$$

The expected frequencies for each of the cells are shown in Table 2 below the observed frequencies.

Step 3: Calculate the quantity $(O - E)^2/E$ for each cell. For cell 1, this quantity is

$$\frac{(20 - 12.5)^2}{12.5} = \frac{56.25}{12.5} = 4.50$$

Step 4: Find the value of χ^2 by summing the $(O - E)^2/E$ values found in step 3. The calculations for obtaining χ^2 for the example data are shown in Table 2.

Significance of Chi-Square

The significance of the obtained χ^2 value can be evaluated by consulting a table of critical values of χ^2. The critical χ^2 values indicate the value that the *obtained* χ^2 must equal or exceed to be significant at the .10 level, the .05 level, and the .01 level. A table of critical χ^2 values is easy to obtain (e.g., http://www.itl.nist.gov/div898/handbook/eda/section3/eda3674.htm).

To be able to use the table of critical values of χ^2 as well as most other statistical tables, you must understand the concept of *degrees of freedom* (df). The critical value of χ^2 for any given study depends on the degrees of freedom. Degrees of freedom refers to the number of scores that are free to vary. In the table of categories for a chi-square test, the number of degrees of freedom is the number of cells in which the frequencies are free to vary once we know the row totals and column totals. The degrees of freedom for chi-square is easily calculated:

$$df = (R - 1)(C - 1)$$

where R is the number of rows in the table and C is the number of columns. In our example in Table 2, there are two columns (pessimist; optimist) and three rows (easy; moderate; difficult), so there are 2 degrees of freedom. In a study with three rows and three columns, there are 4 degrees of freedom, and so on.

In a table of critical χ^2 values, find the correct degrees of freedom and then determine the critical value of χ^2 necessary to reject the null hypothesis at the chosen significance level. With 2 degrees of freedom, the obtained χ^2 value must be *equal to* or *greater than* the critical value of 5.991 to be significant at the .05 level. There is only a .05 probability that a χ^2 of 5.991 would occur if only random error is operating. Because the obtained χ^2 from our example is 26.22, we can reject the null hypothesis that there is no relationship between optimism and task preference.

There is an easy alternative method of determining if your obtained χ^2 is significant: Use an application that provides the exact null hypothesis probability of your χ^2 value. Such an application is located at http://vassarstats.net/tabs.html#csq. Simply input your obtained χ^2 value and degrees of freedom and the output is the probability.

Effect Size for the Chi-Square Statistic

Measures of effect size indicate the strength of association between variables. Results range from 0.00, which indicates no relationship, to 1.00. Correlations above .50 are considered to show very strong relationships. In much research, expect correlations between about .15 and .40. Correlations between about .10 and .20 are weaker, but can be statistically significant with large sample sizes. They can also be important for theoretical and even practical reasons.

The chi-square (χ^2) test was described previously. In addition to determining whether there is a significant relationship, you want an indicator of effect size to tell you the strength of association between the variables. For the optimism example, a statistic called Cramer's V (or phi) is appropriate. The V coefficient is computed after obtaining the value of chi-square. The formula is

$$V = \sqrt{\frac{\chi^2}{N(k - 1)}}$$

In this formula, N is the total number of cases or subjects and k is the smaller of the rows or columns in the table (thus, in our example in Table 2, there are three rows for levels of task difficulty and two columns for level of optimism, and the value of k is 2, the lower value).

The value of V for the example in Table 2 is

$$V = \sqrt{\frac{26.22}{100(2 - 1)}} = \sqrt{.262} = .51$$

Because the significance of the chi-square value has already been determined, no further significance testing is necessary.

Concluding Remarks   The chi-square test is extremely useful and is used frequently in all of the behavioral sciences. The calculational formula described is generalizable to expanded studies in which there are more categories on either of the variables. One note of caution, however: When both variables have only two categories, so that there are only two rows and two columns, the formula for calculating chi-square changes slightly. In such cases, the formula is

$$\chi^2 = \Sigma \frac{(|O - E| - .5)^2}{E}$$

where $|O - E|$ is the absolute value of $O - E$, and .5 is a constant that is subtracted for each cell.

Analysis of Variance (F Test)

The analysis of variance, or F test, is used to determine whether there is a significant difference between groups that have been measured on either interval or ratio scales. The analysis of variance may be used with either independent groups or repeated measures designs. Procedures for calculating F for both types of designs are presented.

Analysis of Variance: One Independent Variable

To illustrate the use of the analysis of variance, let's consider a hypothetical experiment on physical distance and self-disclosure. You think that people will reveal more about themselves to an interviewer when they are sitting close to the interviewer than they will when sitting farther away. To test this idea, you conduct an experiment on interviewing. Participants are told that interviewing techniques are being studied. Each participant is seated in a room; the interviewer comes into the room and sits at one of three distances from the participant: close (2 feet, or .61 meter), medium (4 feet, or 1.22 meters), or far (6 feet, or 1.83 meters). The distance chosen by the interviewer is the independent variable manipulation. Participants are randomly assigned to the three distance conditions, and the interviewer's behavior is constant in all conditions. The interview consists of a number of questions, and the dependent variable is the number of personal, revealing statements made by the participant during the interview.

   Fictitious data for such an experiment are shown in Table 3. Note that this is an independent groups (between-subjects) design with five participants in each group. The calculations of the systematic variance and error variance involve computing the *sum of squares* for the different types of variance.

Sum of Squares   Sum of squares stands for the *sum of squared deviations from the mean*. Computing an analysis of variance for the data in Table 3 involves three sums of squares: (1) SS_{TOTAL}, the sum of squared deviations of each

TABLE 3 Data for hypothetical experiment on distance and self-disclosure: Analysis of variance

Distance (A)		
Close (A1)	Medium (A2)	Far (A3)
33	21	20
24	25	13
31	19	15
29	27	10
34	26	14
$T_{A1} = 151$	$T_{A2} = 118$	$T_{A3} = 72$
$n_{A1} = 5$	$n_{A2} = 5$	$n_{A3} = 5$
$\overline{X}_{A1} = 30.20$	$\overline{X}_{A2} = 23.60$	$\overline{X}_{A3} = 14.40$
$\sum X_{A1}^2 = 4623$	$\sum X_{A2}^2 = 2832$	$\sum X_{A3}^2 = 1090$
$T_{A1}^2 = 22801$	$T_{A2}^2 = 13924$	$T_{A3}^2 = 5184$

$$SS_{TOTAL} = \sum X^2 - \frac{G^2}{N} = (4623 + 2832 + 1090) - \frac{(151 + 118 + 72)^2}{15}$$

$$= 8545 - 7752.07 = 792.93$$

$$SS_A = \sum \frac{T_a^2}{n_a} - \frac{G^2}{N} = \left[\frac{(151)^2}{5} + \frac{(118)^2}{5} + \frac{(72)^2}{5}\right] - 7752.07$$

$$= 8381.80 - 7752.07 = 629.73$$

$$SS_{ERROR} = \sum X^2 - \sum \frac{T_a^2}{n_a} = 8545 - 8381.80 = 163.20$$

individual score from the grand mean; (2) SS_A, the sum of squared deviations of each of the group means from the grand mean; and (3) SS_{ERROR}, the sum of squared deviations of the individual scores from their respective group means. The "A" in SS_A is used to indicate that we are dealing with the systematic variance associated with independent variable A.

The three sums of squares are deviations from a mean. (Recall that we calculated such deviations earlier when discussing the variance in a set of scores.) We could calculate the deviations directly with the data in Table 3, but such calculations are hard to work with, so we will use simplified formulas for computational purposes.

The computational formulas are

$$SS_{TOTAL} = \sum X^2 - \frac{G^2}{N}$$

$$SS_A = \sum \frac{T_a^2}{n_a} - \frac{G^2}{N}$$

$$SS_{ERROR} = \sum X^2 - \sum \frac{T_a^2}{n_a}$$

You might note here that $SS_{TOTAL} = SS_A + SS_{ERROR}$. The actual computations are shown in Table 3.

SS_{TOTAL} The formula for SS_{TOTAL} is

$$\Sigma X^2 - \frac{G^2}{N}$$

ΣX^2 is the sum of the squared scores of all subjects in the experiment. Each of the scores is squared first and then added. Thus, for the data in Table 3, ΣX^2 is $33^2 + 24^2 + 31^2$ and so on until all of the scores have been squared and added. If you are doing the calculations by hand or with a pocket calculator, it may be convenient to find the ΣX^2 for the scores in each group and then add these up for your final computation. This is what I did for the data in the table. The G in the formula stands for the grand total of all of the scores. This involves adding up the scores for all subjects. The grand total is then squared and divided by N, the total number of subjects in the experiment. When computing the sum of squares, you should always keep the calculations clearly labeled, because you can simplify later calculations by referring to these earlier ones. Once you have computed SS_{TOTAL}, you can calculate SS_A.

SS_A The formula for SS_A is

$$\Sigma \frac{T_a^2}{n_a} - \frac{G^2}{N}$$

The T_a in this formula refers to the total of the scores in Group a of independent variable A. (T_a is a shorthand notation for ΣX in each group. Recall the computation of ΣX from our discussion of the mean. The T_a symbol is used to avoid having to deal with too many Σ signs in our calculation procedures.) The a is used to symbolize the particular group number; thus, T_a is a general symbol for T_1, T_2, and T_3. Looking at our data in Table 3, $T_1 = 151$, $T_2 = 118$, and $T_3 = 72$. These are the sums of the scores in each of the groups. After T_a has been calculated, T_a^2 is found by squaring T_a. Now, T_a^2 is divided by n_a, the number of subjects in Group a. Once the quantity T_a^2/n_a^a has been computed for each group, the quantities are summed as indicated by the Σ symbol.

Note that the second part of the formula, G^2/N, was calculated when SS_{TOTAL} was obtained. Because we already have this quantity, it need not be calculated again when computing SS_A. After obtaining SS_A, we can now compute SS_{ERROR}.

SS_{ERROR} The formula for SS_{ERROR} is

$$\Sigma X^2 - \Sigma \frac{T_a^2}{n_a}$$

Both of these quantities were calculated above in obtaining SS_{TOTAL} and SS_A. To obtain SS_{ERROR}, we merely have to find these quantities and perform the proper subtraction.

TABLE 4 Analysis of variance summary table

Source of variance	Sum of squares	df	Mean square	F
A	SS_A	$a - 1$	SS_A/df_A	MS_A/MS_{ERROR}
Error	SS_{ERROR}	$N - a$	SS_{ERROR}/df_{ERROR}	
Total	SS_{TOTAL}	$N - 1$		
A	629.73	2	314.87	23.15
Error	163.20	12	13.60	
Total	792.93	14		

As a check on the calculations, we can make sure that $SS_{TOTAL} = SS_A + SS_{ERROR}$. The next step in the computation of the analysis of variance is to find the *mean square* for each of the sums of squares. We can then find the value of F. The necessary computations are shown in an analysis of variance summary table in Table 4. Constructing a summary table is the easiest way to complete the computations.

Mean Squares
After obtaining the sum of squares, it is necessary to compute the mean squares. Mean square stands for the *mean of the sum of the squared deviations from the mean* or, more simply, the mean of the sum of squares. The mean square (MS) is the sum of squares divided by the degrees of freedom. The degrees of freedom are determined by the number of scores in the sum of squares that are free to vary. The mean squares are the variances that are used in computing the value of F.

From Table 4 you can see that the mean squares that concern us are the mean square for A (systematic variance) and the mean square for error (error variance). The formulas are

$$MS_A = SS_A/df_A$$
$$MS_{ERROR} = SS_{ERROR}/df_{ERROR}$$

where $df_A = a - 1$ (the number of groups minus one) and $df_{ERROR} = N - a$ (the total number of subjects minus the number of groups).

Obtaining the F Value
The obtained F is found by dividing MS_A by MS_{ERROR}. If only random error is operating, the expected value of F is 1.0. The greater the F value, the lower the probability that the results of the experiment were due to chance error.

Significance of F
To determine the significance of the obtained F value, it is necessary to compare the obtained F to a critical value of F. A table of critical values of F for significance levels of .05 and .01 may be found at http://www.itl.nist.gov/div898/handbook/eda/section3/eda3673.htm. To find the critical value of F, locate on the table the degrees of freedom for the numerator of the ratio (the systematic variance) and the degrees of freedom for the

denominator of the F ratio (the error variance). The intersection of these two degrees of freedom on the table is the critical F value.

The appropriate degrees of freedom for our sample data are 2 and 12 (see Table 4). The critical F value is 3.89 for a .05 level of significance. For the results to be significant, the obtained F value must be equal to or greater than the critical value. Because the obtained value of F in Table 4 (23.15) is greater than the critical value, we conclude that the results are significant and reject the null hypothesis that the means of the groups are equal in the population. A calculator to obtain an exact probability could also be used (e.g., http://vassarstats.net/tabs.html#f).

Effect Size for the F Statistic

After computing an analysis of variance and evaluating the significance of the F statistic, you need to examine effect size. *Eta* is a type of correlation coefficient that can be calculated easily. The formula is

$$\text{eta} = \sqrt{\frac{\text{between group (systematic) variance}}{\text{total variance}}}$$

In the experiment on interpersonal distance and disclosure previously described, the SS_A was 629.73, and the SS_{TOTAL} was 792.93. The value of eta then would be

$$\text{eta} = \sqrt{\frac{629.73}{792.93}}$$
$$= .89$$

This is a very high correlation, reflecting the fact that the data were all generated for ease of computation.

Concluding Remarks   The analysis of variance for one independent variable with an independent groups design can be used when there are two or more groups in the experiment. The general formulas described are appropriate for all such designs. Also, the calculations are the same whether the experimental or the correlational method is used to form the groups. The formulas are also applicable to cases in which the number of subjects in each group is not equal (although you should have approximately equal numbers of subjects in the groups).

When the design of the experiment includes more than two levels of the independent variable (as in our example experiment, which had three groups), the obtained F value does not tell us whether any two specific groups are significantly different from one another. One way to examine the difference between two groups in such a study is to use the formula for SS_A to compute the sum of squares and the mean square for the two groups (the df in this case is $2 - 1$). When doing this, the previously calculated MS_{ERROR} should be used as the error variance term for computing F. More complicated procedures for evaluating the difference between two groups in such designs are available, and easily calculated with statistical software.

Analysis of Variance: Two Independent Variables

In this section, we will describe the computations for analysis of variance with a factorial design containing two independent variables. The formulas apply to an $A \times B$ factorial design with any number of levels of the independent variables. The formulas apply only to a completely independent groups design with different subjects in each group, and the number of subjects in each group must be equal. Once you understand this analysis, however, you should have little trouble understanding the analysis for more complicated designs with repeated measures or unequal numbers of subjects. With these limitations in mind, let's consider example data from a hypothetical experiment.

The experiment uses a 2×2 factorial design. Variable A is the type of instruction used in a course, and variable B is the warmth of the instructor. For variable A, students are randomly assigned to one of two types of instruction: (1) the traditional lecture method, or (2) an individualized learning approach with frequent testing over small amounts of material, proctors to help individual students, and a stipulation that students master each section of material before going on to the next section. The information presented to students in the four classes is identical. For variable B, students are randomly assigned to one of two instructor warmth conditions. In one group, students are sent encouraging, personalized, messages from the instructor (high warmth); in the other group, students are sent messages that note due-dates (low warmth). At the end of the course, all students take the same test, which covers all of the material presented in the course. The score on this examination is the dependent variable.

Table 5 shows fictitious data for such an experiment, with five participants in each condition. This design allows us to evaluate three effects—the main effect of A, the main effect of B, and the $A \times B$ interaction. The main effect of A is whether one type of instruction is superior to the other; the main effect of B is whether students with the high-warmth instructor score differently on the test than do students with the low-warmth instructor; the $A \times B$ interaction examines whether the effect of one independent variable is different depending on the particular level of the other variable.

The computation of the analysis of variance starts with calculation of the sum of squares for the following sources of variance in the data: SS_{TOTAL}, SS_A, SS_B, $SS_{A \times B}$, and SS_{ERROR}. The procedures for calculation are similar to the calculations performed for the analysis of variance with one independent variable. The numerical calculations for the example data are shown in Table 6. We can now consider each of these calculations.

SS_{TOTAL} The SS_{TOTAL} is computed in the same way as the previous analysis formula. The formula is

$$SS_{TOTAL} = \sum X^2 - \frac{G^2}{N}$$

where $\sum X^2$ is the sum of the squared scores of all subjects in the experiment, G is the grand total of all of the scores, and N is the total number of subjects. It is usually easiest to calculate $\sum X^2$ and G in smaller steps by calculating subtotals

TABLE 5   Data for hypothetical experiment on the effect of type of instruction and instructor warmth on exam score: Analysis of variance

	Instructor Warmth (B)		
	Low (B1)	High (B2)	
Traditional lecture (A1)	75	90	
	70	95	
	69	89	
	72	85	
	68	91	
	$T_{A1B1} = 354$	$T_{A1B2} = 450$	$T_{A1} = 804$
	$\sum X^2_{A1B1} = 25094$	$\sum X^2_{A1B2} = 40552$	$n_{A1} = 10$
	$n_{A1B1} = 5$	$n_{A1B2} = 5$	$\overline{X}_{A1} = 80.40$
	$\overline{X}_{A1B1} = 70.80$	$\overline{X}_{A1B2} = 90.00$	
Individualized method (A2)	85	87	
	87	94	
	83	93	
	90	89	
	89	92	
	$T_{A2B1} = 434$	$T_{A2B2} = 455$	$T_{A2} = 889$
	$\sum X^2_{A2B1} = 37704$	$\sum X^2_{A2B2} = 41439$	$n_{A2} = 10$
	$n_{A2B1} = 5$	$n_{A2B2} = 5$	$\overline{X}_{A2} = 88.90$
	$\overline{X}_{A2B1} = 86.80$	$\overline{X}_{A2B2} = 91.00$	
	$T_{B1} = 788$	$T_{B2} = 905$	
	$n_{B1} = 10$	$n_{B2} = 10$	
	$\overline{X}_{B1} = 78.80$	$\overline{X}_{B2} = 90.50$	

separately for each group in the design. The subtotals are then added. This is the procedure followed in Tables 5 and 6.

SS_A The formula for SS_A is

$$SS_A = \frac{\sum T_a^2}{n_a} - \frac{G^2}{N}$$

where $\sum T_a^2$ is the sum of the squared totals of the scores in each of the groups of independent variable A, and n_a is the number of subjects in each level of independent variable A. When calculating SS_A, we consider only the groups of independent variable A without considering the particular level of B. In other words, the totals for each group of the A variable are obtained by considering all subjects in that level of A, irrespective of which condition of B the subject may be in. The quantity of G^2-/N was previously calculated for SS_{TOTAL}.

TABLE 6   Computations for analysis of variance with two independent variables

$$SS_{TOTAL} = \sum X^2 - \frac{G^2}{N} = (25094 + 40552 + 37704 + 41439)$$
$$- \frac{(354 + 450 + 434 + 455)^2}{20}$$
$$= 144789 - 143312.45$$
$$= 1476.55$$

$$SS_A = \frac{\sum T_a^2}{n_a} - \frac{G^2}{N} = \frac{(804)^2 + (889)^2}{10} - 143312.45$$
$$= 143673.70 - 143312.45$$
$$= 361.25$$

$$SS_B = \frac{\sum T_b^2}{n_b} - \frac{G^2}{N} = \frac{(788)^2 + (905)^2}{10} - 143312.45$$
$$= 143996.90 - 143312.45$$
$$= 684.45$$

$$SS_{A \times B} = \frac{\sum T_{ab}^2}{n_{ab}} - \frac{G^2}{N} - SS_A - SS_B = \frac{(354)^2 + (450)^2 + (434)^2 + (455)^2}{5}$$
$$- 143312.45 - 361.25 - 684.45$$
$$= 144639.40 - 143312.45 - 361.25 - 684.45$$
$$= 281.25$$

$$SS_{ERROR} = \sum X^2 - \frac{\sum T_{ab}^2}{n_{ab}} = 144789 - 144639.40$$
$$= 149.60$$

SS_B The formula for SS_B is

$$SS_B = \frac{\sum T_b^2}{n_b} - \frac{G^2}{N}$$

SS_B is calculated in the same way as SS_A. The only difference is that we are calculating totals of the groups of independent variable B.

$SS_{A \times B}$ The formula for $SS_{A \times B}$ is

$$SS_{A \times B} = \frac{\sum T_{ab}^2}{n_{ab}} - \frac{G^2}{N} - SS_A - SS_B$$

The sum of squares for the $A \times B$ interaction is computed by first calculating the quantity $\sum T_{ab}^2$. This involves squaring the total of the scores in each of the ab conditions in the experiment. In our example experiment in Table 5, there are four conditions; the interaction calculation considers *all* of the groups. Each of the group totals is squared, and then the sum of the squared totals is obtained. This sum is divided by n_{ab}, the number of subjects in each group. The other quantities in the formula for $SS_{A \times B}$ have already been calculated, so the computation of $SS_{A \times B}$ is relatively straightforward.

SS_{ERROR} The quantities involved in the SS_{ERROR} formula have already been calculated. The formula is

$$SS_{ERROR} = \sum X^2 - \frac{\sum T_{ab}^2}{n_{ab}}$$

These quantities were calculated previously, so we merely have to perform the proper subtraction to complete the computation of SS_{ERROR}.

At this point, you may want to practice calculating the sums of squares using the data in Table 5. As a check on the calculations, make sure that $SS_{TOTAL} = SS_A + SS_B + SS_{A\times B} + SS_{ERROR}$.

After obtaining the sums of squares, the next step is to find the mean square for each of the sources of variance. The easiest way to do this is to use an analysis of variance summary table like Table 7.

Mean Square   The mean square for each of the sources of variance is the sum of squares divided by the degrees of freedom. The formulas for the degrees of freedom and the mean square are shown in the top portion of Table 7, and the computed values are shown in the bottom portion of the table.

Obtaining the F value   The F value for each of the three sources of systematic variance (main effects for A and B, and the interaction) is obtained by dividing the appropriate mean square by the MS_{ERROR}. We now have three obtained F values and can evaluate the significance of the main effects and the interaction.

Significance of F   To determine whether an obtained F is significant, we need to find the critical value of F from http://vassarstats.net/textbook/apx_d.html. For all of the Fs in the analysis of variance summary table, the degrees of freedom are 1 and 16. Let's assume that a .01 significance level for rejecting the null hypothesis was chosen. The critical F at .01 for 1 and 16 degrees of freedom is

TABLE 7   Analysis of variance summary table: Two independent variables

Source of variance	Sum of squares	df	Mean square	F
A	SS_A	$a-1$	SS_A/df_A	MS_A/MS_{ERROR}
B	SS_B	$b-1$	SS_B/df_B	MS_B/MS_{ERROR}
$A \times B$	$SS_{A\times B}$	$(a-1)(b-1)$	$SS_{A\times B}/df_{A\times B}$	$MS_{A\times B}/MS_{ERROR}$
Error	SS_{ERROR}	$N-ab$	SS_{ERROR}/df_{ERROR}	
Total	SS_{TOTAL}			
A	361.25	1	361.25	38.64
B	684.45	1	684.45	73.20
$A \times B$	281.25	1	281.25	30.08
Error	149.60	16	9.35	
Total	1476.55	19		

8.53. If the obtained F is larger than 8.53, we can say that the results are significant at the .01 level. By referring to the obtained Fs in Table 7, you can see that the main effects and the interaction are all significant. I will leave it to you to interpret the main effect means and to graph the interaction. If you do not recall how to do this, you should review the material in the chapter "Complex Experimental Designs."

Analysis of Variance: Repeated Measures (Within Subjects)

The analysis of variance computations considered thus far have been limited to independent groups (between-subjects) designs. This section considers the computations for analysis of variance of a repeated measures (within-subjects) design with one independent variable.

Fictitious data for a hypothetical experiment using a repeated measures design are presented in Table 8. The experiment examines the effect of a job candidate's physical attractiveness on judgments of the candidate's competence. The independent variable is the candidate's physical attractiveness; the dependent variable is judged competence on a 10-point scale. Participants in the experiment view two videotapes of different females performing a mechanical aptitude task that involved piecing together a number of parts. The two females do equally well, but one is physically attractive and the other is unattractive. The order of presentation of the two tapes is counterbalanced to control for order effects.

The main difference between the repeated measures analysis of variance and the independent groups analysis described earlier is that the effect of subject differences becomes a source of variance. There are four sources of variance in the repeated measures analysis of variance, and so four sums of squares are calculated:

$$SS_{TOTAL} = \sum X^2 - \frac{G^2}{N}$$

$$SS_A = \frac{\sum T_a^2}{n_a} - \frac{G^2}{N}$$

$$SS_{SUBJECTS} = \frac{\sum T_s^2}{n_s} - \frac{G^2}{N}$$

$$SS_{ERROR} = SS_{TOTAL} - SS_A - SS_{SUBJECTS}$$

The calculations for these sums of squares are shown in the lower portion of Table 8. The quantities in the formula should be familiar to you by now. The only new quantity involves the calculation of $SS_{SUBJECTS}$. The term T_s^2 refers to the squared total score of each subject—that is, the squared total of the scores that each subject gives when measured in the different groups in the experiment. The quantity $\sum T_s^2$ refers to the sum of these squared totals for all subjects. The calculation of $SS_{SUBJECTS}$ is completed by dividing $\sum T_s^2$ by n_s and then subtracting by G^2/N. The term n_s refers to the number of scores that each subject gives. Because our hypothetical experiment has two groups, $n_s = 2$, the total for each subject is based on two scores.

TABLE 8 Data for hypothetical experiment on attractiveness and judged competence: Repeated measures analysis of variance

Subjects (or subject pairs)	Condition (A)		T_S	T_s^2
	Unattractive candidate (A_1)	Attractive candidate (A_1)		
#1	6	8	14	196
#2	5	6	11	121
#3	5	9	14	196
#4	7	6	13	169
#5	4	6	10	100
#6	3	5	8	64
#7	5	5	10	100
#8	4	7	11	121
	$T_{A1} = 39$	$T_{A2} = 52$	$\sum T_S^2 = 1067$	
	$\sum X_{A1}^2 = 201$	$\sum X_{A2}^2 = 352$		
	$n_{A1} = 8$	$n_{A2} = 8$		
	$\overline{X}_{A1} = 4.88$	$\overline{X}_{A2} = 6.50$		

$$SS_{Total} = \sum X^2 - \frac{G^2}{N} = (201 + 352) - \frac{(39 + 52)^2}{16}$$

$$= 553 - 517.56$$

$$= 35.44$$

$$SS_A = \frac{\sum T_a^2}{n_a} - \frac{G^2}{N} = \frac{(39)^2 + (52)^2}{8} - 517.56$$

$$= 528.13 - 517.56$$

$$= 10.57$$

$$SS_{SUBJECTS} = \frac{\sum T_s^2}{n_s} - \frac{G^2}{N} = \frac{1067}{2} - 517.56$$

$$= 533.50 - 517.56$$

$$= 15.94$$

$$SS_{ERROR} = SS_{TOTAL} - SS_A - SS_{SUBJECTS} = 35.44 - 10.57 - 15.94$$

$$= 8.93$$

An analysis of variance summary table is shown in Table 9. The procedures for computing the mean squares and obtaining F are similar to our previous calculations. Note that the mean square and F for the subjects' source of variance are not computed. There is usually no reason to know or care whether subjects differ significantly from one another. The ability to calculate this source of variance does have the advantage of reducing the amount of error variance—in an independent groups design, subject differences are part of the error variance. Because there is only one score per subject in the independent groups design, it is impossible to estimate the influence of subject differences.

TABLE 9 Analysis of variance summary table: Repeated measures design

Source of variance	Sum of squares	df	Mean square	F
A	SS_A	$a - 1$	SS_A/df_A	MS_A/MS_{ERROR}
Subjects	$SS_{SUBJECTS}$	$s - 1$	—	
Error	SS_{ERROR}	$(a - 1)(s - 1)$	SS_{ERROR}/df_{ERROR}	
Total	SS_{TOTAL}	$N - 1$		
A	10.57	1	10.57	8.26
Subjects	15.94	7	—	
Error	8.93	7	1.28	
Total	35.44	15		

You can use the summary table and the table of critical F values to determine whether the difference between the two groups is significant. The procedures are identical to those discussed previously.

Analysis of Variance: Conclusion

The analysis of variance is a very useful statistical procedure that can be extended to any type of factorial design, including those that use both independent groups and repeated measures in the same design. The method of computing analysis of variance is much the same regardless of the complexity of the design. A section on analysis of variance as brief as this cannot hope to cover all of the many aspects of such a general statistical technique. However, you should now have the background to compute an analysis of variance and to understand the more detailed discussions of analysis of variance in advanced statistics texts.

Pearson Product-Moment Correlation Coefficient

The Pearson product-moment correlation coefficient (r) is used to find the strength of the relationship between two variables that have been measured on interval or ratio scales.

Example Suppose you want to know whether travel experiences are related to knowledge of geography. In your study, you give a 15-item quiz on North American geography, and you also ask how many states and Canadian provinces participants have visited. After obtaining the pairs of observations from each participant, a Pearson r can be computed to measure the strength of the relationship between travel experience and knowledge of geography.

Table 10 presents fictitious data from such a study along with the calculations for r. The calculational formula for r is

$$r = \frac{N\Sigma XY - \Sigma X\Sigma Y}{\sqrt{N\Sigma X^2 - (\Sigma X)^2}\sqrt{N\Sigma Y^2 - (\Sigma Y^2)}}$$

TABLE 10   Data for hypothetical study on travel and knowledge of geography: Pearson r

Subject identification number	Travel score (X)	Knowledge score (Y)	XY
01	4	10	40
02	6	15	90
03	7	8	56
04	8	9	72
05	8	7	56
06	12	10	120
07	14	15	210
08	15	13	195
09	15	15	225
10	17	14	238
	$\Sigma X = 106$	$\Sigma Y = 116$	$\Sigma XY = 1302$
	$\Sigma X^2 = 1308$	$\Sigma Y^2 = 1434$	
	$(\Sigma X^2) = 11236$	$(\Sigma Y^2) = 13456$	

Computation:

$$r = \frac{N\Sigma XY - \Sigma X \Sigma Y}{\sqrt{N\Sigma X^2 - (\Sigma X)^2}\sqrt{N\Sigma Y^2 - (\Sigma Y)^2}}$$

$$= \frac{10(1302) - (106)(116)}{\sqrt{10(1308) - 11236}\sqrt{10(1434) - 13456}}$$

$$= \frac{13020 - 12296}{\sqrt{13080 - 11236}\sqrt{14340 - 13456}}$$

$$= \frac{724}{\sqrt{1844}\sqrt{844}}$$

$$= \frac{724}{1276.61}$$

$$= .567$$

where X refers to a subject's score on variable X, and Y is a subject's score on variable Y. In Table 10, the travel experience score is variable X, and the geography knowledge score is variable Y. In the formula, N is the number of paired observations (that is, the number of participants measured on both variables).

The calculation of r requires a number of arithmetic operations on the X and Y scores. ΣX is simply the sum of the scores on variable X. ΣX^2 is the sum of the squared scores on X (each score is first squared and then the sum of the squared scores is obtained). The quantity $(\Sigma X)^2$ is the square of the sum of the scores: The total of the X scores (ΣX) is first calculated and then this total is squared. It is important not to confuse the two quantities, ΣX^2 and $(\Sigma X)^2$. The same calculations are made, using the Y scores, to obtain ΣY, ΣY^2, and $(\Sigma Y)^2$. To find ΣXY, each participant's X score is multiplied by the score on Y; these values are then summed for all subjects. When these calculations have been made, r is computed using the formula for r given above.

At this point, you may wish to examine carefully the calculations shown in Table 10 to familiarize yourself with the procedures for computing r. You might then try calculating r from another set of data, such as the seating pattern and exam score study shown in the chapter "Understanding Research Results: Description and Correlation," Table 2.

Significance of r The null hypothesis is that the population correlation coefficient is in fact 0.00. To test this hypothesis, you can consult a table of critical values of r or use a simple calculator application to provide the probability of obtaining your correlation value if the null hypothesis is true. Let's use the calculator at http://vassarstats.net/tabs.html#r. Here you input your obtained r (.567) and the total number of paired observations (10). The output shows the degrees of freedom ($N - 2$) and the p value associated with $r = .567$. In this case, $p = .087$ (2-tailed). If the alpha for significance is .05, we cannot reject the null hypothesis. If using a table of critical values of r, you would find that the .05 critical value is .632; because the obtained correlation coefficient is .567, you would conclude that the correlation is not significant.

Notice that we do not reject the null hypothesis in this case, even though the magnitude of r is fairly large. Recall the discussion of nonsignificant results from the chapter "Understanding Research Results: Statistical Inference." It is possible that you would obtain a significant correlation if you used a larger sample size or more sensitive and reliable measures of the variables.

Glossary

alpha level The probability of incorrectly rejecting the null hypothesis that is used by a researcher to decide whether an outcome of a study is statistically significant (most commonly, researchers use a probability of .05).

alternate forms reliability Assessment of reliability by administering two different forms of the same measure to the same individuals at two points in time.

alternative explanation Part of causal inference; a potential alternative cause of an observed relationship between variables.

analysis of variance *See F* test.

APA Ethics Code The American Psychological Association code of general ethical principles. Including: beneficence and nonmaleficence; fidelity and responsibility; integrity; justice, and; respect for people's rights and dignity. The code was last updated in 2017.

APA PsycInfo A digital database of abstracts of articles in psychology, indexed by topic, updated weekly and maintained by the American Psychological Association.

applied research Research that addresses questions that have immediate practical implications.

archival research The use of existing sources of information for research. Sources include statistical records, survey archives, and written records.

attrition The loss of subjects who decide to leave an experiment. *See* mortality.

authority A way of knowing something. Specifically, relying on another person with perceived expertise to know something.

bar graph A visual presentation that uses bars to depict frequencies of responses, percentages, or means in two or more groups.

baseline In a single case design, the subject's behavior during a control period before introduction of the experimental manipulation.

basic research Research that addresses fundamental questions about behavior.

behavioral measures Measures that require participants to engage in a specific behavior.

Belmont Report The Belmont Report, published in 1979 by the National Commission for the Protection of Human Subjects of Biomedical and Behavioral Research, is an important foundational document guiding ethical research with human subjects. It includes three basic principles: beneficence, respect for persons (autonomy), and justice.

between-subjects design An experiment in which different subjects are assigned to each group. Also called independent groups design or between-persons design.

carryover effect A problem that may occur in repeated measures designs if the effects of one treatment are still present when the next treatment is given.

case study A descriptive account of the behavior, past history, and other relevant factors concerning a specific individual.

ceiling effect Failure of a measure to detect a difference because it was too easy (*also see* floor effect).

central tendency A single number or value that describes the typical or central score among a set of scores.

closed-ended questions Questions with response options provided for the research participants to choose from.

cluster sampling A probability sampling method in which existing groups or geographic areas, called clusters, are identified. Clusters are randomly sampled and then everyone in the selected clusters participates in the study.

coding system A set of rules used to categorize observations.

cohort A group of people born at about the same time and exposed to the same societal events; cohort effects are confounded with age in a cross-sectional study.

cohort effects In developmental research using a cross-sectional approach, differences among age groups attributed to social, cultural, economic, or political differences rather than to the effect of age.

conceptual replication A type of replication of research using different procedures for manipulating or measuring the variables.

conclusion validity The accuracy of the conclusions drawn from the results of a research investigation (sometimes called *statistical conclusion validity* when conclusions are drawn from statistical results).

concurrent validity The construct validity of a measure is assessed by examining whether groups of people differ on the measure in expected ways.

confederate A person posing as a participant in an experiment who is actually part of the experiment.

confidence interval An interval of values within which there is a given level of confidence (e.g., 95%) where the population value lies.

confidentiality When data collected from subjects is identifiable such that names or other identifying information is attached to responses or measurements, the data are only accessible to people with permission.

confounding variable A variable that is not controlled in a research investigation. In an experiment, the experimental groups differ on both the independent variable and the confounding variable.

construct validity The extent to which an operational definition of a variable accurately reflects underlying theoretical variable. Applies to both measured and manipulated variable.

In the context of measurement, the degree to which a measurement device accurately measures the theoretical construct it is designed to measure.

content analysis Systematic analysis of records.

content validity An indicator of construct validity of a measure in which the content of the measure is compared to the universe of content that defines the construct.

control series design An extension of the interrupted time series quasi-experimental design in which there is a comparison or control group.

convenience sampling Selecting subjects because they are easy to obtain (a convenient or haphazard manner), usually on the basis of availability, and not with regard to having a representative sample of the population; a type of nonprobability sampling. Also known as "haphazard" sampling.

convergent validity An assessment of the construct validity of a measure via examination of the extent to which scores on the measure are related to scores on other measures of the same construct or similar constructs.

correlation coefficient An index of how strongly two variables are related to each other.

counterbalancing A method of controlling for order effects in a repeated measures design by either including all orders of treatment presentation or randomly determining the order for each subject.

covariation of cause and effect Part of causal inference; observing that a change in one variable is accompanied by a change in a second variable.

criterion variable The variable/score that is predicted based upon an individual's score on another variable (the predictor variable). Conceptually similar to a dependent variable.

Cronbach's alpha An indicator of internal consistency reliability assessed by examining the average correlation of each item (question) in a measure with every other question.

cross-sectional method A developmental research method in which persons of different ages are studied at only one point in time; conceptually similar to an independent groups design.

curvilinear relationship A relationship in which changes in the values of the first variable are accompanied by both increases and decreases in the values of another variable.

day reconstruction method (DRM) A research procedure for studying what people do, feel, and think during their daily lives. It consists in asking individuals to provide diary-like descriptions of events that occurred during the previous day.

debriefing Explanation of the purposes of the research that is given to participants following their participation in the research.

deception In a research study, intentionally providing participants with misinformation (active deception) or withholding information from a participant (passive deception).

Declaration of Helsinki An ethical code of conducted developed by the World Medical Association in 1964 that is broader in its application than the Nuremberg Code. It requires that published journal research conform to its ethical principles.

degrees of freedom A concept used in tests of statistical significance; the number of observations that are free to vary to produce a known outcome; abbreviated *df*.

demand characteristics Cues that inform the subject how he or she is expected to behave.

dependent variable The variable that is the subject's response to, and dependent on, the level of the manipulated independent variable.

descriptive statistics Statistical measures that describe the results of a study; descriptive statistics include measures of central tendency (e.g., mean), variability (e.g., standard deviation), and correlation (e.g., Pearson *r*).

discriminant validity An assessment of the construct validity of a measure by means of examining the extent to which scores on the measure are not related to scores on conceptually unrelated measures.

double-blind experiment An experimental method originating in drug research wherein research participants and experimenters are unaware of participant status in the experimental or control conditions. *See* single-blind experiment, expectancy effects.

effect size The extent to which two variables are associated. In experimental research, the magnitude of the impact of the independent variable on the dependent variable.

electroencephalogram (EEG) A measure of the electrical activity of the brain.

electromyogram (EMG) A measure of the electrical activity of muscles, including muscle tension.

empiricism Use of objective, verifiable observations to answer questions and draw conclusions.

error variance Random variability in a set of scores that is not the result of the independent variable. Statistically, the variability of each score from its group mean.

exact replication A type of replication of research using the same procedures for manipulating and measuring the variables that were used in the original research.

exempt review research Research can undergo an exempt review by the IRB in one of several exempt categories, including: educational settings without adverse effect on learning opportunities, cognitive tests and surveys, benign behavioral interventions, and secondary data.

expectancy effects The impact an experimenter's expectations can have on the outcome of a research study. Also called experimenter bias.

expedited review A review required for research that is minimal risk research, but does not match the exempt research categories.

experience sampling method (ESM) A research procedure for collecting data on what people are doing and experiencing at random times across days.

experimental control Eliminating the influence of an extraneous variable on the outcome of an experiment by keeping the variable constant in the experimental and control groups.

experimental method A method of determining whether variables are related, in which the researcher manipulates the independent

variable and controls all other variables either by randomization or by direct experimental control.

external validity The degree to which the results of an experiment may be generalized.

extraneous variables Variables in a study other than the variables being investigated. *Also see* third variable.

***F* test (analysis of variance)** A statistical significance test for determining whether two or more means are significantly different. *F* is the ratio of systematic variance to error variance.

face validity The degree to which a measurement device appears to accurately measure a variable.

factorial design A design in which all levels of each independent variable are combined with all levels of the other independent variables. A factorial design allows investigation of the separate main effects and interactions of two or more independent variables.

falsifiability The principle that a good scientific idea or theory should be capable of being shown to be false when tested using scientific methods.

fatigue effect Deterioration in participant performance with repeated testing.

field experiment An experiment that is conducted in a natural setting rather than in a laboratory setting.

filler items Items included in a questionnaire measure to help disguise the true purpose of the measure.

floor effect Failure of a measure to detect a difference because it was too difficult (*also see* ceiling effect).

focus group An interview strategy wherein multiple respondents are encouraged to interact in a group interview.

fraud Fabrication of data.

frequency distribution An arrangement of a set of scores from lowest to highest that indicates the number of times each score was obtained.

frequency polygon A graphic display of a frequency distribution in which the frequency of each score is plotted on the vertical axis, with the plotted points connected by straight lines.

functional magnetic resonance imagery (fMRI) A method of measuring blood flow to areas of the brain as a way to provide an image of electrical activity in different areas of the brain while the subject is alert.

galvanic skin response (GSR) The electrical conductance of the skin, which changes when sweating occurs.

generalization The process of applying the procedures and findings of a specific study to other situations and populations

graphic rating scale A rating scale that uses a graphical representation of a numerical dimension.

histogram Graphic representation of a frequency distribution using bars to represent each score or group of scores.

history effect As a threat to the internal validity of an experiment, refers to any outside event that is not part of the manipulation that could be responsible for the results.

hypothesis A statement of the way in which variables are predicted to be related.

IACUC Institutions that conduct research with certain nonhuman animals must have an Institutional Animal Care and Use Committee (IACUC). The IACUC is composed of at least one scientist, one veterinarian, and a community member and is charged with reviewing animal research procedures and ensuring that all regulations are adhered to.

independent groups design An experiment in which different subjects are assigned to each group. Also called between-subjects design or between-persons design.

independent variable The variable that is manipulated to observe its effect on the dependent variable.

inferential statistics Statistics designed to determine whether results based on sample data are generalizable to a population.

informed consent In research ethics, the principle that participants in an experiment be informed in advance of all aspects of the research that might influence their decision to participate.

Institutional Review Board (IRB) An ethics review committee established to review research proposals. The IRB is composed of scientists, nonscientists, and legal experts.

instrument decay As a threat to internal validity, the possibility that a change in the characteristics of the measurement instrument, including human observers, is responsible for the results.

interaction Situation in which the effect of one independent variable on the dependent variable changes, depending on the level of another independent variable.

internal consistency reliability Reliability assessed with data collected at one point in time with multiple measures of a psychological construct. A measure is reliable when the multiple measures provide similar results.

internal validity The certainty with which results of an experiment can be attributed to the manipulation of the independent variable rather than to some other, confounding variable.

interrater reliability An indicator of reliability that examines the agreement of observations made by two or more raters (judges).

interrupted time series design A design in which the effectiveness of a treatment is determined by examining a series of measurements made over an extended time period both before and after the treatment is introduced. The treatment is not introduced at a random point in time.

interval scale A scale of measurement in which the intervals between numbers on the scale are all equal in size.

interviewer bias Intentional or unintentional influence exerted by an interviewer in such a way that the actual or interpreted behavior of respondents is consistent with the interviewer's expectations.

intuition A way of knowing something. Specifically, the ability to know something instinctively rather than through conscious reasoning or systematic observation.

item-total correlation The correlation between scores on individual items with the total score on all items of a measure.

Latin square A technique to control for order effects without having all possible orders.

limited review An IRB review that includes benign behavioral interventions for which sensitive data are collected from adult participants under circumstances where participates would need to be identified.

literature review A written summary and evaluation of the existing literature on a specific topic.

longitudinal method A developmental research method in which the same persons are observed repeatedly as they grow older; conceptually similar to a repeated measures design.

main effect The direct effect of an independent variable on a dependent variable.

manipulation check A measure used to determine whether the manipulation of the independent variable has had its intended effect on a subject.

matched pairs design A method of assigning subjects to groups in which pairs of subjects are first matched on some characteristic and then individually assigned randomly to groups.

maturation effect As a threat to internal validity, the possibility that any naturally occurring change within the individual is responsible for the results.

mean A measure of central tendency, obtained by summing scores and then dividing the sum by the number of scores.

measurement error The degree to which a measurement deviates from the true score value.

median A measure of central tendency; the middle score in a distribution of scores that divides the distribution in half.

meta-analysis An analytics technique that allows researchers to draw statistical conclusions from multiple studies of a single research question.

minimal risk the risks of harm to participants are no greater than risks encountered in daily life or in routine physical or psychological tests.

mixed factorial design A design that includes both independent groups (between-subjects) and repeated measures (within-subjects) variables.

mode A measure of central tendency; the most frequent score in a distribution of scores.

mortality The loss of subjects who decide to leave an experiment. Mortality is a threat to internal validity when the mortality rate is related to the nature of the experimental manipulation.

MRI (magnetic resonance imagery) The use of magnetic fields and radio waves to scan body structures, including the brain, to create images.

multiple baseline design Observing behavior before and after a manipulation under multiple circumstances (across different individuals, different behaviors, or different settings).

multiple correlation A correlation between one variable and a combined set of predictor variables.

multiple regression A statistical technique that combines two or more predictor variables to predict a criterion variable outcome.

naturalistic observation Descriptive method in which observations are made in a natural social setting. Also called field observation.

nay-saying A response set in which a respondent consistently disagrees with a set of questions. *See also* yea-saying.

negative linear relationship A relationship in which increases in the values of the first variable are accompanied by decreases in the values of the second variable.

nominal scale A scale of measurement with two or more categories that have no quantitative (numerical) properties. Variables with nominal scale properties are sometimes termed *qualitative* or *categorical* variables.

nonequivalent control group design A quasi-experimental design in which nonequivalent groups of subjects participate in the different experimental groups, and there is no pretest.

nonequivalent control group pretest-posttest design A quasi-experimental design in which nonequivalent groups are used, but a pretest allows assessment of equivalency and pretest-posttest changes.

nonexperimental method Use of measurement of variables to determine whether variables are related to one another. Also called correlational method.

nonprobability sampling A sampling procedure in which one cannot specify the probability that any member of the population will be included in the sample.

null hypothesis The hypothesis, used for statistical purposes, that the variables under investigation are not related in the population, that any observed effect based on sample results is due to random error.

Nuremberg Code The legal document that resulted from the trials of Nazi doctors and scientists that outlines 10 rules of research designed to prevent future research atrocities. The Nuremberg Code is an important foundational document for ethical research.

one-group posttest-only design A quasi-experimental design that has no control group and no pretest comparison; a very poor design in terms of internal validity.

one-group pretest-posttest design A quasi-experimental design in which the effect of an independent variable is inferred from the pretest-posttest difference in a single group.

open-ended questions Questions that give research participants the opportunity to provide free-form responses in their own words.

operational definition Definition of a concept that specifies the method used to measure or manipulate the concept.

order effect In a repeated measures design, the effect that the order of introducing treatment has on the dependent variable.

ordinal scale A scale of measurement in which the measurement categories form a rank order along a continuum.

panel study Research in which the same sample of subjects is studied at two or more points in time,

usually to assess changes that occur over time.

paraphrasing plagiarism Paraphrasing another person's ideas without attribution. Compare with *word-by-word plagiarism.*

participant (subject) variable A characteristic of the research participant such as gender, age, personality, or ability.

participant observation A technique of observing a situation wherein the observer takes an active role in the situation.

Pearson product-moment correlation coefficient A type of correlation coefficient used with interval and ratio scale data. In addition to providing information on the strength of relationship between two variables, it indicates the direction (positive or negative) of the relationship.

peer review The process of judging the scientific merit of research through review by other scientists with the expertise to evaluate the research.

physiological measures Measures of physiological activity (e.g., heart rate, brain cell activity).

pie chart Graphic display of data in which frequencies or percentages are represented as "slices" of a pie.

pilot study A small-scale study conducted prior to conducting an actual experiment; designed to test and refine procedures.

placebo group In drug research, a group given an inert substance to assess the psychological effect of receiving a treatment.

plagiarism Misrepresenting another's work as your own.

population The defined group of individuals from which a sample is

drawn (also termed *population of interest*).

positive linear relationship A relationship in which increases in the values of the first variable are accompanied by increases in the values of the second variable.

posttest-only design A true experimental design in which the dependent variable (posttest) is measured only once, after manipulation of the independent variable.

power The probability of correctly rejecting the null hypothesis.

practice effect Improvement in participant performance with repeated testing.

prediction A statement of the expected outcome of a research investigation.

predictive validity The construct validity of a measure is assessed by examining the ability of the measure to predict a future behavior or outcome.

predictor variable A variable that is used to make a prediction of an individual's score on another variable (the criterion variable). Conceptually similar to an independent variable.

pretest-posttest design A true experimental design in which the dependent variable is measured both before (pretest) and after (posttest) manipulation of the independent variable.

principle of beneficence Ethical principle of the Belmont Report and APA Code that researchers should maximize the well-being of participants while minimizing harm or distress.

principle of fidelity and responsibility "Psychologists establish relationships of trust with those with whom they work. They are aware of their professional and scientific responsibilities to society and to the specific communities in which they work." (APA Ethics Code)

principle of integrity "Psychologists seek to promote accuracy, honesty and truthfulness in the science, teaching and practice of psychology. In these activities psychologists do not steal, cheat or engage in fraud, subterfuge or intentional misrepresentation of fact." (APA Ethics Code)

principle of justice Ethical principle of the Belmont Report and APA Code that researchers adhere to fairness in the selection of participants so that any risks to not apply to one social group but not another; similarly, any benefits should be applied in a fair and just manner to people of different social groups.

principle of respect for persons (autonomy) Ethical principle of the Belmont report and APA Code that researchers respect the autonomy of individuals to make informed decisions about whether to participate in research. Moreover, persons with impaired autonomy deserve special protection. Participants can expect to be treated with respect in conduct of the research.

privacy In the context of research, privacy refers to participants' ability to maintain control of the information they provide and behaviors that may be observed.

probability The likelihood that a given event (among a specific set of events) will occur.

probability sampling A sampling procedure in which one is able to specify the probability that any member of the population will be included in the sample.

program evaluation Research designed to assess procedures (e.g., social reforms, innovations) that are designed to produce certain changes or outcomes in a target population.

propensity score matching A method of pairing individuals for assignment to a treatment and control condition based upon a combination of scores on participant variables.

pseudoscience The use of seemingly scientific terms and demonstrations to substantiate claims that have no basis in scientific research.

psychobiography A type of case study in which the life of an individual is analyzed using psychological theory.

purposive sampling A type of convenience sampling conducted to obtain predetermined types of individuals for the sample.

quasi-experimental design A type of design that approximates the control features of true experiments to infer that a given treatment did have its intended effect.

quota sampling A sampling procedure in which the sample is chosen to reflect the numerical composition of various subgroups in the population. A convenience sampling technique is used to obtain the sample.

random assignment Use of a random "chance" procedure (such as a random number generator or coin toss) to determine which condition an individual will participate in.

randomization Controlling for the effects of extraneous variables by ensuring that the variables operate in a manner determined entirely by chance.

range A measure of variability. The difference between the highest score and the lowest score.

rating scale A measure used to assign scores along some numerical dimension (such as, indicate current level of hunger).

ratio scale A scale of measurement in which there is an absolute zero point, indicating an absence of the variable being measured. An implication is that ratios of numbers on the scale can be formed (generally, these are physical measures such as weight or timed measures such as duration or reaction time).

reactivity A problem of measurement in which the measure changes the behavior being observed.

regression equation A mathematical equation that allows prediction of one behavior when the score on another variable is known.

regression toward the mean Also called statistical regression; the principle that extreme scores on a variable tend to be closer to the mean when a second measurement is made.

reliability The degree to which a measure is consistent.

repeated measures design An experiment in which the same subjects are assigned to each group. Also called within-subjects design or within-persons design.

replication Repeating a research study to determine whether the results can be duplicated.

research hypothesis The hypothesis that the variables under investigation are related in the population—that the observed effect based on sample data is true in the population.

research question A description of the broad topic of study, in question form.

respect for People's Rights and Dignity (APA) Ethical researchers respect the dignity and worth of all people, and their rights to privacy, confidentiality, and self-determination.

response rate The percentage of people selected for a sample who actually completed a survey.

response set A pattern of responses to questions on a self-report measure that is not related to the content of the question.

restriction of range A problem when scores on a variable are limited to a small subset of their possible values; this makes it more difficult to identify relationships of the variable to other variables of interest.

reversal design A single-case design in which the treatment is introduced after a baseline period and then withdrawn during a second baseline period. It may be extended by adding a second introduction of the treatment. Sometimes called a "withdrawal" design.

risk-benefit analysis The examination of potential risks and benefits that are likely to result from the research.

sample The members of a population selected to participate in a research investigation.

sampling distribution Theoretical distribution of the frequency of all possible outcomes of a study conducted with a given sample size.

sampling error The potential deviation from the true population value of a value obtained using sample data (e.g., a sample mean).

sampling frame The individuals or clusters of individuals in a population who might actually be selected for inclusion in the sample.

scatterplot Graphic representation of each individual's scores on two variables. The score on the first variable is found on the horizontal axis and score on the second variable is found on the vertical axis.

selection differences Differences in the type of subjects who make up each group in an experimental design. One way such differences can arise is by allowing participants to choose which group they will be assigned to.

self-reports Measures that require participants to describe themselves (e.g., their own characteristics, past or planned behaviors, reactions to stimuli).

semantic differential scale A type of rating scale used to measure participants' cognitive understanding of a concept (such as a topic or behavior). Scale items differentiate three dimensions—evaluation, activity, and potency.

sensitivity The ability of a measure to detect differences between groups.

sequential method A combination of the cross-sectional and longitudinal design to study developmental research questions.

simple main effect In a factorial design, the effect of one independent variable at a particular level of another independent variable.

simple random sampling A sampling procedure in which each member of the population has an equal probability of being included in the sample.

single blind experiment An experimental method originating in drug research wherein research participants do not know whether they are in the experimental group or the control group. *See* double-blind experiment, expectancy effects.

single-case experimental designs Experimental designs that allow cause-and-effect inferences based on data from one or a small number of research participants. Also called single-subject design and small-N design.

skepticism Doubt regarding the truth of something.

snowball sampling A nonprobability sampling procedure in which research participants are asked to recruit or identify potential research participants; the new participants may then asked to recruit.

social desirability A response set in which respondents answer questions to present themselves favorably.

Solomon four-group design Experimental design in which the experimental and control groups are studied with and without a pretest.

split-half reliability A reliability coefficient determined by the correlation between scores on half of the items on a measure with scores on the other half of a measure.

staged manipulation Manipulation of the independent variable, using complex situations, often simulating real-life social interactions. Also called event manipulation.

standard deviation The average deviation of scores from the mean (the square root of the variance).

statistical significance Rejection of the null hypothesis when an outcome has a low probability of occurrence (usually .05 or less) if, in fact, the null hypothesis is correct.

straightforward manipulation Manipulation of the independent variable through the use of direct stimulus presentations, types of instructions, and other simple procedures.

stratified random sampling A probability sampling method in which a population is divided into subpopulation groups called strata; individuals are then randomly sampled from each of the strata.

strength of manipulation The potential amount of impact of the independent variable on the dependent variable.

structural equation modeling Statistical techniques that are used to evaluate a proposed set of relationships among variables.

survey research Research method in which samples of people are asked questions using written questionnaires or interviews that are administered via telephone, mail and group distribution, face-to-face, or internet.

systematic observation Observations of one or more specific variables, usually made in a precisely defined setting.

systematic variance Variability in a set of scores that is the result of the independent variable; statistically, the variability of each group mean from the grand mean of all subjects.

***t*-test** A statistical significance test used to compare differences between means.

temporal precedence Part of causal inference; the cause occurs before the effect.

test-retest reliability A reliability coefficient determined by the correlation between scores on a measure given at one time with scores on the same measure given at a later time.

testing effect A threat to internal validity in which taking a pretest changes behavior without any effect on the independent variable.

theory A systematic, coherent, and logical set of ideas about a particular topic or phenomenon that serves to organize and explain data and generate new knowledge.

third variable In descriptions of the relationship between two variables, a third variable is any other variable that is extraneous to the two variables of interest. True experiments control for the possible influence of third variables.

third-variable problem An observed relationship (correlation) between two variables may be due to correlations between each of the two variables and a third variable. True experiments control for the possible influence of third variables.

true score An individual's actual score on a variable being measured, as opposed to the score the individual obtained on the measure itself.

Type I error An incorrect decision to reject the null hypothesis when it is true.

Type II error An incorrect decision to accept the null hypothesis when it is false.

variability The amount of dispersion of scores about some central value.

variable Any event, situation, behavior, or individual characteristic that varies—that is, has at least two values.

variance A measure of the variability of scores about a mean; the mean of the sum of squared deviations of scores from the group mean.

within-subjects design An experiment in which the same subjects are assigned to each group. Also called repeated measures design or a within-persons design.

word-for-word plagiarism A writer commits word-for-word plagiarism when he or she copies a section of another person's work word for word without placing those words within quotation marks to indicate that the segment was written by somebody else, and without citing the source of the information. This is contrasted with *paraphrasing plagiarism.*

yea-saying A response set in which a respondent consistently agrees with a set of questions. Also called acquiescence. *See also* nay-saying.

References

Agerström, J., Carlsson, M., & Strinić, A. (2021). Intersected groups and discriminatory everyday behavior. *Social Psychology, 52*(6), 351–361. https://doi.org/10.1027/1864-9335/a000464

Ajzen, I. (1991). The theory of planned behavior. *Organizational Behavior and Human Decision Processes, 50,* 179–211.

Ajzen, I. (1991). The theory of planned behavior. *Organizational Behavior and Human Decision Processes, 50*(2), 179–211. https://doi.org/10.1016/0749-5978(91)90020-T

Ajzen, I. (2011). The theory of planned behaviour: Reactions and reflections. *Psychology & Health, 26*(9), 1113–1127. https://doi.org/10.1080/08870446.2011.613995

Akins, C. K., Panicker, S., & Cunningham, C. L. (2005). *Laboratory animals in research and teaching: Ethics, care, and methods.* American Psychological Association. https://doi.org/10.1037/10830-000

Albright, L., & Malloy, T. E. (2000). Experimental validity: Brunswik, Campbell, Cronbach, and enduring issues. *Review of General Psychology, 4*(4), 337–353. https://doi.org/10.1037/1089-2680.4.4.337

Altman, D. (2020, Oct. 14). Black Americans are more skeptical of a coronavirus vaccine. https://www.axios.com/black-americans-coronavirus-vaccine-skepticism-ce338845-0263-4cc9-a88e-1125900533fd.html

American Psychological Association (2017). *Multicultural guidelines: An ecological approach to context, identity, and intersectionality.* https://www.apa.org/about/policy/multicultural-guidelines.pdf

American Psychological Association. (2020a). Concise guide to APA style (7th ed.).

American Psychological Association (2020b). *Publication Manual of the American Psychological Association* (7th ed.). https://doi.org/10.1037/0000165-000

American Psychological Association. (2021b). *Inclusive language guidelines.* https://www.apa.org/about/apa/equity-diversity-inclusion/language-guidelines.pdf

American Psychology Association. (2021). *Equity, diversity, and inclusion framework.* https://www.apa.org/about/apa/equity-diversity-inclusion/framework.pdf

Anderson, C. A., & DeLisi, M. (2011). Implications of global climate change for violence in developed and developing countries. In J. P. Forgas, A. W. Kruglanski, & K. D. Williams (Eds.), *The psychology of social conflict and aggression.* (Vol. 13, pp. 249–265). Psychology Press.

Anderson, C. A., Lindsay, J. J., & Bushman, B. J. (1999). Research in the psychological laboratory: Truth or triviality? *Current Directions in Psychological Science, 8,* 3–9. https://doi.org/10.1111/1467-8721.00002

Anderson, C. J., Bahník, Š., Barnett-Cowan, M., Bosco, F. A., Chandler, J., Chartier, C. R., & ... van der Hulst, M. (2016). Response to comment on "Estimating the reproducibility of psychological science." *Science, 351*(6277), 1037c. https://doi.org/10.1126/science.aad9163

Andreou, G., & Raxioni, K. (2022). Language development, reading and word learning in autism spectrum disorder (asd): A review on eye tracking studies. *International Journal of Developmental Disabilities.* https://doi.org/10.1080/20473869.2021.2024404

An, W., & Winship, C. (2017). Causal inference in panel data with application to estimating race-of-interviewer effects in the General Social Survey. *Sociological Methods & Research, 46*(1), 68–102. https://doi.org/10.1177/0049124115600614

Aram, J., Johnson, N. J., Lee, M.-L. T., & Slopen, N. (2020). Drug overdose mortality is associated with employment status and occupation in the national longitudinal mortality study. *The American Journal of Drug and Alcohol Abuse.* https://doi.org/10.1080/00952990.2020.1820018

Arnett, J. J. (2008). The neglected 95%: Why American psychology needs to become less American. *American Psychologist, 63*(7), 602–614. https://doi.org/10.1037/0003-066x.63.7.602

Asch, S. (1956). Studies of independence and conformity: A minority of one against a unanimous majority. *Psychological Monographs: General and Applied, 70*(9) (Whole No. 416).

Aseltine, Jr., R. H., Schilling, E. A., James, A., Murray, M., & Jacobs, D. G. (2008). An evaluation of National Alcohol Screening Day. *Alcohol & Alcoholism, 43*(1), 97–103.

Auh, S., Salisbury, L. C., & Johnson, M. D. (2003). Order effects in customer satisfaction modelling. *Journal of Marketing Management, 19*(3–4), 379–400. https://doi.org/10.1362/026725703321663700

Aurino, E., Wolf, S., & Tsinigo, E. (2020). Household food insecurity and early childhood development: Longitudinal evidence from Ghana. *PLoS ONE, 15*(4). https://doi.org/10.1371/journal.pone.0230965

Avila, J. F., Rentería, M. A., Witkiewitz, K., Verney, S. P., Vonk, J. M. J., & Manly, J. J. (2020). Measurement invariance of neuropsychological measures of cognitive aging across race/ethnicity by sex/gender groups. *Neuropsychology, 34*(1), 3–14. http://dx.doi.org/10.1037/neu0000584

Bakeman, R. (2000). Behavioral observation and coding. In H. T. Reis & C. M. Judd (Eds.), *Handbook of research methods in social and personality psychology* (pp. 138–159). Cambridge University Press.

Bakeman, R., & Brownlee, J. R. (1980). The strategic use of parallel play: A sequential analysis. *Child Development, 51*(3), 873–878. https://doi.org/10.2307/1129476

Bandura, A. (1977). Self-efficacy: Toward a unifying theory of behavioral change. Psychological Review, 84(2), 191–215. https://doi.org/10.1037/0033-295X.84.2.191

Bangerter, A., & Heath, C. (2004). The Mozart effect: Tracking the evolution of a scientific legend. *British Journal of Social Psychology, 43,* 605–623. https://doi.org/10.1348/0144666042565353

Barlow, D. H., Nock, M. K., & Hersen, M. (2009). *Single case experimental designs: Strategies for studying behavior change* (3rd ed.). Allyn & Bacon.

Baron, R. M., & Kenny, D. A. (1986). The moderator–mediator variable distinction in social psychological research: Conceptual, strategic, and statistical considerations. *Journal of Personality and Social Psychology*, 51(6), 1173.

Bedwell, S. A. (2016). Opinion: Why research using animals is important in psychology. *The Psychologist, 29,* 624–627. https://thepsychologist.bps.org.uk/volume-29/august/why-research-using-animals-important-psychology

Benedict, M. E., & Hoag, J. (2004). Seating location in large lectures: Are seating preferences or location related to course performance? *Journal of Economic Education, 35,* 215–231.

Bertola, L., Benseñor, I. M., Barreto, S. M., Moreno, A. B., Griep, R. H., Viana, M. C., Lotufo, P. A., & Suemoto, C. K. (2020). Measurement invariance of neuropsychological tests across different sociodemographic backgrounds in the Brazilian Longitudinal Study of Adult Health (ELSA-Brasil). *Neuropsychology, 34*(2), 227–234. http://dx.doi.org/10.1037/neu0000597

Bird, S. J., & Parlee, M. B. (2000). Of mice and men (and women and children): Scientific and ethical implications of animal models. *Progress in Neuro-Psychopharmacology & Biological Psychiatry, 24*(8), 1219–1227. https://doi.org/10.1016/S0278-5846(00)00139-1

Blanchflower, D. G., & Oswald, A. J. (2008). Is well-being U-shaped over the life cycle? *Social Science & Medicine, 66*(8), 1733–1749. https://doi.org/10.1016/j.socscimed.2008.01.030

Blass, T. (2004). *The man who shocked the world: The life and legacy of Stanley Milgram.* Basic Books.

Bodenlos, J. S., & Wormuth, B. M. (2013). Watching a food-related television show and caloric intake: A laboratory study. *Appetite, 61*(1), 8–12. doi:10.1016/j.appet.2012.10.027

Borchgrevink, C. P., Cha, J., & Kim, S. (2013). Hand washing practices in a college town environment. *Journal of Environmental Health, 75*(8), 18–24.

Borenstein, M., Hedges, L. V., Higgins, J. P. T., & Rothstein, H. R. (2009). *Introduction to meta-analysis.* Wiley.

Bortnik, K., Henderson, L., & Zimbardo, P. (2002). The Shy Q, a measure of chronic shyness: Associations with interpersonal motives and interpersonal values. http://www.shyness.com/documents/2002/SITAR-2002poster_handout.pdf

Bowman, L. L., Levine, L. E., Waite, B. M., & Gendron, M. (2010). Can students really multitask? An experimental study of instant messaging while reading. *Computers & Education, 54*(4), 927–931. https://doi.org/10.1016/j.compedu.2009.09.024

Boynton, M. H., Portnoy, D. B., & Johnson, B. T. (2013). Exploring the ethics and psychological impact of deception in psychological research. *IRB: Ethics & Human Research, 34*(2), 7–13.

Brodeur, M. B., Guérard, K., & Bouras M. (2014). Bank of Standardized Stimuli (BOSS) phase II: 930 new normative photos. *PLoS One, 9*(9), e106953. https://doi.org/10.1371/journal.pone.0106953

Brooks, C. I., & Rebata, J. L. (1991). College classroom ecology: The relation of sex of student to classroom performance and seating preference. *Environment and Behavior, 23,* 305–313.

Brothers, T., & Traxler, M. J. (2016). Anticipating syntax during reading: Evidence from the boundary change paradigm. *Journal of Experimental Psychology: Learning, Memory, and Cognition, 42*(12), 1894–1906. https://doi.org/10.1037/xlm0000257

Brown, A. S., & Rahhal, T. A. (1994). Hiding valuables: A questionnaire study of mnemonically risky behavior. *Applied Cognitive Psychology, 8*(2), 141–154.

https://doi.org/10.1002/acp.2350080205

Brown, C. (2016). *The evidence-based practitioner: Applying research to meet client needs.* F. A. Davis.

Brown, N. A., Blake, A. B., & Sherman, R. A. (2017). A snapshot of the life as lived: Wearable cameras in social and personality psychological science. *Social Psychological and Personality Science, 8*(5), 592–600. https://doi.org/10.1177/1948550617703170

Bruins, J., & Barber, A. (2000). Crowding, performance, and affect: A field experiment investigating mediational processes. *Journal of Applied Social Psychology, 30,* 1268–1280. https://doi.org/10.1111/j.1559-1816.2000.tb02520.x

Buchanan, N. T., Perez, M., Prinstein, M. J., & Thurston, I. B. (2021). Upending racism in psychological science: Strategies to change how science is conducted, reported, reviewed, and disseminated. *American Psychologist, 76*(7), 1097–1112. https://doi.org/10.1037/amp0000905

Buchanan, T., & Williams, J. E. (2010). Ethical issues in psychological research on the Internet. In S. D. Gosling & J. A. Johnson (Eds.), *Advanced methods for conducting online behavioral research* (pp. 255–271). American Psychological Association.

Buchanan, T., & Williams, J. E. (2010). Ethical issues in psychological research on the Internet. In S. D. Gosling & J. A. Johnson (Eds.), *Advanced methods for conducting online behavioral research* (pp. 255–271). American Psychological Association. https://doi.org/10.1037/12076-016

Buhrmester, M. D., Talaifar, S., & Gosling, S. D. (2018). An evaluation of Amazon's Mechanical Turk, its rapid rise, and its effective use. *Perspectives on Psychological Science, 13*(2), 149–154. https://doi.org/10.1177/1745691617706516

Buhrmester, M., Kwang, T., & Gosling, S. D. (2011). Amazon's Mechanical Turk: A new source of inexpensive, yet high-quality, data? *Perspectives on Psychological Science, 6*(1), 3–5. https://doi.org/10.1177/1745691610393980

Burger, J. M. (2009). Replicating Milgram: Would people still obey today? *American Psychologist, 64*(1), 1–11. doi:10.1037/a0010932

Bushman, B., Wang, M., & Anderson, C. (2005). Is the curve relating temperature to aggression linear or curvilinear? Assaults and temperature in Minneapolis reexamined. *Journal of Personality and Social Psychology, 89*(1), 62–66. https://doi.org/doi.org/10.1037/0022-3514.89.1.62

Bushman, B. J., & Wells, G. L. (2001). Narrative impressions of the literature: The availability bias and the corrective properties of meta-analytic approaches. Personality and Social Psychology Bulletin, 27, 1123–1130. https://doi.org/10.1177/0146167201279005

Buss, D. M. (2011). *Evolutionary psychology: The new science of the mind* (4th ed.). Allyn & Bacon.

Byrne, G. (1988, October 7). Breuning pleads guilty. *Science, 242,* 27–28.

Cacioppo, J. T., & Tassinary, L. G. (1990). Inferring psychological significance from physiological signals. *American Psychologist,*

45(1), 16–28. https://doi.org/ 10.1037/0003-066X.45.1.16

Cacioppo, S., & Cacioppo, J. T. (2020). *Introduction to social neuroscience*. Princeton University Press.

Cain, G. E., Kalu, N., Kwagyan, J., Marshall, V. J., Ewing, A. T.,... & Scott, D. M. (2016). Beliefs and preferences for medical research among African-Americans. *Journal of Racial and Ethnic Health Disparities, 3*(1), 74–82. https://doi.org/10.1007/ s40615-015-0117-8

Campbell, D. T. (1968). Quasi-experimental design. In D. L. Gillis (Ed.), *International encyclopedia of the social sciences* (Vol. 5). Macmillan and Free Press.

Campbell, D. T. (1969). Reforms as experiments. *American Psychologist, 24,* 409–429.

Campbell, D. T., & Stanley, J. C. (1966). *Experimental and quasi-experimental designs for research*. Rand McNally.

Carroll, M. E., & Overmier, J. B. (Eds.). (2001). *Animal research and human health: Advancing human welfare through behavioral science*. American Psychological Association.

Chambless, D. L., Sanderson, W. C., Shoham, V., Bennett, S. B., Pope, K. S., Crits-Christoph, P.,... & McCurry, S. (1996). An update on empirically validated therapies. *Clinical Psychologist, 49,* 5–18.

Chandler, J. (2017). Pulling back the curtain: Using Mechanical Turk for research. https://www. mathematica.org/commentary/ crowdsourcing-samples

Chang, H., & Beilock, S. L. (2016). The math anxiety–math performance link and its relation to

individual and environmental factors: A review of current behavioral and psychophysiological research. *Current Opinion in Behavioral Sciences, 1033–1038.* https://doi.org/10.1016/j. cobeha.2016.04.011

Chastain, G. D., & Landrum, R. E. (Eds.). (1999). *Protecting human subjects: Department subject pools and institutional review boards.* American Psychological Association.

Chmielewski, M., & Kucker, S. C. (2020). An MTurk crisis? Shifts in data quality and the impact on study results. *Social Psychological and Personality Science, 11*(4), 464–473. https://doi.org/ 10.1177/1948550619875149

Chrisler, J. C., Fuentes, C. D. L., Durvasula, R. S., Esnil, E. M., McHugh, M. C., Miles-Cohen, S. E., ... & Wisdom, J. P. (2013). The American Psychological Association's Committee on Women in Psychology: 40 years of contributions to the transformation of psychology. *Psychology of Women Quarterly, 37*(4), 444–454. https://doi.org/ 10.1177%2F0361684313505442

Clark, K. B., & Clark, M. P. (1947). Racial identification and preference in Negro children. In T. M. Newcomb & E. L. Hartley (Eds.), *Readings in social psychology.* Holt, Rinehart & Winston.

Clark, M. M., Warren, B. A., Hagen, P. T., Johnson, B. D., Jenkins, S. M., Werneburg, B. L., & Olsen, K. D. (2011). Stress level, health behaviors, and quality of life in employees joining a wellness center. *American Journal of Health Promotion, 26*(1), 21–25. https://doi.org/10.4278/ ajhp.090821-QUAN-27

Clay, R. A. (2010). Psychology's voice is heard. *APA Monitor, 41*(7), 22.

Cohen, J. (1988). *Statistical power analysis for the behavioral sciences*. Erlbaum.

Cohen, J. (1992). A power primer. *Psychological Bulletin, 112*(1), 155–159. https://doi.org/10.1037/ 0033-2909.112.1.155

Cohen, J. (1994). The earth is round ($p < .05$). *American Psychologist, 49,* 997–1003.

Cohen, J. (2016). A power primer. In A. E. Kazdin (Ed.), *Methodological issues and strategies in clinical research*, 4th ed. (pp. 279–284). American Psychological Association. https://doi.org/ 10.1037/ 14805-018

Cook, T. D., & Campbell, D. T. (1979). *Quasi-experimentation: Design and analysis issues for field settings*. Houghton Mifflin.

Corbett, J., & Savarimuthu, B. T. R. (2022). From tweets to insights: A social media analysis of the emotion discourse of sustainable energy in the United States. *Energy Research & Social Science, 89,* 102515. https://doi. org/10.1016/j.erss.2022.102515

Corbie-Smith, G., Thomas, S. B., Williams, M. V., & Moody-Ayers, S. (1999). Attitudes and beliefs of African Americans toward participation in medical research. *Journal of General Internal Medicine, 14*(9), 537–546. https://doi.org/ 10.1046/j.1525-1497.1999. 07048.x

Corder, G. W., & Foreman, D. I. (2014). *Non-parametric statistics for non-statisticians: A step-by-step approach* (2nd ed.). Wiley.

Corona, K., Senft, N., Campos, B., Chen, C., Shiota, M., & Chentsova-Dutton, Y. (2020).

Ethnic variation in gratitude and well-being. *Emotion, 20*(3), 518–524. http://dx.doi.org/10.1037/emo0000582

Cramer, S., Mayer, J., & Ryan, S. (2007). College students use cell phones while driving more frequently than found in government study. *Journal of American College Health, 56,* 181–184. https://doi.org/10.3200/JACH.56.2.181–184

Credé, M., Roch, S. G., & Kieszczynska, U. M. (2010). Class attendance in college: A meta-analytic review of class attendance with grades and student characteristics. *Review of Educational Research, 80,* 272–295.

Creswell, J. W. (2013). *Qualitative Inquiry and Research Design: Choosing Among Five Approaches* (3rd Ed.). Sage.

Creswell, J. W., & Poth, C. N. (2018). *Qualitative inquiry & research design: Choosing among five approaches* (4th ed.). SAGE.

Cushing, C., & Bodner, G. E. (2022). Reading aloud improves proofreading (but using Sans Forgetica font does not). *Journal of Applied Research in Memory and Cognition.* https://doi.org/10.1037/mac0000011.supp

Danner, D. D., Snowden, D. A., & Friesen, W. V. (2001). Positive emotions in early life and longevity: Findings from the Nun Study. *Journal of Personality and Social Psychology, 80,* 804–813.

Davis, R. E., Couper, M. P., Janz, N. K., Caldwell, C. H., & Resnicow, K. (2010). Interviewer effects in public health surveys. *Health Education Research, 25*(1), 14–26. https://doi.org/10.1093/her/cyp046

DeGroot, J. M., Young, V. J., & VanSlette, S. H. (2015). Twitter use and its effects on student perception of instructor credibility. *Communication Education, 64*(4), 419–437. https://doi.org/10.1080/03634523.2015.1014386

Deutsch, D. (2021). Speech to song illusion. https://deutsch.ucsd.edu/psychology/pages.php?i=212

De Vita, M. J., Maisto, S. A., Gilmour, C. E., McGuire, L., Tarvin, E., & Moskal, D. (2021). The effects of cannabidiol and analgesic expectancies on experimental pain reactivity in healthy adults: A balanced placebo design trial. *Experimental and Clinical Psychopharmacology.* Advance online publication. https://doi.org/10.1037/pha0000465

Devlin, B., Daniels, M., & Roeder, K. (1997). The heritability of IQ. *Nature, 388*(6641), 468–471.

Di Lieto, M. C., Pecini, C., Castro, E., Inguaggiato, E., Cecchi, F., Dario, P., Cioni, G., & Sgandurra, G. (2020). Empowering executive functions in 5- and 6-year-old typically developing children through educational robotics: An RCT study. *Frontiers in Psychology, 10.* https://doi.org/10.3389/fpsyg.2019.03084

Dill, C. A., Gilden, E. R., Hill, P. C., & Hanslka, L. L. (1982). Federal human subjects regulations: A methodological artifact? *Personality and Social Psychology Bulletin, 8,* 417–425. https://doi.org/10.1177/0146167282083005

Dillman, D., Smyth, J., & Christian, L. (2014). *Internet, mail, and mixed-mode surveys: The tailored design method* (4th ed.). Wiley.

Does, S., Ellemers, N., Dovidio, J. F., Norman, J. B., Mentovich, A., van der Lee, R., & Goff, P. A. (2018). Implications of research staff demographics for psychological science. *American Psychologist, 73*(5), 639–650. https://doi.org/10.1037/amp0000199

Donde, S. D., Ragsdale, S. K. A., Koss, M. P., & Zucker, A. N. (2018). If it wasn't rape, was it sexual assault? Comparing rape and sexual assault acknowledgement in college women who have experienced rape. *Violence Against Women, 24*(14), 1718–1738. https://doi.org/10.1177/1077801217743339

Douglas, B. D., McGorray, E. L., & Ewell, P. J. (2021). Some researchers wear yellow pants, but even fewer participants read consent forms: Exploring and improving consent form reading in human subjects research. *Psychological Methods, 26*(1), 61–68. https://doi.org/10.1037/met0000267

Duckworth, A. L., & Quinn, P. D. (2009). Development and validation of the Short Grit Scale (GRIT–S). *Journal of Personality Assessment, 91*(2), 166–174. https://doi.org/10.1080/00223890802634290

Duncan, G. J., Ziol-Guest, K. M., & Kalil, A. (2010). Early-childhood poverty and adult attainment, behavior, and health. *Child Development, 81*(1), 306–325. https://doi.org/10.1111/j.1467–8624.2009.01396.x

Duncan, S., Rosenberg, M. J., & Finklestein, J. (1969). The paralanguage of experimenter bias. *Sociometry, 32*(11), 207–219. https://doi.org/10.2307/2786264

Dunn, A. L., Trivedi, M. H., Kampert, J. B., Clark, C. G., & Chambliss, H. O. (2005). Exercise treatment for depression. *American Journal of Preventive Medicine, 28*(1), 1–8. https://doi.org/10.1016/j.amepre.2004.09.003

Eagan, M. K., Stolzenberg, E. B., Ramirez, J. J., Aragon, M. C., Suchard, M. R., & Rios-Aguilar, C. (2016). The American freshman: Fifty-year trends, 1966–2015. Higher Education Research Institute, UCLA. https://www.heri.ucla.edu/monographs/50YearTrendsMonograph2016.pdf.

Ejelöv, E., & Luke, T. J. (2020). "Rarely safe to assume": Evaluating the use and interpretation of manipulation checks in experimental social psychology. *Journal of Experimental Social Psychology, 87*. https://doi.org/10.1016/j.jesp.2019.103937

Ensor, T. M., Surprenant, A. M., & Neath, I. (2019). Increasing word distinctiveness eliminates the picture superiority effect in recognition: Evidence for the physical-distinctiveness account. *Memory & Cognition, 47*(1), 182–193. https://doi.org/10.3758/s13421-018-0858-9

Eskreis-Winkler, L., Shulman, E. P., Beal, S. A., & Duckworth, A. L. (2014). The grit effect: Predicting retention in the military, the workplace, school and marriage. *Frontiers in Psychology, 5*. https://doi.org/10.3389/fpsyg.2014.00036

Faul, F., Erdfelder, E., Buchner, A., & Lang, A.-G. (2009). Statistical power analyses using G*Power 3.1: Tests for correlation and regression analyses. *Behavior Research Methods, 41*, 1149–1160.

Faul, F., Erdfelder, E., Lang, A.-G., & Buchner, A. (2007). G*Power 3: A flexible statistical power analysis program for the social, behavioral, and biomedical sciences. *Behavior Research Methods, 39*, 175–191.

Faverio, M. (2022, January 13). *Share of those 65 and older who are tech users has grown in the past decade*. Pew Research Center. https://www.pewresearch.org/fact-tank/2022/01/13/share-of-those-65-and-older-who-are-tech-users-has-grown-in-the-past-decade/

Felix, E. D., Janson, M., Fly, J., & Powers, J. (2022). Social-cognitive mediators of the relationship of media exposure to acute mass violence and distress among adolescents. *American Journal of Orthopsychiatry, 92*(1), 1–10. https://doi.org/10.1037/ort0000580

Finkel, S. E., Guterbock, T. M., & Borg, M. J. (1991). Race-of-interviewer effects in a preelection poll: Virginia 1989. *Public Opinion Quarterly, 55*(3), 313–330. https://doi.org/10.1086/269264

Fisher, C. B., & Fyrberg, D. (1994). Participant partners: College students weigh the costs and benefits of deceptive research. *American Psychologist, 49*(5), 417–427. https://doi.org/10.1037/0003-066X.49.5.417

Fiske, S. T., & Taylor, S. E. (2021) *Social cognition From brains to culture* (4th ed). Sage.

Flavell, J. H. (1996). Piaget's legacy. *Psychological Science, 7*, 200–203. https://doi.org/10.1111%2Fj.1467-9280.1996.tb00359.x

Forest, A. L., & Wood, J. V. (2012). When social networking is not working: Individuals with low self-esteem recognize but do not reap the benefits of self-disclosure on Facebook. *Psychological Science, 23*(3), 295–302. https://doi.org/10.1177/0956797611429709

Forrin, N. D., Huynh, A. C., Smith, A. C., Cyr, E. N., McLean, D. B., Siklos-Whillans, J., Risko, E. F., Smilek, D., & MacLeod, C. M. (2021). Attention spreads between students in a learning environment. *Journal of Experimental Psychology: Applied, 27*(2), 276–291. https://doi.org/10.1037/xap0000341.supp (Supplemental)

Fowler, F. J., Jr. (2014). *Survey research methods* (5th ed.). Sage.

Fraundorf, S. H., Hourihan, K. L., Peters, R. A., & Benjamin, A. S. (2019). Aging and recognition memory: A meta-analysis. *Psychological Bulletin, 145*(4), 339–371. doi: 10.1037/bul0000185

Fraundorf, S. H., Hourihan, K. L., Peters, R. A., & Benjamin, A. S. (2019). Aging and recognition memory: A meta-analysis. *Psychological Bulletin, 145*(4): 339–371. https://doi.org/10.1037/bul0000185

Freedman, J. L., Klevansky, S., & Ehrlich, P. R. (1971). The effect of crowding on human task performance. Journal of Applied Social Psychology, 1(1), 7–25. https://doi.org/10.1111/j.1559-1816.1971.tb00350.x

Frick, R. W, (1995). Accepting the null hypothesis. *Memory and Cognition, 25*(1), 132–138. https://doi.org/10.3758/BF03210562

Friedman, H. S., & Martin, L. R. (2011). *The longevity project*. Hudson Street Press.

Fritz, C. O., Morris, P. E., & Richler, J. J. (2012). Effect size estimates: Current use, calculations, and interpretation. *Journal of Experimental Psychology: General, 141*(1), 2–18. https://doi.org/10.1037/a0024338

Fryar, C. D., Carroll, M. D., & Afful, J. (2020). Prevalence of overweight, obesity, and severe obesity among children and adolescents aged 2–19 years: United States, 1963–1965 through 2017–2018. https://www.cdc.gov/nchs/data/hestat/obesity-child-17-18/obesity-child.htm

Funk, F., & Todorov, A. (2013). Criminal stereotypes in the courtroom: Facial tattoos affect guilt and punishment differently. *Psychology, Public Policy, and Law, 19*(4), 466–478. https://doi.org/10.1037/a0034736

García-Vera, M. P., Sanz, J., & Gutiérrez, S. (2016). A systematic review of the literature on posttraumatic stress disorder in victims of terrorist attacks. *Psychological Reports, 119*(1), 328–359. https://doi.org/10.1177/0033294116658243

Gardner, G. T. (1978). Effects of federal human subjects' regulations on data obtained in environmental stressor research. *Journal of Personality and Social Psychology, 34*, 774–781. https://doi.org/10.1037/0022-3514.36.6.628

Gardner, L. E. (1988). A relatively painless method of introduction to the psychological literature search. In M. E. Ware & C. L. Brewer (Eds.), *Handbook for teaching statistics and research methods*. Erlbaum.

Gerlich, R. N., Drumheller, K., Clark, R., & Baskin, M. B. (2018). Mechanical Turk: Is it just another convenience sample? *Global Business Journal, 2*(1), 45–55. https://www.igbr.org/wp-content/uploads/articles/GJBD_Vol_2_No_1_2018-pgs-45-55.pdf

Gernsbacher, M. A. (2018). Writing empirical articles: Transparency, reproducibility, clarity, and memorability. *Advances in Methods and Practices in Psychological Science, 1*(3), 403–414. https://doi.org/10.1177/2515245918754485

Gilbert, D. T., King, G., Pettigrew, S., & Wilson, T. D. (2016). Comment on "Estimating the reproducibility of psychological science". *Science, 351*(6277), 1037. https://doi.org/10.1126/science.aad7243

Gilovich, T. (1991). *How we know what isn't so: The fallibility of human reason in everyday life*. Free Press.

Golder, S. A., & Macy, M. W. (2011). Diurnal and season mood vary with work, sleep, and daylength across diverse cultures. *Science, 333*(6051), 1878–1881. https://doi.org/10.1126/science.1202775

Goldstein, N. J., Cialdini, R. B., & Griskevicius, V. (2008). A room with a viewpoint: Using social norms to motivate environmental conservation in hotels. *Journal of Consumer Research, 35*(3), 472–482. https://doi.org/10.1086/586910

Goodrum, N. M., Masyn, K. E., Armistead, L. P., Avina, I., Schulte, M., Marelich, W., & Murphy, D. A. (2021). A mixed-methods longitudinal investigation of mothers' disclosure of hiv to their children. *Child Development, 92*(4), 1403–1420. https://doi.org/10.1111/cdev.13493

Goodstein, D. (2000). How science works. https://www.nap.edu/read/13163/chapter/4

Goodstein, D. (2000). How science works. http://www.its.caltech.edu/,dg/How-Scien.pdf

Graesser, A. C., Cai, Z., Louwerse, M. M., & Daniel, F. (2006). Question Understanding Aid (QUAID): A web facility that tests question comprehensibility. *Public Opinion Quarterly, 70*(1), 3–22. http://doi.org/10.1093/poq/nfj012

Graesser, A. C., Kennedy, T., Wiemer-Hastings, P., & Ottati, V. (1999). The use of computational cognitive methods to improve questions on surveys and questionnaires. In M. G. Sirkin, D. J. Hermann, S. Schechter, N. Schwarz, J. M. Tanur, & R. Tourangeau (Eds.), *Cognition and survey methods research* (pp. 199–216). Wiley.

Graham, K., Tremblay, P. F., Wells, S., Pernanen, K., Purcell, J., & Jelley, J. (2006). Harm, intent, and the nature of aggressive behavior: Measuring naturally occurring aggression in barroom settings. *Assessment, 13*, 280–296. https://doi.org/10.1177/1073191106288180

Grant, A. M., & Schwartz, B. (2011). Too much of a good thing: The challenge and opportunity of the inverted U. *Perspectives on Psychological Science, 6*, 61–76. https://doi.org/10.1177/1745691610393523

Greenspan, R. L., & Loftus, E. F. (2021). What happens after debriefing? The effectiveness and benefits of postexperimental debriefing. *Memory & Cognition*. https://doi.org/10.3758/s13421-021-01223-9

Greenwald, A. G. (1976). Within-subjects designs: To use or not to use? *Psychological Bulletin, 83*(2), 314–320. https://doi.org/10.1037/0033-2909.83.2.314

Groves, R. M., Fowler, J. J., Couper, M. P., Lepkowski, J. M., Singer, E., & Tourangeau, R. (2009). *Survey methodology* (2nd ed.). Wiley.

Gruber, J., Mendle, J., Lindquist, K. A., Schmader, T., Clark, L. A., Bliss-Moreau, E., Akinola, M., Atlas, L., Barch, D. M., Barrett, L. F., Borelli, J. L., Brannon, T. N., Bunge, S. A., Campos, B.,

Cantlon, J., Carter, R., Carter-Sowell, A. R., Chen, S., Craske, M. G., ... Williams, L. A. (2021). The future of women in psychological science. *Perspectives on Psychological Science, 16*(3), 483–516. https://doi.org/10.1177/1745691620952789

Guiding Principles for Mail and Internet Surveys. (2012). https://www.une.edu/sites/default/files/Microsoft-Word-Guiding-Principles-for-Mail-and-Internet-Surveys_8-3.pdf

Guntzviller, L. M., Williamson, L. D., & Ratcliff, C. L. (2020). Stress, social support, and mental health among young adult hispanics. *Family & Community Health: The Journal of Health Promotion & Maintenance, 43*(1), 82–91. https://doi.org/10.1097/FCH.0000000000000224

Guo, S., & Fraser, M. W. (2010). *Propensity score analysis: Statistical methods and applications.* Sage.

Gustavson, D. E., Reynolds, C. A., Corley, R. P., Wadsworth, S. J., Hewitt, J. K., & Friedman, N. P. (2022). Genetic associations between executive functions and intelligence: A combined twin and adoption study. *Journal of Experimental Psychology: General* (Supplemental). https://doi.org/10.1037/xge0001168.supp

Guthrie, R. V. (2004). *Even the rat was white: A historical view of psychology* (2nd ed.). Pearson Education.

Guyer, J. J., Fabrigar, L. R., & Vaughan-Johnston, T. I. (2019). Speech rate, intonation, and pitch: Investigating the bias and cue effects of vocal confidence on persuasion. *Personality and Social Psychology Bulletin,*

45(3), 389–405. https://doi.org/10.1177/0146167218787805n

Günther, V., Kropidlowski, A., Schmidt, F. M., Koelkebeck, K., Kersting, A., & Suslow, T. (2021). Attentional processes during emotional face perception in social anxiety disorder: A systematic review and meta-analysis of eye-tracking findings. *Progress in Neuro-Psychopharmacology & Biological Psychiatry, 111.* https://doi.org/10.1016/j.pnpbp.2021.110353

Hall, L. Hume, C., & Tazzyman, S. (2016) Five degrees of happiness: Effective smiley face Likert scales for evaluating with children. *Proceedings of the 15th International Conference on Interaction Design and Children.* https://sure.sunderland.ac.uk/id/eprint/6965/7/Hall%20Hume%20Tazzyman%20IDC.pdf

Halstead, M., Reed, S., Krause, R., & Williams, M. T. (2021). Ketamine-assisted psychotherapy for PTSD related to racial discrimination. *Clinical Case Studies, 20*(4), 310–330. https://doi.org/10.1177/1534650121990894

Hamby, S. L., & Koss, M. P. (2003). Shades of gray: A qualitative study of terms used in the measurement of sexual victimization. *Psychology of Women Quarterly, 27,* 243–255. https://doi.org/10.1111/1471-6402.00104

Hammond, L., Ioannou, M., & Fewster, M. (2017). Perceptions of male rape and sexual assault in a male sample from the United Kingdom: Barriers to reporting and the impacts of victimization. *Journal of Investigative Psychology and Offender Profiling, 14,* 133–149. https://doi.org/10.1002/jip.1462

Han, K., Colarelli, S. M., & Weed, N. C. (2019). Methodological and statistical advances in the consideration of cultural diversity in assessment: A critical review of group classification and measurement invariance testing. *Psychological Assessment, 31*(12), 1481–1496. http://dx.doi.org/10.1037/pas0000731

Han, W., Feng, X., Zhang, M., Peng, K., & Zhang, D. (2019). Mood states and everyday creativity: Employing an Experience Sampling Method and a Day Reconstruction Method. *Frontiers in Psychology, 10.* https://doi.org/10.3389/fpsyg.2019.01698

Harris, R. (2002). Anti-plagiarism strategies for research papers. http://www.virtualsalt.com/antiplag.htm.

Harro, J. (2019). Animal models of depression: Pros and cons. *Cell and Tissue Research, 377*(6), 5–20. https://doi.org/10.1007/s00441-018-2973-0

Haskett, M. E., Hall, J. K., Finster, H. P., Owens, C., & Buccelli, A. R. (2022). "It brought my family more together": Mixed-methods study of low-income U.S. mothers during the pandemic. *Family Relations, 71*(3), 1–16. https://doi.org/10.1111/fare.12684

Hauser, D. J., Ellsworth, P. C., & Gonzalez, R. (2018). Are manipulation checks necessary? *Frontiers in Psychology, 9.* https://doi.org/10.3389/fpsyg.2018.00998

Haynes, N. J., Vandenberg, R. J., Wilson, M. G., DeJoy, D. M., Padilla, H. M., & Smith, M. L. (2021). Evaluating the impact of the Live Healthy, Work Healthy program on organizational outcomes: A randomized field experiment. *Journal of Applied*

Psychology. https://doi.org/10.1037/apl0000977

Henle, M., & Hubbell, M. B. (1938). "Egocentricity" in adult conversation. *Journal of Social Psychology, 9,* 227–234. https://doi.org/10.1080/00224545.1938.9921692

Henrich, J., Heine, S., & Norenzayan, A. (2010). The weirdest people in the world? *Behavioral and Brain Sciences, 33*(2–3), 61–83. https://doi.org/10.1017/S0140525X 0999152X

Henry, P. J. (2008). College sophomores in the laboratory redux: Influences of a narrow data base on social psychology's view of the nature of prejudice. *Psychological Inquiry, 19*(2), 49–71. https://doi.org/10.1080/10478400802049936

Hermans, R. C., Engels, R. C., Larsen, J. K., & Herman, C. P. (2009). Modeling of palatable food intake: The influence of quality of social interaction. *Appetite, 52*(3), 801–804. https://doi.org/10.1016/j.appet.2009.03.008

Hertwig, R., & Ortmann, A. (2008). Deception in social psychological experiments: Two misconceptions and a research agenda. *Social Psychology Quarterly, 71*(3), 222–227. https://doi.org/10.1177/019027250807100304

Hies, O., & Lewis, M. B. (2022). Beyond the beauty of occlusion: Medical masks increase facial attractiveness more than other face coverings. *Cognitive Research: Principles and Implications, 7*(1). https://doi.org/10.1186/s41235-021-00351-9

Hilbig, B. E., Thielmann, I., & Böhm, R. (2021). Bending our ethics code: Avoidable deception and its justification in psychological research. *European Psycholo-*

gist. https://doi.org/10.1027/1016-9040/a000431

Hoerger, M., & Currell, C. (2012). Ethical issues in Internet research. In S. J. Knapp, M. C. Gottlieb, M. M. Handelsman, & L. D. VandeCreek (Eds.), *APA handbook of ethics in psychology,* vol. 2: *Practice, teaching, and research.* (pp. 385–400). American Psychological Association. https://doi.org/10.1037/13272-018

Holden, C. (1987). Animal regulations: So far, so good. *Science, 238*(4829), 880–882. https://doi.org/10.1126/science.3672130

Hood, T. C., & Back, K. W. (1971). Self-disclosure and the volunteer: A source of bias in laboratory experiments. *Journal of Personality and Social Psychology, 17*(2), 130–136. https://doi.org/10.1037/h0030380

Hostetler, A. J. (1987, May). Fraud inquiry revives doubt: Can science police itself? *APA Monitor, 1,* 12.

How Search Works (n.d.). Retrieved February 7, 2022 from, https://www.google.com/search/howsearchworks/crawling-indexing/

Huchting, K., Lac, A., & LaBrie, J. W. (2008). An application of the Theory of Planned Behavior to sorority alcohol consumption. *Addictive Behaviors, 33,* 538–551.

Humphreys, L. (1970). Tearoom trade. Aldine.

Hölzel, B. K., Carmody, J., Vangel, M., Congleton, C., Yerramsetti, S. M., Gard, T., & Lazar, S. W. (2011). Mindfulness practice leads to increases in regional brain gray matter density. *Psychiatry Research: Neuroimaging Section, 191,* 36–43. https://doi.org/10.1016/j.pscychresns.2010.08.006

Jacoby-Senghor, D. S., Sinclair, S., & Shelton, J. N. (2016). A lesson in bias: The relationship between implicit racial bias and performance in pedagogical contexts. *Journal of Experimental Social Psychology, 63,* 50–55. https://doi.org/10.1016/j.jesp.2015.10.010

Jacquet, J. (2011). The pros and cons of Amazon Mechanical Turk for scientific surveys. https://blogs.scientificamerican.com/guilty-planet/httpblogsscientificamerican-comguilty-planet20110707the-pros-cons-of-amazon-mechanical-turk-for-scientific-surveys/

Jones, R., & Cooper, J. (1971). Mediation of experimenter effects. *Journal of Personality and Social Psychology, 20*(1), 70–74. https://doi.org/10.1037/h0031700

Jose, P. E. (2013). *Doing statistical mediation & moderation.* Guilford Press.

Kahneman, D. (2012, Sept. 26). A proposal to deal with questions about priming effects. http://www.nature.com/polopoly_fs/7.6716.1349271308!/suppinfo-File/Kahneman%20Letter.pdf

Kahneman, D. (2014). A new etiquette for replication. *Social Psychology, 45*(4), 310–311.

Kahneman, D., Krueger, A. B., Schkade, D. A., Schwarz, N., & Stone, A. A. (2004). Survey method for characterizing daily life experience: The Day Reconstruction Method. *Science, 306*(5702), 1776–1780. https://doi.org/10.1126/science.1103572

Kamin, L. G. (1974). *The science and politics of IQ.* Wiley.

Kane, E. W., & Macaulay, L. J. (1993). Interviewer gender and gender attitudes. *Public Opinion*

Quarterly, 57(1), 1–28. https://doi.org/10.1086/269352

Kaplan, J. S. (2012). The effects of shared environment on adult intelligence: A critical review of adoption, twin, and MZA studies. *Developmental Psychology, 48,* 1292–1298.

Kaplan, S. A., Luchman, J. N., & Mock, L. (2013). General and specific question sequence effects in satisfaction surveys: Integrating directional and correlational effects. *Journal of Happiness Studies, 14*(5), 1443–1458. https://doi.org/10.1007/s10902-012-9388-5

Kazbour, R. R., & Bailey, J. S. (2010). An analysis of a contingency program on designated drivers at a college bar. *Journal of Applied Behavior Analysis, 43*(2), 273–277.

Kazdin, A. E. (1995). Preparing and evaluating research reports. *Psychological Assessment, 7,* 228–237.

Kazdin, A. E. (2013). *Behavior modification in applied settings* (7th ed.). Waveland Press.

Kazdin, A. E. (2021a). Single-case experimental designs: Characteristics, changes, and challenges. *Journal of the Experimental Analysis of Behavior, 115*(1), 56–85. https://doi.org/10.1002/jeab.638

Kazdin, A. E. (2021b). *Single-case research designs: Methods for clinical and applied settings* (3rd ed.). Oxford University Press.

Kennedy, R., Clifford, S., Burleigh, T., Jewell, R., & Waggoner, P. (2020). The shape of and solutions to the MTurk quality crisis. *Political Science Research and Methods, 8*(4), 614–629. https://doi.org/10.1017/psrm.2020.6

Kenny, D. A. (2021). *Mediation.* https://davidakenny.net/cm/mediate.htm

Khurana, A., Bleakley, A., Ellithorpe, M. E., Hennessy, M., Jamieson, P. E., & Weitz, I. (2019). Media violence exposure and aggression in adolescents: A risk and resilience perspective. *Aggressive Behavior, 45*(1), 70–81. doi:https://doi.org/10.1002/ab.21798

Kim, A. S. N., Shakory, S., Azad, A., Popovic, C., & Park, L. (2020). Understanding the impact of attendance and participation on academic achievement. *Scholarship of Teaching and Learning in Psychology, 6*(4), 272–284. https://doi.org/10.1037/stl0000151

Kim, H., Sherman, D., & Taylor, S. (2008). Culture and social support. American Psychologist, *63*(6), 518–526. https://doi.org/10.1037/0003-066X

Kimmel, A. J. (2001). Ethical trends in marketing and psychological research. *Ethics & Behavior, 11*(2), 131–149. https://doi.org/10.1207/S15327019EB1102_2

Kimmel, A. J., Smith, N. C., & Klein, J. G. (2011). Ethical decision making and research deception in the behavioral sciences: An application of social contract theory. *Ethics & Behavior, 21*(3), 222–251. https://doi.org/10.1080/10508422.2011.570166

King Jr, M. L. (1967). *King's challenge to the nation's social scientists.* American Psychological Association. https://www.apa.org/monitor/features/king-challenge

Kintz, N. L., Delprato, D. J., Mettee, D. R., Persons, C. E., & Schappe, R. H. (1965). The experimenter effect. *Psychological Bulletin, 63,* 223–232. https://doi.org/10.1037/h0021718

Kirsch, I. (2010). *The emperor's new drugs: Exploding the antidepressant myth.* Basic Books.

Kitayama, S., Markus, H. R., Matsumoto, H., & Norasakkunkit, V. (1997). Individual and collective processes in the construction of the self: Self-enhancement in the United States and self-criticism in Japan. *Journal of Personality and Social Psychology, 72*(6), 1245–1267. https://doi.org/10.1037/0022-3514.72.6.1245

Klein, E. G., Czaplicki, L., Berman, M., Emery, S., & Schillo, B. (2020). Visual attention to the use of #ad versus #sponsored on e-cigarette influencer posts on social media: A randomized experiment. *Journal of Health Communication, 25*(12), 925–930. https://doi.org/10.1080/10810730.2020.1849464

Kline, R. B. (2016). *Principles and practice of structural equation modeling* (4th ed.). Guilford Press.

Klonsky, E. D., & May, A. M. (2015). The Three-Step Theory (3ST): A new theory of suicide rooted in the "ideation-to-action" framework. *International Journal of Cognitive Therapy, 8*(2), 114–129. doi: 10.1521/ijct.2015.8.2.114

Korn, J. H. (1997). *Illusions of reality: A history of deception in social psychology.* State University of New York Press.

Krahé, B., & Möller, I. (2010). Longitudinal effects of media violence on aggression and empathy among German adolescents. *Journal of Applied Developmental Psychology, 31*(5), 401–409. https://doi.org/10.1016/j.appdev.2010.07.003

Kremer, P., Spittle, M., McNeil, D., & Shinners, C. (2009). Amount of mental practice and performance of a simple motor task. *Perceptual and Motor Skills,*

109(2), 347–356. https://doi.org/10.2466/PMS.109.2.347-356

Krumpal, I. (2013). Determinants of social desirability bias in sensitive surveys: A literature review. *Quality & Quantity: International Journal of Methodology, 47*(4), 2025–2047. https://doi.org/10.1007/s11135-011-9640-9

Kruspe, A., Häberle, M., Kuhn, I., & Zhu, X. X. (2020). Cross-language sentiment analysis of european twitter messages during the covid-19 pandemic. https://arxiv.org/pdf/2008.12172.pdf

Krysan, M., & Couper, M. P. (2003). Race in the live and the virtual interview: Racial deference, social desirability, and activation effects in attitude surveys. *Social Psychology Quarterly, 66*(4), 364–383. https://doi.org/10.2307/1519835

Kühne, S., & Kroh, M. (2021). Interviewer effects in panel surveys. In P. Lynn (Ed.), *Advances in longitudinal survey methodology* (pp. 302–336). Wiley. http://doi.org/10.1002/9781119376965.ch13OI

Lambert, N. M., Stillman, T. F., Hicks, J. A., Kamble, S., Baumeister, R. F., & Fincham, F. D. (2013). To belong is to matter: Sense of belonging enhances meaning in life. *Personality and Social Psychology Bulletin, 39*(11), 1418–1427. https://doi.org/10.1177/0146167213499186

Lana, R. E. (1969). Pretest sensitization. In R. Rosenthal & R. L. Rosnow (Eds.), Artifacts in behavioral research (pp. 119 – 141). Academic Press.

Landrum, R. E. (2020). *Undergraduate writing in psychology: Learning to tell the scientific story* (3rd. ed.). American Psychological Association.

Lane, S. D., Cherek, D. R., Tcheremissine, O. V., Lieving, L. M., & Pietras, C. J. (2005). Clinical research acute marijuana effects on human risk taking. *Neuropsychopharmacology, 30*(4), 800–809. https://doi.org/10.1038/sj.npp.1300620

Langer, E. J., & Abelson, R. P. (1974). A patient by any other name…: Clinical group difference in labeling bias. *Journal of Consulting and Clinical Psychology, 42*(1), 4–9. https://doi/10.1037/h00.org36054

Langer, E. J., & Abelson, R. P. (1974). A patient by any other name…: Clinical group difference in labeling bias. *Journal of Consulting and Clinical Psychology, 42*, 4–9.

Larson, R., & Csikszentmihalyi, M. (2014). The Experience Sampling Method. In M. Csikszentmihalyi, *Flow and the Foundations of Positive Psychology* (pp. 21–34). Springer. https://doi.org/10.1007/978-94-017-9088-8_2

Lasser, J., Ryser, G., Borrego, D., Ham, E., Fierros, K. R., Pruin, J., & Randolph, P. (2020). Contemporary college students' attitudes about deception in research. *Ethics & Human Research, 42*(1), 14–21. https://doi.org/10.1002/eahr500039

Latané, B., Williams, K., & Harkins, S. (1979). Many hands make light the work: The causes and consequences of social loafing. *Journal of Personality and Social Psychology, 37*, 822–832. https://doi.org/10.1037/0022-3514.37.6.822

Lee, S. S., Schwarz, N., Taubman, D., & Hou, M. (2010). Sneezing in times of a flu pandemic: Public sneezing increases perception of unrelated risks and shifts

preferences for federal spending. *Psychological Science, 21,* 375–377. https://doi.org/10.1177/0956797609359876

Lehmiller, J. J., Garcia, J. R., Gesselman, A. N., & Mark, K. P. (2020). Less sex, but more sexual diversity: Changes in sexual behavior during the covid-19 coronavirus pandemic. *Leisure Sciences.* https://doi.org/10.1080/01490400.2020.1774016

Leighton, D. C., Legate, N., LePine, S., Anderson, S. F., & Grahe, J. (2018). Self-esteem, self-disclosure, self-expression, and connection on Facebook: A collaborative replication meta-analysis. *Psi Chi Journal of Psychological Research, 23*(2), 98–109. https://doi.org/10.24839/2325-7342.JN23.2.98

Levine, R. (1997). A geography of time: The temporal misadventures of a social psychologist, or how every culture keeps time just a little bit differently. Basic Books.

Levine, R. V. (1990). The pace of life. *American Scientist, 78,* 450–459.

Levy, K. N., & Kelly, K. M. (2010). Sex differences in jealousy: A contribution from attachment theory. *Psychological Science, 21,* 168–173.

Lewis J., & Sauro, J. (2020). Are face emoji ratings better than numbered scales? https://measuringu.com/numbers-versus-face-emojis/

Lewis, M., Cooper Borkenhagen, M., Converse, E., Lupyan, G., & Seidenberg, M. S. (2020). What might books be teaching young children about gender? *Psychological Science, 33*(1), 33–47. https://doi.org/10.1177%2F09567976211024643

Lilienfeld, S., Lynn, S., & Lohr, J. (Eds.). (2004). *Science and pseudoscience in clinical psychology.* Guilford Press.

Lipchock, S. V., Mennella, J. A., Spielman, A. I., & Reed, D. R. (2013). Human bitter perception correlates with bitter receptor messenger RNA expression in taste cells. *American Journal of Clinical Nutrition, 98*(4), 1136–1143. https://doi.org/10.3945/ajcn.113.066688

Liu, M. (2019). The effect of interviewer evaluation of respondents' attitudes and understanding on future survey participation in a panel study. *International Journal of Social Research Methodology: Theory & Practice, 22*(4), 393–402. https://doi.org/10.1080/13645579.2018.1556379

Lofland, J., Snow, D. A., Anderson, L., & Lofland, L. H. (2006). *Analyzing social settings: A guide to qualitative observation and analysis* (4th ed.). Wadsworth.

Loftus, E. (1979). *Eyewitness testimony.* Harvard University Press.

Luk, J. W., Wang, J., & Simons-Morton, B. G. (2010). Bullying victimization and substance use among US adolescents: Mediation by depression. *Prevention Science, 11*(4), 355–359. https://doi.org/10.1007/s11121-010-0179-0

Luria, A. R. (1968). *The mind of a mnemonist.* Basic Books.

Madigan, R., Johnson, S., & Linton, P. (1995). The language of psychology: APA style as epistemology. *American Psychologist, 50*(6), 428–436. https://doi.org/10.1037/0003-066X.50.6.428

Madigan, S. (2014). Picture memory. In J. C. Yuille (Ed.), *Imagery, Memory and Cognition* (pp. 65–89). Psychology Press.

Ma, D. S., Correll, J., & Wittenbrink, B. (2015). The Chicago face database: A free stimulus set of faces and norming data. *Behavior Research Methods, 47*, 1122–1135. https://doi.org/10.3758/s13428-014-0532-5

Magid, K. H., Ranney, M. L., & Risica, P. M. (2021). Using the theory of planned behavior to understand intentions to perform bystander CPR among college students. *Journal of American College Health, 69*(1), 47–52. https://doi.org/10.1080/07448481.2019.1651729

Manlove, J., Cook, E., Whitfield, B., Johnson, M., Martínez-García, G., & Garrido, M. (2020). Short-term impacts of Pulse: An app-based teen pregnancy prevention program for Black and Latinx women. *Journal of Adolescent Health, 66*(2), 224–232. https://doi.org/10.1016/j.jadohealth.2019.08.017

Marlatt, G. A., & Rohsenow, D. R. (1980). Cognitive processes in alcohol use: Expectancy and the balanced placebo design. In N. K. Mello (Ed.), *Advances in substance abuse* (Vol. 1). JAI Press.

Maruyama, G., & Ryan, C. S. (2014). *Research methods in social relations* (8th ed.). Wiley-Blackwell.

Massey, S. (2021). Using Emojis and drawings in surveys to measure children's attitudes to mathematics. *International Journal of Social Research Methodology.* https://doi.org/10.1080/13645579.2021.1940774

Mastergeorge, A. M., Kahathuduwa, C., & Blume, J. (2021). Eye-tracking in infants and young children at risk for autism spectrum disorder: A systematic review of visual stimuli in experimental paradigms. *Journal of Autism and Developmental Disorders, 51*(8), 2578–2599. https://doi.org/10.1007/s10803-020-04731-w

Matsumoto, D. (1994). *Cultural influences on research methods and statistics.* Brooks/Cole.

Mayer, C. (2019). Exceptional human experiences in the life and creative works of Paulo Coelho: A psychobiographical investigation. *Spirituality in Clinical Practice, 6*(3), 166–181. https://doi.org/10.1037/scp0000180

Maćkiewicz, M., & Cieciuch, J. (2016). Pictorial personality traits questionnaire for children (PPTQ-C)—A new measure of children's personality traits. *Frontiers in Psychology, 7*, Article 498. https://doi.org/10.3389/fpsyg.2016.00498

McBride, S. E., Hammond, M. D., Sibley, C. G., & Milfont, T. L. (2021). Longitudinal relations between climate change concern and psychological wellbeing. *Journal of Environmental Psychology, 78*, 101713. https://doi.org/10.1016/j.jenvp.2021.101713

McCutcheon, L. E. (2000). Another failure to generalize the Mozart effect. *Psychological Reports, 87*, 325–330. https://doi.org/10.2466/PR0.87.5.325-330

McFarland, C., Cheam, A., & Buehler, R. (2007). The perseverance effect in the debriefing paradigm: Replication and extension. *Journal of Experimental Social Psychology, 43*, 233–240. https://doi.org/10.1016/j.jesp.2006.01.010

McGuigan, F. J. (1963). The experimenter: A neglected stimulus. Psychological Bulletin, 60, 421–428. https://doi.org/10.1037/h0039936

McKinney, W. T., Jr., & Bunney, W. E., Jr. (1969). Animal model of depression: I. Review of evidence: Implications for research. *Archives of General Psychiatry, 21*(2), 240–248. https://doi.org/10.1001/archpsyc.1969.01740200112015

Mehl, M. R. (2017). The Electronically Activated Recorder (EAR): A method for the naturalistic observation of daily social behavior. *Current Directions in Psychological Science, 26*(2), 184–190. https://doi.org/10.1177/0963721416680611

Mekawi, Y., Carter, S., Packard, G., Wallace, S., Michopoulos, V., & Powers, A. (2022). When (passive) acceptance hurts: Race-based coping moderates the association between racial discrimination and mental health outcomes among Black Americans. *Psychological Trauma: Theory, Research, Practice, and Policy, 14*(1), 38–46. https://doi.org/10.1037/tra0001077.supp

Melzack, R. (2005). The McGill Pain Questionnaire: From description to measurement. *Anesthesiology, 103,* 199–202.

Meston, C. M., & Buss, D. M. (2007). Why humans have sex. *Archives of Sexual Behavior, 36,* 477–507. https://doi.org/10.1007/s10508-007-9175-2

Midanik, L. T., & Greenfield, T. K. (2008). Interactive voice response versus computer-assisted telephone interviewing (CATI) surveys and sensitive questions: The 2005 National Alcohol Survey. *Journal of Studies of Alcohol and Drug, 69*(4), 580–588. https://doi.org/10.15288/jsad.2008.69.580

Milgram, S. (1963). Behavioral study of obedience. *Journal of Abnormal and Social Psychology, 67,* 371–378.

Milgram, S. (1964). Group pressure and action against a person. *Journal of Abnormal and Social Psychology, 69,* 137–143.

Milgram, S. (1965). Some conditions of obedience and disobedience to authority. *Human Relations, 18,* 57–76.

Milgram, S., (1974). *Obedience to authority: An experimental view.* Harper & Row.

Milich, R., Wolraich, M. L., & Lindgren, S. (1986). Sugar and hyperactivity: A critical review of empirical findings. *Clinical Psychology Review, 6*(6), 493–513. https://doi.org/10.1016/0272-7358(86)90034-6

Miller, A. G. (1986). *The obedience experiments: A case study of controversy in social science.* Praeger.

Miller, C. T., & Downey, K. T. (1999). A meta-analysis of heavyweight and self-esteem. *Personality and Social Psychology Review, 3,* 68–84.

Miller, G. A. (1969). Psychology as a means of promoting human welfare. *American Psychologist, 24*(12), 1063–1075. https://doi.org/10.1037/h0028988

Miller, J. G. (1999). Cultural psychology: Implications for basic psychological theory. *Psychological Science, 10*(2), 85–91. https://doi.org/10.1111/1467-9280.00113

Miller, N. E. (1985). The value of behavioral research on animals. *American Psychologist, 40,* 423–440.

Mio, J. S., Barker, L. A., Domenech Rodríguez, M. M., & Gonzalez, J. (2019). *Multicultural psychology* (5th ed.). Oxford University Press.

Moher, D., Liberati, A., Tetzlaff, J., & Altman, D. G. (2009). Preferred reporting items for systematic reviews and meta-analyses: The PRISMA statement. *PLoS Medicine, 6*(7), e1000097. https://doi.org/10.1371/journal.pmed.1000097

Montee, B. B., Miltenberger, R. G., & Wittrock, D. (1995). An experimental analysis of facilitated communication. *Journal of Applied Behavior Analysis, 28,* 189–200.

Moshe, I., Terhorst, Y., Philippi, P., Domhardt, M., Cuijpers, P., Cristea, I., Pulkki-Råback, L., Baumeister, H., & Sander, L. B. (2021). Digital interventions for the treatment of depression: A meta-analytic review. Psychological Bulletin, 147(8), 749–786. https://doi.org/10.1037/bul0000334

Murray, B. (2002). Research fraud needn't happen at all. *APA Monitor, 33*(2). http://www.apa.org/monitor/feb02/fraud.html

Nagata, J. M., Cortez, C. A., Cattle, C. J., Janson, K. T., Iyer, P., Bibbins-Domingo, K., & Baker, F. C. (2022). Screen time use among US adolescents during the COVID-19 pandemic: Findings from the Adolescent Brain Cognitive Development (ABCD) Study. *JAMA Pediatrics, 176*(1), 94–96. https://doi.org/10.1001/jamapediatrics.2021.4334

National Commission for the Protection of Human Subjects of Biomedical and Behavioral Research. (April 18, 1979). *The Belmont Report: Ethical principles and guidelines for the protection of human subjects of research.* Retrieved from https://www.hhs.gov/ohrp/regulations-and-policy/belmontreport/read-the-belmont-report/index.html

Newman, D. A., Tang, C., Song, Q. C., & Wee, S. (2022). Dropping the GRE, keeping the GRE, or GRE-optional admissions?

Considering tradeoffs and fairness. International Journal of Testing, 22(1), 43–71. https://doi.org/10.1080/15305058.2021.2019750

NICHD Early Child Care Research Network (Eds.). (2005). *Child care and child development.* Guilford Press.

Nicol, A. A. M., & Pexman, P. M. (2010a). *Displaying your findings: A practical guide for creating figures, posters, and presentations* (6th ed.). American Psychological Association.

Nicol, A. A. M., & Pexman, P. M. (2010b). *Presenting your findings: A practical guide for creating tables* (6th ed.). American Psychological Association.

Niven, K. (2015). Can music with prosocial lyrics heal the working world? A field intervention in a call center. *Journal of Applied Social Psychology, 45*(3), 132–138. https://doi.org/10.1111/jasp.12282

Nosek, B. A., Ebersole, C. R., DeHaven, A. C., & Mellor, D. T. (2018). The preregistration revolution. *Proceedings of the National Academy of Sciences, 115*(11), 2600–2606. https://doi.org/10.1073/pnas.1708274114

Olkoniemi, H., & Kaakinen, J. K. (2021). Processing of irony in text: A systematic review of eye-tracking studies. *Canadian Journal of Experimental Psychology/Revue Canadienne de Psychologie Expérimentale, 75*(2), 99–106. https://doi.org/10.1037/cep0000216.supp (Supplemental)

Open Science Collaboration (2015). Estimating the reproducibility of psychological science. *Science, 349*(6251), 716-1–716-8. https://doi.org/10.1126/science.aac4716

Opris, D., Pintea, S., García-Palacios, A., Botella, C., Szamosközi, S., & David, D. (2012). Virtual reality exposure therapy in anxiety disorders: A quantitative meta-analysis, *Depression and Anxiety, 29*(2), 85–93.

Orne, M. T. (1962). On the social psychology of the psychological experiment: With particular reference to demand characteristics and their implications. *American Psychologist, 17*(11), 776–783. https://doi.org/10.1037/h0043424

Orquin, J. L., & K. Holmqvist, K. (2018). Threats to the validity of eye-movement research in psychology. *Behavior Research Methods, 50*(4), 1645–1656. https://doi.org/10.3758/s-z13428-017-0998

Orth, U., Trzesniewski, K. H., & Robins, R. W. (2010). Self-esteem development from young adulthood to old age: A cohort-sequential longitudinal study. *Journal of Personality and Social Psychology, 98,* 645–658. https://doi.org/10.1037/a0018769

Osgood, C. E., Suci, G. J., & Tannenbaum, P. H. (1957). *The measurement of meaning.* Urbana: University of Illinois Press.

O'Brien, E. (2019). Enjoy it again: Repeat experiences are less repetitive than people think. *Journal of Personality and Social Psychology, 116*(4), 519–540. https://doi.org/10.1037/pspa0000147

Palan, S., & Schitter, C. (2018). Prolific.ac—A subject pool for online experiments. *Journal of Behavioral and Experimental Finance, 17,* 22–27. https://doi.org/10.1016/j.jbef.2017.12.004

Pan, S. C., Schmitt, A. G., Bjork, E. L., & Sana, F. (2020). Pretesting reduces mind wandering and enhances learning during online lectures. *Journal of Applied Research in Memory and Cognition, 9*(4), 542–554. https://dx.doi.org/10.1016/j.jarmac.2020.07.004

Park, J., Joshanloo, M., & Scheifinger, H. (2020). Predictors of life satisfaction in Australia: A study drawing upon annual data from the Gallup World Poll. *Australian Psychologist, 55*(4), 375–388. https://doi.org/10.1111/ap.12441

Patrick, M. E., Couper, M. P., Parks, M. J., Laetz, V., & Schulenberg, J. E. (2021). Comparison of a web-push survey research protocol with a mailed paper and pencil protocol in the Monitoring the Future panel survey. *Addiction, 116*(1), 191–199. https://doi.org/10.1111/add.15158

Pattinson, D. (2012). PLOS ONE launches Reproducibility Initiative. http://blogs.plos.org/everyone/2012/08/14/plos-one-launches-reproducibility-initiative/

Paulus, P. B., Annis, A. B., Seta, J. J., Schkade, J. K., & Matthews, R. W. (1976). Crowding does affect task performance. *Journal of Personality and Social Psychology, 34*(2), 248–253. https://doi.org/10.1037/0022-3514.34.2.248

Pawlenko, N. B., Safer, M. A., Wise, R. A., & Holfeld, B. (2013). A teaching aid for improving jurors' assessments of eyewitness accuracy. *Applied Cognitive Psychology, 27*(2), 190–197.

Peer, E., Brandimarte, L., Samat, S., & Acquisti, A. (2017). Beyond the Turk: Alternative platforms for crowdsourcing behavioral research. *Journal of Experimental Social Psychology, 70,* 153–163. https://doi.org/10.1016/j.jesp.2017.01.006

Peer, E., Rothschild, D. M., Evernden, Z., Gordon, A., & Damer, E. (2021). Data quality of platforms and panels for online behavioral research. *Behavior Research Methods*. https://doi.org/10.3758/s13428-021-01694-3

Penilla, C., Tschann, J. M., Pasch, L. A., Flores, E., Deardorff, J., Martinez, S. M., Butte, N. F., & Greenspan, L. C. (2022). Style of meal service and feeding practices among Mexican American fathers and mothers: An analysis of video-recorded children's evening meal-time at home. *Appetite, 169*. https://doi.org/10.1016/j.appet.2021.105851

Perry, G. (2013). *Behind the shock machine: The untold story of the notorious Milgram psychology experiments*. New Press.

Peterson, D. A. M., Biederman, L. A., Andersen, D., Ditonto, T. M., & Roe, K. (2019). Mitigating gender bias in student evaluations of teaching. *PLOS ONE, 14*(5), e0216241. https://doi.org/10.1371/journal.pone.0216241

Peterson, R. A., (2001). On the use of college students in social science research: Insights from a second-order meta-analysis. *Journal of Consumer Research, 28*(3), 450–461. https://doi.org/10.1086/323732

Pettigrew, T. F. (2018). The emergence of contextual social psychology. *Personality and Social Psychology Bulletin, 44*(7), 963–971. https://doi.org/10.1177/0146167218756033

Pew Research Center. (2021). Internet/Broadband Fact Sheet. https://www.pewresearch.org/internet/fact-sheet/internet-broadband/

Pew Research Center. Social Media Use in 2021. https://www.pewresearch.org/internet/2021/04/07/social-media-use-in-2021/

Pfungst, O. (1911). *Clever Hans (the horse of Mr. von Osten): A contribution to experimental, animal, and human psychology* (C. L. Rahn, Trans.). Holt, Rinehart & Winston. (Republished 1965.)

Piaget, J. (1952). *The origins of intelligence in children*. International Universities Press.

Pietri, E. S., Drawbaugh, M. L., Lewis, A. N., & Johnson, I. R. (2019). Who encourages Latina women to feel a sense of identity-safety in STEM? *Journal of Experimental Social Psychology, 84*, 1–7. https://doi.org/10.1016/j.jesp.2019.103827

Pietschnig, J., Voracek, M., & Formann, A. K. (2010). Mozart effect–Shmozart effect: A meta-analysis. *Intelligence, 38*(3), 314–323. https://doi.org/10.1016/j.intell.2010.03.001

Pigliucci, M. (2010). *Nonsense on stilts: How to tell science from bunk*. University of Chicago Press.

Plotnikoff, R. C., Lubans, D. R., Costigan, S. A., Trinh, L., Spence, J. C., Downs, S., & McCargar, L. (2011). A test of the theory of planned behavior to explain physical activity in a large population sample of adolescents from Alberta, Canada. *Journal of Adolescent Health, 49*(5), 547–549. https://doi.org/10.1016/j.jadohealth.2011.03.006

Plous, S. (1996a). Attitudes toward the use of animals in psychological research and education: Results from a national survey of psychologists. *American Psychologist, 51*, 1167–1180.

Plous, S. (1996b). Attitudes toward the use of animals in psychological research and education: Results from a national survey of psychology majors. *Psychological Science, 7*, 352–363.

Popper, K. (2002). *The logic of scientific discovery*. New York: Routledge.

Rahman, A., Sánchez, M., Bursac, Z., Whiting, C. Y., de Dios, M. A., Cano, M., Meek, R., Taskin, T., Shawon, M. S. R., Vazquez, V., Koly, K. N., Ullrich, H. S., & Cano, M. Á. (2022). Ethnic discrimination and psychological stress among Hispanic emerging adults: Examining the moderating effects of distress tolerance and optimism. *International Journal of Intercultural Relations, 86*, 217–226. https://doi.org/10.1016/j.ijintrel.2021.12.005

Ramirez, G., & Beilock, S. L. (2011). Writing about testing worries boosts exam performance in the classroom. *Science, 331*(6014), 211–213. https://doi.org/10.1126/science.1199427

Ramírez-Esparza, N., Mehl, M. R., Alvarez-Bermúdez, J. & Pennebaker, J. W. (2009). Are Mexicans more sociable than Americans? Insights from a naturalistic observation study. *Journal of Research in Personality, 43*(1), 1–7. https://doi.org/10.1016/j.jrp.2008.09.002

Randall, J. G., Zimmer, C. U., O'Brien, K. R., Trump-Steele, R. C. E., Villado, A. J., & Hebl, M. R. (2017). Weight discrimination in helping behavior. *European Review of Applied Psychology / Revue Européenne de Psychologie Appliquée, 67*(3), 125–137. https://doi.org/10.1016/j.erap.2017.02.002

Rathje, S., Hackel, L., & Zaki, J. (2021). Attending live theatre improves empathy, changes attitudes, and leads to pro-social behavior. *Journal of Experimental Social Psychology, 95*. https://doi.org/10.1016/j.jesp.2021.104138

Rauscher, F. H., & Shaw, G. L. (1998). Key components of the Mozart effect. *Perceptual and Motor Skills, 86,* 835–841. https://doi.org/10.2466/pms.1998.86.3.835

Rauscher, F. H., Shaw, G. L., & Ky, K. N. (1993). Music and spatial task performance. *Nature, 365,* 611. https://doi.org/10.1038/365611a0

Ravizza, S. M., Uitvlugt, M. G., & Fenn, K. M. (2017). Logged in and zoned out: How laptop Internet use relates to classroom learning. *Psychological Science, 28*(2), 171–180. https://doi.org/10.1177/0956797616677314

Rentfrow, P., Gosling, S., & Potter, J. (2008). A theory of the emergence, persistence, and expression of geographic variation in psychological characteristics. *Perspectives on Psychological Science, 3,* 339–369. https://doi.org/10.1111/j.1745-6924.2008.00084.x

Reverby, S. M. (2011). "Normal exposure" and inoculation syphilis: A PHS "Tuskegee" doctor in Guatemala, 1946–1948. *Journal of Policy History, 23,* 6–28. https://doi.org/10.1017/S0898030610000291

Reverby, S. M. (Ed.). (2000). *Tuskegee's truths: Rethinking the Tuskegee syphilis study.* University of North Carolina Press.

Rew, L., Slesnick, N., Johnson, K., & Sales, A. (2022). Promoting healthy attitudes and behaviors in youth who experience homelessness: Results of a longitudinal intervention study. *Journal of Adolescent Health.* https://doi.org/10.1016/j.jadohealth.2021.12.025

Rhoades, G., & Stocker, C. M. (2006). Can spouses provide knowledge of each other's communication patterns? A study of self-reports, spouses' reports, and observational coding. *Family Process, 45*(4), 499–511. https://doi.org/10.1111/j.1545-5300.2006.00185.x

Rhodes, N., Roskos-Ewoldsen, D., Eno, C. A., & Monahan, J. L. (2009). The content of cigarette counter-advertising: Are perceived functions of smoking addressed? *Journal of Health Communication, 14*(7), 658–673. https://doi.org/10.1080/10810730903204262

Ring, K., Wallston, K., & Corey, M. (1970). Mode of debriefing as a factor affecting subjective reaction to a Milgram-type obedience experiment: An ethical inquiry. *Representative Research in Social Psychology, 1,* 67–68.

Riordan, C. A., & Marlin, N. A. (1987). Some good news about some bad practices. *American Psychologist, 42,* 104–106.

Roberson, M. T., & Sundstrom, E. (1990). Questionnaire design, return rates, and response favorableness in an employee attitude questionnaire. *Journal of Applied Psychology, 75*(3), 354–357. https://doi.org/10.1037/0021-9010.75.3.354

Roberts, L. D., & Sipes, J. B. A. (2018). Ethical issues in online research. In M. M. Leach & E. R. Welfel (Eds.), *The Cambridge handbook of applied psychological ethics* (pp. 474–492). Cambridge University Press. https://doi.org/10.1017/9781316417287.024

Robinson, J. P., Shaver, P. R., & Wrightsman, L. S. (1991). *Measures of personality and social psychological attitudes* (Vol. 1). Academic Press.

Robinson, J. P., Shaver, P. R., & Wrightsman, L. S. (Eds.). (1999). *Measures of political attitudes.* Academic Press.

Rodriguez-Seijas, C., Eaton, N. R., & Pachankis, J. E. (2019). Prevalence of psychiatric disorders at the intersection of race and sexual orientation: Results from the National Epidemiologic Survey of Alcohol and Related Conditions–III. *Journal of Consulting and Clinical Psychology, 87*(4), 321–331. https://doi.org/10.1037/ccp0000377

Rosen, C. C., Simon, L. S., Gajendran, R. S., Johnson, R. E., Lee, H. W., & Lin, S.-H. (Joanna). (2019). Boxed in by your inbox: Implications of daily e-mail demands for managers' leadership behaviors. *Journal of Applied Psychology, 104*(1), 19–33. https://doi.org/10.1037/apl0000343

Rosenthal, R. (1966). *Experimenter effects in behavior research.* Appleton-Century-Crofts.

Rosenthal, R. (1967). Covert communication in the psychological experiment. *Psychological Bulletin, 67*(11), 356–367. https://doi.org/10.1037/h0024529

Rosenthal, R. (1969). Interpersonal expectations: Effects of the experimenter's hypothesis. In R. Rosenthal & R. L. Rosnow (Eds.), *Artifacts in behavioral research.* Academic Press.

Rosenthal, R., & Jacobson, L. (1968). *Pygmalion in the classroom: Teacher expectation and pupils' intellectual development.* Holt, Rinehart & Winston.

Rosenthal, R., & Rosnow, R. L. (1975). *The volunteer subject.* New York: Wiley.

Rosnow, R. L., & Rosnow, M. (2012). *Writing papers in psychology* (9th ed.). Wadsworth Cengage Learning.

Ryan, C. S., & Hemmes, N. S. (2005). Effects of the contingency for homework submission on homework submission and quiz performance in a college course. *Journal of Applied Behavior Analysis, 38,* 79–88. https://doi.org/10.1901/jaba.2005.123-03

Salgado S., & Kaplitt M. G. (2015). The nucleus accumbens: A comprehensive review. *Stereotactic and Functional Neurosurgery.* https://www.karger.com/article/Fulltext/368279

Sato, S., Dyar K. A., Treebak J. T., Jepsen S. L., Ehrlich, A. M., Ashcroft S. P., Trost, K., Kunzke, T., Prade, V. M., Small, L., Basse, A.L., Schönke, M., Chen, S., Samad, M., Baldi, P., Barrès, R., Walch, A., Moritz, T., Holst, J.J.,... Sassone-Corsi, P. (2022). Atlas of exercise metabolism reveals time-dependent signatures of metabolic homeostasis. *Cell Metabolism.* https://doi.org/10.1016/j.cmet.2021.12.016

Schachter, S. (1959). *The psychology of affiliation.* Stanford University Press.

Schaie, K. W. (1986). Beyond calendar definitions of age, time, and cohort: The general developmental model revisited. *Developmental Review, 6,* 252–277.

Schreer, G. E., Smith, S., & Thomas, K. (2009). "Shopping while Black": Examining racial discrimination in a retail setting. *Journal of Applied Social Psychology, 39*(6), 1432–1444. https://doi.org/10.1111/j.1559-1816.2009.00489.x

Schultz, W. (Ed.). (2005). *Handbook of psychobiography.* Oxford University Press.

Schwartz, B. M., Landrum, R. E., & Gurung, R.A.R. (2020). *An easy guide to APA style* (4th ed.). Sage.

Schwarz, N. (1999). Self-reports: How the questions shape the answers. *American Psychologist,* *54*(2), 93–105. https://doi.org/10.1037/0003-066X.54.2.93

Schwarz, N., Knauper, B., Oyserman, D., & Stich, C. (2008). The psychology of asking questions. In E. Desiree de Leeuw, J. J. Hox, & D. A. Dillman (Eds.), *International handbook of survey methodology* (pp. 18–34). Taylor & Francis.

Scribner, S. (1997). Studying literacy at work: Bringing the laboratory to the field. In E. Torbach, R. J. Falmagne, M. B. Parlee, L. M. W. Martin, & A. S. Kapelman (Eds.), *Mind and social practice: Selected writings of Sylvia Scribner.* Cambridge University Press.

Sears, D. O. (1986). College sophomores in the laboratory: Influences of a narrow data base on social psychology's view of human nature. *Journal of Personality and Social Psychology, 51*(3), 515–530. https://doi.org/10.1037/0022-3514.51.3.515

Shadish, W. R., Cook, T. D., & Campbell, D. T. (2002). *Experimental and quasi-experimental designs for generalized causal inference.* Houghton Mifflin.

Shepard, R. N., & Metzler, J. (1971). Mental rotation of three-dimensional objects. *Science, 171,* 701–703. https://doi.org/10.1126/science.171.3972.701

Sidman, M. (1960). *Tactics of scientific research.* Basic Books.

Sieber, J. E. (2009). Evidence-based ethical problem solving (EBEPS). *Perspectives on Psychological Science, 4*(1), 26–27. https://doi.org/10.1111/j.1745-6924.2009.01087.x

Sieber, J. E., Iannuzzo, R., & Rodriguez, B. (1995). Deception methods in psychology: Have they changed in 23 years? *Ethics and Behavior, 5,* 67–85. https://doi.org/10.1207/s15327019eb0501_5

Siegel, S., & Castellan, N. J. (1988). *Nonparametric statistics for the behavioral sciences.* McGraw Hill.

Silverman, L., & Margulis, S. (1973). Experiment title as a source of sampling bias in commonly used "subject-pool" procedures. *Canadian Psychologist, 14*(2), 197–201. https://doi.org/10.1037/h0082218

Simmons, J. P., Nelson, L. D., & Simonsohn, U. (2013). Life after P-Hacking. Paper presented at the Meeting of the Society for Personality and Social Psychology, New Orleans, LA, January 17–19, 2013. Available at SSRN: https://ssrn.com/abstract=2205186 or http://doi.org/10.2139/ssrn.2205186

Singh, D., Dixson, B., Jessop, T., Morgan, B., & Dixson, A. (2010). Cross-cultural consensus for waist–hip ratio and women's attractiveness. *Evolution and Human Behavior, 31*(3), 176–181. https://doi.org/10.1016/j.evolhumbehav.2009.09.001

Skinner, B. F. (1953). *Science and human behavior.* Macmillan.

Smart, R. G. (1966). Subject selection bias in psychological research. *Canadian Psychologist/Psychologie canadienne, 7*(2), 115–121. https://doi.org/10.1037/h0083096

Smith, R. J., Lingle, J. H., & Brock, T. C. (1978). Reactions to death as a function of perceived similarity to the deceased. *Omega, 9,* 125–138.

Smith, S. M., & Shaffer, D. R. (1991). Celerity and cajolery: Rapid speech may promote or inhibit persuasion through its impact on message elaboration. *Personality and Social Psychology Bulletin, 17,* 663–669. https://doi.org/10.1177/0146167291176009

Snowden, D. A. (1997). Aging and Alzheimer's disease: Lessons from the Nun Study. *Gerontologist, 37,* 150–156.

Sodos, L. M., Hirst, R. B., Watson, J., & Vaughn, D. (2018). Don't judge a book by its cover: Examiner expectancy effects predict neuropsychological performance for individuals judged as chronic cannabis users. *Archives of Clinical Neuropsychology, 33*(7), 821–831. https://doi.org/10.1093/arclin/acx114

Sommet, N., Weissman, D. L., & Elliot, A. J. (2022). Income inequality predicts competitiveness and cooperativeness at school. *Journal of Educational Psychology,* https://doi.org/10.1037/edu0000731

Son, C., Hegde, S., Smith, A., Wang, X., & Sasangohar, F. (2020). Effects of COVID-19 on college students' mental health in the United States: Interview survey study. *Journal of Medical internet Research, 22*(9), e21279. https://doi.org/10.2196/21279

Stabell, A., Eide, H., Solheim, G. A., Solberg, K. N., & Rustoen, T. (2004). Nursing home residents' dependence and independence. *Journal of Clinical Nursing, 13,* 677–686.

Stanley, M., Roycroft, J., Amaya, A., Dever, J. A., & Srivastav, A. (2020). The effectiveness of incentives on completion rates, data quality, and nonresponse bias in a probability-based internet panel survey. *Field Methods, 32*(2), 159–179. https://doi.org/10.1177%2F1525822X20901802

Stanley, M., Roycroft, J., Amaya, A., Dever, J. A., & Srivastav, A. (2020). The effectiveness of incentives on completion rates, data quality, and nonresponse bias in a probability-based Internet panel survey. *Field Methods,*
32(2), 159–179. https://doi.org/10.1177/1525822X20901802

Steele, K. M., Bass, K. E., & Crook, M. D. (1999). The mystery of the Mozart effect: Failure to replicate. *Psychological Science, 10,* 366–369. https://doi.org/10.1111/1467-9280.00169

Stephan, W. G. (1983). Intergroup relations. In D. Perlman & P. C. Cozby (Eds.), *Social psychology.* Holt, Rinehart & Winston.

Stern, M. J., Bilgen, I., & Dillman, D. A. (2014). The state of survey methodology: Challenges, dilemmas, and new frontiers in the era of the tailored design. *Field Methods, 26*(3), 284–301. https://doi.org/10.1177/2F1525822X13519561

Stewart, R. E., & Chambless, D. L. (2009). Cognitive-behavioral therapy for adult anxiety disorders in clinical practice: A meta-analysis of effectiveness studies. *Journal of Consulting and Clinical Psychology, 77,* 595–606. https://doi.org/10.1037/a0016032

Stolzenberg, E. B., Aragon, M. C., Romo, E., Couch, V., McLennan, D., Eagan, M. K., & Kang, N. (2020). *The American freshman: National norms, fall 2019.* Higher Education Research Institute, UCLA. https://www.heri.ucla.edu/monographs/TheAmericanFreshman2019.pdf

Stone, V. E., Cosmides, L., Tooby, J., Kroll, N., & Knight, R. T. (2002). Selective impairment of reasoning about social exchange in a patient with bilateral limbic system damage. *Proceedings of the National Academy of Sciences, 99*(17), 11531–11536. http://www.pnas.org/cgi/content/full/99/17/11531.

Storer, H. L., Casey, E., & Herrenkohl, T. (2016). Efficacy of bystander programs to prevent dating abuse among youth and young adults: A review of the literature. *Trauma, Violence, & Abuse, 17*(3), 256–269. https://doi.org/10.1177/1524838015584361

Stout, S. H., Babulal, G. M., Johnson, A. M., Williams, M. M., & Roe, C. M. (2020). Recruitment of African American and Non-Hispanic White older adults for Alzheimer disease research via traditional and social media: A case study. *Journal of Cross-Cultural Gerontology, 35*(3), 329–339. https://doi.org/10.1007/s10823-020-09405-9

Sue, D. W., Capodilupo, C. M., Torino, G. C., Bucceri, J. M., Holder, A. M. B., Nadal, K. L., & Esquilin, M. (2007). Racial microaggressions in everyday life: Implications for clinical practice. *American Psychologist, 62*(4), 271–286. https://doi.org/10.1037/0003-066X.62.4.271

Sue, V. M., & Ritter, L. A. (2012). *Conducting online surveys* (2nd ed.). Sage. https://doi.org/10.4135/9781506335186

Szabo, A., & Underwood, J. (2004). Cybercheats: Is information and communication technology fueling academic dishonesty? *Active Learning in Higher Education, 5,* 180–199.

Tabachnick, B. G., & Fidell, L. S. (2019). *Using multivariate statistics* (7th ed.). Pearson.

Taylor, S. (2019). *The psychology of pandemics: Preparing for the next global outbreak of infectious disease.* Cambridge Scholars Publishing.

Teo, T. (2009). Psychology without Caucasians. *Canadian Psychology/Psychologie canadienne, 50*(2), 91–97. https://doi.org/10.1037/a0014393

Terman, L. M. (1925). *Genetic studies of genius: Vol. 1. Mental and physical traits of a thousand gifted children.* Stanford University Press.

Terman, L. M., & Oden, M. H. (1947). *Genetic studies of genius: Vol. 4. The gifted child grows up: Twenty-five years' follow-up of a superior group.* Stanford University Press.

Terman, L. M., & Oden, M. H. (1959). *Genetic studies of genius: Vol. 5. The gifted group in mid-life: Thirty five years' follow-up of the superior child.* Stanford University Press.

Thalmayer, A. G., Toscanelli, C., & Arnett, J. J. (2021). The neglected 95% revisited: Is American psychology becoming less American? *American Psychologist, 76*(1), 116–129. https://doi.org/10.1037/amp0000622

Thau, M., Mikkelsen, M. F., Hjortskov, M., & Pedersen, M. J. (2021). Question order bias revisited: A split-ballot experiment on satisfaction with public services among experienced and professional users. *Public Administration, 99*(1), 189–204. https://doi.org/10.1111/padm.12688

Thompson, W. F., Schellenberg, E. G., & Husain, G. (2001). Arousal, mood, and the Mozart effect. *Psychological Science, 12,* 248–251. https://doi.org/10.1111/1467-9280.00345

Tierney, A., Patel, A. D., Jasmin, K., & Breen, M. (2021). Individual differences in perception of the speech-to-song illusion are linked to musical aptitude but not musical training. *Journal of Experimental Psychology: Human Perception and Performance, 47*(12), 1681–1697. https://doi.org/10.1037/xhp0000968

Tipping expert. (2013). Retrieved from http://tippingresearch.com

Toepoel, V. (2016). *Doing surveys online.* Sage.

Trivedi, C., Shukla, S., Adnan, M., Shah, K., & Weiss, L. (2021). Impact of "National Suicide Prevention Week" on digital awareness of suicide prevention: An insight from Google trends. *European Psychiatry, 64,* S404. https://doi.org/10.1192/j.eurpsy.2021.1082

Troller-Renfree, S. V., Costanzo, M. A., Duncan, G. J., Magnuson, K., Gennetian, L. A., Yoshikawa, H., ... & Noble, K. G. (2022). The impact of a poverty reduction intervention on infant brain activity. *Proceedings of the National Academy of Sciences, 119*(5). https://doi.org/10.1073/pnas.2115649119

Tufte, E. R. (1983). *The visual display of quantitative information.* Graphics Press.

Tufte, E. R. (1990). *Envisioning information.* Graphics Press.

Tufte, E. R. (1997). *Visual explanations: Images and quantities, evidence and narrative.* Graphics Press.

Tufte, E. R. (2006). *Beautiful evidence.* Graphics Press.

Twenge, J. M., Sherman, R. A., & Wells, B. E. (2017). Declines in sexual frequency among American adults, 1989–2014. *Archives of Sexual Behavior, 46*(8), 2389–2401. https://doi.org /10.1007/s10508-017-0953-1

Tymula, A., Belmaker, L., Ruderman, L., Glimcher, P. W., & Levy, I. (2013). Like cognitive function, decision making across the life span shows profound age-related changes. *PNAS Proceedings of the National Academy of Sciences of the United States of America, 110*(42), 17143–17148. https://doi.org/10.1073/pnas.1309909110

Ueda, R., & Abe, N. (2021). Neural representations of the committed romantic partner in the nucleus accumbens. *Psychological Science, 32*(12), 1884–1895. https://doi.org/10.1177/09567976211021854

U.S. Census Bureau. (2022, March 10). Census Bureau Releases Estimates of Undercount and Overcount in the 2020 Census [Press Release]. https://www.census.gov/newsroom/press-releases/2022/2020-census-estimates-of-undercount-and-overcount.html

U.S. Department of Health and Human Services (HHS). (1998). OHRP Expedited Review Categories (1998). https://www.hhs.gov/ohrp/regulations-and-policy/guidance/categories-of-research-expedited-review-procedure-1998/index.html

U.S. Department of Health and Human Services (HHS). (2018). 2018 Common Rule. https://www.hhs.gov/ohrp/regulations-and-policy/regulations/45-cfr-46/revised-common-rule-regulatory-text/index.html

U.S. Office of Science and Technology Policy. (2013). Expanding public access to the results of federally funded research. https://obamawhitehouse.archives.gov/sites/default/files/microsites/ostp/ostp_public_access_memo_2013.pdf

Vasquez, E. A., Pedersen, W. C., Bushman, B. J., Kelley, N. J., Demeestere, P., & Miller, N. (2013). Lashing out after stewing over public insults: The effects of public provocation, provocation intensity, and rumination on triggered displaced aggression. *Aggressive Behavior, 39*(1), 13–29. https://doi.org/10.1002/ab.21453

Venturo-Conerly, K., Fitzpatrick, O. M., Horn, R. L., Ugueto, A. M.,

& Weisz, J. R. (2022). Effectiveness of youth psychotherapy delivered remotely: A meta-analysis. *American Psychologist, 77*(1), 71–84. https://doi.org/10.1037/amp0000816

Verfaellie, M., & McGwin, J. (2011). The case of Diederik Stapel. Retrieved from http://www.apa.org/science/about/psa/2011/12/diederik-stapel.aspx.

Wallace, E., & Buil, I. (2020). Hiding Instagram likes: Effects on negative affect and loneliness. *Personality and Individual Differences.* https://doi.org/10.1016/j.paid.2020.110509

Wang, H.L. (2018). What you need to know about the 2020 Census. National Public Radio. https://www.npr.org/2019/03/31/707899218/what-you-need-to-know-about-the-2020-census

Wang, Y., Zhang, J., & Lee, H. (2021). An online experiment during COVID-19: Testing the influences of autonomy support toward emotions and academic persistence. *Frontiers in Psychology, 12.* https://doi.org/10.3389/fpsyg.2021.747209

Wanic, R. A., Goldschmied, N., & Nolan, M. (2019). "I'll show them": Assessing performance in recently traded NBA players facing their former team. *Motivation Science, 5*(4), 357–364. https://doi.org/10.1037/mot0000120

Webb, E. J., Campbell, D. T., Schwartz, R. D., Sechrest, R., & Grove, J. B. (1981). *Nonreactive measures in the social sciences* (2nd ed.). Houghton Mifflin.

Wedel, M. (2015). Attention research in marketing: A review of eye-tracking studies. In J. M. Fawcett, E. F. Risko, & A.

Kingstone (Eds.), *The handbook of attention.* (pp. 569–588). Boston Review.

Weijers, R. J., & de Koning, B. B. (2021). Nudging to increase hand hygiene during the COVID-19 pandemic: A field experiment. *Canadian Journal of Behavioural Science / Revue canadienne des sciences du comportement, 53*(3), 353–357. https://doi.org/10.1037/cbs0000245

Wilkinson, L., & the Task Force on Statistical Inference. (1999). Statistical methods in psychology journals: Guidelines and explanations. *American Psychologist, 54,* 594–604.

Will, P., Bischof, W. F., & Kingstone, A. (2020). The impact of classroom seating location and computer use on student academic performance. *PloS one, 15*(8), e0236131. https://doi.org/10.1371/journal.pone.0236131

Wilson, T. D., Aronson, E., & Carlsmith, K. (2010). The art of laboratory experimentation. In S. T. Fiske, D. T. Gilbert, & G. Lindzey (Eds.), *Handbook of social psychology,* 5th ed., vol. 1 (pp. 51–81). Wiley. https://doi.org/10.1002/9780470561119.socpsy001002

Winograd, E., & Soloway, R. M. (1986). On forgetting the location of things stored in special places. *Journal of Experimental Psychology: General, 115,* 366–372. https://doi.org/10.1037/0096-3445.115.4.366

Wolpe, J. (1982). *The practice of behavior therapy* (3rd ed.). Pergamon.

Wolraich, M. L, Wilson, D. B., & White, J. W. (1995). The effect of sugar on behavior or cognition in children: A meta-analysis. *JAMA, 274*(20), 1617–1621.

https://doi.org/10.1001/jama.1995.03530200053037

Woody, W.D., & Viney, W. (2017). *A History of Psychology: The Emergence of Science and Applications* (6th ed.). Routledge. https://doi.org/10.4324/9781315544403

Yang, B. W., Vargas Restrepo, C., Stanley, M. L., & Marsh, E. J. (2021). Truncating bar graphs persistently misleads viewers. *Journal of Applied Research in Memory and Cognition, 10*(2), 298–311. https://doi.org/10.1016/j.jarmac.2020.10.002

Yechiam, E., Ashby, N. J. S., & Hochman, G. (2019). Are we attracted by losses? Boundary conditions for the approach and avoidance effects of losses. *Journal of Experimental Psychology: Learning, Memory, and Cognition, 45*(4), 591–605. https://doi.org/10.1037/xlm0000607

Yin, R. K. (2018). *Case study research and applications: Design and methods* (6th ed.). Sage.

Zhang, H., Sang, Z., Chan, D. K.-S., & Schlegel, R. (2019). Threats to belongingness and meaning in life: A test of the compensation among sources of meaning. *Motivation and Emotion, 43*(2), 242–254. https://doi-org/10.1007/s11031-018-9737-8

Zimbardo, P. G. (2004). Does psychology make a significant difference in our lives? *American Psychologist, 59*(5), 339–351. https://doi.org/10.1037/0003-066X.59.5.339

Zitek, E. M., Jordan, A. H., Monin, B., & Leach, F. R. (2010). Victim entitlement to behave selfishly. *Journal of Personality and Social Psychology, 98*(2), 245–255. https://doi.org/10.1037/a0017168

Index